# NORTHERN CALIFORNIA BEST PLACES

Restaurants, Lodgings, and Touring

Rebecca Poole Forée

SASQUATCH BOOKS
SEATTLE

Printed in the United States
Distributed in Canada by Raincoast Books Ltd.
Third edition.

00  99          6 5 4 3 2

ISSN: 1095-9769
ISBN: 1-57061-110-6

Interior design: Lynne Faulk
Cover design & interior composition: Kate Basart
City maps: Greeneye Design
Regional maps: Karen Schober

*Special Sales*
Best Places® guidebooks are available at special discounts on bulk purchases for corporate, club, or organization sales promotions, premiums, and gifts. Special editions, including personalized covers, excerpts of existing guides, and corporate imprints, can be created in large quantities for specific needs. For more information, contact your local bookseller or Special Sales, Best Places Guidebooks, 615 Second Avenue, Suite 260, Seattle, Washington 98104, (800)775-0817.

**Best Places®. Reach for it first.**

SASQUATCH BOOKS
615 Second Avenue, Suite 260
Seattle, WA 98104
(206)467-4300
books@sasquatchbooks.com
www.sasquatchbooks.com

# CONTENTS

# Introduction and Acknowledgments

Anxious to learn what's hot, what's not, and what's up-and-coming, friends, family, and other loyal readers of *Northern California Best Places* have been asking me for months when this third edition would hit the bookstores. I have no doubt they'll pore over the book, slap me on the back in congratulations, and then, as before, many will wrap an arm around my shoulders and whisper into my ear: "So, tell me what *your* favorite places are. You know, the ones you *didn't* put in the book."

Which guidebook writer or restaurant critic worth her weight in Napa Valley wine hasn't hesitated before telling the world about that special little place hidden in that hard-to-find little corner of you-know-where? None of them, that's who. But the truth is that while we may *hesitate*, we always cave in and put it all in print. Why? Because we know how competitive the hotel, B&B, and restaurant businesses are, and if they don't attract enough customers to keep their doors open and cash registers ringing, we'll all lose out, right? Suffice it to say that what you have in your hands is a candid, honest tally of Northern California's best places—the very places we'd whisper into the ears of our inquiring friends.

I spent the better part of a year editing this travel tome and writing many of the reviews, but several sections of the book were penned by a talented team of writers to whom I owe a major debt of gratitude: Matthew R. Poole, Mary Anne Moore, Maurice Read, Mona Behan, Maria Behan, and Jean Linsteadt. I couldn't have done it without them.

Many others contributed their opinions and observations to this all-new third edition, and deserve to be recognized here: Gary Anspach, Dr. Jeffrey Culver, Susan L. Davis, Stephanie Irving, Erika Lenkert, Terri Leonard, Ken Linsteadt, Sandy McNab, RJ Muna, Susan Organ, Dave Peattie, Susan Stone, Dana Topping, Moses Vaughan, Jenifer Warren, and the readers who sent me their thoughtful evaluations of the previous edition (keep writing!).

Kudos to the Sasquatch staff who helped put this enormous project together, including publisher Chad Haight, editor Kate Rogers, assistant editor Meghan Heffernan, and managing editor Joan Gregory. To copy editor Noelle Sullivan, proofreader Cynthia Rubin, and fact-checkers Thomas A. Knight and Elizabeth Renshaw, I'd like to say bravo and thanks for such splendid work. I am also deeply grateful to Nancy Leson McCarthy and Janean Selkirk, devoted friends who were there when I needed them. And finally, I dedicate this book to the memory of Misha, my 17-year-old Siamese cat: the two of us spent many mornings sitting side by side, staring at my computer screen, trying to make sense of the 250,000 words that make up this book. She made the job a joy.

—*Rebecca Poole Forée*

# ABOUT BEST PLACES® GUIDEBOOKS

Best Places® guidebooks, which have been published continuously since 1975, represent one of the most respected regional travel series in the country. Each guide is written completely independently: no advertisers, no sponsors, no favors. Our reviewers know their territory, work incognito, and seek out the very best a region has to offer. Because we accept no free meals, accommodations, or other complimentary services, we are able to provide tough, candid reports about places that have rested too long on their laurels and to delight in new places that deserve recognition. We describe the true strengths, foibles, and unique characteristics of each establishment listed.

*Northern California Best Places* is written by and for locals, and is therefore coveted by travelers. It's written for people who live here and who enjoy exploring the region's bounty and its out-of-the-way places of high character and individualism. It is these very characteristics that make *Northern California Best Places* ideal for tourists, too. The best places in the region are the ones that denizens favor: independently owned establishments of good value, touched with local history, run by lively individuals, and graced with natural beauty. With this latest edition of *Northern California Best Places*, travelers will find the information they need: where to go and when, what to order, which rooms to request (and which to avoid).

We're so sure you'll be satisfied with our guide, we guarantee it.

*Note: Readers are advised that places listed in previous editions may have closed or changed management, or may no longer be recommended by this series. The reviews in this edition are based on information available at press time and are subject to change. The editors welcome information conveyed by users of this book. A report form is provided at the end of the book, and feedback is also welcome via email: books@sasquatchbooks.com.*

# HOW TO USE THIS BOOK

This book is divided into nine major regions, encompassing Big Sur and Yosemite National Park, and all areas north to the Oregon border. All evaluations are based on numerous reports from local and traveling inspectors. Best Places® reporters do not identify themselves when they review an establishment, and they accept no free meals, accommodations, or any other services. Final judgments are made by the editors. Every place featured in this book is recommended.

**Stars** Restaurants and lodgings are rated on a scale of zero to four stars, based on uniqueness, loyalty of local clientele, performance measured against goals, excellence of cooking, cleanliness, value, and professionalism of service. Reviews are listed alphabetically within each star rating.

| | |
|---|---|
| ★★★★ | The very best in the region |
| ★★★ | Distinguished; many outstanding features |
| ★★ | Excellent; some wonderful qualities |
| ★ | A good place |
| (no stars) | Worth knowing about, if nearby |

&#9855; Appears after listings with wheelchair-accessible facilities.

**Price Range**  Prices for lodgings are based on high-season rates (off-season, rate changes vary but can be significantly less). Call ahead to verify, as all prices are subject to change.

$$$   Expensive (more than $80 for dinner for two, including tip; more than $120 for one night's lodgings for two)

$$   Moderate (between expensive and inexpensive)

$   Inexpensive (less than $35 for dinner for two, including tip; less than $70 for one night's lodgings for two)

**Phone Numbers**  Many area codes in Northern California are undergoing major changes. We have made every attempt to provide the most up-to-date area code information. Check the beginning of each chapter for additional information about changes in that region. If you have a problem reaching an establishment, call the operator.

**Email and Web Site Addresses**  With the understanding that more people are using email and the World Wide Web to access information and to plan trips, Best Places® has added email and Web site addresses of establishments, where available. Please note that the World Wide Web is a fluid and evolving medium, and that web pages are often "under construction" or, as with all time-sensitive information, may no longer be valid.

**Checks and Credit Cards**  Most establishments that accept checks also require a major credit card for identification. Credit cards are abbreviated in this book as follows: American Express (AE); Diners Club (DC); Discover (DIS); Master-Card (MC); Visa (V).

**Maps and Directions**  Each chapter in this book begins with two regional maps that show the general area being covered. Throughout the book, basic directions are provided with each entry. Whenever possible, call ahead to confirm hours and location.

**Bed and Breakfasts**  Many B&Bs have a two-night minimum-stay requirement during the peak season, and several do not welcome children. Ask about a B&B's policies before you make your reservation.

**Smoking**  Most establishments in California do not permit smoking inside, although some lodgings have rooms reserved for smokers. Call ahead to verify an establishment's smoking policy.

**Indexes**  All restaurants, lodgings, town names, and major tourist attractions are listed alphabetically at the back of the book. Restaurants in the San Francisco Bay Area are also indexed by location at the beginning of that chapter.

**Reader Reports**  At the end of the book is a report form. We receive hundreds of reports from readers suggesting new places or agreeing or disagreeing with our assessments. They greatly help in our evaluations. We encourage you to respond.

**Money-Back Guarantee**  Please see page 552.

# SAN FRANCISCO BAY AREA

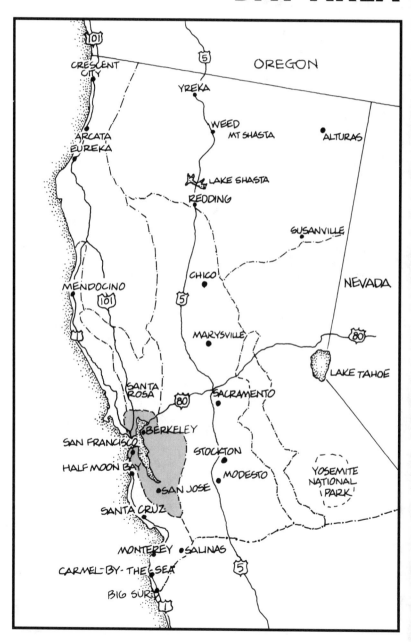

CRESCENT CITY

OREGON

YREKA

WEED
MT SHASTA

ALTURAS

ARCATA
EUREKA

LAKE SHASTA

REDDING

SUSANVILLE

MENDOCINO

CHICO

NEVADA

MARYSVILLE

LAKE TAHOE

SANTA ROSA

SACRAMENTO

BERKELEY

SAN FRANCISCO

STOCKTON

HALF MOON BAY

MODESTO

YOSEMITE NATIONAL PARK

SAN JOSE

SANTA CRUZ

MONTEREY    SALINAS

CARMEL-BY-THE-SEA

BIG SUR

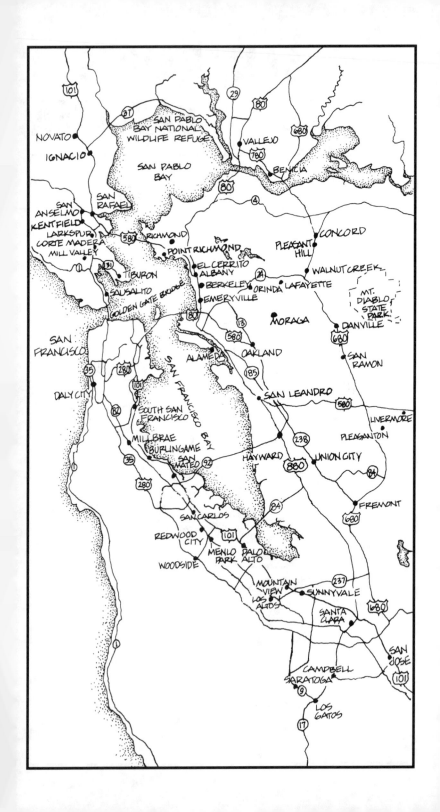

# San Francisco Bay Area Restaurant Index

## SAN FRANCISCO

**The Castro**
Mecca

**Chinatown**
House of Nanking

**Civic Center**
Jardinière
Zuni Cafe

**Cole Valley**
Eos Restaurant & Wine Bar

**The Embarcadero**
Boulevard
Il Fornaio
One Market

**Financial District**
Aqua
The Garden Court
Harbor Village Restaurant
Kyo-ya
Rubicon
Yank Sing

**Fisherman's Wharf**
Chez Michel

**The Haight**
Thep Phanom

**Japantown**
Cafe Kati

**The Marina**
Betelnut
Greens
PlumpJack Cafe

**The Mission**
Bruno's
Flying Saucer
La Taqueria
The Slanted Door
Woodward's Garden

**Nob Hill**
The Dining Room at the
Ritz-Carlton

**Noe Valley**
Firefly

**North Beach**
Cypress Club
Helmand
Rose Pistola

**Pacific Heights**
Pane e Vino

**Polk Gulch**
Acquerello
Swan Oyster Depot

**Potrero Hill**
42 Degrees

**The Richmond**
Alain Rondelli
Hong Kong Flower Lounge
Ton Kiang

**Russian Hill**
Antica Trattoria
Harris'
La Folie

**South of Market (SoMa)**
Bizou
Fringale
Hawthorne Lane
Infusion Bar & Restaurant
Yank Sing

**Union Square**
Campton Place
Farallon
Fleur de Lys
Masa's
Postrio
Scala's Bistro

## MARIN COUNTY

**Corte Madera**
Il Fornaio

**Kentfield**
Half Day Cafe

**Larkspur**
Lark Creek Inn
Left Bank

**Mill Valley**
Buckeye Roadhouse
El Paseo
Jennie Low's Chinese
Cuisine
Piazza D'Angelo

**Novato**
Hilltop Cafe
Jennie Low's Chinese
Cuisine

**San Anselmo**
Bubba's Diner
Creekside Bistro
Insalata's

**San Rafael**
Las Camelias
Panama Hotel
The Rice Table
Royal Thai

**Sausalito**
Mikayla
Sushi Ran

**Tiburon**
Guaymas
Tutto Mare

## EAST BAY

**Alameda**
Tied House Cafe and
Brewery

**Albany**
Britt-Marie's
Christopher's Nothing
Fancy Cafe

**Benicia**
The Union Hotel, Bar, and
Restaurant

**Berkeley**
Ajanta
Bette's Oceanview Diner
Café Fanny
Café Rouge
Cambodiana's
Chez Panisse
Fatapple's
Kirala
Lalime's
O Chamé
Panini
Picante Cocina Mexicana
Rivoli
Venezia

**Danville**
Blackhawk Grille
Bridges

**El Cerrito**
Fatapple's

## Emeryville
Bucci's
Hong Kong East Ocean
    Seafood Restaurant

## Lafayette
Kaffee Barbara
Lisa's Tea Treasures
Miraku
Tourelle Restaurant

## Livermore
Wente Vineyards
    Restaurant

## Oakland
Asmara Restaurant and Bar
Bay Wolf Restaurant
Caffe 817
Citron
Cuckoo's Nest
El Taco Zamorano
Flint's
Jade Villa
Mama's Royal Cafe
Nan Yang Rockridge
Oliveto Cafe and Restaurant
Pho Anh Dao
Pizza Rustica
Sabina India Cuisine
Soizic Bistro-Cafe
Spettro
Tsing Tao
Vi's Restaurant
Yoshi's
Zatis

## Orinda
Amforafino Caffe and Bar

## Pleasanton
Pleasanton Hotel
Tong's

## Point Richmond
Hidden City Cafe

## San Ramon
Bighorn Grill
Mudd's Restaurant

## Walnut Creek
Lark Creek Cafe
Prima

## PENINSULA/
## SOUTH BAY

## Burlingame
Ecco
Kuleto's
Tavern Grill

## Campbell
Chez Sovan Restaurant
Lisa's Tea Treasures

## Los Altos
Beauséjour
Chef Chu's

## Los Gatos
Café Marcella
Cafe Trio
I Gatti
Lisa's Tea Treasures
Los Gatos Brewing
    Company
Pigalle

## Menlo Park
Bistro La Luna
Carpaccio
Dal Baffo
Flea Street Café
Gombei Restaurant
Lisa's Tea Treasures
Vietnam Restaurant

## Millbrae
Hong Kong Flower Lounge

## Mountain View
Amber India Restaurant
Chez T. J.
Hangen
Michaels at Shoreline
Tied House Cafe and
    Brewery
Tony & Alba's Pizza and
    Italian Food

## Palo Alto
Beppo
Bistro Elan
Blue Chalk Cafe
Evvia
Higashi West
Il Fornaio
L'Amie Donia
MacArthur Park
Maddalena's Continental
    Restaurant
Osteria
Peninsula Fountain & Grill
Spago Palo Alto

## Redwood City
The Redwood Cafe & Spice
    Company
2030

## San Carlos
Creo La.

Kabul Afghan Cuisine
Ristorante Piacere

## San Jose
Agenda
Bella Mia
California Sushi and Grill
Chez Sovan Restaurant
Eight Forty North First
Emile's
Gombei Restaurant
Henry's World Famous
    Hi-Life
Il Fornaio
La Forêt French Restaurant
La Pastaia
La Taqueria
Orlo's
Paolo's
San Jose Tied House Cafe
    and Brewery
71 Saint Peter
Tony & Alba's Pizza and
    Italian Food

## San Mateo
Barley & Hopps
Bogie's at the Theatre
Buffalo Grill
Gibson
Lark Creek Cafe
Ristorante Capellini
Spiedo Ristorante
231 Ellsworth
Viognier

## Santa Clara
Birk's

## Saratoga
Bella Saratoga
Le Mouton Noir
Sent Soví

## South San Francisco
Pasta Moon

## Sunnyvale
Il Postale
Kabul Afghan Cuisine
The Palace

## Woodside
Buck's
John Bentley's Restaurant
The Village Pub

# San Francisco Bay Area

*A tour of San Francisco, followed by excursions to Marin County, the East Bay, the South Bay, and the Peninsula.*

## SAN FRANCISCO

San Franciscans know they are uniquely blessed. In no other city in the country is the meeting of land and sea so spectacular. The late afternoon sun flashes off the dark blue bay and lights up the orange towers of the Golden Gate Bridge, and the magnificent sails of boats and Windsurfers add color in brilliant flashes. Almost every evening the fog pours in from the Pacific, spilling over the towers of downtown like a white wave. Lovers of all persuasions kiss on street corners. Poets still scribble in coffee shops. No wonder this is one of the world's favorite cities.

Over the years, however, San Franciscans have begun to view this magnetism as something of a liability. Drawn by the city's fabled beauty, cuisine, art, and culture, newcomers from around the globe have poured into this hilly, 46-square-mile oasis. Housing prices have soared, forcing many middle-class families to move to distant suburbs. On bad days, it seems the city is entirely populated by frazzled workaholics, grumpy long-distance commuters, and legions of the homeless—but even on those days, most people are still smiling.

### THE ARTS

**TIX Bay Area** sells half-price tickets to many of San Francisco's dance, music, and theater events on the day of the performance only (tickets for Sunday and Monday events are sold on Saturday). You must purchase the tickets in person and pay in cash or with travelers' checks. Advance full-price tickets are sold here, too, and may be purchased with Visa, MasterCard, or cash; call (415)433-7827 for recorded information (which half-price tickets are available is not announced on the phone). TIX Bay Area is located at 251 Stockton Street, between Post and Geary Streets on the east side of Union Square. Tickets to most dance and theater events are also sold by phone through the **City Box Office**, (415)392-4400, and **BASS Ticketmaster**, (510)762-2277.

**Dance** The internationally renowned **San Francisco Ballet**, led by artistic director Helgi Tomasson, kicks off its season in mid-December with the classic *Nutcracker*, and dances to more

## San Francisco

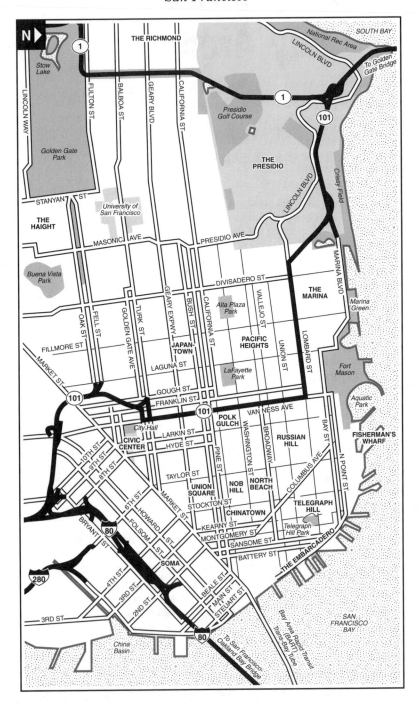

contemporary pieces beginning in February; performances are held at the War Memorial Opera House, 301 Van Ness Avenue at Grove Street, (415)703-9400. Ethnic dance troupes abound in the Bay Area, and they join together in June for the **San Francisco Ethnic Dance Festival**; for more information, call (415)474-3914. For modern and contemporary performances, see the **ODC/San Francisco** dance troupe, (415)863-6606, and for contemporary ballet, **Lines** is a local favorite and often performs at Yerba Buena Gardens' Center for the Arts, 701 Mission Street at Third Street, (415)863-3040, www.pav.org/lines. Modern dance recitals also are frequently held at **Theater Artaud**, 450 Florida Street at 17th Street, (415)621-7797.

**Film** The **San Francisco International Film Festival** attracts film fanatics for a fortnight every spring; screenings are held at various venues in San Francisco, Berkeley, and Marin County, (415)931-3456. Another popular event is the **San Francisco International Lesbian and Gay Film Festival**, which takes place in June, (415)703-8650. Movie buffs also flock to **Spike and Mike's Festival of Animation**, held every spring (generally in April) at various venues including the Palace of Fine Arts at 3601 Lyon Street, between Jefferson and Bay Streets; call the festival's headquarters in San Diego at (619)459-8707 for more details. For rare revivals and premieres, check out the palatial **Castro Theatre**, a flamboyant Spanish baroque-style movie palace designed by Timothy Pflueger in 1923, 429 Castro Street off Market Street, (415)621-6120; the funky (but finely programmed) **Roxie Cinema**, 3117 16th Street at Valencia Street, (415)863-1087; and the homey **Red Vic Movie House**, 1727 Haight Street, between Cole and Schrader Streets, (415)668-3994.

**Music** The world-class **San Francisco Opera**, led by Lotfi Mansouri, alternates warhorses with rarities from September through January at the beautiful War Memorial Opera House, which was modeled on Garnier's Paris Opera and first opened on October 15, 1932, with a production of Puccini's *Tosca*. Sixty-five years later, on September 5, 1997, the same Puccini production launched the reopening of this beloved Beaux Arts beauty after an 18-month, $86.5 million renovation that included seismic retrofitting, regilding the 530 rosettes on the lobby's barrel-vaulted ceiling, and replacing the stage curtain with an elaborate 3,000-pound gold silk organza curtain. Subscribers grab up most of the newly cushioned seats, but fans with smaller bankrolls can stand in line early on performance mornings to buy one of the 200 standing-room tickets, which go on sale at 10am (50 of these inexpensive tickets are also sold two hours before the performance); 301 Van Ness Avenue at Grove Street, (415)864-3330 (box office) or (415)861-4008 (general information). The **San Francisco Symphony** performs from September through July at the modern Louise M. Davies Symphony Hall, a gorgeous $38 million concert hall with a wraparound glass facade; 201 Van Ness Avenue at

Grove Street, (415)431-5400. Other classical groups include **The Women's Philharmonic**, (415)437-0123, and the **San Francisco Early Music Society**, (510)528-1725.

On summer Sundays, families and couples tote blankets and picnic baskets to free outdoor performances (everything from jazz to opera and ballet) at the pretty **Stern Grove**; it's located at Sloat Boulevard and 19th Avenue, (415)252-6252. The **San Francisco Jazz Festival**, one of the largest in the country, toots its horn every fall with concerts, dances, films, and lectures; call (415)788-7353, or check the Web site at www.sfjazzfest.org. (For the scoop on the city's best nightclub performances, see Nightlife, below.)

**Theater and Comedy** American Conservatory Theater (ACT), the city's best-known theater company, presents solid productions of new works and classics under the leadership of Carey Perloff from late September to mid-June in the Geary Theater, 415 Geary Street, (415)749-2ACT or www.act-sfbay.org. Broadway shows on tour are performed at the **Golden Gate**, **Curran**, and **Orpheum Theaters**; call (415)551-2000 for the current lineup and ticket information. For off-Broadway acts, contact the **Theatre on the Square**, 450 Post Street, between Powell and Mason Streets, (415)433-9500, and **Marines Memorial Theatre**, 609 Sutter Street at Mason Street, (415)771-6900.

Among the small local theater companies offering wonderful performances are the **Lorraine Hansberry Theatre**, 620 Sutter Street at Mason Street, (415)474-8800 or (415)288-0320; the **Lamplighters Music Theater**, which performs primarily Gilbert & Sullivan comic operas at the Lindland Theatre, Riordan High School, 175 Phelan Avenue near Ocean Avenue, (415)227-4797; and the **Magic Theatre**, Fort Mason Center, Building D, third floor, off Marina Boulevard at Buchanan Street, (415)441-8822. **Theatre Rhinoceros** specializes in gay and lesbian drama; 2926 16th Street at South Van Ness Avenue, (415)861-5079. Summer and early autumn bring free outdoor performances by America's oldest political musical-comedy theater group, the Tony award–winning **San Francisco Mime Troupe**, at various venues, (415)285-1717. The more serious **Shakespeare in the Park** theater group also performs for free in the summer in Golden Gate Park at Liberty Tree Meadow, off John F. Kennedy Drive just west of the Conservatory of Flowers, (415)422-2221. **Beach Blanket Babylon**, the longest-running musical revue in the world, is a cabaret-style show full of silly jokes that's famous for its wild costumes and humongous hats. It remains a favorite of residents and visitors alike, so be sure to reserve seats several weeks in advance; Club Fugazi, 678 Green Street near Powell Street, (415)421-4222.

San Francisco has launched many comedians' careers, including the nation's reigning king and queen of comedy, Robin

Williams and Whoopi Goldberg. See the latest talents at the **Punchline**, 444 Battery Street, second floor, between Clay and Washington Streets, (415)397-7573, and **Cobb's Comedy Club**, in The Cannery, 2801 Leavenworth Street, Building S, courtyard entrance at Beach Street, (415)928-4320.

**Visual Arts** The **San Francisco Museum of Modern Art (SFMOMA)**, now housed in a dramatic new modernist building designed by internationally acclaimed Swiss architect Mario Botta, offers more than 17,000 works of art, including gems by Picasso, Matisse, O'Keeffe, Rivera, Pollock, Warhol, Klee, De Forest, and Lichtenstein, to name just a few; 151 Third Street, between Mission and Howard Streets, (415)357-4000. The **M. H. de Young Memorial Museum** showcases American art from colonial times to the 20th century. It used to host many traveling international exhibits, but the popular museum, damaged by the 1989 earthquake, was declared unsafe for hosting those big shows by the federal government in 1997. De Young supporters are searching for a new home for the museum, and in the meantime all of its upcoming international exhibitions will be transferred to the California Palace of the Legion of Honor (see below); until further notice, the de Young is located in Golden Gate Park, off John F. Kennedy Drive, (415)863-3330. On the west side of the de Young is the **Asian Art Museum**, the largest museum in the Western world devoted exclusively to Asian art, with many masterpieces from the Avery Brundage collection (note: the museum will move to the former San Francisco Main Library building in the Civic Center in the year 2001), (415)668-8921.

The **California Palace of the Legion of Honor**, a three-quarter-scale replica of Paris' grand Palais de La Légion d'Honneur, reopened on November 11, 1997, after three years of extensive renovation and seismic work. The dazzling museum features European paintings (including works by Monet, Rubens, and Rembrandt), sculptures (more than 70 works by Rodin are on display), and decorative art. It also holds ancient art, the Achenbach Foundation collection of works on paper, plus traveling international shows; the museum is in Lincoln Park near 34th Avenue and Clement Street, (415)863-3330 or (415)750-3600. The city has several terrific folk-art museums, most notably the **Mexican Museum**, the first in the United States to feature Mexican and Chicano art; it's located at Fort Mason Center, in Building D, off Marina Boulevard at Buchanan Street (note: the museum will move to a new building in Yerba Buena Gardens—near SFMOMA—in the year 2000), (415)441-0404. Photography buffs should not miss the **Ansel Adams Center for Photography**, where the work of the master himself, Imogen Cunningham, Dorothea Lange, and many other notables is showcased in five exhibition galleries; 250 Fourth Street, between Howard and Folsom Streets, (415)495-7000.

Fantastic **murals** decorate many public spaces in the city, particularly in the **Mission District**, the city's vibrant, primarily Hispanic neighborhood; for maps outlining self-guided walks or for very good two-hour guided tours, contact the **Precita Eyes Mural Arts Center**, 348 Precita Avenue at Folsom Street, (415)285-2287. If you don't have time for a tour, at least stroll down narrow **Balmy Alley** (near Harrison and 25th Streets), which is lined with about 30 incredibly colorful murals and is the birthplace of mural painting in San Francisco. Galleries for established San Francisco artists are located primarily on lower Grant Avenue and near Union Square; up-and-coming artists tend to exhibit in SoMa (the South of Market Street area). For current art and gallery listings, check the *San Francisco Chronicle's* "Datebook" (more commonly known as the "pink section") in the Sunday paper. San Francisco also has several superb science museums; see Major Attractions, below.

## MAJOR ATTRACTIONS

San Francisco, like Paris, is a great walking town, and one of the city's most spectacular and scenic walks is along the **Golden Gate Promenade**, a 4-mile stretch from **Aquatic Park** in front of The Cannery through the beautiful **Marina Green** and **Crissy Field** to the historic **Fort Point**, a four-level fortification built in 1861 that's nestled under the south end of the Golden Gate Bridge. (If you're not too winded at this point, continue your tour with a walk across the blustery—and usually chilly—bridge for a breathtaking view of the Bay Area and the Pacific.) Another gorgeous waterfront stroll follows the Embarcadero north from Market Street, past the landmark **Ferry Building** to the handsome pier opposite Washington Street, where you'll get a good look at **Treasure Island** and the yachts and freighters sailing beneath the San Francisco–Oakland Bay Bridge. Heartier souls should continue walking up the Embarcadero to touristy **Pier 39** to see the hundreds of silly **sea lions** playing, barking, and basking in the sun on the west side of the pier.

The third-most-visited amusement attraction in the nation, **Pier 39** is packed with kitschy shops and overpriced, touristy restaurants, but it boasts beautiful views of Angel Island, Alcatraz, and the bay, and has great entertainment for kids with its **Venetian Carousel**, jugglers, mimes, the "motion theater" Turbo Ride, the fun (but slightly overrated and expensive) **Underwater World** aquarium, and an arcade stocked with every gizmo and quarter-sucking machine the young-at-heart could dream of. Once you've had your fill of the tourist-packed pier, hop aboard a ferry for the surprisingly fascinating audiocassette tour of **Alcatraz** (make advance reservations), a **San Francisco Bay cruise**, or a scenic trip to the pretty little towns across the bay, **Sausalito** and **Tiburon**; for tour information and ferry schedules, call the Blue & Gold Fleet at Piers 39 through 41, (415)705-5444 or (415)773-1188 (recordings), or (415)705-5555 (reservations).

Just a short jaunt west of Pier 39 are the world-famous **Fisherman's Wharf**, **The Cannery**, and **Ghirardelli Square**. They're always mobbed with tourists, but they offer some interesting shops and are riddled with witty, wisecracking, watch-me-pull-a-rabbit-out-of-my-shoe street entertainers. And from mid-November through June, this is also where you'll see the city's highly touted (and delicious) **Dungeness crabs** boiling in large metal pots on the sidewalks lining the wharf. All three attractions are located side by side on the waterfront at the north end of the Embarcadero and next to Aquatic Park; visit their Web site at www.citysearch.com/sfo/fishermanswharf.

While tourists flock to Fisherman's Wharf and Pier 39, locals often head in the other direction to the extraordinary **California Academy of Sciences**, where under one roof you'll find the **Natural History Museum**, **Morrison Planetarium**, the **Laserium**, and the superb **Steinhart Aquarium**, offering one of the most diverse collections of aquatic life in the world—about 14,500 specimens, including seals, dolphins, and alligators; the science complex is located in Golden Gate Park, off Middle Drive East, between John F. Kennedy and Martin Luther King Jr. Drives, (415)750-7145. Another San Francisco favorite is the **Exploratorium**, a unique interactive museum that brings scientific concepts to vivid life—it's a blast at any age. The Exploratorium's marvelous **Tactile Dome**, where visitors must feel their way through a maze of hurdles in total darkness, requires reservations and a certain amount of nerve. The Exploratorium is housed within the magnificent **Palace of Fine Arts**, designed by renowned architect Bernard Maybeck for the 1915 Panama-Pacific International Exposition. Surrounded by a natural lagoon, the Palace is an ideal spot for a picnic and for tossing your leftovers to grateful swans, seagulls, and pigeons; 3601 Lyon Street, between Jefferson and Bay Streets near the on-ramp to the Golden Gate Bridge, (415)561-0360 (Exploratorium), (415)561-0362 (Tactile Dome reservations).

In the southwest corner of the city, near the ocean and Lake Merced, is the popular **San Francisco Zoo**. Don't miss the famed Primate Discovery Center, where several species of apes and monkeys live in glass-walled condos. The zoo also has rare Sumatran and Siberian tigers, African lions (visit during their mealtimes), a children's petting zoo, and even an insect zoo; 45th Avenue and Sloat Boulevard, (415)753-7061. On the other side of the Golden Gate Bridge in Sausalito is the **Bay Area Discovery Museum**, a wonderland of hands-on science, art, and multimedia exhibits designed for kids from toddlers on up; head north across the bridge, exit at Alexander Avenue, and follow the signs to East Fort Baker and the museum, (415)289-7268.

For a sweeping view of the Pacific Ocean, visit the historic **Cliff House**, (415)386-3330, and sip a cocktail at a windowside table, then climb around the neighboring ruins of the once spectacular **Sutro Baths**; 1090 Point Lobos Avenue at the end of Geary Boulevard.

To get an up-close and personal look at some of the city's multi-ethnic neighborhoods and architectural masterpieces, strap on your heavy-duty walking shoes and hike around the **Russian Hill** neighborhood, starting at the top of the crookedest street in the world, **Lombard Street** (at Hyde Street). Wind your way down Lombard's multiple, flower-lined curves and continue east until Lombard intersects with Columbus Avenue, then turn right and stay on Columbus for a tour of charming **North Beach**—a predominantly Italian and Chinese neighborhood where residents practice tai chi in **Washington Square** on weekend mornings or sip espresso as they peruse Proust or the *Bay Guardian's* really racy personal ads (guaranteed to make you blush—or send you running for the nearest pay phone). You can extend this tour by turning right off of Columbus onto Grant Avenue, which will take you through the heart of the ever-bustling and fascinating **Chinatown**—the only part of the city where vendors sell live, 3-foot-long slippery eels next to X-rated fortune cookies and herbs meant to cure whatever ails you.

If you're in need of an aerobic workout, take a different tour: instead of turning off Lombard onto Columbus, keep following Lombard Street east all the way up to **Coit Tower** on the top of **Telegraph Hill**, then reward yourself for making the steep ascent with a trip (*gasp, gasp*) in an elevator to the top of the tower for a panoramic view of the Bay Area; (415)362-0808. Too worried about getting lost on your self-guided walking tour? Then call **City Guides**, which offers numerous guided tours through San Francisco year-round—and they're free to boot; phone (415)557-4266 for details.

▼
**San Francisco**
*Major
Attractions*
▲

If you'd rather ride than walk the hills of San Francisco, an outside perch on one of the city's famed **cable cars** is always a kick. The three cable car routes are named after the streets on which they run (you can take them in either direction) and operate daily from 6:30am to 12:30am, rain or shine. The Powell-Mason line starts at Powell and Market Streets and terminates at Bay Street near Fisherman's Wharf; the Powell-Hyde line also begins at Powell and Market Streets, but ends at Victorian Park near Aquatic Park and the bay, making it the most scenic route; and the California line runs from California and Market Streets through Chinatown to Van Ness Avenue, the widest street in the city. Expect very long lines during peak travel times, especially when the weather is warm. For more information on the cable cars call the Visitor Information Center at (415)391-2000 or MUNI at (415)673-6864.

### ADDITIONAL ATTRACTIONS

**Bars** San Franciscans need something to cut the chill of those long foggy nights, so many head to North Beach, which has more than its fair share of popular watering holes, including **Little City**, a great spot for flirting over drinks and plates of antipasti; 673

Union Street at Powell Street, near Washington Square, (415)434-2900. There's also the pleasant (and semi-secret) **Specs**, an old Beat Generation hangout located on tiny Saroyan Alley off Columbus Avenue, south of Broadway, (415)421-4112; the charming but rough-around-the-edges **Savoy Tivoli**, 1434 Grant Avenue, between Union and Green Streets, (415)362-7023; the atmospheric and beatnik-loving **Vesuvio**, 255 Columbus Avenue just south of Broadway, (415)362-3370; and **Tosca Cafe**, where locals hang out (and celebs hide in the back room) to sip the house specialty: coffeeless cappuccinos made with brandy, milk, and chocolate, 242 Columbus Avenue, between Pacific Avenue and Broadway, (415)391-1244.

When the fog burns off and the weather heats up, grab a chair on the patio of **Cafe Flore** in the Castro District and order a glass of white wine or a latte; 2298 Market Street at Noe Street, (415)621-8579. Or get the full array of spirits on the outdoor decks of such funky local favorites as **The Ramp**, 855 China Basin Street off Third Street, (415)621-2378, and **Pier 23**, on the Embarcadero between Broadway and Bay Street, (415)362-5125. For a more romantic retreat, make your toasts at the **Redwood Room** in the Clift Hotel (see review under Lodgings), 495 Geary Street at Taylor Street, (415)775-4700; the lounge of the **Carnelian Room** restaurant (perched at the top of the 52-story Bank of America skyscraper, it offers a dizzying view of the city when the sky is clear), 555 California Street, between Kearny and Montgomery Streets, (415)433-7500; the plush **Crown Room** in the Fairmont Hotel, which boasts a great panoramic view, 950 Mason Street at California Street, 24th floor, (415)772-5131; the scenic glass-walled **Top of the Mark** lounge in the Mark Hopkins Hotel, 999 California Street at Mason Street, (415)392-3434; or **The Equinox**, the unique revolving rooftop lounge and restaurant at the Hyatt Regency that slowly spins in a circle, giving patrons a 360-degree view of the city, 5 Embarcadero Center, (415)788-1234.

Union Square's best bustling bars are at **Kuleto's** restaurant, 221 Powell Street, between Geary and O'Farrell Streets, (415)397-7720, and the **Compass Rose** on the first floor of the Westin St. Francis Hotel, 335 Powell Street, between Post and Geary Streets, (415)774-0233 or (415)397-7000. For the best Irish coffee in town, the **Buena Vista** near Ghirardelli Square takes top honors, 2765 Hyde Street at the corner of Beach Street, (415)474-5044.

**Nightlife** Great clubs abound in San Francisco, the city that never seems to sleep. Most of San Francisco's clubs offer an ever-changing lineup of bands or recorded music, so call ahead for up-to-date recorded listings at each venue. The **Be-At Line** recorded hotline will also tell you where you can find the night's hot musical acts: (415)626-4087. Locals tend to pick up a copy of the free *San Francisco Bay Guardian* weekly newspaper (available at cafes and most major street corners) for the straight scoop on the city's wild and ever-changing club scene.

For live blues, jazz, and rock, **Slim's** (co-owned by Boz Scaggs) can't be beat; 333 11th Street, between Folsom and Harrison Streets, (415)522-0333. The famous **Fillmore** always books top talents, 1805 Geary Boulevard at Fillmore Street, (415)346-6000, and **Bruno's** is boffo, 2389 Mission Street, between 19th and 20th Streets, (415)550-7455. For hip-hop, rock, purple hair, and nipple rings, venture into the **DNA Lounge**, 375 11th Street at Harrison Street, (415)626-1409. If you wanna dance among the masses, go to **Club 1015**, 1015 Folsom Street at Sixth Street, (415)431-1200. For a mix of live music, the trendy set kicks up its heels at the very smoky **Cafe du Nord**, 2170 Market Street, between Church and Sanchez Streets, (415)861-5016; **Harry Denton's**, in the Harbor Court Hotel, 161 Steuart Street, between Mission and Howard Streets, (415)882-1333; **Johnny Love's**, 1500 Broadway at Polk Street, (415)931-6053; and the rowdy **Last Day Saloon**, 406 Clement Street, between Fifth and Sixth Avenues, (415)387-6343. If you want to shake, rattle, and roll with the high-fashion crowd, put on your best dancin' shoes and go to **Harry Denton's Starlight Room** at the top of the Sir Francis Drake hotel, where you can boogie to a live band while admiring an incredible view of the city; 450 Powell Street, between Sutter and Post Streets, (415)395-8595. Or try the sophisticated tri-level **Essex Supper Club**, which offers dance tunes, live jazz and R&B, and a cigar lounge; 847 Montgomery Street, between Jackson and Pacific Streets, (415)397-5969.

To hear the sounds of the city's new bands, stroll **Haight Street**. Numerous venues line both sides of this famous strip, still populated by drugged youth, the homeless, and various eccentrics. The ornate **Great American Music Hall** hosts hundreds of concerts a year, ranging from Motown, rock, and jazz bands to bluegrass, folk, and zydeco; 859 O'Farrell Street, between Polk and Larkin Streets, (415)885-0750. **Paradise Lounge** offers a stellar lineup of all kinds of music at 11th and Folsom Streets, (415)861-6906. For a blast of the blues, go to the dimly lit **Blues** club, 2125 Lombard Street at Fillmore Street, (415)771-2583, or the candlelit **Biscuits & Blues**, 401 Mason Street at Geary Street, (415)292-2583. Jumpin' jazz joints include **Jazz at Pearl's**, 256 Columbus Avenue just north of Broadway, (415)291-8255, and **Rasselas**, 2801 California Street at Divisadero Street, (415)567-5010.

**Festivals** Every winter, the two-week-long **Chinese New Year** celebration culminates explosively with an electrifying parade that winds through downtown, Union Square, and Chinatown; (415)982-3071 or (415)982-3000. In the summer and spring, **street fairs** that typify their neighborhoods pop up (from upscale Union Street to the still-hairy Haight). Japantown launches its **Cherry Blossom Festival** with a parade in April; the Mission District draws crowds with its **Cinco de Mayo Parade**; and the **San Francisco Lesbian, Gay, Bisexual, Transgender Pride**

Celebration Parade, (415)864-3733, attracts thousands of revelers on the last weekend of June.

All heads turn skyward when the U.S. Navy flaunts its amazing acrobatic flight team—the **Blue Angels**—during **Fleet Week Celebration** in early October. Bands, boat rides, and a parade of ships and submarines on the bay round out the festivities; held near Fisherman's Wharf and Pier 39, (415)705-5500 or (888)358-9335.

**Parks and Beaches** Golden Gate Park, encompassing 1,017 acres of beautiful, lush grounds dotted with magnificent museums, lakes, and ponds, is a masterpiece of park design. For a good introduction to the park's attractions, join one of the **free guided walking tours** held every weekend from May through October; call the Friends of Recreation and Parks for more information at (415)263-0991 or (415)750-5105. Park highlights include the **Strybing Arboretum and Botanical Gardens**, home to 7,500 plant and tree varieties; near Ninth Avenue and Lincoln Way, (415)661-1316. Right next door is the lovely **Japanese Tea Garden**, the oldest Japanese-style park in the United States, which attracts crowds, particularly when the cherry blossoms and azaleas bloom in late March and April (pssst . . . to avoid the hordes, visit when it's raining). Nearby is the spectacular **Conservatory of Flowers**, an 1879 Victorian fairyland hothouse that was full of tropical flora until massive storms destroyed most of this glass-paneled landmark in 1995. It's still an architectural beauty worth admiring from the outside, but it is closed until enough money can be acquired to pay the lofty repair bill; it's on John F. Kennedy Drive near Conservatory Drive, (415)641-7978. West of the Conservatory is lovely **Stow Lake**, where you can rent rowboats, paddleboats, and electric boats and circle the 430-foot-high artificial island known as **Strawberry Hill**, the highest peak in the park. Highlights include the hill's waterfall and Chinese moon-watching pavilion as well as the numerous turtles and ducks that live on the serene lake; call (415)752-0347 for boat rental information. If you have youngsters in tow, don't skip the **Children's Playground**, which has a dazzling, restored Golden Age 1912 carousel (the oldest one in a public park) that's guaranteed to make every child's heart go pitter-patter; located at the intersection of Martin Luther King Jr. and Kezar Drives. Every Sunday, Golden Gate Park's main drag is closed to auto traffic so skaters and joggers can let loose on the tree-lined street. **Skate rentals** are readily available on Fulton Street and on Haight Street.

The city's entire northwest corner is part of the **Golden Gate National Recreation Area (GGNRA)**, the largest urban park in the world. Take a hike along its gorgeous wildflower-laced **Coastal Trail**, which hugs the headlands for more than 10 miles and offers fantastic views of the bay; start at Point Lobos (at the end of Point Lobos Avenue, near the Sutro Baths) and wind your way to the Golden Gate Bridge. **The Presidio**, a lush 1,480-acre former military base, recently became part of the GGNRA and

San Francisco

*Additional Attractions*

offers superb views to hikers (and drivers), as well as historic buildings, a scenic golf course, walking and biking tours, and a national cemetery. Also part of the GGNRA are **Crissy Field**, a fabulous windsurfing spot, and the **Marina Green**, prime kite-flying and jogging territory; both are located off Marina Boulevard, near the on-ramp to the Golden Gate Bridge. For maps and more details on the GGNRA, call the National Park Information Center at (415)556-0560.

In the heart of the city, across from the Museum of Modern Art, is **Yerba Buena Gardens**, San Francisco's new 5-acre urban park featuring a walk-through waterfall leading to a beautiful memorial for Martin Luther King Jr., a sculpture garden, and terrace cafes. In late 1998, look for the new Yerba Buena **Children's Center** with a carousel, ice-skating rink, bowling alley, technology and arts center, and a children's garden, as well as **Sony's Metreon Entertainment Complex**, featuring a 15-screen cinema, an IMAX theater, and a children's play center designed by author/illustrator Maurice Sendak. Tours of Yerba Buena Gardens, located at Mission and Third Streets across from the Moscone Convention Center, are available by appointment for a nominal fee; for more details call (415)541-0312 or send email to YBAlliance@aol.com.

Riptide-ridden and blustery **Ocean Beach** is a haven for seasoned surfers as well as families, dog-walkers, joggers, and lovers who enjoy the long, sandy beach located off the Great Highway. On warm days, sun worshippers prefer to bask at **Baker Beach** while gazing at the stupendous view of the Golden Gate (as at most of the city's beaches, however, swimming is unsafe here). The east side of the beach is a popular gay hangout, where sunbathers bare all; take 25th Avenue west to the end, bear right, then look for signs to Baker Beach. Other scenic spots include **Glen Canyon Park**, which has a playground, on Bosworth Street and O'Shaughnessy Boulevard; the lush **Stern Grove**, on Sloat Boulevard at 19th Avenue; and **Lake Merced**, where you can rent a rowboat, canoe, or paddleboat and fish for trout, located off Harding Road between Highway 35 and Sloat Boulevard, near the zoo. Call (415)753-1101 for information on Lake Merced boat rentals.

**Shops and Bookstores**  The famous and oh-so-trendy **Union Square** area and the nearby **San Francisco Shopping Centre** at Market and Fifth Streets, (415)495-5656, together boast many major department stores (including Macy's, Nordstrom, and Neiman Marcus) and more specialty shops than Imelda Marcos has shoes. A short walk away is the chichi **Crocker Galleria**, a 70-foot-high glass-domed trilevel shopping mall (with Ralph Lauren, Versace, and similar boutiques), which was modeled after Milan's 1867 Galleria Vittoria Emmanuelle; it's bounded by Post, Kearny, Sutter, and Montgomery Streets. The vast **Embarcadero Center** is a sophisticated triple-level, open-air neo-mall well worth a spree; it's located between Clay, Sacramento, Battery, and Drumm Streets.

Many famed fashion firms have factory outlets south of Market Street. Among them are **Esprit**, 499 Illinois Street off 16th Street, (415)957-2500, and **Jessica McClintock/Gunne Sax**, 35 Stanford Street off Townsend Street, (415)495-3326. Outdoor enthusiasts should check out **The North Face** outlet for skiwear, sweaters, sleeping bags, and other high-quality outdoor gear; 1325 Howard Street, between Ninth and Tenth Streets, (415)626-6444.

Stroll down **Sacramento Street** (between Lyon and Locust Streets) for elegant clothing and furnishings. For vintage, cutting-edge, and folksy fashions and crafts, shop on **24th Street** (between Castro and Church Streets), **Castro Street** (between Market and 19th Streets), **Fillmore Street** (between Jackson and Sutter Streets), **Haight Street** (between Masonic Avenue and Schrader Street), and **Union Street** (between Gough and Steiner Streets). The 5-acre **Japan Center** houses several shops selling Japanese crafts, housewares, and books, with numerous sushi bars sandwiched in between; on Post Street, between Laguna and Fillmore Streets, (415)922-6776.

Cosmopolitan cooks can stock up on Asian foodstuffs in **Chinatown** along Stockton Street (between California Street and Broadway) or in **New Chinatown** on Clement Street (between Arguello Boulevard and 10th Avenue, and 18th and 25th Avenues). Shops along Columbus Avenue (between Broadway and Bay Street) in the **North Beach** district sell Italian treats, while **The Mission** district's stores offer Latin specialties on 24th Street (between Mission Street and Potrero Avenue).

Good bookstores include **City Lights**, still Beat after all these years, 261 Columbus Avenue at Broadway, (415)362-8193; **A Clean Well-Lighted Place for Books**, 601 Van Ness Avenue, in Opera Plaza between Golden Gate Avenue and Turk Street, (415)441-6670; **Stacey's Bookstore**, 581 Market Street at Second Street, (415)421-4687; the massive **Borders Books & Music**, 400 Post Street at Powell Street in Union Square, (415)399-1633; and **Green Apple**, 506 Clement Street at Sixth Avenue, (415)387-2272. Not-to-be-missed specialty bookstores include **William K. Stout Architectural Books**, 804 Montgomery Street at Jackson Street, (415)391-6757; **Rand McNally Map & Travel Store**, 595 Market Street at Second Street, (415)777-3131; and **Thomas Bros. Maps and Books** (open weekdays only), 550 Jackson Street at Columbus Avenue, (415)981-7520 or (800)969-3072.

**Sports** Bay Area sports buffs are justly proud of their champion **San Francisco 49ers** football team, which plays home games at **3Com Park** (previously named Candlestick Park, and still called "The Stick" by Bay Area residents); for 49ers ticket info (don't get your hopes up—they're hard to come by), call (415)468-2249.

The **San Francisco Giants** take over The Stick during baseball season until the year 2000, when the construction of their new state-of-the-art **Pac Bell Park** stadium in China Basin is expected to be completed; call (415)467-8000 for more details on the Giants. The **San Francisco Marathon** is usually run in July, but if you'd rather race against two-legged Brillo boxes, centipedes, Snow White and the Seven Dwarfs, and a Whitney Houston clone in drag, sign up for the wild and wacky 7.5-mile **Bay to Breakers race and walk** held in mid-May; call (415)777-7770, ext. 4. (Fans of the **Oakland A's** and the **Golden State Warriors** should turn to the Oakland section in the following pages.)

## GENERAL INFORMATION

**Transportation** Parking in San Francisco can be an ordeal; many neighborhoods limit nonresidents to only 2 hours, and most downtown meters have a maddening maximum time limit of 30 minutes—about the time it takes to get change for the meter. To make things even more frustrating (and to augment the city's coffers), traffic cops are quick, ruthless, and in abundance. If you see a tow-away warning, take it seriously. Public parking garages abound, and if you look hard enough (or ask a local driver), you can find some garages or park-and-pay lots that don't charge Manhattan rates. Major hotels have taxi stands; otherwise, telephone for a cab, since taxis usually only cruise along the most populated streets.

Public transportation reaches every neighborhood, but grows sparse after midnight. The **San Francisco Municipal Railway (MUNI)**—aptly nicknamed the "Muniserable Railway" by the late *San Francisco Chronicle* columnist Herb Caen—includes buses, overground/underground streetcars, and cable cars. Exact change is required ($1 bills are okay), and free transfers (except for cable cars) grant two more rides within the next 1½ to 2 hours (be sure to ask for a transfer as soon as you board the bus). Short-term (one-, three-, and seven-day) and monthly MUNI passes—allowing unlimited rides—are available at the Visitor Information Center (see below) and at City Hall during weekday business hours; call (415)673-6864 for bus route and ticket information. (For information on **cable cars**, see Major Attractions, above.)

**Bay Area Rapid Transit (BART)** is a clean, reliable, high-speed underground commuter train (similar to a subway) that runs through the southeastern side of the city, with routes to Daly City and the East Bay, including Berkeley and Oakland; for schedule and ticket information, call (650)992-2278. If you need transportation to or from the **San Francisco International Airport (SFO)**, reserve a seat with one of the fast, reliable **shuttle services**, such as SuperShuttle, (415)558-8500, and Quake City, (415)255-4899. (A $1.2 billion extension of a BART train line to the airport is currently under construction, but it won't be in service until late 2001.) Be sure to allow plenty of time to arrive at the airport, which is undergoing a $2.4 billion facelift and expansion until early in the next century; delays in traffic are commonplace due to the extensive construction.

**Weather**  Years of propaganda about sunny California have left millions of tourists freezing in the City by the Bay. Although San Francisco's weather is usually mild and temperatures don't change drastically throughout the year (they rarely rise above 70°F or fall below 40°F), it's seldom warm enough to go without a coat or a sweater, especially at night. Spring and fall months are warmest. The summer is usually foggy, except at midday; locals beat the summer morning chills by dressing in layers.

**Visitor Information**  For more details on San Francisco sites and attractions, visit the tremendously helpful staff at the **Visitor Information Center** (open seven days a week, Monday through Friday 9am to 5pm, Saturday and Sunday 9am to 3pm) on the lower level of Hallidie Plaza, at Market and Powell Streets (near Union Square), or call them at (415)391-2000. For a 24-hour recording of the city's current events and activities, call (415)391-2001. You can also get an information packet via mail by sending a check for $3 to San Francisco Convention & Visitors Bureau Information Center, PO Box 429097, San Francisco, CA 94142-9097. To receive free info by fax 24 hours a day, call (800)220-5747. Be sure to inquire about the terrific discount passes to more than 40 of San Francisco's cultural organizations—from museums and symphonies to ballet and theater.

## RESTAURANTS

**Fleur de Lys** ★★★★  Fleur de Lys is definitely a Grand Occasion restaurant, with fantastic food, formal service, breathtaking decor, and a superb wine list. Trained by such French superstars as Paul Bocuse and Roger Vergé, wunderkind chef and co-owner Hubert Keller displays a formidable technique—beautifully prepared ingredients accompanied by surprising garnishes and subtle sauces—and many of his contemporary French dishes are near-miracles. Recent standouts include the terrine of Hudson Valley foie gras in a fresh herb and black pepper gelée with brioche, fresh Atlantic salmon baked in a tender corn pancake topped with Imperial caviar and a watercress sauce, marinated loin of venison with a mustard seed sabayon, and his five-course vegetarian feast, which prompted a flurry of favorable press when it debuted several years ago. Critics sometimes sniff that individual dishes may be too complex, portions may be too small, and prices always loom large, but these are small dents in Fleur de Lys's mighty armor.

The restaurant's decor matches the splendor of its food step for step: the romantic dining area is draped in a luxurious tentlike fashion with 700 yards of rich, red-and-gold hand-painted floral fabrics, and in the center of the room sits a spectacular crown of fresh flowers on a pedestal. Mirrored walls double this visual spectacle while simultaneously allowing you to admire yourself and your glitteringly attired companion. Fleur de Lys isn't always crowded, but reservations are required; this is the sort of establishment that doesn't want to guess who's coming to dinner. ■ *777 Sutter St (between Taylor and Jones Sts), San Francisco; (415)673-7779; $$$; full bar; AE, DC, MC, V; no checks; dinner Mon–Sat.* ᕃ

**Fringale** ★★★★  Chef/co-owner Gerald Hirigoyen, named one of the 10 best chefs in the nation by *Food & Wine* magazine, draws crowds to his tiny, 50-seat boisterous French restaurant tucked away in a charmless section of the city. Behind this restaurant's cheery yellow facade, however, there's plenty of charm emanating from its casual, blond-wood-trimmed interior, petite curved bar, and its friendly, largely French waitstaff. Hirigoyen was born and raised in the Basque country of southwest France, and his origins serve as the abiding inspiration for his gutsy, flavor-packed—and extremely reasonably priced—fare. Outstanding dishes include the frisée salad topped with a poached egg and warm bacon dressing, steamed mussels sprinkled with garlic and parsley, wild mushroom ravioli, rack of lamb, and his signature (and meltingly tender) pork tenderloin confit with onion and apple marmalade. Hirigoyen was originally a pastry chef, and he flaunts his talents with his incredible crème brûlée and rich chocolate Basque cake topped with chocolate mousse. Fringale (French for "a sudden pang of hunger") is perpetually packed with famished folks at dinnertime, so expect a noisy crowd and a wait for a table, even if you've made a reservation. ■ *570 4th St (between Bryant and Brannan Sts), San Francisco; (415)543-0573; $$; full bar; AE, MC, V; no checks; lunch Mon–Fri, dinner Mon–Sat.* ᕃ

▼
▲

**La Folie** ★★★★  After a stingy San Francisco restaurateur fired him for spending too much on ingredients and serving overly generous portions, French-born chef Roland Passot decided to open his own restaurant where he could spend as much as he liked to make the food perfect. The paradisiacal result is the charming, small, family-run La Folie, now glistening after a much-needed interior refurbishing completed in the summer of '97. The intimate, whimsical, and theatrical dining room with white puffy clouds painted on the sky-blue ceiling now has red-patterned carpeting, new chairs, a colorful stained-glass entryway, and even marionettes from Lyon dangling from the wall—an appropriate stage for Passot's creative and exuberant, but disciplined, menu. His Roquefort soufflé with grapes, herbs, and walnut bread is, alone, worthy of four stars. Other memorable starters are the wonderful foie gras dishes; the potato blinis with golden Osetra caviar, salmon, asparagus, and crème fraîche; the rabbit loin stuffed with exquisitely fresh vegetables and roasted garlic; the velvety corn-and-leek soup; the parsley and garlic soup with snails and shiitake mushrooms; and the lobster consommé. For an entree, choose whatever meat or fish suits your fancy, for it surely will be exquisitely prepared. A few favorites include the quail and squab rolled together, wrapped with crisp potato strings, and topped with a truffle sauce; free-range Sonoma duck breast drizzled with a Viognier-based sauce and paired with French brown rice; and roast rack of lamb with a garlic soufflé and oven-roasted tomatoes. To accommodate the growing number of vegetarians, Passot has thoughtfully included a separate Vegetable Lovers' menu. And for those who can't make up their minds about what to order, there's a discovery menu (though it's pricey) that allows you to choose five courses à la carte. For dessert, indulge in clafouti with chocolate sauce or croquettes of chocolate with orange zest sauce. The wine list is extensive but the prices are steep, and while the service is attentive, it's not as seamless as the well-orchestrated staffs at the city's other four-star establishments. ■ *2316 Polk St (between Union and Green Sts), San Francisco; (415) 776-5577; $$$; full bar; AE, DC, DIS, MC, V; no checks; dinner Mon–Sat.* &

**Masa's** ★★★★ No one just drops in for dinner at Masa's. Not only do you have to make a reservation at least three weeks in advance, but it may take that long to arrange the financing: this is probably San Francisco's most expensive restaurant. That said, the prices accurately reflect the precious ingredients, generous portions, stunning presentations, and labor-intensive nature of the elegant French-California cuisine invented by the late Masa Kobayashi and carried on flawlessly by chef Julian Serrano since 1985. Masa's atmosphere is neither glitzy nor snobbish; nor is the ultra-professional service overly intimidating. To get an idea of Serrano's luxurious cooking, take a gander at one recent *menu de dégustation*: sautéed snapper with red wine sauce; foie gras with Madeira truffle sauce; a choice of either medallions of fallow deer with caramelized apples and Zinfandel sauce or mignon of veal rôti; a choice of chocolate-cappuccino trifle with orange sorbet, raspberry-soaked figs in strawberry consommé with vanilla ice cream, or Valrhona bittersweet chocolate terrine with summer berry sorbet; coffee and petits fours. The excellent wines are even more exorbitantly priced than the food; moreover, if you want to bring a special bottle of your own, you should know that the corkage fee is equal to the retail value of a top-flight chardonnay. Two seatings are available nightly (and only two fixed-price menus are offered), and gentlemen are requested to wear a jacket and tie. Although most of Masa's patrons seem to be businessmen trying to impress other businessmen, the dining room was refurbished a few years ago with modern art, upholstered chairs, and walls covered in Flamenco red Italian silk, making it more conducive to a romantic special-occasion splurge. For most of Masa's regular clientele, however, money seems to be no object. At a Meals on Wheels fund-raising event, one devoted fan forked over $6,000 just to have Serrano prepare him a meal at home. Tip included. ■ *648 Bush St (in the Hotel Vintage Court, between Stockton and Powell Sts), San Francisco; (415) 989-7154; $$$; full bar; AE, DC, DIS, MC, V; checks OK; dinner Tues–Sat.* &

**Acquerello** ★★★ Acquerello, which means "watercolor" in Italian, offers contemporary regional Italian cooking in a tranquil, refined setting. Co-owners Suzette Gresham and Giancarlo Paterlini worked together at Donatello during that restaurant's heyday, and they make a great team: Gresham in the kitchen turning out exceptionally flavorful and well-constructed *nuova cucina*; Paterlini in the 60-seat dining room pampering customers and offering expert advice on wines. The small, innovative menu changes often, but expect elegant dishes such as beef carpaccio with hearts of palm and black truffles to start, and pasta selections like triangular ravioli filled with swordfish in a light tomato-caper sauce. Entrees are beautifully presented and might feature grilled quail with fresh oranges and sage or fillet of beef topped with Gorgonzola and walnuts. Gresham composes delicate dishes and light sauces, so you might have room for such knockout desserts as the chocolate "cloud cake" with pralines or the warm zabaglione scented with orange muscat. Housed in a converted chapel, Acquerello provides a serene and soothing setting for this stellar cuisine, with cream-colored walls spanned by a beamed ceiling, dramatic pointed archways, flower-filled planters, and a permanent collection of—what else?—watercolors. Jackets are suggested for gentlemen. ■ *1722 Sacramento St (near Polk St), San Francisco; (415)567-5432; gcp19@aol.com; www.acquerello. com; $$–$$$; beer and wine; AE, DC, DIS, MC, V; checks OK; dinner Tues–Sat.*

**Alain Rondelli** ★★★ A veteran of some of France's greatest kitchens and the former chef of the once-estimable Ernie's in San Francisco, Alain Rondelli found a setting in the Richmond District for his own little French gem in 1993. Tucked among the bustling businesses lining Clement Street, this softly lit, unpretentious restaurant lined with forest-green wood shutters quickly became a favorite among the city's culinary cognoscenti. One nibble of the foie gras with black mission figs and patrons start to swoon; one sip of the oxtail or oyster soup and they begin to slip out of their chairs. The entrees are equally stirring, a delicious blend of California ingredients and French technique: braised veal cheek with *ravigote* broth; Maine lobster in its own glaze with *salticon*; lamb pot-au-feu spiced with fresh oregano, lemon, and horseradish. If diners haven't hit the floor by now due to sensory overload, they dip into one of the dazzling desserts, particularly the apple bread pudding. Rondelli also offers a tasting menu with a selection of 6, 9, 12, or—believe it or not—20 courses (plan to spend 7 or 8 hours at the table to enjoy the "once-in-a-lifetime" 20-course meal, says Rondelli). Rave reviews have kept this restaurant's reservation book full, so call well in advance to add your name to the list. ■ *126 Clement St (between 2nd and 3rd Aves), San Francisco; (415)387-0408; $$$; full bar; MC, V; no checks; dinner Tues–Sun.* ♿

**Antica Trattoria** ★★★ Soon after Antica Trattoria opened its doors in 1996, the surrounding Russian Hill neighborhood was abuzz with talk about chef Ruggero Gadaldi's incredible Italian fare (he previously wore the chef's toque at the now-shuttered Etrusca). Occupying a moderately busy corner on Polk and Union Streets, this simply decorated restaurant with dark wood floors and cream-colored walls has developed a deserved reputation as one of the city's best Italian trattorias. Appetizers might include a purée of potato and vegetable soup seasoned with bacon, and delicate (and divine) slices of beef carpaccio enhanced with capers, arugula, mustard, and Parmesan shavings. A recent rendition of the creamy risotto was prepared with pears and Taleggio cheese, while a memorable pasta called *fidellini* featured chestnut angel hair dressed with leeks and a smoked-chicken cream sauce. Main dishes might include a savory monkfish wrapped in pancetta, potatoes, and wild mushrooms, or a perfectly grilled pork tenderloin with Gorgonzola, crispy pancetta, and polenta. It's not some of the most surprising Italian fare in the city, but it's some of the most well-prepared and reasonably priced. Top it off with the trattoria's terrific tiramisu. ■ *2400 Polk St (at the corner of Union St), San Francisco; (415)928-5797; $$; beer and wine; AE, DC, MC, V; no checks; dinner Tues–Sun.* &

**Aqua** ★★★ When it opened in September 1991, Aqua was the first restaurant in the city to elevate the humble fish house to a temple of haute cuisine. Huge flower arrangements punctuate its attractive, sleek-as-a-shark dining room, where slipcovers on the chairs change with the seasons and the large mirrors and dramatic lighting reflect a well-heeled Financial District crowd. They're usually oohing and aahing over chef Michael Mina's creations, which are marked by a refreshingly light touch with herbs and sauces. You might begin with a savory mussel soufflé or roasted spot prawns stuffed with spicy crabmeat—or, if you're really feeling flush, you could shell out 60 to 80 bucks for a parfait of Russian caviar. Segue into Hawaiian swordfish au poivre with pancetta-wrapped shrimp dumplings, grilled tuna draped with a layer of foie gras, or cabbage-wrapped king salmon. The dessert list is sure to include such delights as blackberry coffee cake, pumpkin cheesecake, and soufflés. A few non-seafood entrees are always available, and Mina demonstrates his tolerance for culinary landlubbers by offering a five-course vegetarian tasting menu alongside the regular six-course sampler. ■ *252 California St (at Battery St), San Francisco; (415)956-9662; $$$; full bar; AE, DC, DIS, MC, V; no checks; lunch Mon–Fri, dinner Mon–Sat.* &

**Bizou** ★★★ Bizou means "a little kiss" in French, but San Francisco foodies seem to have planted a big fat wet one on this lively bistro with the rustic Mediterranean menu. Since April 1993, chef/owner Loretta Keller (formerly of Stars) has seduced even normally conservative diners into eating such exotica as beef cheeks, parsnip chips, cod ravioli, and house-cured anchovies (with the heads on, no less), winning them over with her deceptively simple, flavorful preparations. There are plenty of less adventurous items, to be sure, including a wonderful salad of pear, Gorgonzola, radicchio, frisée, and toasted walnuts; day-boat scallops with wild mushrooms, endive, and balsamic vinegar; stuffed young chicken with celeriac, grilled apples, and goat cheese; and desserts like French cream with persimmon and fig sauces and a Seville orange and Meyer lemon curd cake. Housed in a 1906 building, the corner storefront restaurant has an updated bistro feel, with window boxes, vintage light fixtures, weathered mustard-colored walls, large windows, and an oak bar. A few caveats, though: the tables are packed tightly together, the place can get very noisy, and the service can range from boffo to beastly. ■ *598 4th St (at Brannan St), San Francisco; (415) 543-2222; $$; full bar; AE, MC, V; no checks; lunch Mon–Fri, dinner Mon–Sat.* &

**Boulevard** ★★★ Nancy Oakes, a self-taught chef whose cooking career began in 1977 at a scruffy San Francisco saloon, teamed up with nationally renowned restaurant designer Pat Kuleto in 1993 and created this glittering jewel that sits squarely in the center of the city's culinary crown. Hailed as one of the nation's 10 best chefs by *Food & Wine* magazine and a "Chef of the Year" by *San Francisco Focus* magazine, Oakes has come a long way from her days of dishing out saloon-style grub to an audience of longshoremen. These days her patrons tend to be well-heeled gastronomes who have been fans of her culinary talents since she opened the doors of her first restaurant, L'Avenue, in 1988. Five years later she shut down the petite L'Avenue and moved uptown to open big, bustling Boulevard, where she now serves hearty American-style cuisine with French and Italian influences. Before you indulge in her fabulous fare, feast your eyes on Kuleto's fantastic Parisian-inspired interior design, which he has dubbed "industrial art nouveau." After a spin through the revolving entrance door, you'll find yourself standing under an impressive domed brick ceiling offset by a dizzying array of details including pressed-tin wainscoting, floors and windows lined with thousands of brightly colored mosaic tiles, white-and-amber-streaked hand-blown glass sconces, and a sea of decorative ironwork that blends elegantly with dark wood walls and chairs. This visual extravaganza is capped with a sweeping view of the Embarcadero and the Bay Bridge at the end of the long, narrow dining room.

If you can wrest your eyes from all the Kuleto glitz and take a look at the seasonal menu, you'll find a well-chosen mix of dishes. Oysters, giant beluga caviar, and fresh sautéed Sonoma foie gras served on an apple and fig strudel top the extensive appetizer list. Main courses might include a boneless rabbit stuffed with fresh chicken-and-sun-dried-tomato sausages, roasted to perfection in the wood-fired oven, and served on a gratin of Yukon Gold potatoes with chives and Gruyère cheese; asparagus risotto accompanied by roasted prawns and shiitake mushrooms filled with herbed goat cheese; and oven-roasted northern halibut resting on a large bed of wilted baby spinach sprinkled with chanterelle mushrooms and a side of buttery potato-chive fritters. For dessert, the ganache-mousse tart with fresh raspberries or pecan pie topped with vanilla ice cream and chocolate sauce push the sated diner over a blissful edge. ■ *1 Mission St (in the Audiffred Building, at the Embarcadero, on the corner of Steuart St), San Francisco; (415)543-6084; blvd@sirius.com; www.kuleto.com/boulevard; $$$; full bar; AE, DC, DIS, MC, V; no checks; lunch Mon–Fri, dinner every day.* ⅙

**Bruno's** ★★★ You wouldn't know it by looking at the rather modest facade, but Bruno's has had a facelift that would make even Liz Taylor envious. The open kitchen and counter that held steaming plates of spaghetti and veal cutlets in the 1930s have been replaced with a swanky 1950s supper-club–style dining room with giant cherry-red U-shaped booths that seem to be custom-made for snuggling up to your honey. Cylindrical lights hang from the ceiling of the dimly lit room and a solitary white candle flickers at each table. It's so romantic you'll wish you could put down your martini and swing your partner to the tune of an old crooner. But ambience isn't the only thing that makes the born-again Bruno's such a hot spot. Chef James Ormsby (an East Bay native who has worked in two dozen kitchens, including Aqua's and the Lark Creek Inn's) offers a marvelous—and very modern—French and Italian menu. Plan on savory soups, which might include a delightful purée of wild mushrooms and garlic or a summer tomato gazpacho, and highly textured salads, most notably the warm duck-leg confit with Moroccan spices, dried apricots, and a pomegranate vinaigrette, or the smoked Atlantic salmon with warm buckwheat blinis, crème fraîche, and a precious dollop of golden caviar. Most of Ormsby's entrees are equally engaging, and the terrifically tender red-wine-braised oxtails, which may be paired with either parsnip mashed potatoes or ricotta-spinach ravioli, have left many diners swooning with joy. Bruno's bar scene has become as popular as the restaurant, and the live music draws crowds into the wee hours of the night Monday through Saturday. ■ *2389 Mission St (between 19th and 20th Sts), San Francisco; (415)550-7455; www.sfbruno.com; $$$; full bar; DC, MC, V; no checks; dinner Tues–Sat.* ⅙

**Cafe Kati** ★★★ Cafe Kati may not have the elbow room of some of San Francisco's other top restaurants, but there are few chefs on the West Coast who can match Kirk Webber—a California Culinary Academy graduate—when it comes to culinary artistry. Obscurely located on a residential block off Fillmore Street, this tiny, modest, 60-seat cafe has garnered a monsoon of kudos for Webber's weird and wonderful arrangements of numerous cuisines. Even something as mundane as a caesar salad is transformed into a towering monument of lovely romaine lettuce leaves arranged upright on the plate and held in place by a ribbon of thinly sliced cucumber. Fortunately, it tastes as good as it looks. Though the menu changes monthly, his dishes always span the globe: miso-marinated Chilean sea bass saddled with tempura kabocha squash; pancetta-wrapped pork tenderloin bathed in a ragout of baby artichokes and chanterelle mushrooms; walnut-crusted chicken with Gorgonzola; crispy duck confit with sweet potato polenta and wild mushrooms. Complete the gustatory experience with the to-die-for butterscotch pudding. When making a reservation, request a table in the front room—and don't make any plans after dinner because the kitchen takes its sweet time preparing your objet d'art. ▪ *1963 Sutter St (near Fillmore St), San Francisco; (415)775-7313; katikwok@aol.com; www.cafekati.com; $$; beer and wine; MC, V; no checks; dinner Tues–Sun.*

**Campton Place** ★★★ Just off the lobby of a small, European-style luxury hotel, Campton Place pairs an ambience steeped in serene, old-money traditionalism with a kitchen that delights in inventive, newfangled ideas. Since its unveiling in 1983, the pricey restaurant has been the proving ground for such noteworthy chefs as Bradley Ogden (who went on to Lark Creek Inn fame) and Jan Birnbaum (now the proud owner of Catahoula in Calistoga). Current chef Todd Humphries has been at his post since 1994, and he's devised an artful menu of New American cuisine laced with Asian and European accents. Starters may include tuna tartare with American caviar and lotus root, beef carpaccio with shallots and a Vietnamese herb salad, or a buckwheat blini with caviar and smoked salmon. Entrees range from roasted lobster with corn risotto and truffles to pan-roasted beef tenderloin with ginger-braised greens and wild American ginseng sauce. Prix-fixe dinners are a good value. Desserts are as decadent as one would expect from this lush brand of cuisine. The service is quietly attentive, and the decor is a study in understated elegance. Campton Place also serves a superb breakfast. ▪ *340 Stockton St (in the Campton Place hotel, near Sutter St), San Francisco; (415)955-5555; reservations@campton.com; www.citysearch7.com; $$$; full bar; AE, DC, DIS, MC, V; no checks; breakfast, lunch, dinner every day.* ᕦ

**Chez Michel** ★★★ Owner Michel Elkaim revived his namesake restaurant in 1994, seven years after closing the first Chez Michel, which he ran for 21 years. Sophisticated without being pretentious, this new incarnation has blond-wood paneling, plantation shutters on the windows, and a sleekly tailored look. Elkaim's new chef de cuisine Daniel Schaffhauser, an Alsatian who worked at the Ritz-Carlton in Atlanta, has propelled Chez Michel back into the limelight with his superb French cuisine. Schaffhauser's menu always offers an interesting roster of dishes, which might include such appetizers as Sonoma Valley duck foie gras *en ballotine* with passion-fruit coulis and the seven-bean soup with oven-dried tomato croutons. Entrees range from the seared Sichuan pepper-dusted halibut fillet with smoked yellow tomatoes and yucca chips to the rack of lamb with a sweet-potato galette with fresh pea coulis. Complete the meal with the warm Valrhona chocolate cake with vanilla-honey ice cream. The pleasing food and the knowledgeable, helpful staff make Chez Michel so inviting that it has even lured locals into the Fisherman's Wharf area for dinner—no mean feat in this often snobbish restaurant town. ■ *804 North Point (at Hyde St), San Francisco; (415) 775-7036; $$$; full bar; MC, V; no checks; dinner Tues–Sun.* ⅙

**The Dining Room at the Ritz-Carlton** ★★★ For those special occasions or when the other person is buying, few restaurants go the extra distance to spoil you rotten like the Dining Room at the Ritz-Carlton hotel. No less than five tuxedoed waitstaff are at your beck and call, surreptitiously attending to your needs as you bask in your evening of opulence. The setting is, as one would expect, sumptuous and regal and was redecorated in the fall of '97: cushy high-backed chairs, rich brocade, crystal chandeliers, elegant table settings, and live harp music provide a definite air of formality (though the waitstaff will lighten up if you prod them with humor). Unfortunately, celebrity chef Gary Danko left the Ritz in the summer of 1996 to open Viognier in San Mateo (reviewed in the following pages). His replacement, chef Sylvain Portay (a Frenchman from the famed Le Cirque restaurant in New York), continues the Ritz-Carlton tradition of using only the finest, freshest ingredients from around the world, though he brings a more modern style of French cooking to the table than his predecessor did. The seasonal menu is strictly prix fixe, offering a choice of three-, four-, or five-course dinners, the latter of which includes wine pairings per course by master sommelier Emmanuel Kemiji (one of only 31 master sommeliers in the United States) for a hefty additional fee. Notable dishes have included the frothy crayfish bisque, risotto with butternut squash and roasted squab, sweetbreads with scallions and bok choy, a juicy roasted rack of Colorado lamb, and grilled John Dory (a New Zealand fish) spiked with basil and olives. For the finale, indulge in the ultimate French dessert: dark chocolate soufflé with bitter almond ice cream. The Dining Room also features a unique rolling cheese cart, laden with at least two dozen individually ripened cheeses. ■ *600 Stockton St (at California St, on Nob Hill), San Francisco; (415) 296-7465; www.ritzcarlton.com; $$$; full bar; AE, DC, DIS, MC, V; no checks; dinner Mon–Sat.* ⅙

**Eos Restaurant & Wine Bar** ★★★ One of the most talked-about new restaurants in the city, Eos has everyone asking, "Where is Cole Valley?" It's not so much the menu—the Euro-Asian fusion theme is hardly original—as it is the portions (generous) and presentations (brilliant) that have brought throngs of visitors and residents to this once little-known San Francisco neighborhood nestled near the southeast corner of Golden Gate Park. Owner/chef Arnold Wong, a California Culinary Academy graduate and a former architecture student, has taken the art of arrangement to a whole new level: every dish is masterfully crafted to take full advantage of the shape, color, and texture of each ingredient. And—egad!—it's a desecration simply to dig into the culinary artwork, though one's guilt is soon assuaged after the assault begins, particularly when it's upon the tender breast of Peking duck, smoked in ginger-peach tea leaves and served with a plum-kumquat chutney. Other notable dishes are the almond-encrusted soft-shell crab appetizer dipped in spicy plum ponzu sauce, shiitake mushroom dumplings, blackened Asian catfish atop a bed of lemongrass risotto, five-pepper calamari, and the red curry-marinated rack of lamb. Desserts are as fetching as the entrees, particularly the Bananamisu (akin to tiramisu) with caramelized bananas and the warm bittersweet chocolate soufflé cake. Unfortunately, a quiet, romantic dinner is out of the question here, since the stark deco-industrial decor merely amplifies the nightly cacophony. After dinner, adjourn to the restaurant's popular wine bar around the corner, which stocks more than 400 bottles—many at reasonable prices—from around the globe. Nearly 50 red and white wines are available by the glass, too. ■ *901 Cole St (at Carl St), San Francisco; (415)566-3063; $$–$$$; beer and wine; AE, MC, V; no checks; dinner every day.* ⟡

**Farallon** ★★★ Diving into the undersea world of chef Mark Franz (of Stars restaurant fame) and designer Pat Kuleto can leave one breathless. In the fall of 1997, the two co-owners opened a dazzling $4 million, 160-seat restaurant offering seafood dishes that are as innovative as Kuleto's elegant aquatic-themed decor. Giant hand-blown jellyfish chandeliers with glowing tentacles seemingly float beneath a sea-blue ceiling in the Jelly Bar cocktail lounge, which is punctuated with sculpted strands of kelp climbing up illuminated pillars. Even the stylish bar stools are reminiscent of octopuses, and the sweeping staircase leading to the main dining room is embedded with 50,000 indigo-blue caviar-shaped marbles. Upstairs, the marine motif continues with huge sea-urchin chandeliers dangling from the painted mosaic ceiling that arches over a sea of tables draped in white linen—it's all a dramatic but enchanting stage for Franz's excellent coastal cuisine.

For starters, consider oysters on the half shell with house-made caviar and Champagne mignonette; a delectable asparagus bisque with cardamom cream; truffled mashed potatoes with crab and salmon caviar artfully stuffed into a real sea-urchin shell; or Maine lobster and wild-mushroom gnocchi with a leek, tarragon, and Champagne lobster sauce. Entrees from the daily changing menu might include ginger-steamed salmon and sea-scallop pillows with a prawn mousse, savoy cabbage, and foie gras coulis or sautéed gulf prawns with potato risotto, English peas, pearl onions, and truffle portobello coulis. While Franz's forte is fish, he also has a flair for meats and offers a few every night, such as a juicy grilled fillet of beef served with a portobello mushroom and potato galette, haricots verts, and black truffle aioli. Desserts are the creation of Emily Luchetti, one of the city's best pastry chefs, and Darcy Tizio, and standouts have included the chocolate peppermint pattie with chocolate custard sauce and the warm chocolate fudge cake with scoops of malted-milk-ball ice cream. The 300-item wine list fits in swimmingly with the menu (though prices are high); two dozen wines are even available by the glass. The attentive staff, which is well-versed on wine and can make sound recommendations, helps make Farallon a deep-sea affair to remember. ▪ *450 Post St (between Powell and Mason Sts, 1 block W of Union Square), San Francisco; (415) 956-6969; $$$; full bar; AE, DC, DIS, MC, V; no checks; lunch Mon-Sat, dinner every day.* ⅋

**Flying Saucer** ★★★ A few weeks after landing in the outer Mission District, Flying Saucer owner/chef Albert Tordjman tossed a well-known restaurant critic out onto the sidewalk. Why? Because Tordjman hates critics. The reviewer wrote a rave anyway, and the legend of Flying Saucer (supposedly named after the wacky spaceship-shaped bumper car hanging over the door) was launched. This hip bistro dominated by a giant *Phantom of the Opera*-esque mask specializes in attitude as well as excellent food. And the credentials Tordjman brings to his enterprise are top-flight: an apprenticeship in his native Lyon, followed by jobs at such high-profile restaurants as London's Dorchester, New Orleans' Commander's Palace, and Napa Valley's Auberge du Soleil. Tordjman's menu can be quite eccentric and changes often, but most of it works rambunctiously well. The entrees are complicated, intense in flavor, and baroque in presentation: duck confit with black chanterelles on coconut-curry lentils, Creole mustard-crusted lamb chops with a chestnut-yam mash cake and Rainwater Madeira demiglace, and crisp-skin salmon topped with a tangerine-basil sauce. Desserts are out of this world, too, so don't leave Tordjman's planet without one. Unfortunately, the Saucer's bad attitude sometimes extends to the service, which can be maddeningly rude. But that doesn't seem to stop city slickers from eating here—at least once. ▪ *1000 Guerrero St (at 22nd St), San Francisco; (415) 641-9955; $$–$$$; beer and wine; MC, V; no checks; dinner Tues–Sat.* ⅋

**42 Degrees** ★★★ Like Caffe Esprit, the former occupant of this bayside site hidden behind a thick line of hedges, 42 Degrees is popular with a relentlessly hip crowd of young professionals and boasts a spare, high-tech warehouse look, with a soaring ceiling and acres of concrete, metal, and glass. As night falls, however, candlelight, table linens, and strains of live jazz soften the effect, transforming the stark 100-seat space into an appealing supper club. The name refers to the latitude of Provence and the Mediterranean Sea, and Montreal-native chef/owner James Moffat's ever-changing menu reflects this sun-splashed influence with starters like watercress salad with duck confit, walnuts, and pomegranates; Medjool dates with Parmesan and celery; and grilled artichokes with Meyer lemons. Entrees might include risotto with shaved truffles and mushrooms, pan-roasted chicken with lemon and black olive sauce, calf's liver with grilled onions and mustard greens, and grilled pancetta-wrapped salmon. Lighter eaters can look to the chalkboard for a lineup of small plates, such as the pizzettas, Iberian blood sausage, and herb-roasted potatoes with aioli. Desserts include a sublime chocolate pot de crème, milk chocolate crème brûlée, and a warm apple Napoleon with vanilla ice cream and huckleberry sauce. The service is courteous and professional, the mezzanine-level windows afford a view of the bay, and there's a large, pleasant courtyard patio for dining alfresco on warm days. ▪ *235 16th St (off 3rd St, next to the Esprit outlet), San Francisco; (415)777-5559; $$–$$$; full bar; MC, V; no checks; lunch Mon–Fri, dinner Wed–Sat.* &

**Hawthorne Lane** ★★★ When Hillary Clinton was in town to promote *It Takes a Village*, she ate a late dinner at Hawthorne Lane. Probably learned about it from hubby Bill, who supped here the year before and might have raved about the miso-glazed black cod with sesame spinach rolls, the special lobster tempura, the roasted Sonoma lamb with butternut squash and Parmesan risotto, or the house-made fettuccine with chanterelle mushrooms. Ever since it opened in June 1995, Hawthorne Lane has been one of the city's hottest restaurants, its popularity fueled by its lovely design, its proximity to the happening SoMa scene, and the pedigree of owners/chefs David and Anne Gingrass (formerly of Spago and Postrio fame). The dining room is a refined, beguiling space, with wrought-iron cherry blossoms, a massive skylight, giant urns with dazzling fresh floral displays, and light-colored woods lending it an air of perennial spring. In keeping with the cheery ambience, the personable staff is utterly without the attitude that often afflicts other hot-ticket restaurants, making it easy to enjoy the contemporary American menu with Asian and Mediterranean influences. Hawthorne also wins raves for its varied selection of wonderful breads and desserts, both of which are the work of pastry chef Nicole Plue, who worked at the Sheraton Palace, Eric's, and One Market before landing here. Don't miss her warm strawberry-rhubarb shortcake with buttermilk-orange ice cream or the rich butterscotch pots de crème with vanilla bean beignets. If you can't get a reservation, snag one of the seats at the long, oval bar, where you can order from the dining room menu, or sign up for one of the many tables set aside for walk-in patrons. ▪ *22 Hawthorne St (off Howard St, between 2nd and 3rd Sts), San Francisco; (415)777-9779; dcg@hawthorne lane.com; www.hawthornelane.com; $$$; full bar; DC, DIS, MC, V; checks OK; lunch Mon–Fri, dinner every day.* &

**Helmand** ★★★ An oasis of good taste on Broadway's less-than-tasteful topless strip, Helmand serves delicious renditions of Afghan cuisine in a pretty room lit by brass chandeliers and small table lanterns. The restaurant's light and variously spiced house-made yogurts (a staple of Afghani cooking) dress several favorite appetizers including *mantwo* (a house-made dumpling filled with sautéed onions and beef, topped with a carrot, yellow split pea, and beef sauce, and served on yogurt) and *kaddo borawni* (sweet baby pumpkin that's pan-fried, then baked, and tempered by a piquant yogurt-garlic sauce). For a main course, try the *chowpan*—a tender, juicy half rack of lamb marinated like a fine Armenian shish kabob, then grilled and served with sautéed eggplant and rice pallow. Other fine choices include *sabzi challow* (a wonderfully seasoned mixture of spinach with lamb), *mourgh challow* (chicken sautéed with split peas and curry), and *koufta challow* (light, moderately spicy meatballs with sun-dried tomatoes, peppers, and peas), each served with a ramekin of flavorful fresh cilantro sauce and aromatic white or brown rice. Servers are personable (if sometimes slightly scattered), and the wine list is well chosen and well priced. Parking spaces in this neighborhood are few and far between, so take advantage of the validated parking at the lot down the block. ▪ *430 Broadway (between Kearny and Montgomery Sts), San Francisco; (415) 362-0641; $$; full bar; AE, MC, V; no checks; dinner every day.* &

**Infusion Bar & Restaurant** ★★★ Trendy, noisy, alcohol oriented— these rather damning adjectives apply to Infusion, a relatively new SoMa bar and restaurant that nevertheless manages to establish itself as a place that's serious about good food. It was named after the house specialty, vodka-based infusions flavored with assorted fruits and vegetables—everything from jalapeño to pineapple, watermelon to cucumber (they have more than 50 flavors in stock). You can admire eight of them in their decanters behind the handcrafted Honduran mahogany bar that stretches along one side of the long, narrow room—or up close in an ice-cold martini glass, of course. The spare, modern furnishings, including a row of light-wood tables and chairs, simple light fixtures, and a few colorful framed prints, stand in dramatic contrast with the intense, spicy complexity of the food. European, Asian, Mexican, and Caribbean influences add interesting grace notes to self-taught chef David Fickes' New American fare, with starters that range from guava empanadas with Brie to a ginger-cured tuna accented with wasabe-infused oil and tangerine essence. There are always a few imaginative pasta dishes, such as fusilli with chicken and chipotle chile sauce (Fickes has a fondness for chiles), and entrees that include a crisp walnut-crusted salmon with chardonnay-pear sauce, peppered filet mignon flamed with Wild Turkey, thick-cut pork chop brined and marinated in spicy apple-barbecue sauce, and chicken roasted with tangerines and rosemary. Fickes sometimes misses his mark with his innovative recipes, but when he hits it, he's incredible. Top off the fine feast

▼

San Francisco

*Restaurants*

▲

with white-chocolate–bourbon mousse with pistachio shortbread or chocolate pecan pie. At 9:30pm Thursday through Saturday a live band performs on the loft stage. ■ *555 2nd St (between Bryant and Brannan Sts), San Francisco; (415)543-2282; infusn@aol.com; www.citysearch.com/sfo/infusion; $$; full bar; AE, DC, MC, V; no checks; lunch Mon–Fri, dinner every day.* ⌖

**Jardinière** ★★★   A native Californian, chef Traci Des Jardins worked in many notable restaurants in France, New York, and Los Angeles as well as San Francisco's now-closed Elka before she joined forces with popular New York restaurateur Drew Nieporent in March 1994 to open Rubicon restaurant in San Francisco, which launched her culinary reputation nationwide. A year later, Des Jardins won the prestigious James Beard Rising Star Chef of the Year award and was named one of *Food and Wine* magazine's Best New Chefs in America. With those kudos under her belt, it was no wonder that the opening of her own restaurant, Jardinière (pronounced zhar-dee-NAIR), was a smashing success as soon as the highly stylized glass doors swung open in September 1997. With award-winning designer/restaurateur Pat Kuleto as her business partner, Des Jardins was assured of an impressive setting for her French-California cuisine. Located in the former home of Kimball's restaurant and jazz club, the 135-seat, two-story brick building is elegantly framed with violet velvet drapes, and the focal point is the central oval mahogany and marble bar, frequently mobbed with patrons of the arts (the symphony hall and opera house are across the street) as well as a sophisticated see-and-be-seen set, including such local politicos as the mayor. Above the bar is a large open space that rises two stories to a dramatic glowing glass dome ceiling.

Appetizers are Des Jardins's strong point, especially the flavor-packed lobster, leek, and chanterelle strudel and the delicate kabocha squash ravioli with chestnuts and sage brown butter. Some of her best entrees thus far have included the crisp chicken with chanterelles and applewood-smoked bacon, herbed lamb loin with cranberry beans and tomato confit, and pan-roasted salmon with lentils, celery root salad, and red wine sauce. After your meal, consider the chef's selection of domestic and imported cheeses, which are visible in the temperature-controlled cheese room on the main floor. The ever-changing dessert roster earns mixed reviews, though the classic apple tart with green-apple sorbet is memorable. Jardinière's wine list is strong, with more than 200 selections including some hard-to-find bottles. Service is excellent, and the live entertainment makes this restaurant ideal for that special night on the town. ■ *300 Grove St (at Franklin St, behind Davies Symphony Hall), San Francisco; (415)861-5555; jardin1997@aol.com; $$$; full bar; AE, DC, DIS, MC, V; no checks; lunch Mon–Fri, dinner, late-night menu every day.* ⌖

**Kyo-ya** ★★★  This elegantly austere restaurant in the Palace Hotel serves some of the best sushi and sashimi in town. Catering to well-heeled business execs visiting from the other side of the Rim, Kyo-ya's food is fresh, authentic, and delicious. Sit at the sushi bar or settle into one of the dining room's black-lacquered chairs flanked by a glossy wood table set with a simple arrangement of fresh flowers. Order a decanter of sake (there are more than a dozen to choose from) and some *toro* (tuna belly), *ebi* (shrimp), *hotate* (scallops), or any other item on Kyo-ya's extensive list of sushi offerings—it's sure to be some of the finest you've ever had. While the sushi and *nabemono* (one-pot dishes cooked tableside) are undeniably expensive, several other dishes, including some wonderful appetizers such as steamed clams in sake and complete tempura and teriyaki dinners, are more reasonably priced. ▪ *2 New Montgomery St (in the Palace Hotel, off Market St, between 2nd and 3rd Sts), San Francisco; (415)392-8600; toshi_matsumura@ittsheraton.com; $$$; full bar; AE, DC, DIS, MC, V; no checks; lunch Tues–Fri, dinner Tues–Sat.* ♿

**Pane e Vino** ★★★  Well hidden on the outskirts of posh Pacific Heights, this dark-wood-trimmed trattoria framed by a cream-colored awning is a local favorite. The two tiny, simply furnished dining rooms with small white-clothed tables fill up fast, and as waiters spouting rapid-fire Italian dart back and forth between the kitchen and their customers, folks waiting for a table are often left frantically searching for a place to stand out of the way of the melee. It's all enchantingly reminiscent of the real *ristorante* scene in Italy, which is perhaps one of the reasons people keep coming back. Newcomers unaccustomed to the hustle and bustle may be a bit disconcerted at first, but after a sip or two of wine the whole scene becomes rather entertaining. And once you're led to your table, the boisterous kitchen scene becomes a faded memory as you take in the first-rate service and rustic Italian fare. Although you might think that nothing could be better than this restaurant's wonderful *pane e vino* (Italian for "bread and wine"), do yourself a favor and indulge in the amazing chilled artichoke appetizer, stuffed with bread and tomatoes and served with a vinaigrette—it's divine! Follow that lead with one of the perfectly prepared pastas, ranging from the simple but savory capellini tossed with fresh tomatoes, basil, garlic, and extra-virgin olive oil to the zesty *bucatini* (hollow straw pasta) smothered with pancetta, hot peppers, and a tomato sauce. The excellent entrees vary from rack of lamb marinated in sage and rosemary to the whole-roasted fresh fish of the day. Before you raise your napkin to your lips for the last time, dive into the delightful *dolci*: a luscious crème caramel, assorted gelati, and a terrific tiramisu are the standouts. ▪ *3011 Steiner St (at Union St), San Francisco; (415)346-2111; $$; beer and wine; AE, MC, V; no checks; lunch Mon–Sat, dinner every day.* ♿

**PlumpJack Cafe** ★★★ Co-owned by Bill Getty (son of billionaire Gordon Getty) and wine-connoisseur-cum-politician Gavin Newsom, this exotic California-Mediterranean bistro is one of San Francisco's leading restaurants, with consistently excellent food and (thanks to its companion wine store a few doors away) a surprisingly extensive wine list with fine bottles offered at near-retail prices. Executive chef Maria Helm, a graduate of the California Culinary Academy and former chef at the Sherman House hotel, has been lauded as one of the top culinary talents in the city. While her seasonal menu is primarily French-inspired, there are a few nods to Asian cuisine and plenty of Italian influences. Helm's appetizers are often the highlight of the menu, including her bruschetta, which might be topped with roasted beets, goat cheese, and garlic one night, and eggplant, sweet peppers, and chèvre the next. Don't miss her remarkable risottos, richly flavored with artichokes, applewood-smoked bacon, and goat cheese, or perhaps smoked salmon and shiitake mushrooms, or her superbly executed roast herb chicken breast with foie gras, hedgehog mushrooms, and spinach, or—Helm's signature dish—roast duck breast and leg confit with French green lentils, barley, parsnip chips, and a sour cherry jus. While the restaurant's highly stylized, handcrafted interior design is unique— gold-leafed lights, chairs with medieval-shield-shaped backs, curved metal screens at the windows, a massive wooden wine rack—the taupe and olive color scheme ensures that what really stands out is the food. Another branch of this popular cafe has been opened in Squaw Valley near Lake Tahoe (see review in the Sierra Nevada chapter). ■ *3127 Fillmore St (between Greenwich and Filbert Sts), San Francisco; (415)563-4755; $$$; beer and wine, AE, MC, V; no checks; lunch Mon–Fri, dinner Mon–Sat.* ♿

**Postrio** ★★★ Owned by Southern California superstar chef Wolfgang Puck and the Kimpton Hotel group, Postrio is a splashy slice of Hollywood set in the heart of San Francisco, with superglitzy decor à la restaurant designer Pat Kuleto, delightful culinary combinations, and the perpetual hope of catching sight of some celeb at the next table. One enters through a spiffy street-level bar that serves tapas and little Puckish pizzas to the unreserving; from there a grand sculpted-iron and copper staircase—on which everybody can at least play a star—descends dramatically into a crowded, pink-lighted dining room ringed with paintings and plants. It's a lovely, sophisticated setting for some terrific food, prepared by Mitchell and Steven Rosenthal, who proved themselves capable successors when founding chefs Anne and David Gingrass jumped ship to open Hawthorne Lane in '95. Working closely with Puck, the brothers Rosenthal have crafted an exciting hybrid of California/Asian/Mediterranean cuisine that includes such creations as grilled quail accompanied by spinach and a soft egg ravioli with port wine glaze; sautéed salmon with plum glaze, wasabe mashed potatoes, and miso vinaigrette; Chinese duck with mango sauce; and roasted leg of lamb with garlic potato purée and Niçoise olives. Tempting choices, indeed, but be sure to save room for one of Postrio's sensational desserts. The dessert menu offers an array of showstoppers—from the potato-pecan pie to the caramel pear tart with Grand Marnier crème fraîche and the chocolate soufflé cake with Irish coffee ice cream. You can overindulge and order the dessert sampler, a stunning smorgasbord of sweets that's almost too pretty to sink your fork into. Postrio's talented chefs are on display in the large exhibition kitchen and their performance is usually first-rate (although when crowds are thick, slip-ups are not unheard of). The wine list is excellent, the service professional, and the reservations essential, usually several weeks in advance. ■ *545 Post St (in the Prescott Hotel, between Mason and Taylor Sts), San Francisco; (415)776-7825; www.postrio.com; $$$; full bar; AE, DC, DIS, MC, V; no checks; brunch Sat–Sun, breakfast, lunch Mon–Fri, dinner every day.* &

**Rose Pistola** ★★★ A new star has been born in North Beach, and her name is Rose Pistola. The brainchild of Midas-like chef/restaurateur Reed Hearon (who launched the reputations of LuLu and Cafe Marimba, then left both successful enterprises), this sleek and sexy addition to the Columbus Avenue promenade is as pleasing to behold as it is to dine in (it's actually named after a popular octogenarian North Beach restaurateur). If you prefer to oversee the preparation of your meal, you may sit at the counter overlooking the grill, but the family-style meals are best enjoyed in the large dining room's comfy booths; tables on the sidewalk offer an alfresco option. The food is rustic Italian with a California flair (less fats, more flavors) inspired by the cuisine of Liguria: roast rabbit with fresh shell bean ragout and polenta, pumpkin-filled ravioli, or roast pork chop with *panzanella*, an Italian bread salad infused with onions, basil, and tomatoes. Any of the pastas, seafood, thin-crust wood-fired pizzas, and hot and cold antipasti are also very well prepared, but the fish dishes (particularly the whole roasted fish) are Hearon's specialty. For night owls a late night menu is served until 1am on weekends. The only flaws to this otherwise outstanding restaurant are its desserts, which don't always measure up to what is arguably the best Italian fare in San Francisco. ■ *532 Columbus Ave (between Green and Union Sts), San Francisco; (415)399-0499; $$–$$$; full bar; AE, DC, MC, V; no checks; lunch, dinner every day.* &

**Rubicon** ★★★ Thanks to Rubicon's star-studded cast of financial backers—Robert De Niro, Robin Williams, and Francis Ford Coppola—this Financial District restaurant received so much advance publicity that San Franciscans were setting dates to eat here long before the seismic reinforcements were bolted to the floorboards. Chances are slim that you'll see any Tinseltown talent sitting at the table next to you, but if you want to catch a rising star, keep an eye out for Rubicon's young chef, Scott

Newman. A native New Yorker who once studied acting, Newman swapped Broadway aspirations for the culinary stage. After graduating from the California Culinary Academy he worked with famed chef Julian Serrano at Masa's and Rubicon's founding chef, Traci Des Jardins (who left to launch her own restaurant, Jardinière). Newman's superb opening acts have included pan-seared rouget (a mild, pink-fleshed French fish) with ratatouille vegetables in a lobster broth and a luscious lobster ravioli with spinach and chervil butter. Main courses on the French-inspired menu may include a crispy polenta cake with wild mushrooms, roasted pork loin with black-eyed peas, and halibut with chanterelles and cranberry beans. Newman also offers a pair of prix-fixe menus and a tasting menu. The excellent, extensive, and expensive wine list is presented by Larry Stone, one of the nation's premier sommeliers. ■ *558 Sacramento St (between Montgomery and Sansome Sts), San Francisco; (415) 434-4100; www.cuisine.com; $$$; full bar; AE, DC, MC, V; no checks; lunch Mon–Fri, dinner Mon–Sat.* &

**Scala's Bistro** ★★★ Opened in 1995, Scala's Bistro immediately won an enthusiastic following by offering exceptional rustic Italian and country French cooking in a lovely, welcoming setting. Co-owners Donna and Giovanni Scala, who operate Napa's Bistro Don Giovanni, installed a golden bas-relief ceiling, amber walls, and lead-pane windows, along with brass wall sconces and Craftsman-type chandeliers that cast a warm glow reminiscent of a Mediterranean sunset. (A remarkable transformation indeed, considering this spot in the Sir Francis Drake hotel used to be a dingy sports bar with the singularly unappetizing name of Crusty's.) Standout appetizers include grilled portobello mushrooms, crispy calamari, and sautéed veal sweetbreads. Pastas range from a dynamite persillade tagliatelle with artichokes, wild mushrooms, and truffle oil to rigatoni with veal meatballs in an oregano and tomato sauce. The seared salmon fillet with buttermilk mashed potatoes and the grilled pork loin with Yukon Gold mashed potatoes and rosemary oil are two excellent entrees, and a selection of risottos, salads, and pizzas round out the menu. Portions are generous, but do try to save room for desserts such as the Chocolate I.V. (layers of chocolate ice-cream cake and mousse encased in a toasted butter-pecan crust) and the Bostini cream pie (creamy vanilla custard topped with orange chiffon cake and a warm chocolate glaze). ■ *432 Powell St (in the Sir Francis Drake hotel, between Post and Sutter Sts), San Francisco; (415) 395-8555; $$; full bar; AE, DC, DIS, MC, V; no checks; breakfast, lunch, dinner every day.* &

**Thep Phanom** ★★★ Thailand's complex, spicy, cosmopolitan cuisine has always been adaptive, incorporating flavors from India, China, Burma, Malaysia, and, more recently, the West. San Francisco boasts dozens of Thai restaurants; virtually all of them are good, and many (including Khan Toke Thai House and Manora's

Thai Cuisine) are excellent. Why, then, does Thep Phanom alone have a permanent line out its front door even though it takes reservations? At this restaurant, a creative touch of California enters the cultural mix, resulting in sophisticated preparations that have a special sparkle. The signature dish, *ped swan*, is a boneless duck in a light honey sauce served on a bed of spinach—and it ranks with the city's greatest entrees. Tart, minty, spicy *yum plamuk* (calamari salad), *larb ped* (minced duck salad), coconut chicken soup, and the velvety basil-spiked seafood curry served on banana leaves (available Wednesday and Thursday only) are superb choices, too. Service is charming and efficient; the tasteful decor, informal atmosphere, eclectic crowd, and discerning wine list are all very San Francisco. ■ *400 Waller St (at Fillmore St, near Haight St), San Francisco; (415)431-2526; $$; beer and wine; AE, DC, DIS, MC, V; no checks; dinner every day.* &

**Woodward's Garden** ★★★ In what is arguably one of the least desired commercial spaces in the city stands what is certainly one of the Bay Area's best restaurants. Woodward's Garden is tucked under a busy highway overpass on a gritty, windy, noisy corner of Mission Street at Duboce Avenue. But that doesn't deter those who reserve one of the diminutive restaurant's 11 tables at least a couple of weeks in advance for a weekend night (there are four seatings per night). To say Woodward's Garden has an open kitchen is putting it mildly—the kitchen takes up at least half the room and the handful of tables are lined up around it. You can not only see and smell your food being prepared, you can feel the heat of the flames! Chef/owners Margie Conard (from Postrio) and Dana Tommasino (from Greens) offer an American/Mediterranean-influenced menu featuring five appetizers and five entrees. The menu changes weekly. A recent visit started with a savory sweet-potato–ginger soup with a dollop of crème fraîche, smoked trout bruschetta with Romesco sauce and arugula, and perfectly sautéed scallops served with endive, Meyer lemon beurre blanc, and caviar. The entrees were equally delightful: a fork-tender lamb shank braised with fennel and orange was nestled on a bed of saffron risotto with asparagus and Reggiano, and a duck breast was roasted to perfection and paired with grilled polenta, a cherry-onion marmalade, and braised chard. Bravo! ■ *1700 Mission St (at Duboce Ave, under the highway overpass), San Francisco; (415)621-7122; $$$; beer and wine; MC, V; checks OK; dinner every day.*

**Betelnut** ★★ A member of the Real Restaurants company (which includes such successes as Tra Vigne and Bix), this sumptuously decorated Asian "beerhouse" has the ever-so-slightly tarty feel of an exotic 1930s Shanghai brothel. Named after a popular seed that is chewed throughout Asia for its intoxicating side effects, Betelnut became a huge success in a short time, and is still on everyone's list of places to try (though, alas, the namesake nut is not offered here). Styled in sensual colors of red, orange, and gold with moody pink lighting, the decor evokes a bygone era straight out of *The Last Emperor*. Tall glass doors facing Union Street are opened on warm evenings to provide alfresco dining, and mechanized bamboo fans sway languorously above the busy bar. The mixed menu is Pan-Asian, with an array of authentic dishes from Vietnam, Singapore, China, Thailand, Indonesia, and Japan. While the unusual concept entices diners, the reality is not always up to par. With more than a dozen cooks in the kitchen on busy nights, results can vary. Some dishes consistently get raves, including the spicy coconut chicken with eggplant, lemongrass, and basil; the crunchy tea-smoked duck; the succulent short ribs; and the sun-dried anchovies with peanuts, chiles, and garlic. But the green papaya salad gets mixed reviews, and Betelnut's dumplings can be downright disappointing. Be sure to order a draft beer with your meal—there's even a rice ale among the offerings. For dessert, select tapioca pudding layered with coconut cream. And beware of the often snooty attitude of the hosts who seem to revel in telling you that a dinner reservation between 6:30pm and 9:30pm is impossible, even if you call two weeks in advance. ■ *2030 Union St (near Buchanan St), San Francisco; (415)929-8855; www.citysearch7.com; $$; full bar; DC, DIS, MC, V; no checks; lunch, dinner every day.* &

**Firefly** ★★ Hidden in a cluster of homes on the west end of 24th Street is Noe Valley's best restaurant—just look for a giant metal sculpture of its namesake nocturnal insect perched above a lime green and sizzling yellow door. Inside, an eclectic array of modern art surrounds small tables laden with an equally eclectic display of food, which might include steaming bowls of bouill-abaisse de Marseilles bubbling over with monkfish, prawns, scallops, and bass; shrimp-and-scallop pot-stickers accompanied by a spicy sesame-soy dipping sauce (the Firefly's signature appetizer); and a portobello mushroom Wellington served with linguine that's swirled with fresh vegetables. Chef/co-owner Brad Levy and co-owner Veva Edelson, both formerly of Embarko, dub it "home cooking with few ethnic boundaries." They also proudly announce on every menu that their meat comes from the well-known Niman–Schell Ranch, home of "happy, drug-free animals with an ocean view," which leaves politically correct Noe Valley carnivores smiling as they savor the spicy pork stew. The changing roster of desserts is as good as it looks, especially the not-too-sweet strawberry shortcake and the banana bread pudding with caramel Anglaise. ■ *4288 24th St (near Douglass St), San Francisco; (415)821-7652; $$–$$$; beer and wine; AE, MC, V; checks OK; dinner every day.* &

**The Garden Court** ★★ Dining at the Garden Court, showpiece of the grand 1875 Palace Hotel, is like entering a Victorian romance novel. One can almost picture scads of beauteous heroines perching straight-backed on the plush settees here, blushing as they avert their eyes from the steady gaze of roguish but tenderhearted young blades jostling each other near the potted palms. Ah, we digress—but you see what magic this incredibly romantic, old-fashioned room can work on you. Blame it on the soaring marble and gilt columns, the opulent furnishings, the mirrored doorways, or the rows of crystal chandeliers descending from the high, intricately patterned, domed ceiling of amber-stained glass. The food hasn't always lived up to the regal surroundings, but recently management has made it a priority, and executive chef Peter DeMarais presents an interesting California menu with European flourishes. Starters might include a French butter pear salad with Stilton cheese and a cracked-pepper vinaigrette or a velvety crab bisque; entrees range from grilled rack of lamb with sweet onions and basil mashed potatoes to freshwater prawns and rock shrimp served on a pumpkin risotto to grilled swordfish with Japanese sweet potato purée and ginger-butter sauce. In addition to lunch and dinner, the Garden Court serves an elegant afternoon tea to the strains of live harp and a lavish (and costly) Sunday brunch. ■ *2 New Montgomery St (in the Palace Hotel, off Market St, between 2nd and 3rd Sts), San Francisco; (415)546-5010 or (415)512-1111; $$$; full bar; AE, DC, DIS, MC, V; no checks; brunch Sun and holidays, breakfast, lunch every day, tea Wed–Sat, dinner Tues–Sat.* ♿

**Greens** ★★ As Le Tour d'Argent in Paris is to the dedicated duck fancier and as the Savoy Grill in London is to the roast beef connoisseur, so is Greens at Fort Mason to the vegetarian aesthete. Not only is the food politically correct here, it's often so good that even carnivores find it irresistible. Part of the Greens treat is visual: located in a converted barracks in the historic Fort Mason Center, the enormous, airy dining room is surrounded by huge windows with a spectacular view of the Golden Gate Bridge, and a gigantic sculpted redwood burl serves as a Buddhist-inspired centerpiece. Yes, Greens is owned and operated by the Zen Center—but this is a restaurant, not a monastery. The menu changes daily and you can expect to see such dishes as mesquite-grilled polenta; filo turnovers filled with mushrooms, spinach, and Parmesan cheese; pizza sprinkled with onion confit, goat cheese, and basil; and fettuccine with mushrooms, peas, goat cheese, and crème fraîche. Greens' baked goods no longer come from the popular Tassajara Bakery (it's been sold); now the restaurant serves wonderful Acme bread and makes most of its own cakes, cookies, and pastries. All of these baked goods are sold at **Greens To Go**, a takeout counter inside the restaurant that also sells savory soups, sandwiches, and black bean chili. An à la carte dinner menu is offered at Greens Monday through Friday; guests may only order from the prix-fixe five-course dinner menu on Saturday. The restaurant is also open for late-night desserts, coffee, and wine from Monday through Saturday 9:30pm to 11pm. If you were expecting to be deprived of a delicious meal for your own good here, think again. ■ *Fort Mason*

*Center, Building A (off Marina Blvd at Buchanan St), San Francisco; (415) 771-6222; $$–$$$; beer and wine; DIS, MC, V; local checks only; brunch Sun, lunch Tues–Sat, dinner Mon–Sat.* &

**Harbor Village Restaurant** ★★ A favorite of prosperous Pacific Rim businesspeople, middle- and upper-class Chinese-American families, and downtown office workers out for a lunchtime treat, this giant Hong Kong–style seafood and dim sum restaurant has great food, but it misses top honors because of minor inconsistencies in cooking and major flaws in service. Lunch is a state-of-the-art dim sum extravaganza, with master chefs from Hong Kong turning out plate after plate of sublime morsels in vast, interesting variety. At dinner, you can choose from an enormous Cantonese menu that includes dishes rarely found on this edge of the Rim, among them prized varieties of shellfish, kept alive in tanks until the moment they're ordered and served with exquisite simplicity (albeit at an exorbitant cost). Many of the more affordable seafood dishes are just as marvelous, though some of the standard Chinese dishes suffer from perfunctory preparation, and all too often entire orders are piled simultaneously on the undersized tables by the standoffish staff. Still, the food and upscale decor (this is one of San Francisco's prettiest Chinese restaurants) might make you forgive these lapses. So be adventurous: go with a gang and get a large table, order only a few dishes at a time, and then order more when the food is nearly gone. And in keeping with Chinese tradition, save the steamed whole fish for last—it's a Cantonese symbol of good luck. ■ *4 Embarcadero Center (at Drumm and Clay Sts), San Francisco; (415) 781-8833; $$$; full bar; AE, DC, DIS, MC, V; no checks; lunch, dinner every day.* &

▼

**Harris'** ★★ Not just another steak house, Harris' is a living monument to the not-quite-bygone joys of guiltless beef-eating. You can even get a sneak preview of your meal by peering at the deep-pink slabs in the showcase window facing the street. The hushed, formal club setting boasts dark wood paneling, plush carpets, large brown tufted booths, well-spaced white-draped tables, and chairs roomy enough to accommodate the most bullish build. Jackets are appreciated (though no longer required). Harris' choice Midwestern beef, impeccably dry-aged for three weeks on the premises, bears the same relation to supermarket beef as foie gras bears to chicken liver; the tender steaks, grilled to order, can even be chosen by cut and by size. The larger bone-in cuts (such as the Harris Steak and the T-bone) have the finest flavor, but the pepper steak and the rare prime rib are great, too. Those who prefer calf brains to these sanguine beauties will find a flawless version here. You might want to skip the usual steak-house appetizers in favor of Harris' excellent caesar salad. For true-blue traditionalists, the exemplary martini—served in a carafe placed in a bucket of shaved ice—makes an excellent starter course. ■ *2100 Van Ness Ave (at Pacific Ave), San Francisco; (415) 673-1888; www.*

*citysearch7.com; $$$; full bar; AE, DC, DIS, MC, V; no checks; dinner every day.* &

## Hong Kong Flower Lounge ★★

See the review of this restaurant's original (and more popular) Millbrae location in the following pages. ■ *5322 Geary Blvd (between 17th and 18th Aves), San Francisco; (415)668-8998; $$; full bar; AE, DC, DIS, MC, V; no checks; lunch, dinner every day.* &

## House of Nanking ★★

The dinnertime waiting line outside this tiny, greasy, wildly popular hole-in-the-wall starts at 5:30pm; by 6pm, you may face a 90-minute wait for a cramped, crowded, itsy-bitsy table with a plastic menu that lists only half of the best dishes served here. Lunchtime crowds make midday eating just as problematic. Here's a solution: arrive for a late lunch or a very early dinner (between 2:30pm and 5pm) and walk right in. When owner/chef/head-waiter Peter Fang can give you his full attention, he'll be glad to apprise you of the day's unlisted specials: succulent chicken or duck dumplings, an exotic shrimp-and-green-onion pancake with peanut sauce, or tempuralike sesame-battered Nanking scallops in a spicy garlic sauce. If Fang and his helpers are too busy to give you a rundown (frequently the case), take a look at what the diners sandwiched around you are eating and point to what looks good (it's hard to go wrong here, anyway). Nanking, Fang's hometown, is at the inland end of the Shanghai Railroad, making it an exchange point for foods from Sichuan, Peking, Guangdong, and the local coast. Fang is famous for concocting wily revisions of many traditional dishes, mingling different regional cuisines with his own inventions. While Nanking's food is outstanding and the prices are some of the most reasonable in the city, the service is downright terrible, often forgetful (you may not get your beer until 10 minutes after you've started eating), and it's the main reason this restaurant doesn't earn three stars. ■ *919 Kearny St (between Jackson St and Pacific Ave), San Francisco; (415)421-1429; $; beer and wine; no credit cards; no checks; lunch Mon–Sat, dinner every day.*

## Il Fornaio ★★

Il Fornaio began as a baker's school in Milan, a project started by the Veggetti family to collect regional recipes and save the disappearing art of Italian baking. In the late 1980s the Veggettis expanded their operation to include several retail bakeries, wholesale bakeries, and restaurants in California (there are now 16 restaurants) and plan openings soon in several Pacific Northwest cities. The San Francisco and Palo Alto restaurants were the first to make it to these shores, and although the staffs occasionally suffer from a too-sexy-for-my-hat attitude (particularly in the Palo Alto branch), there's no denying that Il Fornaio serves fantastic baked goods and good Northern Italian food in an airy, stylish setting. Breads and bread sticks, served with pungent, extra-virgin olive oil, provide simple and unpretentious proof of bread as art form. The antipasti are generally very good (give the grilled eggplant with goat cheese, sun-dried tomatoes, sweet onions, and capers a whirl), and the pizzas and calzones are universally delightful, crisp and smoke-flavored from the wood-burning oven. Interesting pasta choices include *paglia e fieno con gamberetti* (spinach and egg linguine tossed with marinated rock shrimp, garlic, and parsley) and *ravioli di verdura* (pasta stuffed with spinach, Swiss chard, pine nuts, and basil in a rich baby artichoke and tomato sauce). The meats from the rotisserie—duck, rabbit, chicken, turkey, rack of veal—are consistently well prepared. Dessert tortes, cakes, and cookies offer further proof of the skills of Il Fornaio's bakers. Many of the Il Fornaio restaurants in the Bay Area boast pretty patio dining, and the San Francisco branch offers one of the most pleasant outdoor dining areas in the city. The San Francisco and San Jose locales have garnered more favorable reviews than their siblings. ■ *1265 Battery St (in Levi's Plaza), San Francisco; (415)986-0100; www.ilfornaio.com; $$; full bar; AE, DC, MC, V; no checks; breakfast, lunch, dinner every day.* &

**La Taqueria** ★★ Among colorful fruit stands, thrift shops, and greasy panhandlers lining bustling Mission Street sits La Taqueria, the Bay Area's best burrito factory. Its lackluster interior is brightened only by a vibrant mural depicting south-of-the-border scenes and a shiny CD jukebox pumping out merry Mexican music, all of which could only mean one thing: people come here for the food. Don't expect a wide variety of fare, for the folks behind the counter just churn out what they do best: burritos, tacos, and quesadillas. It's all fresh, delicious, and guaranteed to fill you up—for little more than pocket change. The moist meaty fillings include grilled beef, pork, sausage, beef tongue, and chicken (and you won't find any rice in these burritos), and the *bebidas* vary from beer and soda to cantaloupe juice and even horchata (a sweet rice drink). Stand in line to place your order and pay, then take a seat at one of the shared, long wooden tables and wait for someone to bellow out your number (somehow they just *know* whether to say it in Spanish or English). To find La Taqueria among all the neighboring taquerias (and there are plenty of them), look for the white stucco facade and the bright red sign. A second location of this successful bean emporium is in San Jose. ■ *2889 Mission St (at 25th St), San Francisco; (415)285-7117; $; beer only; no credit cards; local checks only; lunch, dinner every day.* &

**Mecca** ★★ Mecca is a magnet for those who want an abundance of atmosphere with hearty American bistro fare—and this sexy, silver Mission Street supper club lined with chocolate brown velvet drapes delivers. Start with one of the sassy cocktails (how about a She's-a-Bad-Girl Mecca-rita with Cuervo, Cointreau, and lime?) at the slick, zinc-topped bar inset with multicolored fiber-optic lights, and enjoy the moody music, which is often provided by live jazz and R&B ensembles on the small stage. Chef Lynn Sheehan, former sous chef at Rubicon and a graduate of Madeleine Kamman's School for American Chefs, creates wonderful appetizers, including a caesar salad topped with shavings of Parmi-giano-Reggiano, a warm Catalan spinach salad with toasted pine nuts and chicken confit, and a roasted beet and goat cheese tart with mizuma, walnuts, and beet chips. Sheehan's wood-burning oven turns out great cornmeal-crust pizzas, and although some entrees have been more successful than others, the fish dishes are delicious, including seared salmon with a French lentil vinaigrette and boneless Idaho trout with roasted tomatoes and hazelnuts in a sherry-vinegar browned butter. And unlike most San Francisco restaurants, the glamorous Mecca serves dinner until midnight Thursday through Saturday. ■ *2029 Market St (between 14th and Dolores Sts, across from Safeway), San Francisco; (415)621-7000; www.sfmecca.com; $$$; full bar; AE, DC, MC, V; no checks; dinner every day.* ਟ੍ਰ

**One Market** ★★ Celebrity chef Bradley Ogden became a household name among Bay Area gastronomes when he opened San Francisco's chichi Campton Place restaurant in 1983, serving the fanciest versions of American food many people had ever seen. Although a number of folks couldn't afford to taste his exorbitantly priced though highly touted cuisine, they still knew he was making waves in the nation's sea of culinary celebrities. Then in 1989 he left the city and the Campton for the suburbs of Marin County, where he opened the more affordable and less pretentious Lark Creek Inn, which quickly became the county's best restaurant (see the Larkspur restaurant's review). Spurred by the great success of the Lark Creek, Ogden decided to branch out, coming back to the city in 1993 with One Market—a much larger venue for his fresh-from-the-farm-style cooking. From the start, the fare at One Market was surprisingly inconsistent, resulting in both bravos and boos from major restaurant critics. Recently, however, the enterprising (and over-extended) Ogden made the wise decision to hire chef George Morrone (of Aqua fame) to rule over the kitchen, and now things are on the upswing (though, as with most high-volume restaurants, the cooks occasionally miss their mark).

One Market's seasonal menus are still influenced by Ogden's midwestern roots, but it's Morrone's contemporary American fare—especially his excellent fish dishes—that dominates. On the list of starters you'll likely see George's Signature Sonoma Quail prepared with smoked bacon truffle jus as well as Bradley's Caesar Salad tossed with garlic-Parmesan croutons. Main courses might include a delightful potato-crusted rainbow trout, delicately seared local sand dabs, rack of pork (for two) with a pomegranate glaze, and Prince Edward Island mussels steamed with garlic and andouille sausage. Best bets on the made-from-scratch dessert menu are the incredible Tahitian vanilla bean ice cream served with a trio of warm sauces (caramel, hot fudge, and strawberry) and Ogden's signature dessert, chocolate brioche custard bread pudding with chocolate-bourbon sabayon. The dozens of waiters and waitresses clad in matching designer togs and ties dart from one end of the vast dining room to the other trying to keep as many as 230 customers satisfied, and while some succeed, others suffer from an abundance of arrogance. But the pretty restaurant makes up for such disappointments with its very good (and sometimes excellent) fare, not to mention the 500-bottle American wine list (one of the city's best) and live jazz piano music that filters through the cavernous dining room every evening. ■ *1 Market St (at Steuart St, across from the Ferry Building), San Francisco; (415)777-5577; $$$; full bar; AE, DC, MC, V; no checks; lunch Mon–Fri, dinner Mon–Sat.* &

**The Slanted Door** ★★ Thank goodness chef Charles Phan abandoned his original plan to build a crêpe stand in San Francisco, because otherwise we never would have had the opportunity to sink our teeth into his superb green papaya salad or stir-fried caramelized shrimp. When Phan and his large extended family discovered a vacant (and affordable) space on a slightly run-down stretch of Valencia Street, they ditched the crêpery plan in late 1995 and transformed the high-ceilinged room into a small, bilevel restaurant specializing in country Vietnamese food. Phan's design talents (he's a former UC Berkeley architecture student) are evident from the moment you enter the stylish, narrow dining room and take a seat at one of his green-stained wood tables. But even more impressive is Phan's unique fare, which attracts droves of people for lunch and dinner. The dinner menu changes weekly to reflect the market's offerings, but look for the favored spring rolls stuffed with fresh shrimp and pork; crab and asparagus soup; caramelized shrimp; curried chicken cooked with yams; "shaking" beef sautéed with onion and garlic; any of the terrific clay pot dishes; and, of course, Phan's special Vietnamese crêpes. When business is booming, the service gets slow, but if you order a pinot gris from the very good wine list, you won't mind so much. For dessert, the hands-down favorite is the all-American chocolate cake. Go figure. ■ *584 Valencia St (near 17th St), San Francisco; (415)861-8032; eat@slanteddoor.com; $–$$; beer and wine; MC, V; no checks; lunch, dinner Tues–Sun.* &

**Ton Kiang** ★★ Ton Kiang has established a solid reputation in San Francisco as one of the best Chinese restaurants in the city, particularly when it comes to dim sum and Hakka cuisine (a mixture of Chinese cuisines—sometimes referred to as "China's soul food"—developed by a nomadic Chinese tribe). There are two Ton Kiangs on Geary Boulevard, located about a mile apart from each other, but the smaller, more modern 22nd Avenue branch is far, far prettier than its ugly-duckling sister at Spruce, which doesn't serve dim sum. Ton Kiang's dim sum is phenomenal—fresh, flavorful, and not the least bit greasy (tip: on weekends ask for a table by the kitchen door to get first dibs from the dim sum carts). Other proven dishes on the regular menu are the ethereal steamed dumplings, chicken wonton soup, house special beef

▼
**San Francisco**
*Restaurants*
▲

and fishball soup (better than it sounds), fried spring rolls, steamed salt-baked chicken with a scallion and ginger sauce (a famous—though quite salty—Hakka dish), and any of the stuffed tofu or clay pot dishes (aka Hakka casseroles). Prices are slightly higher than the going rate in these parts, but definitely worth it. ■ *5821 Geary Blvd (between 22nd and 23rd Aves), San Francisco; (415)387-8273; $$; beer and wine; AE, DC, MC, V; no checks; lunch, dinner every day.* &

**Yank Sing** ★★ Living on the edge of the Pacific Rim has its advantages. For example, the best dim sum in the United States is probably served in the Bay Area. Yank Sing's fare is as good as any dim sum you'll get in Hong Kong, and the prices (and service) are much better than in nearby Harbor Village (see review, above). Numerous servers wander past your table with carts bearing steamer-baskets, bowls, and tureens. If you want some, just nod. Yank Sing serves more than 90 varieties of dim sum, including such standards as pot-stickers, spring rolls, plump shrimp, crab, fried eggplant, and *bao* (steamed buns stuffed with aromatically seasoned minced meat). The barbecued chicken (moist, aromatic, and wrapped in aluminum foil) is a house specialty, although some find it too sweet; other favorites are Peking duck (served by the slice), minced squab in lettuce cups, and soft-shell crab. The adventurous can nibble on the likes of braised chicken feet, marinated jellyfish, and steamed beef tripe. Make reservations or prepare to wait and wait and wait, especially for a weekend brunch. Take-out is available, too, and it costs much less. Another (though less popular) branch of Yank Sing is located in the SoMa district. ■ *427 Battery St (between Clay and Washington Sts), San Francisco; (415)781-1111 or (415)362-1640; www.yanksing.com; $$; full bar; AE, DC, MC, V; no checks; lunch every day.* & ■ *49 Stevenson St (near 1st St), San Francisco; (415)541-4949; www.yanksing.com; $$; beer and wine; AE, DC, MC, V; no checks; lunch Sun–Fri.* &

**Zuni Cafe** ★★ Before it got famous, Zuni was a tiny Southwestern-style lunch spot in a low-class neighborhood. When Chez Panisse alumna Judy Rodgers came on board as chef and co-owner, the cafe became so popular it had to more than double its size. Today, with its roaring copper-topped bar, grand piano, and exposed-brick dining room, it's nearly as quintessential a San Francisco institution as Dungeness crab and sourdough bread, though many loyal patrons miss the days when it was little more than a hole in the wall. It wouldn't be stretching the truth to say that one reason the neighborhood started improving was Zuni's Mediterranean-influenced upscale food, as divinely simple as only the supremely sophisticated can be. Picture a plate of mild, house-cured anchovies sprinkled with olives, celery, and Parmesan cheese; polenta with delicate mascarpone; a terrific caesar salad; a small, perfectly roasted chicken for two on a delicious bed of Tuscan bread salad; a grilled rib-eye steak accompanied by sweet white corn seasoned with fresh basil. At lunchtime and after 10pm, you can get some of the best burgers in town here, too, served on focaccia with aioli and house pickles (and be sure to order a side of the great shoestring potatoes). Service is first-rate for regulars and those who resemble them. ■ *1658 Market St (between Franklin and Gough Sts), San Francisco; (415)552-2522; $$; full bar; AE, MC, V; no checks; lunch, dinner, late dinner Tues–Sun.* ⅄

**Cypress Club ★** Reviews of the Cypress Club invariably begin with descriptions of its dining room, and for good reason: everything in this sumptuous restaurant is over the top. Bulging archways are lined in hammered copper; glass light fixtures look like huge sundaes or a woman's breasts (you choose); low, serpentine partitions snake through the room; plump burgundy velvet covers booths and chairs; and columns resemble giant urns. It's almost as if a particularly impish animator, instead of an interior decorator, had gotten the design commission and decided to fashion a luxury restaurant that would be just as at home in Toontown as San Francisco. All this visual drama could easily overshadow the food, and in some cases it does, depending on who's the chef that month. Unfortunately, the Cypress Club suffers from a revolving door of chefs and other personnel, leaving it difficult for patrons to know exactly what to expect when they take a seat in the plush dining room. At the time this book went to press, Stephen Janke, who previously worked in the kitchen at Aqua, had just donned the chef's hat and introduced his brand of California cuisine with a nod to the French. So far, standout entrees include his monkfish baked with heirloom pear tomatoes in a saffron lobster broth, herb-kissed loin of lamb with roasted baby beets and potato purée, and a whole oven-roasted trout stuffed with lemon, sage, and foie gras. Dinner comes to a rousing finale with temptations like warm lemon cake with white chocolate-poppyseed ice cream, dark chocolate and hazelnut timbale with Tahitian vanilla cream and chocolate sauce, and almond crème brûlée topped with honey-whipped cream. Be sure to scan the room as you dine, because you'll likely find yourself with some interesting dinner companions—everyone from TV talkshow host Conan O'Brien to fashion designer Isaac Mizrahi and actor Don Johnson have graced the Cypress Club's velvet-cushioned chairs. ■ *500 Jackson St (between Columbus Ave and Montgomery St), San Francisco; (415)296-8555; www.citysearch7.com; $$–$$$; full bar; AE, DC, MC, V; no checks; lunch Mon–Fri (in Dec only), dinner every day.* ⅄

**Swan Oyster Depot ★** This is where diehard San Francisco shellfish fans gleefully slurp down fresh blue point oysters, cherrystone clams, and delicious bowls of Boston clam chowder in between swigs of Anchor Steam beer. It's a one-of-a-kind San Francisco experience, the type of place tourists tend to unknowingly walk past. You won't find white linen tablecloths at this oyster bar—in fact, you won't even find any tables. Since 1912, patrons have balanced themselves on the 19 hard, rickety stools lining the long, narrow marble counter cluttered with bowls of oyster crackers, fresh-cut lemons, napkin holders, Tabasco sauce, and other seasonings. On the opposite side stands a quick-shucking team of some of the most congenial men in town, always ready and eager to serve. Other lunch specialties are the sizable salads (crab, shrimp, prawn, or a combo), seafood cocktails, cracked Dungeness crab, lobster, and smoked salmon and trout. If you want to take home some fish for supper, take a gander at all the fresh offerings in the display case: salmon, swordfish, delta crawfish, red snapper, trout, shrimp, lingcod, and whatever else the boat brought in that day. ▪ *1517 Polk St (at California St, next to See's Candies and the Royal Theatre), San Francisco; (415)673-1101; $$; beer and wine; no credit cards; checks OK; lunch Mon–Sat (open 8am-5:30pm).*

## LODGINGS

**Campton Place Kempinski Hotel** ★★★★ Almost as soon as the Campton Place reopened after an extensive restoration in 1984, its posh surroundings, stunning objets d'art, superlative service, and elegant accommodations began swaying the loyalties of the carriage trade away from traditional San Francisco hotels. The lobby, reminiscent of a gallery with its domed ceiling, miles of marble, crystal chandeliers, and striking Asian art, is worth the price of admission alone. The 117 guest rooms are very comfortable, and the Henredon armoires, custom-built chairs, and handsome desks help create a pervasive air of luxury. The travertine-marble bathrooms are equipped with telephones, terrycloth robes, hair dryers, French-milled soaps, and bath scales. For the best views, ask for one of the larger double-deluxe corner rooms on the upper floors (room 1501, which overlooks Union Square, is particularly stunning). A staff member will lend you a hand in packing and unpacking your wardrobe, and someone will tidy up after you at least twice a day. For help with your laundry, dry cleaning, shoeshine, or even baby-sitting, just pick up the phone and you'll be accommodated *tout de suite*. The concierge will make any and all of your arrangements (a reservation for the hotel's limo, perhaps?), and 24-hour room service will deliver whatever you're craving from the menu at the well-regarded **Campton Place** restaurant, one of the city's prettiest—and priciest—dining establishments (see review, above). There's also a small open-air atrium/roof garden overlooking Union Square where guests may recline in the sunshine, and a full line of services to meet your business needs. Should there be anything else your heart desires, the accommodating staff is sure to provide it—and at these prices, why shouldn't they? ▪ *340 Stockton St (between Sutter and Post Sts, at Union Square), San Francisco, CA 94108; (415)781-5555 or (800)235-4300; reserve@campton.com; $$$; full bar; AE, DC, MC, V; checks OK (for lodgings only); brunch Sun, breakfast, lunch Mon–Sat, dinner every day.* ♿

**Clift Hotel** ★★★★ As you step up to the entrance of this resplendent 17-story mansion, a doorman will politely usher you into the lobby, a vast gilded chamber replete with sparkling chandeliers and fine Oriental carpets. Stroll across the room to the source of the piano music and you'll discover this hotel's crowning jewel: the **Redwood Room**. Built entirely from a single 2,000-year-old Northern California coastal redwood, this romantic, dimly lit room is considered by many the most beautiful cocktail lounge in the city, with carved redwood panels polished to a high gloss, art deco lamps, and gorgeous reproductions of Gustav Klimt paintings adorning the walls. Settle into one of the cozy love seats, order a martini, and nibble on nuts as you listen to the talented pianist perform everything from Bach to Scott Joplin, and you'll soon be bewitched by the Redwood Room's charms. But this isn't the only beautiful room in the house. Each of the 326 individually designed guest rooms boasts luxurious hardwood furnishings, an abundance of Brunschwig & Fils fabric, attractive armoires that conceal TVs (and VCRs upon request), marble bathrooms complete with plush robes and hair dryers, and well-stocked honor bars. As with most of San Francisco's high-rise hotels, the higher the floor, the better the view (and, yes, it costs a few more bills, but at these rates you'll hardly notice the difference).

You'll find all the usual high-class perks at the Clift: 24-hour room service, a complimentary limo to transport you to the Financial District, overnight shoe shines, a concierge, a fitness center, and an exemplary business center. Families will love the Clift's VIK (Very Important Kids) program, which offers younger guests (and their grateful parents) a staggering array of services and supplies ranging from pacifiers, strollers, and diapers to Disney movies, video and board games, and activities for older children. This is also one the few hotels in the city that allows pets. **The French Room**, the Clift's opulent restaurant decorated with immense crystal chandeliers, Louis XV furnishings, and flamboyant floral arrangements, serves fine California fare with a French flair. All this, combined with the hotel's prime theater district location and its proximity to Union Square and Chinatown, explains why the Clift is regarded as one of the grandest hotels in San Francisco. ■ *495 Geary St (at Taylor St, 1½ blocks from Union Square), San Francisco, CA 94102; (415)775-4700 or (800)332-3442; $$$; full bar; AE, DC, MC, V; checks OK; brunch Sun, breakfast, lunch Mon–Sat, dinner every day.* &

**Hotel Monaco** ★★★★ "Wow!" is a common exclamation among first-time guests of Hotel Monaco, one of San Francisco's hottest new hotels in a city that's brimming with top-notch accommodations. After a $24-million renovation, Monaco opened in June 1995 and has received nothing but kudos for its sumptuous, stunning decor. Expect a melding of modern European fashion with flourishes of the American Beaux Arts era—the trademark of award-winning designer Cheryl Rowley, who envisioned the 201-room hotel as a "great ship traveling to the farthest reaches of the world, collecting exotic, precious treasures and antiquities." Hence the guest rooms bedecked with canopy beds, Chinese-inspired armoires, bamboo writing desks, old-fashioned decorative luggage, and profusion of bold stripes and vibrant colors. The entire hotel is truly a feast for the eyes, particularly the **Grand Cafe** with its 30-foot ceilings, cascading chandeliers, plethora of stately columns, and many art nouveau frills—all vestiges of its former incarnation as the hotel's grand ballroom. A chic be-and-be-seen crowd typically fills the impressive dining room, noshing on trendy Mediterranean fare. Unfortunately, the kitchen's creations are often inconsistent; best bets include the polenta soufflé, duck confit, steamed mussels with saffron and leeks, and filet mignon au poivre vert.

Of course there are the requisite hotel toys (health club, steam room, whirlpool spa, sauna), services (massages, manicures, valet parking, business and room service), and complimentary perks (newspaper delivery, morning coffee, evening wine reception). You'll also like the location: in the heart of San Francisco's theater district, a mere two blocks from Union Square and the cable cars. Is it expensive as it sounds? Comparatively, no: standard rooms start at about $190, which is only slightly above the city's average hotel rate of $178—a fair price for such a rococo retreat. ∎ *501 Geary St (at Taylor St), San Francisco, CA 94102; (415) 292-0100 or (800) 214-4220; $$$; full bar; AE, DC, DIS, MC, V; no checks; breakfast, lunch, dinner every day.* &

**The Ritz-Carlton, San Francisco** ★★★★ In 1991, after a four-year, multimillion-dollar renovation, this 1909 17-columned neoclassical beauty—formerly the Metropolitan Life Insurance Company building—reopened as the Ritz-Carlton hotel. Since then, it's been stacking up heady accolades, including a seventh-place ranking in *Condé Nast Traveler*'s 1997 list of the top 25 hotels in North America (and a first-place ranking in San Francisco). It's fashionable to a fault: as you arrive by car, prepare to be assaulted by valets in top hats rushing to park your car while a gaggle of natty, nimble young men leap to usher you through the entryway (some folks find the kowtowing a bit annoying, but others are wild about the Ritz for just this type of service). The hotel's lobby is breathtaking, with a series of enormous, high-ceilinged lounges, gigantic floral arrangements, an abundance of museum-quality paintings and antiques, and crystal chandeliers at every turn. The spectacular **Lobby Lounge** is *the* place to mingle over an afternoon tea or sushi, and live piano performances perk up the scene every day.

The 336 guest rooms were the hotel's only downfall (rather drab, to say the least), but a more recent renovation has spruced things up considerably, though high fashion they are not: If it's GQ Casual you're after, try the Hotel Monaco. Regardless, they're sinfully plush and loaded with high-society amenities such as spiffy marble bathrooms, fully stocked honor bars, thick terrycloth robes, in-room safes, phones, and remote-control TVs. Some (though not many) have wonderful views of the city and the bay, but your best bets are the quieter rooms overlooking the landscaped courtyard. Business services abound, with a range of conference and meeting rooms and a limo to whisk you off to the Financial District or Union Square. The hotel's ritzy fitness center has an indoor lap pool, whirlpool, sauna, a fully equipped training room, and massage services. Two restaurants are located in the hotel: the formal **Dining Room at the Ritz-Carlton**, one of the top restaurants in the city (see review, above), and the more casual **Terrace**, serving excellent Mediterranean fare and sensational desserts in a pleasant dining room adorned with handsome oil paintings. When the weather is warm, sit on the Terrace's beautiful, flower-bedecked brick courtyard, the only alfresco dining area offered by a San Francisco hotel. ■ *600 Stockton St (at California St, on Nob Hill), San Francisco, CA 94108-2305; (415) 296-7465 or (800) 241-3333 (reservations only); www.ritz-carlton.com; $$$; full bar; AE, DC, DIS, MC, V; no checks; Terrace: jazz brunch Sun, breakfast, lunch, dinner every day; Dining Room: dinner Mon–Sat.* &

**The Sherman House** ★★★★ Once the home of musical-instrument magnate and opera buff Leander Sherman, this 1876 Victorian mansion has housed such luminaries as Lillian Russell and Enrico Caruso, who sang to privileged guests in the house's private three-story recital hall. Although the Sherman House survived the 1906 quake, the poorly maintained edifice seemed destined to remain just another tired historical landmark (a status that saved it from demolition) until art historian Vesta Mobedshahi and her hotelier husband Manou bought it in 1980. With the help of designer William Gaylord, the couple spent four years and a small fortune restoring the 4½-story mansion to its original splendor—and *then* some. The stunning decor is based on a French Second Empire motif with fine antiques and choice custom replicas, richly upholstered sofas and chairs, and gorgeous carpets covering polished hardwood floors. The huge, skylit recital hall still has a grand piano, but now the room serves as a luxurious lobby guarded by a bevy of musically minded finches. Most of the eight guest rooms and the six one-bedroom suites feature gilded bronze chandeliers, brocaded bed hangings, rich tapestries, and beautifully crafted wainscoting. A few rooms even have such extras as a private garden, bay view, and rooftop deck, and all but one have a wood-burning marble fireplace (ask for one of the upstairs rooms, which have broad bay windows, plush window seats, and views of the bay). If you prefer more contemporary surroundings, take the cobblestone path behind the house through the English-style garden and past its gazebo, fountains, and greenhouse to the Carriage House, which contains three luxury suites decorated with silk floral fabrics and French Country furnishings. The concierge, butler, valet parking, and

24-hour room services are superb. Guests are also given exclusive seating at the **Sherman House Restaurant**—a grand dining establishment, though it's now closed to nonguests due to pesky zoning laws and irate neighbors who complained about the traffic. The leaded-glass solarium offers a sunny setting for breakfast, and afternoon tea is served in an upstairs gallery reminiscent of a Second Empire salon. ■ *2160 Green St (between Fillmore and Webster Sts, 1 block S of Union St), San Francisco, CA 94123; (415)563-3600; www.integra.fr/relaischateaux/sherman; $$$; beer and wine; AE, DC, MC, V; checks OK; breakfast, lunch, dinner every day for guests only (reservations required).*

## The Archbishop's Mansion ★★★

This stately Belle Epoque mansion, built in 1904 for San Francisco's archbishop, is an exercise in Victorian splendor and excess: a three-story staircase winds beneath a gorgeous, 16-foot-tall stained-glass dome, and the surrounding redwood Corinthian columns, crystal chandeliers, Oriental carpets, and gorgeous antiques create an aura of almost papal splendor. The 15 large rooms and suites, each named after a famous opera, are decorated with lush fabrics, embroidered linens, and 19th-century antiques. All have partial canopied beds and private baths with stacks of plush towels and French-milled soaps. Many rooms have a fireplace, Jacuzzi tub, and a view of the park, and some have a parlor and sitting area. The posh, rose-colored Carmen Suite has a claw-footed bathtub in front of a fireplace, a comfortable sitting room with yet *another* fireplace, and a pretty view of Alamo Park. The ultra-luxurious Don Giovanni Suite boasts a cherub-encrusted antique four-poster bed imported from a French castle, as well as a parlor with a palatial fireplace and a lavish seven-head shower in the bathroom. You may breakfast in bed on scones and croissants, then, after spending the day strolling through the park admiring the neighborhood's cherished Victorian homes, return in the afternoon for wine in the French parlor, which is graced by a grand piano that once belonged to Noël Coward. In the evening, ask the concierge to line up a limo to whisk you away to the nearby War Memorial Opera House or Davies Symphony Hall. ■ *1000 Fulton St (at Steiner St), San Francisco, CA 94117; (415)563-7872 or (800)543-5820; www.sftrips.com; $$$; AE, MC, V; checks OK.*

## El Drisco ★★★

If you're a fan of San Francisco's Ritz-Carlton hotel, you'll adore El Drisco. The recent resortation of this magnificent Pacific Heights accommodation started out as mainly a real estate investment for a small group of partners but soon escalated into a labor of love. The six-story structure, perched on one of the most coveted blocks in San Francisco, was originally built in 1903 as a boardinghouse for neighborhood servants. After surviving the great fire of 1906, it was converted into a hotel in the mid '20s but eventually fell into major disrepair. Combining the financial might of hotelier Tom Callinan (Meadowood, the Inn at Southbridge) and the interior design skills of Glenn Texeira

(Ritz-Carlton, Manila), El Drisco's proprietors transformed years of blood, sweat, and greenbacks into one of the finest small hotels in the city. The 24 rooms and 19 suites are bathed in soothing shades of alabaster, celadon, and buttercup yellow and feature rich fabrics, quality antiques, and superior mattresses. Standard amenities include a two-line phone with a modem hookup, a CD player, a discreetly hidden TV with a VCR, and a minibar; suites include a handsome sofa bed, an additional phone and TV, and terrific views. The spacious marble-clad bathrooms are equipped with hair dryers, plush robes, and (in most units) bathtubs. Room 304A—a corner suite with an extraordinary view of Pacific Heights mansions and the surrounding bay—is a favorite. An extended continental breakfast is served in one of the three quiet, comfortable common rooms. Although El Drisco's service isn't nearly as polished as that of the ultra-efficient staff at the Ritz-Carlton, the hotel's management is trying hard to change that. If it succeeds, El Drisco may very well earn a highly coveted four-star ranking. ■ *2901 Pacific Ave (at Broderick St), San Francisco, CA 94115; (415)346-2880 or (800)634-7277; $$$; AE, DC, DIS, MC, V; no checks.* &

**Hotel Diva ★★★** When it first opened in 1985, Hotel Diva was the prima donna of San Francisco's modern hotels, winning Best Hotel Design from *Interiors* magazine for its suave, ultramodern design. The hotel's facade is a veritable work of art, a fashionable fusion of cement, steel, and glass that is *très chic*. But the design works don't stop here: even the 111 guest rooms are works of art, decorated with handsome Italian modern furnishings. Standard luxury amenities in each room include an individually controlled air conditioner, a remote-control television with interactive multimedia and VCR, two telephones with extra-long cords, a data port, voice mail, and a personal safe. Guest services include a complimentary breakfast of fresh fruit, breads, yogurt, coffee, and orange juice delivered to your boudoir, room service via the neighboring California Pizza Kitchen, a concierge, a 24-hour fitness center, and a business center offering free use of computers, software, and a laser printer. Best of all, the Diva is in a prime location, just around the corner from Union Square. Insider tip: reserve one of the rooms ending in "09," which have extra-large bathrooms with vanity mirrors and makeup tables. ■ *440 Geary St (between Mason and Taylor Sts), San Francisco, CA 94102; (415)885-0200 or (800)553-1900; $$$; AE, DC, DIS, MC, V; checks OK.* &

**Hotel Triton ★★★** The Hotel Triton has been described as modern, whimsical, sophisticated, chic, vogue, neo-Baroque, ultra-hip, and retro-futuristic—but the words just don't do justice to this unique hostelry-cum-art-gallery that you'll simply have to see to appreciate. The entire hotel, from the bellhop's inverted-pyramid-shaped podium to the iridescent throw pillows on the beds and the ashtrays ringed with faux pearls, is the original work of four imaginative (some might say wacky) San Francisco artisans. For a preview of what's behind the bedroom doors, peek into the lobby, where you'll see curvaceous chairs shimmering in gold silk taffeta, an imposing duo of floor-to-ceiling pillars sheathed in teal, purple, and gold leaf, and a pastel mural portraying mythic images of sea life, triton shells, and human figures—all that's missing are Dorothy, Toto, and the ruby slippers. Add to this visual extravaganza all the amenities you'd find in any luxury hotel, including a concierge, valet parking (essential in this part of town), room service, complimentary wine and coffee, business and limousine services, and even a fitness center. The 133 rooms and seven designer suites (designed by such celebs as Carlos Santana, Joe Boxer, and the late Jerry Garcia) continue the modern wonderland theme: walls are splashed with giant, hand-painted yellow and blue diamonds, king-size beds feature navy-and-khaki-striped camelback headboards, and armoires that hide remote-control TVs are topped with golden crowns. The tree-hugger in all of us can embrace the EcoFloor, the Triton's environmentally conscious seventh floor where almost everything is made from recycled, biodegradable, or organically grown materials, and the air and water is passed through fancy filtration systems. Heck, the Triton is so utterly hip, even the elevator swings to Thelonious Monk. ■ *342 Grant Ave (at Bush St, near the gateway to Chinatown), San Francisco, CA 94108; (415)394-0500 or (800)433-6611; www.hotel-tritonsf.com; $$$; AE, DC, DIS, MC, V; checks OK.* ♿

**Huntington Hotel** ★★★ The small, modest lobby of this imposing Nob Hill landmark belies its lavish interiors. The Huntington is graced with a remarkable array of antiques, plush sofas, and museum-quality objets d'art; the doorman is subdued and genteel but always seems delighted to see you; and the staff maintains a professional attitude and at the same time treats you like a favored guest. These things—along with superb security—explain why the Huntington has long been a favorite of many of San Francisco's visiting dignitaries and celebrities, from Archbishop Desmond Tutu to Robert Redford. The 12-story hotel's 140 rooms are spacious and lavish, with imported silks, 17th-century paintings, and stunning views of the city and the bay. The rooms are individually decorated, and some are so handsome they have been featured in *Architectural Digest.* Several flaunt gold velvet sofas and fringed, tufted hassocks surrounded by antiques, while others boast modern leather couches, faux-leopard-skin hassocks, and marble bars. Guests are treated to a formal afternoon tea and complimentary sherry, nightly turn-down service, and a morning paper. Valet parking and room service also are available, along with a full range of business services and access to the Nob Hill Club, a top-of-the-line fitness center one block away. Yes, Virginia, it's expensive, but special offers such as the Romance Package (including free champagne, sherry, and limousine service) make the Huntington worth considering for that special occasion.

San Francisco
Bay Area

San Francisco

*Lodgings*

The Huntington hotel's handsome restaurant, **The Big Four** (named after a quartet of railroad tycoons), offers seasonal continental cuisine in a dining room harking back to the age of robber barons. Thick leather chairs and benches, sparkling beveled glass, and an impressive array of early California memorabilia add to the restaurant's rich, clubby atmosphere (hence the aroma of cigar smoke emanating from the bar). Chef Gloria Ciccarone-Nehles is known for her wild game dishes, such as caribou, smoked squab, venison, and wild boar. ■ *1075 California St (at the top of Nob Hill, across from Grace Cathedral), San Francisco, CA 94108; (415) 474-5400 or (800) 652-1539 (in California only), and (800) 227-4683 (outside California only); $$$; full bar; AE, DC, DIS, MC, V; checks OK; breakfast every day, lunch Mon–Fri, dinner every day.*

**Mandarin Oriental** ★★★ The rooms at the award-winning Mandarin Oriental offer some of the most remarkable views in the city. Because it's perched high in the sky (on the top 11 floors of the 48-story First Interstate Building, San Francisco's third tallest skyscraper), you're not only guaranteed a bird's-eye view of the city, you'll be gazing at the *entire* Bay Area. The Mandarin Oriental's 158 rooms are comfortable and deceptively austere: well hidden among the simple blond-wood furniture and fine Asian artwork are all the latest luxury amenities: three two-line speaker phones with facsimile hookups, remote-control televisions with access to video movies, and fully stocked minibars and refrigerators, as well as jumbo marble bathrooms with stall showers and extra-deep soaking tubs (you can even admire the city's skyline from some of the bathtubs). Once settled in your room, you'll be treated to jasmine tea and Thai silk slippers. Contrary to the policy of many other hotels, the room rates at the Mandarin don't vary according to scenery, so request one of the corner rooms (room numbers ending with 6 or 11), which offer the best views. Additional perks include access to numerous business services, valet parking, a continental breakfast served in the lounge, shoe shines, 24-hour room service, and a state-of-the-art fitness center.

The hotel's restaurant, **Silks**, may be the Maytag repairman of luxury restaurants; it's all gussied up and anxious to serve, but a tad lonely and underappreciated. This flagship restaurant has never managed to catch on with local foodies despite a decade of critical acclaim for what was once exceptional California–Pacific Rim cuisine. Perhaps its in-hotel location has hampered its popularity (although that hasn't been the case with Postrio, *et al.*), or maybe it's the three remodels that hint at a decor identity crisis, or the frequent passing of the chef's toque. At press time, an executive chef had not yet been hired and the menu had made a dramatic shift to contemporary American fare. Visually, the last remodel attempted to make the elegant dining room a bit more amiable, with dramatic modern art, wood-latticed windows, recessed lighting, soaring floral arrangements, and thick carpeting.

■ *222 Sansome St (between Pine and California Sts, in the Financial District), San Francisco, CA 94104-2792; (415) 885-0999 or (800) 622-0404; mosfo@aol.com; www.mandarin-oriental. com; $$$; full bar; AE, DC, DIS, MC, V; checks OK (for lodgings only); breakfast, lunch, dinner every day.* ᕇ

**Palace Hotel** ★★★ Reminiscent of more romantic times, this opulent hotel built in 1875 (and, like most everything else in the city, rebuilt after the big quake and fire of 1906) has housed such luminaries as Thomas Edison, D. H. Lawrence, Amelia Earhart, Winston Churchill, and Joe Montana, as well as 10 American presidents and numerous aristocrats and royalty from around the world. Hoping to attract a similarly high-class clientele in the future, the management closed the Palace in 1989 for 27 months and poured $170 million into restoring it to its original splendor. And splendid it is. The downstairs decor is truly breathtaking, from the multiple sparkling Austrian-crystal chandeliers, the double row of white Italian marble Ionic columns, and the 80,000 panes of stained glass that make up the Garden Court's exquisite dome, to the three grand ballrooms and the commissioned paintings and early 19th-century French tapestry that adorn the Palace's walls. Unfortunately, all this impressive glitz comes to a screeching halt when you open the door to one of the 551 guest rooms. Although comfortable and attractive, the rooms are more akin to gussied-up generic hotel rooms than to any palace chamber. However, you will find all the standard luxury-hotel perks here, including a concierge, 24-hour room service, valet parking, and an elaborate business center, plus a new, palm-embellished health club with an exercise room, coed sauna, whirlpool, and stunning white-tiled lap pool capped by a dome of clear glass.

▼

The Palace has an embarrassment of riches when it comes to restaurants: the sky-lit **Garden Court**, one of the world's most spectacular dining rooms, is famous for its elaborate breakfast buffet and elegant afternoon tea (see review, above); **Kyo-ya**, a rather austere Japanese dining room with black lacquer chairs and glossy wood tables, serves the best (and most expensive) sushi and sashimi in town (see review, above); the masculine **Maxfield's** (named in honor of Maxfield Parrish), with its sophisticated men's club ambience and stained-glass ceiling, serves traditional San Francisco grill fare; and the small, comfortable **Pied Piper Bar** is dominated by a stunning, $2.5 million, 1909 Maxfield Parrish painting of the Pied Piper of Hamelin leading a band of 27 children. Even if you don't have the resources to recline or dine here, like most palaces, this one is worth a self-guided tour.

■ *2 New Montgomery St (on Market St, next to the Montgomery BART station), San Francisco, CA 94105; (415) 392-8600 or (800) 325-3535 (reservations only); www.sheraton.com; $$$; full bar; AE, DC, DIS, MC, V; checks OK (for lodgings only); breakfast, lunch, dinner every day.* ᕇ

**The Prescott Hotel** ★★★ Booking a room at the Prescott simply to gain access to a table at the hotel's adjoining restaurant is not unheard of. After all, not just any hotel can boast the extraordinary cuisine of Wolfgang Puck's famous (and perpetually booked) **Postrio** (see review, above). Opened in 1989 by San Francisco hotel magnate Bill Kimpton, the Prescott has put pressure on Union Square's neighboring luxury hotels by offering first-rate accommodations at a fairly reasonable price. This, combined with dining privileges at one of the city's most talked-about restaurants, superlative service from an intelligent, youthful staff, and a prime location in the heart of San Francisco, places the Prescott at the top of the Union Square hotel list. The rooms, decorated with custom-made cherry-wood furnishings, black-granite-topped nightstands and dressers, and silk wallpaper, have rich color schemes of hunter green, deep purple, cerise, taupe, and gold. The Prescott offers 154 rooms, including numerous suites and a wildly posh penthouse complete with a grand piano, a rooftop Jacuzzi, a formal dining room, and twin fireplaces. For an additional $20 per night, you may gain "Club Concierge Level" status, which grants you access to a plush lounge (complete with a complimentary premium bar), an hors d'oeuvres reception, and a continental breakfast, as well as a host of other privileges—not a bad investment for 20 bones. Standard perks include limo service to the Financial District, overnight shoe shine, valet parking, laundry service, a daily newspaper delivered to your room, and access to the adjacent fitness facility. ■ *545 Post St (between Taylor and Mason Sts), San Francisco, CA 94102; (415)563-0303 or (800)283-7322; $$$; full bar; AE, DC, DIS, MC, V; checks OK (for lodgings only); brunch Sat–Sun, breakfast, lunch Mon–Fri, dinner every day.* ♿

**The Bed and Breakfast Inn** ★★ San Francisco's first bed and breakfast maintains the convincing illusion that it's a charming old English inn in a picturesque mews somewhere in Cornwall. The main difference, of course, is that you're not surrounded by verdant countryside dotted with horses and sheep munching on grassy meadows and wildflowers. Instead, this B&B tucked into a cul-de-sac is just steps away from the popular boutiques, bars, and restaurants lining Union Street, one of the city's most popular shopping areas. The three adjoining green Victorian buildings— graced with twining ivy, window boxes bursting with bright red geraniums, and a birdhouse bobbing from a tree out front—offer 11 enchanting guest rooms, each individually decorated with antiques, floral prints, and appealing personal touches (ask for a room that opens directly onto the alluring back garden). The least expensive rooms have shared baths. Of the two sunny penthouses, the Mayfair offers a living room, kitchen, latticed balcony, and spiral staircase leading to a bedroom loft with a king-size bed; the Garden Suite, popular with groups of four, has a king-size bed in the master bedroom, a double bed in the loft, a

Mendocino

fully stocked kitchen, a living room with a fireplace, two bathrooms (one with a Jacuzzi tub), and French doors leading to a private atrium and garden. You may enjoy your simple continental breakfast in your room, the garden, or the diminutive English tearoom. ■ *4 Charlton Court (in a cul-de-sac off Union St, between Buchanan and Laguna Sts), San Francisco, CA 94123; (415)921-9784; $$; no credit cards; checks OK.*

**Commodore International Hotel** ★★ Hotelier Chip Conley, a rising star in San Francisco's brutally competitive accommodations business, has a knack for niches—hence his relatively new 113-room Commodore International Hotel, a fun and surprisingly affordable hostelry. The Commodore actually helps guests explore the city by offering a free staff-created tour book that highlights San Francisco's top insider attractions; if after reading it you're still baffled about what to do next in this city of plenty, spin the gimmicky but fun Wheel of Fortune located in the hotel's sexy lobby and let it choose an only-in-San-Francisco activity for you. The hotel's lower Sutter Street location means that all the hot tourist spots—Chinatown, Union Square, the Financial District—are within walking distance. And after a day of exploring, you can cool your tired dogs here at the wickedly hip **Red Room**, a dazzling bar and cocktail lounge that reflects no other spectrum of light but ruby red. Also adjoining the lobby is an art deco–style diner serving inexpensive buckwheat griddle cakes, big burgers, tofu sandwiches, and similar fare. If you're on a tight budget, stick with the plain but pleasant rooms on the first four floors; otherwise, break out an extra Jackson and live it up near the top, where the interiors echo the neo-Deco theme. All guest rooms feature a large walk-in closet, a tub and shower, cable TV, and a phone with a data port. There's also access to a full-service health club, room service via Waiters on Wheels (a company that delivers from numerous restaurants in the city), and nearby parking for an extra fee. ■ *825 Sutter St (between Jones and Leavenworth Sts), San Francisco, CA 94109; (415)923-6800 or (800)338-6848; commodore@worldnet.att.net; www.joiedevivre-sf.com; $$; AE, DC, DIS, MC, V; no checks.*

**Hotel Bohème** ★★ Hopelessly chic is perhaps the best way to describe the Hotel Bohème, one of the sexiest small hotels in the city and a favorite retreat of visiting writers and poets. Hovering two stories above Columbus Avenue—the Rue St. Michelle of San Francisco streets—the Bohème artfully reflects North Beach's bohemian flair dating from the late 1950s and early 60s. The time trip starts with a gallery of moody black-and-white photographs lining the hallways and segues into the 15 guest rooms decorated in soothing shades of sage green, cantaloupe, lavender, and black. The rooms feature handmade light fixtures crafted from glazed collages of jazz sheet music, Ginsberg poetry, and old menus and headlines, as well as black iron beds with sheer canopies, European armoires, bistro tables, wicker chairs, and

Barnes, Picasso, and Matisse prints. Modern amenities abound, including private baths, remote-control cable TV, and telephones with modem jacks. A couple of minor caveats: most rooms are quite small, and those facing Columbus Avenue aren't kind to light sleepers (though views of the ever-bustling cafes and shops are entrancing). Otherwise, Hotel Bohème's engaging amalgamation of art, poetry, and hospitality will forever turn you away from America's cookie-cutter corporate hotels. ■ *444 Columbus Ave (between Vallejo and Green Sts), San Francisco, CA 94133; (415)433-9111; AK@hotelboheme.com; www.hotelboheme.com; $$; AE, DC, DIS, MC, V; no checks.*

**The Hotel Majestic ★★** An orgy of Victorian grandeur, this five-story Edwardian building, located in a residential neighborhood near Japantown, was one of San Francisco's earliest grand hotels. Marble steps and ornate beveled-glass doors open onto a magnificent, cozy lobby featuring dark green marble pillars, black-and-burgundy floral carpeting, plush rose-colored sofas, chairs and pillows cloaked in silk-tasseled brocades, a white marble fireplace topped with a precious 19th-century bronze clock, and numerous antique fixtures. Upstairs, the 51 guest rooms and eight luxury suites are individually decorated with a mixture of French Empire and English antiques, custom-made matching furniture (including large, hand-painted, four-poster canopied beds), as well as modern amenities such as televisions, private baths, direct-dial phones, and individually controlled thermostats. For maximum charm, request a deluxe room or suite; these rooms have wonderful semicircular bay windows as well as fireplaces and queen-size beds. Concierge services, business facilities, valet service, a limousine, and valet parking are also available. The adjacent **Cafe Majestic**, one of the city's more romantic restaurants, serves very good seasonal dishes ranging from sautéed coho salmon with fresh peach salsa to a mixed grill of lamb chop, quail, and sausage with polenta. After dinner, sip a *digestif* at the handsome 19th-century French mahogany bar and note the fascinating framed butterfly collection displayed on the dark turquoise walls. ■ *1500 Sutter St (at Gough St), San Francisco, CA 94109; (415)441-1100 or (800)869-8966; $$$; full bar; AE, DC, MC, V; no checks; breakfast, dinner Tues–Sat.* &

**Jackson Court ★★** Tucked away behind a brick archway and a white-trellised garden courtyard, this three-story brownstone is set in the heart of the exclusive Pacific Heights residential neighborhood. The living room of the sedate manse is comfortably grand, with Oriental carpeting, gilt-framed mirrors, and a striking, oversized fireplace adorned with figures of wind sprites and storm gods. All 10 blissfully quiet guest rooms have handsome architectural details, pleasantly spare high-quality antiques, telephones, cable television, and private baths; two rooms have fireplaces. Particularly noteworthy is the luxurious Garden Court suite, originally the mansion's dining room, which boasts handcrafted wood paneling and cabinets, an antique chandelier, period furnishings, a king-size bed, and a private garden patio. After dining downstairs on the expanded continental breakfast, spend the day browsing through the numerous boutiques along bustling Union Street and return in time for the late afternoon tea served in the living room. ■ *2198 Jackson St (at Buchanan St, in Pacific Heights), San Francisco, CA 94115; (415)929-7670; $$$; AE, MC, V; checks OK.*

**Petite Auberge** ★★ Located a few blocks from Union Square, the Petite Auberge is a romanticized version of a French Country inn with terra-cotta tile floors, Pierre Deux fabrics, oak furniture, lace curtains, and dried floral wreaths adorning the walls. You'll also see lots of teddy bears on parade, vintage children's toys on shelves and mantels, and a carousel horse cantering in the lobby—not everyone's taste, for sure. In truth, the 26 rooms are small but sweet, with inviting window seats; most have fireplaces. (Rooms on the upper floors toward the back tend to be the quietest.) Honeymooners should splurge on the Petite Suite, which has its own private entrance, deck, and spa tub. Guests are supplied with terrycloth robes, and shoes are shined overnight and delivered with the morning paper; nightly turn-down service includes a chocolate on your pillow. A generous buffet breakfast is served downstairs in a quaint breakfast room with French doors that open onto a small garden. In the afternoon, you may sip tea or wine and snack on hors d'oeuvres in a lounge where a horde of teddy bears on gingham-checked couches face off with a row of rabbits in front of the fireplace. Guests who need to work may use the business services at the White Swan Inn (owned by the same people) just two doors away. ■ *863 Bush St (between Taylor and Mason Sts, near Union Square and Nob Hill), San Francisco, CA 94108; (415)928-6000; $$$; AE, DC, MC, V; checks OK.*

**Savoy Hotel** ★★ Originally built in 1913 for the Panama-Pacific Exposition, this seven-story hotel has had its ups and downs over the years—mostly downs. It was rescued, however, by the same couple who saved the opulent Sherman House when it too was little more than a ramshackle structure. Thanks to the Mobedshahis, who have since sold it, the Savoy is now a posh French Country–style inn with a gorgeous facade of richly veined black marble, beveled glass, mahogany, and polished brass. It's ideally located in the center of the theater district and just 2½ blocks from Union Square. The 83 guest rooms and suites are small but beautifully appointed, with reams of *toile de Jouy* fabrics, heavy French cotton bedspreads, imported Provençal furnishings, plump feather beds, goose-down pillows, two-line telephones with modem jacks, and minibars. A few of the suites come with Jacuzzi tubs. The most tranquil rooms are on the northeast corner (farthest from the traffic noise) facing a rear courtyard. Guests are nurtured with a continental breakfast and afternoon tea and sherry; a full breakfast is also available. Additional amenities include an overnight shoe shine and room service from the hotel's popular **Brasserie Savoy**. This restaurant is a replica of an authentic French brasserie right down to the zinc bar, black-and-white marble floors, comfy banquettes, woven-leather chairs, and a staff clad in long, starched white aprons. Its air of casual sophistication, reasonable prices, and generally very good food—foie gras pâté, filet mignon with truffle sauce, crispy sweetbreads, duck confit—make it a reliable bet, especially for a meal before show time (ask about the well-priced three-course dinner special offered from 5pm to 8pm daily). ■ *580 Geary St (between Taylor and Jones Sts), San Francisco, CA 94102; (415)441-2700 or (800)227-4223; www.masteryellowpages.com; $$; full bar; AE, DC, DIS, MC, V; no checks; breakfast, dinner every day.* ♿

**Tuscan Inn** ★★ Located in the heart of Fisherman's Wharf, San Francisco's most popular tourist attraction, and just a skip away from Ghirardelli Square, the Embarcadero, and the cable car lines, it's no wonder the low-key Tuscan Inn is the favored hideout of many of Hollywood's actors and producers. You won't find the glitz of San Francisco's downtown hostelries or even a terrific view here, but the Tuscan's 221 attractive guest rooms (including 12 deluxe suites) offer every creature comfort one could need. Burgundy floral-print bedspreads, armchairs, writing desks, honor bars, remote-control TVs, direct-dial phones, and private bathrooms are standard features of every room. And, typical of a hotelier Bill Kimpton enterprise, a room at the Tuscan comes with a plethora of complimentary services: a concierge, coffee and biscotti served in the lobby every morning, weekday limousine service to the Financial District and the Moscone Convention Center, an evening wine reception, room service, valet parking, and same-day laundry service. The Tuscan also offers guest privileges at several popular San Francisco fitness centers, including a 24 Hour Nautilus just a block away. Adjoining the hotel is the glittering **Cafe Pescatore**, a classic Italian trattoria serving very good fresh fish and pasta dishes as well as a variety of pizzas baked in a wood-fired oven. When weather permits, the Pescatore opens its floor-to-ceiling windows to allow for prime people-watching and quasi-alfresco dining. ■ *425 North Point St (at Mason St), San Francisco, CA 94133; (415)561-1100 or (800)648-4626; $$$; full bar; AE, DC, DIS, MC, V; checks OK; breakfast, lunch, dinner every day.* ♿

**The Washington Square Inn** ★★ The Washington Square Inn's prime location in the middle of the historic North Beach district—just a short walk from Fisherman's Wharf, Ghirardelli Square, the Embarcadero, and Chinatown—is its best asset. And behind the inn's plain, inconspicuous facade is a delightful European-style bed and breakfast. The 15 comfortable, modest rooms are furnished with European antiques, bright flower-print drapes and matching bedspreads, and vases of fresh flowers. The least expensive rooms share a bath; the priciest units are the larger corner rooms with private baths and bay windows where you can sit and watch the hustle and bustle in the tree-lined square. In the morning you'll find a local newspaper and your freshly polished shoes waiting outside your door. The expanded continental breakfast can be served in your room or in front of the lobby fireplace, although you may want to stroll over to one of the many nearby Italian cafes for a frothy cappuccino or latte instead. Guests are treated to crisp cucumber sandwiches, freshly baked cookies, and tea every afternoon, as well as wine and hors d'oeuvres in the evening. Parking in North Beach is virtually impossible, so take advantage of the hotel's valet parking services. ■ *1660 Stockton St (at Filbert St, in North Beach), San Francisco, CA 94133; (415)981-4220 or (800)388-0220; $$$; AE, DIS, DC, MC, V; checks OK.*

**White Swan Inn** ★★ Perhaps the only hotel in San Francisco more adorable than the White Swan is its nearby sister inn, Petite Auberge. The theme here also harks back to a cozy English garden bed and breakfast, embellished with teddy bears piled on steps, shelves, and couches, as well as a colorful carousel horse in the small lobby. The 1903 building with curved bay windows has 26 rooms with fireplaces and private bathrooms, and each chamber is charmingly decorated with colorful prints, comfy armchairs, antiques, and floral-print wallpaper. Some rooms have inviting bay windows where you can sit and read or gaze out at the garden, and each has a refrigerator, TV, phone, and wet bar. For peace and quiet, ask for a room in the back overlooking the sunny, tree-lined courtyard. If you have business matters to tend to, data ports, a fax machine, and a conference room with audio/video machines are available. Guests are treated to a big breakfast, morning newspaper, afternoon tea, and home-baked cookies. The cozy library, often warmed by a roaring fire, is an ideal spot to curl up and read a novel in the company of—surprise!—more teddy bears. ■ *845 Bush St (between Taylor and Mason Sts, near Union Square and Nob Hill), San Francisco, CA 94108; (415)775-1755; $$$; AE, MC, V; checks OK.*

**San Francisco**

*Lodgings*

▲

**Inn on Castro** ★ This convivial bed-and-breakfast inn, catering to the gay and lesbian community for nearly two decades, has developed an ardent following—hence the intriguing collection of more than 100 heart-shaped boxes on the sideboard in the hallway, trinkets left behind by a legion of wistful patrons who can say they left their hearts in San Francisco. The restored Edwardian exterior is painted in a pleasing medley of blue, rose, and green, with gilded details and dentils. The interior is equally festive, with contemporary furnishings, original modern art, exotic plants, and elaborate flower arrangements. There are eight individually decorated guest rooms ranging from a small single to a suite with a deck; every room has a private bath and a direct-dial phone. Avoid the sunny but noisy rooms facing Castro Street.

TVs are available (but noses tend to wrinkle if you ask for one). An elaborate breakfast is served in the dining room, and may feature a fresh fruit salad, house-made muffins, fruit juice, and scrambled eggs, French toast, or perhaps pancakes. After your repast, relax in the cozy living room with its fireplace and deeply tufted Italian couches or head out for a stroll in the colorful, ever-bustling Castro. ■ *321 Castro St (½ block N of Market St), San Francisco, CA 94114; (415)861-0321; nobhill@nbn.com; www. nobhill.com; $$; MC, V; checks OK.*

**Nob Hill Inn** ★ Any well-appointed bed and breakfast ought to have a resident ghost or two. This elegant establishment—housed in a four-story Edwardian mansion built in 1907—has three: a wispy woman who likes to linger in room 12, a well-bred gentleman in room 21, and a winsome lass who wanders through the inn's Louis XIV– and Louis XV–style decor at whim. Take the etched-glass English elevator upstairs to the 21 rose-and-pink, antique-filled guest rooms, which have TVs tucked inside wardrobes and armoires. The low-end rooms are small, so splurge on a spacious suite. Downstairs, ceiling fans turn slowly above the wicker furniture in the parlor and dining nook, where a continental breakfast is served. You may sip wine or sherry among the racks in the atmospheric wine cellar or lounge on the sun deck or in the hot tub on the roof. Add to this an afternoon tea and nightly turn-down service, and it's little wonder that even the ghosts don't want to leave. ■ *1000 Pine St (at Taylor St), San Francisco, CA 94109; (415)673-6080; nobhill@nbn.com; www. nobhill.com; $$$; AE, DC, MC, V; checks OK.*

▼
San Francisco

Lodgings

▲

**San Remo Hotel** ★ Hidden in a quiet North Beach neighborhood between bustling Washington Square and Fisherman's Wharf, the San Remo is within easy walking distance of San Francisco's main attractions, including Chinatown, the Embarcadero, Pier 39, and one of the main cable car stations. Combine the locale with an inexpensive price tag, and you have one of the best room bargains in the city. This well-preserved, charming three-story Italianate Victorian building originally served as a boardinghouse for dock workers displaced by the great fire of 1906. Space was at a premium, so the hotel's 62 rooms are rather small, the bathrooms are shared, and the walls are thin. If you can live with these minor inconveniences, however, you're in for a treat. The rooms are reminiscent of a European pensione, modestly decorated with brass or iron beds, pedestal sinks, wicker furniture, and oak, maple, or pine armoires; most have ceiling fans. Rooms 42 and 43, which overlook Mason Street, are the favorites. The old-fashioned bathrooms, spotlessly clean and restored to their original luster, have brass pull-chain toilets with oak tanks, showers, and claw-footed tubs. The penthouse suite is one of the best deals in town, and offers a private bath, a small deck, and a 360-degree view of the city. The hotel's lobby and hallways are awash with antiques, leaded-glass windows, and plants bathed by sunlight filtering through stained-glass skylights. You can count on the friendly, city-savvy staff to help you plan your day touring San Francisco's abundant attractions. ■ *2237 Mason St (at Chestnut St), San Francisco, CA 94133; (415)776-8688 or (800)352-REMO; info@sanremohotel.com; $; AE, DC, DIS, MC, V; checks OK.*



**Union Street Inn** ★ Owners Jane Bertorelli and David Coyle have lent such a pleasant personal touch to the period decor, and the staff is so convivial, that this delightful bed and breakfast wins a prize for overall ambience. Although the two-story Edwardian mansion is situated amid the bustle of trendy Union Street, it's set high above the traffic at the top of a steep set of stairs. The five large guest rooms and a deluxe carriage house across the garden have private baths (some feature Jacuzzis), king- or queen-size beds, telephones, terrycloth robes, fresh cut flowers, and televisions (for those who can't survive the Edwardian era without a media fix). Each room has its own theme and color scheme, enhanced by bay windows, patterned wallpaper, Oriental carpets, antiques, and comforters. The best rooms, such as the Wildrose, face the flourishing back garden. The parlor downstairs is furnished with a fireplace, a beguiling range of period finds, and a 24-hour coffee/tea/buffet station. Start your day with a full breakfast in the beautiful English garden, in the parlor, or in bed; spend the afternoon strolling through Union Street's ever-popular boutiques, bars, and cafes; then return by 5pm for a pre-dinner snack of wine and cheese. ■ *2229 Union St (between Fillmore and Steiner Sts), San Francisco, CA 94123; (415)346-0424; www.unionstreetinn.com; $$$; AE, MC, V; checks OK.*



## SAUSALITO

### *RESTAURANTS*

**Sushi Ran** ★★★ To the loyal patrons of this south Marin culinary landmark sushi is not just food—it's a way of life. Tacked to the wall near the cash register is the smiling image of a portly gentleman who patronized the establishment more than 400 times in one year. (Folks, that's more than once a day.) The sushi served here is impeccable, prepared with aplomb and served with a flourish. The fish is glisteningly fresh, and the rice is warm and sticky. The kamikaze roll is stuffed with yellowfin tuna, bright flying-fish roe, and crunchy green onions; the spider roll enfolds a delicate tempura-fried soft-shell crab. Rice-wine lovers can choose from 17 sakes, including two from nearby Napa County, and, surprisingly for such a little restaurant, there is a mighty fine wine list offering 100 bottles. ■ *107 Caledonia St (next to the Marin Theater), Sausalito; (415)332-3620; $$; beer, wine, and sake; AE, DIS, MC, V; no checks; lunch Mon–Fri, dinner every day.* ♿

**Mikayla** ★★ On the side of a terraced hill and just beyond the red-brick, rose-lined path of the Casa Madrona hotel stands sophisticated Mikayla. In a bright, pleasant interior designed by artist Laurel Burch, patrons are treated to the hotel's famous views of Belvedere and Angel Island. It's all very romantic and engaging, and fortunately there's now a chef at the helm who is able to enhance the experience with his American, French-influenced fare. Chef Terry Lynch, who previously cooked at Masa's, Auberge du Soleil, and Mustards, updates his menu daily based on the season's latest bounty. Memorable dishes have included the foie gras "club sandwich" served on brioche with pancetta, frisée, and grape salsa; grilled lamb chops with horse-radish potatoes and oil-cured black olives; and poached salmon with butter lettuce, English peas, and a champagne sauce. ■ *801 Bridgeway (downtown), Sausalito; (415)331-5888; www. casamadrona. com; $$$; beer and wine; AE, DC, DIS, MC, V; no checks; brunch Sun, dinner every day.*

## LODGINGS

**Casa Madrona ★★★★** There are two Sausalitos—the tourist-trampled waterfront area and the exclusive residential region in the hills—and the Casa Madrona is where they meet. The entrance to this unique hotel complex is on boutique-lined Bridgeway, where natives never venture and visitors love to shop. Step into the Madrona's cramped elevator and you'll quickly be transported into Sausalito's enclave of multimillion-dollar mansions and panoramic bay views. Once you're ensconced in one of the lavish rooms, there's really no reason to step out the front door again until you're ready to check out. The hotel offers every-thing you could possibly desire: sweeping bay vistas, an outdoor Jacuzzi, all the amenities of a citified hotel, plus a very good restaurant (see review of **Mikayla**, above). Each of Casa Madrona's 34 rooms is unique; the rooms in the Victorian cottages, which dot the landscaped hillside, and in the 110-year-old mansion on top of the hill are more rustic than those in the 15-year-old blue stucco building below. For greater privacy, choose one of the charming cottages; the Upper and Lower Bungalows have gigantic decks. The best room in the mansion is the Fireside Suite, which features a wood-burning fireplace and a private veranda. The rooms in the newer building tend to be more posh; the favorite is the Rose Chalet, which has rose-colored walls, pine furniture, a fireplace, a private deck, and a great view of the yacht harbor that you can enjoy from the comfort of your bed. Directly below is the slightly less expensive Lord Ashley's Lookout, with an understated Old English decor and a fine view of the water. Artists might request the Artist's Loft, which comes complete with an easel, paints, and brushes as well as a fireplace, a large deck, and a bay view. ■ *801 Bridgeway (downtown), Sausalito, CA 94965; (415)332-0502 or (800)567-9524; www.casamadrona.com; $$$; beer and wine; AE, DC, DIS, MC, V; no checks; brunch Sun, dinner every day.* &

*RESTAURANTS*

**Guaymas** ★★ Mexican food is as elaborate and nuanced as any of the world's great cuisines, with its mixture of indigenous, Spanish, and French flavors (French soldiers occupied Mexico from 1852 to 1857, and the only good that came of it was some new recipes). Guaymas's chef Francisco Cisneros prepares Mexican classics such as posole, a hearty stew from his native Jalisco, as well as California-inspired variations like the *sopes con pato*— crisp, deep-fried corn shells filled with braised duck, pasilla peppers, onions, and garlic. The piping-hot white-corn tortillas are served with three sauces: a tangy salsa verde; a sweet and tantalizing salsa chipotle with smoked jalapeños, pineapples, and carrots; and a more pedestrian salsa cruda with tomatoes, onions, cilantro, and garlic. For an appetizer try the tender, marinated slices of nopales (cactus) with onion and Mexican cheese or the pico de gallo, a large plate of fresh fruit served with wedges of lime and a dish of hot red pepper and other seasonings. Once your palate is warmed up, move on to the spicy tamales, the marinated shrimp, or the seafood platter of grilled octopus, squid, shrimp, and salmon. When the weather is favorable, dine on the deck and take in the incredible view of the bay, Angel Island, and the San Francisco skyline as you sip one of the mighty margaritas. Guaymas boasts one of the best views in the Bay Area—the main reason the place is always packed. However, rainy days can be just as pleasant here, especially if you sit by the fireplace and sip a tequila *añejo*, aged with all the flavor and subtlety of a fine Scotch. ■ *5 Main St (on Tiburon Harbor at the ferry landing), Tiburon; (415) 435-6300; $$; full bar; AE, DC, MC, V; no checks; lunch, dinner every day.* ⅊

**Tiburon**

*Restaurants*

**Tutto Mare** ★★ Picture this: an unobstructed view of the sparkling bay, wealthy yacht owners anchoring their glistening sailboats on the pier below your feet, a chilled negroni martini in hand, and a plate of thinly sliced Parma prosciutto with fresh melon at your fingertips. Ahh . . . the sweet life. And we're not talking about life in Portofino—we're talking about the upper deck of Tutto Mare in Tiburon, a sibling of the company that owns ever-popular Guaymas next door. Although Tutto Mare's Italian-inspired fare doesn't always live up to its astounding view, does it really matter? When the weather is warm and you have a choice seat on the deck, even pretty good food is a bonus. Chef Tony D'Onofrio offers wood-fired pizzas and lighter fare in Tutto Mare's causal downstairs *taverna*; upstairs in the more formal and very chic *ristorante* he prepares whole roasted fish, grilled meats, pizzas, and house-made pastas. Some of his standouts include the pear and pecorino cheese salad with walnuts, frisée, and radicchio; crisp-crust pizza with wild mushrooms and mozzarella; linguine with clams, mussels, and shrimp; and mesquite-grilled rib-eye steak. ■ *9 Main St (on the waterfront), Tiburon; (415)435-4747; $$; full bar; AE, DC, MC, V; no checks; brunch Sun, lunch, dinner every day.* ♿

## MILL VALLEY

### RESTAURANTS

**Buckeye Roadhouse** ★★★ The decor at the Buckeye Roadhouse combines a reserved elegance with over-the-top Marin kitsch— lofty ceilings, mahogany beams, glass chandeliers and sconces, a massive stone fireplace, a huge stuffed yellowfin tuna, and a moose head. The cuisine, likewise, is both classic and eclectic. For an appetizer try oysters on the half shell served with a tasty cocktail sauce; Buckeye's memorable caesar salad; a tangled mound of thin, sweet onion rings cooked in a feathery batter and served with house-made ketchup; or the house-smoked Atlantic salmon. Entrees include barbecued baby back ribs served with coleslaw; smoked Sonoma duck with wild rice and huckleberry sauce; and a sweet, tender, marinated grilled pork chop with to-die-for garlic mashed potatoes. Top off your meal with one of the old-time desserts such as butterscotch crème brûlée or a piece of the S'more Pie, an innovative variation on the campfire classic. If you want to be part of the Marin scene, belly up to the bustling bar and order a pint of Anchor Steam. ■ *15 Shoreline Hwy (from Hwy 101 take the Stinson Beach–Mill Valley exit), Mill Valley; (415)331-2600; e-mail@103064, 245.com; $$; full bar; DC, DIS, MC, V; no checks; brunch Sun, lunch Mon–Sat, dinner every day.* ♿

▼
**Mill Valley**
Restaurants
▲

**El Paseo** ★★ It's comforting to know that little romantic jewels like Mill Valley's El Paseo are still around in a time when noisy, exhibition kitchens and warehouse-size spaces seem to be de rigueur for successful restaurants. El Paseo is Spanish for "the passageway," but don't expect to find paella or fajitas at the end of the red-brick path leading to the restaurant's front door. For a quarter of a century, classic French fare has been served in El Paseo's intimate, dimly lit dining room, where little beaded lamps glow on tables cloaked in red linen. It's the perfect atmosphere for exchanging knowing glances at your significant other over a delicious plate of escargots de Bourgogne and roasted lamb chops wrapped with minced vegetables or perhaps filet mignon flamed with brandy and ginger. El Paseo's wine list is outstanding and includes many wonderful French wines and California cabernets at reasonable prices. Service is attentive and the tables next to the small-paned windows are choice. ■ *17 Throckmorton Ave (follow the narrow passageway just beyond the Sequoia Movie Theater), Mill Valley; (415)388-0741; $$$; beer and wine; AE, DC, DIS, MC, V; local checks only; dinner every day.* ♿

**Jennie Low's Chinese Cuisine** ★★ Jennie Low, author of *Chopsticks, Cleaver and Wok*, a '70s bible of Chinese cooking, opened this fine restaurant in pastoral Mill Valley in 1987. Inspired by Cantonese,

Mandarin, Hunan, and Sichuan cooking styles, Low's very personal cuisine features simple, home-style dishes with velvety textures and sweet, subtle sauces—no MSG, of course. Start out with her rich rainbow chowder, a colorful mix of shrimp, crab, baby corn, green onions, carrots, and cellophane noodles. For entrees, anything preceded by the word "Jennie's" is a guaranteed treat. Other favored dishes include the crisp hot and spicy green beans sautéed in a garlic sauce, and the Snow White Chicken with mushrooms, snow peas, and spicy eggplant. Low also offers several "light creations"—dishes prepared without oil and with less salt. Expect a crowd. This place is perpetually packed, but Low and her family do a fine job managing the chaos. A second branch is located in Novato. ■ *38 Miller Ave (at E Blithedale Ave), Mill Valley; (415)388-8868; $; beer and wine; AE, MC, V; no checks; lunch Mon–Sat, dinner every day.* ₺

**Piazza D'Angelo**  When owners Paolo and Domenico Petrone renovated this restaurant in 1990, Piazza D'Angelo became one of Mill Valley's most popular restaurants—and it still is, with large (often noisy) crowds of Marinites packing the pleasant, airy bar. They don't necessarily come for the food, mind you, but for the charged atmosphere, which most enjoy more than the elegant but somewhat staid Italian newcomer in town, Frantoio. D'Angelo's Italian menu abounds with familiar though not always well-executed fare, including numerous pasta plates—spaghetti sautéed with kalamata olives, chili pepper, baby spinach, onions, sun-dried tomatoes, white wine, and pecorino cheese is one of the better choices—and several juicy entrees from the rotisserie. The calzones, stuffed with fresh ingredients like ricotta, spinach, caramelized onions, mozzarella, and sausage, come out of the pizza oven puffy and light, and the pizzas make a good lunch. Desserts are made fresh daily, and if there's a crème brûlée on the tray, don't let your server take it away. The extensive wine list features a respectable selection of California and Italian labels (about 150 bottles), including 10 wines poured by the glass. ■ *22 Miller Ave (on the square), Mill Valley; (415)388-2000; $$; full bar; AE, DC, MC, V; no checks; brunch Sat–Sun, lunch Mon–Fri, dinner every day.* ₺

▼

**Mill Valley**

*Lodgings*

▲

## LODGINGS

**Mountain Home Inn** ★★  Much has changed at the remote Mountain Home Inn since it opened in 1912 as a Bavarian restaurant, but what has stayed constant through the years is the stunning view. On clear days you can see the Marin hills, San Francisco Bay, the East Bay hills, and even Mount Diablo at the edge of the Central Valley. Perched high above Mill Valley on the side of Mount Tamalpais, the inn now has 10 guest rooms decorated in what might best be described as Marin Modern, with plush carpeting and wood-paneled walls. All of the rooms have private baths. The standard rooms have small wooden balconies and a couple have wood-burning fireplaces, but your best bet is one of the three deluxe rooms with a fireplace, deck, king-size bed, and oversize tub with Jacuzzi jets. The New American cuisine served in the dining room is adequate, but you'd be better off bringing a picnic or making the winding 15-minute drive down the mountain to a restaurant in one of the neighboring towns. Mountain Home Inn becomes a madhouse on sunny weekends, when hikers and mountain bikers descend for après-trek drinks and snacks or a late brunch on the deck. A full breakfast is included with your stay. ▪ *810 Panoramic Hwy (call for directions), Mill Valley, CA 94941; (415)381-9000; $$$ (hotel), $$ (restaurant); beer and wine; AE, MC, V; no checks; brunch Sat–Sun, breakfast every day (Mon–Fri for guests only), lunch, dinner every day (restaurant closed Mon from Nov 1 to Apr 30).*

## CORTE MADERA

### *RESTAURANTS*

**Il Fornaio** ★★ This handsome branch of the popular restaurant chain offers well-prepared Italian standards, especially those items that come from the rotisserie. See the review of the San Francisco location. ▪ *223 Corte Madera Town Center (from Hwy 101, take the Paradise Dr exit), Corte Madera; (415)927-4400; www.ilfornaio.com; $$; full bar; AE, DC, MC, V; no checks; brunch Sat–Sun, lunch Mon–Fri, dinner every day.* ♿

## LARKSPUR

### *RESTAURANTS*

**Left Bank** ★★★ Roland Passot, chef/owner of La Folie (long-regarded as one of San Francisco's best restaurants), has transformed Larkspur's historic Blue Rock Inn into a fun, vibrant restaurant with a phenomenal French bistro-style menu. Sink your teeth into his leek and onion tart studded with applewood-smoked bacon or the roasted duck breast garnished with a sour cherry sauce, and *le Tour Eiffel* looms. The menu changes seasonally, prompting Passot's happy patrons to return again and again for the latest rendition of his wonderful, traditionally prepared French fare. And you'll love the mood as much as the food. Dine on the covered L-shaped veranda hugging the front of the restaurant and you just might believe you've been transported to Paris (especially if you've given the terrific fruit-infused vodkas a generous taste test). For the grand finale, indulge in the warm tarte Tatin topped with thick caramelized apple slices and a scoop of vanilla-bean ice cream. *Incroyable!* ▪ *507 Magnolia Ave (at Ward St), Larkspur; (415)927-3331; www.leftbankdine.com; $$; full bar; AE, MC, V; no checks; lunch, dinner every day.* ♿

**Lark Creek Inn** ★★ When famed Bay Area chef Bradley Ogden took over the Lark Creek Inn in 1989, he faced the unique task of creating a restaurant around a well-established local landmark.

This beautiful century-old two-story Victorian inn, nestled in a stately redwood grove along Lark Creek, demanded a strong presence—and Ogden, fresh from worldwide acclaim at San Francisco's Campton Place, met the challenge. He soon opened what many have considered for years the best restaurant in Marin County; now that Ogden has launched several other Bay Area restaurants, however, Lark Creek has been suffering from his absence and food critics have been stripping the inn of its once untouchable four-star status. Yet when things are going well in the kitchen, the dishes can still be wildly imaginative and successful, and they are always rooted in Ogden's superb mastery of basic American cooking. For instance, Ogden marries a tender Yankee pot roast with roasted vegetables and horseradish mashed potatoes; he roasts a free-range chicken with a tang of lemon and herbs and serves it with mashed red potatoes; and he grills the thickest, most perfect pork chop and enhances it with sweet braised red cabbage. Instead of potatoes au gratin, you might find root vegetables au gratin. And if shoestring potatoes accompany a succulent grilled rabbit, they will likely be made from sweet potatoes. For dessert, a devil's food cake is blessed with chocolate malt ice cream, and the classic strawberry short-cake gets a scoop of cheesecake ice cream for a kick. The glass ceiling creates a wonderfully airy atmosphere, while extensive windows give the restaurant a chance to show off the gardens outside. Those gardens make a great place for the inn's summer Sunday brunch, which features sumptuous fare such as fresh corned-beef hash, banana–sour cream pancakes, and home-fried doughnuts. Stick to Ogden's specialties, and keep your fingers crossed that the high quality we've come to expect from him will be back in no time. ■ *234 Magnolia Ave (on the northern edge of downtown), Larkspur; (415)924-7766; $$$; full bar; AE, DC, MC, V; no checks; brunch Sun, lunch Mon–Fri, dinner every day.* ⛄

## KENTFIELD

### *RESTAURANTS*

**Half Day Cafe** ★★ Breakfast in this beautifully renovated, plant-filled mechanic's garage features a number of first-rate dishes including fluffy omelets stuffed with a variety of fresh fillings, jumbo orange-currant scones, and fine, dark espresso. The only complaint is that you may have to wait a stomach-growling hour for a table on a busy weekend morning, and even longer if you have your eye on the sunny patio. At lunchtime, the College of Marin's ravenous crowds pack the place for fresh salads and sandwiches. As with most good businesses, the half days didn't stay that way. Now the restaurant is open a full day, serving dinner dishes such as ahi tuna seasoned with white wine, garlic, chile flakes, and rosemary; grilled chicken served with garlic mashed potatoes and gravy; and, on some Fridays, the popular slow-baked country-style meat loaf. Take-out is available, too.

■ *848 College Ave (across from the College of Marin), Kentfield;
(415)459-0291; $; beer and wine; MC, V; local checks only; brunch
Sat–Sun, breakfast, lunch Mon–Fri, dinner every day (closed for
dinner Mon–Tues in the winter).* ♿

## SAN ANSELMO

### RESTAURANTS

**Bubba's Diner** ★★ There's nothing on the menu at Bubba's that
you probably couldn't make at home, but chances are you just
couldn't make it as well. Lark Creek Inn alumni Stephen and Elizabeth Simmons offer classic diner food with decor to match: red
Naugahyde booths, a black-and-white tile floor, colorful modern
art, a big Bubba's clock, and a daily special board. People stand
in line to get a taste of their hearty breakfast offerings, including
chunky corned-beef hash, honey whole-wheat flapjacks, and eggs
prepared however you like 'em with home fries and a big, delicious, freshly baked biscuit. For lunch or dinner choose from a
selection of salads, including a crunchy caesar with grilled
chicken or seasonal fried green tomatoes (coated with cornmeal),
or order from an equally delicious if slightly less health-conscious
list of sandwiches, such as the burger slathered with Swiss
cheese or the terrific meat-loaf sandwich smothered in barbecue
sauce. After 5:30pm you can indulge in chicken-fried steak with
red-eye gravy, pot roast and mashed potatoes, crisp fried chicken,
and similar fare. And since you've totally blown your Jenny Craig
diet by now, celebrate your newfound freedom with a real milk-
shake or malt, tapioca pudding, or a slice of banana-butterscotch
pie. Bubba's doesn't take reservations for parties of fewer than
six, so prepare to stroll boutique-lined San Anselmo Avenue as
you wait for one of the few booths or a seat at the cluttered
Formica counter. ■ *566 San Anselmo Ave (downtown), San
Anselmo; (415)459-6862; $; beer and wine; MC, V; no checks;
breakfast, lunch Wed–Sun, dinner every day.*

▼
**San Anselmo**

*Restaurants*

▲

**Creekside Bistro** ★★ Chef/owner Morgan Song, who previously
owned Kiss restaurant in San Francisco, has garnered rave
reviews ever since he opened this pretty bistro perched over rip-
pling San Anselmo Creek in the fall of 1996. The Korean-born
chef has a flair for nearly flawless meat and fish entrees, which
might include a juicy, grilled salmon fillet served over delicately
braised leeks or a pork tenderloin paired with an apple-cinnamon
confit and braised cabbage. The succulent plate of portobello
mushrooms served on a saffron-kissed risotto topped with tender
beets will more than satisfy the vegetarians in your group, and
there are other meatless options to choose from. Song will have
you singing with joy when you spoon into his superb soufflés—
the dessert-menu divas (they take extra time to prepare, so be
sure to order them at the beginning of your meal). Lunch at
Creekside is also a treat. When the weather is warm, dine

alfresco on the large, casual patio fronting the bistro. ■ *636 San Anselmo Ave (downtown), San Anselmo; (415)456-2952; $$; beer and wine; AE, DC, MC, V; no checks; brunch Sat–Sun, lunch, dinner Tues–Sun.* ♿

**Insalata's** ★★ In a handsome, mustard-colored building large enough to be a car showroom, chef/owner Heidi Insalata Krahling (formerly of Square One in San Francisco and Butler's in Mill Valley) has chosen to showcase her dazzling Mediterranean fare behind her new restaurant's floor-to-ceiling windows. The sunny, airy dining room is highlighted by paintings of lemons, plums, and pears that are about as large and colorful as the Miatas zooming down Sir Francis Drake Boulevard outside. At tables cloaked in white linen, diners bask in the spaciousness while noshing on the seven-vegetable Tunisian *tagine* served on a bed of fluffy couscous or the savory Genovese fish and shellfish stew simmering in a prosciutto broth seasoned with sage. You'll have no problem finding the perfect wine to accompany your meal from Insalata's good list, and don't hesitate to ask the staff for suggestions. Service is quite friendly and attentive, and once you've paid your bill, head to the back of the restaurant where goodies-to-go are sold and pick up a little bag of biscotti studded with plump golden raisins—a great treat for the drive home. ■ *120 Sir Francis Drake Blvd (at Barber St), San Anselmo; (415)457-7700; $$$; beer and wine; MC, V; no checks; lunch Mon–Sat, dinner every day.* ♿



## SAN RAFAEL

### *RESTAURANTS*

**The Rice Table** ★★★ Decorated with rattan screens and bright batik tablecloths, this small, popular, dimly lit restaurant offers dozens of wonderfully aromatic Indonesian dishes that are a treat for the soul as well as the palate. The menu here is deliberately simple: there are only 11 entrees. For a real Indonesian feast, order the Rice Table Dinner or the Rice Table Special, which, if you order either meal for two or more people, includes a sampling of every entree on the menu. All meals begin with shrimp chips served with a trio of distinctly spiced sauces, followed by mint-tinged coleslaw, a raw-vegetable salad, and *lumpia* (deep-fried Indonesian spring rolls stuffed with shrimp and pork). Favorite entrees include savory satays cooked with peanut sauce, and an assortment of fork-tender curried meats served in coconut milk. If you like your fare fiery hot, dip into the wonderful *sambals* (a paste of hot chile peppers mixed with various spices and lime juice), then cool the flames with an icy cold beer. For dessert, treat yourself to deep-fried bananas, accompanied by an Indonesian coffee or the floral jasmine tea. ■ *1617 4th St (at G St), San Rafael; (415)456-1808; $$; beer and wine; AE, MC, V; no checks; dinner Wed–Sun.* ♿

**Las Camelias** ★★ The delicious, authentic Mexican cuisine dished up at this pleasant, casual cafe comes straight from the recipe file of owner/chef Gabriel Fregoso's mother in Jalisco, Mexico. Grab a chair at one of the oak tables in front of the paned arched windows, and start in with the ceviche if it's available. The house salad (*la ensalada tostada*) features a mound of crisp romaine lettuce topped with tomatoes, tiny flecks of añejo cheese, avocado, and corn chips, and the whole black bean soup is superb. For dinner try the *arroz Mexicana* (a giant plate of rice stir-fried with shrimp, scallops, chicken, and fresh salsa), the grilled tequila-marinated shrimp, or the delicious *pollo en mole*— a clean, unmuddied version of the chocolate-based classic. Several vegetarian plates are offered, too, and the standout is the chiles rellenos *encuerado* (fresh poblano chiles stuffed with caramelized onions, corn, and zucchini). The unadventurous will find well-prepared versions of familiar Mexican favorites on the back of the menu. Instead of splurging on the so-so desserts, reserve those calories for the refreshing house-made sangria.
■ *912 Lincoln Ave (between 3rd and 4th Sts), San Rafael; (415)453-5850; $; beer and wine; AE, MC, V; no checks; lunch Mon–Sat, dinner every day.* &

**Royal Thai** ★★ Now that Thai restaurants have sprouted all over the Bay Area, it takes something special to lure people away from their neighborhood favorite. Royal Thai, housed in a restored Victorian frame house underneath Highway 101, lures Thai aficionados from far and wide with an array of classics and innovative variations. Owner/chef Jamie and co-owner Pat Disyamonthon's dishes are expertly prepared and beautifully presented, but what really distinguishes this restaurant is its range. In addition to thick coconut-milk curries and perfect phad Thai, it turns out a kaleidoscope of beef and chicken sautés sparkling with ginger paste, chile oil, nuts, and fresh mint, basil, and garlic. Roll up the *miang kham* (dried shrimp, peanuts, small chunks of fresh lime, red onion, baked coconut, ginger, and chile) in butter lettuce leaves and dip it in a sweet tamarind sauce, or explore the *somtum* salad, a wonderfully textured combination of shredded green papaya mixed with carrots, green beans, tomatoes, and ground peanuts. Other favorites are the salmon in red curry sauce and the barbecued squid. There's a second branch of Royal Thai in San Francisco. ■ *610 3rd St (at Irwin St), San Rafael; (415)485-1074; $$; beer and wine; AE, DC, MC, V; no checks; lunch Mon–Fri, dinner every day.* &

**Panama Hotel** ★ This airy dining room, decorated with a clutter of old collectibles ranging from hats and black-and-white photographs to Mexican ceramic teacups and floral-print lamp shades, offers a mix of cuisines that changes seasonally. Typical dishes include a spicy blackened Panama burger, a grilled vegetable sandwich with chayote squash and artichoke hearts, eggplant Parmesan, and jerk chicken. Service is slow and a bit too casual, but then most folks at the Panama don't seem to be too hurried. ■ *4 Bayview St (at the end of B St, 3 blocks W of 2nd St), San Rafael; (415)457-3993 or (800)899-3993; $$; beer and wine; AE, MC, V; no checks; continental breakfast every day, brunch Sun, lunch Mon–Fri, dinner Tues–Sun.*

## LODGINGS

**Panama Hotel ★★** With slowly churning ceiling fans, balconies lined with old wicker chairs, and an eclectic collection of mismatched antiques, the Panama Hotel looks as if it should be the backdrop for a noir detective film. Indeed, Hollywood folks like this place, and they often drop by for an extended stay when they're in town on a shoot. There are a total of 15 individually decorated guest rooms located in two 1910 vintage homes connected by a tropical garden patio; the small and medium-size economy rooms share baths and a communal kitchen, and many of the suites, bungalows, and patio apartments have private kitchens and bathrooms with claw-footed tubs. Ask for Mimi's Bungalow, which has a sitting room with a wet bar and a sunny deck with a table and chairs, or Rosie's Room, with its queen-size canopy bed, glassed-in sun porch with a microwave oven, claw-footed tub, and wraparound balcony. There is no air conditioning here, but ceiling fans spin in every room and are usually sufficient for beating the summer heat. A good expanded continental breakfast comes with the room from the restaurant (see review, above). ■ *4 Bayview St (at the end of B St, 3 blocks W of 2nd St), San Rafael, CA 94901; (415)457-3993 or (800)899-3993; $$; beer and wine; AE, MC, V; no checks; continental breakfast every day, brunch Sun, lunch Mon–Fri, dinner Tues–Sun.*

Novato

*Restaurants*

▲

## NOVATO

### RESTAURANTS

**Jennie Low's Chinese Cuisine ★★** See the review of the Mill Valley branch in the previous pages. ■ *120 Vintage Way (in Vintage Oaks mall), Novato; (415)892-8838; $; beer and wine; AE, MC, V; no checks; lunch Mon–Sat, dinner every day.*

**Hilltop Cafe ★** Many diners are too enraptured by the sweeping vista of the Marin hills to notice what they're eating at the Hilltop Cafe. But Novato's culinary cognoscenti, while acknowledging the panorama, have a better reason to head for this spacious house on the hill: they come to sample its competently prepared Italian and red-meat dishes and to enjoy the friendly, efficient service. While you should avoid anything that smacks of California cuisine on the eclectic 85-item menu, be sure to hail a caesar salad, and don't miss the garlic soup served in a hollowed round of sourdough bread (the Hilltop claims to have originated this now ubiquitous soup-in-a-loaf dish). Also good are the eggplant

Parmesan and the linguine with fresh clams. This is an ideal place to visit for a late lunch, since the afternoon meal is offered until 5pm Monday through Saturday. For dessert, you can't go wrong with the marvelous mud pie: espresso ice cream smothered with chocolate fudge and toasted almonds on a crumbled-Oreo-cookie crust. ■ *850 Lamont Ave (between Redwood Blvd and Hwy 101 at the top of the hill), Novato; (415) 892-2222; brewald@htnet.com; www.htnet.com; $$; full bar; AE, DC, DIS, MC, V; no checks; brunch Sun, lunch Mon–Sat, dinner every day.* ♿

## SAN PABLO BAY

### *LODGINGS*

**East Brother Light Station** ★★★ If basking in the sun on a remote, tiny island far from the madding crowd is your idea of paradise on earth, the East Brother Light Station bed-and-breakfast inn may be the Bay Area retreat you've been dreaming of. This renovated, gingerbread-trimmed light station on tiny East Brother Island at the northern end of the bay houses four simply decorated guest rooms. Each has a queen-size brass bed and comforter, hardwood floors, fresh flowers, a few antiques, and incredible views of the bay, Mount Tamalpais, and the San Francisco skyline. The two downstairs rooms share a bath; the two upstairs rooms have private baths. You won't find TVs, radios, phones, faxes, or even traffic here—just the squawking of seagulls and the continual bleep of the electronic foghorn, which operates every minute for 30 seconds, 24 hours a day between October 1st and April 1st (some guests find the foghorn's blare a romantic attraction and say it lulls them to sleep, while not-so-sound sleepers scramble to insert the earplugs provided by the innkeepers). Most folks pack a few books and perhaps a fishing pole and bait for their short stay here; others are content to simply gaze at the passing freighters, listen to the foghorn, and relax on the diminutive 1-acre island. Since water supplies are limited, showers are available only to guests staying more than one night. A good four-course candle-lit dinner and a hearty breakfast are included in the rate (about $300 per couple, which includes transportation to and from the island), and guests eat together at a long table in the historic dining room. East Brother Light Station was constructed in 1873-74 and was meticulously restored to its original splendor in 1979. It is now on the National Register of Historic Places. Make reservations about six months in advance, especially if you want to stay here in the summer. ■ *On East Brother Island in San Pablo Bay (400 yds off the mainland N of the San Rafael–Richmond Bridge; 10 mins via boat from Point San Pablo Yacht Harbor); (925) 820-9133; mail: 117 Park Place, Point Richmond, CA 94801; www.ebls.org/; $$$; wine only; AE, MC, V; checks OK in advance only; breakfast, dinner included in the rate, lunch available by prior arrangement for guests staying more than 1 night (closed Mon–Wed).*

*RESTAURANTS*

**The Union Hotel, Bar, and Restaurant** ★★ There is something vaguely sad about walking into the lovely dining room at the Union Hotel because it makes you nostalgic for the time when all of California looked like this—before the era of strip malls, drive-through restaurants, and tract housing. Still, it's nice to sit amid the stained glass, ivory walls, and hand-sponged teal wainscoting of this 1882 establishment and savor the feeling for a few hours. Chef Frank Vella is as much a throwback as the hotel is; he uses fresh, local ingredients in his dishes but adds a bit of frontier resourcefulness. The New York steak, for example, gets an extra kick from a Jack Daniels–peppercorn sauce. On the other hand, the golden roast Petaluma duck (an occasional special) is served with wild rice and strawberry salsa, a rendition that might not have gone over well on the wagon train. Other dishes to sample are the popular Union Caesar Salad (made with your choice of either baby spinach or hearts of romaine), fresh-from-the-sea oysters on the half shell, tiger shrimp cakes with papaya-lime salsa and sherry aioli, and fusilli with cauliflower, anchovies, garlic, and hot pepper flakes. A major Union Hotel attraction is the bar, which bustles with locals on weekend nights and features live jazz, rock, or pop Wednesday through Saturday nights (some folks even kick up their heels in the small dancing area). If you happen to eat, drink, and get a little too merry at the Union and decide you'd be better off bedding down here for the night, there are 12 guest rooms. Many of the rooms are small (this hotel once did time as a brothel, and the quantity—not the quality or size—of the rooms was what counted); the George III, the Ritz, and the Mei Ling Rooms are the largest and most elegant, with Jacuzzis and views of the bay. ■ *401 1st St (at D St), Benicia, CA 94510; (707) 746-0100; $$; full bar; AE, DC, DIS, MC, V; no checks; brunch Sat–Sun, lunch Tues–Fri, dinner Tues–Sun.*

Benicia

*Lodgings*

*LODGINGS*

**Captain Walsh House** ★★★ This gorgeous pre-Victorian gothic revival bed and breakfast made its debut on the cover of *Better Homes & Gardens* in the summer of '94, and the inn is definitely worth a journey here—even if you don't have any business in this small-town-turned-sprawling-suburb on the bluffs above the Carquinez Strait. Architect Reed Robbins and her husband Steve (an escapee from the computer industry) have done a masterful job of restoring this exquisite home, which was originally built in Boston, dismantled, and shipped around the horn in 1849. Every room is startlingly original. The living room and dining room feature subtly painted hardwood floors and hand-sponged walls with elaborate hand-painted stripes. Gothic window treatments blend with unusual antique pieces such as the square grand piano and a churchman's vestment rack. There are five guest rooms. The favorite is Epifina's Room, a beautiful rose, gold, and ivory chamber with a soaring ceiling, a massive four-poster canopy bed, and a view of the water. The newest room, the Captain's Den, is another dazzler, with its sea-captain's motif, separate sitting room, antique Belgian walnut furnishings, hand-built model ships, and an antique game table for playing checkers or chess. The almost-hidden Library Room sports a real zebra carpet, a terrific reading loft (accessible via a ladder), floor-to-ceiling bookshelves filled with interesting tomes, a stuffed armadillo, and a Murphy bed behind a trompe l'oeil bookcase. In the morning you'll find coffee or tea, served in an antique silver tea service decorated with a twist of ivy and a fresh garden rose, outside your door. Downstairs, the full-time chef prepares an elaborate, hearty breakfast that might include a grilled shrimp soufflé with a chive-cream sauce or a home-smoked fowl and game omelet with fresh mango chutney, as well as fresh fruit and house-baked scones or muffins. Captain Walsh House is also a popular place for exchanging wedding vows—a testament to the Robbins' ability to keep this inn in top form year after year. ■ *235 East L St (at 2nd St), Benicia, CA 94510; (707) 747-5653; cwhinn@aol.com; $$$; AE, MC, V; checks OK.*

## WALNUT CREEK

*RESTAURANTS*

**Lark Creek Cafe** ★★ See the review of this restaurant's San Mateo branch in the following pages. ■ *1360 Locust St (near Mt Diablo Blvd), Walnut Creek; (925) 256-1234; $$; full bar; AE, DIS, MC, V; no checks; brunch Sun, lunch Mon–Sat, dinner every day.* ♿

**Prima** ★★ When Italophiles Michael and Janet Verlander first offered sidewalk dining outside their restaurant on Walnut Creek's tree-lined Main Street, the city had laws against it. City politicos soon wised up, however, so now you can people-watch to your heart's content while savoring chef Giuseppe Ferrara's fine repertoire of northern Italian specialties. Start off with a generous hunk of thick rosemary focaccia dipped in olive oil, then move on to a perfectly al dente tagliolini with fresh seafood, shellfish, and house-dried organic tomatoes sautéed in a white wine sauce, or sample the risotto of the day. The grilled double-cut veal chop with a caramelized balsamic vinegar sauce and garlic mashed potatoes is worth waiting the extra 20 minutes it takes to prepare this dish, and the wine list is encyclopedic—more than 1,200 California, Italian, and French bottles with several available by the taste or the glass. In addition to the high-quality, freshly made meals, Prima's patrons are treated to live jazz on the grand piano starting at 6:30pm Tuesday through Saturday. ■ *1522 N Main St (downtown, near Lincoln St), Walnut Creek; (925) 935-7780; $$; full bar; AE, DIS, MC, V; no checks; lunch Mon–Sat, dinner every day.* ♿

**The Secret Garden Mansion** ★★★  Formerly known as the Mansion at Lakewood, this lovely bed and breakfast was renamed in early 1997 in memory of a family member who passed away (his favorite book was *The Secret Garden*). It's hard to believe that this luxurious, peaceful Victorian retreat is just three minutes away from downtown Walnut Creek, the nerve center of Contra Costa County's sprawling suburbopolis. Nestled behind elegant white wrought-iron gates at the end of a quiet street, it has seven guest rooms, including Juliet's Balcony, with its lovely garden view, and the Summerhouse, which has a flowered-canopy bed, a sunny porch, and a private entrance. The most extravagant chamber is the romantic Estate Suite, with its private sitting room, terrace overlooking the gardens, antique brass canopy bed, and spectacular black marble bathroom with a Jacuzzi, double vanity, and large shower. Nice touches abound in every room: lace curtains, extraordinary antiques, stacks of soft towels and fluffy robes in the private bathrooms, and fresh flowers everywhere. Downstairs there's a splendid library and an exquisitely furnished formal dining room. Guests enjoy a full breakfast on Saturday and Sunday in the tea room, and a sumptuous continental breakfast is served on weekdays. Three acres of landscaped gardens add to the aura of luxurious seclusion. ■ *1056 Hacienda Dr (from I-680, take the Ygnacio Valley Rd N exit and turn right on Homestead Ave, then left on Hacienda Dr), Walnut Creek, CA 94598; (925)945-3600; $$$; AE, DIS, MC, V; checks OK.*

▼
Lafayette

*Restaurants*

▲

## LAFAYETTE

### *RESTAURANTS*

**Tourelle Restaurant** ★★★  The beautiful ivy-covered, red-brick Tourelle Restaurant consistently dishes out some of the best fare in Contra Costa County. Chef Stephen Silva's menu includes the requisite house-smoked meats, fresh seafood and pasta, and brick-oven pizzas, but it also reflects his fondness for Mediterranean country dishes. His seasonally inspired menu might include a lovely, moist, house-smoked pork chop—redolent of hardwoods and topped with a sweet relish of fresh tomatoes and sun-dried cranberries—or perhaps grilled lamb chops with garlic-mint oil, balsamic vinegar, and grilled radicchio. The warm goat-cheese salad includes baby greens with applewood-smoked bacon and raisin crostini and is tangy and delicious. For dessert, cross your fingers and hope for the pear poached in wine and served on a slice of slightly sweet white cake with a cinnamon glaze, but if that's not available you'll be quite content with the first-rate vanilla-bean crème brûlée. The lively dining room with its thriving fig trees, slate floor, glass-roofed atrium, colorful original paintings, and open kitchen gives the place an exciting, upbeat feel, enhanced by its energetic staff. On Sunday there's a

CLOSED

superb Mediterranean brunch, best enjoyed on the pretty courtyard patio lined with quaking aspens. ■ *3565 Mt Diablo Blvd (from Hwy 24 E, take the Central Lafayette exit, turn right on Oak Hill Rd, then right on Mt Diablo Blvd), Lafayette; (925)284-3565; www.tourelle.com; $$$; full bar; AE, DIS, MC, V; local checks only; brunch Sun, lunch Mon–Fri, dinner every day.* ♿

**Miraku** ★★ Don't let the drab blue and white exterior of this Japanese restaurant perched high on a hill fool you: inside there's an elegant, airy dining room lined with sea-blue padded booths and a sushi bar brightened by several large Oriental good luck statues. The sushi and other traditional Japanese dishes are topnotch, whether you indulge in the teriyakis, tempuras, or such specialties as the *beef shabu-shabu*, thinly sliced prime beef that's cooked tableside with fresh Napa cabbage, spinach, bamboo shoots, mushrooms, green onions, tofu, and yam noodles and served with a pair of dipping sauces. A generous selection of combination plates is offered, too. And you can rest assured that no MSG enters any of the authentic cuisine at Miraku (Japanese for "joy of the taste"). ■ *3740 Mt Diablo Blvd (next to the Hillside Inn & Suites on the W side of town), Lafayette; (925)284-5700; $$; full bar; AE, DC, DIS, MC, V; no checks; lunch Mon–Fri, dinner every day.* ♿



**Kaffee Barbara** ★ If you linger over the morning newspaper at Kaffee Barbara on a weekday you'll see locals mingling easily with out-of-town executives wrapping up leisurely breakfast meetings. This quaint cafe, housed in a white Bavarian-style cottage with an exterior playfully painted with a cow, a mouse, and butterflies, serves simple, satisfying breakfasts (starting at 7am) and lunches. The morning meal features competently executed standards: fluffy omelets, golden waffles, eggs Benedict—all served with fresh fruit. During the day you'll find house-made soups and an assortment of salads and sandwiches including a standout Reuben and an unbelievably overpriced bagel with lox and cream cheese. The service is ebullient and efficient. During the warm weather, dine alfresco on the pleasant red-brick patio covered with fragrant star jasmine vines, trumpet vines, roses, bougainvillea, nasturtiums, and numerous planters bursting with other colorful garden flowers. ■ *1005 Brown Ave (from Hwy 24, take the Central Lafayette exit and drive 1 mile E on Mt Diablo Blvd), Lafayette; (925)284-9390; $; DC, MC, V; checks OK; breakfast, lunch Mon–Sat.*

**Lisa's Tea Treasures** ★ See the review of this establishment's Menlo Park branch in the following pages. ■ *71 Lafayette Circle (at Mt Diablo Blvd), Lafayette; (925)283-2226; $; beer and wine; MC, V; checks OK; full tea service offered at 12pm, 2pm, and 4pm Tues–Sun.*

## *LODGINGS*

**Lafayette Park Hotel** ★★ Set at the end of a cobblestone drive on a hill on the east side of town, this golden ersatz French château is a briskly efficient operation catering to the booming Contra

Costa corporate scene. In keeping with its upscale image, rates are steep for this part of the Bay Area (about $175 to $400), but the 139 rooms—half of which are designated nonsmoking—are suitably commodious, with attractive furnishings that include cherry-wood desks and armoires, down-filled duvets on firm beds, wet bars, refrigerators, and remote-control TVs with a selection of movies. Wood-burning fireplaces and vaulted ceilings adorn the more luxurious rooms and suites; bathrooms are equipped with Italian granite counters, hair dryers, ironing boards, and telephones (three in every room). *USA Today* is delivered to each room and shoe shines are complimentary. An inviting 50-foot heated lap pool, a Jacuzzi, a redwood sauna, and a fitness center are also available to guests 24 hours a day. The hotel's cushy **Duck Club Restaurant** overlooks the pretty fountain courtyard and offers a small, pricey menu featuring filet mignon, fresh fish, pasta, and the namesake General Lafayette's roasted half duckling. The hotel's **Bistro at the Park**—reminiscent of an erudite men's club lounge—is a great place for a drink, especially when the weather is cool and you can cozy up to the roaring fireplace. ■ *3287 Mt Diablo Blvd (from Hwy 24, take the Pleasant Hill Rd S exit and turn right on Mt Diablo Blvd), Lafayette, CA 94549; (925)283-3700 or (800)368-2468, ext. 6 (reservations only); lph@woodsidehotels.com; www.woodsidehotels. com; $$$; full bar; AE, DC, DIS, MC, V; checks OK; brunch Sun, breakfast, lunch Mon–Fri, dinner every day.* &

## ORINDA

### *RESTAURANTS*

**Amforatino Caffe and Bar** ★★ The staff is as exuberant as the decor in this bustling Italian-Mediterranean cafe (formerly known as Alexander Ristorante), where a shocking bolt of blue neon runs across the width of the dining room, colorful modern paintings hang on the walls, and the recently remodeled glass-enclosed dining room allows patrons to watch the passersby on Orinda's quaint main street. Kick off your meal with the house-cured salmon rolled with cream cheese, capers, and garlic and served on toasted bread, or the Roma tomato salad with portobello mushrooms and basil drizzled with a pancetta vinaigrette. For the *secondi* course, chef Mark Regulski (who worked for several years at Piatti's in Carmel and La Jolla before moving north) offers at least a dozen pasta dishes, including a savory tagliatelle with rock shrimp, kalamata olives, grilled endive, and a sun-dried tomato wine sauce. Heartier entrees on his seasonal menu range from grilled Atlantic salmon with eggplant sauce and risotto cakes to grilled free-range veal chop with roasted-garlic mashed potatoes. Other good bets include the meats hot off the rotisserie. ■ *65 Moraga Way (in town, next to the Union 76 gas station), Orinda; (925)253-1322; $$; full bar; AE, DC, DIS, MC, V; no checks; lunch Tues–Fri, dinner every day.* &

# DANVILLE

## *RESTAURANTS*

**Bridges** ★★★ Japanese businessman Kazuo Sugitani was so happy with the education his son received at Danville's famed Athenian prep school that he wanted to give something back to the town. Blending the best of East and West cuisine, Bridges is a pretty nifty gift. Beautifully landscaped grounds and an inviting outdoor terrace encircle a building that mingles the brown-shingled architectural influence of Morgan and Maybeck with soaring angles and interior spaces reminiscent of 17th-century Kyoto. Chef Kevin Gin, who took over in 1993, has continued the Bridges tradition of using fresh ingredients and ingenuity to create a wide array of savory dishes including a grilled marinated pork tenderloin with a ginger–Fuji apple butter served with a crispy sweet-potato pancake; lemon and chive fettuccine with rock shrimp, wild mushrooms, baby tomatoes, and plum wine; and delicately pan-seared sea scallops with a pink grapefruit-vanilla sauce accompanied by braised greens, Chinese sausage, and garlic rice. The respectable wine list includes an extensive collection of dessert wines to match such sweet delights as the Tahitian vanilla-bean crème brûlée, the lemon blueberry swirl ice cream with blueberry compote, or the popular go-ahead-and-splurge dessert sampler for two. ■ *44 Church St (from I-680, take the Diablo Rd exit, go W to Hartz Ave, turn left on Hartz Ave and drive 2 blocks to Church St), Danville; (925)820-7200; $$$; full bar; AE, DC, MC, V; no checks; lunch Fri only, dinner every day.* ⟺

**Blackhawk Grille** ★★ In the exclusive community of Blackhawk, this glamorous, offbeat 7,000-square-foot restaurant is a testament to California's adoration of the automobile. There's almost always a vintage beauty on display in the middle of the dining room (on loan from the Behring Auto Museum at the other end of the plaza), and the booths are covered in the gold-flecked vinyl coveted by '50s hot-rodders. The Grille's exotic interior glows with brushed stainless steel, gleaming copper, and verdigris. Lighting fixtures are stylized hubcap sconces, and the bar is topped with fiber-optic-etched glass. In the midst of this glitz, there's an eclectic but down-to-earth menu of wood-fired pizzas, satisfying pastas such as the porcini ravioli with mascarpone cheese and English peas, and competently prepared entrees including an herb-cured Atlantic salmon with black beluga lentils, mussels, leeks, and crispy artichokes. Better yet, compose a meal from the wide range of smaller dishes like the smoked jumbo prawns with mango chutney, sweet crab cakes, and smoked chicken and shiitake mushroom spring rolls with papaya barbecue sauce and arugula pesto. The wine list is vast (enophiles should take a peek at the wine room through the picture windows in the banquet hall) and focuses on California vintners. Desserts, like everything else about this place, are excessive and fluctuate in quality: try pastry chef Maria Specht's White Russian Torte, a sinful combination of dark and white chocolate mousses with Kahlua and crème de cacao layered with flourless chocolate cake and raspberry coulis. ▪ *3540 Blackhawk Plaza Circle (from I-680, take the Crow Canyon exit, head E on Crow Canyon, drive 7 miles to Camino Tassajara, and bear right to Blackhawk Plaza Circle), Danville; (925)736-4295; $$$; full bar; AE, DC, DIS, MC, V; no checks; brunch Sat–Sun, lunch Mon–Fri, dinner every day.* &

## SAN RAMON

### *RESTAURANTS*

**Bighorn Grill** ★★ As the name suggests, this pleasant Western-themed restaurant attracts big beef eaters, who come for baby back pork ribs slathered with a watermelon barbecue sauce, meat loaf topped with country gravy and mashed sweet potatoes, and a 14-ounce garlic-roasted Black Angus New York steak, to name just a few of the meaty entrees. Freshly tossed salads and pasta and fish dishes are also on the menu, though the Bighorn primarily beckons to carnivores who like their meat grilled, smoked, or hot off the rotisserie and in generous quantities. Designed by popular San Francisco Bay Area restaurateur Pat Kuleto (think Farallon, Kuleto's, and Boulevard), the Bighorn's large, airy, lodgelike dining room has antler chandeliers, horn-shaped hooks on the walls, and a bronze bighorn sheep's head hanging over the long bar, where urban cowboys and business execs sip frosty beers or martinis with jalapeño-stuffed olives. Families love the Bighorn, too, and a Just for Kids menu caters to the young buckaroo wannabes. ▪ *2410 San Ramon Valley Blvd (near Crow Canyon Rd), San Ramon; (925)838-5678; $$; full bar; AE, DC, MC, V; no checks; lunch Mon–Fri, dinner every day.* &

**Mudd's Restaurant** ★★ During the height of the summer harvest, nearly half of Mudd's fruits and vegetables are grown in the 7-acre municipal garden just outside its dining-room windows—the bright idea of founder and former owner Virginia Mudd. Fresh herbs from the garden complement every aspect of the cooking, from the unique flavorings to the delicate, edible herb-and-flower garnishes adorning every plate. Innovative chef Tim Wetzel (formerly of San Francisco's Splendido and Livermore's Wente Vineyards Restaurant) took over the helm in the summer of 1997, turning out his brand of American-style fare that's often inspired by the garden's yields. A recent meal started with a fabulous garden leek tart with smoked salmon, tarragon beurre blanc, and Osetra caviar, followed by a juicy grilled New York steak with spiced cauliflower purée, roast onions, and salsa verde. The meal was topped off with a baked galette made with Ashmeeds Colonel apples (just picked), Brie, and truffled caramel sauce. The best time to eat here is on warm summer days, when the vegetables are at their peak and you can enjoy them on the patio. ▪ *10 Board-*

*walk (just off Crow Canyon Rd and Park Pl, 1 mile W of I-680), San Ramon; (925)837-9387; $$; full bar; AE, DC, MC, V; no checks; brunch Sun, lunch Mon–Fri, dinner every day.* ౬

## LIVERMORE

### RESTAURANTS

**Wente Vineyards Restaurant** ★★★  The Wente family couldn't have devised a better way to showcase its wines than with this exquisite neo–Spanish colonial restaurant set among the vineyards and rolling hills of the 1,200-acre Wente estate. The interior is all glass and glowing wood, and for warm summer nights there's a fine broad patio overlooking the vineyards. Chef Kimball Jones's daily changing menu is a pleasant blend of traditional and experimental, showcased by fresh Hog Island oysters on the half shell served with a sparkling wine mignonette, and roasted butternut squash soup with crème fraîche and sage. House-smoked meats and fresh fish are presented with intriguing, tangy sauces and exotic chutneys, and Wente's trademark beef dishes, such as rib-eye steak with a fire-roasted onion and portobello mushroom relish, are delicious. While it's unfortunate that the Wente wines don't usually measure up to the food, the good news is that the restaurant sells other wines, too. Reservations are strongly advised. The winery is open for tours and tastings seven days a week, and as of April 1998, visitors can tee off at the estate's 18-hole Greg Norman–designed golf course, which is in full view of the restaurant. ■ *5050 Arroyo Rd (follow L St until it turns into Arroyo Rd, about 4½ miles S of town), Livermore; (925)456-2450 (restaurant), (925)456-2400 (estate); www.wentevineyards.com; $$$; wine and wine-based spirits; AE, DC, MC, V; checks OK; brunch Sun, lunch Mon–Sat, dinner every day.* ౬

## PLEASANTON

### RESTAURANTS

**Tong's** ★★  In quaint, peaceful downtown Pleasanton you'll find locals flocking to Tong's for a taste of the area's best Chinese food. If you're craving Peking duck, Tong's terrific rendition is seasoned with spices, dipped in honey, blown dry, then barbecued in a smoke oven and served with cilantro, scallions, and hoisin sauce (you may order a half or a whole duck). Tong's also smokes duck in Chinese tea leaves, and serves it with lotus buns. Maine lobster, Dungeness crab, and steamed whole fish are prepared here, too. Those who desire less elaborate Chinese dishes won't be disappointed: everything from pot-stickers and sizzling rice soup to kung pao prawns and Mongolian beef is dished out with aplomb. ■ *425 Main St (between W Angela and Neal Sts), Pleasanton; (925)462-2800; $-$$; beer and wine; AE, MC, V; local checks only; lunch, dinner Tues–Sun.* ౬

**Pleasanton Hotel** ★ An oasis in the surrounding fast-food desert, the graceful, turn-of-the-century Pleasanton Hotel is the sort of place that makes you want to linger over lunch or dinner. Starters vary from a delicious apple-cured salmon with goat cheese–caper toast points to roasted mussels served with a grilled garlic baguette, in addition to a few freshly tossed salads. The preparation of the hearty entrees varies in consistency but is generally good; try any of the daily specials or the standard menu's maple-cured pork loin with apple–golden raisin chutney, the sesame-crusted ahi tuna with a Niçoise olive and cherry tomato vinaigrette, or the linguine with Manila clams, sweet corn, pancetta, and roasted peppers. The wine list includes many selections from local vineyards, and the staff's advice is usually dependable. The adjoining bar features live rock music for dancing away all those extra calories Friday through Sunday. Blues are offered on the patio (weather permitting) on Tuesday and Thursday, and you can swing to big band or live jazz tunes on Sunday. The Pleasanton Hotel also hosts group winemaker and murder mystery dinners. ■ *855 Main St (from I-580, take the Santa Rita exit and head S for 2 miles), Pleasanton; (925)846-8106; $$$; full bar; AE, DC, DIS, MC, V; local checks only; brunch Sun, lunch Mon–Sat, dinner every day.* ᕱ

San Francisco Bay Area

### LODGINGS

**Evergreen** ★★ High in the emerald hills of Pleasanton stands the grand, flower-rimmed Evergreen inn. A contemporary bed and breakfast, this recently renovated two-story cedar house is lined with windows, decks, and skylights so you can see the sky and treetops at nearly every turn. Evergreen offers four comfortable, pretty guest rooms, including the coveted Grand View, with a private outdoor deck overlooking the garden and valley, a huge white-tiled bathroom with a Jacuzzi tub for two, a fireplace, and an antique king-size sleigh bed that overlooks the trees. Breakfast is served on bistro tables in the aptly named sun room or on the deck, and after the morning repast guests can walk right out the door for a great hike through neighboring Augustin Bernal Park and along panoramic Pleasanton Ridge. ■ *9104 Longview Dr (from Hwy 680, take the Bernal Ave W exit, turn left on Foothill Rd and drive ¼ mile, then turn right on Longview Dr), Pleasanton, CA 94588; (925)426-0901; $$$; AE, MC, V; checks OK.*

**Plum Tree Inn** ★ As you speed past all those shimmering, neo–Silicon Valley glass buildings along Interstate 580, it's hard to believe that Pleasanton has a, well, pleasant turn-of-the-century core. Located smack in the middle of old town, Joan and Bob Cordtz's restored 1890s Victorian has six unique suites—each with its own private bath, a tasteful collection of antiques, a TV, and a phone. Ask for one of the rooms overlooking the patio in back, especially the Cherry Room, which features a giant cherry-wood four-poster bed. Business travelers seeking refuge from all

Pleasanton

*Lodgings*

▲

83

those glass towers will find hookups for faxes and computers in every room. Breakfast is served in the dining room or on the sunny deck of the innkeepers' home next door. Plead for their Belgian waffles. ■ *262 W Angela St (just W of Main St), Pleasanton, CA 94566; (925) 426-9588; $$; AE, MC, V; checks OK.*

## POINT RICHMOND

### RESTAURANTS

**Hidden City Cafe** ★★ Like the pretty little enclave of Point Richmond itself, this neighborhood cafe is a hidden jewel tucked next to the industrial sprawl of Richmond. The local artists and business execs who crowd in here for breakfast and lunch don't come for the decor—they come for the food. In the morning, order the polenta scrapple with bacon, red onion, and two eggs, the yellow cornmeal pancakes, or the fabulous French toast sprinkled with cinnamon, ginger, and quatre épices (a French four-spice powder) and served with real maple syrup. Supplement your breakfast with some house-made fennel sausages. The lunch menu might include a good organic Niman-Schell Ranch hamburger with house-made french fries and a first-rate Atlantic salmon sandwich with fresh salsa verde and melted Jack cheese served on the cafe's own focaccia. The kitchen usually whips up something fresh for dessert, such as apricot and blackberry cobbler on a crumbly multigrain shortcake topped with vanilla ice cream. Unfortunately, the service can be flakier than the shortcake. ■ *109 Park Place (at Washington Ave and the Point Richmond Triangle), Point Richmond; (510) 232-9738; $; beer and wine; no credit cards; checks OK; breakfast, lunch Tues–Sat.*

### LODGINGS

**Hotel Mac** ★★★ Who would have thought there'd be a handsome three-star hotel nestled in the quaint village of Point Richmond, a remote hamlet straddling the edge of the city of Richmond. Hotel Mac is completely sheltered from the hustle and bustle of the East Bay's larger cities and is a 10-minute drive over the Richmond–San Rafael Bridge to the Larkspur–San Francisco ferry. Built in 1911, this imposing three-story, red-brick edifice on the National Register of Historic Places was remodeled in 1995 and now offers seven lovely guest rooms (including two deluxe suites) that cost half as much as what you'd pay for a similar room in San Francisco. Each unit is individually decorated with rich, colorful fabrics and brass light fixtures, and the windows are framed with handsome white plantation shutters. Every room also has a queen- or king-size bed, cable TV with a VCR, a small refrigerator, terrycloth robes, and a safe for storing valuables; four rooms have gas fireplaces that you can turn on with the flick of a light switch.

Colorful stained-glass windows line the Hotel Mac's dining room, where a respectable mix of cuisine—ranging from risotto

with Florida rock shrimp to rack of lamb and chicken cordon bleu—is served. But the hotel's highlight is the spacious, high-ceilinged oak and mahogany bar, an ideal place for an aperitif with your mate and a comfortable spot to mingle with a group of friends. A continental breakfast is included in the room rate.
■ *10 Cottage Ave (at Washington Ave), Point Richmond, CA 94801; (510)235-0010; hotelmac@pointrichmond.com; www.pointrichmond.com/hotelmac; $$; full bar; AE, MC, V; checks OK; breakfast Mon–Fri (Sat–Sun guests only), dinner every day.* &

## EL CERRITO

### RESTAURANTS

**Fatapple's** ★ When local carnivores hear the call of the wild and nothing but a big, rare burger will do, they head for this comfortable, informal spot. Fatapple's makes its burgers with exceptionally lean, high-quality ground beef and serves them on house-made multigrain rolls with a variety of toppings, including five very good cheeses (ask for the creamy crumbled blue cheese). The soups, such as the rich beef barley or creamy corn chowder, are usually winners, as is the delicious spinach salad tossed with feta, walnuts, red onions, marinated black beans, and a tart vinaigrette. Standout desserts include the flaky olallieberry or pecan pie, thick jumbo milk shakes (seven flavors, ranging from mocha to olallieberry) served in icy stainless-steel mixer containers, and cheese puffs (ethereal pastry pillows stuffed with baker's cheese and dusted with powdered sugar). Fatapple's is also famous for its all-American breakfasts: fluffy egg dishes, waffles, pancakes, and the like. There's also a popular Berkeley branch. ■ *7525 Fairmount Ave (at Colusa St), El Cerrito; (510)528-3433; $; beer and wine; MC, V; no checks; breakfast, lunch, dinner every day.* &

Albany

*Restaurants*

## ALBANY

### RESTAURANTS

**Britt-Marie's** ★★ As inviting as a pair of favorite slippers, Britt-Marie's offers comfort food from many corners of the globe. Partisans of the Portuguese sandwich—garlic-rubbed toast topped with salt cod and potatoes—would revolt if it were to disappear from the menu, as would avid fans of the cucumbers in garlicky sour cream, the roast chicken with herbs, and the pork schnitzel with buttered noodles. Two Greek restaurateurs took over Britt-Marie's in 1987, six years after its founding, and enhanced a good thing by adding a few native dishes, including an incredible spanakopita, as well as a California-style menu to supplement the roster of European classics (the fresh fish and risotto items are especially good). Sweet-toothed patrons can top off their meal with desserts like bourbon-pecan tart or chocolate cake with a thin layer of marzipan tucked under the chocolate frosting. With its impressionist paintings, oilcloth-covered tables, and imposing antique wooden bar, Britt-Marie's recalls the sort of European wine bar where intellectuals gather to talk politics ad infinitum. ■ *1369 Solano Ave (between Ramona and Carmel Sts), Albany; (510)527-1314; $$; beer and wine; no credit cards; checks OK; lunch Tues–Sat, dinner Tues–Sun.*

**Christopher's Nothing Fancy Cafe** ★ The exterior of this Mexican restaurant is as humble as the name, but inside lies an amiable dining room with a pleasant south-of-the-border feel. In keeping with its health-conscious environs, Christopher's concentrates on fresh ingredients and a style of cooking that's lower in fat, salt, and calories than your typical Mexican fare. Try the grilled chicken taco salad, the vegetarian burritos, the beef or shrimp fajitas, or the peppy nachos. If it's a nice day, angle for a seat on the pretty outdoor patio with its mosaic tiles and gurgling fountain; if the wind is blowing up from the bay, snag a seat inside near the fireplace. ■ *1019 San Pablo Ave (near Marin St), Albany; (510)526-1185; $; beer and wine; AE, MC, V; local checks only; lunch Mon–Sat, dinner every day.* ৬

## BERKELEY

You can still buy tie-dyed "Berserkley" T-shirts from vendors on **Telegraph Avenue**, but the wild days of this now middle-aged, upper-middle-class burg are gone. Although hot-button issues can still spark a march or two at the **University of California at Berkeley**, these days most UC Berkeley students seem more interested in cramming for exams than in mounting a protest in People's Park. In some respects, the action has moved from the campus to City Hall, where the town's residents—many of them former hippies, student intellectuals, and peace activists—rage on against everything from Columbus Day (Berkeley celebrates Indigenous People's Day instead) to the opening of a large video store downtown (too lowbrow and tacky). The *San Francisco Chronicle* recently called Berkeley the "most contentious of cities," and it's a mantle most of its inhabitants wear with pride.

If you're a newcomer to Berkeley, start your tour of the town at the world-renowned UC Berkeley campus (also known as Cal), the oldest and second-largest of the nine campuses comprising the UC system. Driving through the university is virtually impossible, so park on a side street and set out on foot. The campus isn't so huge that you'd get hopelessly lost if you wandered around on your own, but without a guide you might miss some of the highlights, such as **Sproul Plaza**, **Sather Gate**, and the **Hearst Mining Building**. So pick up a self-guided walking packet at the **UC Berkeley Visitor Information Center** (open Monday through Friday), or attend one of the free 1½-hour tours offered Monday through Friday at 10am (meet at the visitor center) and on Saturday at 10am and Sunday at 1pm (meet in front of the Campanile in the heart of the campus); the visitor

center is at 2200 University Avenue at Oxford Street, University
Hall, Room 101, (510)642-5215 or (510)642-INFO.

*ART AND CULTURE*

**Literature**  Most folks around here agree that if you can't find something good to read at **Cody's Books**, Berkeley's best bookstore, it probably isn't worth reading; 2454 Telegraph Avenue, (510)845-7852. Almost every night, nationally known literary and political writers appear at Cody's and at **Black Oak Books**, a popular purveyor of new and used books; 1491 Shattuck Avenue, (510)486-0698. The four-story **Moe's Books** specializes in used tomes and remainders, 2476 Telegraph Avenue, (510)849-2087, and a **Barnes & Noble** megastore, complete with a high-tech fountain and park benches for on-the-spot reading, offers discounts on *New York Times* bestsellers and hard-cover books and stocks hundreds of periodicals; 2352 Shattuck Avenue, (510)644-0861.

**Museums**  The **University Art Museum** has a small permanent collection of modern art and frequently hosts peculiar but riveting exhibitions by artists such as Robert Mapplethorpe; 2626 Bancroft Way, (510)642-0808. The **Judah L. Magnes Museum**, the third-largest Jewish museum in the West, offers numerous exhibitions of Jewish art and culture, including a Holocaust show and a display of modern Jewish paintings; 2911 Russell Street, (510)849-2710. A vast array of anthropological artifacts is showcased at the **Phoebe Hearst Museum of Anthropology**, located in UC Berkeley's Kroeber Hall, at the corner of College Avenue and Bancroft Way, (510)643-7648. Hands-on exhibits exploring everything from bats to holograms are featured at the **Lawrence Hall of Science**; while you're there, duck outside to hear (and see) the giant, eerie wind chimes and take a peek at the Stonehenge-like solar observatory; located in the hills above UC Berkeley on Centennial Drive, (510)642-5133.

**Berkeley**

*Art and Culture*

**Music**  The **Berkeley Symphony** blends new and experimental music with the classics at Zellerbach Hall on the UC Berkeley campus; for tickets call (510)841-2800. Modern rock, funk, and acid jazz are blasted at **Blake's**; 2367 Telegraph Avenue, (510)848-0886. For Latin jazz and R&B, visit **Mr. E's**; 2286 Shattuck Avenue, (510)848-0260. If you're feeling a bit more mellow, take a seat at the **Freight & Salvage** coffeehouse, a prime Euro-folkie hangout; 1111 Addison Street, (510)548-1761. Live rock, jazz, folk, reggae, and other concerts are frequently held at UC Berkeley's intimate, open-air **Greek Theatre**, a particularly pleasant place for sitting beneath the stars and listening to music on warm summer nights; located on Gayley Road off Hearst Avenue, (510)642-9988. **Cal Performances** presents up-and-coming and established artists of all kinds—from the Bulgarian Women's Chorus to superstar mezzo-soprano Cecilia Bartoli; the concerts are held at various sites on the UC Berkeley campus, (510)642-9988.

**Theater and Film**  The **Berkeley Repertory Theatre** has a national reputation for experimental productions of the classics and innovative new works, 2025 Addison Street, (510)845-4700, and the **Black Repertory Group** offers a range of plays, dance performances, and art by African Americans; 3201 Adeline Street, (510)652-2120. Every summer the **California Shakespeare Festival** performs in an outdoor theater in the Berkeley hills near Orinda (bundle up 'cause it's usually freezing); 100 Gateway Boulevard, (510)548-3422. Film buffs will appreciate the **UC Theater**, a revivalist movie house where the flicks change every night, 2036 University Avenue, (510)843-6267, and the **Pacific Film Archive**, which shows underground avant-garde movies as well as the classics; 2625 Durant Avenue, (510)642-1412. For up-to-date listings of cultural events, pick up a free copy of *The Express*, the East Bay's alternative weekly, available at cafes and newsstands throughout the city.

*ADDITIONAL ATTRACTIONS*

**Shopping**  With its recent profusion of chichi stores and upscale outlets (Smith & Hawken, Crate & Barrel, Dansk, Sur la Table, Pottery Barn, The Garden, Sweet Potatoes, et cetera), the **Fourth Street** area has become a shopping mecca—a somewhat ironic development considering the city's traditional disdain for conspicuous consumption. Another favorite shopping area is in south Berkeley, near the Berkeley/Oakland border, in the small **Elmwood** neighborhood, which stretches along College Avenue and crosses over Ashby Avenue. Poke your head into the tiny **Tail of the Yak** boutique for a look at the fabulous displays of Central American and other art treasures, 2632 Ashby Avenue, west of College, (510)841-9891, then stroll along College, where you can pet the lop-eared baby bunnies and squawk back at the beautiful parrots at **Your Basic Bird**, 2940 College Avenue, north of Ashby, (510)841-7617; dip into the huge candy jars at **Sweet Dreams**, 2901 College Avenue at Russell, (510)549-1211; munch on fantastic fresh-fruit cheese danish at **Nabolom Bakery**, 2708 Russell Street at College, (510)845-BAKE; shop for clothes at numerous boutiques; and indulge in **Bott's** freshly made ice creams, 2975 College Avenue, south of Ashby, (510)845-4545. For fresh pasta salads and sandwiches, try **Ultra Lucca Delicatessen**, 2905 College Avenue, north of Ashby, (510)849-2701, or **Espresso Roma**, where you can sip strong coffee drinks, teas, fresh lemonade, beer on tap, or wine by the glass, and eat some good calzones and sandwiches, 2960 College Avenue at Ashby, (510)644-3773. On the other side of Berkeley, where the northwest border meets the little town of Albany, is **Solano Avenue**, a popular mile-long street lined with shops and cafes frequented by locals.

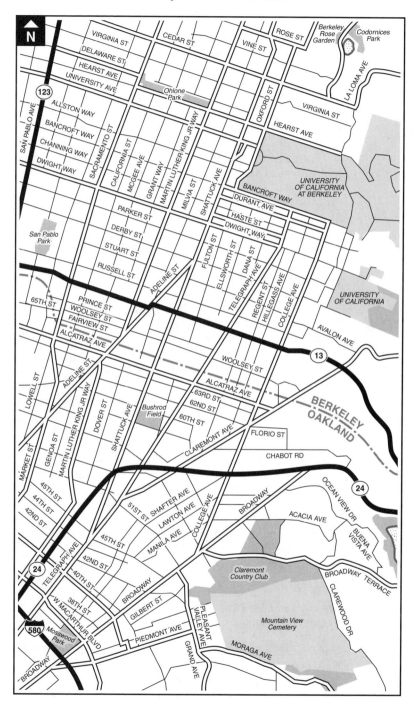

**Parks** For more pastoral diversions, stroll through the **Berkeley Rose Garden**, a terraced park with hundreds of varieties of roses and a great view of San Francisco; it's located on Euclid Avenue, between Bay View and Eunice Streets. Or visit the 30-acre **University of California Botanical Garden**, where you'll see a spectacular collection of cacti from around the world, a Mendocino pygmy forest, and a Miocene-era redwood grove; located in Strawberry Canyon on Centennial Drive, (510)642-3343. The gigantic **Tilden Regional Park**, set high in the hills above town, offers miles of hiking trails plus a steam train, a merry-go-round, and a farm and nature area for kids; it's off Wildcat Canyon Road, (510)843-2137. Tilden also boasts a beautiful **Botanical Garden** specializing in California native plants; (510)841-8732.

**Bread and Bagels** For some of the best bread in the Bay Area, go to Steve Sullivan's famous **Acme Bread Company**, 1601 San Pablo Avenue, (510)524-1327, or the **Cheese Board**, a collectively owned bakery and vast gourmet cheese shop; 1504 Shattuck Avenue, (510)549-3183. If you're a bagel lover, two Berkeley bagel shops rival Brooklyn's best: **Noah's Bagels**, 3170 College Avenue, (510)654-0944, and 1883 Solano Avenue, (510)525-4447; and **Boogie Woogie Bagel Boy** (formerly Brothers' Bagels), 1281 Gilman Street, (510)524-3104.

**Coffee, Beer, and Sake** Like many university towns, this one seems to run on coffee. **Peet's Coffee & Tea**, with its sizable selection of beans and teas, is the local favorite; 2124 Vine Street, (510)841-0564; 2916 Domingo Avenue, (510)843-1434; and 1825 Solano Avenue, (510)526-9607. For an outdoor latte beneath the trees, try **Caffè Strada**, 2300 College Avenue, (510)843-5282, or the hip, crowded, college-hangout **Cafe Milano**; 2522 Bancroft Way, (510)644-3100. **Caffé Mediterraneum** churns out excellent cappuccinos and captures the bohemian flavor of Telegraph Avenue, still a haunt of students, street people, runaways, hipsters, professors, tarot readers, and street vendors; 2475 Telegraph Avenue, (510)549-1128. Or check out the homemade pastries and tasty lunch fare at **Café Intermezzo**, a popular Berkeley haunt; 2442 Telegraph Avenue, (510)849-4592. Some of the best beer in the Bay Area is brewed at the frat-packed **Triple Rock Brewery**, 1920 Shattuck Avenue, (510)843-2739, and the hipper, more experimental **Bison Brewing Company**, which has such unusual offerings as honey-basil ale on tap and chocolate stout in magnums, not to mention hearty bistro food; 2598 Telegraph Avenue, (510)841-7734. In 1997, the **Pyramid Brewery & Ale House** joined the fray with a state-of-the-art brewery and refined pub fare; 901 Gilman Street, (510)528-9880. For something completely different, treat your taste buds to a tour of **Takara Sake USA**, a sake factory that provides tastings of sake and plum wine; 708 Addison Street, (510)540-8250.

**Chez Panisse** ★★★★ In the heart of Berkeley's gourmet ghetto, the most famous restaurant in Northern California is almost invisible from the street. Good-food lovers know where to find it, though; they just look for the small hand-carved sign in front of the vine-covered fence. Owner and chef Alice Waters has been at the forefront of the California cuisine revolution since 1971, when she started cooking simple French-influenced meals for groups of friends, then opened her legendary restaurant. Waters has never specialized in the showier, sometimes downright bizarre, culinary creations that characterize so much of modern California cuisine these days. Instead, she concentrates on simple, exquisitely orchestrated meals using the finest natural ingredients available, making Chez Panisse a major source of support for several small organic enterprises in Northern California (in fact, Chez Panisse may be the only restaurant that pays a "forager" to find the best of everything).

Chez Panisse is divided into a fantastic (albeit expensive) prix-fixe dining room downstairs and a lighthearted (and more reasonably priced) upstairs cafe. Downstairs, the daily changing dinner menu might begin with a bowl of olives and warm Acme bread, followed by aromatic, seasonal dishes such as an appetizer of thin-sliced salmon flash-cooked on a hot plate and served with an herbed flower butter, or a smooth corn-and-garlic soup flavored with a subtle touch of leek. An entree of boneless pigeon wrapped and grilled in vine leaves has a lovely smoky quality with a hint of mint and shallots, and a simple but sensational mixed-greens salad cleanses the palate before the appearance of a beautiful kirsch-infused Bavarian pudding topped with red currant sauce and fresh raspberries.

**Berkeley**

*Restaurants*

The warm, bustling upstairs cafe has a fine wine bar and seldom enough seats to go around. For an appetizer, try the baked Sonoma goat-cheese salad or the antipasto of prosciutto, baked ricotta, and roasted red peppers. The wildly popular pizzas and calzones, baked in a wood-burning oven, often feature ingredients such as squid and roasted onion or simply mozzarella and the finest vine-ripened tomatoes in the state. The pasta station highlights seasonal vegetables in dishes like whole-wheat fettuccine with greens, and the grill cooks do wonders with fresh fish and meats. The cafe's delectable desserts include house-made ice creams and sherbets, fruit cobblers, tarts, and pies. ■ *1517 Shattuck Ave (between Cedar and Vine Sts), Berkeley; (510) 548-5525 (restaurant), (510) 548-5049 (cafe); $$$ (restaurant), $$ (cafe); beer and wine; AE, DC, DIS, MC, V; local checks only; restaurant: dinner Mon–Sat, cafe: lunch, dinner Mon–Sat. & restaurant only*

**O Chamé** ★★★ Even jaded Berkeley food fanatics are bewitched by the fare in this exotic restaurant. Chef David Vardy spent years studying Buddhist-Taoist cooking in Taiwan, as well as Kansai and Kaiseki cuisine in Japan. (Kansai is the regional cuisine of Osaka; Kaiseki, created to complement the Japanese tea ceremony, consists of small dishes that can be consumed in a couple of bites.) Vardy developed an ardent local following when he opened the Daruma Teashop in North Berkeley in 1988, serving an intriguing assortment of teas, bento box lunches, and his popular Nambu teacakes—thin, sesame-based biscuits flavored with nuts or seeds. These and more elaborate works of culinary art may now be found at O Chamé, a soothing cafe crafted in the style of a rustic wayside inn from Japan's Meiji period. The à la carte menu changes often, but typical dishes include a very fresh vinegared wakame seaweed, cucumber, and crab salad, tofu dumplings with burdock and carrot, grilled river eel with endive and chayote, and soba noodles with shiitake mushrooms and daikon sprouts. O Chamé also offers a range of delicately flavored teas and sakes, as well as four good beers. The dining room is casual enough for jeans and running shoes, and the waitstaff is composed of interesting artsy types. Vardy's gracious wife, Hiromi, clad in kimonos she designs, greets guests on weekends. ■ *1830 4th St (near Hearst Ave), Berkeley; (510)841-8783; $$; beer and wine; AE, DC, MC, V; no checks; lunch, dinner Mon–Sat.* ⅍

**Rivoli** ★★★ Chef Wendy Brucker first came to the attention of East Bay diners in 1992 when she took over the kitchen of the dining room at Berkeley's Shattuck Hotel. That venue was too stiff and formal for her California sensibilities—honed at places such as San Francisco's now-shuttered Square One and the eclectic City Restaurant in L.A.—so she transferred her talents to a much more suitable place: her own, where she could have the freedom to present her relaxed yet refined ideas about California-Mediterranean cuisine. Start your meal with bruschetta topped with goat cheese, sun-dried tomatoes, and basil (a cliché, perhaps, but a wonderfully tasty one) or (definitely not a cliché) the expertly fried portobello mushrooms with arugula and aioli (superb!). Her braised lamb shank with white beans and rosemary aioli (offered in the winter) is the essence of good country cooking. Along with her husband and partner, Roscoe Skipper, Brucker deserves kudos for assembling a tantalizing menu that changes every two weeks and features numerous entrees for less than $14; the wine list offers several good choices under $20. Rivoli has been dinged in the past for its noise level, odd layout, and funky decor, but a remodeling was under way in late 1997 to reconfigure the quirky space, improve the acoustics, and install wood wainscoting and other upgrades. Despite these changes, Skipper promises that the lovely back garden (complete with bowls laden with scraps for a few feral cats) and moderate prices will remain. ■ *1539 Solano Ave (between Peralta Ave and Neilson St), Berkeley; (510)526-2542; rivoli@rivolirestaurant.com; www. rivolirestaurant.com; $$; beer and wine; MC, V; local checks only; dinner every day.* ⅍

**Ajanta** ★★ This brightly lit and attractive restaurant was voted the Bay Area's best Indian restaurant in *San Francisco Focus* magazine's 1996 readers' poll. Part of its appeal, no doubt, lies in its policy of presenting specialties from different regions of India each month, allowing intrepid diners to forge beyond the usual curries and tandoori meats. The dining room is a serene and exotic space, with intricate woodwork, golden fabrics, and graceful reproductions of murals found in India's Ajanta cave temples. The lamb rib chops, *murg ularthu* (boneless chicken simmered in a sauce made with onions, mustard seeds, fennel, garlic, and ginger), and the prawn curry are a few of the standout dishes usually featured, and there are always about half-a-dozen vegetarian dishes to choose from, including the wonderful *baigan ki boorani* (pan-fried eggplant slices topped with a garlic-lemon-yogurt sauce). ■ *1888 Solano Ave (near The Alameda), Berkeley; (510)526-4373; $$; beer and wine; AE, DC, DIS, MC, V; local checks only; lunch, dinner every day.*

**Bette's Oceanview Diner** ★★ The charm of Bette's Oceanview Diner doesn't have anything to do with the ocean (there's not even a view here). What this small, nouveau-'40s diner does have is red booths, chrome stools, a checkerboard tile floor, hip waitresses, the best jukebox around, and darn good breakfasts. On weekends expect a 45-minute stomach-growling wait, but consider the payoff: enormous, soufflé-style pancakes stuffed with pecans and ripe berries, farm-fresh eggs scrambled with prosciutto and Parmesan, outstanding omelets, corned beef hash, and the quintessential huevos rancheros with black beans. If you can't bear the wait, pop into **Bette's-to-Go** (BTG) next door for a pre-breakfast snack. Later in the day, BTG offers superlative focaccia sandwiches and California pizzas. ■ *1807-A 4th St (between Virginia St and Hearst Ave), Berkeley; (510)644-3230; $; beer and wine; no credit cards; local checks only; breakfast, lunch every day.*

**Café Fanny** ★★ Alice Waters' diminutive corner cafe can handle fewer than a dozen stand-up customers at once, but that doesn't deter anyone. On sunny Saturday mornings the adjacent parking lot fills with the overflow, with the luckier customers snaring a seat at one of the few tiny outdoor cafe tables. They don't come for the view—the cafe faces busy San Pablo Avenue—but for a simple, inexpensive breakfast or lunch in the inimitable Waters style. Named after Waters' daughter, this popular spot recalls the neighborhood cafes so dear to the French, but Fanny's food is much better. Breakfast on crunchy Café Fanny granola, jam-filled buckwheat crêpes, or perfect soft-boiled eggs served on sourdough toast with a side of house-made jam, and sip a café au lait from a big authentic French handleless bowl. The morning meal is served until 11am and all day on Sunday. For lunch, order one of the seductive sandwiches, such as egg salad on sourdough

Berkeley

*Restaurants*

toast with sun-dried tomatoes and anchovies or the simple but delicious grilled eggplant with olive paste. Many fans combine a visit here with a stop at Fanny's illustrious neighbors: Acme Bread Company on one side and Kermit Lynch Wine Merchant on the other. ■ *1603 San Pablo Ave (between Cedar and Virginia Sts), Berkeley; (510)524-5447; lesliewilson_cafefanny@msn.com; www.onlygourmet.com/; $; beer and wine; V, MC; checks OK; breakfast, lunch every day.* ᕋ

**Café Rouge** ★★ Opened in 1996, this Fourth Street bistro offers everything from duck braised in white wine and smoked trout with frisée and leeks to hot dogs and cheeseburgers. Maybe it all makes a little more sense when one realizes that those aforementioned burgers and franks are the creations of Niman-Schell Ranch, so they're the most upscale versions you're likely to have. In fact, chef/owner Marsha McBride and co-chef Kelsie Kerr (both Zuni Cafe alumni) insist upon high quality in all their ingredients, so it's hard to go wrong with anything on the small but beguiling menu. Their passions are oysters and charcuterie, but there are also creative salads and pastas, great grilled steaks, and juicy spit-roasted chicken. Desserts are absolute knockouts, including a seasonal warm quince bread pudding and a Jonathan apple puff pastry tartlet. Many of the house-smoked charcuterie items are available in the market in the back of the airy, bilevel restaurant, which boasts a long, curved zinc counter, skylights, and gold walls punctuated by red paper wall sconces and modern artwork. ■ *1782 4th St (between Hearst Ave and Delaware St), Berkeley; (510)525-1440; $$$; full bar; AE, MC, V; no checks; lunch every day, dinner Tues–Sun.* ᕋ

**Cambodiana's** ★★ There aren't many Cambodian restaurants in Cambodia, where wayfarers rely on teahouses and noodle shops, and traditional dishes may be sampled only in private homes. It took a forward-thinking Assyrian priest—Father Nazarin—to convince the local immigrant community that a Cambodian restaurant could be a hot property. Cambodiana's is the best of the bunch. Owner Sidney Sok Ke and his wife Carol Bopha Ke, the restaurant's talented chef, have assembled a menu organized around six regional sauces (based on tamarind, ginger, lemongrass, lamb juice, curry, and anchovy), each designed to complement delectable renditions of chicken, salmon, rabbit, lamb, prawns, quail, beef, and trout. Try the deboned quail stuffed with ground pork, shrimp, and garlic or the wonderful grilled lamb chops marinated in a mixture of garlic, lemongrass, galangal, paprika, and soy sauce. The country-style smoky eggplant, roasted and tossed with pork, shrimp, green onion, and garlic, also wins raves. The place is usually packed, so make reservations, especially on weekend evenings. ■ *2156 University Ave (between Shattuck Ave and Oxford St), Berkeley; (510)843-4630; $$; beer and wine; AE, DC, MC, V; checks OK; lunch Mon–Fri, dinner every day.* ᕋ

**Kirala** ★★ A no-reservations policy often means a long wait at this small restaurant with the down-at-the-heels facade and plain-Jane decor. Once you snag a seat, however, get ready to taste some of the best Japanese food in town. The sushi is fresh and ready in a flash of talented chef Akira Komine's knife, the gyoza and other appetizers are first-rate, and the skewers of seafood, vegetables, and meats emerging from the robata grill are cooked to perfection and seasoned with a delicate hand. ■ *2100 Ward St (near Shattuck Ave), Berkeley; (510)549-3486; $$; beer and wine; AE, MC, V; no checks; lunch Tues–Fri, dinner every day.* ⅙

**Lalime's** ★★ It's hard to pass Lalime's at night without stopping to stare at the goings-on through its fishbowl front window: the radiant, pale-pink dining room boasts high ceilings, colorful collages on the walls, and a crush of sleek patrons leaning intimately over candle-lit, white-linen-cloaked tables. The menu changes nightly, but if they're serving the soup made with Finn potatoes, golden beets, and ginger, or the roast garlic and shiitake mushroom ravioli, don't hesitate—they're always delicious. Desserts, such as the creamy house-made anise ice cream, mango flan, and chocolate cake with brandied cherries, are equally splendid. The entrees, while generally well prepared, rarely measure up to the courses surrounding them. Lalime's prix-fixe dinners are often a good bet: one might feature seared spearfish marinated in fresh lime and curry and served with a blood-orange and fennel salad, followed by grilled chicken breast accompanied by crisp polenta triangles and a sweet onion, red pepper, and raisin relish, and, for dessert, a crisp candied pecan tart with a buttery crust. The witty, efficient, and exceptionally knowledgeable staff can direct you to the gems on Lalime's extensive beer and wine list. ■ *1329 Gilman St (between Neilson and Peralta Sts), Berkeley; (510)527-9838; www.lalimes.com; $$$; beer and wine; MC, V; checks OK; dinner every day.* ⅙

**Picante Cocina Mexicana** ★★ Energetic and invested with an engaging neighborhood feel, Picante Cocina Mexicana (literally "spicy Mexican kitchen") packs 'em in because of both the *muy bueno* food and the *muy pequeño* prices. Jim Maser, owner of Café Fanny and brother-in-law of Alice Waters, studied cooking extensively in Mexico before taking over Picante in 1994 from the previous owners. His research shines in every bite. Just about everything on the menu shows his passion for fresh ingredients and careful cooking, from tortillas made by hand throughout the day to the variety of savory sauces. The chiles rellenos are outstanding, as are the two types of tamales: a chicken version bathed in a tomatillo sauce and a vegetable tamale with butternut squash and roasted poblano chiles. The two brightly colored dining areas are always bustling, as customers catch the latest football scores on TV, listen to the occasional live-music performance, and chase after wandering toddlers. Service is efficient and amiable, and a wide variety of domestic, Mexican, and European beers is available.

Best seats in the house are at one of the big, comfortable booths or outdoors on the patio on a pleasant day. ■ *1328 6th St (just S of Gilman St), Berkeley; (510)525-3121; $; beer and wine; MC, V; local checks only; brunch Sun, lunch, dinner every day.* 𝕃

**Fatapple's** ★ See this restaurant's review in the El Cerrito section. ■ *1346 Martin Luther King Jr. Way (at Rose St), Berkeley; (510)526-2260; $; beer and wine; no credit cards; no checks; breakfast, lunch, dinner every day.* 𝕃

**Panini** ★ A delicious, cost-effective way to savor the fruits of Berkeley's obsession with all things gourmet, Panini's lunch menu offers an ever-changing array of creative sandwiches served on anise- and sesame-seeded baguettes: look for exotic collages such as prosciutto, sliced pears, creamy blue-veined Cambozola (similar to blue cheese), and basil, or a mix of melted mozzarella, capocollo (a thinly-sliced dry-cured ham), tomatoes, chopped olives, greens, pesto, and sun-dried tomatoes. Fresh soups and a variety of salads round out a menu that also includes fresh-squeezed juices, strong espresso, and luscious pastries. Panini is operated with the efficiency of an assembly line, but the surroundings are sufficiently inviting to encourage lingering in either the airy dining room or the ivy- and trumpet-vine-laced courtyard. ■ *2115 Allston Way (in Trumpetvine Ct, between Shattuck Ave and Oxford St), Berkeley; (510)849-0405; $; no alcohol; no credit cards; checks OK; lunch Mon–Fri.*

**Venezia** ★ Children love Venezia—the trompe l'oeil murals depicting an Italian piazza complemented by a real fountain and clothesline, the amiable hustle and bustle of the dining room, and the free crayons and coloring menu all add up to a pleasurable family dining experience. Even if you don't come with little ones in tow, the Disneyland-like ambience is a lot of fun, but some folks grumble that the food was better at Venezia's more humble previous location. Indeed, the menu is wildly uneven, with wonderful soups and salads emerging from the kitchen, while the house-made pastas tend to be a bit on the doughy side and the meats are often overdone. Desserts, however, remain mighty fine, and prices are reasonable. ■ *1799 University Ave (at Grant St), Berkeley; (510)849-4681; $$; beer and wine; AE, DC, MC, V; local checks only; lunch Mon–Fri, dinner every day.* 𝕃

*LODGINGS*

**The Claremont Resort and Spa** ★★★ With its towers and cupolas gleaming white against the green and golden Berkeley hills, this proud prima donna of a hotel holds fast to its Edwardian roots. It's hard to hurry here: the posh lobby with its plush furniture, crystal chandeliers, and extensive art collection is made for loitering and gaping, while the 22 acres of gorgeous grounds—with flower beds, rows of exotic palms, and even a modern sculpture garden—invite leisurely strolling. The only folks scurrying about are those rushing the net on the Claremont's 10 championship tennis courts or feeling the burn in one of the spa's aerobics classes. In spring 1997, a $6 million renovation resulted in the addition of a new wing, boosting the hotel's inventory to 279 spacious and attractively decorated guest rooms, all with views of eucalyptus-covered hills or the San Francisco Bay. Amenities include everything you'd expect in a grand hotel, including concierge and room service, a fully equipped business center, and extensive spa facilities. Parking at the hotel and transportation to the airports and San Francisco are available for a fee. In addition to the tennis courts, guests have access to fitness classes, beauty treatments, two heated pools, saunas, and a hot tub.

Three restaurants grace the premises: the **Presto Cafe** for coffees, pastries, soups, salads, and sandwiches; the **Bayview Cafe**, which is located by the pool and serves sandwiches, salads, and grilled fare; and the recently remodeled **Jordan's** (formerly known as the Pavilion), the Claremont's California-Mediterranean flagship restaurant, which serves breakfast, lunch, and dinner in a casually elegant setting known for its stupendous views. The resort's staff—influenced, no doubt, by the aristocratic environs—has at times been known to act irritatingly haughty, but after a massage or two, you just might not care. ■ *41 Tunnel Rd (at the intersection of Ashby and Domingo Aves), Berkeley, CA 94705; (510)843-3000 or (800)551-7266; www.claremont.com; $$$; full bar; AE, DC, DIS, MC, V; checks OK; breakfast, lunch, dinner every day.* &

**Berkeley**

*Lodgings*

**Gramma's Rose Garden Inn** ★★ This attractive bed and breakfast surrounded by beautifully landscaped lawns started out as a restored Tudor-style mansion furnished with wonderful old furniture and period antiques; then it swallowed the house next door and added a couple of cottages and a carriage house, giving Gramma's empire enough space for 40 guest rooms. The best rooms are in the Fay House, which has glowing hardwood walls and stunning stained-glass windows. All of the rooms in the Garden and Carriage houses have fireplaces and overlook the inviting English country garden in back (room 4 in the Carriage House is the best). Of course, the rooms facing away from Telegraph Avenue are the most tranquil. Each guest room has a private bath, a color TV, and a phone; some have balconies and views of San Francisco. Complimentary wine and cheese are served in the evening. ■ *2740 Telegraph Ave (between Ward and Stuart Sts), Berkeley, CA 94705; (510)549-2145; $$; AE, DC, DIS, MC, V; local checks only.* &

**The Berkeley City Club** ★ Julia Morgan called this lovely edifice with the grand Moorish flourishes her "little castle" (her "big castle" was San Simeon, the crowning achievement of her architectural career). The 1927 building, with hallways graced by soaring buttresses, tall lead-paned windows, garden courtyards, and handsome sandstone-colored facade, was designed as a women's club and Morgan wanted it to rival the poshest male enclave. Today both genders are welcome through its stately portals, not only as members who enjoy the club's fitness and social activities but as bed-and-breakfast guests. The club's 40 rooms are simply appointed, small, and old fashioned (if the rooms were as grand as the public areas, this would be a three-star hotel), but all have private baths and many boast views of the bay, the nearby UC campus, or the Berkeley hills. If you need a bit more elbow room, try to book one of the two suites. Overnight guests have access to the club's dining room and fitness facilities, including a 25-yard-long indoor pool that even William Randolph Hearst wouldn't mind taking a dip in. Daily rates include a buffet breakfast; weekly and monthly arrangements are available, too. ■ *2315 Durant Ave (between Dana and Ellsworth Sts), Berkeley, CA 94704; (510)848-7800; berkctyclb@aol.com; $$; full bar; MC, V; checks OK; breakfast every day, lunch Mon–Fri, dinner Mon–Tues and Thurs–Sat for members and B&B guests only.*

**Hillegass House** ★ This rustic, three-story, redwood-shingle-clad 1904 house is located on a quiet street close to UC Berkeley and is enhanced by a large, shaded side porch, a lovely backyard, and a well-manicured front lawn. The four big, high-ceilinged guest rooms are awash with light. Ask for one of the corner rooms, which have tall windows framing the trees outside. Proprietor Richard Warren occupies the third floor but keeps a low profile; guests are given a private code to the front-door lock and have access to the sauna. A sumptuous yet health-conscious breakfast is included and can be enjoyed in the dining room or the garden. ■ *2834 Hillegass Ave (between Russell and Stuart Sts, 2 blocks E of Telegraph Ave), Berkeley, CA 94705; (510)548-5517 or (800)400-5517; $$; AE, MC, V; checks OK.*

**Hotel Durant** ★ Despite extensive renovations, this modestly appointed 1928 hotel's strongest suit is still its proximity to UC Berkeley. The lobby—with comfortable armchairs, handsome paneling, and stained-glass windows—and the adjacent restaurant, **Henry's Publick House & Grille**, succeed in imparting an aura of ersatz Old World charm, but the halls and the 140 rooms and suites have a faintly generic, institutional ambience. Still, the rooms are a bit larger than those found in other old-time Berkeley hotels, and they all have private baths and cable TVs. In a neighborhood known for nightmarish traffic, the hotel's valet parking is a blessing (spaces are limited, so sign up for a parking spot when you reserve your room). The moderately priced, frequent shuttle service to both the San Francisco and Oakland airports is another bonus, as is the free continental breakfast. Henry's bar stays open till midnight, but it's a madhouse on football weekends (especially if the Cal Bears have prevailed). ■ *2600 Durant Ave (at Bowditch St, 1 block from UC Berkeley), Berkeley,*

▼
**Berkeley**

*Lodgings*

▲

CA 94704; (510)845-8981 or (800)2-DURANT; hotdur@ix. **San Francisco**
netcom.com; $$; full bar; AE, DC, DIS, MC, V; no checks; breakfast, **Bay Area**
lunch, dinner every day. &

**The French Hotel**   Because it's situated in the heart of Berkeley's
famed gourmet ghetto, with Chez Panisse across the street and a
staggering array of specialty food purveyors on all sides, you
could begin and end your trip to the Bay Area right here at the
French Hotel. Simply haul an unending stream of goodies up to
your room and stagger downstairs every now and then to quaff
an espresso at the hotel's cafe, where you can relax at a sidewalk
table while wondering what twist of fate turned this town from a
hotbed of radicalism into a world-renowned culinary center in
just a few short years. The French Hotel offers 18 guest rooms
with modern, comfortable furnishings, large bathrooms, and
either a small balcony or patio with a table and chairs. Avoid the
noisy first-floor rooms facing Shattuck Avenue (the back room on
the third floor is the quietest). Room service is efficient and the
concierge is quite friendly. ■ *1538 Shattuck Ave (between Cedar
and Vine Sts), Berkeley, CA 94709; (510)548-9930; $$; AE, DC,
DIS, MC, V; checks OK.* &

## EMERYVILLE

**Emeryville**

───────────

*Restaurants*

▲

This tiny town slivered between Oakland, Berkeley, and the bay
was once a dowdy industrial area, but a dozen years of manic
redevelopment has turned it into one of the most intriguing urban
centers in the Bay Area; computer jockeys, artists, and biotechies
now abound here in their live-work spaces. Emeryville's town
center is a nouveau ultramall called the **Emerybay Public
Market**. The center offers great ethnic food stands, stores, a 10-
screen cinema, and the hot **Kimball's East**, (510)658-2555, a jazz
and blues club with national headliners; take the Powell Street
exit from Interstate 80.

### RESTAURANTS

**Hong Kong East Ocean Seafood Restaurant ★★★**   With its green
pagoda-style tile roof topped with writhing gold dragons and its
white imperial lions guarding the front door, Hong Kong East
Ocean looks more like a temple than a restaurant. Indeed, its worshippers are legion, thanks in large part to its superior dim sum.
Set at the very tip of the Emeryville Marina, the sleek, modern
dining room has a magnificent view of the Bay Bridge and San
Francisco. For the full dim sum treatment, come on the weekend,
when the dining room swarms with dozens of carts pushed by
Chinese waitresses who have a limited grasp of English, and
when most of your fellow diners will be well-heeled Chinese.
(During the week, you order the dim sum from a menu—an efficient but boring departure from the traditional method.) Best
bets are the crystal buns (delicate steamed dumplings filled with

plump shrimp, chopped water chestnuts, cilantro, and ginger); crisp, baked *bao* (buns) filled with sweet red pork and topped with crunchy sesame seeds; and shrimp embedded in a noodle-dough crêpe served in a savory sauce. Besides dim sum, Hong Kong East Ocean offers authentic and exquisitely prepared Cantonese-style lunches and dinners: try the whole black cod dressed in a satiny soy-ginger-garlic sauce; the addictive, peppery deep-fried squid topped with chopped chiles and scallions; or anything that includes the feathery egg noodles. ▪ *3199 Powell St (at the end of the Emeryville Marina), Emeryville; (510)655-3388; $$; full bar; AE, MC, V; no checks; lunch, dinner every day.* &

**Bucci's** ★★ Located in a beautifully restored former warehouse, Bucci's is all brick and glass, with soaring ceilings, an open kitchen, and a small patio garden. At lunch biotech execs and multimedia artists nosh on rich focaccia sandwiches and crisp thin-crust pizzas topped with prosciutto, roasted peppers, provolone, mozzarella, and cherry tomatoes. Dinner offers more elaborate fare from a daily changing menu, which might include a tender roast duck served with a rich butternut-squash risotto or delicate cannelloni stuffed with spinach, walnuts, roasted red peppers, and cheese and served in a lemon cream sauce. The desserts and espressos are topflight, and the full bar specializes in classic cocktails. ▪ *6121 Hollis St (between 59th and 61st Sts), Emeryville; (510)547-4725; $$; full bar; MC, V; checks OK; lunch Mon–Fri, dinner Mon–Sat.* &

## OAKLAND

Several years ago, in an effort to improve Oakland's image, the mayor of Oakland ordered the city to change all of the vaguely threatening "Entering Oakland" signs to read "Welcome to Oakland." Some folks scoffed at the effort and said improving the city's wretched schools or cutting its alarming murder rate would be a better way to improve the city's reputation, but others appreciated the gesture. Most residents agree that Oakland has gotten a bad rap. While the media keep close tabs on the body count, few seem to notice Oakland's peaceful, integrated neighborhoods and richly diverse cultural life.

Oakland's premier tourist destination is **Jack London Square**, a sophisticated seaside spread of boutiques, bookstores, restaurants, hotels, cinemas, and saloons that is refreshingly void of the touristy schlock that pervades San Francisco's Pier 39. Must-see stops along the promenade include **Heinold's First and Last Chance Saloon**, 56 Jack London Square, (510)839-6761, a decidedly funky little bar crammed with faded seafaring souvenirs, and the recently overhauled **USS Potomac**, the 165-foot presidential yacht that served as FDR's "Floating White House." For information on tours of the ship or the bay, call (510)839-8256.

## ART AND CULTURE

**Dance** The **Oakland Ballet** jumps and twirls at the beautiful art deco Paramount Theatre, 2025 Broadway, (510)465-6400, and at various Oakland venues dozens of innovative contemporary and African dance troupes kick up their heels, including **Dimensions**, (510)465-3363, and the **Fuadia Congo Dance Company**, (510)562-0831.

**Film and Theater** Downtown's **Paramount Theatre**, a restored architectural masterpiece built in 1931 and restored in 1973, offers everything from organ concerts and rock concerts to plays and films from Hollywood's Golden Age. Guided tours of the 3,000-seat theater are given the first and third Saturday of each month, excluding holidays. No reservations are necessary—just show up at 10am at the box office entrance at 2025 Broadway at 21st Street, (510)893-2300. The **Grand Lake Theatre**, a beautifully restored Egypto-Deco movie palace, shows new films, which are kicked off on the weekends by a live organist's dazzling performance; 3200 Grand Avenue, (510)452-3556.

**Museums** The sunken building that holds the **Oakland Museum**, a spectacular specimen of modern architecture designed by Kevin Roche in 1969, features innovative displays of the art, history, and ecology of California, and also boasts beautiful terraced gardens; 1000 Oak Street between 10th and 12th Streets, (510)238-3401.

**Music** The highly regarded **Oakland Symphony** offers classical and choral concerts at the Paramount Theatre, 2025 Broadway, and the Calvin Simmons Theater, 10 10th Street; call (510)446-1992 for symphony schedules. You can catch the hottest jazz in town at **Yoshi's** (see review, below), 510 Embarcadero West in Jack London Square, (510)238-9200; the bluest blues at **Eli's Mile High Club**, 3626 Martin Luther King Jr. Way, (510)655-6661; and a little of both at the **Fifth Amendment**, 3255 Lake Shore Avenue, (510)832-3242. Gospel acts abound in the East Bay, but often they're hard to find; try calling Reid's Records in Berkeley at (510)843-7282, which has a bulletin board where folks post the latest local musical events.

**Sports** Those hotshot boys of summer, the **Oakland A's**, are usually knocking 'em dead at the Oakland Coliseum (from Interstate 80 take the Coliseum exit or, better yet, avoid the freeway crawl by taking a BART train); for tickets call (510)638-0500. And the sparkling Oakland Coliseum Arena—recently renovated to the tune of $102 million—is the home of the tall guys: the **Golden State Warriors**, (510)986-2200.

## ADDITIONAL ATTRACTIONS

**Outdoor Entertainment** Pretty **Lake Merritt**, one of the largest saltwater tidal lakes in the world, is home to flocks of migrating ducks, geese, and herons and provides a great place for a leisurely stroll or jog; the lake is bounded by Grand Avenue, Lake Shore Avenue, and Lakeside Drive. It is also the site of the popular **Festival at the Lake**, an annual celebration of dance, arts, and music held at the beginning of June, (510)286-1061. For fun on the water, rent a sailboat, rowboat, paddleboat, or canoe at the lake's **Sailboat House**, (510)444-3807. Tots will get a kick out of Lake Merritt's **Children's Fairyland**, a kid-sized amusement park that supposedly inspired Walt Disney to construct Disneyland; it's located off Grand Avenue, (510)452-2259. Youngsters will also thrill to the beasts at the **Oakland Zoo**; 9777 Golf Links Road, (510)632-9525. For the ultimate urban escape, head for the hills to **Redwood Regional Park**, where miles of fern-trimmed trails wind through redwood groves and oak woodlands; it's located off Joaquin Miller Road, (510)635-0135.

**Shops, Suds, and Snacks** In genteel North Oakland, the Rockridge neighborhood running along College Avenue boasts numerous bookstores, cafes, antique stores, expensive clothing boutiques, and a gourmet's paradise that rivals North Berkeley. Stroll through the **Rockridge Market Hall**, a chic multivendor market offering fresh pastas, gourmet cheeses, chocolates, fresh cut flowers, delicious deli sandwiches and salads, breads from the great **Grace Baking Company**, exquisite produce, and a wide selection of wine; 5655 College Avenue at Shafter Avenue, across from the Rockridge BART station, (510)655-7748. Grittier but just as interesting is downtown Oakland's **Chinatown** (tour the area between 7th and 10th Streets and Broadway and Harrison), which is not as congested (with cars or tourists) as San Francisco's Chinatown. An assortment of Mexican bakeries and taquerias tempt passersby along East 14th Street, between 2nd and 13th Avenues. The **Pacific Coast Brewing Company** offers a lively bar scene and good microbrews; 906 Washington Street, (510)836-2739. On the other side of town are your best bets for books and coffee near Oakland's downtown: **Walden Pond Books**, 3316 Grand Avenue, (510)832-4438, and the **Coffee Mill**, 3363 Grand Avenue, (510)465-4224.

### RESTAURANTS

**Bay Wolf Restaurant** ★★★ Located in an attractive Victorian house with dark wood wainscoting and pale yellow walls, the Bay Wolf first became a local favorite under the direction of co-owner and executive chef Michael Wild. Head chef Lauren Lyle is continuing Wild's tradition of subdued Mediterranean-California cuisine. Don't look for bizarre flights of food fancy here; fresh ingredients and careful preparation take the place of culinary acrobatics. Typical first courses might include a spiced scallop and endive salad or a rich, smoky asparagus and hazelnut soup with lemon cream. Main courses vary from tender braised lamb shanks with white beans, artichokes, and rosemary to a flavorful seafood stew bubbling with cracked Dungeness crab, prawns, rockfish, and mussels. For dessert indulge in the sweetly spiced peach pie topped with a scoop of house-made cinnamon ice cream, or the chocolate-topped profiteroles stuffed with white moons of freshly made almond ice cream. The extensive, well-chosen wine list offers a number of moderately priced vintages. Service is efficient but a little stiff in the evening; the staff loosens up in the afternoon. ■ *3853 Piedmont Ave (between 40th St and MacArthur Blvd), Oakland; (510)655-6004; $$$; beer and wine; MC, V; checks OK; lunch Mon–Fri, dinner every day.*

**Citron** ★★★ An immediate hit when it opened in 1992, Citron has settled in for the long run. The intimate dining room, which, true to its French name, is bathed in soothing shades of lemon yellow, sets the stage for chef Chris Rossi's equally small menu of contemporary French-Mediterranean fare. Rossi's menu changes every two weeks. Recent appetizers included a grilled quail salad nestled on warm savoy spinach with almonds, oranges, and parsley root chips; a mix of pretty garden lettuces laced with fresh herbs with tomato-rubbed toast; and a delicate corn soup topped with a roasted garlic-sage butter and fried sage leaves. One taste of the chicken with 40 garlic cloves and you'll think you've been transported to Provence. Then again, if it's Italian fare you're craving, look for Rossi's wild mushroom cannelloni with chanterelles, ricotta, and Swiss chard, or the osso buco of lamb served on a bed of flageolet bean and sun-dried tomato ragout with a sprinkling of pistachio gremolata garnish. Go Rossi! ■ *5484 College Ave (between Taft and Lawton Sts), Oakland; (510)653-5484; $$; beer and wine; AE, DC, DIS, MC, V; local checks only; dinner every day.*

**Oliveto Cafe and Restaurant** ★★★ Oliveto has always been a top East Bay destination, thanks in part to chef Mike Tusk's and chef/owner Paul Bertolli's obvious passion for the Italian table and careful interpretations of Italy's rustic cuisine. Trimmed with granite, olive-wood, and custom ironwork, the restaurant has the air of a Florentine trattoria, and the well-dressed, well-heeled stockbroker-and-filmmaker crowd cements the impression. House specialties include the fresh fish dishes, such as petrale sole piccata served on a bed of sautéed spinach and topped with a caper, white wine, and butter sauce, and the rotisserie-roasted meats, ranging from Watson Farm's lamb to the house-made pork sausage and grilled rabbit.

Downstairs, the more casual cafe draws a crowd of commuters (a BART station is across the street) and neighbors from morning till night. You may have to knock someone over the head to get a table, but so be it—the cuisine and the scene, especially at peak commute hours, are worth the effort. You'll see tense-but-chic workaholic singles sizing each other up over small, crisp

**San Francisco Bay Area**

**Oakland**

*Restaurants*

pizzas and sophisticated salads like the panzanella with cherry tomatoes and fresh mozzarella. New additions such as a wood-burning oven, flame-broiled rotisserie, and high-end liquor cabinet (i.e., hard alcohol, but no mixed drinks) will only add to Oliveto's popularity. Flirt with your neighbor over awe-inspiring desserts such as the brioche bread pudding with apricot sauce, the divine rhubarb crisp with crème fraîche, or the dark chocolate torte with poached sour cherries and whipped cream. Excellent espressos, good wines by the glass, exotic beers, expensive Scotch, and sidewalk tables add to the appeal of this European-style cafe. ■ *5655 College Ave (at Shafter Ave, across from the Rockridge BART station), Oakland; (510)547-5356; $$; beer and wine; AE, DC, MC, V; no checks; cafe: light breakfast, lunch, dinner every day; restaurant: lunch, dinner every day.* &

**Soizic Bistro-Cafe** ★★★ Just two blocks from Jack London Square in the produce and fishmonger districts, this handsome converted warehouse with 18-foot ceilings and a second-floor loft dining room is owned and operated by Hisuk and Sanju Dong, former owners of the now-closed (but it was wonderful) Cafe Pastoral in Berkeley. Hisuk is an architect, and Sanju is a painter and the head chef. They've created a Paris salon straight out of *The Moderns*, with warm, golden colors and rich details, including a large crusader tapestry on the main dining room wall, striped paneling behind the bar, marble-top cafe tables, and a gallery of paintings upstairs. Named after a French friend of the owners, Soizic (SWA-zik) offers a wonderful mix of Mediterranean-style cuisine: a terrific eggplant entree is layered with sun-dried tomatoes, goat cheese, and mushrooms and is served on a bed of polenta topped with a balsamic-kissed tomato sauce; tender smoked-chicken sandwiches are dressed with sun-dried tomatoes, watercress aioli, and spinach; and a hefty bowl of fresh New Zealand mussels is served steaming in a savory saffron broth with diced tomatoes. The fare is quite memorable and reasonably priced, too. Celebrate the occasion with the bistro's legendary dessert: a creamy ginger custard. ■ *300 Broadway (near Jack London Square), Oakland; (510)251-8100; $$; beer and wine; MC, V; local checks only; lunch Tues–Fri, dinner Wed–Sun.* &

**Yoshi's** ★★★ Business at this jazz-club-cum-Japanese-restaurant—once a premier destination for live jazz on the West Coast—hit a sour note in the early '90s, and the owners were ready to permanently close its doors. Then along came the City of Oakland to the rescue. Fronting a sizable chunk of the $5.1 million construction bill, the Oakland Redevelopment Agency and the Port of Oakland lured Yoshi's from its humble though pleasant Rockridge neighborhood to a glitzy new spread at Jack London Square. The only downside of this otherwise terrific venue is its location on the bottom floor of a seven-story parking garage perched next to rumbling Amtrak rails, although a small fortune was invested in sound-dampening materials to keep things cool and quiet inside. Architect Hiroshi Morimoto has fused traditional Japanese materials and elements with a sleek, modern design and the results are fantastic ($375,000 was spent on furnishings alone). Equal attention was paid to the separate 300-seat amphitheater, a semicircular room equipped with a state-of-the-art sound system—there's nary a bad seat in the house. And then there's the food: textbook Japanese all the way, including sukiyaki, tempura, seafood, vegetarian cuisine, and a sophisticated ash-wood sushi bar. Prices are reasonable, particularly for combo dinner specials that include an appetizer, rice, miso soup, and an entree.

But let's be honest: you're here to see America's top jazz and blues bands, as well as occasional big-name talents such as Herbie Hancock and John Lee Hooker, right? Right. Here's the scoop: there are typically two gigs every night at 8pm and 10pm, and ticket prices range from about $15 to $22. Monday-night headliners are local artists trying to hit the big time, which in the past have included jazz heavies Charlie Hunter, Miles Perkins, and Joshua Redman. ■ *510 Embarcadero West (1 block W of Broadway), Oakland; (510)238-9200; yoshis@yoshis.com; www.yoshis.com; $$; full bar; AE, DC, DIS, MC, V; no checks; lunch, dinner every day.* &

**Zatis** ★★★ Zatis is a real find, discreetly tucked into a narrow spot near a bagel shop and Peet's coffeehouse on Piedmont Avenue. It's hardly noticeable during the day; only at night does the elegant ice-blue neon light entice you to step through the doors, where the aroma of roasted garlic and olive oil will certainly convince you to take a seat and stay for a while. The light seduces, and the jazz soothes. Think intimate (about 15 tables), and think Valentine's Day. Got the picture? Start with the smoked mozzarella and vegetable quesadilla spiced with a zingy guacamole, or dip into the roasted garlic with Gorgonzola and flatbread. Then try the vegetarian eggplant entree stuffed with kalamata olives, jalapeños, and artichoke hearts and baked in a spicy tomato sauce, the herb-crusted fillet of red snapper served with red potatoes and fresh seasonal vegetables, or any of the chef's specialties of the day. ■ *4027 Piedmont Ave (between 40th and 41st Sts), Oakland; (510)658-8210; $$$; beer and wine; AE, MC, V; no checks; lunch, dinner Mon–Sat.* &

**Caffe 817** ★★ Visit the downtown Oakland farmers market on Friday morning, then rest your weary bag-laden arms at Caffe 817. This tiny restaurant bears the stamp of its design-conscious owner, Alessandro Rossi, an electrical engineer who saw potential in this high-ceilinged space and hired local craftspeople to fashion its avant-garde furnishings. Despite its lofty decor, the cafe has modest ambitions: cappuccino and pastries are mainstays in the morning, and Italian sandwiches, simple salads, and fresh soups and stews are on the midday menu. The sandwich fillings are what you might call contemporary Italian-American: roast beef with arugula, grilled mozzarella with artichokes, prosciutto with herb butter and pears. But the rice-and-borlotti-bean soup is a classic Tuscan dish. If all this good fare inspires you to make your own Italian classics at home, head next door to G. B. Ratto International Grocers, a favorite East Bay source for Arborio rice, olive oil, beans, and other imported foodstuffs. ■ *817 Washington St (between 8th and 9th Sts), Oakland; (510) 271-7965; $; beer and wine; no credit cards; checks OK; breakfast, lunch Mon–Fri.* ♿

**Cuckoo's Nest ★★** Oakland's produce district is hardly the place you'd expect to find an artisan-crafted cafe filled with fine design details, but custom-made mahogany tables, whimsical light fixtures, and a vivid mural painted in tropical colors by local artist Margitta Dietrick breathe style and life into this former produce warehouse. There's hardly a kitchen to speak of, but the cooks make do, turning out delightful sandwiches (don't miss the grilled egg salad with fontina and pancetta), creative salads, and a wonderfully creamy polenta studded with mushrooms and sun-dried tomatoes. Stop by in the morning for a cappuccino and pastry or some delicious slow-scrambled eggs before trekking through the nearby Barnes & Noble mega-bookstore. ■ *247 4th St (between Jackson and Alice Sts), Oakland; (510) 452-9414; $; beer and wine; MC, V; local checks only; brunch Sun, breakfast, lunch, dinner Mon–Sat.* ♿

**Jade Villa ★★** Ever since Lantern restaurant closed, the title of Oakland's top dim sum house has been transferred to Jade Villa, a behemoth of a restaurant that takes up nearly a quarter block in Oakland's Chinatown. During the lunch hour the place is packed with Chinese families sitting at large, round tables. The ornate dining room offers a tempting array of dinners, but the real reason you should come here is for the dim sum, served from early morning to midafternoon. Sip a cup of aromatic tea as servers circulate through the room pushing carts laden with assorted delicacies. They'll pause by your table and lift the lids of tiered metal steamers to let you inspect the barbecued pork buns, stuffed dumplings, wedges of green pepper filled with shrimp, and lots of other tasty treats. Hold out for at least one order of the steamed prawns-in-shell, their best dish. You'll be charged by the plate, and you can afford to experiment here—two people can eat with abandon for about 20 bucks. ■ *800 Broadway (at 8th St), Oakland; (510) 839-1688; $$; beer and wine; MC, V; lunch, dinner every day.* ♿

**Nan Yang Rockridge ★★** When Nan Yang opened in 1983, restaurants offering a full spectrum of Burmese delights were virtually nonexistent; even in Rangoon, hungry travelers had to trudge from festival to festival and from stall to stall to gain any sense of the cuisine. Chef and owner Philip Chu assembled the menu for Nan Yang by tracking down recipes from monasteries, street vendors, festival food booths, and family homes to create the first Burmese restaurant in the Bay Area. His noble efforts have been rewarded with rave reviews and long lines of customers clamoring for his fare—especially his ginger salad, a crunchy, textural delight with 16 ingredients including split peas, fava beans, shredded cabbage, coconut slices, sun-dried shrimp, garlic oil, roasted peanuts, and shredded ginger. The generous curry dishes come with giant chunks of beef, chicken, or fish; there are also plenty of seductive vegetarian variations. On sunny days opt for a table on the front patio. ■ *6048 College Ave (just S of Claremont Ave), Oakland; (510) 655-3298; $$; beer and wine; MC, V; no checks; lunch, dinner Tues–Sun.*

**Spettro ★★** Would you consider it creepy to savor pasta and pizza amidst the dearly departed? Well, welcome to Spettro (Italian for "spirit"). This restaurant's otherworldly theme is a bit unsettling at first (a skeleton graces the entrance with a cigarette in hand warning patrons not to light up, and there is an assortment of macabre gravestone photography nearby), but your appetite will return once you get a whiff of the dishes being concocted in the kitchen. Then, again, you might lose it once you see the daily changing menu: baby greens tossed in a blueberry vinaigrette? A bacon, cheese, and *peanut butter* pizza? Believe it or not, Spettro's has many devotees. Run by the owners of the defunct Topless Pizza, Spettro has given rebirth to some of Topless's pies, and added some Cajun and Brazilian dishes for variety, such as red beans and rice, smoked chicken and oyster gumbo, and Brazilian *feijoada* with black beans and linguiça on a bed of rice. But why the dead theme, you ask? Two of the owners, children of an anthropologist, used to get their kicks as tykes tracing gravestones. Whatever. The chatty staff is very much alive, however, and since the wait for a table can be as long as an hour on the weekend (reservations are not available), they will ply you with cider and wine to raise your own spirits. ■ *3355 Lakeshore Ave (at Trestle Glen St), Oakland; (510) 465-8320; $$; beer and wine; AE, DC, DIS, MC, V; no checks; dinner every day.*

**Asmara Restaurant and Bar ★** Asmara has a split personality: the comfortable restaurant is full of East African kitsch, while the adjacent bar—stark white and brightly lit—is a sterile jolt to the senses. Eritrean expatriates seem to prefer the bar, while locals enjoy the restaurant's African decor. Both groups, however, often get caught up in the communal spirit of the place, sharing their meals with fellow diners and using pieces of spongy injera bread to scoop up tasty *ziggni* (beef marinated in a surprisingly mild berbere sauce made with jalapeño and other chile peppers) and *yegomen alicha* (mustard greens simmered with spices). Make the most of this culinary adventure by getting one of the combination dinners. ■ *5020 Telegraph Ave (at 51st St), Oakland; (510)547-5100; $; full bar; MC, V; no checks; lunch, dinner every day.* ♿

**El Taco Zamorano** ★ Hearty, home-style Mexican cooking draws Latinos to this comfortable oasis in a dreary and violence-prone Oakland neighborhood. You won't want to park too far away, but once inside you can relax and relish the local color. Mexican music floats from a jukebox, and vivid murals depict festive scenes from south of the border. The food tastes like the handiwork of a Mexican grandmother. Don't miss the crusty, tender *carnitas* served with—a rare find—delicious tomato rice, or the spirit-warming fish soup, a spicy broth loaded with vegetables that actually still have texture. The restaurant makes its own tortillas, so the tacos here are divine. Try the *taco al pastor*, made with spicy shredded pork, and ask for whole (not refried) beans on the side. The same tortilla dough, pressed into thick patties, forms the foundation for wonderful *sopes* topped with shredded chicken, lettuce, tomatoes, and sour cream. The restaurant's whole fried fish, deeply scored and aggressively seasoned, makes a satisfying dinner, too. ■ *4032 Foothill Blvd (at Rosedale Ave), Oakland; (510)536-3146; $; beer and wine; AE, DC, DIS, MC, V; no checks; lunch, dinner every day.*

**Flint's** ★ If you've got a hankering for a sinful serving of juicy barbecued ribs doused in a sinus-blasting sauce, this is the place for you. Owned by the Flintroy family, this nitty-gritty rib joint has red-eye hours (open till 2am on the weekends) and the best barbecue in town. The lip-smacking pork ribs and hot links retain their succulent juiciness after slowly cooking in the massive black oven (but skip the stringy, dried-out chicken). The sweet, thick, mahogany sauce comes in mild, medium, or incendiary (back off if your taste buds are timid). Everything is piled onto a flimsy paper plate, covered with butcher paper, and shoved into a paper sack. Grab plenty of napkins—you'll need 'em. ■ *6609 Shattuck Ave (at 66th St), Oakland; (510)653-0593; $; no alcohol; no credit cards; no checks; lunch, dinner every day.*

**Mama's Royal Cafe** ★ Diehard regulars don't even question the 40- to 60-minute wait required on weekends to get a seat at this 20-year-old Oakland landmark known simply as Mama's. A combination of good food served in large portions and a schizo decor (picture a '40s-style diner/noodle house with pagoda door frames and Rosie-the-Riveter–era ads on Formica tabletops) attracts the bohemian/boomer crowd in Doc Martens and Tevas for some of the heartiest breakfasts in the East Bay. Unfortunately, the prices are kinda expensive, the service is suhlooooow (leave the antsy kids at home), and the waiters sometimes serve up a little attitude with your home-fries, but who cares when the menu includes 31 types of omelets and such breakfast specials as fresh fruit crêpes and burritos with chipotle tortillas? Of course, a place like this has to have its own lingo—"cowboy with spurs" is the name for a western omelet with fries, and "wax" is sliced American cheese—as well as a legend. Rumors abound of a ghost who haunts the third dining room, which purportedly was once a former barber shop where a local mobster was cut down midshave. ■ *4012 Broadway (at 40th St), Oakland; (510)547-7600; $; beer and wine; no credit cards; no checks; breakfast, lunch every day.* ♿

**Pho Anh Dao** ★ Essentially a one-dish restaurant, Pho Anh Dao specializes in *pho*, the Hanoi anise-scented beef and noodle soup that many Vietnamese eat almost every day. This aromatic meal-in-a-bowl has everything in its favor: it's cheap (less than $4), delicious, plentiful, and healthful. The essential garnishes arrive on the side: Asian basil, sliced green chiles, a lime or lemon wedge, and bean sprouts. Add as much of them as you like and then, with chopsticks in one hand and a soupspoon in the other, dive in. Pho aficionados ask for raw beef so they can "cook" it in the hot broth a slice at a time. Good *pho* takes hours to make, and Pho Anh Dao does it right. ■ *280 E 18th St (between 2nd and 3rd Aves), Oakland; (510)836-1566; $; beer only; no credit cards; no checks; breakfast, lunch, dinner every day.* ♿

**Pizza Rustica** ★ Housed in a white postmodern building with red Corinthian columns, this jazzy nouveau pizza joint has a cramped, noisy dining room with tiny, knee-bruising tables, bright pop art on the walls, and California pizzas made with a light, crunchy cornmeal crust or a traditional peasant-bread crust. The traditional Mediterranean-style pizzas are impeccable, but pizza adventurers should try one of the more exotic offerings: the Thai pizza is prepared with roasted chicken in a spicy ginger and peanut sauce, mozzarella, julienned carrots, scallions, daikon, peppers, and sesame seeds, and the Ambrosia features sun-dried tomatoes, artichoke hearts, roasted garlic, kalamata olives, and a mix of fontina, mozzarella, and Parmesan cheeses. The desserts aren't particularly inspired, but sometimes there's a chocolate-dipped crisp rice and marshmallow bar that's an upscale version of those Rice Krispies treats you loved so much as a kid. ■ *5422 College Ave (between Kales and Manila Sts), Oakland; (510)654-1601; $; beer and wine; MC, V; local checks only; lunch, dinner every day.* ♿



**Sabina India Cuisine** ★ The Singh family now owns and operates this gracious North Indian restaurant in a fanciful space that used to be a tile store. The restaurant's narrow, columned facade is covered with handsome ceramic work, and there's a tile fountain in the dining room. Sabina's specialties are mildly spiced Indian comfort foods: tempting renditions of tandoori dishes, curries, and vegetarian entrees, all served with wonderfully aromatic basmati rice. Start your meal with the crisp samosas and pakoras, followed by the chicken *pasanda* (chunks of tender roasted white chicken served in a cashew cream sauce). The bargain buffet lunch allows you to sample 19 dishes and refill your plate as often as you want—all for less than the cost of admission to a movie. ▪ *1628 Webster St (at 17th St, 2 blocks W of Broadway), Oakland; (510)268-0170; $; beer and wine; DC, DIS, MC, V; checks OK; lunch Mon–Sat, dinner every day.* ⅃

**Tsing Tao ★** A favorite Sunday-night destination for local Chinese-American families, Tsing Tao delivers high-quality Cantonese cooking. It's a far cry from fancy (would you believe fluorescent pink walls dotted with cheap chandeliers?), but it's a definite step up in quality and service from many Oakland Chinatown restaurants. Avoid the standard dishes that seem aimed mostly at non-Chinese, and ask about the chef's specials of the day—that's where you'll find the good (i.e., authentic) stuff. For the Chinese equivalent of Mom's meat loaf, try the steamed pork patty flavored with heavily salted fish, and pair it with the tender mustard-green hearts glazed with a rich broth. Another winning combo: stir-fried crab with scallions and ginger (ask the price first—it can be high here) and stir-fried baby pea shoots, a springtime delicacy. The fish tanks sometimes hold live sturgeon, a bony fish the kitchen subjects to a two-part preparation: the bones and head are turned into a milky broth, and the fillets are steamed. ▪ *200 Broadway (at 2nd St), Oakland; (510)465-8811; $$; full bar; AE, MC, V; no checks; lunch, dinner every day.* ⅃

**Vi's Restaurant ★** Look closely at your fellow diners slurping up Vi's famous braised duck noodle soup (which is actually a bit bland), and you may notice a few familiar faces from some of Berkeley and Oakland's top restaurants. This is where the professionals from places like Chez Panisse come to get their fix of Vietnamese steamed rolls, five-spice barbecued chicken, and a sophisticated beef stew that's seasoned with cinnamon and warm curry spices and spooned over egg noodles. The rolls, made with a rice noodle crêpe, are stuffed with dried mushrooms, onions, ground pork, and shallots, and come with bean sprouts and Vietnamese pork sausage. At lunchtime many Vietnamese customers begin their meals with a soft, floppy steamed rice noodle stuffed with ground pork, black mushrooms, and onions that's served with a dipping sauce. Located on a bustling street in the heart of Chinatown, the place is generally full and parking can be difficult, but the turnover is quick and the inexpensive prices are worth the short wait. ▪ *724 Webster St (in Chinatown, between 7th and 8th Sts), Oakland; (510)835-8375; $; beer and wine; no credit cards; no checks; lunch, dinner Fri–Wed.* ⅃

## LODGINGS

**Lake Merritt Hotel Clarion Suites ★★** This art deco masterpiece standing right next to downtown Oakland looks out over Lake Merritt—a large, landscaped lake that's a mecca for joggers, walkers, and rowers. Built in 1927, the vintage white-stucco hotel was restored several years ago to its original opulence with stunning light fixtures, richly patterned carpeting, plush furniture, and lush flower arrangements. Most of its 50 rooms are standard suites appointed in the charming manner of studio apartments circa 1930 (with a modern-day nod to microwaves and coffee-makers). The deluxe suites with separate living rooms are a bargain at less than $200 per night. Every room has cable TV, a modern bathroom, a stocked minibar, and a phone, and some units face the lake. Other amenities include fax and copy services, a concierge, weekly wine tastings, and a full breakfast (included in the room rate) served downstairs in the Terrace Room, which is adorned with scenes of Lake Merritt during the mid-'50s. If you're a business exec, you'll be happy to know the hotel provides a complimentary shuttle to whisk you to the nearby Oakland Financial District. ■ *1800 Madison St (at Lakeside Dr), Oakland, CA 94612; (510) 832-2300 or (800) 933-HOTEL (in California only); www. choicehotel.com; $$$; full bar; AE, DC, DIS, MC, V; no checks; breakfast (for guests only), lunch Mon–Fri, dinner every day.* &

**Waterfront Plaza Hotel** ★★ Our top recommendation for an Oakland-based lodging is this small luxury hotel perched on the water's edge at Jack London Square. Granted, it's not the fanciest hotel you'll ever stay in, but it comes with all the essential amenities at a reasonable price *and* it's next to Jack London Square, which is brimming with great stores, restaurants, and attractions, including the hot new Yoshi's jazz venue. Heck, you can even catch a ferry to San Francisco or a shuttle to downtown Oakland from the lobby. Each of the 144 rooms is attractively outfitted with pinewood furnishings, pleasing prints, quilted comforters, and color schemes of beige, copper, and blue. Be sure to request a room with a deck and a view of the harbor (an extra $20), and in the winter months ask for a unit with a fireplace. All rooms are equipped with coffee-makers, VCRs, voice mail, minibars, in-room safes, and hair dryers. Additional perks include business and fax services, a fitness center, and a heated pool and sauna overlooking the harbor. Adjacent to the hotel is Jack's Bistro, where you can munch on wood-fired meats in a dining room overlooking the marina. ■ *10 Washington St (at Jack London Square), Oakland, CA 94607; (510) 836-3800 or (800) 729-3638; www.waterfrontplaza. com; $$$; full bar; AE, DC, DIS, MC, V; no checks; breakfast, lunch, dinner every day.* &

Alameda

*Restaurants*

## ALAMEDA

### *RESTAURANTS*

**Tied House Cafe and Brewery** ★ See the review of this restaurant's San Jose location in the following pages. ■ *On Triumph St (on the water, next to the Oakland Yacht Club), Alameda; (510) 521-4321; $$; beer, wine, and limited spirits; AE, DC, DIS, MC, V; no checks; lunch, dinner every day.* &

*LODGINGS*

**Garratt Mansion** ★★ Surrounded by lush gardens and located just four blocks from the beach, this three-story, 1893 colonial revival manse is a picture-perfect example of Victoriana, with gorgeous stained-glass windows, hand-carved interior woodwork, and a wealth of wonderful architectural details. All seven spacious guest rooms have sitting areas, and five have private baths and phones. Favored boudoirs include Diana's Room, a large second-floor suite with a fireplace, a separate sitting room, a bamboo canopy bed, and a private bath with a claw-footed tub and stall shower, and the Captain's Room, which sports a nautical motif in blue and gold, with gold stars on the ceiling, a Venetian mask on the wall, leopard-print chairs, and a cigar-box collection. On the third floor, Martha's and Angela's Rooms enchant with seating alcoves nestled under dormer windows that look out over the treetops and a sheltered lagoon. Innkeeper Betty Gladden serves guests a full breakfast with fresh OJ and coffee and lays out platters of home-baked cookies in the late afternoon. ■ *900 Union St (between Encinal and Clinton Aves), Alameda, CA 94501; (510)521-4779; garrattm@pacbell.net; www.innformation.com/ ca/garrattmansion; $$; AE, DC, MC, V; checks OK.*

## FREMONT

*LODGINGS*

**Lord Bradley's Inn** ★★ Rebuilt after the devastating earthquake of 1868 that flattened large sections of the East Bay, this atmospheric Victorian-style hotel offers a good sense of what it must have been like to live in the Bay Area during the 19th century (though it's considerably more comfortable). Separated from historic Mission San Jose by a row of ancient olive trees, the inn faces oak- and grass-covered hills that look much as they did in the time of the great ranchos. The eight individually decorated guest rooms have antique bedsteads and private baths, and a few of them were recently redecorated from floor to ceiling. The spacious Lady Jennifer attic room is the fave—a pretty bridal suite with a pitched roof that's decorated in hues of soft beige and green. It offers a queen-size bed draped with Battenburg lace, a charming bathroom with a one-of-a-kind hand-painted floor featuring little ladybugs and butterflies, and a cushy window seat from which you can see Mission Peak. In the morning you'll be treated to a breakfast of fresh and dried fruit, croissants, and muffins with orange butter. During your stay, hike up Mission Peak—the highest prominence hereabouts, with panoramic views of the South Bay. Lord Bradley's also hosts outdoor weddings among the olive trees and roses, and has a spacious second-floor room with a view in the Victorian next door, available for business meetings or special events. ■ *43344 Mission Blvd (at*

*Washington Blvd, just past Mission San Jose), Fremont, CA 94539; (510)490-0520; $; AE, DC, DIS, MC, V; checks OK.* &

## SAN JOSE

All the boomers who grew up with Dionne Warwick's "Do You Know the Way to San Jose," a paean to the relaxed small-town San Jose of yesteryear, may be shocked to see the city's newly gentrified chrome, glass, and pastel downtown and its sprawling, freeway-locked suburbs. Some may mourn the loss of the orchards and the sleepy, mañana attitude, but most San Joseans seemed puffed up with understandable pride at the city's energetic new look and feel. First-class restaurants, a state-of-the-art light rail system, a flourishing arts scene, and a dazzling sports arena (go Sharks!) have all contributed to the city's revitalization, helping it emerge at last from the long cultural shadow cast by San Francisco, its cosmopolitan neighbor to the north.

### ART AND CULTURE

**Museums** The newly renovated **San Jose Museum of Art** provides a handsome setting for contemporary European and American art; 110 South Market Street, (408)294-2787. The **Egyptian Museum and Planetarium**, run by the mystical Rosicrucian order, presents a collection of Egyptian artifacts, mummies, and re-creations of tombs in a pyramidlike structure (the British Museum it's not, but it's educational, funky, and fun); located at the corner of Park Avenue and Naglee Street, (408)947-3636. The lively and ever-so-loud **Children's Discovery Museum**, painted in Easter-egg purple, offers kids the opportunity to explore exhibits of urban life: traffic lights, fire engines, a post office, a bank, and even a sewer (spanking clean and minus any errant rats or Ninja turtles). A Wells Fargo stagecoach, a farmhouse, and rural diversions like corn-husk doll-making help youngsters experience what the valley was like when it produced major crops instead of microchips; 180 Woz Way, (408)298-5437. The **Tech Museum of Innovation** is a terrific hands-on science museum where adults and kids alike can play with robots, gain insight into genetic engineering, or design a high-tech bicycle; it's located across from the Convention Center, 145 West San Carlos Street, (408)279-7150. (Ground has been broken for the Tech Museum's new site at the corner of Park Avenue and Market Street. Slated to open in the fall of 1998, the new three-story building will feature six times the exhibit space of the old museum and contain an IMAX theater and 250 interactive exhibits.) Fans of the supernatural might enjoy a tour of the **Winchester Mystery House**, an odd, rambling mansion with an intriguing history: after inheriting $20 million from her husband's repeating-rifle company, Sarah Winchester became convinced that the ghosts of people killed by Winchester rifles were coming back to haunt her. Her paranoia led her to have additions built to her home 24 hours a day for 38 years to house their restless spirits. The lovely if somewhat unorthodox Victorian mansion is a 160-room labyrinth of crooked corridors, doors opening into space, and dead-end stairways; 525 South Winchester Boulevard, (408)247-2101.

**Theater, Dance, and Music**  San Jose has a thriving community of theater, ballet, and opera groups, most of which may be found at the **San Jose Center for the Performing Arts**; 255 Almaden Boulevard at Park Avenue, (408)277-3900. The **San Jose Civic Light Opera**, (408)453-7108, puts on musicals and other frothy diversions, while **Opera San Jose**, (408)437-4450, the **San Jose Cleveland Ballet**, (408)288-2800, and the **San Jose Symphony Orchestra**, (408)288-2828, offer more classical cultural enrichments. **Los Lupeños de San Jose** dance company reflects the Spanish heritage of the city; 34 North First Street, (408)292-0443. For drama, the **San Jose Repertory Theatre** offers innovative productions of new works and classics; 1 North First Street, (408)291-2255. The **San Jose Stage Company**, 490 South First Street, (408)283-7142, primarily showcases American contemporary drama and comedy, while the **City Lights Theatre** follows the more experimental route; 529 South Second Street, (408)295-4200.

### ADDITIONAL ATTRACTIONS

**Nightlife**  Once the red-light district, the area around Market and First Streets has gradually developed into a clean, hip home for many nightclubs and a slightly more alternative scene. If you gotta dance, you'll find live rock and recorded dance tunes in the **Cactus Club** at 417 South First Street, two blocks south of the Fairmont hotel, (408)491-9300, and in the **B Hive** (formerly the Ajax Lounge), 372 South First Street above Olympia Restaurant, (408)298-2529. For live jazz and a bit of alternative rock, head to **Agenda** at the northwest corner of South First Street and East San Salvador Street, (408)287-4087. Live rock, dance classics, and cheap draft beer are featured at **Toons**; 52 East Santa Clara Street at Second Street, (408)292-7464. For a mix of music—modern rock, swing bands, DJ-spun rock, and '70s disco—check out **The Usual**; 400 South First Street, (408)535-0330, www.theusualnight club.com. Coffee and attitude are dished out at **Cafe Matisse**, 371 South First Street, (408)298-7788, and if you want a little bit of everything, visit the **Pavilion**, where under one roof you'll find a deluxe, eight-screen movie theater, a virtual-reality theme park, and a smattering of shops, bars, and restaurants, as well as **San Jose Live**, a popular nightspot with two dance floors, a sports bar with 11 big-screen TVs, a cafe serving California fare, a cigar and martini bar, dueling piano players on baby grands, an arcade, pool tables, and even a basketball court; 150 South First Street, (408)294-5483.

**Parks** **Kelley Park** is a pleasant place for a picnic and a stroll around the **Japanese Friendship Garden**, complete with a koi pond and a teahouse; it's located at the corner of Senter Road and Keyes Street, (408)277-4193. If you have little ones in tow, they're sure to be beguiled by the old-fashioned, low-tech charms of **Happy Hollow** next door, a zoo and amusement park aimed at the toddler-through-early-grade-school set. **Guadalupe River Park** is undergoing extensive renovations to set up picnic areas and paved walkways that will stretch from the Children's Discovery Museum to near Highway 880 and the San Jose Airport. Part of the project is already completed; call the San Jose Department of Parks and Recreation for more information at (408)277-4573.

## *RESTAURANTS*

**Agenda** ★★★ At this chic and beautifully designed restaurant in the city's SoMa district (yes, San Jose's got one, too), stylish types sip cosmopolitans at the sculptured wood bar, Silicon Valley execs talk IPOs at tables flanked by arty souls discussing the NEA, and jazz buffs check out the live (and very loud) band. A giant androgynous angel presides over all, stretching its da Vinci-esque flying-machine wings across an exposed brick wall. If you turn your attention away from your surroundings, however, you'll notice the eclectic food is what *really* takes flight here. That's apparent as soon as you spread a piece of feather-light focaccia with a delectable basil- and olive-infused tapenade, a secret recipe from chef Christian Raia's Sicilian grandmother. The kitchen displays impressive breadth with dishes ranging from exotic vegetable empanadas to delicate seafood ravioli to barn-burning pot-stickers to comfort food like to-die-for garlic mashed potatoes. Just about everything on the menu is exquisitely prepared, judiciously seasoned, and fetchingly presented. Portions are generous, but try to save room for dessert; choices that seem passé on paper such as cherries jubilee and crème caramel turn out to be retro revelations, especially the air-spun milk chocolate mousse served in a tulip of dark chocolate. Service is savvy but a bit slow, which gives you a chance to soak up the scene and consider the rest of the evening. On Thursday evenings, the cellar hosts screenings of 16mm movies, often by local auteurs; other nights, a DJ serves up funk, disco, or a "full-sweat session." Upstairs is the cigar/pool-table lounge, where 24 beers are on tap along with live acid jazz, reggae, and even Sunday-evening poetry readings. ■ *399 S 1st St (at San Salvador St), San Jose; (408)287-3991; $$; full bar; AE, MC, V; no checks; dinner Tues–Sat.* &

**Emile's** ★★★ Catering to an older, well-heeled crowd and expense-account execs, Emile's has been one of San Jose's finest restaurants for nearly three decades. Chef/owner Emile Mooser offers a California version of the cuisine he learned in his Swiss homeland, and his menu features classic French, Swiss, and

Italian preparations as well as *cuisine minceur* (a somewhat leaner style of French cooking). Using fine stocks and the best seasonal ingredients available, the kitchen does a particularly good job with fish and game. Consider its splendid grilled pistachio-crusted scallops on a bed of baby spinach drizzled with a citrus vinaigrette, or its peppered and seared Sonoma foie gras with poached pears and an arugula salad. Entrees on the seasonal menu may include a giant open-faced ravioli with prawns, scallops, and fish in a lobster-brandy sauce, fillet of beef with a roasted garlic and cabernet sauvignon sauce, or even such exotica as wild boar with fresh fruit compote. The *roesti*—a crunchy Swiss version of hashbrowns—is wonderful. Almost everything is made on the premises, from the house-cured gravlax to flawless desserts like the justly celebrated Grand Marnier soufflé. Emile's wine cellar contains more than 300 selections, ranging from the very reasonable to the very, very expensive. The restaurant was remodeled a few years ago, forsaking some of its romantic European charm for a sleeker, more open look. ■ *545 S 2nd St (between Williams and Reed Sts), San Jose; (408) 289-1960; emiles@emiles.com; $$$; full bar; AE, DC, DIS, MC, V; no checks; lunch Fri, dinner Tues–Sat.* &

**La Forêt French Restaurant** ★★★  Located in an old two-story hotel overlooking Los Alamedos Creek, this picturesque and pricey restaurant offers unusual wild game that's flown in daily. Chef Vazgen "Ken" Davoudi can always be counted on to create superb sauces for the day's special, which might be tender medallions of wild boar marinated in shallots, balsamic vinegar, brandy, and cumin and topped with an outstanding pink peppercorn sauce, paired with medallions of elk in an equally masterful tarragon cream sauce. Davoudi's prowess isn't limited to game; he also works well with seafood, including a perfectly poached salmon served with a port wine sauce. Appetizers might feature fusilli with olive oil, herbs, garlic, wild mushrooms, and Gouda cheese or escargot with garlic butter and Pernod. The dessert list features a selection of cakes, cheesecakes, and exotic soufflés. ■ *21747 Bertram Rd (from the Almaden Expwy take the Almaden Rd exit, go S for 3 miles, turn left at Almaden Way, and cross the small bridge to Bertram Rd), San Jose; (408) 997-3458; www.menusonline.com; $$$; full bar; AE, DC, DIS, MC, V; no checks; brunch Sun, dinner Tues–Sun.* &

**Orlo's** ★★★  Faith healer Mary Hayes Chynoweth built a gorgeous 41,000-square-foot Mediterranean revival–style mansion in 1905 as a base of operations for her ministry. Unfortunately, the wealthy do-gooder passed away four months before the house was completed, and the grand estate fell into disrepair years later. These days, the restored and sensitively modernized mansion, which once hosted the likes of Teddy Roosevelt and Herbert Hoover, is a home-away-from-home for Silicon Valley professionals attending meetings at the Hayes Conference Center. Most of the healing going on here now takes place in the health spa, but one might also reap salubrious benefits from a meal at Orlo's, an innovative restaurant open to the public. Housed in the former family dining room, the elegant space has floral-fabric-and-wood-covered walls, green and maroon carpeting, ornate metal table bases, and built-in Mission furniture. Service is a bit formal, which seems right for the setting, and the seasonal menu, which stresses fresh, first-rate ingredients, stops just short of fussy. Appetizers include Oyster Orlo's (oysters baked with house-made venison ham, crimini mushrooms, and sun-dried-tomato pesto), and a splendid salad of baby greens with a walnut-balsamic vinaigrette and Amish blue cheese. Entrees are notable for unusual renderings of traditional fare, such as the mixed seafood grill with honey-lavender sauce or the Kona coffee–roasted rack of lamb. Some of the bewitching items on the dessert tray look better than they taste (try the chocolate opera cake, which is ethereally light and boasts a liquory bite). All in all, if dining on new American cuisine in a splendid Old World setting appeals, Orlo's is well worth the drive from downtown San Jose. ■ *200 Edenvale Ave (from Hwy 101, turn W on Blossom Hill Rd, then right on Lean Ave, which turns into Edenvale Ave), San Jose; (408) 226-3200; $$$; full bar; AE, DC, DIS, MC, V; no checks; lunch Mon–Fri, dinner every day.* &

**San Jose**

*Restaurants*

**Paolo's** ★★★ A longtime San Jose institution, Paolo's moved to expensive new digs in 1991, and while the handsome facility may have a bit of a Corporate America feel, the flavorful food remains authentically Italian. Look for unexpected little flourishes that give even the most tried-and-true dishes an interesting twist: veal scaloppine, for example, is served on a bed of wilted spinach, while Paolo's gnocchi is baked with truffle butter and Fontina Val D'ostra cheese. Other outstanding items include *tortelli di zucca* (pasta stuffed with pumpkin and cheese, tossed with brown butter and sage), roasted quail with white raisins and grappa, and an intriguing appetizer of grilled Tuscan cheese wrapped in chard served with roasted peppers and eggplant. Service can be a little brusque at times, especially if you're not a silver-haired CEO on his or her lunch hour, but it's always efficient. The wine list could bring a tear of joy to Bacchus' eye—the 50-page tome encompasses an outstanding variety of domestic and European selections. A patio for alfresco dining lets you take advantage of all those balmy San Jose days. ■ *333 W San Carlos St (between Woz Way and Almaden Blvd), San Jose; (408) 294-2558; www.acoates. com/paolos; $$$; full bar; AE, DC, DIS, MC, V; no checks; lunch Mon–Fri, dinner Mon–Sat.* &

**California Sushi and Grill** ★★ This chic sushi spot is popular with the downtown crowd, who want something fast and delicious and don't mind parting with a chunk of change to get it. The recently remodeled and expanded venue is attractive, with the grill and chef in full view of the small sushi bar and a large (and more sedate) upstairs loft. The creative, unerringly fresh sushi preparations range from classics such as ebi and nori-wrapped yellowfin tuna to provocative specials like spider rolls (half a deep-fried soft-shell crab with slices of buttery avocado and crisp cucumber rolled inside sticky rice and seaweed). The miso soup is a standout, as is the delicious seaweed salad tossed with a few slices of sashimi, smoked salmon, or crab. The teriyaki entrees, particularly the rare beef and salmon, are expertly rendered and delicious. Another branch is located in San Jose's Doubletree Hotel. ■ *1 E San Fernando St (between 1st and 2nd Sts), San Jose; (408)297-1847; $$; beer and wine; AE, MC, V; no checks; lunch Mon–Fri, dinner Mon–Sat.* & ■ *2050 Gateway Pl (in the Doubletree Hotel), San Jose; (408)436-1754; $$; beer and wine; AE, MC, V; no checks; lunch Mon–Fri, dinner Mon–Sat.* &

**Chez Sovan Restaurant** ★★ See the review of this restaurant's Campbell location in the following pages. ■ *923 Old Oakland Rd (near 13th St), San Jose; (408)287-7619; $; beer and wine; AE, MC, V; no checks; lunch Mon–Fri.*

**Eight Forty North First** ★★ This restaurant with the no-nonsense name caters to the San Jose power elite—say, isn't that the mayor exchanging pleasantries with a justice from the municipal court? The setting for all this gastronomic moving and shaking boasts a lean, sophisticated design, with comfortable armchairs in maroon and gray fabrics, abstract oil paintings, and an eclectic collection of modern light fixtures. The food is equally eclectic, with Italian and Asian touches influencing the contemporary American menu. Starters include a spicy sauté of honey prawns nesting on a bed of Chinese cabbage; a vegetable quesadilla with pepper Jack cheese, guacamole, and salsa; and a curried spinach salad with apples, peanuts, and golden raisins. Entrees include pastas (such as linguine with chicken and broccoli topped with a creamy sun-dried tomato sauce and a sprinkle of feta and walnuts), grilled sea scallops on wilted spinach and other temptations from the deep, and a panoply of meat and poultry dishes ranging from venison medallions to a chicken breast topped with goat cheese, spicy pecans, and a poached pear. By now, you've probably gotten the idea that chef/co-owner John Petricca takes chances here; sometimes he hits the mark and sometimes he misses. Still, his concoctions are always interesting, and you can wash them down with a selection from the extensive (and pricey) wine list. ■ *840 N 1st St (between Mission and Hedding Sts), San Jose; (408)282-0840; $$$; full bar; AE, DC, DIS, MC, V; no checks; lunch Mon–Fri, dinner Mon–Sat.* &

▼ **San Jose**
*Restaurants*
▲

**Gombei Restaurant** ★★ Among the many worthy restaurants in San Jose's Japantown, tiny, lively Gombei stands out with its unparalleled noodle dishes and the near-volcanic energy of its devoted patrons and youthful staff. The menu offers everything from teriyaki and donburi to Gombei's renowned *udon*—the Japanese equivalent of Jewish chicken soup, which arrives in a huge ceramic bowl filled with fat wheat noodles, loads of tender strips of chicken, ribbons of egg, green onion, and a sheaf of dried seaweed. Be sure to check the specials board for such irresistible nibbles as deep-fried oysters or cold chicken salad served on buckwheat noodles. ■ *193 E Jackson St (between 4th and 5th Sts), San Jose; (408)279-4311; $; beer and wine; no credit cards; no checks; lunch, dinner Mon–Sat.* ■ *1438 El Camino Real (near Glenwood), Menlo Park; (650)329-1799; $; beer and wine; no credit cards; no checks; lunch Mon–Fri, dinner every day.*

**Il Fornaio ★★** See the review of this restaurant's San Francisco location in the previous pages. ■ *302 S Market St (inside the Hyatt Sainte Claire, at San Carlos St), San Jose; (408)271-3366; www.ilfornaio.com; $$; full bar; AE, DC, MC, V; no checks; breakfast, lunch, dinner every day.* ⌖

**La Taqueria ★★** See the review of this taqueria's San Francisco branch in the previous pages. ■ *15 S 1st St (at Santa Clara St), San Jose; (408)287-1542; $; beer only; no credit cards; no checks; lunch, early dinner every day (closes at 5pm Mon–Thurs and 7pm Fri–Sun).* ⌖

**71 Saint Peter ★★** Chef and co-owner Mark Tabak has attracted a loyal following with this tiny and romantic Mediterranean bistro. The Spanish floor tiles, flowers, exposed brick walls, and crisp linens help create a feeling of rustic elegance, a theme echoed by Tabak's robust yet refined cuisine. Outstanding starters include duck liver pâté with mustard and toast points, steamed New Zealand clams simply seasoned with tomato, basil, and garlic, and a bevy of interesting salads. For your entree, you'd do well to consider the roasted duck cloaked in a raspberry–black pepper demiglace, the seafood linguini in a spicy tomato broth, or any of the fresh fish dishes. Tabak is justly proud of his crème brûlée, which was voted the best in Santa Clara Valley in a recent newspaper poll. The sensibly priced wine list includes French and Italian selections as well as the usual California suspects. ■ *71 N San Pedro St (between Saint John and Santa Clara Sts), San Jose; (408)971-8523; $$; beer and wine; AE, DC, DIS, MC, V; checks OK; lunch Mon–Fri, dinner Tues–Sat.* ⌖

**Bella Mia ★** A large and lovely brick patio and a lively bar scene are two of the principal draws at this cheery Italian restaurant. The downstairs dining area is equipped with comfortable booths decked out in shades of green, gold, and rust, an impressive mahogany bar, and vintage photographs of the city that look decidedly quaint in the polished, modern setting. Upstairs, the restaurant has the feel of an Old West hotel, with high ceilings, wallpaper, wood wainscoting, floral carpeting, and frosted glass-

and-brass light fixtures. The menu encompasses everything from wood-grilled meats to flatbread pizzas, fresh pasta to ambitious salads. Kids will like the crayons and coloring menu. ▪ *58 S 1st St (at San Fernando St), San Jose; (408)280-1993; www.bellamia. com; $$; full bar; AE, DC, DIS, MC, V; no checks; brunch Sat–Sun, lunch Mon–Fri, dinner every day.* &

**Henry's World Famous Hi-Life** ★ Before there was Silicon Valley, before there was gentrification, before folks began anxiously watching their cholesterol count, there was Henry's Hi-Life. The exterior of this carnivores' paradise has a Depression-era look, while the interior is a cross between a bordello and the stage set for *Li'l Abner.* Formica tables are outfitted with paper place mats and candles wrapped in plastic netting that do little to shed light on the joint's cavernous darkness. None of this, however, has stopped office workers, college students, and laborers from queuing up each day for the best barbecued ribs, steaks, and chicken in town, all cooked in a white-oak barbecue pit and accompanied by a tangy, sweet sauce. Dinners come with a basket of garlic bread, a huge baked potato heaped with cheese, butter, and chives, and an insignificant salad. The bar's jukebox offers selections by such vintage crooners as the Ink Spots and Ella Fitzgerald. ▪ *301 W Saint John St (at Almaden Blvd, near Hwy 87), San Jose; (408)295-5414; $$; full bar; AE, MC, V; no checks; lunch Tues–Fri, dinner every day.*

**San Jose Tied House Cafe and Brewery** ★ This better-than-average brewery restaurant draws crowds with its high-quality beers and something-for-everyone menu. Like the original Tied House in Mountain View, the San Jose establishment has a noisy, boisterous atmosphere that may prove a little wearing if you enjoy hearing yourself think. This microbrewery pours eight beers produced right on the premises, and the menu features traditional pub fare (ribs, burgers, and fish 'n' chips) along with some unusual renditions of seafood, pasta, and vegetarian dishes. Appetizers include Cajun popcorn shrimp, sautéed tequila prawns and scallops, and egg roll towers. Indulge in the peanut butter mud pie with a cookie-crumb crust or the cookie-dough cheesecake for dessert. On warm days, grab a seat on the outdoor patio. There is also a branch of Tied House in Alameda. ▪ *65 N San Pedro St (between Santa Clara and Saint John Sts), San Jose; (408)295-2739; www.redwoodcoast.com: $$; beer, wine, and limited spirits; AE, DC, DIS, MC, V; no checks; lunch, dinner every day.* &

**Tony & Alba's Pizza and Italian Food** ★ See the review of this restaurant's Mountain View location in the following pages. ▪ *3137 Stevens Creek Blvd (at Winchester Blvd), San Jose; (408)246-4605; $; beer and wine; AE, DC, DIS, MC, V; local checks only; lunch, dinner every day.* & ▪ *864 Blossom Hill Rd (in the shopping plaza, at Santa Theresa Blvd), San Jose; (408)227-8669; $; beer* *and wine; AE, DC, DIS, MC, V; local checks only; lunch, dinner every day.* ☺

## LODGINGS

**The Fairmont** ★★★ President Clinton's done it. So have Al Gore, Luciano Pavarotti, Neil Diamond, Mike Wallace, George Bush, and a host of other celebs—slipped between the Supercale cotton sheets of San Jose's Fairmont, that is. Twenty stories high in the heart of downtown, the city's most luxurious hostelry has become one of the best known features of the skyline. Massive crystal chandeliers, golden marble columns, and plush furnishings set a tone of gracious elegance in the lobby, and the Fairmont offers every possible service a VIP-on-the-go could desire: 24-hour room service, multilingual staff, concierge, foreign currency exchange, complimentary health club, teleconferencing facilities, and a palm-tree-shaded pool. The 541 guest rooms (as well as the public areas) recently have been refurbished and feature such niceties as marble bathrooms, plush robes, electric shoe polishers, desks, walk-in closets, custom-made mattresses, minibars, and nightly turn-down service. In keeping with the Silicon Valley setting, they also contain an arsenal of tech toys such as high-speed modem links for computers and fax machines and interactive TV sets that let a guest do everything from ordering up a movie to checking out of the hotel.

Three well-regarded restaurants stand ready to serve peckish travelers: the **Pagoda** serves Chinese food at lunch and dinner; the **Fountain** is a casual spot for breakfast, lunch, dinner, spectacular ice-cream creations, and late-night snacks; and the poolside **Gazebo Bar and Grill** offers cocktails and light fare in the summer and fall, weather permitting. In addition, an elegant afternoon tea is served daily in the hotel's lobby. ■ *170 S Market St (between San Fernando and San Carlos Sts), San Jose, CA 95113; (408)998-1900 or (800)527-4727; www.fairmontsj.com; $$$; full bar; AE, DC, DIS, MC, V; checks OK; brunch Sun, breakfast, lunch, dinner every day.* ☺

**Hotel De Anza** ★★★ Renovations that took 10 months and $10 million brought this 1931 grande dame back to life after years of decay. The richly colored Moorish ceilings in the De Anza Room and the Hedley Club are art deco jewels, and the same design influence can be felt in the guest rooms. Each of the 99 rooms has a multiple-line desk phone with a dedicated data line and fax port, an armoire with an honor bar, and a TV with a VCR (you can check out movies gratis from the video library downstairs). Ask for one of the south-facing rooms to enjoy a sweeping view of downtown. T he hotel's flagship restaurant, **La Pastaia**, serves some of the best Italian food in town, and the place is always packed with locals as well as hungry travelers. The stately **Palm Court Terrace** is a favorite place to meet for drinks in the warmer months, and a live jazz trio performs in the **Hedley Club** on Wednesday through Saturday nights. One especially nice touch: the De Anza has a "Raid Our Pantry" program, in which guests are invited to partake of complimentary late-night munchies. When you're poking around the second-floor pantry, take a look at your fellow midnight snackers; many National Hockey League players stay here when they're in town to tangle with the San Jose Sharks, and stars ranging from Eddie Murphy to Tony Bennett have sampled the hotel's charms. ■ *233 W Santa Clara St (at Almaden Blvd), San Jose, CA 95113; (408)286-1000 or (800)843-3700; deanza@ix.netcom.com; $$$; full bar; AE, DC, MC, V; checks OK; breakfast, lunch, dinner every day.* 🕭

**Hyatt Sainte Claire** ★★★ This gracious Spanish revival–style hostelry was built in 1926 by the same architectural firm responsible for the Mark Hopkins Hotel in San Francisco. The 170 recently refurbished guest rooms (including 14 one-bedroom suites and one grand suite boasting two fireplaces and a library) feature feather beds, dual phone lines with high-speed modems, safes, and minibars among the other usual first-class amenities. In addition, some of the rooms have whirlpool tubs and fireplaces, and 80 percent are equipped with laser printers and IBM-compatible computers with Internet access. A small exercise room with a treadmill and an exercise bike stands ready to help guests work out any knots or kinks resulting from sessions at those computers. And the Hyatt has a pleasant coffee shop, the **Panetteria**, serving Italian sandwiches and pastries, as well as a top-rated branch of **Il Fornaio** restaurant (see the review of this restaurant's San Francisco branch). ■ *302 S Market St (at San Carlos St), San Jose, CA 95113; (408)885-1234 or (800)233-1234; $$$; full bar; AE, DC, DIS, MC, V; checks OK; breakfast, lunch, dinner every day.* 🕭

**The Hensley House** ★★ Close to museums, theaters, and restaurants, this stately Queen Anne is a haven for corporate visitors and child-weary couples. Proprietors Toni Contreras and Ron Evans recently restored the landmark building, lightening the interior and decorating it with crystal chandeliers, attractive antiques, and crisp linens. They added four more rooms, including three units in the lovely craftsman-style house across the street. Each of the guest rooms has a queen-size feather bed, private bath, TV with VCR, and a telephone. If you're ready to splurge, try the Judge's Chambers, with its wet bar, whirlpool bath for two, hand-painted ceiling and walls, and fireplace. (By the way, the ghost of the room's namesake, Superior Court Judge Perley Gosbey, one of the home's original owners, is rumored to pay a friendly visit now and then.) Guests are treated to a full breakfast. High tea is available to guests and the public on Thursday and Saturday afternoons by appointment only. ■ *456 N 3rd St (at Hensley St), San Jose, CA 95112; (408)298-3537 or*

*(800)498-3537 (in California only); henhouse@ix.netcom.com;
www.virtualcities.com/~virtual/ons/ca/b/cab3603.htm; $$–$$$;
AE, DC, DIS, MC, V; checks OK.*

## SANTA CLARA

### RESTAURANTS

**Birk's** ★★ Despite its office-park setting and rather stern exterior, Birk's is a handsome American grill with a spirited atmosphere. Design features such as multilevel dining areas, a long mahogany bar, brass and amber-glass light fixtures, an open kitchen, and a massive wood-burning oven mark Birk's as a Pat Kuleto creation, and the hearty food reflects the vaguely men's-club feel of the place. Appetizers might include steak bits with béarnaise sauce, a grilled artichoke with garlic-lemon aioli, or oysters Rockefeller. For a main course, you can choose from all manner of grilled and smoked meat, fish, and fowl. Standouts include the popular smoked prime rib, the pan-seared duck breast with bourbon and maple-syrup sauce, and grilled lamb chops marinated in oregano, lemon, garlic, and olive oil. Lighter eaters might enjoy one of the imaginative salads, such as the teriyaki salmon with cabbage slaw, sprouts, noodles, and dried apricots served with a light sake dressing. If you still have room for dessert, Birk's offers a dynamite chocolate cake, berry crisp à la mode, and other oh-I'll-diet-tomorrow temptations. The wine list reflects a good range of California vintners, and you'll find an excellent selection of single-malt Scotches and beers on tap, many from local microbreweries. ■ *3955 Freedom Circle (at Hwy 101 and Great America Pkwy), Santa Clara; (408)980-6400; www.birksrestaurant.com; $$$; full bar; AE, DC, DIS, MC, V; no checks; lunch Mon–Fri, dinner every day.* &

Santa Clara

*Lodgings*

### LODGINGS

**Madison Street Inn** ★★ Two gigantic pepper trees and a white picket fence studded with roses guard this restored Victorian house just minutes from downtown. The six guest rooms are small and quaint. The Monroe Room, overlooking the garden, has a queen-size brass bed and a claw-footed tub for two; the Madison Room (often used as a honeymoon suite) features a four-poster bed with a lace coverlet. If the smallness of the rooms begins to get to you, you can stretch out upstairs in the spacious living room and parlor decorated with Oriental rugs and lace curtains, or lounge by the pool and hot tub. The inn's hearty breakfast, prepared in a restaurant-size kitchen, might feature omelets, Belgian waffles, or eggs Benedict, accompanied by fresh-baked muffins and breads. By prior arrangement, proprietors Ralph and Theresa Wigginton will whip up masterful California cuisine dinners. ■ *1390 Madison St (at Lewis St), Santa Clara, CA 95050;*

*(408)249-5541 or (800)491-5541; madstinn@aol.com; $$; full bar; AE, DC, DIS, MC, V; checks OK; dinner by appointment only.*

## CAMPBELL

### RESTAURANTS

**Chez Sovan Restaurant ★★** An upscale cousin of the San Jose original, Chez Sovan's Campbell branch features the same authentic Cambodian cuisine and exceptionally friendly service. The stars of the menu are the *samlaws*, Cambodian stews. *Samlaw korko* is a brothy concoction that combines tender chicken with an exotic array of vegetables. Several catfish dishes are offered, too, including a dynamite version with black beans, green onions, vinegar, and loads of fresh ginger. Skip the house specialty, *amok*—chicken or fish marinated in coconut milk and wrapped in a banana leaf (it may be a little too authentic for untutored Western palates). The fresh salads are packed with cilantro, mint, shredded Napa cabbage, bell peppers, and carrots, plus your choice of chicken, pork, or beef. ■ *2425 S Bascom Ave (near Dry Creek Rd), Campbell; (408)371-7711; $; beer and wine; AE, DIS, MC, V; no checks; lunch, dinner every day.* &

**Lisa's Tea Treasures ★** See the review of this restaurant in the Menlo Park section in the following pages. ■ *1875 S Bascom Ave (Ste 165, in the Pruneyard shopping center, at Campbell Ave), Campbell; (408)371-7377; $; no alcohol; MC, V; checks OK; full tea service offered at 11:30am, 2pm, and 4pm Mon–Sat, 12pm and 3pm Sun.* &

## LOS GATOS

### RESTAURANTS

**Café Marcella ★★★** This sophisticated little side-street bistro's flavorful California-Mediterranean cuisine has won a loyal following. A long wood-and-marble bar dominates the sparse, Eurocafe setting, while bold prints depicting food and contented diners (appropriate enough subjects) add a splash of color. The small but provocative menu features individual pizzas, pastas, and a handful of entrees, all supplemented by an ever-changing list of weekly specials. Starters range from duck pâté with whole-grain mustard and chutney to wild mushroom risotto. Entrees include such interesting fare as pork medallions with sun-dried cherries, swordfish steaks with celery cream and eggplant relish, and rabbit with orange-mustard sauce. And no matter how full you are, order dessert—many locals would argue that Café Marcella's are the best around (how about a terrine of three chocolates with raspberry coulis and crème Anglaise, or perhaps rhubarb shortcake with hot caramel sauce?). The cafe is also known for its wine list, which offers a host of selections from both local vineyards and European boutique wineries. The service can suffer from an overabundance of attitude, and the ambience from an overabundance of noise, but all in all, this is one of the most exciting restaurants in the area. ■ *368 Village Lane (between Santa Cruz and University Aves), Los Gatos; (408) 354-8006; $$$; beer and wine; AE, MC, V; no checks; lunch Tues–Sat, dinner Tues–Sun.* ᕙ

**Cafe Trio** ★★★ Jack and Rosemary Edwards are the duo behind this engaging California bistro that opened in 1993. The black-and-white floor tiles, green marbleized wallpaper, and crisp table linens give the restaurant an uptown feel that triumphs over its shopping-center locale. Rosemary presides out front, ensuring friendly and knowledgeable service, while Jack, an alumnus of the Hotel De Anza's La Pastaia restaurant in San Jose, toils in the kitchen. He infuses the essentially California menu with French and Italian touches, and his predilection for spicy food keeps things interesting. Signature dishes include an appetizer of grilled Anaheim peppers stuffed with goat cheese, bread crumbs, and salsa, as well as entrees such as penne with chicken, tomatoes, pine nuts, and basil, and a delectable pork loin stuffed with herbs, dried cranberries, and fresh horseradish. Once a month or so, Cafe Trio hosts a popular four-course wine dinner designed to showcase the products of a specific vintner; call for dates and prices. ■ *15466 Los Gatos Blvd (in the Village Square shopping center, between Lark Ave and Los Gatos–Almaden Rd), Los Gatos; (408) 356-8129; $$$; beer and wine; AE, DC, MC, V; no checks; lunch Mon–Fri, dinner Mon–Sat.* ᕙ

**I Gatti** ★★★ With its sponge-painted mustard and red-brown walls, weathered wooden shutters, and terra-cotta floor tiles, I Gatti (the Italian counterpart to Los Gatos, Spanish for "the cats"—get it?) evokes a Tuscan patio on a sunny afternoon. A moss-colored banquette lines one wall, burlap and rope swags adorn the windows, and ceiling fans turn overhead, further enhancing a feeling of rustic comfort. I Gatti serves a variety of refined and intensely flavorful Italian dishes, and the kitchen has a particular flair for pasta and fish. Terrific appetizers are *scampi al vino blanco*, goat-cheese ravioli with a rich Chianti-wine glaze, and gnocchi (which can be a little doughy) with a first-rate creamy tomato–vodka sauce. There's a selection of both traditional and unusual salads (try the mixed greens with berries, leeks, and pistachios drizzled with a blackberry vinaigrette), well-prepared pizzas, and *secondi piatti* that include roasted filet mignon with a Barolo-wine and wild mushroom sauce, braised lamb shank, and *pollo modo mio* (lightly breaded breast of chicken served with a champagne, lemon-herb, and caper sauce). ■ *25 E Main St (near University Ave), Los Gatos; (408) 399-5180; $$$; beer and wine; AE, MC, V; checks OK; lunch Tues–Fri, dinner Tues–Sun.* ᕙ

**Pigalle** ★★ Playing off its name, some Los Gatos residents have affectionately dubbed this French bistro "Pig Alley" because of the generous, reasonably priced portions served here. Although the owners probably wouldn't appreciate that version of their moniker, they can't quibble with the loyalty their topnotch French Country cuisine inspires. Named after Paris's red-light district (a mural of a Parisian street scene sets the mood), Pigalle offers a small, interesting menu that changes seasonally. Lunch offerings may range from a seafood fettuccine with scallops and prawns to a chicken pie made with artichoke hearts, mushrooms, and cream sauce. For dinner, crisp roast duck in a caramelized raspberry sauce, classic beef Wellington, or braised rabbit with a mustard cream sauce may be among the tempting entrees. Dessert specialties include soufflés and fruit concoctions such as poached pears drenched in a port wine sauce. ■ *27 N Santa Cruz Ave (near Main St), Los Gatos; (408)395-7924; $$; beer and wine; MC, V; local checks only; lunch, dinner every day.*

**Lisa's Tea Treasures** ★ See the review of this restaurant in the Menlo Park section in the following pages. ■ *330 N Santa Cruz Ave (at Hwy 9/Saratoga–Los Gatos Blvd), Los Gatos; (408)395-8327; $; wine and champagne only; MC, V; checks OK; full tea service offered at 11:30am, 2pm, and 4pm Tues–Sun.* ᕇ

**Los Gatos Brewing Company** ★ This cheery, upscale techno-barn of a restaurant has something for everyone: good, house-made beers and ales for the thirsty, a lively singles scene for the action-oriented, crayons and coloring books for the wee ones, and, most important, good pub fare for the hungry. Executive chef Jim Stump (who formerly graced Le Mouton Noir in Saratoga and Birk's in Santa Clara) has created an ambitious menu encompassing everything from pizzas and fresh oysters on the half shell to rotisserie chicken. You can indulge in a dainty charred tuna carpaccio salad or give your arteries a workout with rib-eye steak in a red wine reduction sauce accompanied by garlic mashed potatoes, sautéed green beans, and buttermilk onion rings. In-house brewskis include special seasonal brews ranging from nut-brown ale to a German-style wheat beer. ■ *130-G N Santa Cruz Ave (at Grays Lane), Los Gatos; (408)395-9929; $$; beer and wine; AE, DC, DIS, MC, V; no checks; brunch Sun, lunch, dinner every day.* ᕇ

## SARATOGA

### *RESTAURANTS*

**Sent Soví** ★★★★ When Sent Soví opened in 1995, many long-established and well-regarded Saratoga restaurants watched enviously as it inspired purple prose from the pens of dazzled restaurant critics and caused foodies from all over the Bay Area to clamor for reservations. Why all the fuss? Well, co-owner

Aimee Hebert is one of those charming hostesses who treats every customer like a VIP, the service is big-city polished, and the dining room is a study in understated elegance, with copper wainscoting, dramatic dried flower-and-fruit garlands framing the windows, and stained-glass light fixtures. But Sent Sovi's principal draw is the contemporary French cuisine of chef/co-owner David Kinch, whose résumé includes stints at Ernie's and Silks in San Francisco as well as some of the finest restaurants in Europe. A passion for the best and freshest ingredients and a knack for coaxing a complex medley of flavors to work together characterize everything from house-made wine infusions to frozen soufflés. The best way to sample Kinch's inspired cuisine is to order the six-course tasting menu; it changes nightly, but a recent menu included the following sumptuous lineup: an *amuse bouche* (a tiny taste to stimulate your palate) of chicken salad, duck foie gras with corn bread and quince sauce, creamy soup of wild mushrooms and black truffles, venison medallions with apples and dates, spiced cranberry soup with fresh fruit and granitas, and frozen passion fruit soufflé with champagne sabayon. If someone in your party balks at ordering the tasting menu (unfortunately, the entire table must elect this option), don't despair; à la carte selections might include such treasures as risotto with black truffles and turkey, braised lamb shank with a cumin-scented carrot confit, and duck breast glazed with a spiced honey, raspberry, and verbena sauce. ■ *14583 Big Basin Way (at 5th St), Saratoga; (408)867-3110; www.sentsovi.com; $$$; beer and wine; AE, MC, V; no checks; dinner Tues–Sun.*

**Le Mouton Noir** ★★★ For a small town, Saratoga has more than its fair share of good French restaurants, but the sheer inventiveness of Le Mouton Noir's kitchen has always set it apart from its competitors. Recently there's been an upheaval in both ownership and kitchen staff, but new chef Jason Siccone (an alumnus of San Francisco's La Folie and Los Gatos' Café Marcella) continues to turn out the superb French-California fare that has made Le Mouton Noir a destination restaurant. The cozy dining room is reminiscent of a refined country house, with mauve, pink, and white Laura Ashley prints and sprays of dried flowers to create a romantic mood, and the service is courtly. The menu changes seasonally, but specialties include such appetizers as escargots served on new potato skins, wild mushrooms and goat cheese encased in a pastry shell, and duck pâté with pistachios and sun-dried cranberries. Entrees may feature boneless, pan-roasted quail with pheasant sausage and risotto stuffing, salmon with an almond-citrus crust, and rack of lamb perched on a parsnip gratin. Duck remains a house specialty, with a rotating repertoire of preparations. Desserts may include such ethereal creations as a flourless mocha cake surrounded by crème Anglaise, a banana-bread pudding with warm caramel sauce, and a frangipane pear tartlette. The pricey wine list features a wide range of French and California offerings, with a good selection from nearby Santa Cruz mountain wineries. Patio dining is available when the weather cooperates. ■ *14560 Big Basin Way (between 4th and 5th Sts, near Hwy 9), Saratoga; (408) 867-7017; $$$; full bar; AE, DC, MC, V; no checks; lunch Sat, dinner every day.* &

**Bella Saratoga** ★★ A pretty two-story Victorian house in the center of town is the homey setting for this popular Italian restaurant that changed hands in 1995 (the founding family continues to operate Bella Mia in San Jose). Pasta is its forte, with such offerings as salmon ravioli in a creamy tomato-dill sauce; lasagne layered with ground beef, sausage, salami, and cheese; and linguini and clams. Starters include fried calamari, artichokes with roasted garlic aioli, and bruschetta with mozzarella, pesto, and peppers. You'll also find a selection of salads, pizzas, and meat and poultry items. On balmy Sundays, Bella Saratoga serves a brunch with live music ranging from an accordion player to a jazz trio. ■ *14503 Big Basin Way (between 3rd and 4th Sts), Saratoga; (408) 741-5115; $$; full bar; AE, DC, DIS, MC, V; no checks; breakfast Sat, brunch Sun, lunch Mon–Fri, dinner every day.*

## LODGINGS

**The Inn at Saratoga** ★★ Tucked into a tranquil, parklike setting, this small, modern hotel is a comfortable haven catering mostly to the business traveler. The five-story inn has 45 spacious rooms decorated in dark greens and beiges with large picture windows overlooking pretty Saratoga Creek. All the usual touches demanded by peripatetic execs are here: sitting area, minibar, desk, complimentary newspaper, whirlpool bath, remote-control cable television with VCR, computer gizmos, and, of course, a telephone in the john. A continental breakfast is included in the room rate, and the hotel is a pleasant stroll away from many fine restaurants and shops. ■ *20645 4th St (just off Big Basin Way), Saratoga, CA 95070; (408) 867-5020 or (800) 543-5020 (in California only) or (800) 338-5020 (outside California); $$$; AE, DC, MC, V; no checks.* &

## SUNNYVALE

### RESTAURANTS

**The Palace** ★★★ The Palace is an apt enough name for this amazing endeavor, but owner Greg Eaton really should have dubbed it The Mirage. Picture this: You are in Sunnyvale, driving past legions of modest tract homes, circling a giant mall, when, lo and behold, you stumble onto one of the few vestiges of the city's former downtown. It's a remarkable-looking edifice peeking out from the storefronts, a terra-cotta confection with the soaring lines of an art nouveau movie palace. You enter, sidling past the tuxedo-clad bouncer, and, honey, you're not in Kansas, er, Sunnyvale, any more. The cavernous, 13,000-square-foot interior, with its artful meld of Italianate, art nouveau, and modern design influences, has the feel of a grand movie set, and the dressed-to-the-nines crowd has that "I'm ready for my close-up, Mr. DeMille" look. The rows of seats that once filled this 1930s movie house have been ripped out to make way for a huge dance floor flanked by dining areas on several levels and two bars.

Perhaps the biggest surprise is the quality of the food. Joey Altman, who took over the kitchen in August 1993 after tenures at Stars and Miss Pearl's Jam House in San Francisco, has created an inventive tapas menu. Consider the possibilities: spring rolls with a chile-mint dipping sauce, succulent crayfish in a spicy garlic-ginger broth, and filet mignon with foie gras, black chanterelles, and Armagnac sauce. Don't be afraid to experiment here—Altman has a sure hand with all this exotica, and everything is as delicious as it is beautifully presented. Dessert includes such wonders as a milk chocolate mousse torte with white chocolate ganache. With food this good, it's a shame the management allows the dance crowd to take over as the evening progresses; if you're lolling at a floorside table after 9:30pm or so, expect to have the service slow to a crawl while the booze-and-boogie hordes press in from all sides. But perhaps you'll want to join them: the Palace features a jazz trio Tuesday through Thursday and a DJ spins disco, funk, and techno grooves Friday through Sunday. ■ *146 S Murphy Ave (between Washington and Evelyn Aves), Sunnyvale; (408) 739-5179; $$; full bar; AE, MC, V; no checks; dinner Tues–Sat.*

**Sunnyvale**

*Restaurants*

**Il Postale** ★★ Set in Sunnyvale's old post office (hence the name), Il Postale is an airy, attractive trattoria with brick walls hung with large framed prints of Italian postal stamps, dark wood bistro furniture set with white linens, and an open kitchen. Although owner Joe Antuzzi insists that his welcoming little restaurant serves Italian-American bistro food, that designation doesn't begin to describe the ambitious menu. Sure, there are plenty of Italian classics (spaghetti puttanesca, linguine with clams, veal braciola, cheese pizza), but the kitchen seems to delight in putting its own twist on some of the standards, tossing grilled boar sausage in wild mushroom risotto, serving veal scalloppine with a sun-dried tomato, caper, and black-olive sauce, even stuffing agnolotti with garlic mashed potatoes (yikes!). And then there are dishes like grilled prawns with soba noodles, defying inclusion on any Italian-American menu we've ever seen. Most of the time this iconoclastic approach works, resulting in a satisfying, interesting meal at a reasonable price. ■ *127 W Washington St (near Murphy Ave), Sunnyvale; (408) 733-9600; $$; full bar; AE, DC, DIS, MC, V; no checks; lunch Mon–Fri, dinner every day.* ㅎ

**Kabul Afghan Cuisine** ★★  See the review of this restaurant's San Carlos location. ■ *833 W El Camino Real (at Pastoira), Sunnyvale; (408)245-4350; $$; beer and wine; AE, MC, V; checks OK; lunch Mon–Fri, dinner every day.* &

## MOUNTAIN VIEW

### *RESTAURANTS*

**Amber India Restaurant** ★★  Opened in 1995 in a small, unprepossessing shopping center on busy El Camino Real, Amber India offers an escape into a serene, exotic realm. Soft light from brass sconces reflects off rough-textured white stucco walls, partitions and archways divide the space into a series of cozy areas, and wood-and-fabric awnings jut over the central dining room. The staff is solicitous and welcoming, and the food is a cut above the fare typically found in Bay Area Indian restaurants, in terms of both quality and variety. The menu derives its inspiration from several regions of India, resulting in an adventurous selection of exceptionally flavorful yet well-balanced dishes. Appetizers include deep-fried fish pakora, *shami kabab* (lamb patties mixed with lentils and onions), and *reshmi tikka* (marinated and barbecued chicken morsels seasoned with saffron and topped with mint). A large variety of distinctively spiced curries, tandoori selections, and rice dishes rounds out the menu; come with a group so you can order enough items to experience the kitchen's impressive breadth. Intrepid diners can top off their meal with *kulfi* (saffron-flavored ice cream with pistachios) or *gulab jamun* (deep-fried cheese balls drizzled with honey). One quibble: the service can be a bit erratic at times. In one recent visit, the appetizer and two entrees were served simultaneously and, after a 45-minute wait, the remaining entrees and the bread (wonderful buttered naan and onion *kulcha*) made their appearance. ■ *2290 El Camino Real (between Rengstorff and Ortega Aves), Mountain View; (650)968-7511; $$$; full bar; AE, DC, DIS, MC, V; no checks; lunch, dinner every day.* &

**Chez T. J.** ★★  Founding chef Thomas J. McCombie's masterful cooking established this homey little restaurant on a quiet Mountain View street as one of the best French restaurants in the Bay Area. After McCombie passed away several years ago, Chez T. J. seemed to lose some of its luster, but current chef Andrew Trice III is determined to revive its flagging reputation. Located right around the corner from Mountain View's bustling Castro Street, Chez T. J.'s four dining rooms are decorated with colorful modern artwork, and each table has its own unique blown-glass lamp. The prix-fixe menus feature traditional French cuisine with California touches; they change every three to four weeks. Meals range from the four-course *menu petit* to the formidable seven-course *menu gastronomique.* A recent feast featured a warm salad of guinea hen confit, seared scallops with a delicate potato crust and chive sauce, cassis sorbet in champagne, roasted pork tenderloin with candied ginger beurre blanc, a well-chosen selection of cheeses, and two house-made desserts. Each course is a visual work of art and a shame to destroy, but once the exquisite aromas reach you, you'll find your fork has a mind of its own. An extensive wine list allows you to select the perfect accompaniment. ■ *938 Villa St (between Castro St and Shoreline Blvd), Mountain View; (650)964-7466; $$$; beer and wine; AE, MC, V; checks OK; dinner Tues–Sat.*

**Hangen** ★★ Mountain View's Castro Street is undeniably saturated with Asian restaurants of all descriptions, but chef Neng Wang's delicate and tasty Sichuan fare still has managed to carve out a distinctive niche. At lunch, Hangen caters to its workday crowd by offering multicourse menus entitled the Executive Lunch and the Business Lunch, both of which provide several choices. At dinner, the chef spreads his culinary wings, and the far-ranging menu includes delights such as Emerald Shrimp (shrimp with a spinach-wine sauce perched on a bed of orange slices and lettuce), deep-fried whole fish in a spicy sauce, beef satay, conch salad, tea-smoked duck, and mushrooms in a tangerine zest sauce. Some non-Asian customers grumble about being given a different, smaller menu than their Chinese counterparts, but they're still assured of plenty of delicious options. ■ *134 Castro St (just W of the Central Expwy), Mountain View; (650)964-8881; $$; beer and wine; AE, DC, MC, V; no checks; lunch, dinner every day.* ♿

Mountain
View

*Restaurants*

**Michaels at Shoreline** ★ On a warm, sunny day, an alfresco lunch at this upscale cafeteria is like a mini-vacation. Watch golfers chase their little white balls or ducks light on the water hazards at the Shoreline golf course while you munch on a garden burger on a sesame bun, penne with chicken and spinach, or a hot roast beef sandwich with Swiss cheese and fries. The food, while nothing fancy, is quite good, and the setting wonderfully relaxing (except for the occasional presence of some persistent crumb-chasing birds). Afterwards, you can work off the calories on the nearby biking and jogging trails, or maybe take a spin on a paddleboat on Shoreline's scenic man-made lake. ■ *2960 N Shoreline Blvd (near Rengstorff House), Mountain View; (650)962-1014; $; full bar; AE, MC, V; no checks; breakfast, lunch, late-afternoon light fare every day.* ♿

**Tied House Cafe and Brewery** ★ See the review of the San Jose Tied House Cafe and Brewery. ■ *954 Villa St (between Shoreline Blvd and Castro St), Mountain View; (650)965-BREW; $$; beer and wine; AE, DC, DIS, MC, V; no checks; lunch, dinner every day.* ♿

**Tony & Alba's Pizza and Italian Food** ★  When newly arrived East Coast transplants start complaining about California's dearth of good pizza joints, one way to shut them up is to spirit them to Tony & Alba's, where they'll be confronted with a pie so laden with goodies and endowed with such a pleasing, hand-spun crust that they just might have to quit their bellyaching. Year after year this friendly, family-run restaurant with its huge brick oven wins awards for its heavenly pizzas. Inspired creations include Tony's Special (pepperoni, salami, onion, bell peppers, mushrooms, Italian sausage, and linguiça), Alba's Special (fresh garlic, clams, tomatoes, and herbs), and the wonderful Bianca (four cheeses, sun-dried tomatoes, olive oil, fresh herbs, and garlic). The specialty sandwiches—meatball, veal cutlet, chicken, et cetera—are huge, and there are always a few pasta dishes to choose from. This place is extremely popular and noisy, so if you want a little peace with your pizza, order a pie to go. The original Tony & Alba's has been a Mountain View institution since 1982; in 1990 the family began opening other branches in the South Bay. ■ *619 Escuela Ave (between El Camino Real and Latham St), Mountain View; (650) 968-5089; $; beer and wine; AE, DC, DIS, MC, V; local checks only; lunch, dinner every day.* &

## LOS ALTOS

### *RESTAURANTS*

**Beauséjour** ★★★  A downtown gem, Beauséjour (bow-zay-ZHUR, French for "a beautiful visit") presents French cuisine in a charming old building with a European country house feel. The atmosphere may be a little prim, but the food is executed with rare skill and precision. Traditional favorites are well covered, including escargots in puff pastry, sautéed sweetbreads, and beef bourguignon, but the menu also branches out into unusual, lighter fare. Starters might include pan-seared prawns on a bed of Parmesan mashed potatoes or duck mousse pâté with truffles. The soups are excellent, and the salads range from a very simple medley of mixed baby greens to a tiger-prawns salad with grapefruit and red potatoes. The inviting entrees include medallions of venison with bok choy and curry-potato fritters, calamari steak in a lemon-caper sauce, and filet mignon with an herb sauce and goat cheese ravioli. Beauséjour is also known for its duck with raspberry sauce and lamb with mint sauce and potato timbale. Whatever you order, you can count on everything being perfectly cooked, attractively presented, and served with polite efficiency. A reasonably priced prix-fixe dinner is offered daily and includes soup or salad, entree, and dessert. ■ *170 State St (between 3rd and 4th Sts), Los Altos; (650) 948-1382; www.menusonline.com; $$$; full bar; AE, DC, MC, V; no checks; lunch Mon–Fri, dinner every day.* &

**Chef Chu's** ★★ Take a culinary tour of mainland China without ever leaving your table. Feast on dim sum from Guangzhou, banquet dishes from Shanghai and Beijing, dumplings and stretched noodles from Xian, and spicy favorites from Sichuan and Hunan—all from the kitchen of Lawrence Chu, a chef who's been expanding the culinary horizons of Los Altos for more than two decades. Chef Chu does all the standards well and offers some delicious innovations of his own, such as crisp salmon rolls (tender salmon mixed with Chinese herbs, wrapped in sheets of dried tofu and deep-fried). Munch on jumbo prawns with candied pecans in a mild mustard sauce. The Peking duck, which must be ordered in advance, is crisp and flawless, with virtually all the fat melted away. ▪ *1067 N San Antonio Rd (at El Camino Real), Los Altos; (650)948-2696; $$; full bar; AE, DC, MC, V; no checks; lunch, dinner every day.*

## PALO ALTO

The home of **Stanford University**, notable restaurants, fine-art galleries, foreign-movie houses, great bookstores, a thriving theater troupe, and some of the best shopping this side of heaven, Palo Alto is a beacon of cosmopolitan energy shining on the suburban sea. Much of the fuel for this cultural lighthouse comes, of course, from the university, which offers tours of its attractive campus on a fairly regular basis. Highlights of the university include the **Main Quad**, **Hoover Tower** (there are great views from its observation platform), the huge bookstore, and gorgeous **Memorial Church**; call the campus at (650)723-2560 for more tour information. If you'd like to try to glimpse some atom smashing, visit the nearby **Stanford Linear Accelerator Center**; call (650)926-3300 to arrange a tour.

**Palo Alto**

If you didn't find the tome you were looking for at the Stanford bookstore, Palo Alto and its neighbors contain many other outlets for bibliophiles. **Kepler's Books and Magazines**, 1010 El Camino Real, Menlo Park, (650)324-4321, is a wonderland for serious bookworms, and you'll find a healthy selection of mind food at **Printer's Inc.**, 310 California Avenue, Palo Alto, (650)327-6500; **Borders Books**, 456 University Avenue, Palo Alto, (650)326-3670; **Stacey's**, 219 University Avenue, Palo Alto, (650)326-0681; and **Books Inc.**, at the Stanford Shopping Center, on El Camino Real near University Avenue, (650)321-0600. You'll probably need to follow that literary excursion with a cup of joe. Some of the bookstores, such as Printer's Inc. and Borders, serve coffee and light snacks, but for authentic coffeehouse atmosphere and great espresso try **Caffè Verona**, 236 Hamilton Avenue, Palo Alto, (650)326-9942, or **Cafe Borrone**, located right next to Kepler's, 1010 El Camino Real, Menlo Park, (650)327-0830. If you'd like to surf the Web while you sip your cappuccino, head to

**Cybersmith**, where you can connect to the Internet, try out the latest software, or don a helmet and gloves for a voyage into virtual reality; 353 University Avenue, Palo Alto, (650)325-2005.

Moviegoers have a broad range of choices. The beautifully restored **Stanford Theater**, which showcases classic flicks, is especially worth a visit; 221 University Avenue, Palo Alto, (650)324-3700. If you prefer your performances live, check out the local **Theatreworks** troupe, (650)463-1950, the **Lively Arts** series at Stanford University, (650)725-2787, or the top-name talents currently appearing at the **Shoreline Amphitheater**, 1 Amphitheater Parkway, Mountain View, (650)967-3000. If you have nothing to wear for the show (or, indeed, if you have any other shopping need), Palo Alto won't let you down. University Avenue and its side streets contain a plethora of interesting stores. The **Stanford Shopping Center**, just north of downtown on El Camino Real, (650)617-8585, is a sprawling, beautifully landscaped temple of consumerism (stores include Bloomingdales, Macy's, Nordstrom, Ralph Lauren, The Gap, Imaginarium, Crate & Barrel, the Disney Store, and many more). Good places to eat in this shoppers' paradise include **Bravo Fono**, **Bok Choy**, **Max's Opera Cafe**, and **Cafe Andrea** (avoid the handsome but substandard branch of Piatti).

▼ *RESTAURANTS*

**Palo Alto**

▲

**Bistro Elan** ★★★ The Palo Alto restaurant explosion recently has spread from downtown to other sections of the city, and this natty little bistro, open since 1995, is one of the best and brightest to emerge in the California Avenue area. Its forte is a small, ever-changing repertoire of carefully crafted, subtly flavored dishes that respect the integrity of each of their wonderfully fresh components. Although many of the offerings would be at home in any classic French bistro (duck confit, grilled pork tenderloin, lamb ragout), chef/co-owner Ambjörn Lindskog is not adverse to taking cues from California cuisine. You'll find such seemingly disparate appetizers as smoked salmon with wonton wrappers and wasabe, seared Sonoma foie gras on brioche with oranges and arugula, and a poached egg with sevruga caviar, spinach, caramelized shallots, and prosciutto. Entrees might range from duck confit with beet risotto to pan-seared Hawaiian pink snapper with red endive and spinach and a red wine-shallot sauce. Desserts might include such diverse creations as a stellar warm chocolate tart with whipped cream, a trio of tropical fruit ice creams topped with vanilla-butter sauce, or fresh-baked cookies and cupcakes. The storefront dining room is decked out in that spare Parisian neighborhood-bistro style, and there's a lovely back patio nestled in an herb and rose garden. ■ *448 California Ave (just off El Camino Real), Palo Alto; (650)327-0284; $$; beer and wine; AE, DC, MC, V; no checks; lunch Tues–Fri, dinner Tues–Sat.* ⅙

**Evvia** ★★★ This warm and welcoming restaurant has a sun-drenched, Mediterranean feel. Colored bottles, ceramic plates, and copper pots line the walls and the mantel of an imposing fireplace, beaded light fixtures cast a golden glow, and wooden beams and a planked oak floor add handsome rustic accents. Traditional Greek dishes have succumbed to California's culinary charms here, resulting in an emphasis on fresh produce and interesting twists on traditional dishes such as moussaka and Greek salad. Fish and pasta dishes are other good choices, and if leg of lamb is offered as a special, order it—the meat is exceptionally tender and juicy and comes flanked by some fine roasted potatoes and vegetables. Good desserts include the baklava and the chocolate torte. Order a traditional Greek coffee to top off your meal. ■ *420 Emerson St (between Lytton and University Aves), Palo Alto; (650) 326-0983; $$; full bar; MC, V; no checks; lunch Mon–Fri, dinner every day.* &

**L'Amie Donia** ★★★ One of the first superstar chefs to desert San Francisco for the Peninsula, Donia Bijan, whose résumé includes the Sherman House and Brasserie Savoy, opened this amiable, bustling French bistro and wine bar in the summer of 1994. Expect traditional favorites such as onion soup, galantine of duck, and steak bordelaise with pommes frites dished up in a pleasant space that's dominated by a zinc bar and a battery of banquettes covered in burgundy and green fabric reminiscent of a wine-country harvest. In keeping with her reputation, Bijan renders her traditional fare with a light touch, allowing diners to save room for one of her superb desserts such as the celebrated tarte Tatin with sweet vanilla cream. She has instituted an imaginative wine list, equally divided between California and French varietals, with about half of the well-priced choices offered by the glass. Two small patios are open for alfresco dining and the kitchen offers a two-course prix-fixe lunch and a three-course dinner at quite reasonable prices. ■ *530 Bryant St (between University and Hamilton Aves), Palo Alto; (650) 323-7614; $$$; beer and wine; AE, DIS, MC, V; no checks; lunch Tues–Fri, dinner Tues–Sat.* &

**Maddalena's Continental Restaurant** ★★★ If your mood is romantic, your culinary craving continental, and your wallet well padded, it's time to slip on your glad rags and head over to Maddalena's. This longtime favorite of Palo Alto's haves and have-mores is a splendid example of a dying breed: an unapologetically classic continental restaurant. The lush decor exudes an Old World formality, and waiters in tuxes hover about, ready to spring into service. Chef Jieme Maciel excels with veal dishes and such opulent fare as crisp duck with juniper berries and cassis, delicate poached salmon with a mustard-and-white-wine cream sauce, pheasant with Grand Marnier, and steak au poivre. If it's pasta you fancy, try the Fettuccine Chef Maciel (with smoked duck, spinach, and garlic in a light Roma tomato sauce) or fettuccine

▼
**Palo Alto**
*Restaurants*
▲

with lobster. The desserts, as rich and decadent as you'd expect, include a wonderful house-made cheesecake and a three-layer chocolate mousse cake. The wine list, tipped toward expensive vintages, offers mostly Italian and California selections. For a romantic surprise, book the beautifully appointed art deco private room for two upstairs. If you'd like to sample this Palo Alto classic but your bankroll is a little thin, try **Cafe Fino**, the less-expensive Italian bistro next door, which has the same management and shares Maddalena's kitchen. ■ *544 Emerson St (between University and Hamilton Aves), Palo Alto; (650)326-6082; $$$; full bar; AE, DC, MC, V; checks OK; lunch Tues–Fri, dinner Mon–Sat.* ら

**Spago Palo Alto** ★★★ When Jeremiah Tower and his business partners opened Stars Palo Alto in 1995, it was an undeniable signal that the increasingly sophisticated Peninsula/South Bay restaurant scene had truly come of age. But plagued by management problems, poor service, uneven food, and a dizzying succession of short-lived head chefs (Tower left after just a few months), Stars Palo Alto never quite caught on. Enter Wolfgang Puck. Puck apparently took one look at the dazzling restaurant— and the bulging wallets of the Silicon Valley culinary cognoscenti—and declared that he at last had found the perfect site for his first Northern California outpost since unveiling the highly regarded Postrio in San Francisco in 1989. Spago Palo Alto opened in December 1997, boasting a new exhibition kitchen, a remodeled formal dining room, a separate casual cafe and bar area, and a menu featuring American cuisine with European and Asian influences. This is the seventh Spago in Puck's ever-expanding restaurant empire, which also contains a battalion of informal Wolfgang Puck Cafes and Expresses. And, as at most Puck enterprises, you won't see the celebrity chef in the kitchen very often; instead, Puck-trained executive chef Michael French, who was previously executive sous chef at Postrio, is the man at the helm. French's menu changes daily, and some of his standouts have included an appetizer of oven-roasted calamari stuffed with shrimp and Chinese black-bean sauce, and main courses such as Puck's popular Chinese-style duck with citrus-chile-glazed kumquats and curried vegetables, and an oven-roasted monkfish saddle with brussels sprouts and balsamic brown butter. Be sure to top off the memorable meal with the superb bittersweet-chocolate truffle cake. ■ *265 Lytton Ave (between Bryant and Ramona Sts), Palo Alto; (650)833-1000; $$$; full bar; AE, DC, DIS, MC, V; no checks; lunch Mon–Sat, dinner every day.* ら

**Beppo** ★★ At one end of the Italian restaurant spectrum lie the sophisticated Northern Italian restaurants with their Euro-sleek decor; at the other stand the Southern Italian family-style restaurants with their posters of the Leaning Tower of Pisa and "Eat, you look too skinny" waitstaffs. Then there's Beppo, a young Palo

Alto establishment that manages to sidestep this continuum. Picture Alice in Wonderland meets the Knights of Columbus. Picture a place where you enter through the kitchen and wander through a maze of eating areas drenched in Christmas lights, statues glazed in neon colors, and hundreds and hundreds of photos featuring everything from the Spanish Steps to Sophia Loren striking poses in skimpy lingerie. There's a candlelit shrine to Frank Sinatra, naughty pictures in the rest rooms, and an upstairs parlor in which a portrait of a beaming pope overlooks a little throne under a domed ceiling adorned with kitschy cherubs. Connie Francis, Dean Martin, and Ol' Blue Eyes himself belt out tunes over the sound system and the exuberant, young waitstaff often sing along as they plunk down huge serving platters on the red-and-white-checked tables. The small, traditional menu, which is inscribed on the walls, is as eccentric as the decor: the quantities are so huge and the prices so high ($16.95 for spaghetti with meatballs; $19.95 for chicken cacciatore), you had better come with a big group of people who all like to eat the same food—otherwise you end up with a shopping bag full of leftovers and a bill that's just as hefty. Even with this limited menu there are a few culinary land mines: the pasta is often overcooked and the eggplant Parmigiana tends to be dry and oddly seasoned. But the salads, wafer-thin-crusted pizza, green beans, veal piccata, and tortellini usually are quite good. Whatever you do, be sure to save room for the spumoni—Beppo manages to elevate this humble ice cream concoction to a creamy and complex gourmet's delight. It's so good, it almost makes you forgive the crazy reservations policy (too baffling to detail here; call and let the staff try to explain it to you). ■ *643 Emerson St (between Forest and Hamilton Aves), Palo Alto; (650)329-0665; $$; full bar; AE, DC, MC, V; local checks only; dinner every day.* ⃝

▼

**Palo Alto**

*Restaurants*

▲

**Higashi West** ★★ It's East meets West at this small, slick restaurant, where lamb chops are marinated in shallots and plum wine, mashed potatoes are infused with wasabe, and ravioli comes bathed in an herb-miso cream sauce. Some people will delight in the experimentation (the success of the wasabe mashed potatoes is an especially happy surprise); others might wonder what the heck they're smoking in the kitchen. The space is a bit loud and cramped and service can be slow, but adventuresome eaters will forgive all that. The murmur of the wall-mounted sculptural fountain, the stands of black bamboo, and the modern paintings help create a pleasing, sophisticated setting for the unusual fare. There's an excellent but expensive sushi bar, and about a dozen varieties of sake to sip. ■ *636 Emerson St (between Hamilton and Forest Aves), Palo Alto; (650)323-WEST; $$; beer and wine; AE, DIS, MC, V; no checks; dinner Mon–Sat.* ⃝

**Il Fornaio** ★★  See the review of this restaurant's San Francisco branch. ■ *520 Cowper St (in the Garden Court Hotel, just S of University Ave), Palo Alto; (650)853-3888; www.ilfornaio.com; $$; full bar; AE, DC, MC, V; no checks; breakfast, lunch, dinner every day.* &

**MacArthur Park** ★★  One look inside this attractive Julia Morgan–designed building reveals that the clientele here has a conservative Stanford spin: lots of blue blazers and dresses with big bows and pearls. Not your usual ribs fans, true, but devotees nonetheless. They come for the lean, tender, oak-smoked ribs and first-rate mesquite-grilled steaks. The rest of the menu seems more appropriate considering the crowd: fish, chops, and fowl sporting respectable California-style sauces such as fresh tomato chutney, jalapeño jelly, and orange-tamarind glaze—but the ribs are the raison d' être. For dessert, try the killer mud pie. The excellent wine list is rich in California cabernets, the single-malt Scotch list is a classy touch, and the roster of dessert wines is long and interesting enough to keep you there late into the evening. Patio seating and private dining rooms are available, too. ■ *27 University Ave (just off El Camino Real, near the train depot), Palo Alto; (650)321-9990; $$; full bar; AE, DC, MC, V; no checks; brunch Sun, lunch Mon–Fri, dinner every day.* &

**Osteria** ★★  Folks either love this ever-crowded regional Northern Italian restaurant or don't understand what all the fuss is about. One thing is certain, however: if noise, tightly packed tables, and a rather limited menu disqualify a restaurant for you, Osteria won't be your cup of tea—er, cappuccino. The pastas are house-made and the sauces are competently prepared, if a little too straightforward; this is not the kind of place where the chef often feels like pushing the culinary envelope. The tortellini with prosciutto, cream, and peas or the simple but tasty capellini al pomodoro are good bets. Osteria usually has a nice way with veal and fish, and, if they're on the menu, try the huge, juicy prawns in a light lemon cream sauce with a fan of steamed vegetables. For a pleasant finale, indulge in the rich hazelnut flan. ■ *247 Hamilton Ave (at Ramona St), Palo Alto; (650)328-5700; $$; beer and wine; AE, MC, V; no checks; lunch Mon–Fri, dinner Mon–Sat.* &

**Blue Chalk Cafe** ★  Although a taste of California and even the Far East sneak into the menu now and then, this engaging cafe's culinary strength lies in its satisfying Southern comfort food: mufalata sandwiches, chicken with garlic mashed potatoes, spicy prawns on a bed of creamy grits, pan-seared catfish with sautéed greens, and pecan rice. The bar menu also takes a page from the South, offering such treats as Farmstand Punch (Midori, Absolut Kurant, and fresh juices poured over chilled melon), a Hurricane (the potent blend of rum and fruit juices that's the mother's milk of Mardi Gras), and a peach-flavored mint julep that will soon have you singing *Georgia on My Mind*. A young waitstaff dishes out playful but efficient service in a high-energy atmosphere. A sea of blue felt pool tables stand ready for a friendly game or two, and there's a cozy pub area in back and a small, flower-bedecked patio out front, both remnants from the building's former life as an English restaurant. ■ *630 Ramona St (between Hamilton and Forest Aves), Palo Alto; (650)326-1020; www.ispot.com/bluechalk; $$; full bar; AE, MC, V; no checks; lunch Mon–Fri, dinner every day.* ♿

**Peninsula Fountain & Grill** ★ After its recent remodeling, this longtime downtown favorite looks suspiciously like those faux-'50s diners cropping up all over the place, but make no mistake about it: this is the genuine article. Hearty, basic breakfasts ensure a long queue of hungry folks when the doors open, and satisfying burgers, fries, sandwiches, and other diner fare keep the joint jumping throughout the day. As the pile-up of strollers will attest, this is a terrific place to bring the kids—they love the booths and the bustle, and you can always get them to finish their grilled cheese sandwiches by bribing them with one of the Fountain's legendary milk shakes. ■ *566 Emerson St (at Hamilton Ave), Palo Alto; (650)323-3131; $; beer and wine; DIS, MC, V; local checks only; breakfast, lunch, dinner every day.* ♿

## LODGINGS

**The Garden Court Hotel** ★★★ If you like elegance, pampering, and a happening location (well, some people may not), this is a darn good place to stay. A flower-laden courtyard, providing the balcony view for most of the 62 rooms, is surrounded by Italianate architecture draped with arches and studded with colorful tile work and hand-wrought-iron fixtures. The Mediterranean modern rooms are tinted in pastel shades of green, peach, and violet; all have four-poster beds, white faux-marble furniture, and thick, cushioned couches. The suites approach decadence; the penthouse, for example, has a fireplace, a whirlpool bath, and a wet bar. All the little details are covered in style, from an exercise room to terrycloth robes to complimentary copies of the *Wall Street Journal*. The hotel is in a good shopping and nightlife area, just off University Avenue, and room service is available from **Il Fornaio** restaurant, which shares the building (see review of its San Francisco branch). ■ *520 Cowper St (between University and Hamilton Aves), Palo Alto, CA 94301; (650)322-9000 or (800)824-9028; raimee@gardencourt.com; www.gardencourt.com; $$$; AE, DC, MC, V; checks OK.* ♿

## MENLO PARK

### RESTAURANTS

**Bistro La Luna** ★★ Flickering candlelight, not *la luna bonita*, illuminates the spare, golden-hued dining room, but the kitchen's what really shines at this small restaurant. The engaging owner,

Ali Elsafy, constantly updates the globe-trotting fare, which melds Italian, French, and California flavors with a heavy dose of *sabor Latino*. The menu might include chicken flautas or shrimp soup with corn and potatoes for starters, followed by a simply prepared but tasty roasted trout or chile pepper linguine with chicken and green onions. Vegetarians (or anyone in the mood for a light dish) might try the transportingly delicious roasted red bell pepper with basmati rice and tomato-corn sauce, accompanied by expertly cooked and seasoned spinach and mushrooms. There's a good selection of wines by the glass, but the dessert menu's limited, consisting mostly of basics like rice pudding, flan, and chocolate cake with vanilla ice cream. ▪ *1137 Chestnut St (between Santa Cruz and Oak Grove Aves), Menlo Park; (650)324-3810; $$; full bar; AE, MC, V; local checks OK; lunch Mon–Fri, dinner Mon–Sat.* &

**Carpaccio ★★** Carpaccio was started by the same folks responsible for the wildly successful Osteria in Palo Alto, but a parting of the ways has left this restaurant to evolve along its own lines. Carpaccio holds tightly to its Northern Italian roots, as evidenced by such dishes as the grilled polenta with tomatoes and pesto and the restaurant's namesake dish, served with onions, capers, lemon, and mustard, plus a grating of grana cheese and a drizzle of olive oil. The angel hair pasta sports a lively pomodoro sauce made from sweet, vine-ripened tomatoes and fresh basil. The real treat here is the free-range veal: the scaloppine features veal medallions and mushrooms, but those in search of the platonic veal ideal should choose the simple grilled chop. Also keep an eye out for the prosciutto-wrapped grilled prawns with garlic and shallots in a smooth lemon-cream sauce. The wood-burning oven (with bricks imported from Italy) turns out divine pizzas with premium toppings laced together with fresh mozzarella, Gorgonzola, and fennel sausage on wonderful smoke-flavored crusts. ▪ *1120 Crane St (between Oak Grove and Santa Cruz Aves), Menlo Park; (650)322-1211; $$; full bar; AE, DC, MC, V; no checks; lunch Mon–Fri, dinner every day.* &

**Dal Baffo ★★** A dignified fixture on the Peninsula dining scene for more than 20 years, Dal Baffo serves classic continental cuisine in a plush, old-fashioned setting. This is the type of place where tuxedo-clad waiters whip up caesar salads tableside while the kitchen delights traditionalists with its competent renderings of classic French and Italian dishes. The pasta, lamb, and beef entrees tend to be especially good; if you're in the mood for a magnificent hunk of meat, knife into the filet mignon with foie gras and a black truffle–wine sauce. The award-winning wine list is 4 inches thick and contains rare (not to mention incredibly expensive) selections that will make a connoisseur's heart go pitter-patter. ▪ *878 Santa Cruz Ave (at University Dr), Menlo Park;*

▼

**Menlo Park**

*Restaurants*

▲

*(650)325-1588; $$$; full bar; AE, DC, MC, V; no checks; lunch Mon–Fri, dinner Mon–Sat.* ♿

**Gombei Restaurant** ★★   See the review of this restaurant's San Jose location. ■ *1438 El Camino Real (3 blocks off Santa Cruz Ave), Menlo Park; (650)329-1799; $; beer and wine; no credit cards; no checks; lunch Mon–Fri, dinner every day.* ♿

**Flea Street Café** ★   Flea Street has come a long way since it was accused years ago of serving tasteless organic food. Now it wins respect for its unique brand of feisty California cuisine. Organic ingredients are still the rule, but the kitchen proves wholesome items can be put to innovative use. The appealing first courses might include a green onion–noodle cake with rock shrimp and shiitake mushrooms in a spicy Thai-style sauce, Dungeness crab cakes with crispy leeks and sun-dried peppers, and incredibly fresh salads. The Wild, Wild Pasta (fettuccine with mushrooms, wild rice, sun-dried tomatoes, and feta in an olive oil, oregano, and garlic sauce that comes mild or spicy, according to customer preference) and the smoked pork chop with dried cherry conserve and chile corn bread–andouille stuffing are two of the hearty entrees that demonstrate the kitchen's ability to meld diverse ingredients into a well-balanced entity. Vegetarians will also be happy here; there always a few interesting veggie dishes on the menu, and the kitchen will substitute tofu or another vegetarian filling for the meat in a number of other selections. ■ *3607 Alameda de las Pulgas (near Santa Cruz Ave), Menlo Park; (650)854-1226; $$; beer and wine; MC, V; checks OK; brunch Sun, lunch Tues–Fri, dinner Tues–Sun.* ♿

▼

▲

**Lisa's Tea Treasures** ★   This cozy little house by the train station is so precious, so neo-Victorian, and so pink that (if we can indulge in a bit of stereotyping here), most men probably would run screaming from the place. However, fans of Jane Austen, the British royal family, and anyone who likes a nice cuppa will feel right at home. Afternoon tea is served from late morning to late afternoon, and coordinated selections of flavored teas, savories, and sweets are centered around themes that sound as if they've been lifted straight out of a romance novel. The Duchess' Delight, for example, features a pot of boysenberry tea, a scone with Devonshire cream and preserves, cucumber tea sandwiches, shepherd's pie, and a lemon tart. (If it sounds as though the duchess really likes to chow down, keep in mind that we're talking about dainty portions of the aforementioned goodies.) The Venetian's Romance pairs amaretto-flavored tea with mini-calzones, pesto-and-nut sandwiches, and tiramisu, while My Lady's Respite favors Earl Grey tea, an assortment of delicate sandwiches, a petite herb soufflé, a scone, a little cheesecake, a petit four, and a tea cookie. There's even a fat-free spread (The Marquis' Light Delight) and one for children (The Court Jester's

Surprise). Extremely polite waitresses mince about in classic black-and-white maids' uniforms, and you get to ring a little china bell if they fail to anticipate your every desire. Yes, it's all a bit contrived, but Lisa's Tea Treasures does manage to whip up some tasty treats and make you feel pleasantly pampered. ■ *1145 Merrill St (between Santa Cruz and Oak Grove Aves), Menlo Park; (650)326-8327; $; no alcohol; MC, V; checks OK; full tea service offered at 11:30am, 2pm, and 4pm Tues–Sun.* ᏸ

**Vietnam Restaurant** ★   Yes, the walls could use a coat of paint, some new linoleum wouldn't hurt, and those paper lanterns have seen better days, but this family-run restaurant is still one of the best spots on the Peninsula for Vietnamese food. The spring rolls, available in both vegetarian and pork-filled versions, are to die for, and the earthen-pot rice, barbecue beef in grape leaves, and marinated grilled shrimp are highly recommended. If you're in doubt about what to order, the combination plate offers a harmonious selection of house specialties. ■ *1010 Doyle St (at Menlo Ave), Menlo Park; (650)326-2501; $; beer and wine; DIS, MC, V; no checks; lunch, dinner Tues–Sun.* ᏸ

## LODGINGS

**Stanford Park Hotel** ★★★   Cedar shingles, dormer windows, serene courtyards, and a copper-clad gabled roof distinguish this gracious low-rise hotel near Stanford University, just a credit card's throw from the wonderful Stanford Shopping Center. A massive brick fireplace and a sweeping oak staircase accent the attractive decor in the skylight-lit lobby. Some of the 163 rooms have fireplaces, balconies, vaulted ceilings, courtyard views, or parlors, and all are appointed with handsome English-style furniture and splashed with accents of green and mauve—a pleasant change from the timid beige-and-pastel color schemes found in so many other executive-class hotels. The Stanford Park provides a fitness room, a sauna, a heated pool, and a spa for its guests, as well as complimentary newspapers, morning coffee, turn-down service, fresh-baked cookies, and shuttle service within the Menlo Park–Palo Alto area. **The Duck Club** restaurant serves good American regional cuisine and, appropriately enough, duck is the specialty of the house. ■ *100 El Camino Real (just N of University Ave), Menlo Park, CA 94025; (650)322-1234 or (800)368-2468; www.wlodging.com; $$$; full bar; AE, DC, DIS, MC, V; checks OK; brunch Sun, breakfast, lunch, dinner every day.* ᏸ

## WOODSIDE

## RESTAURANTS

**John Bentley's Restaurant** ★★★   Housed in Woodside's first firehouse, John Bentley's resembles a snug cabin inside and out. But this is a classy kind of rustic, with wood paneling on the ceiling and walls, a potbelly stove, dangling light fixtures with ribbed-glass shades, chair backs fashioned out of verdigris wrought-iron leaves, and a brown-and-green color scheme that heightens the mountain-retreat mood. There's even an enclosed porch out back that's illuminated by strings of white lights in the evening. In keeping with the atmosphere of backwoods elegance, chef/owner John Bentley serves fare that's bold yet refined and generously laced with rarefied ingredients: lobster-ginger wontons in a delicate broth, ravioli stuffed with artichokes and caramelized onions, medallions of venison with shiitakes and braised red cabbage. With options like apple tart with sun-dried cherry ice cream and a milk chocolate crème brûlée so smooth it seemingly lacks molecules, desserts are a must here. ■ *2991 Woodside Rd (between Highway 280 and Cañada Rd), Woodside; (650)851-4988; $$$; beer and wine; AE, MC, V; local checks only; lunch Tues–Fri, dinner Tues–Sun.* &

**The Village Pub** ★★★ Don't let the name mislead you: this pub in the hills of Woodside is hardly typical of the genre—unless you're used to encountering a parking lot full of Mercedeses, Jaguars, and BMWs in front of your favorite watering hole. You won't exactly find bangers and mash on the menu either—think hearty California cuisine served in a classy, modern setting. Chef Kirke Byers's starters include Thai shrimp ravioli, wild mushrooms sautéed with pears served over goat cheese polenta with huckleberry essence, and raw tuna with wasabe coleslaw. Entrees cover a wide range of standards to suit the pickiest of eaters (seafood, steak, chicken, and pasta), and Byers goes out on a limb with a few creative specials every night. Some intriguing choices include fillet of salmon with a mustard-seed crust and brandy mashed potatoes, Australian lamb with figs and dried cherry pinot sauce, and wild mushroom pasta in a tarragon cream sauce. ■ *2967 Woodside Rd (½ mile west of Hwy 280), Woodside; (650)851-1294; $$$; full bar; AE, DC, DIS, MC, V; no checks; lunch Mon–Fri, dinner every day.* &

**Buck's** ★★ Since it opened in 1991, Jamis MacNiven's cheery and eccentric restaurant has become one of the most unlikely spots for power breakfasts in all of Silicon Valley. Where else can you find high-profile execs, entrepreneurs, and venture capitalists cutting deals as they chow down on huevos rancheros and silver-dollar pancakes under brightly painted cowboy hat lamps while life-size marlin figurines, a 6-foot plaster Statue of Liberty, and a flying horse look on? Most of the design touches—including palomino-colored walls, rows of natty cowboy boots, and a portrait of Mona Lisa decked out in a Stetson and bandanna—play into a tongue-in-cheek Western motif, a good fit in this wealthy, horsey community. The food, however, is a cut above chuck-wagon fare. Breakfast includes tasty and well-prepared renditions of the usual muffins, waffles, egg dishes, et cetera; lunch ranges from chili to hot Dungeness crab sandwiches; and dinner features a freewheeling menu that has everything from Yankee pot roast to chicken piccata "so tender it will sing you to sleep" (it says so right on the mock-newspaper-style menu). ■ *3062 Woodside Rd (near Cañada Rd), Woodside; (650) 851-8010; $$; full bar; AE, MC, V; no checks; breakfast, lunch, dinner every day.* &

## REDWOOD CITY

### *RESTAURANTS*

**The Redwood Cafe & Spice Company** ★★ This pretty blue Victorian house with lovely gardens is a welcome surprise in the midst of a rather gritty section of downtown. Celebrated for its wonderful breakfast dishes, the cafe serves soul-satisfying morning fare such as Swedish oatmeal pancakes with lingonberries or house-made applesauce; house-made muffins and scones; and 10 varieties of country egg scrambles, including a smoked salmon, spinach, and cream cheese mélange dubbed the Northern Lights. The cafe also attracts a sizable lunch crowd, drawn by the patio outside or the cozy atmosphere inside as much as by the homemade soups and tasty salads. Sandwiches range from comfortable old standards like chicken salad to more unusual offerings such as Nashelle's Shrimp Sandwich, which features tiny shrimp, creamy dill dressing, and cheddar cheese grilled on sourdough bread. On weekends, there's a well-priced prix-fixe brunch (you may bring your own champagne, if you're so inclined) offering a range of egg dishes as well as sweeter treats like Belgian waffles and pecan pancakes. Whatever the meal, the ingredients are always fresh, the service friendly, and the value outstanding. ■ *1020 Main St (at Middlefield Rd), Redwood City; (650) 366-1498; rwcafe@aol.com; $; no alcohol; AE, DC, DIS, MC, V; checks OK; breakfast Tues–Fri, brunch Sat–Sun, lunch Tues–Fri.* &

**2030** ★★ Wide, brick-parquet sidewalks, a bevy of attractive restaurants with outdoor cafe seating, and a parade of spiffed-up storefronts announce that gentrification has come to Redwood City, at least along this stretch of Broadway. One of the best spots to grab a bite on this handsome block is 2030, a stylish restaurant serving generous portions of California and American regional food. At lunchtime you'll find diners on the patio soaking up the rays along with imaginative salads, focaccia sandwiches, and entrees ranging from chicken potpie to agnolotti filled with chicken and prosciutto in an alfredo sauce. Dinners, which include a big bowl of soup and a salad, feature an exciting lineup of ever-changing entrees, which might include steak with a five-pepper crust and Cognac-chive butter, Dungeness crab cakes on linguine tossed with cayenne cream and corn, a double-thick pork chop with sweet potato sauce and pear ginger chutney, and smoked salmon ravioli with asparagus cream and sun-dried tomatoes. In the unlikely event you have room for dessert (portions are huge here), delicacies such as white chocolate cheesecake with warm chocolate sauce, almond brittle with Jamoca Almond Fudge ice cream, and berry shortcake with whipped cream await to sabotage any vestige of self-control. ■ *2030 Broadway (between Jefferson and Main Sts), Redwood City; (650) 363-2030; $$; full bar; AE, DIS, MC, V; no checks; lunch Mon–Fri, dinner every day.* ♿

### LODGINGS

**Hotel Sofitel San Francisco Bay** ★★★  This gray behemoth perched in a corporate park is distinguished by its pretty setting on a man-made lagoon and Gallic touches provided by the French management: filigreed ironwork above the entrance, old-fashioned Parisian street lamps scattered throughout the property, and a staff endowed with charming accents. The 319 spacious guest rooms are decorated in a French country motif and feature blond-wood furniture and amenities such as desks, remote-controlled TVs, voice mail, imported toiletries, minibars, and turn-down service. The lobby and restaurants boast a large sweep of windows that take full advantage of the Sofitel's waterfront location, and the hotel is equipped with a workout room, a parcourse, a health and beauty spa, and an outdoor pool. French regional food is served all day at the casual **Gigi Brasserie**, while the formal and well-regarded **Baccarat** restaurant specializes in classic French cuisine. ■ *223 Twin Dolphin Dr (turn on Shoreline Dr to reach the hotel's entrance), Redwood City, CA 94065; (650) 598-9000 or (800) SOFITEL; $$$; full bar; AE, DC, MC, V; checks OK; brunch Sun, breakfast, lunch, dinner every day.* ♿

## SAN CARLOS

### RESTAURANTS

**Creo La.** ★★★  It took awhile for this restaurant serving terrific New Orleans–style food to catch on in San Carlos, but now that the culinary cognoscenti know to ignore its inauspicious El Camino Real location and humble facade, Creo La. is coming into its own. Co-owner/chef Bud Deslatte has four other, similar restaurants to his credit—two in Atlanta and one each in New Orleans and San Diego—and he knows how to craft a menu that ably represents the new, lighter side of Creole and Cajun cooking. Deslatte goes right to the source for many of his dishes, flying out andouille sausage, gulf shrimp, and several other topnotch ingredients from Louisiana. For appetizers, try the Shrimp Bourbon Street (lightly battered, flash-fried prawns served with a tangy orange marmalade–horseradish sauce), Satchmo's Special (red beans and rice with andouille sausage rings), or the crawfish hush puppies with rémoulade sauce. Interesting salads are served, too, including a caesar topped with bacon-wrapped fried oysters, and the list of entrees includes everything from alligator piccata and pan-blackened catfish to chicken with corn-bread stuffing and crawfish étouffée. For a real taste of the bayou, go for the zesty Cajun Indulgence, a five-course sampler featuring red beans and rice, gumbo, salad, jambalaya, and bread pudding. Creo La.'s lineup of desserts includes a not-to-be-missed silky Cajun Velvet Pie with a light-as-air peanut butter mousse filling. ■ *344 El Camino Real (just N of Holly St), San Carlos; (650)654-0882; $$; beer and wine; AE, DC, DIS, MC, V; no checks; dinner Tues–Sat.* ♿

**Kabul Afghan Cuisine ★★** Afghanistan's national cuisine has roots ranging from the Mediterranean to Southeast Asia. This family-run establishment re-creates these tastes for Northern California with the highest-quality ingredients, including well-marbled meats and spices that the owners procure on trips to Asia and the Middle East. Set in a corner of a small shopping center, Kabul's spacious interior is unexpectedly atmospheric, with glimmering, candle-lit, whitewashed stucco walls studded with bright Afghani tapestries and costumes; pink and white tablecloths; and the low whine of sitar music humming discreetly in the background. The management and servers are charming and attentive (even when you wander in with children—the true test of a place's friendliness quotient). A few dishes shouldn't be missed: the fragrant char-broiled lamb chops marinated in yogurt, olive oil, fresh garlic, and black and white pepper; the splendid sautéed pumpkin topped with yogurt and a tomato-based ground-beef sauce; and *aushak* (leek-and-onion-filled dumplings topped with yogurt and a meat sauce). First-timers might enjoy Kabul's combination platter for lunch—a generous sampler of three popular appetizers. Another Kabul restaurant run by the same family is located in Sunnyvale. ■ *135 El Camino Real (in the San Carlos Plaza, between Holly St and Harbor Blvd), San Carlos; (650)594-2840; $$; beer and wine; AE, MC, V; checks OK; lunch Mon–Fri, dinner every day.* ♿

▼
**San Carlos**

*Restaurants*

▲

**Ristorante Piacere ★★** A welcome addition to downtown San Carlos, this mid-sized restaurant serves good Northern and Southern Italian cuisine in an attractive, modern setting that somehow manages to be stylish enough for a special night out yet friendly enough for family dining. Start your meal with *gamberi Piacere* (sautéed prawns with tomatoes, garlic, white wine, and mushrooms), grilled eggplant rolled with Gorgonzola cheese and tomato sauce, or imported prosciutto with fresh asparagus. Pastas include fettuccine with prawns and roasted garlic, and linguine enlivened by fresh mussels, tomato, garlic, and basil. The *secondi piatti* are particularly strong here, with such offerings as a zesty Italian sausage with vegetables and polenta, wood-fired pizzas, and *spiedini di gamberoni* (prawns cloaked in a light and lemony white wine sauce). Top off your meal with an espresso drink and one of Piacere's traditional Italian desserts, such as caffè affagato, gelato, and cheesecake. ■ *727 Laurel St (near*

## SAN MATEO

### RESTAURANTS

**Gibson** ★★★ Named after the onion-garnished classic cocktail and owned by the same folks who run the popular Rumpus in San Francisco, Gibson opened its doors in late 1996 and immediately made the A-list of Peninsula gourmets. Lively and sophisticated, the corner restaurant is fronted by plate glass windows on two sides, affording diners a prime see-and-be-seen perch on busy Third Avenue. Inside, large oil paintings punctuate the peach-colored walls, banquettes and chairs are swathed in a tapestrylike fabric bearing images culled from the Golden Age of Hollywood (think preening starlets and reels of film), and a row of stylized leaded-glass windows and iron-and-glass light fixtures lend art deco touches. Service is polished and professional from the moment you walk in the door, and, refreshingly, the staff isn't hesitant to offer knowledgeable opinions about the wine or the food when asked. Head chef Benjamin Davis, whose credits include stints at San Francisco's Cypress Club and Burlingame's Tavern Grill, specializes in a gutsy brand of California cuisine enhanced by Mediterranean and Asian influences. On one of his seasonal menus, stellar starters included squash ravioli with cranberries, sage, pistachios, and spinach; oysters on the half shell with fennel mignonette; and spicy gulf prawns coyly poised on dollops of white-bean purée. The salads featured marvelously fresh produce, and the entrees included such unusual fare as a moist and tender fillet of halibut steamed in a fragrant broth infused with lemongrass, ginger, and Thai chiles (absolutely wonderful!); slices of perfectly seared tuna accompanied by simmered burdock root; and marinated duck breast flanked by mustard spaetzle and Swiss chard. Desserts run the gamut from a classic crème brûlée to a marvelous, subtly flavored chèvre cheesecake. The far-ranging wine list is reasonably priced and as imaginative as the food. ■ *201 E 3rd Ave (at Ellsworth St), San Mateo; (650)344-6566; $$$; full bar; AE, DC, MC, V; local checks only; brunch Sun, lunch Mon–Fri, dinner every day.* &

▼

**San Mateo**

*Restaurants*

▲

**231 Ellsworth** ★★★ This upscale restaurant caters to the refined palates and well-padded wallets of old-money Peninsulites from Hillsborough and other tony suburbs. The pink-and-aqua color scheme seems a little dated, but it's still a pleasant stage for the ever-changing, predominantly French menu. Appetizers might include smoked rabbit with pear brûlée, oysters on the half shell with lemon-pepper ice and vodka, or a selection of forest mushrooms (a specialty here, since the owner also heads a mushroom company). A fillet of beef with hazelnut gnocchi, sweetbreads with black truffles and apple cider, and a roasted, marinated salmon topped with fresh chanterelle cream sauce are typical of the complex, compelling entrees. Primo desserts from celebrated pastry chef Phil Ogiela include an unusual and utterly delicious coriander soufflé and a delicate warm chocolate cake accompanied by a nest of chocolate curls holding a scoop of gelato and sorbet—heaven on a plate. The prodigious cellar offers more than 200 fine wines from Europe and California. Service is usually impeccable, although when the restaurant gets packed, the pace of the meal can sometimes be measured in geologic time. You'll also find a two-course prix-fixe lunch and a four-course dinner that are not outrageously priced. ■ *231 Ellsworth St (between 2nd and 3rd Aves), San Mateo; (650)347-7231; $$$; beer and wine; AE, DC, MC, V; checks OK; lunch Mon–Fri, dinner Mon–Sat.* &

**Viognier** ★★★ Among the many conundrums raised by the opening of Viognier—how to pronounce its name (roughly vee-on-YAY, a type of Rhône varietal), why an urbane, four-star chef like Gary Danko decided to set up a post in the 'burbs, et cetera—perhaps none is more vexing than figuring out exactly what to wear to dinner. The stylish ambience, the refined cuisine, and Danko's stature (former chef at San Francisco's Ritz-Carlton, the James Beard Foundation's 1995 Best Chef in California) all point toward somewhat formal attire. But, darn it all, one does feel just a tad foolish puttin' on the ritz for a restaurant plopped right in the middle of a supermarket, even one as upscale as Draeger's Market Place. However, once you've decided upon some sort of suitable outfit (maybe a running suit draped with an Hermès scarf?) and slid into one of Viognier's many comfortable booths, you'll relax and settle down to the more important matter at hand: choosing from the intriguing and wide-ranging menu.

Danko drew upon his 27 years of cooking experience to design a vigorous and wide-ranging brand of cuisine for his restaurant, which he describes as "Mediterranean with global influences." You'll find everything from the simple comforts of a perfectly roasted chicken and mashed potatoes to more rarefied delights like chilled lobster salad with mustard-tarragon vinaigrette or grilled quail with creamy polenta, arugula, pine nuts, and wild mushroom sauce. There are usually a couple of lamb dishes (Danko has always had a way with our woolly friends), as well as a roster of imaginative vegetarian dishes and specialties from the wood-burning oven such as smoked trout pizza with mozzarella and crème fraîche. Hearty eaters are hereby warned that portions can be so dainty they'd make a supermodel whine for more, so consider ordering one of the terrific side dishes—sautéed vegetables, roasted red potatoes with aioli, rosemary-flecked polenta—along with your entree. You'll probably still have room for dessert, which may include a frozen almond soufflé with warm chocolate sauce, port-roasted figs and peaches with raspberries and vanilla gelato, or polenta bread pudding with black-berries and lemon sauce. The light and airy 160-seat dining room echoes the menu's Mediterranean theme, with garlands of dried flowers and herbs, polished ash floors, a dramatic central fire-place of rough-hewn limestone bricks, windows outfitted with hand-loomed, raffialike shades, and an open kitchen. Patrons also have a view of Draeger's glass-enclosed culinary center, and when a cooking class is in full swing, Danko says he loves "the added sense of bustle and celebration of food it adds to the dining experience." Service is courteous and professional, and Viog-nier's award-winning sommelier, Joseph Stein, is happy to guide your selection from the extensive and extremely well-priced wine list. ■ *222 4th Ave (at B St), San Mateo; (650)685-3727; $$$; full bar; AE, DIS, MC, V; local checks only; brunch Sat–Sun, breakfast, lunch Mon–Fri, dinner every day.* &

**Bogie's at the Theatre** ★★ Although this amiable restaurant bills itself as an intimate 1940s-style joint where Bogart and Bacall could trade wisecracks and smoldering looks, the most adven-turous aspect to Bogie's may be the hunt to find it (it's hidden at the end of an arcade). This is an old-fashioned restaurant in the nicest sense of the word, serving well-prepared continental cuisine with a flourish of courtly service against an atmospheric back-drop of dark wood, mirrors, and posters of classic film stars. The seasonal menu might include pasta filled with fennel-flavored veal sausage, roasted breast of duck with spiced pears, wiener schnitzel with potato pancakes, and medallions of venison as meltingly tender as Bambi's glances at Faline. The well-chosen wine list leans toward expensive vintages. And don't forget dessert, which can be spectacular. ■ *60 E 3rd Ave (between El Camino Real and San Mateo Dr; look for the passageway near the Ben Franklin Hotel), San Mateo; (650)579-5911; $$; full bar; AE, DC, MC, V; no checks; lunch Tues–Fri, dinner Tues–Sun.* &

**Buffalo Grill** ★★ Here a Kuleto, there a Kuleto, everywhere a Kuleto—sometimes it seems that no one designs restaurants in the Bay Area these days except Pat Kuleto. Still, there's no denying the appeal that his sophisticated and playful South-western decor lends to this mallside restaurant. Good American regional cuisine—and plenty of it—is dished up in a friendly, high-voltage atmosphere. Chef Keith Lord, formerly of the Lark Creek Inn in Marin County, serves some interesting dishes, such as buffalo carpaccio, maple-cured pork chops with corn spoon-bread, and other robust, neo-heartland fare (the roast chicken with garlic mashed potatoes is exceptional). Desserts are smashing (the 10-mile-high devil's food cake with white choco-late ice cream is one perpetual favorite) and so gigantic you'll need help polishing off a serving. For some reason the quality of the food at lunchtime can be uneven, but the kitchen almost always shines at dinner. ■ *66 31st Ave (in the Hillsdale Mall, off El*

*Camino Real), San Mateo; (650)358-8777; $$; full bar; AE, DC, MC, V; no checks; lunch Mon–Sat, dinner every day.* &

**Lark Creek Cafe** ★★  In 1996, *uber* chef Bradley Ogden expanded his Lark Creek Inn empire by opening this inviting, casual-chic cafe on San Mateo's main drag. Chef John Mitchell continues the Lark Creek tradition of serving what Ogden likes to call "seasonal farm-fresh American fare," a concept that translates into updated versions of such stick-to-your-ribs dishes as chicken and dumplings, meat loaf and mashed potatoes, and spiral pasta with green beans, pesto, and goat-cheese ricotta. You'll also find burgers, pizza, sandwiches, salads, and Ogden's justly celebrated onion rings with blue-cheese dipping sauce. Every evening, a different American classic is featured—grilled liver with bacon and onions on Wednesday, a New England lobster and shellfish bake on Friday, prime rib on Saturday, et cetera. Portions are generous, and Lark Creek prides itself on scouring the local produce markets for the best raw ingredients. The smartly designed dining room, with its whimsical collection of gaily painted birdhouses, lark-bedecked light fixtures, roomy booths, and long bar counter, sports an inviting country-sophisticate look, and service is polished and friendly. The wine list is carefully chosen and concentrates on California selections. Another branch of this cafe is located in Walnut Creek. ■ *50 E 3rd Ave (near El Camino Real, in the Benjamin Franklin Hotel), San Mateo; (650)344-9444; $$; full bar; AE, DC, MC, V; no checks; lunch, dinner every day.* &

**Ristorante Capellini** ★★  Opened in 1990, this dapper, trilevel restaurant designed by (who else?) Pat Kuleto was one of the first to bring big-city sophistication to San Mateo's dining scene. Contemporary Northern Italian cuisine is served in a sumptuous setting characterized by a generous use of polished mahogany and an autumn-in-the-wine-country palette of burgundy, green, and gold; the best seats are the comfortable booths or the tables on the mezzanine level, which offer a bird's-eye view of the bustling bar scene. The antipasto, fried calamari, and *insalata con pera* (a seasonal salad of pears, endive, radicchio, arugula, pine nuts, and Gorgonzola in a champagne-shallot vinaigrette) make excellent starters. You might move on to one of the imaginative, thin-crusted pizzas or entrees such as sole piccata, veal Milanese, and steak with a merlot-mushroom sauce. The pasta is usually excellent here, light and cooked al dente; the long lineup includes linguine with assorted seafood, four-cheese ravioli in a lemon-pesto cream sauce, and penne with pancetta, tomatoes, garlic, mushrooms, and smoked mozzarella. The creamy tiramisu ranks as the most popular dessert, but the *torta di limone* and the warm bread pudding served with brandy hard sauce and a scoop of vanilla gelato also are winners. ■ *310 Baldwin Ave (at the corner of South B St), San Mateo; (650)348-2296; www.capellinis.com; $$$; full bar; AE, DC, MC, V; no checks; lunch Mon–Fri, dinner every day.* &

**Spiedo Ristorante** ★★  Good Italian regional fare is served in an attractive, modern setting at this family-friendly restaurant. The owners are justly proud of their mesquite-fired rotisserie, from which emerge herb-kissed and succulent chicken, game hen, rabbit, and duck. Savvy choices from the grill include the salmon, lamb chops, and pork cutlets. The kitchen also has a pleasant way with pasta, turning out delicate noodles flavored by interesting sauces; the agnolotti with smoked salmon and the *tortelloni di ànitra* (hat-shaped pasta filled with duck and zucchini in a sun-dried tomato and wild mushroom cream sauce) are two winners. Pizzas are quite good here, too. When it comes time for dessert, forsake the unremarkable gelato and opt for the tiramisu—the raspberry sauce gives this old standard an unexpected twist.
■ *223 4th Ave (between Ellsworth and B Sts), San Mateo; (650)375-0818; $$; full bar; AE, DC, MC, V; no checks; lunch, dinner every day.* ⅄

**Barley & Hopps** ★  This handsome trilevel restaurant and microbrewery in a historic brick building is one happening place. At lunchtime, a stylish professional crowd comes in for the all-American comfort food, such as tangy pulled-pork sandwiches, smoked chicken caesar salads, pizzas, ribs, and hot links. At nighttime, fun and games are also on the menu, as this something-for-everyone establishment hosts a blues club, a gaming parlor with pool tables, darts, and shuffleboard courts, and a thriving sports bar/singles scene in addition to the restaurant operation. Portions are huge, service is friendly, and the house brews—everything from oatmeal stout to root beer—are mighty fine. Children's menus are available, and families (along with everyone else who wants to hear themselves think) often opt for the quieter tables on the mezzanine. ■ *201 South B St (at 2nd Ave), San Mateo; (650)348-7808; barley@barleyhopps.com; www.barleyhopps.com; $$; full bar; AE, DC, MC, V; no checks; lunch Tues–Sat, dinner every day.* ⅄

## BURLINGAME

### RESTAURANTS

**Ecco** ★★  Recently remodeled and expanded, this California-continental restaurant with high ceilings and peach-painted walls caters to business types during lunch and an older, moneyed crowd at dinner. Although the overall ambience is one of formal comfort, the old-pro waitstaff dissipates any whiff of stuffiness with its exuberant, eccentric service. In one recent visit, for example, things were going a bit slow in the kitchen, so a couple of the waiters employed everything from free glasses of merlot to impromptu magic tricks with the napkins to help peckish customers while away the time. The food can be very good here, but sometimes, especially at dinner, it consists of the overblown, curiously flavorless fare that gives continental cuisine a bad rep. ■ *322*

*Lorton Ave (near Burlingame Ave), Burlingame; (650)342-7355; $$$; beer and wine; AE, DC, DIS, MC, V; no checks; lunch Mon–Fri, dinner Mon–Sat.* ⟨⟩

**Kuleto's** ★★  A spinoff of the popular San Francisco restaurant that bears the same name, this Burlingame branch immediately became one of the area's see-and-be-seen places when it opened in 1993. The sophisticated decor (which isn't, believe it or not, a product of the restaurant's namesake, designer Pat Kuleto) is bright and lively, with expanses of polished wood, a smattering of booths swathed in handsome fabrics, a large wood-burning oven, and a multilevel dining area. Alas, the Northern Italian food is not always as winning as the decor—it's not uncommon to see a diner swooning with ecstasy over a meal while her companion complains about his disappointing dish. However, the staff is often helpful about steering you through the menu's shoals, and the pizzas, salads, and many of the roast meats and pasta selections are noteworthy. ▪ *1095 Rollins Rd (just W of Hwy 101), Burlingame; (650)342-4922; $$; full bar; AE, DC, DIS, MC, V; no checks; lunch Mon–Fri, dinner every day.* ⟨⟩

▼

**Burlingame**

*Restaurants*

▲

**Tavern Grill** ★★  This upscale bar and grill opened in 1995 and immediately won raves for its stylish ambience and chef Benjamin Davis's delicious Cal-Med-American fare. Davis left a year later to head up the kitchen at San Mateo's Gibson, but his successor, Vince Nannini, is doing a fairly good job maintaining the quality of the food. Nannini has shifted the menu's focus to American bistro dishes, with starters such as smoked salmon on a corn and green-apple pancake with chive crème fraîche, andouille-crusted prawns, and smoked chicken ravioli on sweet-onion confit. Main courses include jambalaya with prawns, chicken, and sausage; grilled flatiron steak with balsamic syrup and horseradish mashed potatoes; and herb-crusted lamb chops with apple-mint relish and Creole mustard. The mango crème brûlée and the bittersweet chocolate torte are two stars on the dessert roster. The dining room has a California-meets-England feel, with a two-story bar, a large stone fireplace, wainscoting, and a Victorian-style lantern at the entrance. The bar scene is always hopping, and a wide variety of both live and recorded music is offered most nights; call for the entertainment lineup. If the noise level in the small, cramped dining area gets to you—it's loud even when a band isn't playing—head for the enclosed patio area in back with its heat lamps and drape of ivy. Service can range from charming to downright surly, efficient to space-cadetish. ▪ *1448 Burlingame Ave (4 doors E of El Camino), Burlingame; (650)344-5692; $$; full bar; AE, MC, V; no checks; dinner every day.* ⟨⟩

**Embassy Suites San Francisco–Airport–Burlingame** ★★★ This hotel's a towering pink-and-aqua spectacle more typical of the sunny Southland than Northern California. In front, a cobblestone drive encircles a Spanish-style fountain; just inside, another fountain gurgles in front of the junglelike atrium. Each of the 340 suites has a private bedroom and a separate living room complete with a refrigerator, wet bar, coffee-maker, microwave, two color televisions, two telephones, and a pull-out sofa bed. Ask for a room overlooking San Francisco Bay. You can amuse yourself by lounging in the indoor swimming pool or by checking out the action at **Bobby McGee's**, a popular singles bar and restaurant specializing in hearty fare like steaks, ribs, and chops. ■ *150 Anza Blvd (just off Hwy 101), Burlingame, CA 94010; (650)342-4600 or (800)EMBASSY; www.embassysuites.com; $$$; full bar; AE, DC, DIS, MC, V; checks OK; lunch Mon–Sat, dinner every day.* &

## MILLBRAE

*RESTAURANTS*

**Hong Kong Flower Lounge** ★★★ Hong Kong, probably the world's most competitive culinary arena, has hundreds of excellent restaurants vying to produce the freshest, subtlest, and most exciting flavors. In 1987 Alice Wong, whose family owns four Flower Lounges in and around that city, expanded their empire to California with a small restaurant on Millbrae's main drag. Its success prompted her to open another fancier branch on Millbrae Avenue, followed by another location in San Francisco (although the city branch doesn't win quite the same raves). Fortunately, the food at the Millbrae locations has remained legendary, thanks largely to the Hong Kong chefs, who continue to produce cuisine according to the stringent standards of their home city. The red, gold, and jade decor is pure Kowloon glitz (although the patrons are comfortably informal), and the service is outstanding. Among the best dishes on the vast menu are the exquisite minced squab in lettuce cups, the delicate crystal scallops in shrimp sauce, the fried prawns with walnuts, and any fish fresh from the live tank. An excellent Peking duck is served at a moderate price. ■ *51 Millbrae Ave (at El Camino Real), Millbrae; (650)878-8108 or (650)692-6666; $$; full bar; AE, DC, DIS, MC, V; no checks; lunch, dinner every day.* & ■ *1671 El Camino Real (at Parks Blvd), Millbrae; (650)588-9972; $$; beer and wine; AE, DC, DIS, MC, V; no checks; lunch, dinner every day.* &

**Millbrae**

*Restaurants*

## SOUTH SAN FRANCISCO

### *RESTAURANTS*

**Pasta Moon** ★★ See the review of this restaurant's Half Moon Bay location in the Central Coast chapter. ■ *425 Marina Blvd (take the Oyster Pt Blvd exit off Hwy 101, head toward the bay, and turn right at Marina Blvd), South San Francisco; (650) 737-7633; www.erslodging.com; $$$; full bar; AE, DC, DIS, MC, V; checks OK; lunch Mon–Fri, dinner Mon–Sat.* ♿

### *LODGINGS*

**Oyster Point Marina Inn** ★★ This small, pleasant hotel works hard to accentuate the positive (attractive, well-appointed rooms, a spectacular bay setting) and diminish the negative (the fact that you have to wade through an industrial park to get here). In keeping with its marina setting, the modern, Cape Cod–style inn is decked out in a snappy nautical-looking blue-and-white color scheme, and the 30 guest rooms have bay views and tile fireplaces. Some rooms come equipped with saunas, feather beds, and VCRs. A continental breakfast is included in the price of the room, and there's free shuttle service to nearby San Francisco International Airport (by prior arrangement). A branch of the popular **Pasta Moon** restaurant occupies part of the first floor, and its deck overlooks the marina and is a great place for lunch on a warm day (see review in the Half Moon Bay section of the Central Coast chapter). ■ *425 Marina Blvd (take the Oyster Pt Blvd exit off Hwy 101, head towards the bay, and turn right at Marina Blvd), South San Francisco, CA 94080; (650) 737-7633; www.erslodging.com; $$$; full bar; AE, DC, DIS, MC, V; checks OK; lunch Mon–Fri, dinner Mon–Sat.* ♿

# CENTRAL COAST

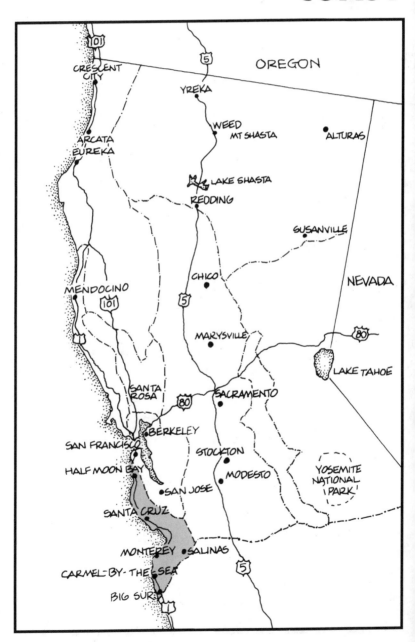

CRESCENT CITY
101
OREGON
5
YREKA
WEED
MT SHASTA
ALTURAS
ARCATA
EUREKA
LAKE SHASTA
REDDING
SUSANVILLE
MENDOCINO
CHICO
NEVADA
101
5
MARYSVILLE
80
LAKE TAHOE
SANTA ROSA
80
SACRAMENTO
BERKELEY
SAN FRANCISCO
STOCKTON
YOSEMITE NATIONAL PARK
HALF MOON BAY
MODESTO
SAN JOSE
SANTA CRUZ
MONTEREY
SALINAS
CARMEL-BY-THE-SEA
5
BIG SUR

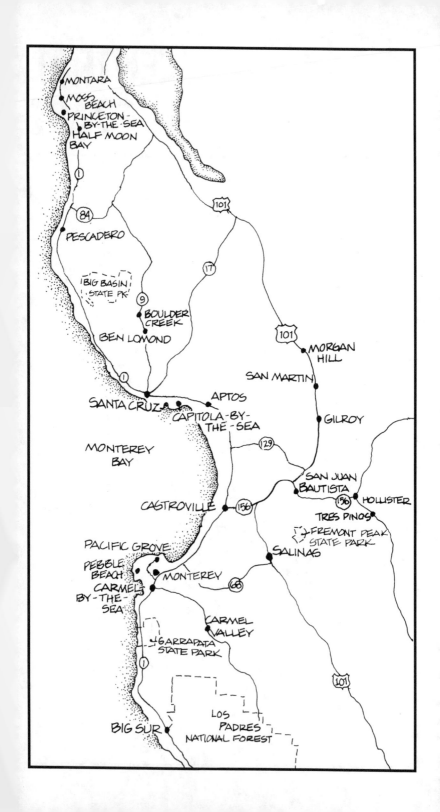

# Central Coast

*From Pacifica south along Highway 1 to Big Sur, with detours inland from Morgan Hill to Pinnacles National Monument, plus highlights of the Central Coast wine country. Note: The 831 area code in this chapter goes into effect July 11, 1998. Until that date, use area code 408.*

## PACIFICA

### *RESTAURANTS*

**Invitation House** ★★ Set on Rockaway Beach, this large, two-level restaurant serves very good Korean and Japanese food in a modern setting softened by Asian artifacts. Part of the restaurant has been transformed into a traditional tatami room with pillow-strewn straw mats and low-slung tables equipped with barbecue grills, and the rest of the airy, light-filled space features western-style blond-wood tables and chairs. The neon sign dangling over the sushi bar and the ceiling of angled fiberglass panels add vibrant dashes of color. The menu has some unexpected touches, too, with traditional Japanese appetizers such as gyoza (pork- and vegetable-filled pot-stickers) and robata yaki (grilled skewers of vegetables, seafood, and lamb) offered alongside a Western-style romaine salad and spinach crêpes filled with crab and leeks. Entrees range from tender tandoori dishes and fresh, expertly prepared sushi to Korean barbecue items like calamari and beef short ribs. Reasonably priced lunch specials are available on weekdays, though the chefs do a much better job with dinner than the midday meal. "Little prince and princess specials" will keep tots happy as they munch on pot-stickers or perhaps beef dumplings, while bigger kids might enjoy a turn at the karaoke machine. The service is as welcoming as the restaurant's name suggests. ■ *270 Rockaway Beach Ave (just W of Hwy 1), Pacifica; (650) 738-8588; $$; full bar; AE, DC, MC, V; no checks; lunch, dinner every day.* ♿

## MOSS BEACH

### *RESTAURANTS*

**Moss Beach Distillery** ★★ Used by bootleggers during Prohibition to store their illicit wares, this coastal grande dame was treated to a $2 million facelift in 1997, and the old gal's never looked better. With its blue-painted walls, cozy dining alcoves, and massive patio and windows affording magnificent ocean views, the cliff-side landmark still has its beguiling 1920s beach-house atmosphere, but new state-of-the-art kitchens have been installed, the old dirt parking lot paved, a downstairs dining area added, and the decor enhanced with mahogany ceilings, discreet spot lighting, and some rather racy stained-glass tableaux featuring celebratory bare-breasted women. The food has gotten considerably better, too, with new chef Scott Monfils (formerly of San Francisco's Fog City Diner) in charge of the kitchen. Gone is the pedestrian surf-and-turf fare that used to be the Distillery's lot; in its place are tasty, creative California-Mediterranean dishes such as grilled portobello mushrooms with cabernet sauce, shrimp tempura with a ginger vinaigrette, and a fork-tender pork chop enlivened by a mustard-shallot sauce and leek-buttermilk mashed potatoes. If the views, historical setting, and good food weren't enough, the Distillery also lays claim to a couple of resident ghosts, including the famous Blue Lady, a flapper-era beauty who's said to haunt the place searching for her faithless lover. If you're not in the mood for a complete meal, grab a seat on the patio at sunset, curl up in one of the blankets the management thoughtfully provides, and enjoy a drink and some treats from the bar menu as the sun slowly sinks into the Pacific. ■ *On Beach Way at Ocean Blvd (from Hwy 1, take the Cypress Ave turnoff and turn right on Marine Blvd, which turns into Beach Way), Moss Beach; (650) 728-5595; $$; full bar; DC, DIS, MC, V; no checks; brunch Sun, lunch Mon–Sat, dinner every day; patio menu available all day, every day.* &

### LODGINGS

**Seal Cove Inn** ★★★ Karen Brown Herbert (of *Country Inns* guidebook fame) knows what makes a superior bed and breakfast, and she didn't miss a trick when she and her husband, Rick, set up their own several years ago. The result is a gracious, sophisticated B&B that somehow manages to harmoniously blend California, New England, and European influences in a spectacular seacoast setting. The large, vaguely English-style country manor has 10 bedrooms that overlook a colorful half-acre wildflower garden dotted with birdhouses. All of the rooms have wood-burning fireplaces, fresh flowers, antique furnishings, original watercolors, grandfather clocks, hidden televisions with VCRs, and refrigerators stocked with free beverages. One thing's for sure: you won't starve here. Early in the morning, you'll find coffee and a newspaper outside your door, and later Herbert serves a full breakfast, wherever you prefer to eat. In the afternoon, wine and hors d'oeuvres are offered in the dining room, and at night, chocolates appear on the pillows of your turned-down bed.

The inn's extravagant backyard garden fronts open parkland with seaside meadows and a miniforest of cypress trees. On the other side of the park, about a quarter-mile away, is the Fitzgerald Marine Reserve, one of the area's best spots for exploring tide pools. Nearby are some interesting local restaurants, horseback riding on the beach, and a seaside bike trail. ■ *221 Cypress Ave (6 miles N of Half Moon Bay on Hwy 1, then W on Cypress Ave), Moss Beach, CA 94038; (650) 728-7325; sealcove@coastside.net; $$$; AE, DIS, MC, V; checks OK.* &

### RESTAURANTS

**Barbara's Fish Trap** ★ To get any closer to the ocean than Barbara's Fish Trap, you'd have to get your feet wet. Situated on stilts above the beach, the Fish Trap has indoor and outdoor dining with panoramic views of Half Moon Bay. The decor is classic fish 'n' chips style (complete with checkered plastic tablecloths, fishnets on the walls, and a wooden fisherman by the door), but the food is a cut above. Barbara's Fish Trap offers a selection of deep-fried seafood (calamari, rockfish, scallops, and prawns) as well as broiled fish such as Cajun-spiced snapper. The garlic prawns and steamed mussels are other good bets, and the french fries are fat and tasty. Kids can order from the children's menu, while adults may choose from more than 50 kinds of beer. ■ *281 Capistrano Rd (4 miles N of Half Moon Bay on Hwy 1, and W on Capistrano Rd), Princeton-by-the-Sea; (650) 728-7049; $$; beer and wine; no credit cards; checks OK; lunch, dinner every day.*

### LODGINGS

**Pillar Point Inn** ★★ Located on a bustling harbor with a commercial fishing fleet, sport-fishing and whale-watching charters, a few popular restaurants, and a busy pier, this modern inn is surprisingly quiet. Cheery and reminiscent of Cape Cod, the inn's 11 sunny, smallish rooms have harbor views, private baths, gas fireplaces, feather beds, and televisions with VCRs. Breakfast, served in the common room, includes coffee, juice, warm muffins, granola, and a hot dish such as waffles, scrambled eggs, or crêpes. Guests who request a spot of afternoon tea can enjoy it by the fire in the living room or outside on the sun deck. ■ *380 Capistrano Rd (4 miles N of Half Moon Bay on Hwy 1, then W on Capistrano Rd), Princeton-by-the-Sea; (650) 728-7377 or (800) 400-8281; mail: PO Box 388, El Granada, CA 94018; $$$; AE, MC, V; checks OK.*

▼

**Half Moon
Bay**

▲

## HALF MOON BAY

Old Victorian houses and small boutiques line downtown Half Moon Bay, the oldest city in San Mateo County, while produce stands, U-pick farms, and well-stocked nurseries ring its perimeter (artichokes, broccoli, and pumpkins are the town's prime crops). There are plenty of good beaches nearby, too: **Montara Beach** and **Saint Francis Beach** are arguably the most beautiful. Surfers congregate at (where else?) **Surfer's Beach** in El Granada and **Mavericks**, which is just south of Princeton-by-the-Sea and is known for its challenging (and sometimes lethal) waves. **Venice Beach** and **Dune Beach** are among the least crowded. For the best tide pools, explore the **Fitzgerald Marine Reserve** at nearby **Moss Beach** (and, if you can tear yourself away from the starfish, follow the south-side cliff trail to the eerily beautiful cypress forest and go down the rough-hewn stairs to another lovely little stretch of beach). Look for the signs on Highway 1 announcing the reserve; for more information call (650)728-3584. For seasonal **whale watching** (approximately December through March), call Huck Finn's Sport Fishing Tours, (650)726-7133, or Captain John's, (650)726-2913; both are located on Pillar Point Harbor, about 4 miles north of Half Moon Bay.

Every October, thousands of Bay Area families make their yearly pilgrimage to this picturesque seacoast town in search of the ultimate Halloween pumpkin. The **Half Moon Bay Pumpkin Festival** features all manner of squash cuisine and crafts, as well as the World Heavyweight Pumpkin Championship, a weigh-in contest won recently by a 375-pound monster. During the spring and summer months, the **weekend flower market** is a big draw, while year-round the city's fine restaurants lure folks from "over the hill" (the Coastsiders' term for inland San Mateo County). For specifics on the Pumpkin Festival and other local happenings, call the chamber of commerce at (650)726-5202.

## RESTAURANTS

**Pasta Moon ★★** Recent renovations have left this popular establishment spruce and spacious but, alas, the Moon's kitchen may be on the wane. It was once widely regarded as the area's best coastside restaurant, but the nouveau-Italian fare hasn't been up to past standards lately (perhaps executive chef Sean David Lynd needs to spend more time personally manning the stove). Fortunately, the baked-on-the-premises focaccia is still heavenly and the house-made pasta seldom disappoints; tempting possibilities include squash ravioli in sage butter sauce and tagliatelle with spicy Calabrese sausage and mushrooms. *Secondi piatti* might include roasted chicken and Tuscan potatoes or a braised lamb shank with garlic mashed potatoes. Pizza lovers can select from a wide range of thin-crust creations, including a daily special, cooked in the open kitchen's wood-burning oven. ■ *315 Main St (in the Tin Palace, at the N end of Main St, near Hwy 92), Half Moon Bay; (650)726-5125; $$; beer and wine; AE, DC, DIS, MC, V; local checks only; brunch Sun, lunch, dinner every day.* ♿ ■ *425 Marina Blvd (in the Oyster Point Marina Inn, off Oyster Pt Blvd), South San Francisco; (650)876-7090; $$; beer and wine; AE, DC, DIS, MC, V; local checks only; lunch Mon–Fri, dinner Mon–Sat.* ♿

**San Benito House ★★** A pastel blue Victorian on Half Moon Bay's Main Street, San Benito House has a candle-lit dining room that's one of the prettiest on the Central Coast, decorated with country antiques, vases of fresh flowers, and paintings by local turn-of-the-century artists. At lunch, the deli cafe turns out top-notch sandwiches on very fresh house-made bread—perfect to eat in the garden or on one of the nearby beaches. A trio of chefs—owner Greg Regan, Carol Mickelsen, and Lidia Machado—presides over the kitchen at dinnertime, turning out such interesting California-Mediterranean fare as homemade ravioli stuffed with fennel, fontina, and toasted almonds with creamy leek sauce, fillet of beef with Gorgonzola and herb butter, and salmon topped with a lemon-caper vinaigrette on a bed of lentil ragout. Desserts are terrific here, and may include such caloric wonders as a strawberry-rhubarb crêpe served with crème Anglaise and strawberry sauce, chocolate-espresso custard with Chantilly cream, and a pear poached with ginger and port wine. Too stuffed to move? Consider spending the night upstairs in one of the dozen modest but cheerful guest rooms (the one above the garden is the best). ■ *356 Main St (at Mill St), Half Moon Bay, CA 94019; (650) 726-3425; $$; full bar; AE, DC, MC, V; no checks in the restaurant, advance checks OK in the hotel; lunch (deli cafe only) every day, dinner (main restaurant only) Thurs–Sun.*

**Sushi Main Street** ★★ The food is Japanese, the decor is Balinese, and the background music might be anything from up-tempo Latin to bebop American. Hard to envision, yes, but these elements come together beautifully at Sushi Main Street, a funky yet tranquil oasis in the heart of town. The alluringly offbeat ambience blends Eastern elements such as the intricately carved wooden door and assorted Indonesian antiques with contemporary Western details like spot lighting, towering flower arrangements, and even a surfer-dude waiter complete with a Dobie Gillis goatee. Grab a seat at the L-shaped sushi bar, pull up a chair at one of the rust-colored asymmetrical slate tables or, if you're feeling limber, plunk yourself down at the large, low table designed for traditional cross-legged dining. You might want to tickle your tonsils with a drop of the special sake (served room temperature in a traditional wooden box) or nosh on a kelp salad (a crisp, sesame-laden mixture of Japanese seaweeds) before diving into your main course.

You can choose from a wide range of sushi and sashimi, from arctic surf clams to marinated mackerel. (For 40 cents extra, they'll even toss some uncooked quail eggs into your sushi rice.) Frankly, you're better off sticking to sushi and sashimi here—other typical Japanese dishes such as beef teriyaki and shrimp tempura are on the menu, but the kitchen doesn't seem to have the same enthusiasm for their preparation. For a Zen sense of wholeness, top off your meal with green-tea ice cream or a dessert roll with papaya, plum paste, sesame seeds, and teriyaki sauce. ■ *696 Mill St (just off Main St), Half Moon Bay; (650) 726-6336; www.SushiMainSt.com; $$; beer and wine; MC, V; checks OK; lunch Mon–Sat, dinner every day.* ዼ

**2 Fools Cafe and Market** ★★ Opened in 1993, this small, pleasantly modern restaurant has become a favorite with locals and visitors alike. Breakfast includes waffles and breakfast burritos, while the lunch menu concentrates on wonderfully fresh salads and sandwiches made with tasty, unusual breads. Dinner entrees

▼

**Half Moon Bay**

*Restaurants*

▲

run the gamut from a tangy buttermilk-roasted free-range chicken to an unusually subtle meat loaf (vegetarians can opt for the nut loaf alternative) to a simple but satisfying fried calamari with herb aioli. There's a special menu for tykes, and on warm days, diners of all ages might find the patio out back an inviting option. Everything on the menu may be ordered to go, and an ever-growing array of wines, teas, olives, jellies, and organically grown goodies is available for purchase. ■ *408 Main St (near Mill St), Half Moon Bay; (650) 712-1222; $$; beer and wine; MC, V; local checks only; breakfast, lunch every day, dinner Tues–Sun.* ♿

## LODGINGS

**Cypress Inn on Miramar Beach** ★★★ With Miramar Beach literally 10 steps away, this wonderful modern inn is *the* place to commune with the ocean along the Peninsula coast. From each of its 12 rooms you not only see the ocean, you hear it, smell it, even feel it when a fine mist drifts in with the morning fog. The cheerful wooden building, set at the end of a residential block, has beamed ceilings, skylights, terra-cotta tiles, colorful folk art, and warm, rustic furniture made of pine, heavy wicker, and leather—sort of a Santa-Fe-meets-California effect. Each room has a feather bed, a gas fireplace, its own bath, and an unobstructed ocean view. Most have private balconies, and the enormous penthouse also boasts a two-person soaking tub. Proprietors Dan Floyd and Suzie Lankes, who also own the stylish Inn at Depot Hill in Capitola, added a conference room, an outdoor hot tub, and four guest rooms that have such amenities as built-in stereo systems and hidden TVs. (The older rooms don't come with televisions, but the obliging innkeepers will put one in your room if you ask.)

The sidebar:

▼

**Half Moon Bay**

*Restaurants*

▲

The Cypress Inn's breakfast is far above the standard B&B fare—expect fresh juices, croissants, a fruit parfait, and made-to-order entrees such as eggs Benedict and the inn's signature peaches-and-cream French toast. In the afternoon you'll find an elaborate feast of wine and hors d'oeuvres (perhaps prosciutto and melon, freshly baked quiche, and fresh fruit pie) in the common room. And if the proximity to the sea, engaging decor, great food, and flawless service aren't enough to relax you, make a reservation for the tender ministrations of the in-house masseuse. ■ *407 Mirada Rd (drive 3 miles N of the junction of Hwys 92 and 1, turn W on Medio Rd, and follow it to the end), Half Moon Bay, CA 94019; (650) 726-6002 or (800) 83-BEACH; www. cypressinn.com; $$$; AE, MC, V; checks OK.* ♿

**Mill Rose Inn** ★★ One of the oldest bed and breakfasts on the Peninsula coast, the Mill Rose Inn fancies itself an old-fashioned English country house, with an extravagant garden and flower boxes as well as all the requisite lace curtains, antique beds, and nightstands. Romantics may love it here, but the inn's profusion of fabric flowers and slightly garish wallpapers (think William

Morris on LSD) take it over the top for many folks; frankly, the overall effect is more Harlequin romance than authentic British country manor. But, heck, that can be fun, too—and the rooms are spacious and chock-full of creature comforts, the hosts are friendly, and the Jacuzzi, tucked inside a frosted-glass gazebo, is quite enjoyable on a chilly coastal evening. The six guest rooms have private entrances and private baths, king- or queen-size feather beds, fireplaces (with the exception of the Baroque Rose Room), and views of the garden. They also have telephones, televisions with cable and VCRs, well-stocked refrigerators, fresh flowers, chocolates, and liqueurs. Two rooms, the Bordeaux and Renaissance Suites, have sitting rooms as well. In the morning, you'll find a newspaper outside your door and a full breakfast that you can enjoy in the dining area or in the privacy of your room. ■ *615 Mill St (1 block W of Main St), Half Moon Bay, CA 94019; (650) 726-9794; www.millroseinn.com; $$$; AE, DIS, MC, V; checks OK.*

**The Zaballa House** ★★ The oldest building in Half Moon Bay, this 1859 pastel blue Victorian offers a few amenities that go beyond the usual B&B offerings—including the ghost that reportedly walks through the wall in room 9 now and then. Homey, pretty, and unpretentious, the nine guest rooms in the main house are decorated with understated wallpaper and country furniture. Some have fireplaces, vaulted ceilings, or garden views. None have telephones, but three rooms have TVs.

**Half Moon Bay**

*Lodgings*

The gardens that once surrounded the building have been sacrificed for a recent addition (designed and painted to mimic this historic structure) housing stores, offices, and three attractive (and costlier) private-entrance suites. These new suites may lack spooks, but they offer some appealing extras: kitchenettes, double Jacuzzis, VCRs, and private decks. Each is decorated differently: *Casablanca*-inspired number 10 is a charming, airy room with skylights, ceiling fans, and light wood-and-wicker furniture; number 11 has a French country look; while room 12—the most opulent—uses red velvet and plaster pillars, busts, and cornices to create an over-the-top classical look that will thrill some and be Greek to others. Whether you're staying in the annex or the original structure, in the evening you may partake of wine, hors d'oeuvres, and cookies by the fireplace in the main house's snug, antique-filled living room. Come morning, guests are treated to a lavish buffet breakfast. ■ *324 Main St (at the N end of town), Half Moon Bay, CA 94019; (650) 726-9123; www.whistlere.com/zaballa; $$–$$$; AE, DIS, MC, V; checks OK.*

**Old Thyme Inn** ★ A comfortable and informal B&B, this 1899 Victorian house sits on the quiet southern end of Main Street. Floral wallpapers and bedspreads, rustic antiques, and lots of teddy bears grace the seven cozy guest rooms, each of which is named after one of the fragrant herbs in the inn's garden. The Thyme

Room has a double whirlpool tub, a fireplace, and a queen-size canopy bed. Behind the main house is a spacious detached unit, the Garden Suite, with a queen-size four-poster bed, a fireplace, a double whirlpool tub under a skylight, a TV with a VCR, and a refrigerator stocked with complimentary beverages. Hosts George and Marcia Dempsey are eager to please and knowledgeable about the area's attractions and restaurants. A full breakfast, served in the parlor, includes such items as Swedish egg cake, quiche, cinnamon-raisin scones, and seasonal fruit; refreshments are also provided in the evening. ■ *779 Main St (near Filbert St), Half Moon Bay, CA 94019; (650) 726-1616; oldthyme@coastside.net; www.inntraveler.com/oldthyme; $$–$$$; AE, MC, V; checks OK.*

## SAN GREGORIO

### *LODGINGS*

**Rancho San Gregorio** ★★ This Spanish Mission–style bed and breakfast, with its terra-cotta tile floors, heavy oak antiques, and redwood-beamed ceilings, is a well-tended, unpretentious home-away-from-home. The four guest rooms, decorated in Native American, Southwestern, and Early California motifs, boast such niceties as wood-burning stoves and stained-glass windows. Two of the rooms (San Gregorio and Corte Madera) have private decks overlooking farmland and wooded hills. The tranquil and lovely 15-acre grounds include a creek, an apple orchard, a gazebo, and flower and herb gardens. Ebullient and welcoming hosts Bud and Lee Raynor are eager to indoctrinate guests into the quiet wonders of the rural locale they call home. They also serve a mean "harvest breakfast feast" featuring ranch-grown organic produce, Lee's fresh baked breads, and deliciously hearty fare like artichoke frittata or Swedish egg cake. The away-from-it-all feeling is reinforced by the absence of TVs and phones in the rooms, although guests have access to a phone and a VCR with a 500-video movie library. ■ *5086 San Gregorio Rd (about 5 miles inland on Rte 84), San Gregorio; (650) 747-0810; mail: PO Box 21, San Gregorio, CA, 94074; rsgleebud@aol.com; $$–$$$; AE, DC, DIS, MC, V; checks OK.*

## PESCADERO

### *RESTAURANTS*

**Duarte's Tavern** ★★ Duarte's (pronounced "DO-arts") is a rustic gem, still owned and operated by members of the family that built it in 1894. Back then it was a place to buy a 10-cent shot of whiskey on the stagecoach ride from San Francisco to Santa Cruz. Now Duarte's is half bar, half restaurant, though it's still set in an Old West–style wood-and-stucco building near Pescadero's general store. The bar is dark and loud, filled with locals drinking beer, smoking, and spinning tales. The unassuming restaurant next door has checkered tablecloths and terrific coastal fare. Most of the fruits and vegetables come from the Duartes' own farms. Start with the flavorful cream of artichoke or green chile soup. The salads are a bit unimaginative, but the greens are fresh. For your entree, there are about a dozen kinds of fresh fish daily, as well as a selection of sandwiches, chops, and steaks. Portions are generous, but save room for dessert—the fruit pies are the stuff of local legend. After your meal, walk down the road to visit the oldest church on the Northern California coast and the interesting old graveyard just beyond it. ■ *202 Stage Rd (at Pescadero Creek Rd), Pescadero; (650)879-0464; $$; full bar; AE, MC, V; local checks only; breakfast, lunch, dinner every day.* &

## AÑO NUEVO STATE RESERVE

You're not the only one having fun in the sun: for a seaside sex show, pull off Highway 1 between the coastal towns of Pescadero and Davenport (22 miles north of Santa Cruz) at Año Nuevo State Reserve, a unique and fascinating breeding ground for **northern elephant seals**. A close encounter with a 16-foot-long, 2½-ton male elephant seal waving his humongous schnoz is an unforgettable event. Even more memorable is the sight of two males fighting and snorting (they can be heard for miles) over a harem of a few dozen females. The seals are named after the male's dangling proboscis, which can grow up to a couple of feet long. The reserve is open year-round, but you'll see hundreds of these marine mammals during their mating season, which starts in December and continues through March. To access the reserve during the mating season you must have a reservation on one of the 2½-hour naturalist-led tours (held rain or shine from December 15 through March 31). The tours are terrific and tickets are cheap, but they sell out fast, so plan about two months ahead (and don't forget to bring a jacket). Call ParkNet for tickets at (800)444-4445; for more information call (650)879-0227.

## DAVENPORT

### *LODGINGS*

**The Davenport Bed & Breakfast Inn** ★★ This pretty, rustic spot has a simple charm befitting this laid-back region of the coast. Artist-owners Bruce and Marcia McDougal have decorated the dozen rooms in a pleasing mélange of Native American, Victorian, and country motifs. If you're not likely to be bothered by traffic sounds from Highway 1 or music drifting up from the restaurant below, opt for one of the eight rooms in the main building. All have private baths and open onto a narrow wooden porch commanding inspiring views of ocean and cliffs; the grandest, Captain Davenport's Retreat, features two walls of windows framing the splendid vista. If it's peace and quiet you're after, forgo the view and settle down in one of the four slightly smaller rooms in the annex next door. The room rate includes a full breakfast and a complimentary drink at the **New Davenport Cash Store Restaurant**, an attractive, Old West–style bar and dining establishment serving well-prepared American and Mexican fare. ■ *31 Davenport Ave (right off Hwy 1), Davenport; (831)425-1818 or (800)870-1817; mail: PO Box J, Davenport, CA 95017; inn@ swanton.com; www.swanton.com; $$; full bar; inn: AE, MC, V, checks OK; restaurant: MC, V, no checks; breakfast, lunch, dinner every day.*

## BOULDER CREEK

### *RESTAURANTS*

**The White Cockade Public House** ★ Named for the white rosette that Bonnie Prince Charlie wore on his cap, the White Cockade earns high marks for authenticity in the pub department. Owners Barbara Stanford and Tom Cramer opened it in 1987 after returning from England and Scotland, and they have succeeded in transforming this once rough-and-tumble bar into a homey watering hole where there's always a cozy fire and a friendly game of darts in progress. Note their vast list of fine imported British ales, lagers, and stouts—there's not a single domestic beer in sight. This is also the place for some of the Bay Area's best genuine pub food: bangers and mash, house-made meat pies, and the like. ■ *18025 Hwy 9 (about 15 miles S of Saratoga, and 4½ miles N of town), Boulder Creek; (831)338-4148; $; beer and wine; no credit cards; local checks only; dinner Tues–Sun.*

## BEN LOMOND

### *RESTAURANTS*

**Ciao! Bella!!** ★★ This exuberant restaurant, nestled in a mountain redwood grove, serves what owner Tad Morgan describes as "new California-Italian" cuisine. In addition to nightly specials, there are always about a half-dozen pasta dishes, ranging from Tutto Mare (prawns, clams, calamari, and fresh fish sautéed in cream and white wine) to Penne alla Napoletana (penne with tomatoes, basil, garlic, and mozzarella tossed in a marinara sauce). *Secondi piatti* include scampi as well as chicken with prosciutto, mozzarella, and spinach, topped with a sauce of basil, tomatoes, and garlic. The staff is friendly and eager to please. ■ *9217 Hwy 9 (just S of town), Ben Lomond; (831)336-9221; $$; beer and wine; AE, DIS, MC, V; no checks; lunch Fri–Sun in the summer, dinner every day year-round.* ⅃

**Tyrolean Inn** ★★  Button up your lederhosen, raise your beer stein, and shout *"Gruss Gott!"* That's Austrian slang for "hello" and "good-bye." As you pass the plaster sculptures of rotund Teutons in the entryway, you'll be greeted by real live Austrians—the Wolf family—who will serve you amid the Tyrolean's fire-lit copper coziness and the unmistakable perfume of smoked pork. The generous portions of sauerbraten, goulash, sausage, and various schnitzels are served with sides of red cabbage and potato pancakes or noodles. Wash it all down with a European beer, some *Glühwein* (hot spiced wine), or even a shot of schnapps. ■ *9600 Hwy 9 (at Mill St), Ben Lomond; (831)336-5188; $$; full bar; AE, DC, DIS, MC, V; no checks; dinner Wed–Sun.*

*LODGINGS*

**Chateau des Fleurs** ★★  Owners Lee and Laura Jonas are some of the most down-to-earth folks you're likely to meet, yet their three-room B&B is full of elegant little surprises: huge, supersoft towels in every bathroom, billowy down comforters, hypnotic ceiling fans, and even a gazebo trimmed with little white fairy lights out front. The gabled 1879 Victorian home was once owned by the Bartlett family, and their legendary pear trees still line the drive. The Orchid Room has a small private deck outfitted with wicker furniture and surrounded by tall, fragrant redwoods. The Rose Room's appointments include a claw-footed bathtub regally displayed on a raised platform. Both rooms boast new fireplaces, and the Jonases also recently installed a pressed-tin ceiling in the dining room and a bay window in the common room, which is equipped with a wide-screen TV, a dart board, afternoon wine and hors d'oeuvres, books, magazines, musical instruments, and a trampoline. The inn's lush breakfasts might include velvety little soufflés, hot popovers with jam, and fresh fruit laced with mint. ■ *7995 Hwy 9 (just S of town), Ben Lomond, CA 95005; (831)336-8943 or (800)596-1133, ext. 5679; $$; AE, DIS, MC, V; checks OK.*

▼
**Central Coast Wine Country**
▲

## SCOTTS VALLEY

*RESTAURANTS*

**Tony & Alba's Pizza and Italian Food** ★  See the review of the Mountain View branch in the San Francisco Bay Area chapter. ■ *226 E Mount Herman Rd, Scotts Valley; (831)439-9999; $; beer and wine; AE, DC, DIS, MC, V; local checks only; lunch, dinner every day.* ♿

## CENTRAL COAST WINE COUNTRY

Back before the wine boom of the '70s and '80s, going on a wine-tasting trip was something of an adventure. However, Napa and, to a lesser degree, Sonoma have become major-league tourist stops in recent decades, and their wineries have put together elaborate tasting rooms and slick tours. But along California's Central Coast, it's still possible to find wineries on narrow backroads with nothing more than a small sign out front to indicate their presence. Once inside, you'll likely be greeted by the owner/winemaker who conducts tastings at a leisurely pace, with plenty of talk about winemaking. It's always a good idea to call ahead because you may need detailed directions to many of the tucked-away wineries, and tasting hours are often limited and sometimes quite irregular.

**Ridge Vineyards**, one of California's original "boutique" wineries, earned its reputation making superb zinfandel and cabernet; 17100 Montebello Road, Cupertino, (408)867-3233. **Sunrise Winery** uses grapes from its century-old vines to produce highly regarded estate zinfandel and pinot noir; 13100 Montebello Road, Cupertino, (408)741-1310. Bear Creek Road off Highway 17 is narrow and twisting, and features incredible vistas as you drive the 5 miles to **David Bruce Winery**; 21439 Bear Creek Road, Los Gatos, (408)354-4214 or (800)397-9972. Dr. Bruce makes wines with names like "Old Dog Red" and "Mr. and Mrs. Baggins," but his pinot noir and chardonnay are seriously good. A bit farther down the road is **Byington Winery and Vineyard**, which makes hearty cabernets in a big estatelike building overlooking a redwood forest and has a picnic area with an ocean view; 21850 Bear Creek Road, Los Gatos, (408)354-1111.

It's easy to get lost on your way to **Roudon-Smith Winery**, but its estate-grown chardonnay is worth the risk; 2364 Bean Creek Road (near Scotts Valley), Santa Cruz, (408)438-1244. If you want to find out why winemaker Randall Grahm named his Rhône-style red wine after a "flying cigar," visit **Bonny Doon Vineyard**; 10 Pine Flat Road, Santa Cruz, (831)425-3625. You'll have to make an appointment to try **Santa Cruz Mountain Vineyard's** pinot noir, cabernet sauvignon, merlot, and chardonnay; 2300 Jarvis Road, Santa Cruz, (831)426-6209. **Hallcrest Vineyards**, secreted away behind a residential neighborhood, is an easy-to-miss winery, but you won't want to miss its riesling; 379 Felton Empire Road, Felton, (831)335-4441.

The Hecker Pass Highway (aka State Route 152) in Gilroy is home to a number of wineries, some new, some old. **Solis Winery**, offering chardonnay and merlot as well as more unusual European varietals, is located in a refurbished 1917 winery building; 3920 Hecker Pass, Gilroy, (408)847-6306. **Fortino Winery** makes hearty, old-style reds, and has a wonderfully kitschy gift shop; 4525 Hecker Pass, Gilroy, (408)842-3305. **Thomas Kruse Winery** is owned by an enologist with a sense of humor and little tolerance for wine snobbery or hype. Read his back labels and laugh, but do try his chardonnay and zinfandel; on Dryden Road (call for directions), Gilroy, (408)842-7016. Back on Highway 101 at the intersection of Highway 25 is the **Rapazzini Winery**, which makes garlic wine, garlic jelly, and, believe it or not, garlic ice cream—

all of which taste better than they sound; 4350 Monterey Road,
Gilroy, (408)842-5649.

South of Salinas, the wine country continues. **Chalone Vineyards**, producers of legendary chardonnay and pinot noir, is located near Pinnacles National Monument on Stonewall Canyon Road at Highway 146, Soledad, (408)678-1717. **Smith and Hook Winery** is so far up a dirt road that after a while you'll think you made a wrong turn. But be patient—there's good cabernet and merlot just ahead, as well as a network of hiking and biking trails and a picnic area; 37700 Foothill Road, Soledad, (408)678-2132. **Jekel Vineyard** makes wonderful riesling and chardonnay a short distance away from homes and shopping centers; 40155 Walnut Avenue, Greenfield, (831)674-5522. Over in the Carmel Valley, **Château Julien** makes 60,000 cases of wine a year and has a pleasant tasting room and patio. Try the private reserve chardonnay and merlot; 8940 Carmel Valley Road, Carmel Valley, (831)624-2600.

## SANTA CRUZ

Santa Cruz is a chimerical place, skittering from diamond-bright beach to swampy slough to moody redwood grove to cafe society to rustic farm in just about the time it takes to say "Surf's up, dude!" The city rings the north end of Monterey Bay and is bisected by the San Lorenzo River, which spills into the sea. Santa Cruz (Spanish for "holy cross") was founded by the ubiquitous Father Junípero Serra when he built the **Mission of the Holy Cross** here in 1791. The mission was destroyed by earthquakes in 1857 and 1858, but a half-size replica of the building (built in 1931) is open to the public every day except Monday, offering morning masses and an opportunity to view some of the mission's original books and vestments; on the corner of Emmet and High Streets, (831)426-5686. Despite its holy beginnings, Santa Cruz is now a devil-may-care, saltwater-taffy seaside resort, embodied by both the wet-suit-clad surfer set and the roller-coaster world of the famous Santa Cruz Beach Boardwalk, where the roar of revelers mingles with the plaintive bark of California sea lions. But peer a little closer and you'll see the city's intellectual side, too, bolstered by the town's ultraliberal politics and a handsome **University of California** campus situated in a pretty, woodsy environment near town (you can visit the school's Web site at www.ucsc.edu).

Santa Cruz attracts more than three million visitors each year, and most of them flock to the half-mile-long, 100-year-old **Santa Cruz Beach Boardwalk**, the last remaining beachfront amusement park on the West Coast. Take a spin on the famous **Giant Dipper**, one of the best and oldest wooden roller coasters in the country (with a great view at the top), then grab a seat on one of the intricately hand-carved horses on the 1911 **Looff Carousel** (both rides are listed on the National Register of Historic Places). Of course, the Boardwalk (now a cement walk) also caters to hard-core thrill-seekers who yearn for those state-of-the-art, whirl-and-twirl rides that do their best to make you lose your lunch. Buy the reasonably priced day pass and stand in line for rides like Riptide and the Bermuda Triangle, and you won't be disappointed. If you're among the crowds here on a Friday night in the summer, don't miss the Boardwalk's free concerts, featuring the likes of the Shirelles, Chubby Checker, and Sha Na Na. The Boardwalk is at 400 Beach Street; call (831) 423-5590 for current prices and events.

Beaches are Santa Cruz's other crowning glory. At the western edge of the city, on the north end of West Cliff Drive, is **Natural Bridges State Beach**, named after archways carved into the rock formations here by the ocean waves (only one of the three original arches still stands). The beach is popular with surfers, windsurfers, tide-pool trekkers, and sunbathers, as well as fans of the migrating **Monarch butterflies** that roost in the nearby eucalyptus grove from late October through February. On the south end of West Cliff Drive is **Lighthouse Field State Beach**, the reputed birthplace of American surfing. This beach has several benches for sitting and gazing, a jogging and bicycling path, and a park with picnic tables, showers, and even

*Santa Cruz*

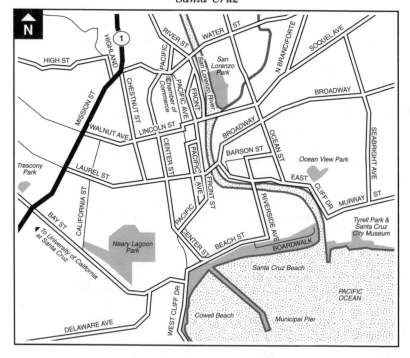

plastic-bag dispensers for cleaning up after your dog (it's one of the few public places in town where canines are allowed). The nearby brick lighthouse is now home to the tiny **Santa Cruz Surfing Museum** (the first of its kind in the world), which is chock-full of hang-ten memorabilia (admission is free); located on West Cliff Drive at Lighthouse Point, (831)429-3429.

Between the lighthouse and the Boardwalk is that famous strip of the sea known as **Steamers Lane**, the summa cum laude of California surfing spots (savvy surfers say *this*—not Southern California—is the place to catch the best breaks in the state). Watch the dudes ride the gnarly waves, then head over to the marvelous (but often crowded) white-sand **Santa Cruz Beach** fronting the Boardwalk. The breakers are tamer here, and free volleyball courts and barbecue pits make this a favorite spot for sunbathing, swimming, picnicking, and playing volleyball on the sand courts. In the center of the action is the 85-year-old **Municipal Wharf**, where you can drive your car out to the shops, fish markets, and seafood restaurants.

The **Pacific Garden Mall** (aka **Pacific Avenue**) is Santa Cruz's main shopping district, and until the Loma Prieta earthquake hit in 1989, it was a charming amalgam of Victorian houses, street musicians, bag ladies and gentlemen, inexpensive restaurants, bookstores, antique shops, and New Age head shops. It's recuperating slowly from the apocalypse (the earthquake's epicenter was only 10 miles away), but there's still plenty to gawk at. As you make your way down the mall, look for the **Octagon Building**, an ornate, eight-sided Victorian brick edifice built in 1882 that has survived numerous quakes. The building once served as the city's Hall of Records and is now part of the **McPherson Center for Art and History**, where museums showcase 10,000 years of the area's past as well as contemporary art of the Pacific Rim; 705 Front Street at Cooper Street, (831)429-1964. Next door is the excellent **Visitor's Information Center**; 701 Front Street, (800)833-3494.

▼

**Santa Cruz**

▲

The nearby **Bookshop Santa Cruz** has an inventory worthy of any university town, with a particularly good children's section, an adjacent coffeehouse, and plenty of places to sit, sip, and read a bit of your prospective purchase; 1520 Pacific Avenue, (831)423-0900. For great organically grown produce and other picnic-basket goodies, shop at the **Farmer's Market**, held Wednesday from 2:30pm to 6:30pm on Lincoln Street, between Pacific Avenue and Cedar Street. Another town highlight is the small aquarium and marine exhibits at the **Joseph M. Long Marine Laboratory**, where you can handle mollusks and other small sea creatures. You can also see scientists studying dolphins and sea lions in the lab's marine mammals pools; 100 Shaffer Road, (831)459-4308, www.ucsc.edu/mb/lml/.

For some serious hiking and mountain biking, drive about 23 miles north to the 18,000-acre **Big Basin Redwoods State Park**,

California's first state park (established in 1902) and its second-largest redwood preserve. Big Basin is home to black-tailed deer and mountain lions, and 80 miles of trails wind past 300-foot-high redwoods and many waterfalls. Some trails even access the long golden strand of **Waddell Creek Beach**; 21600 Big Basin Way, off Highway 236, 9 miles north of Boulder Creek (call for recorded directions), (831)338-8860.

Locomotive lovers, kids, and fans of Mother Nature should hop aboard the historic narrow-gauge **Roaring Camp Train** for a 6-mile round-trip excursion up some of the steepest grades in North America. The steam-powered train winds through stately redwood groves to the summit of **Bear Mountain**. Another train, called the **Big Trees Railroad**, offers an 18-mile round-trip ride through mountain tunnels and along ridges with spectacular views of the San Lorenzo River before stopping at the Santa Cruz Beach Boardwalk. To reach the **Roaring Camp and Big Trees Narrow-Gauge Railroad** center, take Highway 17 to the Mount Herman Road exit, then turn on Graham Hill Road (near the town of Felton). Train schedules vary seasonally; call (831)335-4400 for more details.

## RESTAURANTS

**O'mei Restaurant** ★★★ Named after a mountain in the Sichuan province of China, this acclaimed Chinese restaurant is a wondrous little paradox tucked into one of Santa Cruz's many strip malls. Owner/chef Roger Grigsby is not Chinese, nor are any of his cooks, but his food caters less to American sensibilities than do most Chinese restaurants. While you may order predictable northern Chinese offerings such as Mongolian beef and mu-shu pork, those with adventurous palates are better served if they forgo the old standbys. Pushing the envelope of Chinese cuisine, O'mei offers tasty provincial curiosities such as litchi chicken, leg of lamb sautéed with hot-and-sour cabbage, and an enchanting black sesame ice cream. Another plus: O'mei boasts a limited but well-chosen wine list, with all wines available by the glass. ■ *2316 Mission St (near Fair Ave), Santa Cruz; (831)425-8458; $$; beer and wine; AE, MC, V; no checks; lunch Mon–Fri, dinner every day.* ⅟

**Oswald** ★★★ Thanks to chef Charlie Deal's adept cooking, reverence for fresh produce, and restrained spicing and saucing that let the flavors of the principal ingredients sing out loud and clear, this small California-French bistro will remind you of Berkeley's celebrated Chez Panisse. The dining room has a spare, arty look, with bold still-life paintings on the brick and pale yellow-painted walls, high ceilings, wooden banquettes, and a petite wrought-iron-railed balcony set with a couple of tables. Chef Deal's small seasonal menu is supplemented nightly by a roster of specials that take good advantage of the best meats and veggies in the markets that day (organic whenever possible). Expect starters such as plump pork and shrimp raviolis nestled in broth flecked with slivers of asparagus and mushrooms, steamed mussels with fried bread and aioli, and a butter lettuce salad with shaved fennel, delicate wedges of citrus, and green olives. Entrees might include savory Gruyère bread pudding with asparagus and leeks, buttermilk-fried chicken with an herbed potato and carrot chowder, and seared ahi tuna with scallion-potato cakes and a roasted beet and endive salad. There's always a very reasonably priced three-course vegetarian tasting menu, and desserts often feature seasonal fruit—two more indications of Deal's love affair with exceptional produce, no doubt fostered during his previous stint at San Francisco's famous Greens restaurant. The servers are knowledgeable and solicitous, and the wine list features a good lineup of both California and French offerings. ■ *1547 Pacific Ave (use the parking lot on Cedar St and enter the restaurant through the courtyard), Santa Cruz; (831)423-7427; www.oswald. com; $$; beer and wine; AE, DC, MC, V; local checks OK; dinner every day.* &

**Ristorante Avanti ★★★** Newcomers who take one look at this unpretentious restaurant set in a humble strip mall may be forgiven for thinking, "Three-star restaurant? I don't think so." Ah, but wait until they've tasted the food and sampled the considerate, professional service—they'll be sorry for doubting our stellar designation. In keeping with the Santa Cruz lifestyle, Avanti prides itself on serving "the healthiest meal possible" (think fresh, organic produce and free-range chicken, veal, and lamb). The modern, casual decor, with a long wooden counter dominating one of the small rooms and posters of Italy scattered throughout, provides a welcome setting for aromatic, seasonal dishes such as sweet squash ravioli with sage butter, lasagne primavera, spaghetti with wild-mushroom and shallot duxelles, and orecchiette with salmon, Italian greens, mushrooms, and sun-dried tomatoes. The grilled lemon chicken, salmon with roasted garlic cream sauce, and balsamic-vinegar-marinated lamb chops also demonstrate the kitchen's skillful and delicate touch, and you simply can't go wrong with the daily specials. The ample and reasonably priced wine list contains selections from California, Spain, and Italy, and don't even think about skipping dessert— any of the ever-changing selections is worth an extra 20 minutes on the Stairmaster. ■ *1711 Mission St (near Bay St), Santa Cruz; (831)427-0135; $$; beer and wine; AE, MC, V; local checks only; breakfast, lunch, dinner every day.* &

**Santa Cruz**

*Restaurants*

▲

**Casablanca Restaurant ★★** There's nothing very Moroccan about this boardwalk bastion of California-continental cuisine, except, perhaps, the palpable air of romance. Soft music fills the candle-lit dining room, and stars wink on the water outside the window—you know, the sort of place where you get the urge to hold hands across the table. Chef Scott Cater, who worked here in the '80s and recently returned to Casablanca, has crafted a regional American menu with European accents. Starters include fried calamari with a spicy lime dipping sauce, lobster chowder, and fried brie served with jalapeño jelly and toast rounds. Entrees range from grilled Hawaiian swordfish served on a bed of garlic-herb linguine to a cilantro-marinated chicken breast with garlic whipped potatoes and sun-dried-tomato pesto. Local wines share a book-length wine list with selections from Italy, Germany, France, and Australia. ▪ *101 Main St (at Beach St, on the waterfront), Santa Cruz; (831)426-9063; $$$; full bar; AE, DC, DIS, MC, V; checks OK; brunch Sun, dinner every day.*

**El Palomar** ★★ Even on a rainy day, this lovely, vibrant restaurant hidden at the back of a former '30s hotel manages to create a sunny atmosphere. Maybe it's the tall vaulted-and-beamed ceiling painted in the Spanish manner, the huge mural depicting a Mexican waterfront village scene, or all the plants in big ceramic urns, but something about the place puts you in a good frame of mind even before the food shows up. When it does, your disposition is sure to be further enhanced. Peruse the imaginative, extensive menu while sipping an Ultimate Margarita and munching on delicate tortilla chips still warm from the oven. El Palomar is known for its seafood dishes, which are topped with exotic sauces, but traditional Mexican favorites such as burritos and tacos are also outstanding. A casual new sister restaurant, **Cafe El Palomar**, serves breakfast, lunch, and "taco cafe" fare beside the Santa Cruz harbor from 7am to 7pm. ▪ *1336 Pacific Ave (in the Pacific Garden Mall, near Soquel Ave), Santa Cruz; (831)425-7575; $$; full bar; AE, DIS, MC, V; local checks only; brunch Sun, lunch, dinner every day.* ♿ ▪ *Cafe El Palomar: 2222 E Cliff Dr (at the Santa Cruz Harbor), Santa Cruz; (831)462-4248; $; beer and wine; MC, V; no checks; breakfast, lunch, early dinner every day.* ♿

**Crow's Nest** ★ This large, multilevel seaside restaurant offers a heated, glassed-in deck that's an uncommonly pleasant place to watch boats cruise in and out of Santa Cruz Harbor. The food at the Crow's Nest isn't exactly gourmet, but the steaks, seafood, chicken, and salads are competently prepared and tasty. The staff is friendly and efficient, and there's a bar area for drinks and light eats. Young mateys can choose from a bargain-priced children's menu, then top off their meal with a little toy from the treasure chest. All in all, it's hard to think of a more relaxing and scenic place for a casual repast. ▪ *2218 E Cliff Dr (at the Santa Cruz Harbor), Santa Cruz; (831)476-4560; $$; full bar; AE, DC, DIS, MC, V; no checks; lunch, dinner every day.* ♿

**Tony & Alba's Pizza and Italian Food** ★ See the review of this restaurant's Mountain View branch in the San Francisco Bay Area chapter. ▪ *817 Soquel Ave, Santa Cruz; (831)425-8669; $;*

*beer and wine; AE, DC, DIS, MC, V; local checks only; lunch,*
*dinner every day.* &

## LODGINGS

**The Babbling Brook Inn** ★★ Secreted in a fantastical garden with
waterfalls, wishing wells, gazebos, and, of course, a babbling
brook, Santa Cruz's oldest B&B offers 13 rooms, mostly named
after famous artists. The mauve-and-blue Van Gogh Room has a
private deck, a fireplace, a beamed ceiling, and a whirlpool tub for
two. Peach and ivory predominate in the Cézanne Room, with its
generous bath and canopy bed. The blue-and-white Monet Room
has a corner fireplace, a canopy bed, a private deck, and a view of
the waterfall and footbridge. In the morning, chatty and enthusiastic innkeeper Helen King lays out a delectable spread of fruit
compote, banana muffins, croissants, French toast, fresh-
squeezed orange juice, yogurt, fresh coffee, and more. She'll
even whip up dishes for guests with special diets. You may eat in
the luxurious dining room, on the flowery patio, or in your suite.
■ *1025 Laurel St (near California St), Santa Cruz, CA 95060;
(831)427-2437 or (800)866-1131; www.virtualcities.com; $$–$$$;
AE, DC, DIS, MC, V; checks OK.* &

**The Darling House: A Bed and Breakfast Inn by the Sea** ★★ There
are probably no better views (and no softer carpeting) in all of
Santa Cruz than those you'll find at the Darling House, a Spanish
Revival mansion built as a summer home for a Colorado cattle
baron in 1910. From its postcard-perfect location in a posh residential neighborhood, you can see endless miles of gray-blue sea,
boats, seagulls, and the lights of faraway towns. On chilly days
you'll always find a fire crackling in the living room's glorious art
deco fireplace. The Pacific Ocean Room, upstairs, is decorated
like a sea captain's quarters, with a telescope and huge polished
seashells. Across the hall, the Chinese Room features brightly
colored lanterns and an exotic canopied Chinese wedding bed.
The cottage out back has a kitchenette, a wood-burning stove,
a living room, a claw-footed tub, and a queen-size canopy bed.
Owners Darrell and Karen Darling have worked hard to preserve
the house's intricate woodwork and have outfitted all eight guest
rooms with museum-quality antiques. There's a hot tub in the
backyard, and there are fluffy white robes in every closet. The
incredibly attentive Darrell will even call to make sure a restaurant's evening menu is to your liking. Karen's breakfasts include
fresh fruit, homemade granola made with walnuts from the Dar-
lings' farm, and oven-fresh breads and pastries. ■ *314 W Cliff Dr
(between the pier and the lighthouse), Santa Cruz, CA 95060;
(831)458-1958 or (800)458-1958; $$$; AE, DIS, MC, V; checks OK.*

**Cliff Crest Bed and Breakfast Inn** ★ History, the allure of an
antique-laden Victorian house, and views of the Santa Cruz
Boardwalk and the bay beyond are all a part of this welcoming

five-room B&B. With grounds designed by Golden Gate Park architect John McLaren, this 1887 Queen Anne inn is the former home of Lieutenant Governor William Jeter and his even more formidable wife, Jenny. Mrs. Jeter, who lived here until her death at age 99, reportedly used her cane to keep unruly nieces and nephews in line and insisted on driving her horse and buggy into town until the authorities prevailed upon the 89-year-old dowager to desist in 1949. These days, guests are greeted by the charming and, rest assured, far more easygoing hosts Bruce and Sharon Taylor. They'll invite you into their cozy sitting room/breakfast nook, complete with fireplace, antique furniture, old-time Jeter family photos—and a view of the Boardwalk's Hurricane roller coaster. Some painting and minor carpentry wouldn't be amiss, but the lack of these doesn't really detract from the feeling of old Santa Cruz charm fostered by the inn's intricate woodwork, stained glass, intriguing nooks, claw-footed tubs, and converted gaslight fixtures. The Rose Room boasts bay views, a sitting area, and an Eastlake bed, while the more modest Jenny's Room offers a window seat and a shower reputedly large enough for three (Aunt Jenny must be turning in her grave). Two other guest rooms have fireplaces. All the rooms are equipped with telephones, TVs are available upon request, and the complimentary full breakfast may be served in bed or on the garden terrace outside. ■ *407 Cliff St (near 3rd St), Santa Cruz, CA 95060; (831) 427-2609; innkpr@cliffcrestinn.com; $$–$$$; AE, MC, V; checks OK.*

## CAPITOLA-BY-THE-SEA

Just east of Santa Cruz sits Capitola-by-the-Sea, a tiny, very popular resort town nestled around a small bay. The intimate downtown is only a few blocks long; it's a quaint, jumbled mix of restaurants, gift shops, and beachwear boutiques reminiscent of resort towns of yesteryear. Capitola's broad, sandy beach attracts lots of sun worshipers, primarily because it's sheltered from the wind; it's also bordered by a charming promenade. At the west end of town is the bustling 867-foot-long **Capitola Pier**—a great place to hang out, admire the view of the town, and, on weekends, listen to live music. Many **anglers** come here to try their luck at reeling in the big one (and you don't need a license to fish from a pier in California). If you'd rather try your luck out at sea, visit Capitola Boat & Bait at the end of the pier. Even if you don't know an outboard from a Ouija board, the friendly staff has faith that you'll bring their fishing boats back in one piece. Rates are reasonable and include fuel, safety equipment, and a map of the hot fishing spots. You can also rent fishing gear and purchase one-day licenses, so there's no excuse not to brave the open ocean just for the halibut; closed January to mid-February, 1400 Wharf Road, (831) 462-2208.

**Gayle's Bakery & Rosticceria** ★★ Take a number and stand in line. It's worth the wait at this wildly popular place, which is packed with local folk on weekend mornings. A self-service bakery and deli, Gayle's offers numerous imaginative sandwiches, pastas, casseroles, roasted meats, salads, cheeses, appetizers, breads, and treats. The variety is staggering and the quality topnotch. There's a good selection of wine, beer, bottled water, and espresso drinks, too. Once you've fought your way to the counter, you'll have the makings of a first-class picnic to take to one of the nearby parks or beaches. You can also eat your feast in the cafe's small dining area or on the heated patio. ■ *504 Bay Ave (by Capitola Ave), Capitola-by-the-Sea; (831) 462-1200; $; beer and wine; MC, V; checks OK; open 6:30am-8:30pm every day.* ⅄

**Shadowbrook Restaurant** ★★ While locals are forever undecided about the quality of the food at Shadowbrook, they nevertheless insist that all Santa Cruz visitors dine here at least once in their lives. It's just such a fun place to eat—even its detractors delight in escorting their guests aboard the funicular that runs down through the ferny woods, past a waterfall, to the multistoried, woodsy restaurant bedecked in white lights. Lately, Shadowbrook has been paying more attention to the food, resulting in a well-crafted, seasonal California-Mediterranean menu. Starters might include artichoke hearts with lime-cilantro sauce, tender calamari strips served with a zesty pineapple-chile sauce, or a Tuscan salad with frisée, rock shrimp, pancetta, white beans, and goat-cheese croutons. Some of the better entrees are tender braised lamb shank, bacon-wrapped prawns with creamy polenta, and swordfish. Mud pie and cheesecake remain the most popular desserts. The best seat in the house is at the alfresco tables on the brickwork terraces, nestled romantically among rock gardens and rhododendrons. Management recently remodeled the entryway, allowing diners to eat in the informal bar area with a view of the waterfalls and gardens. ■ *1750 Wharf Rd (near the end of Capitola Rd), Capitola-by-the-Sea; (408) 475-1511; michael@ shadowbrook-capitola.com; $$$; full bar; AE, DC, DIS, MC, V; local checks only; brunch Sun, dinner every day.*

**Capitola-by-the-Sea**

*Lodgings*

**Tony & Alba's Pizza and Italian Food** ★ See the review of this restaurant's Mountain View branch in the San Francisco Bay Area chapter. ■ *1501 41st Ave (at Capitola Rd), Capitola-by-the-Sea; (408) 475-4450; $; beer and wine; AE, DC, DIS, MC, V; local checks only; lunch, dinner every day.* ⅄

*LODGINGS*

**The Inn at Depot Hill** ★★★ Located in a turn-of-the-century train station, the Inn at Depot Hill is a dream of a place, with trompe l'oeil paintings on the walls and soft, sophisticated lighting that bathes everyone in an angelic glow. The 12 guest rooms, lavishly designed to evoke international ports of call, seem to have sprung directly from the pages of *Architectural Digest*. The terra-cotta-walled Portofino Room, patterned after a coastal Italian villa, sports a stone cherub, ivy, frescoes, and a brick patio. No less charming is the Stratford-upon-Avon, a faux English cottage with a cozy window seat. The Paris Room with its toile-covered walls dazzles in black and white, while the rather fussy Côte d'Azur boasts an ornate canopy bed with bronze vines climbing the four-posters. Every room has a TV and a VCR, a built-in stereo system, and a marble-appointed bathroom complete with a mini-TV and a coffee machine. In the morning, there's a buffet of pastries, cereal, and quiche, as well as a hot dish such as French toast or a spinach omelet. In the evening, you'll find sweets and wine in the downstairs parlor. You may also browse along the massive wall-length bookcase for a tome or videotape to borrow. ■ *250 Monterey Ave (near Park Ave, next to the railroad tracks), Capitola-by-the-Sea; (831) 462-3376 or (800) 572-2632; mail: PO Box 1934, Capitola-by-the-Sea, CA 95010; lodging@innatdepothill.com; www. innatdepothill.com; $$$; AE, MC, V; checks OK.* &

| ▼ | APTOS |
|---|---|

*RESTAURANTS*

**Cafe Sparrow** ★★ Chef/owner Bob Montague opened this quaint French Country restaurant in June 1989. Then along came the Loma Prieta earthquake on October 17th (whose epicenter lay just a short distance away), and Montague had little more than a pile of rubble on his hands. Fortunately, he and his wife didn't throw in the towel, and their remodeled restaurant is indeed a gem of a dining spot, acting as a magnet for local gourmets. Two charming rooms, decorated in a casual yet elegant style with country furniture and a tentlike expanse of French printed fabric, provide a romantic backdrop for Montague's spirited culinary creations. Lunch, a pleasant affair, may include a croissant layered with shrimp in lemon, fresh dill, and crème fraîche, or a bowl of creamed spinach with a vinaigrette salad and bread. Dinner, however, is when Montague puts on the ritz. Start with a pâté of fresh chicken livers seasoned with herbs and Cognac, prawns in an orange and pink peppercorn beurre blanc, or a fondue of white wine, herbs, and cheeses, served with vegetables and a baguette. Then progress to such entrees as a grilled chicken breast with pears topped with Brie, lamb chops in a rich red-wine and mint sauce, or pan-sautéed calamari steak with lemon, butter, and capers. Desserts are as decadent as you'd expect from a place that seems intent on spoiling its customers rotten. One unexpected touch: this sophisticated restaurant isn't afraid to be kid-friendly, and dishes tailored to tots are available. The wine list is far-ranging and agreeably priced, and the service is amiable. ■ *8042 Soquel Dr (near Trout Gulch Rd), Aptos; (408)688-6238; $$; beer and wine; MC, V; checks OK; brunch Sun, lunch Mon–Sat, dinner every day.*

## LODGINGS

**Mangels House** ★★ Set on an imposing green lawn in the middle of a redwood forest, this Italianate mansion was built as a summer house for Spreckels sugar magnate Claus Mangels in 1886. British-born Jacqueline Fisher and her husband, Ron, who bought the estate in 1979, have decorated the six guest rooms in a daring, artful, whimsical way that enlivens the house's stately Victorian demeanor. One room sports a huge bed and chocolate-brown walls decorated with masks, shields, and other African souvenirs that sometimes shock guests expecting a more traditional approach to Victorian decoration. Other rooms feature pastel stenciling that dances across the walls and dramatic modern vases atop antique marble sinks. Lavish breakfasts are served in the dining room, featuring such delights as apple-puff pancakes, a spicy chile-cheese fluff, fresh fruit, and homemade scones. All in all, this is a comfortable, homey inn in a glorious natural setting. ■ *570 Aptos Creek Rd (on the road into the Forest of Nisene Marks State Park, ½ mile above town), Aptos; (408)688-7982 or (800)320-7401; mail: PO Box 302, Aptos, CA 95001; $$–$$$; AE, MC, V; checks OK.*

**Seascape Resort** ★★ This new condo-resort complex on 64 cliffside acres offers spacious accommodations and plenty of creature comforts. The more than 200 guest suites (they're still building) are arranged in a cluster of three-story stucco buildings and are available in studio or one- or two-bedroom configurations. Each suite is outfitted with identical beach-house-style furnishings—not especially luxurious but pleasant enough—and comes with a fireplace, a private balcony or patio, a TV, a kitchenette, sitting and dining areas, a modem port, and an ocean view. Largely given over to corporate functions during the week, the complex segues into a haven for couples and families on the weekend. A paved path leads down to the beach, and guests enjoy member privileges at a nearby PGA-rated golf course and the Seascape Sports Club, which offers tennis, swimming, and a fully equipped gym. There's 24-hour room service, a children's program during the summer, and a spa offering massage and beautician services. Fresh seafood is the specialty at **Sanderlings**, the resort's airy, Florida-style restaurant with patio dining and gorgeous ocean vistas. ■ *1 Seascape Resort Dr (at Sumner Blvd), Aptos, CA 95003; (408)688-6800 or (800)929-7727; www.seascaperesort.com; $$$; full bar; AE, DC, MC, V; checks OK; breakfast, lunch, dinner every day.* &

**Bayview Hotel Bed and Breakfast Inn** ★ Built in 1878 on former Spanish land-grant property, the oldest hotel on Monterey Bay combines Old West ambience with up-to-date comfort. The steep staircase, book-lined parlor, and antiques recall Aptos' frontier past, but guests won't feel like they're roughing it. Each of the 11 rooms has its own phone, bath, and firm mattress resting in an antique frame; some have fireplaces and extra-large tubs. Occupying part of the first floor is **The White Magnolia**, a restaurant that opened in late 1997 featuring California cuisine with Pacific Rim accents. ■ *8041 Soquel Dr (at Trout Gulch Rd), Aptos, CA 95003; (408) 688-8654, (800) 4-BAYVIEW or (408) 662-1890 (restaurant); $$–$$$; full bar; AE, MC, V; checks OK; brunch Sun, lunch Tues–Fri, dinner every day.*

## RIO DEL MAR

### *RESTAURANTS*

**Bittersweet Bistro** ★★ In its earlier incarnation as Cafe Bittersweet, this sleek restaurant and wine bar was embraced by Santa Cruz foodies. There have been some changes of late—notably a new name and spacious new digs a few miles down the road in the old Deer Park Tavern. The new location, six times the size of the previous cafe, features a patio for dining alfresco and a stylish mahogany, lacquer, and black granite bar area (diners should opt for the front room rather than the barnlike back room). Chef Thomas Vinolus is still at the kitchen's helm, creating appetizers such as the tasty grilled shrimp served over a bed of greens and white beans, and a varied and generous antipasto sampler. Pasta offerings include freshly made black pepper linguine tossed with olive oil, herbs, pine nuts, kalamata olives, tomatoes, and cheese, as well as a satisfying seafood pasta with garlic, tomatoes, shallots, and a white wine sauce. For a main course, order the grilled, marinated lamb tenderloins with a rosemary-cabernet sauce if it's available—the long, thick strips of lamb look a bit inelegant, but it's a meltingly tender and flavorful dish. Also recommended are the garlic chicken with Madeira and the amazing, fresh, herb-crusted salmon fillet. The rest of the seasonal menu features everything from a robust version of moussaka to a range of pizzas from the wood-fired oven. The pretty-as-a-picture desserts are scrumptious (no surprise, given that the chef's last gig involved whipping up pastries at Carmel's Casanova restaurant). Don't miss his classic version of crème brûlée and the warm bread pudding crowned with toasted almonds, brandied raisins, and crème Anglaise. The wine list is extensive and varied, with some interesting if pricey older vintages among its treasures. ■ *787 Rio Del Mar Blvd (take Hwy 1 south of Santa Cruz to the Rio Del Mar exit), Rio Del Mar; (408) 662-9799; $$$; full bar; AE, MC, V; local checks only; dinner Tues–Sun.* ⅋

▼

**Aptos**

*Lodgings*

▲

### *RESTAURANTS*

**Sinaloa** ★★ Don't let the truck-stop exterior trick you, and once you're inside, pay no attention to the well-worn linoleum, blaring TV, and rather garish murals of fishing-village life. Make no mistake about it—folks don't pack the place for the ambience (although it is kinda fun). They come to Sinaloa for the topnotch Mexican food. You'll know you're in for a treat with your first taste of fresh, light tortilla chips paired with freshly made salsa (this stuff is so good, people bring their own jars for the kitchen to fill). The family-run operation has a sure and uncommonly delicate hand with all the usual favorites—burritos, enchiladas, chimichangas, chiles rellenos—and the sauces never overpower the other ingredients. ▪ *19210 Monterey Rd (about 1 mile N of town), Morgan Hill; (408) 779-9740; $; full bar; MC, V; checks OK; lunch, dinner Tues–Sun.* &

## GILROY

Will Rogers called Gilroy the only town in America where you can marinate a steak just by hanging it out on the line—and, yes, when the wind's blowing in the right direction, the aroma from the area's garlic fields is just about that strong. So it only made sense that the people of Gilroy decided in 1979 to celebrate their odoriferous claim to fame with the now-famous **Garlic Festival**, held the last weekend in July. The three-day-long festivities attract throngs of people eager to try such oddities as garlic ice cream and garlic chocolate and to enter their own stinking-rose recipes in the Great Garlic Cook-Off. You may also buy any number of garlic-based foodstuffs and doodads; call (408) 842-1625 for more festival facts. To find out about Gilroy before the age of garlic, visit the **Gilroy Historical Museum**; located on the corner of Fifth and Church Streets, (408) 848-0470. If bargain hunting, not garlic, happens to set your heart aflutter, be sure to stop at the newly expanded **Pacific West Outlet Center**, with scores of attractive outlets for big-name retailers on Leavesley Road, just east of Highway 101; (408) 847-4155.

Gilroy

*Restaurants*

### *RESTAURANTS*

**Harvest Time Restaurant** ★ The entrance to this former hotel ballroom is dominated by a large horseshoe-shaped bar and a hand-carved stagecoach. Inside you'll find a comfortably elegant Old West decor, with high ceilings, crystal chandeliers, mirrors, fresh flowers, and chairs upholstered in floral chintz. If you've come to Gilroy for the garlic, try the roasted garlic appetizer, the fried garlic calamari, or other tributes to the stinking rose. In general, the menu is a good jumble of American and Continental dishes; pastas, salads, prime rib, and fresh seafood rank high among the offerings. Catering to the local clientele, the restaurant runs frequent specials that are real bargains. ■ *7397 Monterey Rd (at 6th St), Gilroy; (408)842-7575; $$; full bar; AE, DIS, MC, V; checks OK; breakfast Sat–Sun, lunch, dinner every day.* ♿

## SAN JUAN BAUTISTA

This sunny little town is home to one of the most beautifully restored missions in California. Built just 2 feet away from the main trace of the San Andreas Fault, **Mission San Juan Bautista** was nearly destroyed by the 1906 quake, but locals raised the money to rebuild it. With its pretty chapel and gardens, the mission sits on a broad plaza surrounded by other well-preserved Spanish colonial buildings. Fans of Alfred Hitchcock's *Vertigo* will want to explore the bell tower from which Kim Novak's character fell to her death. On the first Saturday of the month, docents dress in period costume and give tours; call (831)623-2127 for more information. San Juan Bautista is also home to the world-famous theater troupe **El Teatro Campesino**; 705 Fourth Street, (831)623-2444. El Teatro Campesino director Luis Valdez left the San Francisco Mime Troupe in the '60s to form this political theater group composed of migrant farmworkers. The group puts on plays throughout the year and is most famous for its Christmas plays, *La Virgen del Tepeyac* and *La Pastorela*, presented at the mission. Hikers, rock climbers, birdwatchers, and other nature lovers will want to explore the cliffs and caves of nearby **Pinnacles National Monument,** a glorious 16,000-acre volcanic park located high in the hills above the Salinas Valley off Highway 101; (831)389-4485.

▼

**San Juan Bautista**

▲

### RESTAURANTS

**Felipe's California & Mexican Cuisine** ★ One of several Mexican places on San Juan Bautista's main street, this crowded storefront restaurant serves all the standard Mexican fare—good chicken mole, pork burritos, and light, freshly made tortilla chips—but its Salvadoran dishes are what set it apart from its neighbors. Especially delicious are the handmade *pupusas* (fat corn tortillas stuffed with cheese) and the *plátanos fritos* (fried plantains) served on a bed of rich, nicely textured, refried pinto beans. The Salvadoran dishes are served with an appropriately tangy pickled-cabbage dish called *curtido*. Felipe's also has several good Mexican beers, as well as espresso and cappuccino. Don't leave without trying the fried ice cream, a house specialty. Vegetarians take note: Felipe's uses no lard. ■ *313 3rd St (between Mariposa and Polk Sts), San Juan Bautista; (831)623-2161; $; beer and wine; MC, V; no checks; lunch, dinner Wed–Mon.* ♿

# TRES PINOS

## *RESTAURANTS*

**Inn at Tres Pinos** ★★  Tres Pinos is one of those blink-and-you'll-miss-it towns, but it's worth keeping your peepers wide open to catch this intriguing restaurant. "Keep it fresh and keep it simple," is owner Mike Howard's philosophy, a credo that executive chef Dave DeMaggio translates into a continental menu with an Italian accent. Popular dishes include filet mignon with green peppercorn sauce, Fettuccine Fantasia (chicken, artichoke hearts, sun-dried tomatoes, olives, herbs, and garlic with a white-wine and cream sauce), and calamari sautéed in chardonnay and butter. Rustic but surprisingly elegant, the inn wins high praise for both its desserts and its romantic atmosphere. ■ *6991 Airline Hwy (5 miles S of Hollister), Tres Pinos; (831)628-3320; $$$; full bar; AE, MC, V; local checks only; lunch Mon–Fri, dinner every day.* ♿

# MOSS LANDING

Nature lovers have long revered Moss Landing's **Elkhorn Slough** as a prime spot to study egrets, pelicans, cormorants, terns, great blue herons, and many other types of aquatic birds, not to mention packs of frolicking harbor seals and otters. Besides hiking or kayaking, one of the best ways to explore this scenic coastal wetland is to embark on an **Elkhorn Slough Safari**. Naturalist guides provide expert and enthusiastic commentary aboard a 26-foot-long pontoon boat, special activities (such as Bird Bingo) are provided for children, binoculars are available for rent, and coffee, soda, and cookies are served on the way back. The two-hour tours operate on a regular basis Friday through Sunday year-round; weekday tours can be arranged for groups of six or more; call (831)424-3939 for details and reservations.

*Moss Landing*

*Restaurants*

## *RESTAURANTS*

**The Whole Enchilada** ★  Fresh seafood is the focus of this upbeat restaurant on Highway 1 with gaily painted walls, folk-art decorations, and leather basket chairs that lend an engaging south-of-the-border ambience. You'll find the usual lineup of burritos, tacos, chiles rellenos, and enchiladas on the comprehensive menu, but go for one of the more exotic regional specialties, such as Oaxacan chicken mole tamales or garlic prawns. Service is warm and efficient, and little touches like crayons and plastic mermaids clinging to the drink cups make this a place your kids will like, too. ■ *7902 Hwy 1 (at Moss Landing Rd), Moss Landing; (831)633-3038; $$; full bar; AE, DC, DIS, MC, V; no checks; lunch, dinner every day.* ♿

If you're looking for the romantically gritty, working-class fishing village of John Steinbeck's *Cannery Row*, you won't find it here. Even though Monterey was the sardine capital of the Western Hemisphere during World War II, overfishing forced most of its canneries to close in the early '50s, and the city began trawling for tourist dollars instead. The low-slung factories of **Cannery Row** and **Fisherman's Wharf** have been turned into tacky clothing boutiques, knickknack stores, and yogurt shops. But the town itself, set on the south end of Monterey Bay, still has more than its fair share of breathtaking seacoast vistas, pretty Victorian buildings, historic adobes, and secret gardens full of succulents, herbs, and native plants. To catch the town at its best, come in the spring or during the sunny Indian summer months; at other times, expect it to be foggy and slightly cool.

The glory of the town is the amazing, high-tech, 221,000-square-foot **Monterey Bay Aquarium**, the largest aquarium in the United States with more than 350,000 fascinating fish and other denizens of the (local) deep. It also boasts one of the world's largest indoor, glass-walled aquarium tanks. The bat-ray petting pool (not to worry, their stingers have been removed) and the two-story sea otter tank will thrill the kids (and adults), particularly when the sea otters get to scarf down a mixture of clams, rock cod, and shrimp at 10:30am, 1:30pm, and 3:30pm every day. Try to visit midweek to escape the crowds that consistently flock to this beloved institution, which plans to open new exhibits showing the mysterious luminous fish of the deep sea in 2001. Reservations are recommended in the summer and on holidays; 886 Cannery Row (follow the signs). Call (800)756-3737 for advance tickets and (831)648-4888 for more information.

To get the flavor of Monterey's heritage, follow the 2-mile **Path of History**, a walking tour of the former state capital's most important historic sites and splendidly preserved old buildings— remember, this city was thriving under Spanish and Mexican flags when San Francisco was still a crude village. Free tour maps are available at various locations, including the **Custom House**, California's oldest public building (at the foot of Alvarado Street, near Fisherman's Wharf), and **Colton Hall**, where the California State Constitution was written and signed in 1849 (on Pacific Street, between Madison and Jefferson Streets); call Monterey State Historic Park at (831)649-7118 for more information. Nautical history buffs should visit the **Maritime Museum of Monterey**, which houses ship models, whaling relics, and the two-story-high, 10,000-pound Fresnel lens used for nearly 80 years at the Point Sur lighthouse to warn mariners away from the treacherous Big Sur coast; 5 Custom House Plaza, in Stanton Center, near Fisherman's Wharf, (831)373-2469.

▼

**Monterey**

▲

The landmark Fisherman's Wharf, the center of Monterey's cargo and whaling industry until the early 1900s, is awash today in mediocre (or worse) restaurants and equally tasteless souvenir shops. Serious shoppers will be better off strolling **Alvarado Street**, a pleasantly low-key, attractive downtown area with a much less touristy mix of art galleries, bookstores, and restaurants. Alvarado Street is also the site of the popular **Old Monterey Farmer's Market and Marketplace**, a good spot for free family entertainment and picnic-basket treats; it's held Tuesday year-round from 4pm to 8pm in the summer and 4pm to 7pm in the winter.

Children will love the **Dennis the Menace Playground**, designed by cartoonist Hank Ketcham himself. He created enough climbing apparatuses to please a monkey; it's at Camino El Estero and Del Monte Avenue, near Lake El Estero. For fun on the water, take your Curious Georges on a paddleboat and pedal around **Lake El Estero**; (831)375-1484. You can rent **bicycles** and **in-line skates** at the **Monterey Bay Recreation Trail**, which runs along the Monterey shore for 18 miles to Lover's Point in Pacific Grove. More adventurous sorts should get a **sea kayak** at one of the rental outlets along Del Monte Avenue and explore the coast. In the winter and spring, **whale-watching trips** sail regularly from Fisherman's Wharf.

For a terrific, toe-tappin' time, visit Monterey on the third weekend in September, when top talents such as Wynton Marsalis, Etta James, and Ornette Coleman strut their stuff at the **Monterey Jazz Festival**, one of the country's best jazz jubilees and the oldest continuous jazz celebration in the world. Tickets and hotel rooms sell out fast—so plan early (die-hard jazz fans make reservations at least six months before show time); call (800)307-3378 for tickets and (831)373-3366 for more information. Monterey also hosts a **Blues Festival** in late June, which attracts a respectable but smaller crowd; (831)649-6544.

You'll find plenty of references to Nobel prize–winning author John Steinbeck (*The Grapes of Wrath, Cannery Row, East of Eden*) all over town, but you'll have to go to the nearby town of **Salinas** to check out the writer's birthplace, **Steinbeck House**, which is now a luncheon restaurant run by the Salinas Valley Women's Guild; 132 Central Avenue, Salinas, (831)424-2735. Also in Salinas, the **John Steinbeck Library** has a large collection of his letters and first editions; 350 Lincoln Avenue at West San Luis Street, Salinas, (831)758-7311.

### RESTAURANTS

**Fresh Cream** ★★★  One of the most highly rated restaurants on the California coast, Fresh Cream has a veritable mountain of rave reviews to its credit. It's easy to see why—from the delightful complimentary caviar-and-onion tartlet that starts each meal to the divine dessert at the end, the food here is exquisitely prepared and presented. Specializing in French cuisine with hints of California, Fresh Cream moved into handsome new quarters several years ago, and some of the tables afford pleasing views of Monterey Bay. Appetizers range from lobster ravioli with gold caviar to escargots in garlic butter with Pernod or a smooth-as-silk goose liver pâté with capers and onions. Executive chef Gregory Lizza's luscious entrees include roasted duck with black currant sauce, the definitive rack of lamb Dijonnaise, and a delicate poached salmon in saffron-thyme sauce. Vegetarians needn't feel left out; the tasty grilled seasonal vegetable plate is a cut above most veggie entrees. For dessert try the Grand Marnier soufflé or the amazing *sac au chocolat,* a dark chocolate sack filled with a mocha milk shake. Service tends to be a bit on the formal side; the wine list is extensive and expensive. Dinner at Fresh Cream isn't cheap, to be sure, but it's worth the splurge. ■ *99 Pacific St (Suite 100C in the Heritage Harbor complex, across from Fisherman's Wharf), Monterey; (831)375-9798; dining@ freshcream.com; www.freshcream.com; $$$; full bar; AE, DC, DIS, MC, V; checks OK; dinner every day.* &

**Montrio** ★★★ It's rare indeed to find a haven where all the rough edges have been smoothed off, but that's the delightful state of affairs at this downtown Monterey hot spot. All's welcoming here, from the curved lines and soft-sculpture clouds that define the decor of this converted 1910 firehouse to the insightful, cordial waitstaff. The only thing even slightly edgy is the food, which has the lusty, rough-yet-refined flavors characteristic of Rio Grill and Tarpy's, two other local favorites founded by Montrio co-owners Tony Tollner and Bill Cox. Indulge in such eloquent dishes as Dungeness crab cakes with spicy rémoulade and duckling with sun-dried cherry sauce. The Tuesday-night special is another standout: a fork-tender fillet of beef on Roquefort ravioli that one must taste to comprehend—the distinct, exquisite flavors create a dish that's strong, yet lilting. The wine list, which received *Wine Spectator* magazine's Award of Excellence, includes a passel of vintages by the glass. Another option is to sample a wee dram of single-malt Scotch or small-batch bourbon—and if it's thrills you seek, try a Black Death Martini, described on the menu as "soooo smooth it's scary." Surprisingly for such a stylish place, a kid's menu and crayons are available, which should keep junior diners as content as their parents. ■ *414 Calle Principal (near Franklin St), Monterey; (831)648-8880; www.critics-choice.com/ restaurants/montrio; $$$; full bar; AE, DIS, MC, V; no checks; brunch Sun, lunch, dinner every day.* &

**Stokes Adobe** ★★★ A historic peach-colored adobe built in 1833 for the eponymous town doctor is the setting for one of Monterey's most engaging restaurants. Co-proprietors Dorothea and Kirk Probasco (Kirk formerly managed Carmel's Rio Grill and Pacific's Edge at the Highlands Inn) didn't miss a trick when they opened Stokes in 1996, snagging Brandon Miller as head chef (think Campton Place and Tra Vigne), assembling a staff that is both well trained and friendly, and overseeing a redesign that is a particularly skillful blend of old and new. The two-story adobe and board-and-batten house is surrounded by lovely gardens and reflects the Spanish character of Old Monterey. Inside, the large space has been divided into several airy, dining rooms, with terra-cotta floors, bleached-wood plank ceilings, Southwestern wooden chairs and tables, and white walls dotted with paintings. It's a soothing and lovely showcase for Miller's terrific food, which he describes as contemporary rustic Mediterranean fare: butternut squash soup with apple cider and maple crème fraîche, roasted spinach gratin with mussels and herbed bread crumbs, grilled lavender-infused pork chops with savory bread pudding and pear chutney, cassoulet of duck confit and homemade currant sausage with chestnut beans. Don't let the "rustic" label fool you; this is extremely refined cooking that respects the individual flavors of the high-quality ingredients. Desserts are wonderful here, and include such winners as a warm apricot clafouti, chocolate espresso crème brûlée, and warm banana-rum bread pudding with vanilla crème Anglaise. A prix-fixe dinner is offered nightly— a real bargain at about $26 (and for another $20 you can get a carefully orchestrated selection of wines). ▪ *500 Hartnell St (at Madison St), Monterey; (831)373-1110; $$; full bar; AE, MC, V; no checks; lunch, dinner every day.* &

**Tarpy's Roadhouse** ★★★ Worth a hop in the car for a spin on Highway 68, this exuberant restaurant features a broad, sunny patio shaded by market umbrellas out front and a handsome Southwestern decor inside, with rustic, bleached-wood furniture, golden stone walls, and whimsical art. The menu indulges in a creative approach to traditional American food. Lunch emphasizes well-prepared sandwiches and salads, but dinner is when Tarpy's really shines. Appetizers might include grilled polenta with mushrooms and Madeira, fire-roasted artichokes with lemon-herb vinaigrette, and Pacific oysters with red wine–jalapeño mignonette. Entrees run the gamut from a bourbon-molasses pork chop or a Dijon-crusted lamb loin to sea scallops with saffron penne or a grilled vegetable plate with succotash. Desserts include lemon and fresh ginger crème brûlée, a triple-layer chocolate cake, and olallieberry pie. The wine list is modest and skewed toward the expensive side, but thoughtfully selected. ▪ *2999 Monterey-Salinas Hwy (at Hwy 68 and Canyon Del Rey), Monterey; (831)647-1444; www.critics-choice.com/restaurants/ tarpys; $$$; full bar; AE, DIS, MC, V; no checks; brunch Sun, lunch, dinner every day.* &

**Cafe Fina** ★★ Many locals swear this is the only restaurant worth dining at on Fisherman's Wharf. And, indeed, Cafe Fina is a refreshing outpost of quality amid all the tourist-carnival trappings. Owner Dominic Mercurio offers fresh fish, mesquite-grilled chicken and beef, salads, house-made pasta with inventive herb sauces, and pizzas hot from the brick oven. Specialties are the seafood and pasta dishes, including the flavorful Pasta Fina (linguine with baby shrimp, white wine, olives, clam juice, olive oil, tomatoes, and green onions). The food is delicious and carefully prepared, the atmosphere is casual and fun, and the view is a maritime dream. ■ *47 Fisherman's Wharf (on the wharf), Monterey; (831)372-5200; $$; full bar; AE, DC, DIS, MC, V; no checks; lunch, dinner every day.*

## LODGINGS

**Hotel Pacific** ★★★ Like a Modigliani looming angular and bold in a gallery full of Fra Angelicos, this somewhat modern, neo-hacienda hotel stands out in the midst of Monterey's authentic old adobes. A sparkling fountain burbles beside the entrance; inside you'll find handwoven rugs, muted Southwestern colors, terra-cotta tiles, and beamed ceilings soaring above rounded walls. Connected by tiled courtyards, arches, and flowered pathways, a scattering of low-rise buildings holds 105 small suites. All rooms have private patios or terraces, fireplaces, goose-down feather beds, three telephones, and two TVs (one in the bathroom). Ask for a room on the fourth level with a panoramic view of the bay, or a room facing the inner courtyard with its large fountain. A deluxe continental breakfast is provided in the morning, and guests may indulge in afternoon tea. Complimentary underground parking is available, too. ■ *300 Pacific St (between Scott St and Del Monte Blvd), Monterey, CA 93940; (831)373-5700 or (800)554-5542; www.travelweb.com; $$$; AE, DC, DIS, MC, V; checks OK.* &

**Old Monterey Inn** ★★★ Even those who feel they've seen it all on the bed-and-breakfast circuit are likely to be awed by the elegantly appointed Old Monterey Inn. Nestled among giant oak trees and gardens filled with rhododendrons, begonias, fuchsias, and ferns, this Tudor-style country inn built in 1929 positively gleams with natural wood, skylights, and stained-glass windows. The 10 beautifully decorated guest rooms, each with a private bath, are filled with lovely antiques and comfortable beds with plump down comforters and huge, fluffy pillows. Most rooms have fireplaces, and although none have TVs or telephones, TVs may be brought into a few of the cable-equipped rooms upon request, and portable phones are available for guests. For the utmost privacy, request the lacy Garden Cottage, which has a private patio, skylights, and a fireplace sitting room. The deluxe Ashford Suite has a sitting area, a separate dressing room, a king-size bed, an antique day bed, and a panoramic garden view. Another standout: the handsome Library guest room, with its book-lined walls, stone fireplace, and private sun deck.

Breakfast, taken in the dining room or *en suite*, might include baked apples, French toast, crêpes, cheese rolls, and curiosities such as coconut-lime muffins. You'll also find a delightful afternoon tea and evening hors d'oeuvres. There are plenty of low-key ways to pamper yourself around here, such as lounging at the picnic tables in the rose garden or strolling around the acre-plus grounds. ■ *500 Martin St (near Pacific St), Monterey, CA 93940; (831)375-8284 or (800)350-2344; omi@oldmontereyinn.com; www. oldmontereyinn.com; $$$; MC, V; checks OK.*

**Spindrift Inn** ★★★ With its soaring four-story atrium and rooftop garden, the Spindrift is an unexpected and elegant refuge amid the hurly-burly tourist world of Cannery Row. Downstairs in this former bordello, plush Oriental carpets muffle your footsteps, and a tall pair of attractive, if politically questionable, Italian blackamoor statues keep you company in the fireside sitting room. Upstairs, all 42 rooms have feather beds (many with canopies) with down comforters, fireplaces, hardwood floors, telephones, and tiled bathrooms with marble appointments. You'll also discover terrycloth robes, cable TVs, and nightly turn-down service. The corner rooms, with their cushioned window seats and breathtaking ocean views, are the best in the house. In the morning there will be a newspaper, a dewy rose, and a delicious breakfast of fruit, orange juice, croissants, and sweet rolls waiting outside your door on a silver tray. In the afternoon you are invited to partake of tea, pastries, wine, and cheese. ■ *652 Cannery Row (at Hawthorne St), Monterey, CA 93940; (831)646-8900 or (800)841-1879; www.spindriftinn.com; $$$; AE, DC, DIS, MC, V; checks OK.* &

Monterey

*Lodgings*

**The Jabberwock** ★★ The Jabberwock, as you may recall, is a fearsome creature that sprang, gnashing its jaws and flashing its claws, from the fertile mind of Lewis Carroll. This inn has none of the menace but lots of the whimsy of his tale. The rooms bear names such as The Toves and Tulgey Woods and the delicious breakfast dishes (written on a board in backwards mirror-writing) are called "razzleberry flabjous" and "snarkleberry flumptious." Set well back from the hubbub of nearby Cannery Row, this 1911 former convent has seven guest rooms, five with private baths. The spacious and grand Borogrove Room boasts wraparound picture windows with views of the town and the inn's garden. The Mome Rath Room has a bed big enough for any beast. The large, beautifully landscaped garden has a pond, a waterfall, a nifty sundial, and, certainly no surprise, a rabbit—who's very late. ■ *598 Laine St (at Hoffman Ave), Monterey, CA 93940; (831)372-4777 or (888)428-7253; $$; MC, V; checks OK.*

Established in 1889 as a retreat for pious Methodists, this beautiful Victorian seacoast village retains its decorous old-town character, though it's loosened its collar a bit since the early days, when dancing, alcohol, and even the Sunday newspaper were banned. Less tourist-oriented than Carmel, less commercial than Monterey, P.G. (as locals call it) exudes peace and tranquillity—there's no graffiti, no raucous revelers, and not even an unleashed dog in sight. Introduce yourself to the town by strolling the 4 miles of trails that meander between the white-sand beaches and rocky tide-pool-dotted coves at **Lover's Point Beach** (off Ocean View Boulevard on the east side of Point Piños) and **Asilomar State Beach** (off Sunset Drive on the west side of Point Piños). Be sure to sit and enjoy the view from the landmark **Lover's Point** (which, by the way, was named for lovers of Jesus Christ, not the more carnal kind).

At the tip of Point Piños (Spanish for "Point of the Pines") stands the Cape Cod–style **Point Piños Lighthouse**, the oldest continuously operating lighthouse on the West Coast, built in February 1855. This National Historic Landmark is open to the public Thursday through Sunday, from 1pm to 4pm, and admission is free; on Asilomar Boulevard at Lighthouse Avenue, (831)648-3116.

**Pacific Grove**

P.G. is famous for its Victorian houses, inns, and churches, and hundreds of them have been declared historically significant by the Pacific Grove Heritage Society. Every October, some of the most beautiful and artfully restored are opened to the public on the **Victorian Home Tour**; call (831)373-3304 for details. If you can't make the tour, you can at least admire the faces of these lavish lovelies clustered along Lighthouse Avenue, Central Avenue, and Ocean View Boulevard.

Pacific Grove bills itself as Butterfly Town, U.S.A., in honor of the thousands of monarchs that migrate here from late October to mid-March. Two popular places to view these lovely orange-and-black insects are the **Monarch Grove Sanctuary** (at Lighthouse Avenue and Ridge Road) and **George Washington Park** (at Sinex Avenue and Alder Street). To learn more about the monarchs, visit the charmingly informal and kid-friendly **Pacific Grove Museum of Natural History**, which has a video and display on the butterfly's life cycle, as well as exhibits of other insects, local birds, mammals, and reptiles (admission is free); located at the intersection of Forest and Central Avenues, (831)648-3116.

For good books and coffee, amble over to the nearby **Bookworks**, which also has an extensive array of magazines and newspapers; 667 Lighthouse Avenue, (831)372-2242. (For tips on touring the famous **17-Mile Drive**, see Pebble Beach in the following pages.)

**Melac's** ★★★ This transplanted slice of France, with its brick fireplace, white-lace cafe curtains, and soldierly rows of wine bottles lining the walls, is a masterly combination of exquisite cuisine and elegant presentation. American chef Janet Melac graduated at the top of her class from Paris' Cordon Bleu cooking school before apprenticing with some of France's most exacting chefs. She invigorates her classic French cuisine with unusual local ingredients and light, delicate sauces; expect offerings such as jumbo sea scallops seared in olive oil with a shallot and red wine sauce on angel hair pasta; smoked salmon and goat cheese on a potato galette with a white wine and dill sauce; veal sweetbreads sautéed on a bed of mushrooms and drizzled with white truffle oil; and foie gras sautéed with a leek crêpe, deglazed with sherry and balsamic vinegar and chives. Melac can be overly restrained with her seasonings, perhaps in deference to the sedate, older crowd the restaurant seems to attract, but she pulls out all the stops with desserts such as tarte Tatin and chocolate mousse cake with pistachio cream sauce. The wine list offers a wide variety of excellent (and pricey) French and California labels as well as ports and sherries. Melac's French-born husband, Jacques, is the charming and attentive dining room host. ■ *663 Lighthouse Ave (at 19th St), Pacific Grove; (831)375-1743; www. critics-choice.com/restaurants/melac; $$$; beer and wine; AE, DC, DIS, MC, V; no checks; lunch Tues–Fri, dinner Tues–Sun.* &

**Pacific Grove**

*Restaurants*

▲

**Old Bath House Restaurant** ★★★ Although many locals are quick to dismiss the Old Bath House as a pricey tourist restaurant (and it is indeed guilty on both counts), the food is meticulously prepared and the setting is undeniably romantic. This former bath house at Lover's Point has a fine view of the rocky coast and a wonderful wood interior with a low, carved ceiling. Chef Jeffrey Jake, formerly at Domaine Chandon in Yountville and Montrio in Monterey, has breathed new life into the continental menu. Expect starters such as truffle-mousse pâté, grilled prawns and wild boar sausage, and artichoke ravioli with a lemon-nutmeg cream sauce; entrees may feature braised petrale sole with fettuccine and chardonnay sauce, veal medallions crusted with pistachios and topped with lime butter, and soy-ginger-glazed filet mignon grilled with shiitakes. Tempting desserts include hot pecan ice-cream fritters and the aptly named Oceans of Chocolate (chocolate ice cream on chocolate pudding cake cloaked in chocolate fudge and white-chocolate chunks). The service is impeccable and the wine list extensive. ■ *620 Ocean View Blvd (at Lover's Point Park), Pacific Grove; (831)375-5195; www.critics-choice.com/restaurants/bath; $$$; full bar; AE, DC, DIS, MC, V; no checks; dinner every day.*

**Taste Cafe & Bistro** ★★★ When it opened several years ago, Taste Cafe quickly developed a loyal and enthusiastic word-of-mouth following that remains the envy of several more established restaurants in town. You'll be hard-pressed to find higher quality food for the same price anywhere else on the coast. Chef/owners Paolo Kautz and Sylvia Medina describe their preparations as a combination of rustic French, Italian, and California cuisines, and they work hard to glean the best and freshest produce, seafood, and meats from local suppliers. Start your meal with house-cured salmon carpaccio, butternut squash agnolotti, or an organic red oak leaf salad with crumbled blue cheese, balsamic dressing, sliced pears, and glazed pecans. Move on to entrees such as tortellini Florentine, marinated rabbit with braised red cabbage, and grilled pork medallions on mashed potatoes with shiitake sauce. Be sure to save room for one of Sylvia's wonderful desserts: warm brioche pudding with apricot coulis and crème fraîche, a hazelnut-chocolate torte, or a country-style apple galette with vanilla-bean ice cream and caramel sauce. Regulars elbow up to the wine and espresso bar. The word is out on this terrific restaurant, so be sure to call well ahead for reservations, especially for weekend dinners. ■ *1199 Forest Ave (at Prescott Ave), Pacific Grove; (831) 655-0324; $$; beer and wine; no credit cards; checks OK; dinner Tues–Sun.* ⅋

▼

**Pacific Grove**

*Restaurants*

▲

**El Cocodrilo Rotisserie and Seafood Grill** ★★ Drawing on the sharp, exotic flavors of the Caribbean and Central and South America, Julio Ramirez's exciting, hybrid-Hispanic cuisine manages to cater to the tender sensibilities of *norteamericanos* without sacrificing authenticity. Lush tropical plants, photographs of Latin America, and dozens of crocodile chatchkas set an appropriate mood for fiery, flavorful, fish-focused meals. Starters include Bahamian seafood chowder, Salvadoran *pupusas* (fat tortillas stuffed with two cheeses and served with black beans and salsa), and, somewhat ironically considering this place's affection for large, toothy reptiles, alligator nuggets with passion-fruit dipping sauce. Specialties include Red Snapper Mardi Gras, smoked West Indian ribs, and spit-roasted Mayan chicken. El Cocodrilo's interesting selection of desserts includes mango cheesecake, chocolate–Brazil nut pie, and *paletas tropicales*, those delicious and refreshing frozen fruit treats so familiar to travelers in Mexico. A light bar menu is served from 4pm to 10pm, and you can chase down all that fiery food with a refreshing (if somewhat insincere) pitcher of Crocodile Tears (aka sangria). ■ *701 Lighthouse Ave (at Congress Ave), Pacific Grove; (831) 655-3311; www.critics-choice.com/restaurants/cocodrilo; $$; beer and wine; AE, DC, DIS, MC, V; no checks; dinner Wed–Mon.* ⅋

**Fandango** ★★ Fandango, the name of a lively Spanish dance, is the perfect moniker for this kick-up-your-heels restaurant specializing in Mediterranean country cuisine. It's a big, sprawling,

▬

colorful place with textured adobe walls and a spirited crowd filling five separate dining rooms; the glass-domed terrace in back, with its stone fireplace and open mesquite grill, is especially pleasant. Start with a few tapas—perhaps spicy sausage, roasted red peppers, or a potato-and-onion frittata. If you're feeling adventurous, order the Veloute Bongo Bongo, an exotic creamy soup with oysters, spinach, and Cognac, or the Couscous Algerois, a 130-year-old family recipe featuring lamb, vegetables, and North African spices. Other selections include the flavorful Paella Fandango (served at your table in a huge skillet), pasta puttanesca, bouillabaisse Marseillaise, osso buco, and a 26-ounce porterhouse steak. Fandango's wine list is one of the best in the area, with an impressive selection of French, California, Spanish, and Italian varietals. For dessert, try the profiteroles filled with chocolate ice cream and topped with hot fudge sauce. *Olé!* ■ *223 17th St (near Lighthouse Ave), Pacific Grove; (831)372-3456; www. critics-choice.com/restaurants/fandango; $$$; full bar; AE, DC, DIS, MC, V; no checks; brunch Sun, lunch, dinner every day.* &

**Gernot's Victoria House ★★** Located in the beautiful Hart Mansion, Gernot's Victoria House has the kind of quiet charm and gracious service that the town's trendier restaurants just can't match (and at comparatively modest prices). All of chef Gernot Leitzinger's continental entrees come with soup, a salad made with local greens in an herby vinaigrette, and hot country rolls. Popular selections include wiener schnitzel with lingonberry compote; rack of lamb Dijon with bread crumbs, herbs, and garlic; and salmon with mango salsa. Daring sorts may want to sample Gernot's wild boar bourguignon. For dessert, there's a luscious Sacher torte and delicate meringue shells topped with ice cream and chocolate sauce. ■ *649 Lighthouse Ave (at 19th St), Pacific Grove; (831)646-1477; www.critics-choice.com/restaurants/ gernot; $$; beer and wine; AE, MC, V; checks OK; dinner Tues–Sun.*

**Pasta Mia ★★** A century-old Victorian house provides a homey backdrop for Pasta Mia's hearty Italian fare. The soup and appetizers tend to be tried-and-true standards, such as minestrone, *mozzarella fresca*, and carpaccio, but the house-made pastas include some intriguing choices. There's black-and-white linguine with scallops, caviar, cream, and chives, for instance, or half-moon pasta stuffed with pesto in a lemon-zest cream sauce dotted with chicken and sun-dried tomatoes. The corkscrew pasta with sausage and chicken in a pink sauce is satisfying and flavorful, as is the scampi in a light champagne cream sauce. *Secondi piatti* include a robust version of osso buco, pounded breast of chicken with a garlic, wine, and rosemary sauce, and a daily fresh fish preparation. Portions are generous in this friendly, informal restaurant. ■ *481 Lighthouse Ave (near 13th St), Pacific Grove; (831)375-7709; $$; beer and wine; AE, MC, V; local checks only; dinner every day.* &

**Red House Café** ★★ A trim, 103-year-old, brick red house in downtown Pacific Grove is the deceptively modest setting for some of the most adroit cooking on the Monterey Peninsula. Opened in 1996 by Laura and Chris D'Amelio (both formerly of Taste Cafe & Bistro), the Red House offers a handful of humble-sounding dishes at breakfast and lunch—items such as Irish oatmeal, Belgian waffles, pastries, a mixed green salad, roast beef on sourdough, a BLT, and eggs any way you like them as long as they're scrambled. Order at the counter, then take a seat on the porch with its smattering of wicker chairs and tables-for-two or in one of the snug, country-cottage dining rooms. After your food is served and you tuck into your warm pine-nut tart or chicken sandwich, you'll realize how even the simplest fare can be transporting if it's prepared by the right hands. Perfectly cooked, every dish demonstrates the kitchen's insistence on first-rate ingredients—heck, even the toast and jam tastes like a gourmet treat here. The Red House has been a locals' favorite ever since it opened, and its popularity is the only rub; traffic can back up at the counter as people wait to place their orders, creating some cramped conditions in the dining areas. ■ *662 Lighthouse Ave (at 19th St), Pacific Grove; (831)643-1060; $; beer and wine; no credit cards; checks OK; breakfast, lunch Tues–Sun.*

▼

**Pacific Grove**

*Restaurants*

▲

**Fishwife** ★ Locals swear by this bustling and casual seaside restaurant. The decor is playful, with cloth parrots and toucans suspended from the ceiling and brightly colored fish-shaped pillows tossed about the waiting area. The long roster of seafood dishes includes fried calamari, grilled Cajun snapper, fillet of sole doré, and prawns Belize, as well as a number of daily specials featuring fresh seasonal fish. The Boston clam chowder is justly famous, as is the Key lime pie. For those who eschew eating our gilled friends, the Fishwife also serves steaks and a couple of pasta dishes such as fettuccine with alfredo or pesto sauce. The reasonable prices and separate kids' menu make this a good choice for folks with children in tow. ■ *1996½ Sunset Dr (in the Beachcomber Inn at Asilomar Beach), Pacific Grove; (831)375-7107; www.critics-choice.com/restaurants/fishwife; $$; beer and wine; AE, DIS, MC, V; no checks; brunch Sun, lunch, dinner Wed–Mon.*

**Peppers** ★ This Pacific Grove hot spot (pun intended) with strings of red chile peppers dangling from the ceiling is known for its house-made tamales and chiles rellenos. The delicately flavored seafood tacos with mahi-mahi, swordfish, or salmon, and the spicy prawns Gonzalez, with tomatoes, chiles, cilantro, and lime juice, are also worth a try. The chips and salsa are dynamite, and a good selection of beers can cool your singed palate. Owner Scott Gonzalez is usually on hand to make sure everything runs smoothly; consequently, the service is always friendly even though the place is usually packed. ■ *170 Forest Ave (by Light-house Ave), Pacific Grove; (831)373-6892; $; beer and wine; AE, DIS, MC, V; local checks only; lunch Mon, Wed–Sat, dinner Wed–Mon.*

## LODGINGS

**Grand View Inn ★★★** Even in a town as rich in resplendent Victorians as Pacific Grove, this pristine and romantic inn stands out. Built in 1910 as the residence of Dr. Julia Platt, a marine biologist who became Pacific Grove's first female mayor, the Grand View was bought by the family that owns the Seven Gables Inn next door (the two inns share the same garden). They lovingly restored this inn and opened it to the public in July 1995. A bit more casual and restrained in decor than its ornate sister, this charmer with the cheerful blue exterior has 10 guest rooms, all with bay views, high plaster ceilings with decorative detailing, eclectic antique furniture and light fixtures, queen-size beds, sitting areas, and beautifully appointed marble bathrooms. A full breakfast is served in the elegant first-floor dining room with its breathtaking view of Lover's Point; later in the day, the same room is the setting for a pleasant afternoon tea. Complimentary off-street parking is available, too. ■ *557 Ocean View Blvd (at Grand Ave), Pacific Grove, CA 93950; (831)372-4341; $$$; MC, V; checks OK.* &

**The Martine Inn ★★★** Perched like a vast pink wedding cake on a cliff above Monterey Bay, this villa with a Mediterranean exterior and a Victorian interior is one of Pacific Grove's most elegant bed and breakfasts. Built in 1899 for James and Laura Parke (of Parke-Davis Pharmaceuticals fame), the inn has 19 spacious guest rooms, all with private baths and gloriously unfussy, high-quality antiques, including interesting beadwork lamps. Most rooms have fireplaces; all have views of the water or the garden courtyard with its delightful dragon fountain. If you feel like splurging, the Parke Room at the very top of the house is outstanding. Originally the master bedroom, it has a magnificent picture window, a four-poster canopy bed, and a massive, white brick fireplace. No matter which room you choose, you'll find a silver basket of fruit and a rose waiting for you upon arrival, and a newspaper at your door in the morning. Several intimate sitting rooms offset three large common areas: the library, the main dining room (with a dazzling view of the bay), and the breakfast parlor. There's also a pool table and an eight-person Jacuzzi in the old conservatory. The Martine serves an elaborate and well-prepared breakfast, and offers wine and hors d'oeuvres in the late afternoon. ■ *255 Ocean View Blvd (4 blocks from Cannery Row), Pacific Grove, CA 93950; (831)373-3388 or (800)852-5588; www.virtualcities.com; $$$; AE, DIS, MC, V; checks OK.* &

**Seven Gables Inn** ★★★ An immaculate yellow mansion built in 1886 and surrounded by gardens, this family-run inn commands a magnificent view of Monterey Bay. Chock-full of formal European antiques, Seven Gables will seem like paradise to those who revel in things Victorian; those who prefer a more restrained, less fussy decor will do better elsewhere. Once you're ensconced in one of the 14 guest rooms, which are divided among the main house, a guest house, and a smattering of cottages, the warm and welcoming Flatley family will see to your every comfort. The beautifully appointed rooms feature ocean views, private baths, and queen-size beds. A pull-out-all-the-stops breakfast is served in the imposing dining room, and tea is set out every afternoon. ■ *555 Ocean View Blvd (at Fountain Ave), Pacific Grove, CA 93950; (831)372-4341; $$$; MC, V; checks OK.*

**The Centrella** ★★ The aptly named Centrella (located smack in the center of town) combines the down-home glow of an Old West boardinghouse with the comfort and attentive service of a modern hotel. The front hallway of this spacious 1886 Victorian inn opens onto a large parlor overlooking a garden courtyard. The main building offers 21 rooms, and all but two have private baths. The upstairs rooms overlooking the garden are particularly attractive and comfortable, as are the two intimate attic suites with skylights and TVs. Outside, a brick path meanders through an old-fashioned garden of gardenias and camellias, leading to five well-equipped private cottages. For breakfast you'll find crisp waffles hot from the antique waffle iron, and in the evening look for dainty hors d'oeuvres served in the parlor. ■ *612 Central Ave (at 17th St), Pacific Grove, CA 93950; (831)372-3372 or (800)233-3372; centrella@aol.com; www.centrellainn.com; $$$; AE, MC, V; checks OK.* &

**Gatehouse Inn** ★★ When State Senator Benjamin Langford built this ocean-view Victorian mansion in 1884, Pacific Grove was less a town than a pious Methodist meeting ground. Swathed in rules and regulations, it was separated from wicked, worldly Monterey by a white picket fence. Langford's domain is now an enticingly eccentric B&B. Decorated in an interesting mix of Victoriana and art deco, the inn's nine guest rooms have private baths and queen-size beds, with the exception of the Cannery Row Room, with its king-size bed. The Langford Suite ranks as the inn's most luxurious, with an ocean-view sitting room, fireplace, and a claw-footed bathtub that's just a step away from the bed and commands a stunning view of the coast (talk about soaking it all in!). You'll find delicious hors d'oeuvres, tea, and wine every evening and a full breakfast buffet in the morning. You can even help yourself to cookies and beverages from the kitchen any time of day or night. ■ *225 Central Ave (at 2nd St), Pacific Grove, CA 93950; (831)649-8436 or (800)753-1881; $$$; AE, DIS, MC, V; checks OK.* &

**Lighthouse Lodge and Suites** ★★ Less than a block from the ocean, the Lighthouse Lodge and Suites is really two entities with rather distinct personalities. The lodge, a Best Western property with a heated pool, consists of 68 motel-like rooms. Those seeking more luxurious accommodations should spring for one of the 31 newer suites down the road. The Cape Cod–style suites, all with beamed ceilings, plush carpeting, fireplaces, vast bathrooms with marble Jacuzzis, large-screen TVs, minikitchens, and king-size beds, glow in peacock hues of purple, green, and fuchsia. The overall effect is a bit nouveau riche, but riche all the same. After a made-to-order breakfast in the fireside lounge, take a morning stroll around the grounds, cleverly landscaped with native plants and fountains. ▪ *1150 and 1249 Lighthouse Ave (at Asilomar Blvd), Pacific Grove, CA 93950; (831)655-2111 or (800)858-1249; www.lhls.com; $$ (lodge), $$$ (suites); AE, DC, DIS, MC, V; no checks.* ♿

**Rosedale Inn** ★ While its name may conjure up images of pink petals and white lace, the Rosedale is more like an upscale motel, with woodsy flourishes such as a huge carved-redwood bear that welcomes guests. Despite a somewhat rustic appearance, each of the inn's 19 rooms is equipped with a wealth of electronic conveniences: multiple TV sets, a couple of phone lines, a Jacuzzi, a clock radio, a microwave, a VCR, and a hair dryer. The rooms are spacious, and some have kitchenettes. Located across the road from the Asilomar Conference Center, the Rosedale is well suited to conference-goers, business travelers, and families. ▪ *775 Asilomar Blvd (at Sinex Ave), Pacific Grove, CA 93950; (831)655-1000 or (800)822-5606; $$; AE, DC, MC, V; no checks.* ♿

**The Asilomar Conference Center** Many of the original buildings at Asilomar, located at the tip of the Monterey Peninsula on a wooded stretch of beach, were designed by famed Bay Area architect Julia Morgan. Donated to the YWCA by Phoebe Apperson Hearst and now owned by the State Division of Beaches and Parks, the Asilomar feels a bit like a grown-up Girl Scout camp, albeit a little more luxurious. Its 105 acres of park-like grounds include a large, heated swimming pool, wooded trails, and a fine beach where you can watch otters, seals, and, depending on the season, whales. There are 314 units in the complex; the older rooms, designed by Morgan, have hardwood floors and are much smaller and more rustic than the newer suites with their wall-to-wall carpeting, fireplaces, and kitchenettes. The apartment-style Guest Inn Cottage and Forest Lodge Suite can accommodate a large group or family. Breakfast is included in the price. There's also a cafeteria-style restaurant on the premises, but you're better off going into town to eat. ▪ *800 Asilomar Blvd (at Sinex Ave), Pacific Grove, CA 93950; (831)372-8016; www.worldint.com/asilomar; $$; MC, V; checks OK.* ♿

How much are a room and a round of golf at Pebble Beach these days? Let's put it this way: if you have to ask, you can't afford it. This exclusive gated community of 6,000 or so residents even requires a $7.25 levy to trod on its gilded avenues. If you have no strong desire to tour corporate-owned hideaways and redundant—albeit gorgeous—seascapes along the famous **17-Mile Drive**, save your lunch money; you're not really missing anything that can't be seen elsewhere along the Monterey coast. Then again, some folks swear that 17-Mile Drive is one of those things you must do at least once in your life, and that the enclave of mansions and manicured golf courses is worth the admission just to contemplate the lifestyles of the very rich.

If you decide to pay the toll, you'll see everything from a spectacular Byzantine castle with a private beach (the Crocker Mansion near the Carmel gate) to several tastefully bland California Nouvelle country-club establishments in perfectly maintained forest settings. Other highlights include the often-photographed gnarled **Lone Cypress** clinging to its rocky precipice above the sea; miles of hiking and equestrian trails winding through groves of native pines and wildflowers, with glorious views of Monterey Bay; and **Bird Rock**, a small offshore isle covered with hundreds of seals and sea lions (bring binoculars). Self-guided nature tours are outlined in a variety of brochures, available for free at the gate entrances and at the Inn at Spanish Bay and the Lodge at Pebble Beach (see reviews, below). And then there are the golf courses. This area is a bit of heaven to golfers, who flock to such famous courses as **Spyglass Hill**, named after a location in Robert Louis Stevenson's *Treasure Island*.

▼

**Pebble Beach**

▲

Pebble Beach has five guarded entrance gates, and the entire drive takes about 3 hours (though you can whiz by the highlights in 30 minutes). The most famous stretch is along the coast between Pacific Grove and Carmel, and your best bet is to avoid the busy summer weekends and come midweek. Visitors may enter the 17-Mile Drive for free on foot or bike, although cyclists are required to use the Pacific Grove gate on weekends and holidays—and must dust off the wheels of their bikes, of course. For more information, contact Pebble Beach Security at (831) 624-6669.

*LODGINGS*

**The Inn at Spanish Bay** ★★★ Set on the privately owned 17-Mile Drive, this sprawling modern inn defines "deluxe." Its 270 luxuriously appointed rooms and suites perched on a cypress-dotted bluff have gas fireplaces, quilted down comforters, and elegant sitting areas. Most have private patios or balconies affording gorgeous views of the rocky coast or the Del Monte cypress forest. Three of the most deluxe suites even come with grand pianos.

The bathrooms, equipped with all the modern conveniences you could want, are appropriately regal. Hotel guests have access to the world-famous Pebble Beach, Spanish Bay, and Spyglass Hill golf courses, as well as eight championship tennis courts, a fitness club, a swimming pool, and miles of hiking and equestrian trails. At sunset a Scottish bagpiper strolls along the golf course and serenades the guests. Relax over a repast at the well-regarded **Bay Club**, serving fashionable northern Italian fare, or at **Roy's**, an exciting newcomer where Hawaiian master chef Roy Yamaguchi serves an artful blend of Asian-Pacific and European cuisine. ■ *2700 17-Mile Dr (near the Pacific Grove entrance), Pebble Beach, CA 93953; (831)647-7500 or (800)654-9300; www.pebblebeach.com; $$$; full bar; AE, DC, MC, V; checks OK; Bay Club: dinner every day; Roy's: breakfast, lunch, dinner every day.* ⏣

**The Lodge at Pebble Beach ★★★** Despite greens fees that top $300, Pebble Beach remains the mecca of American golf courses, and avid golfers feel they have to play it at least once before retiring to that Big Clubhouse in the Sky. Until the rooms in the Lodge were renovated several years ago, this scattered cluster of accommodations surprised many guests with its rather run-down appearance—it was clear that golf and the spectacular natural setting, not the rooms, were Pebble Beach's principal allure. The guest rooms have been tastefully revamped, however, swathed in soothing earth tones and outfitted with a sophisticated, modern decor. There are 161 suites and rooms, most with private balconies or patios, brick fireplaces, sitting areas, and gorgeous views. All the usual upscale amenities are provided, from phones by the commode and honor-bar refrigerators to robes and cable TVs. The whole effect is very East Coast country club. Four restaurants cater to visitors, most notably **Club XIX**, which has been drawing raves since signing up Hubert Keller of San Francisco's Fleur de Lys as executive chef, and the **Cypress Room**, with a menu that offers several excellent methods of preparing fish—everything from poaching them in champagne to searing them in Cajun spices. The Cypress Room is a lovely spot for lunch, too—try the salads. ■ *On 17-Mile Dr (near the Carmel Gate), Pebble Beach, CA 93953; (831)624-3811 or (800)654-9300; www.pebble-beach.com; $$$; full bar; AE, DC, DIS, MC, V; checks OK; Club XIX: lunch, dinner every day; Cypress Room: breakfast, lunch, dinner every day.* ⏣

## CARMEL-BY-THE-SEA

Years ago, Carmel was a quaint little seaside town with a relaxed Mediterranean atmosphere conducive to the pursuit of such arts as photography, painting, and writing. Luminaries such as Robert Louis Stevenson, Robinson Jeffers, Mary Austin, Sinclair Lewis, Edward Weston, Upton Sinclair, and Ansel Adams at one time called Carmel home. Today, though, the very name of this city has become synonymous with a spectacular fall from grace, and antidevelopment folks up and down the coast use the term "Carmelization" with their lips curled in disgust. The charmingly ragtag bohemian village (which once banned skateboards, high heels, and ice-cream cones) has long since given way to a cute but conservative and very wealthy coastal tourist village filled with frozen yogurt stands, T-shirt stores, and chichi house-and-garden marts offering ceramic geese and other essentials. Traffic—both vehicular and pedestrian—can be maddeningly congested during the summer and on weekends, and prices in the shops, hotels, and restaurants tend to be gougingly high.

But if you hit Carmel on the right day—preferably midweek in the off season, when the sun is shining and a good, stiff breeze is blowing in from the sea—you'll discover all the charm that made the burg so famous. Stroll the streets in the early morning or early evening to avoid the crowds and admire the varied, eccentric architecture that gives the town its unique look: Hansel-and-Gretel cottages abut Italian villas, and Spanish haciendas nudge tiny Tudor-style houses that would be right at home in a remote English hamlet. Flowers abound in every season—in pretty little courtyards complete with benches for weary travelers, in window boxes, and even on traffic islands. And then there's the setting: even the city's firmest detractors have to admit that Carmel boasts one of the most beautiful curves of beach on the Central Coast.

Part of Carmel's charm lies in its unusual city ordinances, which ban sidewalks, streetlights, franchises, billboards, and even residential addresses. That's right—no one living within city limits has a numerical street address. Instead, people have homes with names like Periwinkle and Mouse House, and residents go

## Carmel-by-the-Sea

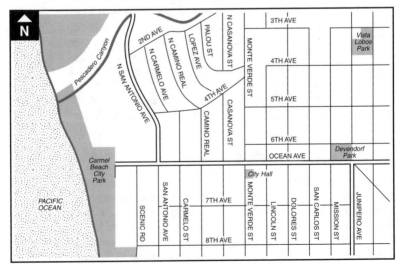

to the post office to pick up their letters and magazines, gossiping all the while about celebrity citizens like former mayor Clint Eastwood, Kim Novak, and Doris Day. If you don't feel like rambling through town on your own, knowledgeable local Gale Wrausmann conducts leisurely, two-hour guided **walking tours** Tuesday through Saturday; call (831)642-2700 for details.

Carmel is also a little bit o' heaven for shoppers. Not only is its downtown packed with interesting little stores, but just outside of town lie two luxe suburban malls: **The Barnyard** (on Highway 1 at Carmel Valley Road) and **The Crossroads** (on Highway 1 at Rio Road). Ocean Avenue has its share of tourist-schlock shops, it's true, but hit the side streets for some fine adventures in consumerland. Intriguing stores include **Ladyfingers** for jewelry (on Dolores Street between Ocean and Seventh Avenues), **Handworks** for beautifully made modern furniture and crafts (two locations, both on Dolores Street, one between Seventh and Eighth Avenues, and one between Fourth and Fifth Avenues), **GJ's Wild West** for Western clothes and accessories (on San Carlos Street between Fifth and Sixth Avenues), the **Dansk II** outlet for housewares (on Ocean Avenue and San Carlos Street), and the **Secret Garden** for pretty garden accessories (on Dolores Street between Fifth and Sixth Avenues).

**Mission Trails Park** supports 5 miles of winding paths, with wildflowers, willows, deer, and redwoods. It's adjacent to the restored **Mission San Carlos Borromeo del Río Carmelo**, better known as the **Carmel Mission**. Established in 1770, this was the headquarters of pioneer priest Father Junípero Serra's famous chain of California missions, and his favorite (Serra is buried in front of the altar in the sanctuary, which is marked with a plaque). The vine-covered baroque church with its 11-bell Moorish tower, completed in 1797, is one of California's architectural treasures. Be sure to see the main altar, with its gothic arch and elaborate decorations, and Serra's restored cell, where he died in 1784. The mission houses three extensive museums, and its surrounding 14 acres are planted with native flowers and trees. The cemetery has more than 3,000 graves of Native Americans who worked and lived in the mission; in place of a gravestone, many plots are marked by a solitary abalone shell; 3080 Rio Road at Lasuén Drive, several blocks west of Highway 1, (831)624-3600.

Other interesting structural landmarks include the **storybook cottages** Hugh Comstock constructed in 1924 and 1925 to indulge his wife's love of fairy tales and dollhouses; the Carmel Business Association can provide a list of the houses if you drop by its office in the Eastwood Building on San Carlos Street, above Hog's Breath Inn, between Fifth and Sixth Avenues, or call (831)624-2522. **Tor House**, the former home of poet Robinson Jeffers, is a rustic granite building that looks as though it were transplanted from the British Isles. Constructed over several

▼

**Carmel-by-the-Sea**

▲

years beginning in 1914, today it's the residence of one of Jeffers' descendants. Even more intriguing is the nearby four-story **Hawk Tower**, which Jeffers built for his wife, Una, with huge rocks he hauled up from the beach below. Guided tours of the house and tower are available for a fee on Friday and Saturday by reservation only (no children under 12 admitted); 26304 Ocean View Avenue at Stewart Way, (831)624-1813.

Carmel has an active theater scene, perhaps best represented by the **Pacific Repertory Theatre** company, which puts on an outdoor musical and Shakespeare festival each summer and performs other classics such as *Amadeus* and *Death of a Salesman* in its indoor theater year-round. Call (831)622-0700 or (831)622-0100 for details. A thick cluster of quality **art galleries** is located between Lincoln and San Carlos Streets and Fifth and Sixth Avenues. Particularly noteworthy is the **Weston Gallery**, which showcases 19th- and 20th-century photographers' works, including a permanent display featuring such famous Carmelites as Edward Weston, Ansel Adams, and Imogen Cunningham; located on Sixth Avenue at Dolores Street, (831)624-4453.

The annual monthlong **Carmel Bach Festival** offers numerous concerts, recitals, lectures, and discussion groups—some are even free. In addition to Bach masterpieces, you'll hear scores by Vivaldi and Scarlatti, and some by those young whippersnappers Beethoven and Chopin. The classical music celebration begins in mid-July; series tickets are sold starting in January, and single-event tickets (ranging from $10 to $50) go on sale in April. Call (831)624-2046 for tickets, and (831)624-1521 for additional festival facts.

Are you ready for a good dose of Mother Nature's great wonders? Then visit one of the town's two beautiful beaches. **Carmel City Beach**, at the foot of Ocean Avenue and the town's shopping district, tends to be overcrowded in the summer (though its chilly aquamarine water is unsafe for swimming), but the gorgeous white sand and towering cypresses are worth the price of sunbathing among the hordes. Or head a mile south on Scenic Drive to spectacular **Carmel River State Beach**, where the locals go to hide from the tourists (though swimming is unsafe here, too). The Carmel River enters the Pacific at this point, and you'll see a bird sanctuary frequented by pelicans, hawks, sandpipers, kingfishers, willets, and the occasional goose. **Middle Beach** and **Monastery Beach** lie beyond. These areas are remarkably scenic, but Mother Nature saved her best efforts for 1,276-acre **Point Lobos State Reserve**, on Highway 1 approximately 3 miles south of Carmel; call (831)624-4909 for park information and (831)624-8413 for scuba-diving reservations, or peruse the park's Web site at www.pt-lobos.parks.state.ca.us/. More than a dozen Point Lobos trails lead to ocean coves, where you might spy sea otters, harbor seals, California sea lions, large colonies of seabirds, and, between December and May, migrating California gray whales. Some trails will even take you to one of the two naturally growing stands of Monterey cypress remaining on earth; the other stand is in Pebble Beach on the 17-Mile Drive. For more nearby hiking recommendations, see the Big Sur section in the following pages. And for tips on touring the famous **17-Mile Drive**, see Pebble Beach in the previous pages.

## RESTAURANTS

**Crème Carmel Restaurant** ★★★ Located in a courtyard behind a liquor store, Crème Carmel is easy to miss. And that's a pity, because this lovely, intimate restaurant decorated with eclectic local art offers some of the most inventive food in town. Chef and co-owner Kenn Leth Madsen has mastered a light, delicate brand of French cooking that makes the most of the region's extraordinary fruits, vegetables, seafood, and meats. Depending on the season, you might see Pacific salmon with roasted leeks and basil sauce, Sonoma foie gras with onion marmalade and puff pastry, or loin of lamb with apple mint chutney, eggplant cannelloni, and roasted garlic sauce. Madsen's originality extends to his nightly vegetarian plate, which might contain a medley of eggplant lasagne, roasted garlic soufflé, and sweet-onion pancakes with mushrooms and fennel mousse. For dessert try the incredible chocolate soufflé with Chantilly cream or the hazelnut pavé layered with mocha and vanilla-bean ice cream. ■ *On San Carlos St (between Ocean and 7th Aves), Carmel-by-the-Sea; (831) 624-0444; $$$; full bar; AE, MC, V; local checks only; dinner Mon–Sat.*

**Pacific's Edge** ★★★ Pacific's Edge, the Highlands Inn's flagship restaurant, is one of the best (and most expensive) dining establishments in the area, serving inspired California cuisine in a luxe setting blessed with panoramic views (reserve well in advance for a table at sunset). Starters might include farm-fresh artichokes with basil mayonnaise, potato-wrapped ahi tuna, or grilled quail with creamy rosemary polenta. Entrees range from grilled Monterey Bay salmon in an onion-rosemary sauce to roasted rack of lamb with white truffle potatoes. Chef Cal Stamenov also offers a nightly Sunset Dinner, a hand-picked selection of courses designed to create a truly memorable meal. ■ *On Hwy 1 (4 miles S of town), Carmel-by-the-Sea; (831) 624-3801 or (800) 682-4811; gm@ highlands-inn.com; www.highlands-inn.com; $$$; full bar; AE, DC, DIS, MC, V; checks OK; brunch Sun, lunch, dinner every day.* ⅙

**Robert Kincaid's Bistro** ★★★ The master chef who created Monterey's ever-popular Fresh Cream restaurant returned to the peninsula in 1995 to open this charming temple to earthy haute cuisine. Wooden beams adorned with hanging dried flowers, golden-hued stucco walls, Provençal furnishings, and not one, but two, roaring stone hearths beckon visitors to relax. The older, moneyed clientele isn't here for the *charmant* French farmhouse atmosphere, though—they've come to sample Kincaid's culinary

▼

▲

magic. His updated bistro fare includes such appetizers as an exceptionally creamy (and delicious) onion tart; delicate and delectable crab dumplings in two sauces (a honey-mustard and a dill sauce); and a baked Brie in white wine–butter sauce that may leave you feeling dangerously like Henry VIII after a state banquet. Main courses include sautéed red snapper Grenobloise (with bay shrimp, capers, and lemon) and a fillet of beef seared with green peppercorns, cream, and brandy. The *San Francisco Chronicle* deemed the roast duckling the best on the Monterey Peninsula, though it may be a mite dry and overcooked for some tastes. Desserts include mind-bendingly delicious treats such as Kincaid's signature chocolate bag with chocolate shake as well as pithivier, a wonderfully light and tasty marriage of flaky puff pastry and almond cream. The service is both warm and impeccable, a rare combination, but the wine list disappoints: it's not as extensive as one would expect at a restaurant of this caliber and it's tipped toward pricier vintages. ▪ *217 Crossroads Blvd (in the Crossroads Shopping Center, at Hwy 1 and Rio Rd), Carmel-by-the-Sea; (831)624-9626; $$$; beer and wine; AE, DIS, MC, V; local checks only; lunch Mon–Fri, dinner Mon–Sun.* ♿

**Sans Souci** ★★★ True to its name, the folks at Sans Souci (French for "without worry") are determined that you'll never have to fret about the food or the service at their charming restaurant, which specializes in both classic and contemporary French cuisine. The candle-lit dining room has a lovely bay window, a fireplace, fresh flowers, decorative wall sconces, and bright, cheery wallpaper bordered by white wainscoting. Despite the traditional white linens, silver, china, and crystal, Sans Souci isn't a bit stuffy. Owner John Williams' infectious sense of humor sets the tone of the place, and the young waitstaff is friendly yet highly professional. Chef Aaron Welsh's changing menu offers a large selection of appetizers, including escargots encased in filo pastry with garlic sauce, portobello mushrooms with spinach and a garlic-walnut vinaigrette, and sautéed foie gras with black currant sauce. Entrees on the seasonal menu might include duck with raspberry sauce, a Roquefort-crusted filet mignon in cabernet sauce, or Dover sole with toasted almonds, hazelnut butter, and parsley. The desserts here put the "d" in decadent: luscious fruit soufflés, a classic tarte Tatin, and crêpes filled with fresh fruit and ice cream flambéed tableside. ▪ *On Lincoln St (between 5th and 6th Aves), Carmel-by-the-Sea; (831)624-6220; $$$; full bar; AE, MC, V; no checks; dinner Thurs–Tues.*

**6th Avenue Grill** ★★★ Formerly known as Prima 6th Avenue Grill, this breezily sophisticated restaurant scored a culinary coup when it recruited noted chef Kurt Grasing in late 1996. Grasing retooled the menu to reflect a more casual version of the contemporary California-Mediterranean cuisine he formerly turned out at tony restaurants like Big Sur's Ventana and San

Mateo's 231 Ellsworth. At lunch, you'll find a smattering of pasta dishes, superb salads, and sandwiches—the charbroiled steak with sautéed onions and garlic aioli on grilled country bread is absolutely delicious. Weekend brunch features such treats as raisin bread French toast with sautéed apples, and eggs scrambled with salmon, sun-dried tomatoes, and mascarpone cheese. Dinner starters might include potato, wild rice, and zucchini pancakes with house-cured salmon and crème fraîche or a savory three-onion tart with a fennel sauce and balsamic syrup; main courses range from wild-mushroom stew with creamy polenta to roast duck with an orange-port glaze. The dining room is a cheerful stage for Grasing's inspired cooking, with its Milano-modern furnishings, textured ocher walls, cathedral ceilings, and witty sculptures and photographs of coffee cups. The wine list is ample and thoughtfully selected, desserts are diet-busting delights, and there's a small patio for dining alfresco. ■ *On 6th Ave (at Mission St), Carmel-by-the-Sea; (831)624-6562; $$; beer and wine; AE, MC, V; local checks only; brunch Sat–Sun, lunch, dinner every day.* ⅃

**Anton & Michel** ★★ This longtime Carmel favorite overlooks the Court of the Fountains with its Louis XV lions and verdigris garden pavilions. Anton & Michel's elegant dining room has pink walls, white wainscoting, and tall, slender pillars topped by elegant curlicue cornices. Despite the interesting decor, the continental cuisine isn't very daring, but chef Max Muramatsu trained at Maxim's in Paris and Tokyo and his food is delicious and extremely well prepared. Standouts include the rack of lamb with an herb-Dijon mustard au jus, grilled veal with a spinach-Madeira sauce, and medallions of ahi tuna with a black-pepper-and-sesame-seed crust and a wasabe-cilantro sauce. Anton & Michel also offers traditional French desserts such as crêpes Suzette, cherries jubilee, and chocolate mousse cake with sauce Anglaise. Service is courtly, and the extensive wine list has garnered many *Wine Spectator* magazine awards. ■ *On Mission St (between Ocean and 7th Aves), Carmel-by-the-Sea; (831)624-2406; www.critics-choice.com/restaurants/anton; $$$; full bar; AE, DC, DIS, MC, V; no checks; lunch, dinner every day.* ⅃

**Casanova Restaurant** ★★ The former home of Charlie Chaplin's cook, this sunny cottage with a Mediterranean feel attracts happy throngs of locals and tourists alike. Casanova specializes in Italian and French Country–style dishes; the pasta creations, such as linguine with seafood served in a big copper pot, are particularly fetching. Lunch on the big patio out back is informal and fun, with heaters keeping patrons warm on chilly afternoons. Inside, the cottage is a jumble of nooks and crannies decked out in rustic European decor. Casanova prides itself on its extensive and reasonably priced wine list, including the well-received Georis merlot and cabernet, produced by one of the restaurant's owners.

Cap off your meal with one of Casanova's superb desserts; the many choices include a Basque-style pear tart and a chocolate custard pie with whipped cream, nuts, and shaved dark and white Belgian chocolates. ■ *On 5th Ave (between San Carlos and Mission Sts), Carmel-by-the-Sea; (831)625-0501; www.casanova-resto.com; $$; full bar; MC, V; no checks; brunch Sun, lunch, dinner every day.* &

**Flying Fish Grill** ★★ Hidden on the ground level of the Carmel Plaza shopping center, this ebullient newcomer is worth seeking out for its fun, stylish atmosphere and its delicious Pacific Rim seafood. The interior is a maze of booths and tables flanked by an expanse of warm, polished wood and crisp blue-and-white banners. Chef/owner Kenny Fukumoto offers such creative dishes as Yin-Yan Salmon (roast salmon on angel hair pasta sprinkled with sesame seeds and served with a soy-lime cream sauce); catfish fillets with fermented Chinese black beans, ginger, and scallions steamed in paper pouches; pan-fried Chilean sea bass with almonds, whipped potatoes, and a Chinese cabbage and rock shrimp stir-fry; and his specialty, rare peppered ahi tuna on angel hair pasta. A few meat dishes and a couple of flavorful clay pot dishes that you cook at your own table round out the menu. There's also a tempting lineup of desserts, including Chocolate Decadence, a warm banana sundae, and an assortment of delicate sorbets. ■ *On Mission St (between Ocean and 7th Aves, in Carmel Plaza), Carmel-by-the-Sea; (831)625-1962; $$; beer and wine; AE, DIS, MC, V; no checks; dinner every day.*

▼
**Carmel-
by-the-Sea**

*Restaurants*

▲

**Il Fornaio** ★★ See the review of this restaurant's San Francisco branch in the San Francisco Bay Area chapter. ■ *On Ocean Ave (at Monte Verde St, in the Pine Inn), Carmel-by-the-Sea; (831)622-5100; www.ilfornaio.com; $$; full bar; AE, DC, MC, V; no checks; breakfast Mon–Fri, brunch Sat–Sun, lunch, dinner every day.* &

**La Bohême** ★★ La Bohême is very small, very cute, and—depending on your luck—very good. The walls of this heart-flutteringly romantic restaurant are painted a pale blue and dotted with cream puff clouds. Two of the most sought-after tables are tucked inside a topsy-turvy little toy house—part of the whimsical street scene mural. La Bohême serves only a prix-fixe menu, which changes nightly. Calendars list the entrees for an entire month, and patrons in the know make it a point to pick up this schedule as soon as they hit town. The three courses include a salad, a bowl of soup, and a main course—perhaps duck with a sherry sauce, filet mignon with a Roquefort-wine sauce, or prawns and scallops in a champagne sauce. The soups, such as salmon bisque, and the salads, with Carmel Valley organic greens, are universally wonderful. The entrees, alas, are less predictable, due to inconsistent meat preparation; cuts can range from splendidly pink and juicy to dull and overcooked. On the other hand, when everything works, La Bohême's cuisine ranks among the best in

Carmel, at bargain prices to boot. At worst, you can console yourself with the rich but fluffy chocolate mousse or the velvety crème brûlée. ▪ *On Dolores St (at 7th Ave), Carmel-by-the-Sea; (831)624-7500; www.carmelnet.com/laboheme; $$; beer and wine; AE, MC, V; no checks; dinner every day.*

**La Dolce Vita** ★★ Marcello Mastroianni and Anouk Aimee might have preferred sleeker surroundings, but those in the mood for authentic Italian food in a casual atmosphere will enjoy this restaurant, a local favorite. The terrace, which overlooks the street, is popular both for sunny lunches and moonlit dinners (heaters take the chill off when necessary). Decorated in an Italian-flag color scheme—green chairs, Astroturf, and plastic red-and-white tablecloths—it's a wonderfully unassuming place to sit back, sip a glass of wine, and revel in *la dolce di far niente*—the joy of doing nothing. The main dining room is a bit more gussied up; it resembles a cozy trattoria with slate floors, light wood furniture, and peach-toned walls bedecked with garlic braids. Specialties include the transporting ravioli alla Rachele (homemade spinach ravioli stuffed with crab and cheese in a champagne cream sauce, topped with scallops and sun-dried tomatoes) and gnocchi della nonna (fresh potato dumplings in either a tomato or gorgonzola-sage-cream sauce—ask for a little of both). A range of individual-size pizzas is also available, along with *secondi piatti* ranging from traditional osso buco to calamari steak drizzled with sun-dried tomato pesto, lemon juice, and crisp Orvieto wine. The waitstaff can be a bit cheeky at times, but hey, with food this *bellissima*, you're not likely to get your feathers ruffled. ▪ *On San Carlos St (between 7th and 8th Aves), Carmel-by-the-Sea; (831)624-3667; $$; beer and wine; MC, V; local checks only; lunch, dinner every day.* ⎕

**Piatti Ristorante** ★★ See the review of this restaurant's Yountville branch in the Wine Country chapter. ▪ *On 6th Ave (at Junípero Ave), Carmel-by-the-Sea; (831)625-1766; $$; full bar; AE, MC, V; no checks; lunch, dinner every day.* ⎕

**Rio Grill** ★★ This noisy Southwestern-style grill is packed with a lively, young crowd from opening to closing. The salads, such as organic mixed greens with aged goat cheese, seasoned walnuts, and curry vinaigrette, are wonderfully fresh, and appetizers like the ever-popular onion rings and fried Monterey Bay squid with orange-sesame dipping sauce draw raves. The tasty barbecued baby back ribs and the herb-crusted chicken with crispy broccoli-corn risotto cakes are good bets for the main course, as is the pumpkin-seed-crusted salmon with chipotle-lime vinaigrette and roasted red-pepper potato cakes. Desserts include a killer olallieberry pie and caramel-apple bread pudding. While the atmosphere may be chaotic, the service isn't, and the grill boasts a large wine list, with many selections available by the glass. ▪ *101 Crossroads Blvd (in the Crossroads Shopping Center, at Hwy 1 and*

Rio Rd), Carmel-by-the-Sea; (831) 625-5436; www.critics-choice.com/ restaurants/riogrill; $$; full bar; AE, DIS, MC, V; no checks; brunch Sun, lunch, dinner every day. &

**Hog's Breath Inn** ★ If rowdy crowds and music blasting so loud you can hardly think are your idea of a good time, then join the dinnertime melee at movie star and ex-Carmel mayor Clint Eastwood's place—just look for the fire-breathing hog out front. You'll always find a horde of tourists and locals cruising, carousing, and plowing their way through the better-than-average pub grub here. Many of the dishes are named after Eastwood's films, like the succulent Dirty Harry burger on a fresh-baked bun, the aptly named For a Few Dollars More 16-ounce New York steak, and the Sudden Impact sandwich, a broiled Polish sausage with Jack cheese and jalapeño peppers on a French roll. (A word to the wise: Prices vary wildly here—most dinner entrees will run you around $15 to $25, but the $7.25 burger or the $9.50 roast chicken might make your day.) Thanks to half-a-dozen heat lamps and fireplaces, you can eat outside on the brick patio, with its immense bucolic mural of Carmel Valley, in just about any weather. ■ *On San Carlos St (between 5th and 6th Aves), Carmel-by-the-Sea; (831) 625-1044; $$; full bar; AE, DC, MC, V; no checks; brunch Sun, lunch Mon–Sat, dinner every day.*

**Carmel-by-the-Sea**

*Restaurants*

▲

**Katy's Place** ★ When Katy's Place is closed for the day, there's no doubt about it—a big sign announces, "Kitchen's closed—this chick's had it!" When it's open, however, Katy's has a reputation for serving the best breakfasts in town. The country-kitchen-style restaurant specializes in comfort foods: big helpings and endless variations of pancakes, waffles, and eggs, including a dynamite eggs Benedict. Eat in the pretty dining room or on the patio under the redwood trees. ■ *On Mission St (between 5th and 6th Aves), Carmel-by-the-Sea; (831) 624-0199; $; beer and wine; no credit cards; local checks only; breakfast, lunch every day.* &

**Patisserie Boissiere** ★ After you've shopped till you dropped in Carmel, this is the place to go to rest those tootsies while you refuel with some of the most divine desserts in town. For more than 30 years, this comfortable, European-style restaurant has turned out a tempting array of masterful cakes, tarts, mousses, and other delights, all displayed in big glass cases so you can visually caress each one before making your selection. Patisserie Boissiere is also a delightful spot for a light lunch or dinner in the pretty Louis XIV dining room. The predominantly French Country cuisine encompasses such offerings as a roasted chicken and spinach salad with jicama, apples, and caramelized walnuts; coquilles St. Jacques; lamb shank; and salmon baked in parchment paper with fresh artichokes and lemon-basil butter. Takeout is available on weekdays, and there's an extensive espresso menu. ■ *On Mission St (between Ocean and 7th Aves), Carmel-by-*

*the-Sea; (831) 624-5008; $$; beer and wine; AE, MC, V; checks*
*OK; breakfast Sat–Sun, lunch every day, dinner Wed–Sun.* &

## LODGINGS

**Highlands Inn** ★★★ This exquisite luxury hotel began as a clutch of cabins in 1916, but its rustic days are long gone. Set high above the rocky coastline south of Carmel with fine views of Yankee Point, the Highlands Inn is now a sprawling modern complex of glowing redwood and soaring glass. In the main lodge, a sky-lit promenade leads to a series of glass-walled salons built for watching sunsets. In the fireside lobby you'll find deep leather settees, a granite fireplace, a grand piano, and elaborate floral displays. Outside, flower-lined walkways connect the cottagelike collection of rooms and suites. Every suite and town-house unit comes with a full parlor, kitchen, and bath with a massive spa tub. The 142 guest rooms were completely refurbished in 1996, and jewel-tone accents in fabrics and carpeting substantially jazzed up the muted earth-tone color scheme. Most rooms have fireplaces, private decks, and fabulous views of the ocean, landscaped grounds, and evergreen-draped hills. Another perk is the inn's elegant three-star restaurant, **Pacific's Edge** (see review, above), and the less formal **California Market**, which boasts lovely coastline views and serves casual, well-prepared California fare.
■ *On Hwy 1 (4 miles S of town), Carmel-by-the-Sea; (831) 624-3801 or (800) 682-4811; mail: PO Box 1700, Carmel-by-the-Sea, CA 93921; gm@highlands-inn.com; www.highlands-inn.com; $$$; full bar; AE, DC, DIS, MC, V; checks OK; Pacific's Edge: brunch Sun, lunch, dinner every day; California Market: breakfast, lunch, dinner every day.* &

**La Playa Hotel** ★★★ Almost regal in its splendor, this imposing 1904 luxury hotel spills down a terraced, bougainvillea-and-jasmine-strewn hillside toward the sea. Paths lit by gas street lamps wind among lush gardens with cast-iron gazebos and past a heated swimming pool festooned with mermaids, La Playa's mythical mascots. The hotel's 75 guest rooms were remodeled in January 1997, and everything from the carpeting and bedspreads to the pillows and window fixtures were replaced. The rooms are lighter now, with Spanish-style furnishings and refinished headboards hand-carved with the hotel's signature mermaids. To do La Playa right, invest in one of the five cottages, some of which are nestled in the gardens. These have varying numbers of rooms, and four of them offer full kitchens, fireplaces, and private patios. The hotel's restaurant, the **Terrace Grill**, has a fine view of the gardens and serves such tasty seasonal fare as artichoke ravioli, grilled shrimp risotto, and chicken breast stuffed with dried cherries, cranberries, and walnuts. ■ *On Camino Real (at 8th Ave), Carmel-by-the-Sea; (831) 624-6476 or (800) 582-8900; mail: PO Box 900, Carmel-by-the-Sea, CA 93921; $$$; full bar; AE,*

DC, MC, V; checks OK; breakfast, lunch Mon–Sat, brunch Sun, dinner every day. ⟨⟩

**Mission Ranch** ★★★ When Clint Eastwood—director, movie star, and former mayor of Carmel—was a young recruit stationed at Fort Ord 40 years ago, he happened to venture onto the Mission Ranch, and it was love at first sight. Once a working dairy farm, the ranch had become a humble roadhouse restaurant and motel—nothing special, perhaps, except for its magnificent natural setting. Nestled in back of the Carmel Mission, the Ranch overlooks a carpet of pastureland that gives way to a dramatic view of Carmel River Beach, with the craggy splendor of Point Lobos stretching just beyond. (Eastwood, by the way, wasn't the first to fall for that view. In 1879, Robert Louis Stevenson, hot in pursuit of his beloved—but inconveniently married—Fanny, was so taken with the vista that he made Point Lobos the setting for *Treasure Island*.)

Alas, over the years, termites, erosion, and lack of management interest had taken their toll on the ranch, and a developer was all set to raze the buildings in the late 1980s when Eastwood rode in to the rescue. He poured a ton of money and a lot of love into restoring the Victorian farmhouse, cottages, bunkhouse, and other buildings, determined to be true to the original spirit of the place. The result is simply wonderful. The peaceful, Western-style spread opened in 1992, offering everything a guest needs to feel comfortable and not a single silly frill. The 31 rooms, distributed among a clutch of pretty, immaculately maintained buildings, are sparsely but tastefully appointed, with props from Eastwood's films, such as the clock from *Unforgiven*, nonchalantly scattered among the furnishings. The 1857 Martin Family Farmhouse is a Victorian charmer, with six bedrooms and a lovely parlor complete with a grand piano and fireplace. Other structures include the old Bunkhouse (which has its own living room with a fireplace, dining room, and kitchen), the aptly named Meadow View Rooms (which are newer and more deluxe), the main barn, and the luxurious Hay Loft Bedroom. Handmade quilts grace the custom-made country-style wooden beds that are so large you literally have to climb into them, and each guest room has its own phone, TV, and bathroom. Rates include a continental breakfast served in the tennis clubhouse. The informal and Western-themed **Restaurant at Mission Ranch**, which operates under separate management, serves hearty American-style fare. The place's only flaw is that the piano bar can get a little rowdy, and guests in the structures closest to the restaurant may find themselves reaching for earplugs in the middle of the night. Otherwise, our Stetson is off to Clint. ■ *26270 Dolores St (at 15th Ave), Carmel-by-the-Sea, CA 93923; (831) 624-6436, (800) 538-8221 or (831) 625-9040 (restaurant); $$–$$$; MC, V; checks OK; brunch Sun, lunch Sat, dinner every day.* ⟨⟩

▼

**Carmel-
by-the-Sea**

*Lodgings*

▲

**Cypress Inn** ★★  This charming Mediterranean-style inn in the center of town recently has been treated to a much-needed renovation that brought it up to date while preserving its Old Carmel charm. The 33 guest rooms received new paint, furniture, carpets, and TVs, and the bathrooms have been outfitted in new ceramic or marble tile. Movie star and animal-rights activist Doris Day owns the inn, and pets, naturally, are more than welcome; the hotel even provides dog beds for its four-footed guests. Service is uniformly professional and courteous, and the rooms contain some thoughtful touches: fresh fruit, bottles of spring water, chocolates left on the pillow at night, and a decanter of sherry. Some have sitting rooms, wet bars, private verandas, and ocean views. There's a spacious Spanish-style living room with a comforting fire and a friendly bar that dishes out coffee and a continental breakfast in the morning, as well as libations of a more spirited kind at night. Posters of Doris Day movies add a touch of glamour and fun to the decor. ■ *On Lincoln St (at 7th Ave), Carmel-by-the-Sea; (831)624-3871 or (800)443-7443; mail: PO Box Y, Carmel-by-the-Sea, CA 93921; $$$; full bar; AE, DIS, MC, V; checks OK.*

**The Happy Landing** ★★  One could easily see Snow White puttering around contentedly in this B&B's garden courtyard, a storybook setting complete with gazebo, fountain, and a passel of stone gnomes. This aptly named pink-and-azure Comstock cottage, built in 1925 as a summer retreat for two lucky sisters from San Francisco, has been divided into seven cozy guest rooms. With private baths and televisions (but no phones), all rooms but one are grouped around the courtyard, and three have fireplaces (have-nots can console themselves with the large adobe-and-stone hearth in the reception room). The best rooms are the two spacious suites, which are equipped with wet bars, but all the rooms boast at least a few charming details befitting a Comstock creation: wood-beamed cathedral ceilings, stained-glass windows, hand-painted sinks, curved archways, and cunning little windows and doors in surprising places. Lovers of pristine modernity may not be comfortable here—some of the furniture is a bit down at the heels and the 1920s-era bathrooms in a few of the quarters might seem a little dowdy. A full breakfast is delivered to guests in the morning, and tea and sherry are served in the grand, antique-laden sitting room every afternoon. ■ *On Monte Verde St (between 5th and 6th Aves), Carmel-by-the-Sea; (831)624-7917; mail: PO Box 2619, Carmel-by-the-Sea, CA 93921; $$–$$$; MC, V; checks OK.*

**San Antonio House** ★★  Built in the late 1920s, this white-painted wood-shingle home with green trim has four cozy, wood-paneled rooms, each with antiques, a fireplace, a private bath, a refrigerator, and a telephone. In the morning, a breakfast of fruit, coffee cake, scones, and juice arrives at your door with the morning paper. Two rooms, the Doll House and the Patio Suite, have separate sitting areas. Stroll the lovely gardens with their interesting little nooks and arbors. Carmel Beach is just one block away. ■ *On San Antonio Ave (between Ocean and 7th Aves), Carmel-by-the-Sea; (831)624-4334; mail: PO Box 3683, Carmel-by-the-Sea, CA 93921; $$$; MC, V; checks OK.*

**The Stonehouse Inn** ★★ This ivy-covered stone structure is one of those inns people return to again and again—and many have been coming back since it opened as a hostelry in 1948. Prior to that, the 1906 building was the home of Nana Foster, and the six prettily decorated guest rooms are named after local writers and artists who were her frequent guests. The Jack London Room has gabled ceilings, a queen-size brass bed, and a ruffled day bed with a sea view. The Sinclair Lewis Room has a king-size bed, a writing desk, and a fine view of the ocean (though who knows what Lewis—that loather of the bourgeois—would think of the giant teddy bears). None except the Ansel Adams and Robinson Jeffers Rooms have private bathrooms—a definite detraction for some folks. Downstairs, you may lounge in the wing chairs before the fireplace and help yourself to wine and cheese in the early evening. Huge bouquets of flowers enliven the house, and antique toy cars line the staircase. ■ *On 8th Ave (between Monte Verde and Casanova Sts), Carmel-by-the-Sea; (831)624-4569 or (800)748-6618; mail: PO Box 2517, Carmel-by-the-Sea, CA 93921; $$; MC, V; checks OK.*

▼

**Carmel-by-the-Sea**

*Lodgings*

▲

**The Green Lantern Inn** ★ Built in 1925, the Green Lantern's rustic buildings are nestled among lush gardens just a few blocks above Ocean Beach. Renovated in 1993, the inn was treated to new wallpaper, carpets, and bathrooms, enhancing the place's Old Carmel charm; in 1996, it became a member of the Best Western hotel chain. Four of the 18 guest rooms have fireplaces, and a recently added mini-suite has a king-size bed, a dining alcove, a private deck, and a refrigerator. The staff is accommodating and a deluxe continental breakfast is served in the morning. ■ *On Casanova St (at 7th Ave), Carmel-by-the-Sea; (831)624-4392; mail: PO Box 1114, Carmel-by-the-Sea, CA 93921; www.travelweb.com; $$; AE, DC, DIS, MC, V; no checks.*

**Carmel River Inn** Families favor these 24 cottages and 19 motel units that offer utilitarian but homey accommodations at reasonable prices. Though the inn's close to the highway, noise isn't a problem because it is set back along the Carmel River and surrounded by a natural buffer of trees. The rustic Sierra-style units were refurbished after the floods of '95, but the cabins remain the best places to stay; a few have full kitchens or kitchenettes, and some have fireplaces and two bedrooms. Guests have use of a heated pool year-round. ■ *On Hwy 1 (at the bridge, S of Rio Rd), Carmel-by-the-Sea; (831)624-1575 or (800)882-8142; mail: PO Box 221609, Carmel-by-the-Sea, CA 93922; $$; MC, V; no checks.* ♿

### LODGINGS

**Stonepine** ★★★★ This exquisite Mediterranean villa (the former country home of the Crocker banking family) rises in terraced splendor against the oak-covered hills of the Carmel Valley. Surrounded by cypress, imported stone pines, and wisteria trailing from hand-carved Italian stone pillars, the inn has 16 guest rooms divided among Château Noel (named after owner Noel Hentschel), the Paddock House, and the idyllic (and astronomically expensive) Briar Rose Cottage, a two-bedroom affair with a private rose garden, living room, dining room, kitchen, and bar. The suites in the main house are studies in formal splendor; all have French antique furnishings, Jacuzzis, down comforters, and fluffy robes, and five of them feature fireplaces. The lavish gray-and-rose living room, with its magnificent medieval-style fireplace, incorporates interesting contemporary furniture with European antiques and a dash of Asian art. The Paddock House is more casual—but casual in the Ralph Lauren–country, not rustic-bunkhouse, sense. The cost of your room includes a big breakfast and an afternoon tea with pastries. For an additional charge you may partake of a wine reception followed by an elegant five-course estate dinner in the Château's dining room. During the day, float in the jewel-like swimming pool, play tennis, explore the ranch's 330 acres, or horse around at the Stonepine Equestrian Center. (Beware: The equestrian staff takes horseback riding mighty seriously, and more than one city slicker has suffered a bruised ego as well as a sore derriere after a turn on the trails.) ▪ *150 E Carmel Valley Rd (13 miles E of Hwy 1), Carmel Valley, CA 93924; (831)659-2245; www.integra.fr/relaischateaux/stonepine; $$$; AE, MC, V; checks OK.*

▼

**Carmel Valley**

*Lodgings*

▲

**Carmel Valley Ranch** ★★★ Nestled on a 1,700-acre spread in bucolic Carmel Valley, this haven for golf and tennis enthusiasts (and corporate retreaters) is about as plush a ranch as you're ever likely to encounter. Outfitted in earth tones, burgundies, and greens, the 100 guest suites are arranged in low-lying, condolike clusters on the rolling hills; each comes equipped with cathedral ceilings, a wood-burning fireplace, a well-stocked refreshment center, two TVs, a trio of phones, a private deck, and a richly appointed bathroom. Some of the pricier suites come with a dining area, a kitchenette, and a private outdoor whirlpool tub (discreetly enclosed, of course). You might need that whirlpool after partaking of the ranch's activities: golf at a newly renovated Pete Dye 18-hole course, tennis on one of a dozen clay and hard-surface courts, guided nature hikes, biking, horseback riding, workouts with a personal trainer at the fitness club, or a dip in one of two swimming pools. When you're ready to relax, indulge in a facial or a manicure, a soak in one of six whirlpool spas, or perhaps a couple's massage followed by champagne and chocolate-covered strawberries. The ranch also offers three restaurants, including the elegant **Oaks**, which serves refined American regional cooking in a formal room graced by Old California antiques, a towering stone fireplace, and a phalanx of windows affording a panoramic view of the oak-covered hills. ■ *1 Old Ranch Rd (off Carmel Valley Rd), Carmel Valley, CA 93923; (831) 625-9500 or (800) 422-7635; $$$; full bar; AE, MC, V; checks OK; breakfast, lunch, dinner every day.* ₺

**Quail Lodge ★★★** This posh resort catering to golfers and tennis players has 100 guest rooms set along winding paths flanking a meticulously kept 18-hole course and a series of pretty little ponds. Comfort, not ostentatious luxury, is the byword here, and Quail Lodge does comfort very well indeed. Decorated in nature-inspired shades of green, yellow, and red, even the least expensive rooms are spacious and have private balconies or patios. Higher-priced units feature fireplaces, Jacuzzis, and separate living rooms. Nice touches abound: all rooms have a coffee-maker, robes, a pants press, room service, a minibar, a refrigerator, cable TV, and a bathroom equipped with every amenity. Two pools and a large hot tub stand ready for your dipping pleasure. The formal **Covey Restaurant**, the pride of executive chef Bob Williamson, offers a blend of European and regional cuisine, such as sautéed sweetbreads, scallops with champagne sauce, duckling with an aromatic fruit sauce, and other fare that reflects his emphasis on fresh local products. Hearty, well-prepared, reasonably priced breakfasts and lunches are served at the clubhouse, a pleasant quarter-mile stroll away. Guests are entitled to reduced greens fees at the private club and use of the tennis courts. ■ *8205 Valley Greens Dr (3½ miles E of Hwy 1, just off Carmel Valley Rd), Carmel Valley, CA 93923; (831) 624-1581 or (800) 538-9516; info@quail-lodge-resort.com; $$$; full bar; AE, DC, MC, V; checks OK; dinner every day.* ₺

**Los Laureles Lodge and Restaurant ★★** Believe it or not, the more than two dozen white clapboard guest rooms here were once actually stables for Muriel Vanderbilt's Thoroughbred racehorses. The hay and the flies have been replaced by knotty pine paneling and country antiques, but the property retains a refreshing ranch house ambience. Los Laureles also has several private places to stay, including the three-bedroom Hill House with its dramatic valley views, the Vanderbilt Cottage (actually a large suite), and the Honeymoon Cottage, which has a hot tub and a view overlooking a canyon. Shaded by ancient oak trees, the original 1890s lodge houses **Los Laureles Restaurant**, which sports a trim, country-club look with plaid fabrics and mementos of early California and equestrian pursuits. The seasonal American regional menu may include venison medallions with red cabbage, wild pig tenderloin with candied bananas, or a Monterey Bay salmon with dill chardonnay sauce. Outside, you'll find a large swimming pool and a patio with a terraced garden—the venue for big weekend barbecues held throughout the summer. ■ *313 W Carmel Valley Rd (10½ miles E of Hwy 1), Carmel Valley; (831)659-2233 or (800)533-4404; mail: PO Box 2310, Carmel Valley, CA 93924; $$–$$$; full bar; AE, MC, V; checks OK; breakfast, lunch every day Apr–Nov; dinner every day year-round.* ᕇ

**Robles del Rio Lodge** ★★  Set on an oak-covered ridge 1,000 feet above Carmel Valley, this classic 1920s Western lodge, constructed of river rock and timber, makes guests feel as if they've stepped back to a time of simple pleasures. Those who fancy sunning and soaking will enjoy the lodge's huge, inviting stone terrace, which boasts a pool and a large, tiled hot tub. Guests who simply want to sit for a spell can do so in style on the lodge's wraparound front porch, complete with comfy Adirondack furniture. Some of the 26 rustic rooms in the original lodge are a bit small, but they're attractively decorated with country furniture. The five private cabins with fireplaces and kitchenettes are especially appealing to families and larger groups. Be advised, though: the furnishings can be a bit worn, and some of the facilities—like the showers and stoves—are antique in a way that's less than charming. An expansive continental breakfast buffet is served in the morning. **The Ridge**, the lodge's award-winning restaurant with spectacular valley views, serves California-French cuisine, drawing customers from as far away as Monterey. During the summer, don't miss Robles del Rio's Sunday terrace barbecues. ■ *200 Punta Del Monte St (from Hwy 1, take the Carmel Valley Rd for about 13 miles to Esquiline Rd, then follow the signs to the lodge), Carmel Valley, CA 93924; (831)659-3705, (800)833-0843 or (831)659-0170 (restaurant); $$–$$$; full bar; AE, MC, V; local checks only; lunch, dinner every day.* ᕇ

## BIG SUR

There isn't exactly a Big Sur in Big Sur . . . not a town by that name, anyway. Originally El Sur Grande (Spanish for "the Big South"), Big Sur encompasses 90 miles of rugged, spectacular coastline stretching south from Carmel to San Simeon. A narrow, twisting segment of Highway 1 (built with convict labor in the 1930s) snakes through this coastal area, and the mist-shrouded forests, plunging cliffs, and cobalt sea bordering the road make the drive one of the most beautiful in the country—if not the world. The region is so scenic that some folks favor giving it national park status; others, however, recoil in horror at the thought of involving the federal government in the preservation of this untamed land and have coined the expression "Don't Yosemitecate Big Sur."

Despite Big Sur's popularity, the area miraculously has remained sparsely populated, and most people journey here for only a few days to camp or backpack—or to luxuriate in the elegant (and, in some cases, exorbitantly priced) resorts hidden in the hills. The bumper-to-bumper traffic on summer weekends is reminiscent of LA's rush hour; to avoid the crowds, come midweek or in the spring, when the gold, yellow, and purple wildflowers brighten the windswept landscape. Check in with the folks at the Big Sur Land Trust, (831) 625-5523, to find out where you can pick up an audiotape offering a guided tour of the region.

Whether you're cruising through for the day or plan to hide out in a resort, be sure to spend some time hiking in the gorgeous **Point Lobos State Reserve** (for more details on the reserve, see Carmel-by-the-Sea in the previous pages). Farther south, Highway 1 crosses Bixby Creek via the 268-foot-high, 739-foot-long **Bixby Bridge** (also known as the Rainbow Bridge), a solitary, majestic arch built in 1932 that attracts lots of snap-happy photographers. Nearby is the automated **Point Sur Lighthouse**, built in 1889 and situated 360 feet above the surf on Point Sur, a giant volcanic-rock island. Inexpensive (though physically taxing) 2½-hour guided lighthouse tours, some under spectacular moonlight, are offered on weekends year-round and on Wednesdays in the summer (be sure to take a jacket, even in the summer months); located off Highway 1, 19 miles south of Carmel, (831) 625-4419.

▼

**Big Sur**

▲

Hikers and bicyclists often head farther south to navigate the many trails zigzagging through the sycamores and maples in 4,800-acre **Andrew Molera State Park**, the largest state park on the Big Sur coast. A mile-long walk through a meadow laced with wildflowers leads to the park's 2-mile-long beach harboring the area's best tide pools. A few miles down Highway 1 on the inland side is one of California's most popular parks, **Pfeiffer–Big Sur State Park**. Here, 810 acres of madrone and oak woodlands and misty redwood canyons are crisscrossed with hiking trails, and many paths provide panoramic views of the sea. The **Big Sur River** meanders through the park, too, attracting anglers and swimmers who brave the chilly waters. Nearby, the unmarked Sycamore Canyon Road (the only paved, ungated road west of Highway 1 between the Big Sur Post Office and Pfeiffer–Big Sur State Park) leads to beautiful but blustery **Pfeiffer Beach**, with its white-and-mauve sands and enormous sea caves; follow the road until it ends at a parking lot, about 2 miles from Highway 1.

If your idea of communing with nature is a comfy chair in the shade, grab a seat on the upper deck of the fabled **Nepenthe** bar and restaurant, perched 800 feet above the roiling Pacific; located on Highway 1, 3 miles south of Pfeiffer–Big Sur State Park, (831) 667-2345. The food at Nepenthe isn't worth the steep prices, but the view merits a pit stop at the bar, particularly at sunset. Sit back and imagine the days when Orson Welles bought this lot in 1944 for his wife, Rita Hayworth.

Four miles south of Nepenthe is the **Coast Gallery**, a showplace for local artists and craftspeople featuring pottery, jewelry, and paintings, including watercolors by author Henry Miller, who lived nearby for more than 15 years. The author's fans will also want to seek out the **Henry Miller Library**. In addition to a great collection of Miller's books and art, the library serves as one of Big Sur's cultural centers and features the art, poetry, prose, and music of locals; it's open Tuesday through Sunday, and is located just beyond Nepenthe restaurant on the east side of Highway 1, (831)667-2574. Seekers of other sorts flock to **Esalen Institute**, the world-famous New Age retreat and home of heavenly massages and hot springs that overlook the ocean; call (831)667-3000 for general information, and (831)667-3047 for hot springs reservations. The springs are accessible to non-guests daily in the wee hours only, from 1am to 3:30am.

At the southern end of Big Sur is beautiful **Julia Pfeiffer Burns State Park**, with 4,000 acres to roam. You'll find some excellent day hikes here, but if you just want to get out of the car and stretch your legs, take the quarter-mile Waterfall Trail to 80-foot-high **McWay Waterfall**, one of the few falls in California that plunges directly into the sea. Keep an eye open for the silly sea otters that play in McWay Cove. And wherever you trek through Big Sur, beware of the poison oak—it's as ubiquitous as the seagulls hovering over the coast.

## LODGINGS

**Post Ranch Inn** ★★★★ *Travel & Leisure* magazine has hailed the 98-acre Post Ranch Inn as "the most spectacular hotel on the Pacific Coast," and that might not be hyperbole. Discreetly hidden on a ridge in the Santa Lucia Mountains, architect Mickey Muennig's redwood complex was completed in April 1992. Muennig supposedly camped out on the property for five months before setting pencil to paper for his design, which had to conform to the strict Big Sur Coastal Land Use Plan. He propped up six of the inn's units (known as the Tree Houses) on stilts to avoid disturbing the surrounding redwoods' root systems, and sank others into the earth, roofing them with sod. The inn's deceptively simple exteriors are meant to harmonize with the forested slopes, while windows, windows everywhere celebrate the breathtaking vista of sky and sea that is Big Sur's birthright. Inside, the lodgepole construction and wealth of warm woods lend a rough-hewn luxury to the rooms. Earth tones, blues, and greens predominate, extending the link between the buildings and their environment.

"Environment," in fact, is a word you'll hear a lot around this place, which was named after William Post, one of the area's early settlers. The Post Ranch Inn is one of the new breed of eco-hotels, where the affluent can indulge in sumptuous luxury and still feel politically correct. The water is filtered; visitors are encouraged to sort their paper, glass, and plastic garbage; and the paper upon which guests' rather staggering bills are printed is recycled.

Despite this more-ecologically-correct-than-thou attitude, the folks behind the Post Ranch Inn haven't forgotten about the niceties of life. The 30 spacious rooms have spare—but by no means spartan—decor, including fireplaces, massage tables, king-size beds, and sideboards made of African hardwoods (nonendangered, naturally). Designer robes hang in the closets, Jacuzzi tubs for two adorn the well-equipped bathrooms, and stereo systems fill the air with ethereal, New Age music. A continental breakfast and guided nature hikes are included in the room rates; the massages, facials, herbal wraps, and yoga classes are not.

The Ranch also boasts a gorgeous, cliff-hugging restaurant that has been hailed as one of the best on the Central Coast. **Sierra Mar** serves a sophisticated brand of California cuisine in a serene expanse of wood and glass that lets you drink in the incredible views along with the costly wine. When you can wrest your eyes from the ocean and focus on the dinner menu, which changes daily, you might see such sumptuous starters as pine-smoked squab with ginger and cilantro, mussel soup with saffron and potatoes, and perhaps a salad of lettuces (organic, of course) mixed with shaved fennel, oranges, Parmesan, and a Campari vinaigrette. Main courses include such bounty as roast rack of venison with glazed chestnuts and huckleberries, truffled fettuccine with asparagus and English peas, and roasted Guinea fowl with potato gnocchi and pearl onions. Finish off your feast with a plate of assorted house-made sweets—proof positive that politically correct need not mean diet deprived. ■ *On Hwy 1 (30 miles S of Carmel), Big Sur; (831)667-2200, (800)527-2200 or (831)667-2800 (restaurant); mail: PO Box 219, Big Sur, CA 93920; $$$; full bar; AE, MC, V; checks OK; lunch, dinner every day.* &

▼

**Big Sur**

*Lodgings*

▲

**Ventana Country Inn Resort** ★★★★ If one casts the Post Ranch as the brash newcomer, the Ventana must be the revered granddaddy of the eco-hotel scene. Not that this stunning resort is showing its age—the Ventana is as fresh and up with the times as it was when it made its debut two decades ago. Set on the brow of a chaparral-covered hill in the Santa Lucia Mountains, this modern, weathered cedar inn is almost too serene and contemplative to be called decadent, yet too luxurious to be called anything else. Its spacious 59 rooms, decorated in an upscale country style and divided among 12 low-rise buildings, look out over the plunging forested hillsides, wildflower-laced meadows, and roiling waters of the Big Sur coast. Three houses are also available to rent; the rooms in the Sycamore and Madrone Houses have large private balconies and some of the best views of the ocean. Several rooms have fireplaces, hot tubs, and wet bars; rates climb in accordance with the amenities offered (peak-season

prices range from approximately $200 to a whopping $900). A  **Central Coast**
sumptuous breakfast is included.

The inn's other big draw is the **Ventana Restaurant**, which delivers panoramic patio views of 50 miles of coastline at prices that can be equally breathtaking. Although critics have been unanimous in praising its aesthetics, a revolving-door parade of chefs has kept them uncertain about the quality of the food since Jeremiah Tower did his star turn here years ago. The current chef, Hamid Borna, serves ambitious dishes such as pan-seared, potato-wrapped salmon, oak-grilled Angus pavé with potato gratin, and chestnut-crusted ahi tuna. ■ *On Hwy 1 (28 miles S of Carmel, 2½ miles S of Pfeiffer–Big Sur State Park), Big Sur, CA 93920; (831)667-2331 or (800)628-6500; $$$; full bar; AE, DC, DIS, MC, V; checks OK; lunch, dinner every day.* ♿

**Deetjen's Big Sur Inn** ★ During the '30s and '40s, travelers making the long journey up or down the coast used to drop in and stay the night with Grandpa Deetjen, a Norwegian immigrant. No doubt weary of houseguests, he constructed a cluster of redwood buildings with 20 rooms to accommodate them. Grandpa's idea of comfort was a bit austere, but then again, he never expected to charge $70 to $150 per night. Located in a damp redwood canyon, most cabins are divided into two units, with dark wood interiors, hand-hewn doors without locks or keys (they can be secured with the hook and eye from within, though), and nonexistent insulation. Some have shared baths, and many are quite charming in a rustic sort of way, but they're definitely not for everyone. If you stay in one of the two-story units (some with fireplaces or wood-burning stoves), be sure to request the quieter upstairs rooms. The cabins near the river offer the most privacy.

**Big Sur**

*Lodgings*

▲

**Deetjen's Big Sur Inn Restaurant**, which has garnered a loyal following, serves good Euro-California cuisine that takes advantage of local produce and seafood. The small menu varies seasonally and features half-a-dozen starters ranging from a warm poached pear stuffed with Stilton cheese and walnuts to the appetizer of roasted garlic, baked goat cheese, and grilled bell pepper served with tapenade and croutons. Several entrees are offered, including a fresh pasta that changes nightly and a roasted, sautéed, grilled, and steamed vegetable platter. Meat eaters will want to knife into such robust fare as the roasted rack of lamb with a honey-mustard and rosemary crust or an oak-grilled rib-eye steak. ■ *On Hwy 1 (3 miles S of Pfeiffer–Big Sur State Park), Big Sur, CA 93920; (831)667-2377 or (831)667-2378 (restaurant); $$; beer and wine; MC, V; checks OK; breakfast, dinner every day.* ♿

**Ripplewood Resort** ★ With its 16 spartan cabins clustered along a rugged section of Highway 1, Ripplewood Resort is a wonderful place to go with a large group of friends. Try to book cabins 1 to 9, which are set on the river far below the highway, where the air

**Central Coast** is sweet with redwood. During the summer the popular units are typically booked four months in advance. **The Ripplewood Cafe** is comfortable and pretty and serves a good breakfast and lunch. The muffins, sticky buns, and pies are house-made, and the cinnamon French toast is a big favorite. For lunch try the marinated bean salad or the grilled Jack cheese sandwich slathered with green chile salsa. ▪ *On Hwy 1 (about 1 mile N of Pfeiffer–Big Sur State Park), Big Sur, CA 93920; (831)667-2242; $$; beer and wine; MC, V; no checks; breakfast, lunch every day.*

# WINE COUNTRY

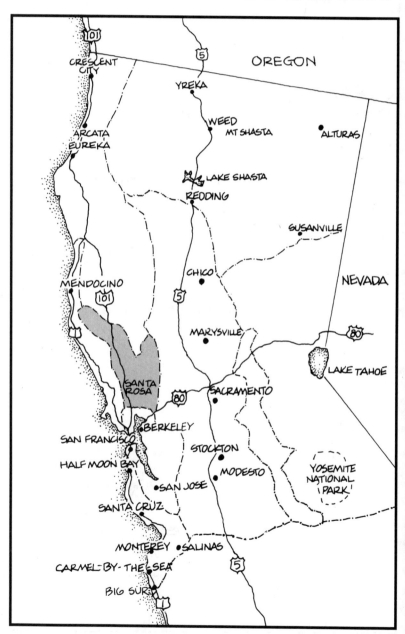

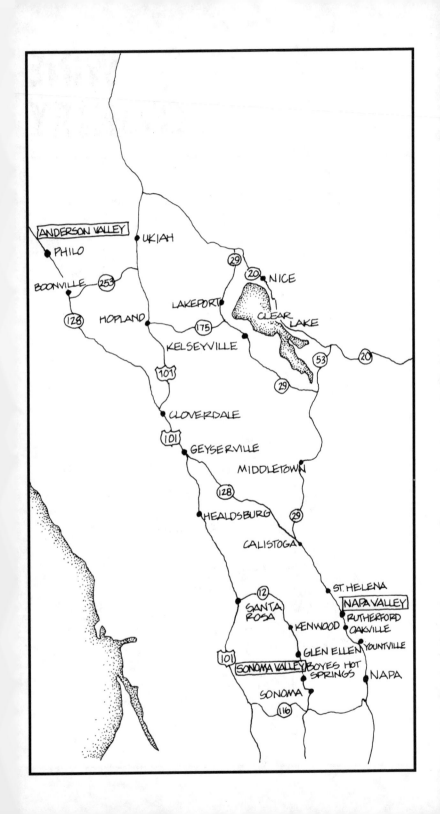

# Wine Country

*A tour from the Napa Valley north to Calistoga and Clear Lake, followed by a trip through the Sonoma Valley up to Ukiah, with a detour to the Anderson Valley via Highway 128 West. Plus, highlights of the area's top wineries.*

## NAPA VALLEY WINE COUNTRY

Despite the plethora of nouveau châteaus, fake French barns, and gimcrack stores selling wine bottles full of cabernet-flavored jelly beans, the Napa Valley is still one of the most magical spots in Northern California. In early spring, the hills are a vibrant green, bright yellow mustard blossoms poke up between the vines, and stands of fruit trees burst into showy flower. In the summer, tourists flood the valley, cranking up the energy level a few notches and conferring a patina of glamour and excitement that some locals delight in and others deplore. Later, after the grape harvest, the vineyards turn a bright autumnal scarlet, and the region's quaint, Old–West-style towns assume a more relaxed, homey atmosphere. At any time of year, Napa is blessed with an abundance of excellent restaurants, scores of welcoming bed and breakfasts, a couple of ultra-luxurious resorts, enough interesting shops to keep gold cards flashing up and down the valley, and recreational opportunities galore: boating, biking, horseback riding, hot-air ballooning, gliding, hiking, soaking in mud baths or hot springs, and exploring historic sites. Diversity is the watchword here. You might grab a map to the region's numerous wineries and work on expanding the contents of your cellar. Or engage in that ultimate food-to-go experience, the **Napa Valley Wine Train**, where passengers sip fine wines and sup on an excellent meal while gazing out at the lush countryside on their cushy three-hour train ride; for dining information and reservations call (707)253-2111 or (800)427-4124. Winery maps and details about parks, hot-air balloon rides, and other recreational pastimes are readily available at many locations, including most hotels and the **Napa Valley Conference and Visitors Bureau** at 1310 Town Center Mall (off First Street) in Napa, (707)226-7459.

### WINERIES

Napa's wineries are mainly clustered along Highway 29 and the Silverado Trail, two parallel roads running the length of the valley. The place is a zoo on weekends—especially in the summer and early fall, when the traffic on narrow Highway 29 rivals rush hour in the Bay Area. With the increased number of visitors, most vintners now charge a small fee to taste their wines and some require reservations for tours (don't let the latter deter you—the smaller establishments just need to control the number of visitors at any one time and make sure someone will be available to show you around). As you whiz along the highway and see the signs announcing some of the most famous wineries in the world, you'll be tempted to pull over and stop at every one. But do yourself a favor and follow a tip from veteran wine tasters: pick out the four or five wineries you're most interested in visiting over the weekend, and stick to your itinerary. Touring more than a couple of wineries a day will surely overwhelm and exhaust even the most intrepid wine connoisseur, although if you really want to see several wineries in a short period, skip the grand tours and just visit the tasting rooms. If you're new to the wine-touring scene, you'll be relieved to know you won't ever be pressured to buy any of the wines you've sampled—the vintners are just delighted to expose you to their line of products (besides, you'll often find much better prices at some of the good wine stores in town). Here's a roster of some of the Napa Valley's most popular wineries, many of which offer free tours of their facilities:

**Beaulieu Vineyards** Nicknamed "BV," this winery is housed in a historic estate and is famous for its cabernet sauvignon; 1960 St. Helena Highway, Rutherford, (707)963-2411.

**Beringer Vineyards** The Napa Valley's oldest continuously operating winery features a stately, old Rhineland–style mansion and good tours of the vineyards and caves. It's well known for its chardonnay and cabernet; 2000 Main Street, St. Helena, (707)963-7115.

**Château Montelena Winery** This stunning French château–style winery is built of stone and is celebrated for its chardonnay. The beautiful setting includes a lake with two islands and wonderful (though hard-to-get) picnic facilities available by reservation only; 1429 Tubbs Lane, Calistoga, (707)942-5105.

**Clos Pegase** Designed by architect Michael Graves, this stunning, modern facility offers grand outdoor sculpture, a "Wine in Art" slide show, and good guided tours of the winery, caves, and art collection; 1060 Dunaweal Lane, Calistoga, (707)942-4982, www. clospegase.com.

**Domaine Chandon** Good sparkling wines come from this winery's handsome building. There's a four-star dining room (see the restaurant's review, below) and fantastic guided tours, too; 1 California Drive, Yountville, (707)944-2280, www.dchandon.com.

**The Hess Collection Winery** A stone winery in a remote, scenic location, the Hess Collection is well known for its cabernet sauvignon and chardonnay. Contemporary-American and European art is showcased in a dramatic building, part of the very good self-guided tour; 4411 Redwood Road, Napa, (707)255-1144.

**Merryvale Vineyards** Within Merryvale's historic stone building are daily tastings and, by appointment only, informative, thorough tasting classes on Saturday and Sunday mornings. The winery is best known for its chardonnay; 1000 Main Street, St. Helena, (707)963-7777.

**Niebaum-Coppola Winery** Filmmaker Francis Ford Coppola now owns this former Inglenook grand château, built in the 1880s. There's a good display on Coppola's film career and Inglenook's history, and a gift shop stocked with wine, pottery, books, T-shirts, and even Coppola's favorite cigars. Daily wine tastings are offered, and tours are by appointment; 1991 St. Helena Highway, Rutherford, (707)963-9099.

**Opus One** In a dramatic bermed neoclassical building, tours and expensive wine tastings ($15 per 4-ounce glass of wine) are offered by appointment at this extraordinary winery; 7900 St. Helena Highway, Oakville, (707)944-9442.

**Robert Mondavi Winery** This huge, world-famous winery, housed in a Mission-style building, offers excellent tours of the facilities and a famous cooking school; 7801 St. Helena Highway, Oakville, (707)963-9611.

**Schramsberg Vineyards** Schramsberg's first-rate sparkling wines are showcased in attractive, historic facilities and extensive caves. Interesting guided tours are available by appointment only; 1400 Schramsberg Road, Calistoga, (707)942-4558.

**Napa**

**Sterling Vineyards** Sterling offers an excellent self-guided tour through its impressive, white Mediterranean-style complex perched on a hill. Access is via an aerial tramway offering splendid views, and there's a vast tasting room with panoramic vistas; 1111 Dunaweal Lane, Calistoga, (707)942-3300.

**ZD** Good tours of the winery are available by appointment. ZD produces fine barrel-fermented chardonnay and powerful reds, too; 8383 Silverado Trail, Napa, (707)963-5188.

## NAPA

About half the residents of the Napa Valley live in this pretty, sprawling town whose name has become synonymous with wine. Napa's downtown has plenty of imposing Victorian structures worth admiring, and you can pick up a walking-tour map at the **Napa Valley Conference and Visitors Bureau**; 1310 Town Center Mall, off First Street, (707)226-7459. For a break, amble over to the **ABC/Alexis Baking Company** for great espresso, pizza, fresh salads, and goodies like chocolate-caramel cake, pumpkin-spice muffins, and pistachio-apricot cake; 1517 Third Street, (707)258-1827. **Napa Valley Roasting Company** is another pleasant place to sip a cup of freshly brewed java; 948 Main Street, (707)224-2233. If you want a good read as you linger over a steamy mug, browse through **Copperfield's** for new and used books at reasonable prices; 1303 First Street, (707)252-8002.

## RESTAURANTS

**Bistro Don Giovanni** ★★★ As the name suggests, Donna and Giovanni Scala (who also opened the wonderful Scala's Bistro in San Francisco's Sir Francis Drake hotel) bring a touch of French bistro to their friendly Italian trattoria. Although the kitchen has been known to stumble in years past, the food is now consistently well prepared, whether you order the penne with green beans and pesto, the ravioli stuffed with fresh basil and ricotta, the juicy "chicken under a brick," or even the side dish of grilled corn on the cob with red pepper butter. The service is remarkably attentive and the atmosphere is joyous. The wine list, although skewed toward expensive California vintages, is extensive and imaginative, and such offerings as watermelon granita and a delectable fresh fruit crisp beckon from the dessert menu. ■ *4110 St. Helena Hwy (on Hwy 29, just N of Salvador Ave), Napa; (707)224-3300; $$; full bar; AE, DC, DIS, MC, V; local checks only; lunch, dinner every day.* &

*Napa*

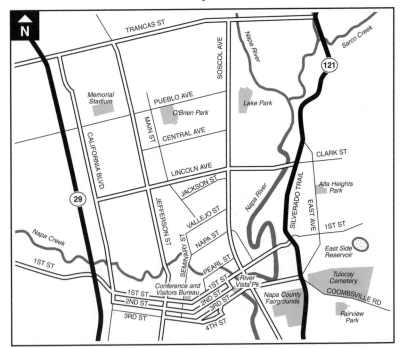

**Foothill Cafe** ★★ Tucked away in a plain-Jane neighborhood shopping center far from the Wine Country's glitzy tourist attractions, the Foothill Cafe earns kudos for its delicious, meticulously prepared food. Chef/owner Jerry Shaffer, a former *chef de parti* at San Francisco's venerable Masa's, concentrates on a small menu of meat, seafood, and vegetarian dishes, with an emphasis on local produce. Expect to find hearty fare such as garlic-thyme roasted chicken, corn cakes topped with smoked salmon and crème fraîche, and Shaffer's signature knock-your-socks-off oak-roasted baby back pork ribs (available as an appetizer or entree). All of the simply but attractively presented main courses are generous in quantity and come with a savory soup or a freshly tossed salad. For dessert, indulge in the superb fresh-fruit cobbler, which might feature fillings of mixed berries or pears and cherries. Service is casual and friendly, and the wine list is well chosen and reasonably priced. The decor borders on whimsical, with papier-mâché animals, oddball salt and pepper shakers, and plaid tablecloths. Now if Shaffer would only do something about that faux-marble linoleum floor.... ■ *2766 Old Sonoma Rd (W of Hwy 29, near Foster Rd), Napa; (707)252-6178; $$; beer and wine; AE, MC, V; checks OK; dinner Wed–Sun.* 占

**La Boucane** ★★ Housed in a restored Victorian, Napa Valley's bastion of classic French cuisine has a small teal-and-rose dining room that glows with candles. The wine list, with its healthy mix of Bordeaux and Burgundian varietals from California's top vintners, is perfectly matched to owner/chef Jacques Mokrani's traditional French fare: crisp roasted duck in a zesty, bittersweet orange sauce; perfect poached salmon in a delicate champagne-cream sauce; and thick, flavorful tournedos forestière in a reduction of game and beef stock with fresh herbs and red wine. All entrees come with a richly flavored soup such as crawfish bisque or cream of turnip, artfully arranged vegetables, a salad, and a divine dessert such as soufflé glacé praline, *mousse au chocolat*, or crème caramel. Despite the restaurant's old-fashioned decor, the atmosphere is delightfully unstuffy; you'll often find Mokrani, a veteran of cruise-ship kitchens, schmoozing with his guests in the dining room. ■ *1778 2nd St (1 block E of Jefferson St), Napa; (707)253-1177; $$$; beer and wine; MC, V; local checks only; dinner Mon–Sat (closed in Jan).*

## LODGINGS

**Churchill Manor** ★★ Churchill Manor is an elegant, meticulously maintained mansion, incongruously set in a modest neighborhood. Built in 1889 by a local banker, it is listed on the National Register of Historic Places. The colonial revival house, which rises three stories above an expanse of beautiful gardens, is graced by stately pillars and a large, inviting veranda. Each of the 10 immaculate guest rooms features antique furnishings, ultra-plush carpeting, and an elegant private bath; among the favorites are Victoria's Room (imposing and spacious, with a king-size bed and a claw-footed tub perched by the fireplace), Rose's Room (originally Mrs. Churchill's bedroom, this bit of Victoriana has a giant tub with 24-karat gold trim that's smack-dab in the middle of the room, as well as a scattering of French antiques including a carved-wood, king-size bed), and Edward's Room (the largest room, Mr. Churchill's former sanctuary also boasts magnificent French antiques and a lavish bath with hand-painted tiles). Rates include a full breakfast served in the marble-floored sun room, fresh-baked cookies and coffee or tea in the afternoon, and a wine-and-cheese reception in the evening. When you're not out touring the local wineries, you may tickle the ivories of the grand piano in the parlor, watch television in the game room, play croquet on the lovely side lawn, or tour Old Town Napa on the inn's tandem bicycles. Owners Brian Jensen and Joanna Guidotti are attentive and welcoming hosts. ■ *485 Brown St (at Oak St), Napa, CA 94559; (707)253-7733; www.virtualcities.com/virtual/ons/ca/w/caw3503.htm; $$; AE, DIS, MC, V; checks OK.*

**La Residence** ★★ Set back in the trees along busy Highway 29, this multimillion-dollar creation of partners David Jackson and Craig Claussen is one of the valley's most luxurious bed and breakfasts. Twenty guest rooms are scattered throughout two houses separated by a heated swimming pool and an elaborate gazebo. The main house, a gothic revival mansion built in 1870 by a former New Orleans riverboat captain, contains nine comfortable guest rooms beautifully decorated with designer fabrics and American antiques. Most have sitting rooms, fireplaces, and private baths. Airier accommodations can be found in the modern French-style barn across the plaza. Filled with simple pine antiques, these spacious rooms have fireplaces, private baths, and French doors that open onto small patios or balconies. A delicious gourmet breakfast is served downstairs in the barn in a cheery, sunny dining room. Although La Residence is undeniably one of the region's loveliest small inns, its location next to the highway detracts from the away-from-it-all feel that B&Bs usually try to cultivate. ■ *4066 St. Helena Hwy (on Hwy 29, next to Bistro Don Giovanni), Napa, CA 94558; (707)253-0337; $$$; AE, DC, MC, V; checks OK.* &

**Silverado Country Club & Resort** ★★ Golfers and tennis players flock to this 1,200-acre estate, and it's easy to see why. The Silverado boasts two perfectly maintained 18-hole golf courses designed by Robert Trent Jones Jr. and the largest tennis complex in North America, with 20 championship courts rimmed with flowered walkways. If you're not into golf or tennis, however, there's little reason to stay here; the 280 unprepossessing rooms seem to have been designed for people who don't plan to spend much time indoors. The standard rooms, in a condolike warren, start at about $135. The one- and two-bedroom suites overlooking the golf course are prettier but equally soulless; they're gleamingly modern with black-marble fireplaces and well-appointed kitchens. A few minutes' drive from the main complex are the more secluded Oak Creek East accommodations, street after street of mind-numbingly similar houses and condominiums owned by country-club members and rented out to guests. Numerous swimming pools dot the extensive grounds—popular spots to cool off on those sweltering summer days.

The resort's clubhouse and restaurants are located in the magnificent colonnaded Southern gothic mansion at the heart of the main complex. **Vintners Court**, a formal dining room dominated by a glittering chandelier and a white grand piano, offers decent Pacific Rim fare. For a more casual meal, order a club sandwich or a hamburger at the **Silverado Bar & Grill**. **The Royal Oak** restaurant, with its exposed wood beams, brickwork, and burnished-copper accents, is a luxurious throwback to the days of elegant club grills. The cuisine here is traditional with a capital T. Seafood (particularly the fresh Maine lobster) and beef are the popular entrees. Ask for a table overlooking the oak groves and the golf course. ■ *1600 Atlas Peak Rd (from Hwy 29 turn onto Trancas St, then turn left on Atlas Peak Rd), Napa, CA 94558; (707)257-0200; www.silveradoresort.com; $$$; full bar; AE, DC, DIS, MC, V; checks OK; breakfast, lunch, dinner every day.* &

**Crossroads Inn** ★   The three most important factors in real estate—location, location, location—make the Crossroads Inn an ideal retreat. Perched on a hillside 500 feet off the valley floor, this modest and homey B&B beats out such stiff contenders as Auberge du Soleil and Sterling Vineyards for Best View in the Wine Country. The four guest rooms, while nothing fancy, are comfortably spacious. Each has a king-size bed, Jacuzzi spa, private bath, and large deck overlooking the spectacular surroundings; one even has a tub for two with an incredible view. The remote inn is positioned on a 23-acre wooded property laced with hiking trails, so you can work off the full breakfast and afternoon tea included in the price of your room. When the weather warms up in the spring and summer, guests can cool down in the new swimming pool and spa, or lounge poolside and take in the valley views. Hosts Nancy and Sam Scott are exceptionally friendly and knowledgeable about the area. ■ *6380 Silverado Trail (1½ miles E of Yountville, at the Yountville Cross Rd), Napa, CA 94558; (707)944-0646; $$$; MC, V; checks OK.*

**Oak Knoll Inn** ★   This French Country–inspired hostelry is blessed with one of the most serene, isolated settings of any Napa Valley B&B: it sits amid 600 acres of spectacular vineyards. The mix of contemporary and antique furniture, stone walls, and huge (albeit a bit motel-like) guest rooms may be just the ticket if you're seeking a respite from Victorian clutter or Wine Country cutesiness. Each of the four high-ceilinged rooms has a fireplace, king-size bed, sitting area, and private bath. Plant yourself in a lounge chair by the swimming pool or sit in the gazebo and gaze at the lush scenery while you enjoy a picnic. There's an outdoor whirlpool tub for chillier days and evenings, and a croquet lawn stands ready for the crack of your mallet. In the morning, hosts Barbara Passino and John Kuhlmann serve a full breakfast in your room, in the dining room, or on the wood deck. ■ *2200 E Oak Knoll Ave (off the Silverado Trail, 3 miles S of Yountville), Napa, CA 94558; (707)255-2200; www.oakknollinn.com; $$$; MC, V; checks OK.*

## YOUNTVILLE

### *RESTAURANTS*

**Domaine Chandon** ★★★★ Napa Valley's culinary reputation was born at this elegant restaurant with its rough-textured walls and wood archways overlooking the winery's manicured gardens and vineyards. Rooted in traditional French techniques enlivened by California innovation, executive chef Robert Curry's creative and delicate cooking style is perfectly matched to Domaine Chandon's sparkling wines (Curry, who worked for a few years as sous chef to Domaine's star chef Phillipe Jeanty, took over as head chef when Jeanty left the restaurant in 1997 after 20 years). Past winners from the ever-changing menu have included an exquisite appetizer of alder-smoked trout served on a bed of curly endive, and a Japanese eggplant soup that arrived not as the customary purée but as a multicolored mélange streaked with basil and red and yellow peppers. Anything from the grill—such as beef, rabbit, or the divine pancetta-wrapped salmon—packs a salt-and-peppery punch, followed by a flavorful unfolding of meltingly tender meat. Simple but superb roasted chicken might be sliced and rearranged in the shape of a pear and served with basil mashed potatoes, a few spears of roasted summer squash, and a tomato-onion coulis. Grand desserts have included such jewels as a ground-almond shortcake with strawberries and a polenta pudding saturated with grappa and topped with fresh raspberries and mascarpone. The extensive wine list features some interesting (mainly California) vintages at surprisingly reasonable prices. Service is gracious and impeccable. Domaine Chandon also offers patio dining during the warm months, making it one of the most pleasant places to lunch in the Wine Country. ■ *1 California Dr (just W of Hwy 29), Yountville; (707)944-2892; www.dchandon. com; $$$; wine only; AE, DC, DIS, MC, V; no checks; lunch every day, dinner Wed–Sun May to Oct; lunch, dinner Wed–Sun Nov to Apr (closed first 2 weeks of Jan).* ⓑ

**The French Laundry** ★★★★ This is the place you dream of stumbling upon in the French countryside: an unassuming old stone house (with no sign announcing its purpose) draped in ivy and surrounded by herb gardens, occupied by a brilliant chef offering magnificent meals, stellar wines, and faultless service. There is nothing accidental about the French Laundry, however. Since taking over the helm in 1994, chef Thomas Keller (named chef of the year in 1997 by the prestigious James Beard Foundation) has created one of the finest—and most expensive—dining experiences in the Napa Valley. His prix-fixe tasting menu offers a choice of five or seven courses that change daily and are always memorable. On one evening, dinner commenced with a chilled English pea soup infused with white truffle oil, followed by Maine lobster poached in sweet butter, pan-seared white quail with braised Adriatic figs and a Mission fig coulis, and an incredible saddle of venison. In true French style the meal was topped off by a cheese course (Neal's Yard Dairy Stilton, pecorino Toscano, maxi bûche chèvre) with French butter pears poached in white wine followed by a divine yellow nectarine sorbet. The service was subtle and perfectly timed, and if your dining partner indulges in all seven courses while you select the smaller menu, your server will be sure to bring you a little something to nibble while you wait for your next course. Such perfection doesn't come quickly *or* cheaply: settle in for the evening, and rest assured that the tab will be as out of this world as the food (dinner is easily more than $250 for two, including wine and tip). The French Laundry (the place was indeed a laundry when it was constructed in the 1890s) also serves a four-course lunch, which is best enjoyed on the patio next to the flower and herb gardens. Reservations are accepted up to two months in advance. ■ *6640 Washington St (at Creek St), Yountville; (707) 944-2380; $$$; beer and wine; AE, MC, V; local checks only; lunch Fri–Sun, dinner every day.* &

**Mustards Grill** ★★★ Some critics call Mustards' feisty American regional cuisine "comfort food," but that's too complacent a description for the vigorous, spicy, vaguely Asian-influenced bistro fare served here. Part of the Cindy Pawlcyn dynasty (which includes such highly successful restaurants as St. Helena's Tra Vigne and Mill Valley's Buckeye Roadhouse), this wildly popular restaurant has a big open kitchen, pale yellow walls, dark wood wainscoting, and a black-and-white checkerboard floor. The starters here are hit-and-miss: the grilled pasilla pepper with tamale stuffing and tomatillo salsa is very popular, but it can be a bit bland; you're better off with the house-smoked salmon served with soft little pasilla-corn pancakes and dill cream cheese. Chef Louise Branch does a masterful job with the giant Mongolian pork chop with braised sweet-and-sour cabbage, and with the smoked Long Island duck served in a pool of curry-almond sauce and topped with a savory mélange of spinach, onions, and mangoes. A side dish of light, crisp onion rings goes great with the grilled Sonoma rabbit in a tomato, white bean, and saffron stew. The desserts, like the menu, often change, but they're always worth the splurge, especially if they include the fresh blueberry crisp with lemon ice cream. Mustards' voluminous international wine list includes a vintage chart, and the restaurant pours a selection of domestic microbrews including a "sassy beer of the day." ■ *7399 St. Helena Hwy (on Hwy 29, just N of town), Yountville; (707)944-2424; $$; full bar; DC, DIS, MC, V; no checks; lunch, dinner every day.* ら

**Brix** ★★ Chef Tod Michael Kawachi's Hawaiian roots infuse the eclectic cuisine at this Napa Valley newcomer, a refreshing addition to a restaurant scene that typically veers towards Mediterranean-style fare. House-smoked salmon pizza with Maui onions, seared ahi tuna with wasabe aioli, and soy-glazed salmon medallions are just a few of the dishes where East melds nicely with West, thanks in part to Kawachi's great sauces. The airy dining room has a crisp, slightly Asian feel. The tables are flanked on one side by a large, open kitchen, and on the other by a wall of windows facing the restaurant's gardens and the rolling vineyards and the Mayacamas Mountains beyond. Be sure to take a minute to meander through the impressive gardens, which on a visit in August were brimming with Japanese eggplant, purple basil, and heirloom tomatoes. ■ *7377 St. Helena Hwy (on Hwy 29, just N of town), Yountville; (707)944-2749; $$$; full bar; AE, DC, DIS, MC, V; local checks only; lunch, dinner every day.* ら

**Ristorante Piatti** ★★ Piatti is a deservedly popular chain of good, chic, nouvelle Italian restaurants with outlets in cute, touristy towns throughout Northern California. And it all started right here in tiny Yountville. Piatti has a large, open kitchen and an L-shaped dining room decorated in soft Mediterranean colors, with terra-cotta tile floors, light woods, and plenty of natural light. Chef Peter Hall (of Tra Vigne and Mustards Grill fame) took over from Renzo Veronese in 1997, bringing his own touch to the kitchen with such dishes as Peter's Rabbit Sausage and homemade potato gnocchi. Kick off your meal with the melt-in-your-mouth sweetbreads sautéed with mushrooms or perfectly grilled vegetables with whole roasted garlic. For a main course, try any of the plump, delicately flavored cannelloni or the risotto of the day: favorites include a creamy risotto packed with artichoke hearts, chicken, and sun-dried tomatoes, and a delicious variation with smoked salmon and fresh asparagus. Grilled items, such as the chicken and rabbit, are also consistently topnotch. Piatti sometimes goes overboard with the seasonings, forsaking balance for blasts of flavor, so select a wine with a lot of backbone. The Italian–

Napa Valley wine list is extensive. ■ *6480 Washington St (S of the Vintage 1870 shopping complex), Yountville; (707)944-2070; $$; full bar; AE, DC, MC, V; no checks; lunch, dinner every day.* &

**The Diner** ★ This is the place to go when you've brought along the kids, want a tasty, informal meal, or have an uncontrollable urge for a buttermilk shake—it tastes just like cheesecake! Terrific, belly-packing breakfasts (don't pass up the huevos rancheros) have secured this restaurant's reputation for years, but lunches and dinners are good, too, with hearty, well-prepared Mexican dishes and seafood specialties supplementing the typical diner fare. ■ *6476 Washington St (near Oak St), Yountville; (707)944-2626; $; beer and wine; no credit cards; checks OK; breakfast, lunch, dinner Tues–Sun.* &

## LODGINGS

**Maison Fleurie** ★★ Built in 1873, this beautiful, ivy-covered brick-and-fieldstone hotel was a bordello and later a 4-H clubhouse before it opened in 1971 as the Napa Valley's first bed-and-breakfast inn. Purchased by the owners of the Four Sisters Inns company (who also run the charming Petite Auberge in San Francisco and Pacific Grove's Gosbey House), the old Magnolia Hotel was reborn as Maison Fleurie in 1994 and endowed with a new, French Country feel. Seven of the guest rooms are located in the main house, with its thick brick walls, terra-cotta tiles, and vineyard views; the remaining six are divided between the old bakery building and the carriage house. All have private baths, and some feature fireplaces, private balconies, sitting areas, and patios. After a long day of wine-tasting, unwind at the pool or soak your tired dogs in the outdoor spa tub. The inn also provides bicycles for tooling around town. ■ *6529 Yount St (at Washington St), Yountville, CA 94599; (707)944-2056; www.foursisters.com; $$$; AE, DC, MC, V; no checks.*

**Vintage Inn** ★★ Spread throughout a 23-acre estate and designed by the same architect who created Big Sur's Ventana Inn, the Vintage Inn provides the Napa Valley traveler with a host of creature comforts in a modern setting. The 80 large, cheery rooms, bathed in soothing earth tones and wood accents, are all equipped with fireplaces, Jacuzzi tubs, refrigerators, patios or verandas, ceiling fans, and plush private baths. Guests may take a dip in the heated pool or outdoor spa, play a game of tennis, order room service, sip a spirit at the bar, or rent the inn's bikes, hot-air balloon, or private limo for a tour of the Wine Country. You'll also be treated to a continental breakfast served with glasses of bubbly. ■ *6541 Washington St (just E of Hwy 29), Yountville, CA 94599; (707)944-1112 or (800)351-1133; www.vintageinn.com; $$$; full bar; AE, DC, DIS, MC, V; checks OK.* &

**Wine Country**

▼

**Yountville**

*Lodgings*

▲

## OAKVILLE

Despite the demise of celebrity chef Jeremiah Tower's Stars Oakville Cafe, the itsy-bitsy town of Oakville is still a destination in itself, thanks to the famous **Oakville Grocery Co.**, which has turned the former Stars restaurant site next door into the **Oakville Grocery Cafe** to keep up with the demand for its tasty deli fare. Although the Oakville Grocery is disguised as an old-fashioned country market complete with a fading "Drink Coca-Cola" sign outside, step inside this extraordinary gourmet deli and you'll find a fine variety of local wines (including a good selection of splits), a small espresso bar tucked in the corner, and pricey but delicious picnic supplies ranging from pâté and caviar to sliced-turkey sandwiches and several freshly made sweets; 7856 St. Helena Highway at the Oakville Cross Road, (707)944-8802.

## RUTHERFORD

### *LODGINGS*

▼
Oakville
▲

**Auberge du Soleil ★★★★** This exclusive 33-acre, 52-unit resort, inspired by the sunny architecture of southern France, is nestled in an olive grove on a wooded hillside above the Napa Valley. Its 11 original cottages have rough-textured adobe-style walls, white French doors and windows, and smashing views of the valley. Set on a winding street on a terraced hillside, each cottage is divided into four guest rooms and suites that have private entrances and balconies designed for maximum privacy. The upstairs rooms with their vaulted, exposed-beam ceilings are particularly posh, but even the humblest accommodations here are sinfully hedonistic, with fireplaces, artful and comfortable furnishings, candles, sitting areas, and tiled floors. Two additional rooms on the top floor of the main building lack fireplaces but have king-size beds and French doors that open onto private terraces. Two new cottages offer you a true 1,800-square-foot home-away-from-home—that is if your home has a Jacuzzi on the terrace, two fireplaces, a living room, den, and master bedroom and bath, not to mention a $1,500-a-night price tag.

The gorgeous Southwestern-style dining room has soaring lodgepole accents, carved wooden chairs, and a kiva fireplace. As lovely as the dining room is, however, most fair-weather diners make a beeline for the patio, which has one of the Wine Country's best panoramic views. Look for classic Wine Country cuisine such as wild mushroom sauté in an herb-garlic filo nest with black peppercorn sauce, or sautéed Sterling salmon with crisp vegetables and pinot noir sauce, followed by an almond tulip filled with Grand Marnier ice cream, fresh berries, and bittersweet chocolate sauce. The bar serves a light menu on the deck from 11am to 11pm. If your wallet isn't thick enough to handle the steep rates at the Auberge, at least come for a cocktail on the terrace and drink in the fabulous view—the same view all those fortunate guests are getting from their lush little villas. ■ *180 Rutherford Hill Rd (N of Yountville; from the Silverado Trail, turn right on Rutherford Hill Rd), Rutherford, CA 94573; (707) 963-1211 or (800) 348-5406; aubergdusolei@aol.com; www.aubergedu-soleil.com; $$$; full bar, AE, DIS, MC, V; checks OK; breakfast, lunch, dinner every day.* &

**Rancho Caymus Inn ★** Resembling a Spanish villa with a central garden courtyard, Rancho Caymus has 26 guest rooms with adobe walls, exposed beams, and rugs and wall hangings from Mexico and Ecuador. The inn was created by local sculptor Mary Tilden Morton (of the Morton Salt family), who built many of its unique features and collected the crafts herself. All rooms have private baths with hand-thrown pottery sinks, and most have an adobe beehive fireplace. Room rates include a continental breakfast in the dining area downstairs with its unusual hammered-copper Spanish chandeliers, peach tablecloths, and large fireplace. Better yet, break your fast on the pleasant flowery patio. ■ *1140 Rutherford Rd (1 block E of Hwy 29), Rutherford; (707) 963-1777; mail: PO Box 78, Rutherford, CA 94573; $$$; beer and wine; AE, MC, V; checks OK; breakfast (for guests only) every day, lunch Mon–Fri.* &

## ST. HELENA

Where else can you find a small farming town that sells $1,600 owl-skin Japanese lanterns? St. Helena has come a long way since its days as a rural Seventh Day Adventist village. On Main Street, with its Victorian Old West feel, farming-supply stores now sit stiffly next to chichi women's-clothing boutiques and upscale purveyors of home furnishings. Just off the main drag you can find more earthy pleasures at such shops as the **Napa Valley Olive Oil Manufacturing Company**, an authentic Italian deli and general store stuffed to the rafters with goodies ranging from dried fruit and biscotti to salami and fresh mozzarella. Be sure to pick up a bottle or two of the very reasonably priced extra-virgin California olive oil; the store is located at the corner of Charter Oak and Allison Avenues, (707) 963-4173. Take your Italian treats to **Lyman Park** (on Main Street between Adams and Pine Streets) and picnic on the grass or in the beautiful little white gazebo where bands sometimes set up for live summer concerts. A more bucolic picnic spot is **Bale Grist Mill State Historic Park**, which still has a 36-foot-tall wooden waterwheel grinding grain into meal and flour; located on Highway 29, 3 miles north of St. Helena. Nearby is St. Helena's popular tree-lined upscale outlet mall, where you'll find discounted designer wares by such familiar names as Donna Karan, Brooks Brothers, London Fog, and Joan & David; 3111 St. Helena Highway, (707) 963-7282.

**Tra Vigne ▪ Cantinetta Tra Vigne** ★★★★ It's become fashionable to trash this now-too-famous Tuscan-inspired temple to food and wine, but if you've never eaten at Tra Vigne, you haven't really done the Wine Country. (And if you have dined here, you're probably glad the winds of culinary fads have blown elsewhere for the moment because it makes it a little easier to get a table.) The vast, exquisitely designed dining room has soaring ceilings, taupe walls covered with big, bright Italian poster art, antique amber-beaded lamps hung low above intimate tables, a partially open kitchen, and a magnificent, towering mahogany bar. On warm days and nights, patrons vie for one of the beautiful patio tables. The food here is exceptionally fresh, and almost everything is made on the premises, including the anise-flecked bread, pasta, cheese, olive oils, smoked meats, and desserts. Appetizers are chef Michael Chiarello's forte. The menu changes seasonally, but you can usually find delicately crisp polenta rounds topped with meaty wild mushrooms in a rich, gamy vinaigrette; wonderfully fresh mozzarella and tomatoes drizzled with basil oil and balsamic vinegar; and a daily seafood selection fried crisp in Arborio rice flour with mustard seed vinegar. Pastas run the gamut from traditional to outrageous—such as ravioli stuffed with puréed pumpkin and sprinkled with fresh cranberries—and pizzas are delicately and expertly rendered. Entrees might include grilled Sonoma rabbit with Teleme cheese-layered potatoes, oven-dried tomatoes, and mustard sauce; ahi tuna grilled on a rosemary skewer and served on a roasted-pepper salad with pea sprouts; and a crisp leg of duck confit on a pea-and-potato purée with spring onion sauce. Desserts are stellar: try the velvety espresso custard with a thin layer of fudgelike chocolate dusted with powdered sugar, served with a crisp hazelnut cookie. Service is knowledgeable, witty, and efficient (although the folks in charge of managing reservations have been known to make mistakes, so be sure to confirm your reservation before making the trek here). The wine list, though not large, includes a carefully chosen array of Italian and Napa Valley bottles. If you'd prefer a light lunch or want your food to go, amble over to the less-expensive **Cantinetta Tra Vigne** out front, which also has patio seating. The cantinetta sells several varieties of focaccia pizza, gourmet sandwiches, interesting soups and salads, pastas topped with smoked salmon and other delights, and a variety of sweets. ▪ *1050 Charter Oak Ave (off Hwy 29), St. Helena; (707) 963-4444 (restaurant) or (707) 963-8888 (cantinetta); $$; full bar; DC, DIS, MC, V; no checks; restaurant: lunch, dinner every day; cantinetta: lunch every day.*

▼

**St. Helena**

*Restaurants*

▲

**Terra** ★★★ Housed in a historic stone building with high ceilings and arched windows, Terra's subdued dining rooms have an ineffable sense of intimacy about them. Fervid tête-à-têtes, however, are more likely to revolve around Terra's fine Southern

French/ Northern Italian food than around *amore*. Yet this isn't the sort of food that screams to be noticed; chef Hiro Sone's cuisine never grandstands. Unusual combinations such as mild duck-liver wontons with an earthy wild mushroom sauce may sound a little forced, but they don't play that way on the palate. Recommended dishes include broiled sake-marinated Chilean sea bass with shrimp dumplings; spaghettini with fresh tomatoes and white bean stew; a grilled veal chop with pinot noir sauce; and strawberries drenched in a cabernet-and-black-peppercorn sauce served with vanilla ice cream. ■ *1345 Railroad Ave (between Adams and Hunt Sts, 1 block E of Main St), St. Helena; (707) 963-8931; $$$; beer and wine; DC, MC, V; local checks only; dinner Wed–Mon.* ঙ্

**Trilogy** ★★★ Despite its humble storefront setting and low-key ambience, Trilogy doesn't have to shout to be heard over the culinary din of Napa Valley's competitive restaurant scene. What it lacks in glitz it more than makes up for with inspired California-French cuisine. Chef/co-owner Diane Pariseau has a deft and delicate way with starters such as smoked salmon and herbed goat cheese with wild rice and onion bread; shaved-cabbage salad with bacon-onion dressing topped by a crumble of blue cheese; and quail with aromatic French lentils. She has an equally sure hand with entrees, which might include grilled salmon with ginger, lemongrass, and a cilantro dressing; duck with pears, brandy, and green peppercorn sauce; or her amazing tournedos of beef with Oregon blue cheese and walnuts. An ever-changing prix-fixe menu is offered daily, which you may elect to have served with a trio of well-chosen wines and liqueurs. ■ *1234 Main St (near Hunt Ave), St. Helena; (707) 963-5507; $$; beer and wine; DC, MC, V; checks OK; lunch Tues–Fri, dinner Tues–Sat.* ঙ্

**Wine Spectator Restaurant at Greystone** ★★★ Don't even think about popping in for a glass of wine and tapas at this wildly popular spot on a summer weekend without reservations—unless you're willing to wait an hour or more for a bar stool. Set in the old Christian Brothers winery building on the first floor of the Culinary Institute of America, the Wine Spectator rates high for authentic Wine Country atmosphere, with old stone walls and deep-set ceiling windows in the dining room. Actually, the blue-and-yellow-tile bar that curves around the exhibition kitchen offers the best seat in the house. From here you can watch chefs in starched white hats bustle among copper pots and state-of-the-art equipment, all orchestrated by executive chef Bill Briwa. The menu cuts a wide swath through the Mediterranean, with a touch of Spain, the south of France, Italy, and Greece. Choose a few dishes from the tasting menu (the mushroom bruschetta is very good) or order a full lunch or dinner (both meals share the same menu). Recent standouts included a seared coriander-crusted halibut served on a bed of potato purée and morel mushrooms,

**Wine Country**

**▼**

**St. Helena**

*Restaurants*

**▲**

and the vegetarian dish of seared ricotta and garlic gnocchi. The restaurant is named for *Wine Spectator* magazine, which donated $1 million to the school's scholarship fund. ▪ *Culinary Institute of America at Greystone, 2555 Main St (at Deer Park Rd), St. Helena; (707)967-1010; www.ciachef.com; $$; full bar; AE, DC, MC, V; local checks only; lunch every day in the summer (call for winter hours), dinner every day year-round.* ♿

**Brava Terrace** ★★ Brava Terrace offers lively French-Mediterranean cuisine in an idyllic setting: the beautiful dining room has vaulted ceilings with exposed wood beams, white walls with bright modern art, glowing hardwood floors and furniture, and a big stone fireplace. Even better are the large, beautifully landscaped terraces, the perfect place for a lazy lunch, a late afternoon snack, or dinner on a warm evening. Owner Fred Halpert breathes life into old classics like cassoulet, but he also has an inviting menu of daily pastas and risottos. The grilled portobello mushrooms with spinach and artichokes topped by a roasted garlic-walnut vinaigrette is a first-rate appetizer, and the pan-roasted chicken with "garlic-smashed" potatoes and rosemary-infused pan juices is a soul-satisfying choice for the main course. Finish with a chocolate chip crème brûlée or one of the exquisite house-made sorbets. There's a lengthy, reasonably priced wine list to boot. ▪ *3010 St. Helena Hwy (on Hwy 29, between St. Helena and Calistoga, next to Freemark Abbey), St. Helena; (707)963-9300; fredbrava@aol.com; $$$; full bar; AE, DC, DIS, MC, V; no checks; lunch, dinner every day May to Oct; lunch, dinner Thurs–Tues Nov to Apr.* ♿

**Pinot Blanc** ★★ Celebrity chef Joachim Splichal (owner of LA's Patina and a trio of other Pinots in Los Angeles) migrated north to open this "country bistro." Inside, the dark wood wainscoting, black leather banquettes, and nouveau ironwork do indeed evoke a French bistro, though the fresco of local wine labels covering two walls is pure Napa Valley. With executive chef Sean Knight in the kitchen, the food usually shines. Don't miss his salmon with a shallot and apple-smoked bacon crust, marinated pork chop with horseradish mashed potatoes, or any of the *plats du jour* (for example, braised Calistoga pig with homemade sauerkraut is served on Sunday, and Provençal-style bouillabaisse with saffron rouille is offered on Friday). You can't miss Splichal's not-so-subtle humor on the menu: "Sure, We Have a Green Salad" is a mix of local garden greens; there's also "High Cholesterol Foie Gras" and a "Daily Spa Special leaning toward lighter fare, with a strong emphasis on flavor." And yes, the wine list suggests trying a bottle of pinot blanc, but it also features more than 350 other possibilities, including a lengthy list of whites for those suffering from chardonnay burnout. ▪ *641 Main St (off Hwy 29), St. Helena; (707)963-6191; $$$; full bar; AE, DC, DIS, MC, V; local checks only; lunch, dinner every day.* ♿

**Meadowood Resort** ★★★★ Rising out of a surreal green sea of fairways and croquet lawns, Meadowood's pearl-gray, New England–style mansions are resolutely Eastern. Winding landscaped paths and roads connect the central buildings with smaller lodges scattered over 256 acres; the lodges are strategically situated near an immaculately maintained nine-hole golf course, two croquet lawns (with a full-time croquet pro on hand), seven championship tennis courts, and a 25-yard lap pool. The 85 exorbitantly priced accommodations range from one-room studios to four-room suites, each with a private porch and a wet bar. The suites tucked back in the woods are the most private, but the Lawnview Terrace rooms are the best with their vaulted ceilings, massive stone fireplaces, and French doors opening onto balconies that overlook the croquet green. The vast bathrooms have hair dryers, magnified makeup mirrors, thick bathrobes, and floors inset with radiant heating to keep your toes cozy as you pad to the cavernous shower. All guests have access to the swimming pool, the outdoor whirlpool, and the well-equipped health spa that offers a weight room, aerobics classes, massages, and numerous other ways to pamper your body.

The octagonal **Restaurant at Meadowood** has a high ceiling and a beautiful balcony overlooking the golf course. Appetizers, like the sweet-bell-pepper ravioli with wild mushrooms in a browned sage butter or the Miyagi oysters on the half shell with champagne sauce and caviar, are consistently very good, though the expensive entrees vary in quality: the herb-encrusted rack of lamb is competently prepared but unexciting, the sweetwater prawns risotto is surprisingly flavorless, but the grilled Cervena venison rib chop with cabernet-huckleberry sauce is superb. The more informal **Grill at Meadowood** offers an elaborate breakfast buffet and sandwiches and salads for lunch. When the weather is mild, dine on the terrace and watch golfers tee off alongside croquet buffs clad from head to toe in their de rigueur whites. ■ *900 Meadowood Lane (off the Silverado Trail), St. Helena, CA 94574; (707) 963-3646 or (800) 458-8080; www.placestostay. com; $$$; full bar, AE, DC, DIS, MC, V; checks OK; brunch Sun, breakfast, lunch, dinner every day.* &

**Inn at Southbridge** ★★★ This new sister to the swanky Meadowood Resort fills the gap between Napa's ultra-luxe digs and its ubiquitous bed-and-breakfast inns. Designed by the late William Turnbull Jr., the 21-room inn is part of a terra-cotta-hued complex that dominates a long block on St. Helena's main drag. At first glance, the complex appears out of scale for St. Helena's historic downtown, but vines are starting to twine around the columns and up the exterior walls, so another season or two of growth should help soften the bulk of the buildings. Inside, the guest rooms are almost Shaker in their elegant simplicity, with white piqué cotton comforters, candles, fireplaces, vaulted ceilings, and French doors opening onto private balconies. Guest privileges are available at the exclusive Meadowood Resort, though the on-site Health Spa Napa Valley offers a plethora of spa treatments, plus its own swimming pool and exercise equipment.

In the courtyard, a big red tomato sets the mood at **Tomatina**, the inn's stylish pizzeria. Sit on one of the tomato-red bar stools facing the open kitchen and order the clam pie, a winning pizza combo. ■ *1020 Main St (between Charter Oak Ave and Pope St), St. Helena, CA 94575; (707) 967-9400, (800) 520-6800 or (707) 967-9999 (pizzeria); www.placestostay.com; $$$; DC, MC, V; checks OK; lunch, dinner every day.* &

**Harvest Inn** ★ If you can't get enough of Merry Olde England but demand all the conveniences of the 20th century, this is the place for you. From its oak-paneled Great Room in the Harvest Centre to its Tudor-inspired architecture with flourishes of impressive brickwork, the Harvest Inn works hard to evoke the spirit of an earlier time and another place. The 54 immaculate guest rooms, many of which boast names such as Camelot, Duchess of Delight, and Earl of Ecstasy, are all outfitted with antiques and televisions, and most have fireplaces, wet bars, patios or balconies, refrigerators, vanities, and separate dressing areas. Swimming pools and outdoor spas await your bathing pleasure, my lord and lady, and in the morning you'll be greeted with a continental breakfast fit for a . . . well, you get the picture. ■ *1 Main St (off Hwy 29), St. Helena, CA 94574; (707) 963-9463 or (800) 950-8466; www.harvestinn.com; $$$; AE, DC, DIS, MC, V; checks OK.* &

**The Ink House Bed and Breakfast** ★ This gorgeous Italianate Victorian inn, built in the shape of an ink bottle by Napa settler Theron Ink in 1884, would merit three stars if it weren't for its no-star location alongside a busy, noisy stretch of Highway 29. The three-story yellow-and-white home has seven sumptuously decorated guest rooms, plus a lavish living room and parlor with an old-fashioned pump organ and a grand piano. The B&B's most interesting architectural feature is the glass-walled belvedere that sits atop the house like the stopper of an inkwell and offers a sweeping 360-degree view of the Napa Valley hills and vineyards. The best (and quietest) room is the spacious, high-ceilinged French Room with its richly carved mahogany bed graced by an elegant half-canopy. Another good choice is the Torino Room, which is filled with family heirlooms, including a charming doll collection. Two of the smaller rooms share a bath. The rooms at the front of the house are for sound sleepers only. Innkeepers David and Diane Horkheimer are incredibly friendly and helpful, and they'll nourish you with a full country breakfast, plus wine and appetizers in the afternoon. ■ *1575 St. Helena Hwy (at Whitehall Lane), St. Helena, CA 94574; (707) 963-3890; inkhousebb@aol.com; www.napavalley.com/inkhouse; $$$; MC, V; checks OK.*

Mud baths, mineral pools, and massages are still the main attractions of this charming little spa town, founded in the mid-19th century by California's first millionaire, Sam Brannan. Savvy Brannan made a bundle of cash supplying miners in the Gold Rush and quickly recognized the value of Calistoga's mineral-rich hot springs. In 1859 he purchased 2,000 acres of the Wappo Indians' hot springs land, built a first-class hotel and spa, and named the region Calistoga (a combination of the words California and Saratoga). He then watched his fortunes grow as affluent San Franciscans paraded into town for a relaxing respite from city life.

Generations later, city slickers are still making the pilgrimage to this city of spas. These days, however, more than a dozen enterprises touting the magical restorative powers of mineral baths line the town's Old West–style streets. You'll see an odd combo of stressed-out CEOs and earthier types shelling out dough for a chance to soak away their worries and get the kinks rubbed out of their necks. While Calistoga's spas and resorts are far from glamorous (you have to go to the Sonoma Mission Inn & Spa—see review, below—for rubdowns in luxe surroundings), many offer body treatments and mud baths you won't find anywhere else in this part of the state. Among the most popular spas are **Dr. Wilkinson's Hot Springs**, where you'll get a great massage and numerous other body treatments in a rather drab setting, 1507 Lincoln Avenue, (707)942-4102, www.napavalley.com/drwilkinson.html; **Calistoga Spa Hot Springs** (a favorite for families with young children), which boasts four mineral pools in addition to several body-pampering services, 1006 Washington Street, (707)942-6269, www.napavalley.com/Calistoga; **Indian Springs** for pricey spa treatments in a historic setting and the best (and largest) mineral pool in the area (you can even see—and hear—the steam from one of the geysers feeding hot mineral water into the pool), 1712 Lincoln Avenue, (707)942-4913; and **Lavender Hill Spa**, which provides aromatherapy facials, seaweed wraps, mud baths, and other sybaritic delights in one of the most attractive settings in town, 1015 Foothill Boulevard (Highway 29), (707)942-4495, www.lavenderhillspa.com.

**Calistoga**

After you've steamed or soaked away all your tensions, head over to the **Calistoga Inn's** pretty outdoor patio for a tall, cool drink; 1250 Lincoln Avenue, (707)942-4101. Try one of their house-brewed beers or ales, but save your appetite for one of the better restaurants in town. Once you're rejuvenated, stroll down the main street and browse through the numerous quaint shops marketing everything from French soaps and antique armoires to silk-screened T-shirts and saltwater taffy. For a trip back in time to Calistoga's pioneer past, stop by the **Sharpsteen Museum and Brannan Cottage**; 1311 Washington Street, (707)942-5911.

Just outside of town you can marvel at **Old Faithful Geyser**, which faithfully shoots a plume of 350-degree mineral water 60 feet into the air at regular intervals; 1299 Tubbs Lane, 2 miles north of Calistoga, (707)942-6463.

Other natural wonders abound at **The Petrified Forest**, where towering redwoods were turned to stone when Mount St. Helena erupted three million years ago (you can read about the fascinating event at the museum at the forest entrance); 4100 Petrified Forest Road, off Highway 128, 6 miles north of town, (707)942-6667, www.petrifiedforest.org. For a splendid view of the entire valley, hike through the beautiful redwood canyons and oak-madrone woodlands in **Robert Louis Stevenson State Park** to the top of Mount St. Helena; located off Highway 29, 8 miles north of Calistoga, (707)942-4575. If you'd rather get a bird's-eye view without exerting so much energy, hop aboard a glider plane for a stunning tour of the Wine Country at the **Calistoga Gliderport**; 1546 Lincoln Avenue, (707)942-5000.

## RESTAURANTS

**Catahoula** ★★★ By playfully dubbing his Wine Country restaurant Catahoula, the name of the Louisiana state dog, chef/owner Jan Birnbaum served notice that he was returning to his Southern roots—a surprise move since Birnbaum's reputation had been built at such bastions of haute cuisine as New York's Quilted Giraffe and San Francisco's Campton Place restaurant. The discrepancy between his formal training and Catahoula's down-home fare turns out to be serendipitous, resulting in a glorious, spirited brand of nouvelle Southern cuisine. Hominy cakes served hot off the griddle are paired with fennel, potatoes, endive, and other veggies coated with a smoked-onion vinaigrette. The cornmeal-fried catfish is laced with lemon-jalapeño meunière and served with slaw, and a thin-crusted pizza is crowned with crayfish and andouille sausage. The menu may read "country Southern" (with other regional American dishes occasionally tossed in), but the execution is unexpectedly delicate and refined. Although plunked in the middle of the **Mount View Hotel**, with its Old-West-meets-art-deco flavor, the dining room has a sophisticated, urban feel, with a colored concrete floor, a found-object mural by San Francisco artist Michael Brennan, and a long granite bar. Birnbaum also offers appetizers and light dinners in the saloon on weekends and serves salads and other tidbits on the poolside patio in the summer. If you overindulge in his tasty creations, you can always chill out at the Mount View's well-appointed and thoroughly professional spa, or sleep it off in one of the hotel's spartan but pleasant guest rooms. ■ *1457 Lincoln Ave (near Washington St), Calistoga; (707)942-2275; $$; full bar;*

▼

**Calistoga**

▲

*DIS, MC, V; local checks only; lunch, dinner Wed–Mon (dinner every day Sept to Oct).* ♿

**All Seasons Café ★★** Many restaurants in Napa Valley have elaborate wine lists, but none compare to this cafe's award-winning roster. The rear of the restaurant—a retail wine store with a tasting bar—stocks hundreds of first-rate foreign and domestic selections at remarkably reasonable prices. If nothing catches your fancy on the restaurant's regular wine list, ask to see the shop's enormous computerized catalog. The All Seasons' menu is even structured around wine: the appetizers, such as crisp, herby bruschetta and creative salads, are recommended to accompany sparklers, chardonnay, and sauvignon blanc; respectable California pizzas and pastas are paired with sauvignon blanc, zinfandel, and Rhône wines; and entrees such as delicate roast quail with walnut-studded polenta, grilled lamb with fresh sprigs of dill, and fish with fruity sauces are matched with an excellent selection of chardonnay, cabernet, and pinot noir. So much emphasis is placed on wine, in fact, that the food sometimes suffers. Great-sounding ingredients often fail to marry, while the consistency of the starches (gnocchi, polenta, potatoes, et cetera) can be downright weird. However, the enthusiastic and opinionated servers can usually steer you safely to the better choices on the changing menu. ■ *1400 Lincoln Ave (at Washington St), Calistoga; (707) 942-9111; $$; beer and wine; MC, V; checks OK; lunch Thurs–Tues, dinner every day.* ♿

**Wappo Bar & Bistro ★★** Husband-and-wife chefs Aaron Bauman and Michelle Matrux opened this zesty bistro in 1993 and immediately began collecting accolades for what Bauman describes as "regional global cuisine." Confused? Well, even Bauman admits their cuisine is hard to pinpoint, merrily skipping as it does from the Middle East to Europe to Asia to South America to the good old USA. The small menu changes often, but this culinary United Nations has embraced such diverse dishes as chicken potpie with a cornmeal-herb crust, fresh sea bass dipped in chickpea flour served with mint chutney and lentil crêpes, and Moroccan lamb stew with dried fruit and couscous. One dish that turns up often due to popular demand: chiles rellenos stuffed with basmati rice, crème fraîche, currants, and fresh herbs, dipped in a blue cornmeal batter, deep-fried, and served on a bed of walnut-pomegranate sauce. This is ambitious, imaginative cooking, and the talented chefs usually pull it off with aplomb. The small dining room is appointed with simple but tasteful furnishings—lots of copper and redwood sprinkled about—and the large, pretty patio out back serves as a tranquil retreat on sunny days. ■ *1226-B Washington St (off Lincoln Ave), Calistoga; (707) 942-4712; $$; beer and wine; AE, MC, V; checks OK; lunch, dinner Wed–Mon.* ♿

**Cottage Grove Inn ★★** If B&B quarters are a little too cozy for comfort, you can't beat the privacy of your very own cottage tucked in a grove of elm trees. Too bad Calistoga's busiest street is a little too close to some of the cottages at this new resort along Lincoln Avenue (though the walls have double layers of Sheetrock to cut down on noise). Still, the 16 gray clapboard structures are storybook sweet, with white wicker rockers and firewood on the porches, two-person Jacuzzi tubs, fireplaces, hardwood floors, TVs with VCRs, CD players, and quaint quilts on the beds. An expanded continental breakfast of pastries, fresh fruit, cereal, coffee, and juice (included in the rate) is served in the guest lounge, and wine and cheese are offered in the evening. ■ *1711 Lincoln Ave (at Wappo Ave), Calistoga, CA 94515; (707) 942-8400 or (800) 799-2284; www.cottagegrove.com; $$$; AE, DC, DIS, MC, V; checks OK.* &

**Quail Mountain Bed and Breakfast ★★** Quail Mountain is a good choice for people who want to escape the bustle of the valley floor but still want to be near the action. A long private drive winds up (and up and up) from Highway 29 through pine and oak woodland to a serene, slate-gray modern house with a gurgling pond and a beautiful patio with a trellised grape arbor out front. Decorated with contemporary furnishings, artwork, and a smattering of antiques, the inn's three rooms open onto the outside balcony through sliding glass doors. During the day, you can read in the glass-enclosed solarium, swim in the small lap pool out back, warm up in the hot tub, chill out in the hammock tucked in the trees on the hill above the house, or stroll through the fruit orchard and nibble on the amazing bounty. Innkeepers Don and Alma Swiers encourage guests to pick their own apricots, apples, peaches, cherries, figs, oranges, kumquats, and more. Some of the harvest always turns up at the table for breakfast, perhaps fresh with yogurt or in a brandy-wine sauce over French toast. The bad news is that this idyllic place is almost always booked; you'd be wise to make reservations several months in advance. ■ *4455 St. Helena Hwy (from Hwy 29 turn left just after Dunaweal Lane and follow the signs), Calistoga, CA 94515; (707) 942-0316; $$$; MC, V; checks OK.*

**Scott Courtyard ★★** Just a short jaunt away from Calistoga's best shops, spas, and restaurants, the Scott Courtyard B&B offers six comfortable suites with private entrances and baths in a quiet, tree-lined residential neighborhood. The three bungalows and downstairs suites are the favored units, although all of the rooms are attractively decorated with antiques and contemporary furnishings. Half of the suites have kitchens and fireplaces. The courtyard swimming pool beckons on those sunny summer days when the temperatures soar near the triple digits, and the Jacuzzi is the place to unwind after the sun sets. You might find proprietors

Lauren and Joe Scott in their open art studio, where guests are welcome to give watercolor painting or pottery-making a try. The Scotts are also well acquainted with the area and will be happy to assist you with your Wine Country itinerary. A hearty breakfast is included with your stay (ask Lauren to prepare her delicious poppyseed French toast). ■ *1443 2nd St (off Washington St), Calistoga, CA 94515; (707)942-0948; www.scottcourtyard.com; $$$; AE, MC, V; checks OK.*

**Indian Springs Resort** ★ This historic inn was built in 1860 by Sam Brannan, the founder of Calistoga, on a site where Native Americans used to erect sweat lodges to harness the region's thermal waters. A procession of 60 palm trees leads to the accommodations—17 rustic and casually furnished wooden cottages with partial kitchens, which appeal to families eager to cavort in the resort's huge hot-springs-fed swimming pool. Indian Springs also offers a playground and the full gamut of spa services (massages, facials, mud baths, and more). The spa is open to the public, but the wonderful pool is now restricted to spa and hotel guests only. ■ *1712 Lincoln Ave (between Wappo Ave and Brannan St, next to the Calistoga Gliderport), Calistoga, CA 94515; (707)942-4913; $$$; DIS, MC, V; checks OK.* &

## MIDDLETOWN

If you're traveling north from Napa Valley to Clear Lake, stop at the well-regarded **Guenoc Winery**, a 23,000-acre estate once owned by British actress Lillie Langtry in the 1880s. In Langtry's memory, the current owners grace their wine labels with her portrait. Take a tour of the winery and taste their buttery chardonnays and the trendy blend of reds called Meritage; 21000 Butts Canyon Road, 6 miles east of Middletown, (707)987-2385, www.guenoc.com. For the lowdown on what to expect up ahead in the Clear Lake region, visit the small branch office of the **Lake County Information and Visitor Center**, open Monday through Friday 10am to 2pm; 21159 Calistoga Street (Highway 29), Middletown, (707)987-0359.

### RESTAURANTS

**Las Conchitas Restaurant** ★ Granted, it's not worth making a detour to Middletown for a taco, but if you happen to be passing through on a wine-tasting tour, stop at this small cantina and sample its crispy tortilla chips and fiery salsa. There's a vast selection of well-prepared Mexican *especialidades*, including spicy chicken enchiladas prepared with soft, freshly made tortillas, and gigantic Super Quesadillas smothered in cheese, guacamole, and sour cream. Since summer temperatures in this region often soar above 100 degrees, owners Paula and Javier Arroyo always make sure there's plenty of Mexican beer in the cooler. ■ *21308 Calistoga*

*St (on Hwy 29), Middletown; (707)987-9454; $; beer and wine; MC, V; checks OK; breakfast Sun only, lunch, dinner every day.*

## CLEAR LAKE

California's largest freshwater lake, Clear Lake once had more than 30 wineries ringing its shore. Prohibition put an end to all that in 1919. The land was converted to walnut and Bartlett pear orchards, and only in the last few decades have the grapes (and the wineries) been making a comeback. This area may one day become as celebrated as Napa and Sonoma, but unlike these trendy stepsisters to the south, there ain't nothin' nouveau about Clear Lake. Country music wafts from pickup trucks, bored (and bared) youths wander the roads aimlessly (perhaps in search of their shirts), and there's generally not a whole lot going on until the weekend boaters and anglers arrive. Clear Lake's big annual blowout is the **Fourth of July Festival**, when thousands of born-again patriots amass (and timorous locals split) for a three-day sunburnt orgy of flag-waving, fireworks, and waterskiing. If you want to dive into the aquatic activities, **boats** of all shapes and sizes, as well as Jet Skis and Wave-Runners, can be rented at Mike's Watersports, 6035 Old Highway 53, Clearlake, (707)994-6267, or from On the Waterfront, 60 Third Street, Lakeport, (707)263-6789.

Clear Lake also draws crowds eager to snag some of its large-mouth bass, catfish, perch, and crappie. Although the lake has earned the title of **Bass Capital of the West**, there aren't any shops renting fishing equipment, so you'll have to tote your own. For a stunning view of the lake and the surrounding mountain peaks, hop aboard a **glider plane** or, if you're a true daredevil (or truly nuts), skydive into the scenery; tours and **skydiving** trips are available through Crazy Creek Soaring, 18896 Grange Road, 3 miles north of Middletown, (707)987-9112. For more information on Clear Lake and its surrounding towns and wineries, call or drop by the **Lake County Visitor Information Center**, at 875 Lakeport Boulevard, Vista Point, Lakeport, (707)263-9544 or (800)LAKESIDE.

## KELSEYVILLE

### LODGINGS

**Konocti Harbor Resort & Spa** ★ The Clear Lake area isn't known for its swanky accommodations and restaurants, but this 250-room mega-resort is the fanciest place around. Located at the foot of Mount Konocti and on the shores of Clear Lake, Konocti Harbor is best known for its live, year-round concerts featuring top talents such as Fleetwood Mac, the Oakridge Boys, James Brown, Charlie Daniels, and Tower of Power. Other major attractions are the eight tennis courts, two swimming pools (and a couple of wading pools), playgrounds, recreation center, miniature golf course, and even a 64-foot Mississippi-style paddlewheel boat that takes visitors on two-hour lake tours. Two golf courses are also nearby. In addition, the resort has all the water toys one could wish for lined up on its private marina, as well as a bait-and-tackle shop and a gas station. For more sensual (and relaxing) pleasures, visit Konocti's multimillion-dollar spa, where you can indulge in an herbal body wrap and a massage, topped off by a trip to the steam room, sauna, or whirlpool.

The resort's accommodations range from standard no-frills rooms to suites, apartments, and beach cottages set on a large lawn that leads down to the lake. Each unit has air conditioning (essential for the desertlike summer months), a phone, cable TV, and access to a barbecue. The **Classic Rock Cafe** offers a wide variety of fare throughout the day. Babysitting can be arranged, and golf, tennis, and fishing packages are available, too. The resort offers discounted room rates for concert-goers. ■ *8727 Soda Bay Rd (off Hwy 29), Kelseyville, CA 95451; (707)279-4281 or (800)660-LAKE; www.konoctiharbor.com; $$; full bar; AE, DIS, MC, V; checks OK; breakfast, lunch, dinner every day.* &

## LAKEPORT

With its small, old-fashioned downtown, Lakeport is the prettiest town on Clear Lake. Formerly known as Forbestown (after early settler William Forbes), the area is usually very peaceful until people from outlying cities pack up their Jeeps and station wagons and caravan out here in the summer for fishing, camping, swimming, and wine-tasting. **Clear Lake State Park**, on the southwest side of the lake, is one of the area's main draws, with its campgrounds, miles of hiking trails, and beaches; the park is located on Soda Bay Road, south of Lakeport, (707)279-4293. Folks also flock to Lakeport every Labor Day weekend for the **Lake County Fair**, featuring 4-H exhibits, livestock auctions, horse shows, and a carnival; it's held at the fairgrounds, 401 Martin Street, (707)263-6181.

### RESTAURANTS

**Park Place** ★★ Ever since the Loon's Nest restaurant in nearby Kelseyville closed, there hasn't been much debate over Lake County's best restaurant. It's Park Place—a small lakeside cafe serving very good Italian food. Owners Barbara Morris and Nancy Zabel make fettuccine every day, and serve it with simple, fresh sauces such as creamy alfredo, zingy marinara, pesto, or *quattro formaggi*. Also highly recommended are Nancy's made-from-scratch soups (particularly the chunky Italian vegetable) and the gourmet pizzas. Save room for the superb cheesecake. ■ *50 3rd St (off Main St, near the lake), Lakeport; (707)263-0444; $$; beer and wine; MC, V; checks OK; lunch, dinner every day.* &

**The Forbestown Inn** ★ Located only a few blocks from the lake, this wisteria-draped, cream-and-brown Victorian house dates back to 1869, when Lakeport was still known as Forbestown. Each of the inn's four guest rooms is pleasantly decorated with fine American antiques, Laura Ashley fabrics, and piles of hand-stitched pillows atop queen- and king-size beds. The mauve-and-cream Anna's Rose Room and the forest-green Bartlett Suite downstairs are the best. The upstairs rooms are small and sweet (the Sayre Room has the inn's only private bath) but can get very hot in the summer. Friendly innkeepers Nancy and Jack Dunne live in the carriage house out back, and in the morning you'll most likely find them puttering around the kitchen in their bathrobes preparing a big breakfast of Grand Marnier French toast stuffed with cream cheese and jam or hearty three-egg omelets served with muffins or a wonderful walnut pie. In the afternoon, wine and home-baked snacks are served on the garden patio by the hot tub and the gorgeous black-bottom swimming pool. Bicycles are available for guests who'd like to pedal around town. ▪ *825 Forbes St (1 block W of Main St, downtown), Lakeport, CA 95453; (707) 263-7858; $$; AE, MC, V; checks OK.*

## NICE

LODGINGS

**Featherbed Railroad Company** ★ Nine cabooses that look as though they would be right at home in Disneyland are spread out underneath a grove of oak trees at this gimmicky but fun bed and breakfast. The freight-train cars are burdened with cutesy names, but they're equipped with quilt-covered feather beds, private baths (some with Jacuzzi tubs), and other amenities that make up for the silliness. Favorite train cars include two new cabooses, the Orient Express (with a private deck) and the Casablanca (complete with a piano and bar), plus the red-and-white Casey Jones Caboose (with two watchman's seats) and the more feminine Lovers and Mint Julep cars. But it's the black-and-maroon La Loose Caboose, tackiest of them all, with a bordello decor and a mirror over the bed, that's always booked. The Rosebud Caboose has two small bunk beds for the kids, and there's only a $10 extra charge per child. Breakfast is served at the Main Station, a century-old ranch house, in front of a cozy fire or on the porch overlooking the lake. A small pool and spa adjoin the house. ▪ *2870 Lakeshore Blvd (off Hwy 20, at the SW end of town), Nice; (707) 274-8378 or (800) 966-6322; mail: PO Box 4016, Nice, CA 95464; $$; AE, MC, V; checks OK.*

## SONOMA VALLEY WINE COUNTRY

Many California enophiles would argue that when it comes to comparing the Sonoma Valley's Wine Country with Napa's, less is definitely more: Sonoma is less congested, less developed, less commercial, and less glitzy than its rival. Smitten with the bucolic charm of the region, Sonomaphiles delight in wandering the area's backroads, leisurely hopping from winery to winery and exploring the quaint towns along the way. Before setting out for this verdant vineyard-laced region, stop at the **Sonoma Valley Visitors Bureau** for lots of free, helpful information about the area's wineries, farmers markets, historic sites, walking tours, recreational facilities, and seasonal events; 453 First Street East, Sonoma, (707)996-1090.

### *WINERIES*

California's world-renowned wine industry was born in the Sonoma Valley. Franciscan fathers planted the state's first vineyards at the Mission San Francisco Solano de Sonoma in 1823 and harvested the grapes to make their sacramental wines. Thirty-four years later, California's first major vineyard was planted with European grape varietals by Hungarian Count Agoston Haraszthy at Sonoma's revered Buena Vista Winery. Little did the count know that one day he would become widely hailed as the father of California wine—wine that is consistently rated as some of the best in the world. Today more than 40 wineries dot the Sonoma Valley, most offering pretty picnic areas and free tours of their winemaking facilities. Here's a roundup of some of Sonoma's best:

**Benziger Family Winery** Tram ride tours take visitors through the vineyards here, and tastings are held in the wine shop. Home to good chardonnay and cabernet sauvignon, Benziger also operates the nearby Sonoma Mountain Brewery; 1883 London Ranch Road, Glen Ellen, (707)935-3000 or (800)989-8890.

**Buena Vista Winery** California's oldest premium winery (founded in 1857) is a large estate set in a forest with picnic grounds. It offers tours of the stone winery and the hillside tunnels, and a gallery features locals' artwork; 18000 Old Winery Road, Sonoma, (707)938-1266.

**Château St. Jean** Follow the self-guided tour through this beautiful 250-acre estate with tastings in the mansion and stunning views from a faux medieval tower. There is also a picnic area; 8555 Sonoma Highway (Highway 12), Kenwood, (707)833-4134.

**Ferrari–Carano Vineyards and Winery** Ferrari–Carano offers good chardonnay, fumé blanc, and cabernet. A cutting-edge facility; 8761 Dry Creek Road, Healdsburg, (707)433-6700.

**Geyser Peak Winery**  This stone winery covered with ivy produces pleasant gewürztraminer and riesling. There are beautiful hiking trails and a great picnic area available by reservation; 22281 Chianti Road, Geyserville, (707)857-9463.

**Gloria Ferrer Champagne Caves**  See interesting subterranean cellars on this excellent tour. Spanish cooking classes are occasionally offered; 23555 Highway 121, Sonoma, (707)996-7256.

**Gundlach–Bundschu Winery**  A grand, historic building set on impressive grounds. This winery is known primarily for its red wines. Picnic facilities are available, too; 2000 Denmark Street, Sonoma, (707)938-5277.

**Kenwood Vineyards**  Renowned for its red wines and quaint wooden barns; 9592 Sonoma Highway (Highway 12), Kenwood, (707)833-5891.

**Korbel Champagne Cellars**  An ivy-covered brick building is set in a redwood forest with a view of the Russian River. Korbel hosts informative tours; the extensive and beautiful flower gardens are open for tours from May through September; 13250 River Road, Guerneville, (707)887-2294.

**Kunde Estate Winery**  This century-old winery set on 2,000 gorgeous acres of rolling hills is one of Sonoma County's largest grape suppliers. It also boasts a nice tasting room; 10155 Sonoma Highway (Highway 12), Kenwood, (707)833-5501.

**Matanzas Creek Winery**  A beautiful drive leads to this winery's attractive facilities. Matanzas offers outstanding chardonnay and merlot as well as guided tours and picnic tables; 6097 Bennett Valley Road, Santa Rosa, (707)528-6464.

**Sebastiani Vineyards**  Sonoma's largest premium-variety winery, Sebastiani Vineyards provides tours of its fermentation room and aging cellar, which includes an interesting collection of carved-oak cask heads. There's also a tasting room and picnic tables; 389 Fourth Street East, Sonoma, (707)938-5532 or (800)888-5532.

**Viansa Winery and Italian Marketplace**  These buildings and grounds modeled after a Tuscan village are owned by the Sebastiani family. They produce good sauvignon blanc, chardonnay, and cabernet, plus gourmet Italian picnic fare and local delicacies perfect for the beautiful hillside picnic grounds; 25200 Highway 121, Sonoma, (707)935-4700.

## SONOMA

Sonoma's slide into gentrification has been slower than Napa's, though just as relentless. Designed by Mexican General Mariano Vallejo in 1835, Sonoma is set up like a Mexican town, with an 8-acre parklike plaza in the center. Several historic adobe buildings hug the perimeter of the plaza, most of which now house wine stores, specialty food shops, quaint boutiques, and restaurants. **Mission San Francisco Solano de Sonoma** (aka the Sonoma Mission), the northernmost and last of the 21 missions built by the Spanish fathers, is on the corner of the square at First Street East and East Spain Street; (707)938-1519. After touring the mission and the plaza, stroll over to **The Coffee Garden** for a good cup of java and a quick bite on the pretty, vine-laced patio hidden in back; 415-421 First Street West (across from the plaza's west side), (707)996-6645. Not far from the plaza, **The General's Daughter** restaurant dishes out very good, moderately priced continental cuisine in the beautifully remodeled Victorian home built in 1878 by General Vallejo's daughter, Natalia; 400 West Spain Street, (707)938-4004.

### RESTAURANTS

**Babette's Restaurant & Wine Bar ★★★★**  In a region where aspiring restaurants put as much, if not more, thought into decor as cuisine, Babette's is proof of the old adage that looks aren't everything. The wine bar, where casual bistro food is served, is a funky mix of paisley, brocade, and even leopard-skin prints, with wine boxes stacked haphazardly around two green sofas, and black plastic chairs on the patio. Casually chic, you ask? Not even close. And when you walk down the dark hall you'll find the more

*Sonoma*

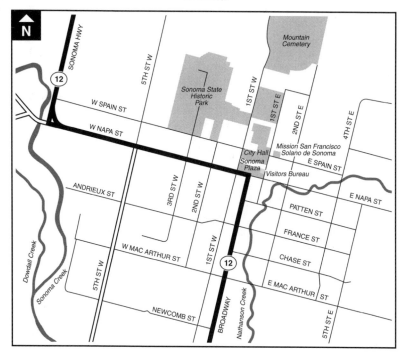

formal but still modest dining room, which fares a bit better aesthetically (at least all the tablecloths are white). But never mind. The wine in those boxes is first-rate, the cuisine is incredible, and the service is superb. Chef Daniel Patterson worked at Domain Chandon and Mustards Grill, and spent childhood summers in France; he and his wife, Elizabeth Ramsey, oversee a dazzling contemporary French five-course prix-fixe menu (with three choices for each course, including a vegetarian entree), plus wine pairings for every dish. Starters might include a silky foie gras or ricotta quenelles with black truffle butter, followed by such entrees as salmon with portobello mushrooms, a seared venison tenderloin, or a ragout of vegetables with handmade morel-stuffed ravioli. The cheese courses are exquisite, and, ahhh—bring on the desserts! Bing cherries in an almond filo basket with lavender ice cream and a warm peach and blueberry napoleon are among the delightful possibilities. The wine bar features a less-expensive bistro-style menu, with everything from pâté de foie gras to heirloom tomato and bread salad and, believe it or not, a very good hamburger. ■ *464 1st St E (down an alley between E Spain and E Napa Sts), Sonoma; (707)939-8921; $$ (wine bar), $$$ (dining room); beer and wine; MC, V; no checks; wine bar: lunch, dinner every day; dining room: dinner Thurs–Sat.* 

**Della Santina's** ★★★ A fixture on the plaza for years, this popular local outpost of the Joe's restaurant dynasty in San Francisco was smart to move down the block into the digs vacated by the late Eastside Oyster Bar & Grill. In addition to the small, trattoria-style dining room, Della Santina's inherited the wonderful vine-laced brick patio tucked in back—*the* place to dine when the weather is warm. The menu includes a good selection of light to heavy house-made pastas (the Gnocchi della Nonna with a tomato, basil, and garlic sauce would impress any Italian grandmother) and wonderful meats from the *rosticceria* (the chicken with fresh herbs is tender and perfectly spiced). Be sure to inquire about the *pasticceria*—and if *panna cotta* (a vanilla cream custard flavored with Italian rum) is among the offerings, nab it. Paired with an espresso, it's the perfect finale to a fine meal. ■ *133 E Napa St (off 2nd St), Sonoma; (707)935-0576; $$; beer and wine; AE, DIS, MC, V; local checks only; lunch, dinner every day.* 

**Ristorante Piatti** ★★ See the review of this restaurant's Yountville location in the preceding pages. ■ *405 1st St W (in El Dorado Hotel, at W Spain St, facing the plaza's W side), Sonoma; (707)996-2351; $$; full bar; AE, MC, V; local checks only; lunch, dinner every day.* 

## LODGINGS

**El Dorado Hotel** ★★ If you've had it with cutesy B&Bs, El Dorado Hotel is a welcome respite, offering 26 moderately priced rooms modestly decorated with terra-cotta tile floors, handcrafted furniture, and down comforters. Renovated by the team that created the exclusive Auberge du Soleil, each room has French doors leading to a small balcony overlooking the town square or the hotel's private courtyard, a pleasant, sunny spot where you can enjoy the complimentary continental breakfast. There's also a heated outdoor lap pool, and concierge service to help you arrange your next Wine Country excursion. ■ *405 1st St W (at W Spain St, on the plaza's W side), Sonoma, CA 95476; (707) 996-2351 or (800) 289-3031; $$; AE, MC, V; checks OK.* &

**Sonoma Chalet** ★★  So close, and yet so far: every room in this secluded Swiss-style farmhouse overlooks the grassy hills of a 200-acre ranch, giving you the impression that you're way out in the country. Fact is, you're at the edge of a suburban neighborhood—three-quarters of a mile from Sonoma's town square. There are four rooms in the two-story 1940s chalet (two of them share a bath) and three adorable private cottages, each with its own little sitting area, feather bed, fireplace or wood-burning stove, and kitchen. All of the rooms have decks or balconies with views, and each boasts an assortment of Western antiques, quilts, and collectibles that complement the rustic surroundings. In the morning proprietor Joe Leese serves pastries, juices, yogurt, and granola in the country kitchen or, if you prefer, in the privacy of your cottage. What's left over from breakfast is fed to the gaggle of ducks, chickens, and ornery geese strutting about the barnyard. If you're looking for a low-key, rustic, and romantic retreat, the Sonoma Chalet is a good choice, particularly if you reserve one of the cottages. ■ *18935 5th St W (follow 5th St W to the end, then continue W on the gravel road), Sonoma, CA 95476; (707) 938-3129; www.virtualcities.com/ons/ca/w/caw4606.htm; $$; AE, MC, V; checks OK.*

**Victorian Garden Inn** ★  This 1870s Greek revival farmhouse with a wraparound veranda has one of the most inviting small gardens you'll ever see: lush bowers of roses, azaleas, and camellias encircle wonderful little tables and chairs, while flowering fruit trees bend low over Victorian benches. The inn's four guest rooms, decorated in white wicker and florals, are pretty, if a bit cloying. The blue and white Top o' the Tower, the inn's most private room, is situated atop an authentic water tower, with its own entrance and private bath, and overlooks the garden. The most requested room is the Woodcutter's Cottage, favored for its comfy sofa and armchairs facing the fireplace and its private entrance and bath. In the evening, owner Donna Lewis pours glasses of wine and sherry in front of the parlor fireplace. Breakfast, served at the dining table, in the garden, or in your room, consists of granola, croissants, gourmet coffee, and fruit picked right from the garden. A big bonus is the large swimming pool in the backyard—a blessing during Sonoma's typically hot summer days. ■ *316 E Napa St (between 3rd St E and 4th St E, 2 blocks from the plaza), Sonoma, CA 95476; (707) 996-5339; VGardeninn@ aol.com; www.victoriangardeninn.com; $$; AE, DC, MC, V; checks OK.*

▼

▲

## BOYES HOT SPRINGS

### LODGINGS

**Sonoma Mission Inn & Spa ★★★** With its ethereally serene grounds and elegant pink stucco buildings, the Sonoma Mission Inn feels a bit like a convent—except that novitiates wear white terrycloth bathrobes or colorful running suits instead of nuns' habits. Chic sportif sorts carry tennis rackets and jog about the grounds looking glisteningly fit; less-athletic types lounge poolside with umbrella-topped fruit drinks. Indulgence, in body and spirit, is the order of the day. The European-style spa offers everything from aerobics classes and Swedish massages to aromatherapy facials, seaweed wraps, and tarot card readings in glamorous surroundings (where the likes of Barbra Streisand, Tom Cruise, and Harrison Ford come to get pampered). You'll also find exercise rooms, saunas, Jacuzzis, a salon, yoga and meditation classes, and a swimming pool filled with artesian mineral water. And as if all that weren't enough, the inn's new Texan owners promise to expand the spa menu over the next few years.

While the luxurious spa is the main draw, the inn's 200 rooms and suites offer every amenity one could want. Bathed in shades of light peach and pink, each room features plantation-style shutters, ceiling fans, and down comforters, and some units have luxe granite bathrooms big enough for an impromptu tango with your partner. Sybarites might opt for a room in the newest wing (completed in 1997), which boasts 30 higher-end suites (limestone and marble bathrooms, larger bottles of shampoo, wood-burning fireplaces). Otherwise, ask for one of the rooms overlooking the inn's swimming pool (a favorite, room 232, is in a turret), which are in the historic building, or book one of the suites in the wing facing the eucalyptus trees shading the front lawn. The inn's two restaurants, **The Grille** and **The Cafe**, are both basic Californian. The pretty Grille is one of the most expensive restaurants in Sonoma; the food is good, but doesn't live up to its high price tag. The less-expensive Cafe offers such California-Mediterranean fare as light pastas, pizzas, and grilled items, as well as hearty breakfasts.
■ *18140 Sonoma Hwy (on Hwy 12, at Boyes Blvd), Boyes Hot Springs; (707)938-9000 or (800)862-4945 (in California only), (800)358-9022 (outside California); mail: PO Box 1447, Sonoma, CA 95476; $$$; full bar; AE, DC, MC, V; checks OK; brunch Sun, breakfast, lunch, dinner every day.* ♿

## GLEN ELLEN

There are more places and things named after Jack London in Sonoma County than there are women named María in Mexico. This cult reaches its apex in Glen Ellen, where the writer built his aptly named **Beauty Ranch**, an 800-acre spread now known as

**Jack London State Historic Park.** London's vineyards, piggery, and other ranch buildings are here, as well as a house-turned-museum containing his art collection and mementos (including a series of rejection letters London received from several publishers, who must have fallen over backwards in their cushy chairs the day they learned London had become the highest-paid author of his time). Ten miles of trails lead through oaks, madrones, and redwoods, including a grove of oaks shading London's grave; 2400 London Ranch Road, off Highway 12 and Arnold Drive, (707)938-5216. If you'd rather ride than walk through London's land, let the friendly folks at the Sonoma Cattle Company saddle up a horse for you. Call for the lowdown on their **guided horseback trips** (reservations are required); located in Jack London State Historic Park, (707)996-8566.

The tiny town of Glen Ellen was also the longtime home of the late celebrated food writer M.F.K. Fisher. It offers a couple of good restaurants, plus wine-tasting and antique-hunting excursions. The **Wine Country Film Festival**, a three-week summer splurge of screenings and parties throughout Napa and Sonoma, is headquartered here; call (707)996-2536 for more information.

### RESTAURANTS

**Glen Ellen Inn** ★★ If you're staying in Glen Ellen, it's nice to know you don't have to go far to find a good meal. In fact, Christian and Karen Bertrand's tiny, romantic restaurant is worth a drive from farther afield. The menu changes frequently, but always features local cuisine at its freshest and in beautiful preparations. Dinner might include a jambalaya of prawns, bay shrimp, chicken, sausage, and honey-smoked ham, simmered in vegetables and fresh-from-the-garden herbs; expertly seared ahi tuna in a wasabe cream sauce with pickled ginger; or tender ricotta and pecorino cheese dumplings in a roasted bell pepper sauce with a garlic-infused tomato-basil salsa. The wine list features strictly Sonoma Valley labels. With just six white-clothed tables in the dining room and eight more outside in the herb garden, service is personal and attentive, almost as if you've been invited into the Bertrands' home. ■ *13670 Arnold Dr (at O'Donnell Lane), Glen Ellen; (707)996-6409; $$; beer and wine; AE, MC, V; local checks only; dinner every day.* &

**Mes Trois Filles** ★★ This wisp of a restaurant in a small, gray clapboard storefront holds its own with the big guys, thanks to owner chef Len Moriyama's skillful rendition of French Country fare with a soupçon of Japanese style. His emphasis on fresh Sonoma Valley ingredients is abundantly clear as soon as you bite into such stellar dishes as the juicy free-range chicken breast served on a coulis of leeks with a wild mushroom and tarragon sauce, or the ragout of organic vegetables baked in parchment with herbed butter and garlic. For dessert, order the perfectly balanced chocolate Grand Marnier mousse or the classic crème brûlée. Nice touches include a single red rose for the ladies. Moriyama, who once worked at San Francisco's Campton Place restaurant, named his establishment after his *trois filles* (French for "three daughters"). ■ *13648 Arnold Dr (at Warm Springs Rd), Glen Ellen; (707)938-4844; $$; beer and wine; MC, V; local checks only; dinner Wed–Sun.*

## LODGINGS

**Beltane Ranch** ★★★ Surrounded by vineyards at the foot of the Mayacamas Mountains, this century-old buttercup yellow and white clapboard farmhouse was a bunkhouse long before it was a bed and breakfast—but certainly the cowhands of old never had it so good. Each of the inn's five rooms is uniquely decorated; all have sitting areas, private baths, separate entrances, and a family antique or two. Ask for one of the upstairs rooms that opens onto the huge wraparound porch equipped with hammocks and a swing. Innkeeper Deborah Mahoney serves a full country breakfast in the garden or on the porch overlooking Sonoma's hillsides. Blissfully calm and beautiful, the whole place makes you feel as though you should be wearing a wide-brimmed hat and sipping a mint julep. Should you tire of lolling Southern belle–style, knock a few balls around the tennis court near the house, pitch horseshoes in the garden, or hike the trails through the estate's 1,600 acres of vineyards and hills. ■ *11775 Sonoma Hwy (on Hwy 12, 2.2 miles past the Glen Ellen turnoff), Glen Ellen; (707)996-6501; mail: PO Box 395, Glen Ellen, CA 95442; $$$; no credit cards; checks OK.*

**Gaige House Inn** ★★★ From the outside, the Gaige House looks like yet another spiffed-up Victorian mansion, inevitably filled with the ubiquitous dusty antiques and family heirlooms. Inside, however, the Victorian theme comes to a screeching halt. All eleven rooms are spectacular, and each is individually decorated with an eclectic mix of modern art. Owners Ken Burnet Jr. and Greg Nemrow have added three new guest rooms, including one with a private Japanese garden and waterfall. An old favorite is the Gaige Suite, which features a king-size four-poster canopy bed; it's also known as the Oh Wow! Room (since that is what everyone instantaneously gasps as they enter the bathroom). The suite has an enormous blue-tiled bathroom centered by a whirlpool tub that could easily fit a party of six (and probably has), as well as a huge wraparound balcony. The three Garden Rooms, slightly smaller and less expensive, open onto a shaded deck and are within steps of a beautiful brick-lined 40-foot swimming pool surrounded by a large, perfectly manicured lawn. All rooms have telephones, king- or queen-size beds, and private bathrooms; a few have fireplaces. Included in the room rate—which is surprisingly affordable considering the caliber of the accommodations—is a two-course gourmet breakfast served at individual tables or on the terrace. ■ *13540 Arnold Dr (from Hwy 12, take the Glen Ellen exit), Glen Ellen, CA 95442; (707)935-0237 or (800)935-0237; gaige@sprynet.com; www.gaige.com; $$$; AE, DIS, MC, V; checks OK.* &

**Glenelly Inn** ★★  A graceful grove of oak trees forms the backdrop for this serene peach-and-cream two-building inn, originally built in 1916 as a lodging for railway travelers. The eight guest rooms, each with private entrances, down comforters, private bathrooms, ceiling fans, and reading lights, open onto the elaborate garden or the veranda, which offers a fine view of the Sonoma Valley and the tree-covered mountains beyond. One building houses six veranda rooms; the Buena Vista—a Victorian delight with a wrought-iron-and-brass bed, a treadle-base sink, and the inn's best view—is the most favored. Two larger suites with small private patios are located in the main house. The better of the pair is the Jack London Suite, with its wooden sleigh bed, wood-burning stove, rattan furniture, and assortment of Jack London memorabilia. Rock away the afternoon in the swing suspended from a 200-year-old oak, or mellow out in the hot tub recessed deep within the garden. A full breakfast is served in the common room. ■ *5131 Warm Springs Rd (off Arnold Dr), Glen Ellen, CA 95442; (707)996-6720; www.vom.com/glenelly; $$; MC, V; checks OK.*

## KENWOOD

### RESTAURANTS

**Kenwood Restaurant and Bar** ★  This large, sun-filled dining room with polished wood floors, a natural-pine ceiling, white linens, and bamboo chairs is the showcase for Swiss-born chef Max Schacher. Although his menu changes often, you can't go wrong if you stick to the meat and poultry offerings, such as Schacher's braised Sonoma rabbit served with mushrooms and polenta, the crisp Petaluma duck, or the calf liver sautéed in onions—each dish is robed in a richly complex sauce. Schacher also offers a vegetarian entree and a great caesar salad. This is a good place to stop for a casual meal or drink, particularly on a sunny day when the umbrellas are set up on the outdoor terrace. ■ *9900 Sonoma Hwy (on Hwy 12, 3 miles past Glen Ellen), Kenwood; (707)833-6326; www.serba.com/kenwood/restaurant; $$; full bar; MC, V; no checks; lunch, dinner Wed–Sun.* &

### LODGINGS

**Kenwood Inn** ★★★  This posh inn, owned by Roseann and Terry Grimm, resembles a centuries-old Italian pensione. The 12 guest rooms are beautifully decorated, each with a fluffy feather bed, a fireplace, and a sitting area. Room 3, bathed in shades of burgundy and green paisley, has a pleasant private patio, and room 6 sports a sitting room with a stereo, Jacuzzi, and balcony overlooking the vineyards and the swimming pool. The six-room, full-service spa pampers with such special treatments as a Mediterranean scrub of lemon rind, rosemary, and salt followed by a massage. The Grimms serve an ample breakfast with fresh fruit, polenta with poached eggs, and buttery house-made croissants. ■ *10400 Sonoma Hwy (on Hwy 12, 3 miles past Glen Ellen), Kenwood, CA 95452; (707)833-1293; www.sterba.com/kenwood/ inn; $$$; AE, MC, V; checks OK.* &

## SANTA ROSA

Santa Rosa is the closest thing Sonoma County has to a big city, but it's more like a countrified suburb. Oddly enough, it's got more than its share of offbeat museums. Botanists, gardeners, and other plant lovers will want to make a beeline to the popular gardens and greenhouse at the **Luther Burbank Home & Gardens**. Burbank, for those struggling to recall their elementary-school history, was a world-renowned horticulturist who created 800 new strains of plants, fruits, and vegetables at the turn of the century; the home is located at the corner of Santa Rosa and Sonoma Avenues, (707)524-5445. Pop culture fans will get a kick out of **Snoopy's Gallery & Gift Shop**, a "Peanuts" cartoon museum with the world's largest collection of Snoopy memorabilia, thanks to donations by the beagle's creator, Charles Schulz, who lives in Santa Rosa; 1665 West Steel Lane, (707)546-3385. The tacky but fun **Robert L. Ripley Memorial Museum**, housed in the historic **Church Built from One Tree**, is filled with wacky displays and information about the late Santa Rosa resident who created the world-famous "Ripley's Believe It or Not" cartoon strip; 492 Sonoma Avenue, (707)524-5233.

For music, magicians, and a plethora of fresh-from-the-farm food, head over to the wildly successful **Thursday Night Farmers Market** on downtown Santa Rosa's Fourth Street, which is closed to traffic every Thursday night for this festive event and draws folks from far and near from Memorial Day through Labor Day; (707)542-2123. Another local crowd-pleaser is the annual **Sonoma County Harvest Fair**, a wine-tasting, food-guzzling orgy held at the fairgrounds from late July to early August; 1350 Bennett Valley Road, (707)545-4200.

### RESTAURANTS

**John Ash & Co.** ★★★★ This casually elegant restaurant, founded by Wine Country cuisine guru John Ash, has topped the list of Santa Rosa's best restaurants for many years. It's pricey, but the service is expert, the food is fabulous, and the serene dining room with cream-colored walls, tall French windows, and a crackling fire will entice you to settle in for a good, long time. The menu, under the direction of executive chef Jeffrey Madura, is a classic California hybrid of French, Italian, Asian, and Southwestern cuisines. A meal might include such glorious dishes as rich corn chowder with firecracker rock shrimp, followed by a sautéed breast of chicken with mango-avocado salsa and orzo pasta with spinach, oranges, and macadamia nuts; a perfectly pink roast loin of lamb in a nutty walnut-thyme sauce; or an expertly poached Bodega Bay salmon with fresh ginger sauce. For dessert, pastry chef Theresa Di Falco makes diners swoon with her signature tiramisu served in a chocolate cup or her port wine crème brûlée with house-made walnut cookies and fresh Sonoma figs. The large, reasonably priced wine list, showcasing Napa and Sonoma wines, also includes a good selection of ports, sherries, and dessert wines. For a taste of John Ash's superb cuisine at one-third the regular price, sit at the bar or on the patio and order from the Vineyard Cafe menu. ■ *4330 Barnes Rd (next door to Vintners Inn, off River Rd, at Hwy 101), Santa Rosa; (707)527-7687; www.johnashco.com; $$$; full bar; AE, MC, V; local checks only; brunch Sat–Sun, lunch Tues–Fri, dinner every day.* ♿

**Willowside Cafe ★★★** Hiding out in a funky roadhouse a few miles from downtown Santa Rosa, Willowside may be Sonoma's best-kept dining secret. Inside, the mood is simple yet sophisticated, with pale yellow walls, copper-topped tables, and fresh flowers—the perfect match for chef/co-owner Richard Hale's highly personal rendition of California-French cuisine. Hale

*Santa Rosa*

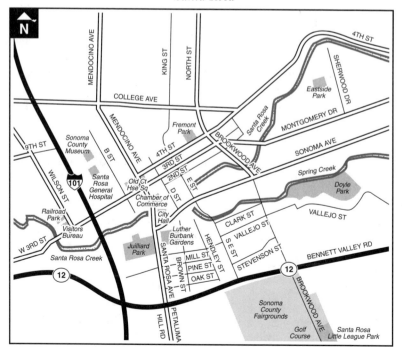

rewrites the menu every week, but it always includes five starters (such as duck breast with red onion marmalade or mussels in mustard sauce) and five entrees (quail with portobello mushrooms, lamb with fava beans and pecorino cheese). Rounding out the trio of culinary talents behind Willowside are co-owners Mike Hale, the maitre d', and his wife, Carole Hale, the pastry chef (don't miss her first-rate cobblers and tarts). A favorite with local winemakers, Willowside offers 200 labels on its wine list, including hard-to-find California, French, and Australian bottles. ■ *3535 Guerneville Rd (at Willowside Rd), Santa Rosa; (707)523-4814; $$; beer and wine; MC, V; local checks only; dinner Wed–Sun.* &

**Lisa Hemenway's** ★★ Don't let the rather drab shopping center setting fool you—centered within this boxy brown shrine to the '70s is a refreshingly light, airy restaurant with alfresco dining and an inviting menu. With cooking skills honed at the venerable John Ash & Co. restaurant, combined with working vacations in Asia and Europe, owner-chef Lisa Hemenway has created an expansive and varied menu: triàngoli with a wild mushroom filling and an eggplant pesto sauce; a skewer of grilled shiitake mushrooms served on sunsprouts and buckwheat noodles with a spicy ginger dressing; vegetable tamales with smoked California chile sauce; Hungarian tortes; and chutney burgers. If all this is too daunting for you, pass on the main menu and ponder the appetizer selection at the wine bar, which proudly boasts numerous Awards of Excellence from *Wine Spectator* magazine. ■ *714 Village Ct (in the Village Court Mall/Montgomery Village, at Farmers Lane and Sonoma Ave), Santa Rosa; (707)526-5111; $$; full bar; DC, DIS, MC, V; checks OK; brunch Sun, lunch Mon–Sat, dinner every day.* &

**Caffe Portofino** ★ Caffe Portofino's handsome oak dining room is always bustling and crowded with patrons. The vast California-Italian menu features more than 30 entrees, including meat, poultry, seafood, and an array of pastas. The quality of the food may vary from day to day, but that doesn't seem to deter locals, who love the place. Two consistently reliable dishes include the Fettuccine Portofino with bite-size bits of pork tenderloin and tender mushrooms in a garlicky red wine sauce, and the prawns tossed in a wine sauce with olives and tomatoes. The grilled fish and chops are also good bets. The wine bar at the cafe's entrance is a popular place to meet friends and sip some of the area's finer vintages. ■ *535 4th St (between Mendocino Ave and B St), Santa Rosa; (707)523-1171; $$; full bar; AE, MC, V; no checks; lunch, dinner Mon–Sat.* &

## LODGINGS

**Vintners Inn** ★★ The Vintners Inn combines the charm of a country inn with the conveniences of a modern hotel. Its four Provençal-style buildings are clustered around a central courtyard set amid vineyards. The inn's 44 newly refurbished rooms have pine beds, plush carpets, antique armoires and desks, and separate sitting areas; many have wood-burning fireplaces, too. French doors open onto a balcony or patio with a view of the vineyards or the landscaped grounds (ask for a room with a vineyard view facing away from Highway 101). The young, courteous staff is very attentive, providing first-class room service. A complimentary breakfast is served in the main building's sunny dining room until 10am on weekdays and 11am on weekends. Though there's also a fine deck for sunning and a Jacuzzi, the inn's best feature is its adjoining four-star restaurant, John Ash & Co. (see review, above). ■ *4350 Barnes Rd (off River Rd, at Hwy 101), Santa Rosa, CA 95403; (707)575-7350 or (800)421-2584; www. vintnersinn.com; $$$; full bar; AE, DC, MC, V; checks OK.* &

**Fountaingrove Inn ★** The Fountaingrove's 84 rooms are elegant to the point of austerity, with gray carpets, gray bedspreads, mirrored walls, and pen-and-ink drawings of horses over the beds. Outside, the swimming pool and Jacuzzi are surrounded by a slate sun deck next to the kind of fountain you usually see in the lobbies of corporate headquarters. It all seems very serious (and very '70s), perhaps because the motel caters more to business travelers than to tourists. But there's no reason you have to take it as seriously as it takes itself. In the morning you can grab a quick continental breakfast in the lobby before heading out for a hard day of wine-tasting. Or, if you have to work, there is a place to hook up your modem. Adjoining the inn is the **Equus Restaurant & Lounge**, a formal dining room of redwood carvings, etched glass, and air-brushed murals that serves reasonably good if uninspired men's club standbys. ■ *101 Fountaingrove Pkwy (at Mendocino Ave), Santa Rosa, CA 95403; (707)578-6101 or (800)222-6101; www.fountaingroveinn.com; $$$; full bar; AE, DC, DIS, MC, V; checks OK; lunch, dinner every day.* &

**The Gables Bed and Breakfast ★** This gothic Victorian is the house of not 7 but rather 15 gables. Innkeepers Judy and Michael Ogne have decorated the eight cheerful guest rooms in this historic landmark with antiques and old-fashioned furnishings. The spacious Brookside Suite, overlooking a creek, has a fireplace and a king-size bed, and the Parlor Suite features a gorgeous Italian marble fireplace and furniture handmade by Michael. The most sought-after accommodation is the small William and Mary's Cottage situated at the edge of the backyard creek. The enchanting little cabin, which includes a Jacuzzi tub for two, has a sleeping loft, a wood-burning stove, and a tiny kitchen. All guest rooms are air-conditioned. The inn has a 3-acre backyard and a roomy wooden deck inhabited by several identical white cats. ■ *4257 Petaluma Hill Rd (4 miles from the Rohnert Park Expwy), Santa Rosa, CA 95404; (707)585-7777; innkeeper@thegablesinn. com; www.thegablesinn.com; $$$; AE, DIS, MC, V; checks OK.*

This is one tourist town whose charm seems completely unforced. Boutiques and bakeries surround a pretty, tree-lined plaza where you can sit and read the newspaper while munching on pastries from the marvelous **Downtown Bakery & Creamery**; 308-A Center Street, (707) 431-2719. In the summer, nothing beats paddling down the glorious **Russian River** past vineyards and secret swimming holes in a canoe rented from W. C. "Bob" Trowbridge Canoe Trips; 20 Healdsburg Avenue, (707) 433-7247 or (800) 640-1386. If you're in need of a respite from your hectic day trips, catch a flick at the **Raven Theater**, the Wine Country's best movie house for new releases and art films; 115 North Street, (707) 433-5448.

## RESTAURANTS

**Bistro Ralph** ★★★ In a town where restaurants have been afflicted with the revolving door syndrome (Tre Scalini and Samba Java were a couple of the latest victims), simple yet stylish Bistro Ralph continues to thrive. Housed in a slender storefront on the square, Ralph Tingle's intimate bistro serves consistently excellent food, with a focus on local ingredients. Nibble on some *focaccini* (balls of sautéed focaccia dough) while perusing the well-rounded dinner menu. Choice starters include grilled portobello mushrooms with white truffle oil and crispy Sichuan pepper calamari. The lamb dishes are always good, particularly the hearty spring lamb stew à la Provençal, and the lamb shanks with crème fraîche–horseradish mashed potatoes. The lunch menu sticks to upscale salads and sandwiches, such as the grilled ahi tuna or salmon sandwich and the popular lamb burger on a fresh roll, all served with a pile of irresistible shoestring fries. The decor has a cozy, slightly industrial feel, with a dozen or so linentopped tables, white brick walls, and a long concrete counter where you can watch Chef Tingle perform culinary magic in the small open kitchen. ■ *109 Plaza St E (on the plaza), Healdsburg; (707) 433-1380; $$; beer and wine; MC, V; local checks only; lunch Mon–Sat, dinner every day.* &

## LODGINGS

**Belle de Jour Inn** ★★★ In a region where rampant Victoriana is all the rage, Belle de Jour's four romantic hillside cottages and large carriage house have a refreshingly spare, uncluttered feel. From the bedroom of the cottage called the Terrace Room, you can savor a fine view of the valley from the comfort of a giant Jacuzzi. Also recommended is the Caretaker's Suite with its lace-canopied four-poster bed, private deck with a vine-covered trellis, and blue-tiled whirlpool tub. The newest suite is the 700-square-foot Carriage House, with vaulted ceilings, a Jacuzzi, and views of Mount St. Helena. All of the accommodations have a fireplace or

▼
**Healdsburg**
▲

a wood-burning stove, ceiling fans, and refrigerators, and are air-conditioned—a big plus around here in the summer. Innkeepers Tom and Brenda Hearn whip up a bountiful country breakfast in their beautiful state-of-the-art kitchen and serve it on the deck of the main house. Also available to guests for an hourly fee is a chauffeured backroads winery tour in the Hearns' 1925 Star touring car—something to consider if wine-tasting makes you tipsy. ▪ *16276 Healdsburg Ave (1 mile N of Dry Creek Rd, across from Simi Winery), Healdsburg, CA 95448; (707)431-9777; $$$; MC, V; checks OK.*

### Healdsburg Inn on the Plaza ★★★

Originally built as a Wells Fargo Express office in 1900, this surprisingly quiet inn on the plaza has high ceilings and a lovely old staircase leading from the ground-floor art gallery to the 10 attractive guest rooms upstairs. The four rooms facing the plaza have beautiful bay windows; particularly engaging is the spacious pale yellow and white Song of the Rose Room, which has a queen-size white iron and brass bed, and a comfy oak rocker set in front of the fireplace. The largest room is the Garden Suite, which has a Jacuzzi, king-size bed, and private patio bedecked with flowers. All 10 rooms have private baths with showers, TVs with VCRs, and air conditioning, and all but three have gas-log fireplaces and claw-footed bathtubs. A full breakfast and afternoon wine and snacks are served at tables for two in the glass-enclosed solarium. ▪ *110 Matheson St (on the plaza's south side), Healdsburg; (707)433-6991 or (800)431-8663; mail: PO Box 1196, Healdsburg, CA 95448; www.healdsburginn. com; $$$; MC, V; checks OK.*

### Haydon Street Inn ★★

This pretty blue 1912 Queen Anne Victorian inn with a large veranda set behind a white picket fence offers eight cheery guest rooms, a few with private baths. But your best bet is to rent one of the two larger rooms in the Victorian Cottage tucked behind the main house. Owner Joann Claus lives on the first floor of the cottage; the upstairs has been turned into two spacious rooms with vaulted ceilings, queen-size beds, high dormer windows, big whirlpool tubs, and loads of charm. In the morning you'll find a full country breakfast featuring such treats as green chile frittatas with basil and cilantro, fresh fruit or baked apples, and plenty of house-made muffins and croissants. ▪ *321 Haydon St (at Fitch St), Healdsburg, CA 95448; (707)433-5228; www.haydon.com; $$; MC, V; checks OK.*

### Madrona Manor ★

Surrounded by lush green lawns, exotic gardens, and a citrus orchard, Madrona Manor looks a lot like a cheerier version of the Addams Family's gothic abode. The inn's 21 rooms and three suites are divided between the main house and the carriage house. Several of the rooms in the main house have their original furnishings, which are somewhat shabbier than you might expect in so pricey an establishment. Oddly enough, this doesn't detract from the charm; instead, it lends a homey sense of authenticity. Most of the rooms have fireplaces, some with delicate hand-painted borders. Rooms 203, 204, and 400 are the most spacious, with French doors opening onto lovely—if somewhat precarious—balconies. All rooms are air-conditioned and have telephones and private bathrooms. A full breakfast is included in the room rate.

The **Madrona Manor Restaurant** offers a five-course prix-fixe or an à la carte menu. Despite the fact that most of the vegetables and herbs are harvested from the manor's own garden and the breads, pastries, and pastas are prepared on the premises, the pricey offerings don't quite measure up to the ambience—or to the restaurant's reputation. ■ *1001 Westside Rd (at Dry Creek Rd), Healdsburg; (707)433-4231 or (800)258-4003; mail: PO Box 818, Healdsburg, CA 95448; www.madronamanor. com; $$$; beer and wine; AE, DC, DIS, MC, V; checks OK; dinner every day.* &

## GEYSERVILLE

### *RESTAURANTS*

**Château Souverain Cafe at the Winery** ★ From the ornate stone-and-wrought-iron archway at the end of the drive to the grand, curving white staircase and the formal gardens leading up to the entrance, the whole design of Château Souverain seems calculated to awe. The winery's cafe, however, is on a much more down-to-earth level. Chef Martin Courtman presides over the brightly painted restaurant, offering a small menu of roast Sonoma chicken, grilled salmon fillet, roast leg of lamb, and a few pasta dishes, soups, salads, and desserts. Although it's not worth going too far out of your way to dine here, it's still a great place for an inexpensive bite to eat while touring the Wine Country. ■ *400 Souverain Rd (S of town; from Hwy 101, take the Independence Lane exit), Geyserville; (707)433-3141; $$; wine only; AE, DIS, MC, V; checks OK; lunch, dinner Fri–Sun.* &

### *LODGINGS*

**Hope–Merrill House** ★★★ Since nearly every mediocre shack built in the late 19th century gets dubbed "Victorian," it's easy to forget the dizzying architectural and design heights reached during this period. This beautifully restored 1870 Eastlake gothic will remind you: the three-story brown and cream Hope–Merrill House has expansive bay windows and a back veranda furnished with comfortable cane chairs. The landscaping is formal and strictly symmetrical, with box hedges and weeping mulberries. Inside, you'll find extravagant silk-screened wallpapers, carved armchairs, and velvet-covered divans (which are just as uncomfortable now as they were in their heyday). The inn offers eight individually decorated guest rooms with private baths and queen-size beds. The fairest is the Peacock Room: gold, rose, and gray-blue peacocks strut around a ceiling border, a wood-burning fireplace dominates one wall, and French doors open into a bathroom with an immense marble-topped whirlpool tub. For the best views, ask for the Vineyard View Room or the Bradbury Room, which have fireplaces, two-person showers, and views of the swimming pool and the pretty gardens. A hearty breakfast is included in the rates. ■ *21253 Geyserville Ave (from Hwy 101, take the Geyserville exit), Geyserville; (707)857-3356 or (800)825-4BED; mail: PO Box 42, Geyserville, CA 95441; $$; AE, MC, V; checks OK.*

**Hope–Bosworth House ★★** Across the street from its showier cousin, the Hope–Merrill House, the 1904 Hope–Bosworth House provides a cheery, informal, and less-expensive place to stay. This Queen Anne–style Victorian inn has four bedrooms, three of which have full baths, including one with a Jacuzzi tub. The downstairs Sun Porch Room has the dry, woody fragrance of a summer cottage, and it reverberates each morning with birdsong from the backyard. Everyone's favorite, however, is the sunny and spacious Wicker Room with its old-fashioned white and pink flowered wallpaper. Guests are treated to the same elaborate breakfast as their neighbors, and they have access to the pool and other facilities at the Hope–Merrill House. ■ *21238 Geyserville Ave (from Hwy 101, take the Geyserville exit), Geyserville; (707)857-3356 or (800)825-4BED; mail: PO Box 42, Geyserville, CA 95441; $$; AE, MC, V; checks OK.*

## CLOVERDALE

### RESTAURANTS

**World Famous Hamburger Ranch and Pasta Farm ★** Rave reviews from satisfied customers all over the world paper the walls of this converted service station, which was voted the purveyor of Sonoma County's Best Burger by readers of the *Santa Rosa Press Democrat*. A typical homage: "Killer burgers. Awesome fries. We asked the locals. And they didn't lie." A favorite with truck drivers and other travelers for more than 50 years, the Hamburger Ranch offers fresh pastas and summer barbecues in addition to great burgers and fries, funky blues music, and friendly service. You can sip a brewski from the nearby Anderson Valley Brewing Company, and dine alfresco under the shade of a large umbrella. ■ *31195 Redwood Hwy (at the N end of town at the top of the hill), Cloverdale; (707)894-5616; $; beer and wine; DC, MC, V; checks OK; breakfast, lunch, dinner every day.*

### LODGINGS

**Vintage Towers Bed and Breakfast Inn ★★** Listed on the National Register of Historic Places, this beautiful mauve mansion located on a quiet residential street has seven air-conditioned guest rooms. The three corner suites have tower sitting rooms (one round, one square, and one octagonal), separate sleeping quarters, and private baths. Particularly unique is the Vintage Tower Suite, which has its own private porch complete with a telescope for stargazing and a spiral staircase that descends to the yard. Scarlet's Room and the Sunroom share a bath. Downstairs you'll find a large dining room with a fireplace, a parlor, and a library. In the morning, friendly innkeepers Cindy and Gus Wolter serve a full gourmet breakfast in the dining room; the veranda is the spot for lemonade and homemade cookies in the afternoon. ■ *302 N Main St (at 3rd St, off Cloverdale Blvd), Cloverdale, CA 95425; (707) 894-4535; www.vintagetowers.com; $$; AE, DIS, MC, V; checks OK.*

## ANDERSON VALLEY WINE COUNTRY

Once noted only for sheep, apples, and timber, Anderson Valley has become the premier producer of cool-climate California wines such as chardonnay, gewürztraminer, and riesling. The enological future of this valley, whose climate is almost identical to that of the Champagne region of France, may also reside in the production of sparkling wine, now that some of France's best champagne-makers have successfully set up shop here.

▼

▲

### WINERIES

Most of Anderson Valley's wineries line the narrow stretch of Highway 28 that winds through this gorgeous, verdant 25-mile-long valley before it reaches the Pacific Coast. Here are some of of Anderson Valley's premier wineries:

**Greenwood Ridge** Known for its white riesling (and cabernet and zinfandel produced in another region), Greenwood is the site of the annual California Wine Tasting Championships (for novices and pros) held on the last weekend of July; it also has a picnic area by a pond and a tasting room; 5501 Highway 128, Philo, (707) 895-2002.

**Handley Cellars** Popular for its chardonnay, Handley has a tasting room and picnic area in a garden courtyard; 3151 Highway 128, Philo, (707) 895-3876.

**Husch Vineyards** The oldest winery in Anderson Valley (founded in 1971), Husch produces chardonnay, pinot noir, gewürztraminer, and wines from its Ukiah vineyards. It offers a small, rustic redwood tasting room and picnic tables; 4400 Highway 128, Philo, (707) 895-3216.

**Navarro Vineyards** This small, family-owned winery pioneered the region's trademark wine (dry, fruity, spicy Alsatian-style gewürztraminer) and produces excellent chardonnay, pinot noir, and white riesling. Navarro wines are sold only at the winery and by mail order. There are picnic tables and a tiny tasting room; 5601 Highway 128, Philo, (707) 895-3686.

**Roederer Estate** A winery established by one of France's most prestigious champagne producers. Inside the low-key, low-slung hillside facility visitors can take tours of the sparkling-wine-making process. The tasting room has an antique French bar topped with zinc where you can sip high-quality sparkling wines; 4501 Highway 128, Philo, (707)895-2288.

**Scharffenberger Cellars** Anderson Valley's first vintner to make sparkling wine in the traditional French way, Scharffenberger produces excellent brut, blanc de blancs, brut rosé, and crémant. The tasting room is in a remodeled farmhouse. Tours are offered, too; 8501 Highway 128, Philo, (707)895-2957.

## BOONVILLE

This speck of a town in the heart of the Anderson Valley is best known for a regional dialect called Boontling, developed by townsfolk at the beginning of the century. No one really speaks Boontling anymore, though a few old-timers remember the lingo. As in most private languages, a large percentage of the words refer to sex, a fact glossed over in most touristy brochures on the topic. Most people don't know what the Boontling word for beer is, but the folks at the **Anderson Valley Brewing Company & Buckhorn Saloon**, a fine little microbrewery across from the Boonville Hotel, probably do. It's at 14081 Highway 128, (707)895-BEER. While you're in town, grab a copy of the *Anderson Valley Advertiser*, a rollicking, crusading (some say muckraking) small-town paper with avid readers from as far away as San Francisco and the Oregon border. **Boont Berry Farm**, an organic-produce market and deli in a small, weathered-wood building, turns out terrific treats; 13981 Highway 128, (707)895-3576.

### LODGINGS

**The Boonville Hotel and Restaurant** ★★★ In the mid-1980s, the Boonville Hotel was the most famous culinary destination in the Northern California outback. Swells from San Francisco and New York flew by private plane to Anderson Valley's tiny airport just to sample the precious culinary creations of former owner Charlotte Rollins. Pressed by debts, she and her partner eventually skipped town in the dead of night, leaving an unpaid staff and a bad taste in the mouths of locals, who had had their doubts about the hotel's ritzy clientele in the first place. The Boonville Hotel languished for a few years until current owner John Schmitt brought it back to life as a quiet little restaurant and inn.

The decor of the Boonville Hotel is pleasantly austere. The beautiful wood bar downstairs and most of the exquisite furniture in the 10 guest rooms are the work of local craftspeople. Half of the rooms have private balconies, although two of them overlook the busy highway. Two newer suites offer spacious separate sitting areas, making them well-suited to those with kids in tow. The smaller rooms at the back of the hotel are quieter and less expensive, but here the inn's austerity shades dangerously close to bareness. Medium-size room 3, with its unique iron bed, is a good compromise of price, spaciousness, and peacefulness. Guests are treated to a continental breakfast in the sunny dining room.

The restaurant in the Boonville Hotel, a gathering spot for local winemakers, is still one of the best north of the Napa Valley. Chef Schmitt (who worked for years cooking with his mother at the beloved French Laundry restaurant in Yountville) offers a fresh mix of California, Southwestern, and backwoods regional cuisine, such as sliced pork tenderloin with cumin, cilantro, and oranges, and chicken breast with roasted tomato-mint salsa. Everyone loves the roasted garlic mashed potatoes, the individual pizzas sprinkled with farm-fresh produce and locally made goat cheese, and the hot crusty bread that makes a terrific sponge for the savory soups. Many of Schmitt's ingredients come from the beautiful 2-acre garden behind the hotel. From May through October, the hotel's parking lot becomes the site of the festive **Boonville Farmers Market** held every Saturday from 9am to noon, where you can purchase wonderful produce, handmade soaps, wool, and even your own billy goat. Reservations are recommended for both the hotel and the restaurant, especially in the summer. ■ *On Hwy 128 (at Lambert Lane, in the center of town), Boonville; (707)895-2210; mail: PO Box 326, Boonville, CA 95415; $$$; beer and wine; MC, V; checks OK; lunch Fri–Sun from June to Sept, dinner Wed–Mon year-round (the hotel and restaurant close the first 2 weeks in Jan and Mon–Thurs from Jan 14 to Feb 14).* &

**The Toll House Inn ★★** Located high in the oak-covered hills on the twisting road between Boonville and Ukiah, this wonderful 1912 Victorian farmhouse set on a 360-acre ranch feels far away from everything. The five individually decorated guest rooms have a modern flair, softened by a few attractive antiques (you won't find any Victorian clutter here). Unfortunately, as with every other roadside inn in the Anderson Valley, the rooms toward the front of the house suffer from truck noise at night. Proprietors Betty Ingram and Barbara McGuinness serve a full breakfast made from the fruit and vegetables grown in their organic garden. Guests are welcome to roam the property, which is also home to two llamas and six sheep. The less adventurous can luxuriate in the hot tub or in the beautifully landscaped backyard. ■ *15301 Hwy 253 (5 miles N of town), Boonville, CA 95415; (707)895-3630; $$$; full bar; DIS, MC, V; checks OK.*

## PHILO

There's not much to see in this hamlet, but about 2 miles west you'll find **Gowan's Oak Tree**, a great family-run roadside fruit-and-vegetable stand with a few picnic tables in back and a swing for road-weary tots; 6350 Highway 128, (707)895-3353.

**Philo Pottery Inn** ★★ This 1888 redwood farmhouse is pure and authentic country—no frilly ruffles, no overdressed dolls, just a lavender-filled English garden in the front yard and bright hand-made quilts and sturdy frontier furnishings in each of the five guest rooms. You may linger in the library downstairs or snooze in the bent-willow loungers on the rustic front porch. Evaline's and Donna's Rooms are the lightest and most spacious, but the favored unit is the cozy one-room cottage with a detached private bath, a wood-burning stove, and a back porch. Owner Sue Chiverton will direct you to all the best hiking and biking trails (ask her about the great 12-mile mountain-bike route) and will happily arrange private tastings at the valley's many small private wineries. She also serves a full breakfast, featuring many homemade treats, in the dining room. For a great snack, ask for her freshly made biscotti. ■ *8550 Hwy 128 (in town), Philo; (707)895-3069; mail: PO Box 166, Philo, CA 95466; $$; MC, V; checks OK.*

## HOPLAND

### *RESTAURANTS*

**Hopland Brewery Brewpub and Beer Garden ■ Mendocino Brewing Company** ★ California's first brewpub since Prohibition (and the second in the nation), the Hopland Brewery is a refreshing break from the crushed-grape circuit. This quintessential brewpub has tasty grub, foot-stomping live music on Saturday (everything from the blues to Cajun), and eight fine beers brewed on the premises. The classic beer garden has long tables shaded by trellised hops, as well as a sandbox to keep the kids amused while you chow down on the large burgers served on house-made buns or the Red Tail Chili—a heavenly mash of fresh vegetables, sirloin steak, and a generous splash of Red Tail Ale. ■ *13351 Hwy 101 (downtown), Hopland; (707)744-1015; www.mendobrew.com; $; beer and wine; MC, V; no checks; lunch, dinner every day.*

**Hopland**

*Lodgings*

### *LODGINGS*

**Thatcher Inn** ★ Built as a stage stop in 1890, this haughty cream-colored combination of gothic spires and gabled windows still looks like a luxurious frontier saloon-hotel, thanks to an $800,000 restoration in 1990. The lobby is dominated by a long, mirrored, polished wood bar, and the gorgeous, dark, wood-paneled library is filled with interesting old books, velvet settees, and shiny brass reading lamps. A wide, curving wood stairway leads from the lobby to 20 charmingly decorated guest rooms on the second and third stories—all with private baths. The quietest rooms with the best views are on the south side of the hotel overlooking the backyard patio with a fountain, wrought-iron lamp posts, and a giant oak tree. A full breakfast, usually served alfresco, is included in the rate. The hotel's **Thatcher Inn Restaurant** serves accept-able but uninspired California cuisine. ■ *13401 Hwy 101 (down-town), Hopland; (707)744-1890 or (800)266-1891; mail: PO Box 660, Hopland, CA 95449; $$$; full bar; AE, MC, V; checks OK; brunch Sun, lunch Wed–Sat, dinner Wed–Sun.*

## UKIAH

Located in the upper reaches of the California Wine Country, Ukiah is still what Napa, Sonoma, and Healdsburg used to be—a sleepy little agricultural town surrounded by vineyards and apple and pear orchards. Peopled by an odd mix of farmers, loggers, and back-to-the-landers, Ukiah is a down-to-earth little burg with few traces of Wine Country gentrification. That doesn't mean there isn't any wine, however. **Jepson Vineyards** produces chardonnay, sauvignon blanc, and sparkling wine, as well as brandy, which is distilled in a copper alembic; 10400 Highway 101, (707)468-8936. Mendocino County's oldest winery, founded in 1932, is **Parducci Wine Estates**, an enterprise that produces a variety of reds and whites; 501 Parducci Road, (707)462-WINE. And if you continue up the road a bit to the Redwood Valley you'll find **Frey Vine-yards**, one of the few wineries in the state that doesn't add sul-fites to its wines and uses certified organically grown grapes. Sample the Frey family's petite sirah, cabernet, and sauvignon blanc; 14000 Tomki Road, off Highway 101, Redwood Valley, (707)485-5177 or (800)760-3739.

Soak away the aches and pains of your long drive (Ukiah is a long drive from almost anywhere) at the clothing-optional **Orr Hot Springs**, 13201 Orr Springs Road, (707)462-6277, or in North America's only warm and naturally carbonated mineral baths at **Vichy Springs Resort** (see review, below). Hikers will want to stretch their legs at **Montgomery Woods State Reserve**, 1,142 acres of coastal redwoods with a self-guided nature trail along Montgomery Creek; it's located on Orr Springs Road, off Highway 101, 15 miles northwest of Ukiah. In town, the main attraction is the **Grace Hudson Museum and Sun House**, fea-turing Hudson's paintings of Pomo Indians and a collection of beautiful Pomo baskets; 431 South Main Street, (707)467-2836.

### RESTAURANTS

**Ellie's Mutt Hut & Vegetarian Cafe** ★ Okay, so nobody travels to Ukiah for the fine dining. There are, however, a few notable places for a good, quick, cheap bite to eat, and this is one of them. Try thinking of the Mutt Hut as the Wienerschnitzel of an alternate universe. It has 11 imaginative variations on the tradi-tional dog (including kraut dogs, Reuben dogs, and—naturally—tofu dogs), plus a cellar full of baked spuds stuffed with every-thing from carrots, broccoli, and cauliflower to tofu cooked in tamari sauce with mushrooms. Owner Ellie Threade also caters to Ukiah's former hippies and small-town yups with her big garden-fresh salads, huge omelets, tofu-and-brown-rice dinners, great fruit smoothies, and potent cappuccinos. Because it's healthy, the Mutt Hut attracts the health-conscious, and because it's cheap (nothing on the menu is more than $6), the Mutt Hut attracts everyone else. You can also get breakfast here as early as 6:30am. ▪ *732 S State St (from Hwy 101, take the Talmadge St exit, then head N on S State St), Ukiah; (707)468-5376; $; beer and wine; no credit cards; local checks only; breakfast, lunch Mon–Sat, dinner Mon–Fri.*

### Schat's Courthouse Bakery and Cafe ★

Schat's Courthouse Bakery has been open in Ukiah since 1990, but its history dates back to Holland in the early 1800s—which is as far back as the fifth-generation baker brothers Zach and Brian Schat can trace the roots of a very long line of Schat bakers. In 1948, the Schat clan emigrated to California, bringing with them the hallowed family recipe for their signature Sheepherder's Bread, a semi-sour, dairy- and sugar-free round loaf that's so popular it's been featured in *Sunset* magazine's "Best of the West" column. What really separates Schat's Courthouse Bakery from the rest are the huge, more-than-you-can-possibly-eat lunch items: made-to-order sandwiches, build-your-own baked potatoes, house-made soups, a tangy caesar salad, and huge slices of vegetarian quiche (served with bread and a salad), all for around five bucks. Located just off Highway 101, this is a great spot to load up on munchies while exploring the Wine Country. Schat's stays open for lunch until 6pm during the week, and 4:30pm on Saturday. ▪ *113 W Perkins St (from Hwy 101 take the Perkins St exit W; ½ block W of State St, across from the courthouse), Ukiah; (707)462-1670; $; no credit cards; local checks only; light breakfast, lunch Mon–Sat.*

### LODGINGS

### Sanford House Bed and Breakfast ★★

There's something indisputably small-town about this tall, yellow Victorian inn on a tree-lined street just west of Ukiah's Mayberry-like downtown. Peaceful, unhurried, and bucolic, Sanford House boasts only one gothic turret, but it does have a big front porch dotted with white wicker chairs and an old-fashioned baby buggy, plus an English garden complete with a koi pond. Inside, antiques grace every room and everything is freshly painted, but it's far too comfortable and unpretentious to be called a showplace. The five guest rooms are named after turn-of-the-century presidents; the Taft Room, with its dark four-poster bed, floral fabrics, and a Princess Di doll in a wedding dress, is the most elegant, but equally pleasant is the spacious cream-and-green Wilson Room with its floral wallpaper, beautiful armoire, and sunny turret sitting area. Innkeeper Dorsey Manogue serves a breakfast feast every morning in the dining room using fresh, mostly organic ingredients, and in the evening she offers homemade biscotti (dipped in white and dark chocolate) and wine in the parlor. ■ *306 Pine St S (from Hwy 101, take the Perkins St exit, head W, and turn left on Pine), Ukiah, CA 95482; (707)462-1653; $$; MC, V; checks OK.*

**Vichy Springs Resort** ★   Although the rejuvenating effect of the naturally carbonated mineral pools at Vichy Springs had been known by the Pomo Indians for hundreds of years, it wasn't until the mid-1800s that others caught on to the idea. Since then, this California Historic Landmark has attracted the likes of Ulysses S. Grant, Teddy Roosevelt, Mark Twain, and Jack London, who all soaked their famous bones in North America's only naturally carbonated mineral baths—baths that have a mineral content identical to the famed pools in Vichy, France. With such a remarkable distinction and luminous history, one would expect the resort to be ringed by four-star accommodations and fancy bathhouses. Ironically, the estate was practically a disaster area for years, littered with rusting cars and machinery, until proprietors Gilbert and Marjorie Ashoff completely refurbished the 700-acre property and reopened it in 1989.

Even with its facelift, the resort is far from posh, though five new creekside rooms, all with private baths, and the new two-bedroom Jack London Cottage bring the accommodations up a notch. Twelve more small, simply decorated guest rooms, all with private baths and most with queen-size beds, line a long ranch-house-style building. If you're visiting with children, consider staying at one of the three private cottages, each fully equipped with a kitchen, a wood-burning stove, and a shaded porch. Built more than 130 years ago, the eight indoor and outdoor baths remain basically unchanged since the first molds were set in pairs, enabling you to chat with a friend while soaking (bathing suits required). Also on the grounds are a nonchlorinated Olympic-size pool filled with the therapeutic bubbly, a modern whirlpool bath, a playground, a barbecue, a small cabin where Swedish massages are administered, and 6 miles of ranch roads available to hikers and mountain bikers. Room rates include an expanded continental breakfast and unlimited use of the pools, which are rarely crowded. The baths are available for day use, too, and the resort has basic services for business travelers. ■ *2605 Vichy Springs Rd (from Hwy 101, take the Vichy Springs Rd exit and head W), Ukiah, CA 95482; (707)462-9515; $$$; AE, DC, DIS, MC, V; checks OK.*

# NORTH COAST

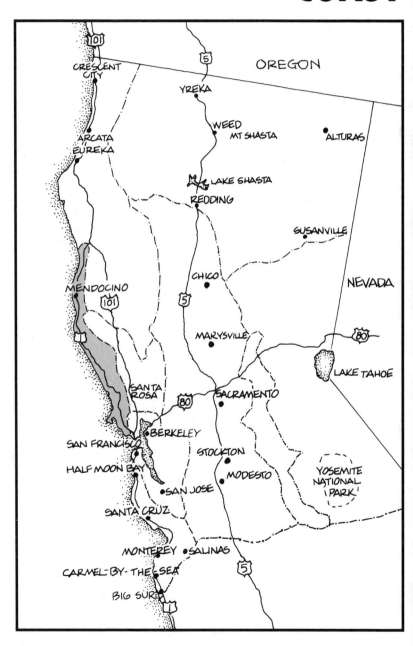

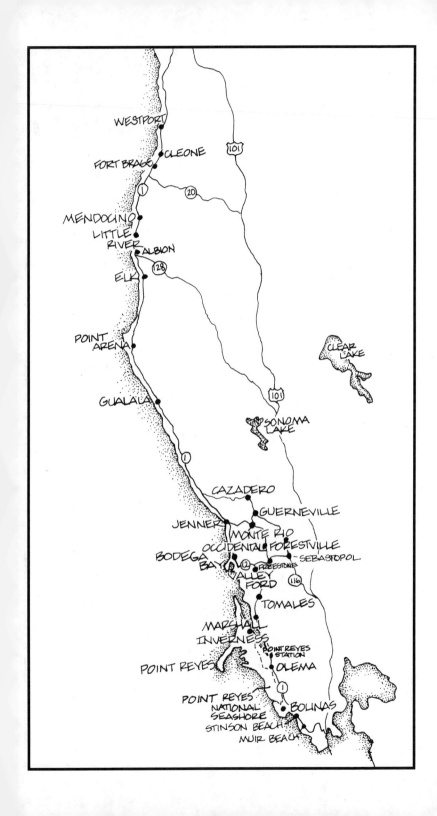

# North Coast

*A south-to-north sweep of the Northern California coastline, beginning north of San Francisco at the Marin coast and ending at Westport, just north of Mendocino and Fort Bragg.*

## MARIN COAST

When you consider that the San Francisco Bay Area has more people than the entire state of Oregon, and that Marin County has the highest per capita income in the nation, you would expect its coastline to be lined with gated communities and fancy resorts. Truth is, you won't find even a Motel 6 along the entire Marin coast, due partly to public pressure but mostly to the inaccessibly rugged, heavily forested terrain (it may *look* like a 15-minute drive from San Francisco on the map, but 90 minutes later you'll probably still be negotiating hairpin curves down the side of Mount Tamalpais). The only downside to the Marin coast's underdevelopment is the scarcity of affordable lodgings; expensive B&Bs reign supreme, which is fine if you don't mind blowing $150 a night or more for a bed and a bagel. Otherwise, the Marin coast is just short of Eden, a veritable organic playground for city-weary 9-to-5ers in search of a patch of green or a square of sand to call their own for a day.

## MARIN HEADLANDS

On a sunny San Francisco day, there's no better place to spend time outdoors than in the Marin Headlands. For more than a century following the Civil War, this vast expanse of grass-covered hills and rocky shore was off-limits to the public, appropriated by the U.S. Army as a strategic base for defending the bay against invaders. Remnants of obsolete and untested defenses—dozens of thick concrete bunkers and batteries recessed into the bluffs—now serve as playground and picnic sites for the millions of tourists who visit each year.

There's a wealth of scheduled activities offered daily within the 15-square-mile **Golden Gate National Recreation Area**—birding clinics, bunker tours, wildflower hunts, geology hikes—but most visitors are satisfied with poking their heads into a bunker or two, snapping a photo of the San Francisco skyline, and driving home. For a more thorough approach, buy the handy $1.50 "Marin Headlands Map and Guide to Sites, Trails and Wildlife," at the Information Center at Fort Barry (follow the signs in the headlands), and plan your day from there. Free hiking, mountain biking, and pet-friendly trail maps are available, too. The center is open daily from 9:30am to 4:30pm; (415)331-1540.

A popular Marin Headlands attraction is **The Marine Mammal Center**, a volunteer-run hospital for injured and abandoned mammals-of-the-sea. It's virtually impossible not to melt at the sight of the cute sea lions and elephant and harbor seals as they lie in their pens (the center's staff, being no dummies, take donations right on the spot). Signs list each animal's adopted name, species, stranding site, and injury—the latter of which is usually human-caused. Located at the east end of Fort Cronkhite near Rodeo Lagoon, the Marine Mammal Center is open daily from 10am to 4pm and admission is free; (415)289-SEAL.

Closed to the public for several years due to storm damage, the precariously perched 1877 **Point Bonita Lighthouse** is once again thrilling those tourists who are brave enough to traverse the long, dark tunnel and seven small footbridges leading to the beacon. (Because the cliffs along the passageway are so steep, one 19th-century lighthouse keeper rigged ropes around his children to prevent them from slipping into the raging sea below.) The reward for such bravery is, among other things, a rare and sensational view of the entrance to the bay. Call for tour times, and be sure to inquire about the full-moon tours, which take place twice a month by reservation only; (415)331-1540.

Also within the Marin Headlands is **Hawk Hill**, one of the most remarkable avian sites in the western United States and the biggest hawk lookout in western North America. Record count in 1992 was more than 20,000 birds, including 21 species of hawks. The best time to visit is during September and October, when thousands of birds of prey soar over the hill each day. The hill is located above Battery 129, where Conzelman Road becomes a one-way street.

For a current schedule of the free ranger-led walks through the Marin Headlands—with topics ranging from birdwatching to wildflowers and war relics—call (415)331-1540.

## MUIR WOODS ▪ MUIR BEACH

When you stand in the middle of **Muir Woods**, surrounded by a canopy of ancient redwoods towering hundreds of feet skyward, it's hard to fathom that San Francisco is less than 6 miles away. It's a den of wooden giants: tourists speak in hushed tones as they crane their necks in disbelief, snapping photographs that don't begin to capture the immensity of these living titans.

Although Muir Woods can get absurdly crowded on summer weekends, you can usually circumvent the masses by hiking up the Ocean View Trail and returning via the Fern Creek trail. Admission is free, but a donation box is prominently displayed to stoke your conscience. Picnicking is not allowed, although there is a snack bar (and gift shop) at the entrance. It's typically cool and damp here, so dress appropriately. Muir Woods is located at the end of Muir Woods Road off the Panoramic Highway (from Highway 101 in Sausalito, take the Stinson Beach/Highway 1 exit and head west); open 8am to sunset, (415)388-2595.

Three miles west of Muir Woods, along Highway 1, is a small crescent-shaped cove called **Muir Beach**. Strewn with bits of driftwood and numerous tide pools, Muir Beach is a more sedate alternative to the beer-'n'-bikini crowds at the ever-popular Stinson Beach up north. If all you're looking for is a sandy, quiet place for some R&R, park your car right here and skip the trip to Stinson altogether (swimming, however, isn't allowed at Muir Beach because of the strong rip currents).

## RESTAURANTS

**The Pelican Inn ★★** One of the better ways to spend a Sunday afternoon in the Bay Area is to take a leisurely drive to this homey little English pub, grab a table at the glassed-in patio or by the fireplace, and gorge yourself proper on a steaming shepherd's pie. Rack of lamb, prime rib, and a few fish dishes are also on the menu, and in the bar you'll find a goodly number of British, Irish, and Scottish beers on tap. After lunch, burn a few calories with a stroll down Muir Beach. ■ *10 Pacific Way (off Hwy 1 at the entrance to the beach), Muir Beach; (415)383-6000; $$; beer and wine; MC, V; no checks; lunch, dinner every day May 1 to Oct 31 and holidays year-round (lunch, dinner Tues–Sun Nov 1 to Apr 30).*

▼

**Muir Woods
Muir Beach**

*Lodgings*

▲

## LODGINGS

**The Pelican Inn ★★** Romantic intentions of a homesick expatriate led to the creation of this 16th-century English Tudor country inn, and by God if it isn't filled with convivial dart-playing chaps chugging pints of bitter as lovebirds snuggle in front of the hearth's glowing fire in the inn's pub (see review, above). The inn, named after Sir Francis Drake's ship *The Pelican*, has seven small yet cozy rooms with canopy beds, leaded-glass windows, heavy brocade curtains, and English antiques (the top pick is room 3 with its authentic Half-Tester bed). There's also a "snug" (i.e., common room) for lounging by the fire or playing the piano. In the morning guests are treated to an authentic English breakfast of bangers and eggs, toast and marmalade, and—but of course—a cuppa. ■ *10 Pacific Way (off Hwy 1 at the entrance to the beach), Muir Beach, CA 94965; (415)383-6000; $$; beer and wine; MC, V; no checks; breakfast (guests only) every day year-round, lunch, dinner every day May 1 to Oct 31 and holidays year-round (lunch, dinner Tues–Sun Nov 1 to Apr 30).*

On those treasured weekend days when the fog has lifted and the sun is scorching the Northern California coast, blurry-eyed Bay Area residents grab their morning paper and beach chairs, pile into their Mazda Miatas and Jeeps, and scramble to the sandy shores of Stinson Beach—the North Coast's nice-try answer to the fabled beaches of Southern California.

Stinson Beach is one of Northern California's most popular beaches, a 3½-mile stretch of beige sand that offers enough elbow room for everyone to spread out beach blankets, picnic baskets, and toys. Swimming is allowed and lifeguards are on hand from May to mid-September, though notices about rip-tides (plus the sea's toe-numbing temperatures and the threat of sharks) tend to discourage folks from venturing too far into the water. For recorded weather and surf conditions at Stinson Beach call (415)868-1922. Joined at the hip with *la playa* is the town of Stinson Beach, which does a brisk summer business serving lunch alfresco at its numerous cafes.

There are plenty of adventurous things to do around Stinson. For example, Scott Tye, a kayak instructor for Off the Beach Boats in downtown Stinson Beach, offers 2-hour lessons on the basics of **sea and surf kayaking**. Rentals are surprisingly cheap (about $25 for 4 hours for surf kayaks), and they even rent a kayak that can hold an entire nuclear family. Call (415)868-9445 or drop by the shop at 15 Calle del Mar next to the Stinson Beach Post Office.

▼

**Stinson Beach**

▲

A short drive north of Stinson Beach on Highway 1 leads to **Bolinas Lagoon**, a placid saltwater expanse that serves as refuge for numerous shorebirds and harbor seals sprawled out on the sandbars. Across from the lagoon is the **Audubon Canyon Ranch's Bolinas Lagoon Preserve**, a 1,014-acre wildlife sanctuary that supports a major heronry of great blue herons. This is the premier spot along the Pacific Coast to watch immense, graceful seabirds as they court, mate, and rear their young, all accomplished on the tops of towering redwoods. Admission is free, though donations are requested; open mid-March to mid-July on Saturday, Sunday, and holidays, 10am to 4pm, and by appointment for groups. Located at 4900 Highway 1, just north of Stinson Beach; (415)868-9244.

And if you head back the other way, about a mile south of Stinson Beach off Highway 1 is **Red Rock Beach**, one of the few nude beaches on the Marin coast. It's easy to miss since you can't see it from the road; park at the first dirt pull-off on your right after leaving Stinson Beach and look for a steep trail leading down to the water.

**The Parkside Café** ★ During the day this popular neighborhood cafe bustles with locals and Bay Area beach-goers who stop for an inexpensive breakfast or lunch before shoving off to Stinson Beach around the corner. Morning favorites are the omelets, blueberry pancakes, and the not-to-be-missed raisin-walnut bread. For lunch there are basics like burgers, grilled sandwiches, and soups, as well as a few daily specials. Once the beach crowd departs, chef Jim White starts preparing the evening menu, which includes a wide variety of dishes ranging from lamb chops and roast chicken to mussel linguine, seafood pizza, and baked eggplant. On sunny days dine alfresco on the brick patio; otherwise, cozy up to the fire. For a quick bite to go, the cafe's snack bar sells great burgers, fries, and shakes daily from March through September, and on weekends from October through February. ■ *43 Arenal Ave (off Calle del Mar downtown), Stinson Beach; (415)868-1272; $; beer and wine; AE, MC, V; local checks only; breakfast, lunch every day, dinner Thurs–Mon.*

## LODGINGS

**Casa del Mar** ★★★ After stints as a lawyer and a fisherman, proprietor Rick Klein jumped headfirst into the B&B business by designing, building, and running the Casa del Mar, a beautiful Mediterranean-style haven that overlooks Stinson Beach. Each of the six sun-drenched rooms has large windows (with views of Mount Tamalpais, the ocean, or the spectacular terraced garden), French doors that open onto a private balcony, and a private bath. The spartan but comfortable furnishings include a few cushy chairs and a platform bed topped with a down comforter and piles of pillows. Fresh flowers and whimsical artwork by local artists brighten the rooms while the sound of the ocean provides the ambience. Breakfast features an ever-changing array of wonders such as fresh fruit compote, spinach and mushroom quiche, Spanish frittata, and fresh baked breads. ■ *37 Belvedere Ave (heading N into Stinson Beach, turn right at the fire station), Stinson Beach; (415)868-2124 or (800)552-2124; mail: PO Box 238, Stinson Beach, CA 94970; Inn@StinsonBeach.com; www.StinsonBeach.com; $$$; AE, MC, V; checks OK if mailed 2 weeks in advance.*

**Stinson Beach**

*Lodgings*

**Stinson Beach Motel** ★ If you can't afford the Casa del Mar, try this place. The Stinson Beach Motel has five small rooms and one apartment nestled in a cute little garden setting, each individually decorated with aging yet homey furnishings and private baths. Rates are quite reasonable, and the small apartment, which sleeps up to four, is a steal, given the prime location in downtown Stinson Beach. Try to reserve room 7, which is separated from the rest and offers the most privacy. ■ *3416 Hwy 1 (at the S end of town near the fire station), Stinson Beach; (415)868-1712; mail: PO Box 64, Stinson Beach, CA 94970; $$; MC, V; checks OK if received 10 days in advance.*

## BOLINAS

A sort of retirement community for aging rock stars, spent novelists, and former hippies, Bolinas is one of the most reclusive towns in Northern California. Residents regularly take down highway signs pointing the way to their rural enclave, an act that ironically has created more publicity for Bolinas than any road sign ever did. As a tourist, you don't have to worry about being chased out of town by a band of machete-wielding Bolinistas, but don't expect anyone to roll out the welcome mat either. The trick is to not *look* like a tourist, but more like a Bay Area resident who's only here to buy some peaches at the **People's Store**.

What's the People's Store, you ask? It's a town landmark that's famous for its locally grown organic produce and exceptional service—the antithesis of the corporate supermarket. It's a little hard to find, hidden at the end of a gravel driveway next to the Bolinas Bakery (don't confuse it with the much larger general store down the street), but it's worth searching out just to see (and taste) the difference between Safeway and the Bolinas way; open 8:30am to 6:30pm daily, (415)868-1433.

Three side trips near Bolinas offer some adventurous exercise. Just before entering downtown Bolinas, turn right (west) on Mesa Road, left on Overlook Road, and right on Elm Road and you'll dead-end at the **Duxbury Reef Nature Reserve**, a rocky outcropping with numerous tide pools harboring a healthy population of starfish, sea anemones, snails, sea urchins, and other creatures that kids go gaga over. If you continue west on Mesa Road you'll reach the **Point Reyes Bird Observatory**, where ornithologists keep an eye on more than 400 feathered species—it's one of the few full-time ornithological research stations in the United States. Admission to the visitors center and nature trail is free, and visitors are welcome to observe the tricky process of catching and banding the birds Tuesday through Sunday mornings, weather permitting, from May through October. It's open daily 15 minutes after sunrise until sunset. Banding hours vary, so call (415)868-0655 for exact times and (415)868-1221, extension 40, for recorded general information. At the very end of Mesa Road is the **Palomarin Trailhead**, a popular hiking trail that leads into the south entrance of **Point Reyes National Seashore**. The 6-mile round-trip trek—one of Point Reyes's prettiest hikes—passes several small lakes and meadows before it reaches

**Alamere Falls**, a freshwater stream that cascades down a 40-foot bluff onto Wildcat Beach.

*LODGINGS*

**Thomas's White House Inn** ★★  This inn is Bolinas personified—charming, offbeat (e.g., the bathroom doubles as an aviary), and surrounded by incredible vistas. Lounging on the immense and beautifully landscaped front lawn—it alone is worth the room rate—you get a sweeping view of the Bay Area coastline from Marin to Half Moon Bay. The two guest rooms are located upstairs and boast cathedral ceilings and window seats ideal for gazing out at the sea. The larger room has a more rustic feel, with old pine furnishings and an antique steamer trunk, while the smaller room is decorated in softer tones with lace and white wicker. Owner Jackie Thomas serves a simple continental breakfast. ■ *118 Kale Rd (call for directions), Bolinas; (415)868-0279; mail: PO Box 132, Bolinas, CA 94924; www.coastallodging.com/thomas/thomas.html/; $$; no credit cards; checks OK.*

## POINT REYES

Think of Point Reyes as Mother Nature's version of Disneyland, an outdoor-lover's playground with one doozy of a sandbox. Hiking, biking, swimming, sailing, windsurfing, sunbathing, camping, fishing, horseback riding, bird-watching, kayaking—all are fair game at this 71,000-acre sanctuary of forested hills, deep green pastures, and undisturbed beaches. Point Reyes is hardly a secret anymore—millions of visitors arrive each year—but the land is so vast and varied that finding your own space is never a problem. (Like the old saying goes: if you want to be alone, walk up.)

▼

**Point Reyes**

▲

There are four towns in and around the **Point Reyes National Seashore** boundary—**Olema**, **Point Reyes Station**, **Inverness Park**, and **Inverness**—but they are all so close together that it really doesn't matter where you stay, because you'll always be within a stone's throw of the park. While the selection of lodging in Point Reyes is excellent, it's also expensive (most rooms cost well over $100 per night). Be sure to make your reservation far in advance for the summer and holidays, and dress warm: Point Reyes gets darn chilly at night regardless of the season. If you're having trouble finding a vacancy here, call the West Marin Network at (415)663-9543 for information on available lodgings.

As soon as you arrive at Point Reyes, stop at the **Bear Valley Visitors Center** on Bear Valley Road (look for the small sign posted just north of Olema on Highway 1) and pick up a free Point Reyes trail map; open weekdays 9am to 5pm and weekends 8am to 5pm, (415)663-1092. On the westernmost tip of Point Reyes at the end of Sir Francis Drake Highway is the **Point Reyes Lighthouse**, the park's most popular attraction. If you loathe lighthouse tours, go anyway. The drive alone is worth the trip, a 45-minute scenic excursion through wind-swept meadows and working dairy ranches (watch out for cows on the road). When the fog burns off, the lighthouse and the headlands provide a fantastic lookout point for spying gray whales and thousands of common mures that inundate the rocks below. Visitors have free access to the lighthouse via a thigh-burning 308-step staircase; open 10am to 4:30pm, Thursday through Monday, weather permitting, (415) 669-1534.

That mighty pungent aroma you smell on the way to the Point Reyes Lighthouse is probably emanating from **Johnson's Oyster Farm**. It may not look like much—a cluster of trailer homes, shacks, and oyster tanks surrounded by huge piles of oyster shells—but that certainly doesn't detract from the taste of fresh-out-of-the-water oysters dipped in Johnson's special sauce. Eat 'em on the spot, or buy a bag for the road—either way, you're not likely to find California oysters as fresh or as cheap anywhere else. The oyster farm resides within **Drakes Estero**, a large saltwater lagoon on the Point Reyes peninsula that produces nearly 20 percent of California's commercial oyster yield. It's located off Sir Francis Drake Boulevard, about 6 miles west of Inverness, and is open 8am to 4pm Tuesday through Sunday; (415) 669-1149.

A popular Point Reyes pastime is **ocean kayaking**. Don't worry, the kayaks are very stable and there are no waves to contend with because you'll be paddling through placid **Tomales Bay**, a haven for migrating birds and marine mammals. Rental prices at Tomales Bay Sea Kayaking start at about $35 for a half-day ($65 for a double-hulled kayak), and you can sign up for a guided day trip, a sunset cruise, or a romantic full-moon outing. Instruction, clinics, and boat delivery are available, and all ages and levels are welcome. The launching point is located on Highway 1 at the Marshall Boatworks in Marshall, 8 miles north of Point Reyes Station. It's open in the summer Friday through Sunday from 9am to 6pm and by appointment; (415) 663-1743.

As most ardent Bay Area mountain bikers know, Point Reyes National Seashore also has some of the finest **mountain-bike trails** in the region. Narrow dirt paths wind through densely forested knolls and end with spectacular ocean views. A trail map is a must (available for free at the Bear Valley Visitors Center) since many of the park trails are off-limits to bikes, and fines are quite steep if you pedal up a bike-free path. If you didn't bring your own bicycle, you can rent a mountain bike at the Bear Valley Inn and Rental Shop, located at the intersection of Bear Valley Road and Highway 1 in Olema; (415) 663-1958.

# OLEMA

## LODGINGS

**Point Reyes Seashore Lodge** ★★  For folks who want the beauty of the countryside combined with the creature comforts of the city, this is the place. Built in 1988, the three-story cedar inn has 21 guest rooms, most of which offer a fireplace, telephone, down comforter, whirlpool bath, and view of the exquisite garden. If price is no object, opt for one of the two-story suites with a sleeping loft, refrigerator, and the perk of having breakfast delivered to your room. One note of caution: the lodge is located on Highway 1, next to a restaurant that does a brisk (read noisy) business. For peace and quiet, ask for a room in the north wing, or reserve the Casa Olema Retreat, a detached cottage that sleeps up to eight and has a hot tub with room for eight as well. A continental breakfast, included in the nightly rate, is served in the lodge's common room. ■ *10021 Hwy 1 (at Sir Francis Drake Blvd), Olema; (415)663-9000 or (800)404-LODG; mail: PO Box 39, Olema, CA 94950; prsl@worldnet.att.net; www.placestostay.com; $$$; AE, DIS, MC, V; checks OK.* ㅤ

**Bear Valley Inn** ★  Ron and JoAnne Nowell's pleasant and reasonably priced bed-and-breakfast inn is an ideal base for exploring Point Reyes. The two-story Victorian home, built in 1899, has three guest rooms and a shared bath (though a detached private bath is available with the Rose Room or King Room during the week). If you want the quietest space, ask for the Rose Room. After breakfast, Ron will be happy to give tips on where to bicycle in the area (he also runs the mountain bike rental shop next door). When you return from your day of exploring, plop yourself onto one of the overstuffed chairs and relax in front of the old wood-burning stove. ■ *88 Bear Valley Rd (at the intersection of Hwy 1 and Bear Valley Rd), Olema, CA 94950; (415)663-1777; $$; AE, MC, V; checks OK.*

# POINT REYES STATION

## RESTAURANTS

**The Station House Café** ★★  For more than two decades the Station House has been a favorite stop for West Marin residents and San Francisco day trippers. The menu changes weekly, but you can count on chef Denis Bold to work daily wonders with local produce, seafood, and organic beef from Niman-Schell Farms. Breakfast items range from French toast made with Il Fornaio bakery's sweet challah to buckwheat pancakes and roasted vegetable frittatas. For dinner, start with a platter of local oysters and mussels, followed by a braised lamb shank (made with Guinness Stout), salmon with roasted yellow pepper sauce, or one of their old standbys such as fish and chips with country fries and cole slaw. There's a good selection of wines, too. If the weather is warm, sit outside in the shaded garden area—particularly if you're eating breakfast here on a sunny day. In the summer barbecued oysters are often served on the patio. ■ *11180 Shoreline Hwy (on Main St, in the center of town), Point Reyes Station; (415) 663-1515; $$; full bar; DIS, MC, V; local checks only; breakfast, lunch, dinner every day.* &

**Point Reyes Roadhouse & Oyster Bar** ★ A popular roadside attraction, the Roadhouse & Oyster Bar is a good spot for a lunch break. First choose from a wide selection of microbrews on tap or local wines by the glass, then order one of the daily specials such as fresh seafood, pasta and pizza. Regular menu items like burgers, salads, sandwiches, and barbecued oysters are also safe bets. Top things off with a chocolate milk shake and you'll be ready to roll. ■ *10905 Hwy 1 (at the S end of town), Point Reyes Station; (415) 663-1277; $; beer and wine; AE, MC, V; no checks; lunch Sat–Sun, dinner every day (Dec and Jan hours may vary).* &

**Taqueria La Quinta** ★ Mexican folk music fills the air and bright colors abound at this exuberant restaurant, where most of the fare costs less than *seis dólares*. La Quinta (Spanish for "the country house") offers a large selection of Mexican-American standards, as well as vegetarian dishes and weekend seafood specials. The service is fast, the food is fresh, the salsa is *muy caliente.* ■ *11285 Hwy 1 (at 3rd and Main Sts), Point Reyes Station; (415) 663-8868; $; beer only; no credit cards; local checks only; lunch, dinner Wed–Mon.*

### LODGINGS

**Knob Hill** ★ Horse trainer Janet Schlitt rents out a cottage that stands atop a small bluff overlooking Point Reyes Mesa. Perfect for couples and horse owners, it comes with a stereo, wood-burning stove, private deck, an optional TV, and, if you brought along your horse, stable service. Schlitt also rents a very small (and very reasonably priced) room that's attached to her house and has a private bath, entrance, and garden area. Be sure to indulge in the optional breakfast of fresh baked goods and fruit, then hit the nearby trailhead to Tomales Bay or sign up for some horseback riding lessons. ■ *40 Knob Hill Rd (from Highway 1 N of Point Reyes Station, turn W on Viento Way), Point Reyes Station; (415) 663-1784; mail: PO Box 1108, Point Reyes Station, CA 94956; $$; no credit cards; checks OK.*

*LODGINGS*

**Blackthorne Inn** ★★★ With its four levels, five rooms, multiple decks, spiral staircase, skybridge, and fire pole, the Blackthorne Inn is more like a tree house for grown-ups than a B&B. The octagonal Eagle's Nest, perched on the top level, has its own sun deck and a 360-degree view of the forest (the bath, however, is located across the skybridge—something of a nuisance on blustery nights); the spacious Forest View and Hideaway Rooms, which share a bath, have sitting areas facing the woods; the outdoor treetop-level hot tub offers a great view of the stars. A country buffet breakfast is included in the room rate and is served on the upper deck when the sun is shining. ■ *266 Vallejo Ave (off Sir Francis Drake Blvd, ¼ mile up Vallejo Ave), Inverness Park; (415)663-8621; mail: PO Box 712, Inverness, CA 94937; susan@blackthorneinn.com; www. blackthorneinn.com; $$$; MC, V; checks OK.*

**Holly Tree Inn** ★★★ Hidden within a 19-acre valley with a meandering creek and wooded hillsides is the blissfully quiet Holly Tree Inn. This family-owned B&B has four cozy guest rooms, each with a private bath (one with a fireplace) and decorated with Laura Ashley prints and country antiques. The large, airy living room has a fireplace and comfortable chairs where guests converse over afternoon tea. If privacy is what you're after, tucked in a far corner of the estate is the Cottage-in-the-Woods, a two-room hideaway with a small fireplace, a king-size bed, and an old-fashioned bathtub from which you can gaze at the garden. Families or honeymooners should inquire about the separate Sea Star Cottage—built on stilts over Tomales Bay—and the two-bedroom Vision Cottage; both have hot tubs. In the morning enjoy a bountiful country breakfast. ■ *3 Silverhills Rd (off Bear Valley Rd, 1 mile from Point Reyes Station), Inverness Park; (415)663-1554; mail: PO Box 642, Point Reyes Station, CA 94956; $$$; AE, MC, V; checks OK.*

**Inverness**

*Restaurants*

## INVERNESS

*RESTAURANTS*

**Manka's Inverness Lodge** ★★★ Half the fun of dining at Manka's is waiting for your table. Sit in the lobby's plush high-backed chairs, warm your toes by the small wood-burning fireplace, and watch in fascination as one of the cooks kneels beside you to grill the house-made wild boar sausages over the fire: it's like being in a freaking Jack London novel. To complement the hunting lodge illusion, Manka's serves "unusual game, local line-caught fish, oysters pulled from the bay, and bounteous greens from down the road and over the hill." Appetizers range from grilled California quail with wild-mushroom sauce to fire-roasted figs with black-pepper syrup. And the entrees? How about pan-seared elk tenderloin, black buck antelope chops with sweet corn salsa, and wild Canadian pheasant with mashed potatoes? The divine desserts—such as the cinnamon-croissant pudding with warm caramel sauce—are made from scratch, and the wine list is longer than the drive to get here. ■ *On Argyle St (off Sir Francis Drake Blvd, 3 blocks N of downtown), Inverness; (415) 669-1034 or (800) 58-LODGE; $$$; beer and wine; MC, V; checks OK; brunch on special occasions only, dinner Thurs–Mon.*

**Vladimir's Czech Restaurant** ★ The first thing you're likely to notice when you walk into this dark, wood-paneled dining room is an old guy neatly dressed in traditional Czech attire. This is Vladimir Nevl, who since 1960 has been entertaining guests with his war stories as they boldly sample the chicken paprikash, Moravian cabbage roll, beef tongue, klobasa, and Hungarian goulash—all of which are served with dumplings. On weekends the place tends to feel like a tourist trap and the service can be lackadaisical, but hey, when you gotta have beef tongue, you gotta have it. ■ *12785 Sir Francis Drake Blvd (downtown), Inverness; (415) 669-1021; $$; full bar; no credit cards; checks OK; lunch Wed–Sun, dinner Tues–Sun.* ⅃

## LODGINGS

**Manka's Inverness Lodge** ★★★★ What a difference a Grade makes. For years Manka's was a mediocre Czech restaurant, but when Margaret Grade and family took over in 1989, things changed. This former hunting and fishing lodge soon became one of the most romantic places to stay in California, as well as a wonderful place to eat (see review, above). Manka's offers a dozen accommodations, including four upstairs guest rooms that look as though they came out of a Hans Christian Andersen fairy tale—small and cozy, with tree-limb bedsteads, down comforters, high ceilings, and old-fashioned bathrooms; rooms 1 and 2 extend out to large private decks overlooking Tomales Bay and have fireplaces and double tubs with showers open to the sky. Manka's also offers four handsome rooms in its Redwood Annex, and two spacious one-bedroom cabins with living rooms, fireplaces, and hot tubs. For the ultimate romantic—or family—retreat, reserve either the fantastic two-level/two-bedroom/two-bath boathouse built out over the bay (equipped with a fireplace, deck, and kitchenette) or the Chicken Ranch, a private 19th-century hunting cabin protected by the wary eye of Duke, Manka's "guard" pony.

Friendly, refreshingly unpretentious, and surprisingly affordable, Manka's Inverness Lodge is *the* idyllic weekend getaway.
■ *On Argyle St (off Sir Francis Drake Blvd, 3 blocks N of downtown), Inverness; (415)669-1034 or (800)58- LODGE; mail:
PO Box 1110, Inverness, CA 94937; $$$; beer and wine; MC, V;
checks OK.*

**Dancing Coyote Beach ★★★**  The local Miwok Indians called
falling stars "dancing coyotes"—something to ponder as you
stare at the heavens through the skylit sleeping lofts of this
bayside bed and breakfast. Hidden in a pine-covered cove and
within easy walking distance of downtown Inverness, the four
adjoining natural-wood cottages are painted in Southwestern
pastels and equipped with simple furniture, private decks, fire-
places, and full kitchens. The Beach Cottage, with its small
upper deck overlooking Tomales Bay, should be your first
choice; Acacia Cottage, which gets a fair amount of traffic
noise, should be your last, although you're allowed to bring
your pooch in this one. The private lawn, beach, and sun
deck are perfect spots for settling down with a good book.
■ *12794 Sir Francis Drake Blvd (just N of downtown), Inver-
ness; (415)669-7200; mail: PO Box 98, Inverness, CA 94937;
$$; no credit cards; checks OK.*

**Ten Inverness Way ★★★**  Follow the curving flagstone path-
way through the garden and under the wisteria-laced entryway to this three-story Inverness bed and breakfast. Inside
you'll find a fir-paneled living room with inviting couches facing
a huge stone fireplace, and five comfortable guest rooms
equipped with plush chairs, patchwork quilts, and private
baths. The best room is the Garden Suite: separated from the
others by an entire floor, it has its own sitting room, kitchen,
and private patio. The terrific breakfast—banana-buttermilk-
buckwheat pancakes, chicken-apple sausages, and fresh fruit—
is prepared by innkeepers Barbara Searles and Mary Davies
and will fortify you for a long day of hiking in the hills. When
you return, soak your sore muscles in the garden hot tub.
■ *10 Inverness Way (off Sir Francis Drake Blvd), Inverness;
(415)669-1648; mail: PO Box 63, Inverness, CA 94937; $$$;
MC, V; checks OK.*

## MARSHALL

### RESTAURANTS

**Tony's Seafood Restaurant**  Don't bother ordering anything
but the barbecued oysters at Tony's—they're so tasty they're
worth the drive to this ramshackle building on the east shore
of Tomales Bay. For more than half a century oysters have
been shucked and barbecued on the patio out back. And for

just as many years folks have been lining up at Tony's to watch the shuckers in action as they wait for their order to come up. ■ *18863 Hwy 1 (1 mile S of town), Marshall; (415)663-1107; $; beer and wine; no credit cards; no checks; lunch, dinner Fri–Sun.*

## TOMALES

Most people don't even know the town of Tomales exists, which is just fine with the handful of people who live here. Comprising not much more than a general store, two churches, and a superb little bakery, the tiny ranching community looks pretty much the same as it did a hundred years ago, which gives you an idea of the pace around here. It's in a prime location, though—only a 30-minute drive from Point Reyes National Seashore, yet far enough away to avoid the traffic and other signs of civilization.

One of the most scenic drives on the Marin coast is along **Dillon Beach Road** from Tomales. The 4-mile drive passes through windswept meadows with wonderful vistas of Tomales Bay, Point Reyes, and the Pacific before ending at the privately owned Dillon Beach campground. For a proper grand finale to the drive, turn right on Oceana Drive in Dillon Beach and continue to a vacant cul-de-sac. On a clear day you can see all the way to Bodega Bay.

▼

**Tomales**

▲

Tomales is also a hugely popular stop for fresh raw and barbecued oysters. Since 1909 the **Tomales Bay Oyster Company** has been selling its wares right off the shore at 15479 Highway 1, just south of Marshall and 5 miles north of Point Reyes Station. The oysters range from bite-size cocktails to big ol' hunkin' cowboys and are sold by the dozen or in sacks of 100, should you be feeling randy enough. Those in the know bring their own knife, lemons, cocktail sauce, and even bags of charcoal for the nearby barbecue pits; open daily from 9am to 5pm, (415)663-1242.

### LODGINGS

**U.S. Hotel** ★ With nothing more to go by than a photograph of the original inn—which burned down in 1920—the owners of the U.S. Hotel built it from the ground up in 1989. The result? This place is so evocative of a bygone era that you could film a Western here and never need a set decorator. The pleasingly plain interiors are a welcome alternative to the typical lace-and-patchwork B&B decor: each of the eight immaculate rooms has high ceilings, a private bath, and simple yet attractive faux-antique furnishings. While the staff could be a bit more accommodating, the reasonable room rates—which include a self-serve continental breakfast—more than compensate. ■ *26985 Hwy 1 (in the center of town), Tomales, CA 94971; (707)878-2742; $$; MC, V; no checks.*

## VALLEY FORD

*LODGINGS*

**The Inn at Valley Ford ★** Writers and poets looking for a fresh source of inspiration should pack their Ouija boards and head for this 1860s Victorian farmhouse-turned-B&B situated in the quiet town of Valley Ford. It's run by the erudite innkeeper, traveler, and poet Sandy Nichols, and four of the five guest rooms are named after significant literary figures of the past, such as Molly Bloom and Virginia Woolf; they are decorated with photographs, poems, and publications (as well as period antiques and some Laura Ashley wallpaper for a dash of color). The inn is small, and the rooms near the front door can be a bit noisy; if you're a light sleeper, ask for the Sun Room or the detached cottage called the Somerset Maugham Room, which offer the most privacy. Each morning Nichols serves a full country breakfast of fresh fruit, homemade scones, and eggs seasoned with herbs from her garden. All in all, it's the perfect place to bring a good book and relax in the warm sunshine that bathes the large wood deck. ■ *14395 Hwy 1 (in the center of town), Valley Ford; (707) 876-3182; mail: PO Box 439, Valley Ford, CA 94972; $$; MC, V; checks OK.*

**The Valley Ford Hotel ★** The pleasant, old-fashioned Valley Ford Hotel, built in 1864 and completely renovated in 1990, is a good choice for travelers who prefer the privacy of a hotel to the more intimate quarters of a B&B. This family-run hotel isn't a spectacular place, but it has its charm; the seven rooms (with private baths) are clean, spacious, and comfortably furnished with cushy chairs and good, hard beds. A complimentary full breakfast is served downstairs. ■ *14415 Hwy 1 (downtown), Valley Ford; (707) 876-3600 or (800) 696-6679; mail: PO Box 329, Valley Ford, CA 94972; $$; full bar; AE, MC, V; checks OK; breakfast (for guests only) every day.* ↓

▼

**Bodega Bay**

▲

## BODEGA BAY

When it comes to fancy restaurants, accommodations, and boutiques, Bodega Bay has a long way to go. As it stands, there is only one three-star lodge and restaurant, and the town's most venerable store sells taffy and kites. This is odd, considering Bodega Bay is only a few hours' drive from the Bay Area—a good 2 to 3 hours closer than Mendocino—and has all the beautiful scenery and golden beaches you could possibly hope for.

Even though it is internationally famous as the setting for Alfred Hitchcock's *The Birds*, things haven't changed much. Spend a few hours meandering through town and it becomes apparent that Bodega Bay is, for the most part, still a working-class fishing town—the sort of place where most people start their day before dawn mending nets, rigging fishing poles, and talking shop. If all you want to do this weekend is breathe in some salty air and couldn't care less about Gucci boutiques and dancing till sunup, come to Bodega Bay—there ain't much here, which is precisely the point.

As you roll into Bodega Bay, keep an eye out for the **Bodega Bay Area Chamber of Commerce**, located in the center of town at 850 Highway 1; (707)875-3422. Load up on free maps, guides, and brochures, including the "Bodega Bay Area Map & Guide," which gives the exact locations of all the town's attractions, including **Bodega Head**, the small peninsula that shelters Bodega Bay. From downtown Bodega Bay, turn west on Eastshore Road, then turn right at the stop sign onto Bay Flat Road and follow it to the end. Here you'll find two superb walking trails that follow the ocean. The first, a 4-mile round-trip trail, starts from Bodega Head's west parking lot, leads past the **Bodega Bay Marine Laboratory**, and ends at the sand dunes of Salmon Creek Beach. An easier, 1½-mile round-trip walk begins in the east parking lot and encircles the edge of Bodega Head, branching off for an optional side trip to the tip of the point for a spectacular 360-degree view. From December through April, Bodega Head is one of the premier whale-watching points along the California coast (don't forget your binoculars).

Then again, why break a sweat? A great way to spend a lazy afternoon in Bodega Bay is at the docks, watching the rusty fishing boats unload their catches. **Tides Wharf Restaurant**, at 835 Highway 1 in Bodega Bay, (707)875-3652, has the most active dock scene, including a viewing room near the processing plant that allows you to witness a fish's ultimate fate—a swift and merciless gutting by deft hands, followed by a quick burial in ice. Just outside, sea lions linger by the dock hoping for a handout.

Linking Bodega Bay and the nearby town of Jenner are the **Sonoma Coast State Beaches**, 16 miles of pristine sand and gravel beaches, tide pools, rocky bluffs, hiking trails, and one heck of a gorgeous drive along Highway 1. Although all the beaches are pretty much the same—divine—the safest for kids is **Doran Park Beach**, located just south of Bodega Bay. When the water's rough everywhere else, Doran is still calm enough for swimming, clamming, and crabbing (an added bonus: the adjacent Doran mud flats are a favorite haunt of egrets, pelicans, and other seabirds). Tide pool trekkers will want to head to the north end of **Salmon Creek Beach** (off Bean Avenue, 2 miles north of town) or **Shell Beach**, a small low-tide treasure trove 10 miles north of Bodega Bay near Jenner. If all you want to do is get horizontal in the sand, deciding which of the 14 beaches along Highway 1 looks the best will drive you nuts; just pick one and park.

Worth half an hour of any Hitchcock fan's day is a quick trip to the town of **Bodega**, a few miles southeast of Bodega Bay off Highway 1. The attraction is a bird's-eye view of the hauntingly familiar Potter School House and St. Teresa's Church, both immortalized in Hitchcock's *The Birds*, filmed here in 1961. The two or three boutiques in downtown Bodega manage to entice a few visitors to park and browse, but most people seem content with a little rubbernecking and finger-pointing as they flip U-turns through the tiny town.

## RESTAURANTS

**The Duck Club** ★★★ Bodega Bay sure took its sweet time coaxing a premier chef to the coast, but now that Jeff Reilly (formerly the executive chef at Lafayette Park in Walnut Creek) is in town, gastronomes up and down the coast are coming to the Bodega Bay Lodge to sample his wares. "Sonoma County Cuisine" best describes Reilly's penchant for local yields, with creations such as roasted Petaluma duck with Valencia orange sauce or a Sonoma-farm-fresh asparagus strudel bathed in a mild curry sauce. *Le poisson du jour* comes straight from the docks down the street. Large windows overlook the bay, so be sure to beg for a table-with-a-view when making the required reservations. The Duck Club offers a lengthy wine list with an extensive selection of Sonoma County labels. ■ *103 Hwy 1 (in Bodega Bay Lodge, at the S end of town), Bodega Bay; (707)875-3525; $$$; beer and wine; AE, DC, DIS, MC, V; no checks; breakfast, dinner every day.* &

**Breakers Café** ★ If you're not exactly crazy about lemon-buttered seafood (see the review below) and can't afford the Duck Club, Bodega Bay's Breakers Café is the answer. For breakfast, park your fanny among the numerous plants in the sun-filled dining room and feast on yummy Belgian waffles topped with hot spiced peaches and whipped cream. Lunch is mostly sandwiches, burgers, and house-made soups, and dinner items range from fresh seafood to chicken, pasta, and low-fat vegetarian dishes. ■ *1400 Hwy 1 (in the Pelican Plaza at the N end of town), Bodega Bay; (707)875-2513; $; beer and wine; MC, V; local checks only; breakfast every day, May 1 to Sept 30, lunch, dinner every day year-round.* &

**Lucas Wharf Restaurant and Bar** ■ **Lucas Wharf Deli** ★ Few tourists come to Bodega Bay for the food, as you'll soon discover if you spend more than a day here. There are only two seafood restaurants in town, Tides Wharf and Lucas Wharf, and both do little to excite the palate. Yes, the fish is fresh off the boats, but the preparations are basic and uninspired. The petrale sole *doré* is served with lemon butter. The red snapper filet is served with lemon butter. And the grilled ling cod? You guessed it: lemon butter. Folks must think the Lucas Wharf Restaurant whips up some pretty darn good lemon butter because the place is always packed (as is the Tides Wharf, which is slightly more expensive and significantly less appealing). Your best bet is to skip both restaurants and go next door to **Lucas Wharf Deli**, pick up a $6 pint of crab cioppino or a big ol' basket of fresh fish 'n' chips, and make a picnic of it on the dock. ■ *595 Hwy 1 (at the S end of town), Bodega Bay. Restaurant: (707)875-3522; $$; full bar; DIS, MC, V; checks OK; lunch, dinner every day. ⅃ Deli: (707)875-3562; $; beer and wine; DIS, MC, V; checks OK; picnic items to go every day. ⅃*

## LODGINGS

**Bodega Bay Lodge** ★★★ Granted, the competition isn't very fierce, but it's safe to say that the Bodega Bay Lodge provides the Sonoma Coast's finest accommodations. It's the view that clinches it: all 78 rooms—recently remodeled in handsome hues of cardinal red and forest green with wood-burning fireplaces and stocked minibars—have private balconies with a wonderful panorama of Bodega Bay and its bird-filled wetlands. Should you ever leave your balcony, a short walk through elaborate flower gardens leads to an outdoor fieldstone spa and heated swimming pool overlooking the bay. A fitness center, sauna, and complimentary morning newspaper are also part of the package. More proof of Bodega Bay Lodge's top standing is its **Duck Club** restaurant (see review, above), easily the Sonoma Coast's best. ■ *103 Hwy 1 (at the S end of town), Bodega Bay, CA 94923; (707)875-3525 or (800)368-2468; bbl@woodsidehotels.com; www.woodsidehotels. com; $$$; AE, DC, DIS, MC, V; checks OK. ⅃*

**Inn at the Tides** ★★ In Bodega Bay the architectural style of most structures is nouveau Californian—wood-shingled boxes with lots of glass—and the Inn at the Tides is no exception. Perched on a hillside overlooking Bodega Bay, it offers 86 units with bay views, spacious interiors, and contemporary (albeit *dated* contemporary) decor, and all with the usual amenities of an expensive resort: terrycloth robes, coffee makers, hair dryers, cable TV, refrigerators, minibars, fresh flowers, continental breakfasts, and access to the indoor/outdoor pool, sauna, and Jacuzzis. A few of the rooms have king-size beds, and most have fireplaces. The Inn at the Tides restaurant, the **Bay View**, is open for dinner only. It offers ocean views and has a romantic, somewhat formal ambience, though it suffers from a so-so reputation. The owners, to their credit, have recently poured a bundle of money into revitalizing it and have hired two new chefs. Call for details about the

▼

▲

monthly gourmet winemaker dinners (advance reservations are required). ■ *800 Hwy 1 (across from the Tides Wharf), Bodega Bay; (707)875-2751 or (800)541-7788; mail: PO Box 640, Bodega Bay, CA 94923; iatt@monitor.net; www.innatthe tides. com; $$$; full bar; AE, DIS, MC, V; checks OK; dinner Wed–Sun.* &

**Bodega Harbor Inn** ★ A homey old-timer in a town of mostly modern accommodations, the Bodega Harbor Inn consists of four clapboard buildings (with a total of 14 guest rooms) set on a large lawn overlooking the harbor. The rooms are small but tidy, with private baths, cable TV, double beds, and access to a private yard where you can kick back in lawn chairs. If you're willing to shell out a few extra dollars, request a room with a partial ocean view and a small deck. The inn also has two reasonably priced two-bedroom suites and rents out seven houses and cottages, including the three-bedroom, two-bath Spyglass home, located on the Bodega Harbour Golf Links and overlooking the ocean. Guests at the inn are treated to a complimentary continental breakfast. ■ *1345 Bodega Ave (off Hwy 1 at the N end of town), Bodega Bay; (707)875-3594; mail: PO Box 161, Bodega Bay, CA 94923; $–$$$; MC, V; checks OK.* &

## FREESTONE

The tiny town of Freestone, a county-designated historic district, boasts a population of 35 people and 10 cute-as-a-button restored Victorian farmhouses. And stirring things up a bit in this sleepy little farming community is the **Osmosis Enzyme Baths**, a spa offering massages and rare Japanese heat-therapy treatments in large wooden boxes filled with hot, fragrant cedar sawdust; 209 Bohemian Highway, (707)823-8231.

### *LODGINGS*

**Green Apple Inn** ★ Rosemary Hoffman bought this picture-perfect little New England farmhouse more than a dozen years ago. Built in the 1860s, the Green Apple is surrounded by 5 green acres, and it's only a 15-minute drive from the coast. From the moment Rosemary and her dog Concierge greet you at the door, you'll know you're in the hands of a woman who truly enjoys her role as innkeeper. Staying here is a bit like staying at the home of a relative you actually like; in fact, much of the inn's appeal is due to the amiable hostess. The main house has four guest rooms with private baths, and the room in the back is the best, with its claw-footed bathtub and a view of the goat pasture. ■ *520 Bohemian Hwy (at the N end of town), Freestone, CA 95472; (707)874-2526; $$; MC, V; checks OK.*

▼

**Freestone**

*Lodgings*

▲

### RESTAURANTS

**The Bohemian Cafe** ★   When in Rome, do as the Romans do, and when traveling the Bohemian Highway, do as Occidental's bohemian crowd does and eat at the Bohemian Cafe. This converted old house is staffed by friendly (though not particularly service-oriented) free-spirit types, who bring artistic expression even to their pizzas, which range from the Athenian (spinach, artichoke hearts, feta, and olives) to the Sonoma (walnut, Brie, pesto, and apples). Bohemian breakfasts include incredibly light "cotton cakes" with real maple syrup; herbaceous frittatas with fresh cilantro, basil, parsley, and garlic; and the Hangtown Fry, an oyster, ham, and eggs combo served with applesauce. Dinner specials, such as the brick-oven-baked Chilean sea bass and the creamy linguine with mussels, scallops, and ling cod, are good enough to attract Occidental's Philistines as well. ■ *3688 Bohemian Hwy (at the S end of town), Occidental; (707)874-3931; $$; beer and wine; MC, V; checks OK; breakfast, lunch Wed–Sun, dinner every day.* ₠

### LODGINGS

▼
**Occidental**
___
*Restaurants*
▲

**The Inn at Occidental** ★★★   Innkeeper Jack Bullard has done a fantastic job remodeling this stately 1887 Victorian into one of the finest B&Bs in the region. Covered porches, wainscoted hallways, antique wicker furniture, walled-in English gardens, and a comfortable sitting parlor are all elegant reminders of the historic days when Occidental was a stopping point on the railroad between San Francisco and the Northwest. The eight individually decorated rooms have private baths and are furnished with the innkeeper's vast collection of heirlooms, antiques, and original artwork. Overlooking the courtyard, gardens, and fountain is the Sandwich Glass Suite, luxuriously appointed with a queen bed and a separate sitting area with a corner fireplace, comfortable chairs, and a spa tub for two. Also overlooking the courtyard is the Marble Room, sumptuously furnished with an antique pine queen bed, a large separate sitting area with a fireplace, comfortable chairs, and a spa tub for two overlooking the hill and woods behind the inn. Guests are treated to a full gourmet breakfast of fresh fruit, juices, homemade granola, freshly baked pastries, and hot entrees such as orange-thyme pancakes or French toast with jam—all served in the dining room or outdoors. Inquire about the inn's Saturday dinners, reserved for guests only. Most of the town's restaurants are just a few blocks away, and it's only a short drive to the coast. ■ *3657 Church St (off the Bohemian Hwy), Occidental; (707)874-1047 or (800)522-6324; mail: PO Box 857, Occidental, CA 95465; innkeeper@innatoccidental. com; www.innatoccidental.com; $$$; AE, DIS, MC, V; checks OK; dinner Sat (for guests only).* ₠

## RESTAURANTS

**Chez Peyo** ★★ As you enter Chez Peyo's foyer you may be greeted by a man whose French accent is so smooth you'll think he's faking it. He's not. This is Pierre Lagourgue, the owner and chef of Chez Peyo (Peyo is the Basque form of Pierre). Sebastopol's most popular French chef, Pierre is renowned for his savory French Country fare such as braised lamb shanks dressed in a pinot noir sauce, and baked salmon with an almond-and-black-pepper crust topped with a citrus beurre blanc. The restaurant's Sunday champagne brunches have been a popular town attraction for years. Granted, Chez Peyo wouldn't survive long on the Champs-Elysées, but for Sebastopol, this is *très bon.* ■ *2295 Gravenstein Hwy (on Hwy 116, 2 miles S of town), Sebastopol; (707)823-1262; $$; beer and wine; MC, V; local checks only; brunch Sun, lunch Tues–Sat, dinner Tues–Sun.* &

## LODGINGS

**The Gravenstein Inn** ★★ This rustic three-story farmhouse has garnered National Historic Landmark status. The inn was built in 1872 and restored in 1989, when it opened as a bed-and-breakfast hotel. Surrounded by six gently sloping acres of apple orchards, the Gravenstein Inn offers four guest rooms upstairs, two of which share a bath. The Gravenstein Suite, the inn's finest (and most expensive), has a wood-burning fireplace and a private sun porch overlooking the orchard. Downstairs is a parlor furnished with comfortable chairs and a Chickering grand piano, and outside are horseshoe pits, a heated swimming pool shaded by a giant sycamore, and barbecue facilities. Breakfast is served in your room, the dining room, or outdoors under the wisteria arbor. ■ *3160 Hicks Rd (off Hwy 116, at Graton Rd, 2¼ miles N of town), Sebastopol, CA 95472; (707)829-0493; gravensteininn.metro.net; www. metro.net/gravensteininn; $$; MC, V; checks OK.*

**▼**

**Forestville**

**▲**

## FORESTVILLE

From this tiny hamlet surrounded by redwoods you can launch an all-day **canoe trip** down the gentle **Russian River**. Set forth from Burke's Canoe Trips from May through September, and someone there will pick you up 10 miles down the scenic, forested river (a haven for turtles, river otters, egrets, and great blue herons) and take you back to your car; (707)887-1222. On Forestville's itty-bitty main drag is **Brother Juniper's Bakery**, the home of the Russian River Valley's best breads; 6544 Front Street, (707)542-9012. Also worth a detour is **Koslowski Farms**, a family farm that has turned into a gourmet-food business. The Koslowski's apple butter, jams, and vinegars are sold in specialty shops throughout Sonoma County; 5566 Gravenstein Highway, (707)887-1587.

## RESTAURANTS

**Topolos Russian River Vineyards Restaurant & Winery ★★** A Greek restaurant on the Russian River? Well, why not—especially when chefs Bob Engel and Christine Topolos prepare the food the same way you'd get it on the Mediterranean. Every meal at this family owned restaurant and winery comes with tzatziki (a garlic-laden cucumber-yogurt dip for bread) and a tomato stuffed with aromatic ratatouille. Follow that with an order of mezes: a plate of dolmathes, tiropita (a cheese-and-egg pie wrapped in scrumptious, flaky filo pastry), marinated eggplant, and feta. Then choose from such main courses as prawns Santorini (prepared with tomato, feta, and dill), souvlakia (a marinated lamb brochette), and spanakopita (spinach and feta cheese baked in filo pastry). Topolos wines are made here, so that's what's served in the dining room (ask your server to pair a different glass of wine with each course of your meal). Dessert, naturally, is a heavy hunk of honey-drenched baklava. After your meal, peruse the tasting room, then look for the largest colony of brown bats in California as they fly out of the eaves of the building around sunset. ■ *5700 Gravenstein Hwy (on Hwy 116, ¼ mile S of town), Forestville; (707)887-1562; $$; wine only; AE, DC, MC, V; checks OK; brunch Sun, lunch, dinner every day.*

## LODGINGS

**The Farmhouse Inn ★** Don't let the Farmhouse Inn's eight guest cottages fool you. At first glance these buildings tucked within a grove of trees look like nothing more than your everyday roadside motel cabins. Take a step inside and you'll see that these little lodges are actually quite luxurious, with plush carpets, fireplaces, saunas, and jumbo Jacuzzis. The grounds—six acres of hills and redwoods—include a large swimming pool, a croquet course, and formal English gardens. Guests gather for breakfast in the restored turn-of-the-century farmhouse, which features country-style furniture and a giant fireplace. Expect to be treated to a breakfast of fruit, cereal, and hot dishes such as huevos rancheros or eggs Florentine, as well as homemade croissants, scones, and pastries. ■ *7871 River Rd (at Wohler Rd), Forestville, CA 95436; (707)887-3300 or (800)464-6642; innkeep@sonic.net; www.sonic.net/farmhouse; $$$; AE, MC, V; checks OK.*

Local boosters of this blink-and-you'll-miss-it town have put a gigantic banner over the main street announcing that you are indeed in Monte Rio. Earlier this century, Monte Rio and nearby Cazadero were destinations on the old Northern Pacific Railroad, which took thousands of vacationers from the San Francisco Bay Area to the Russian River each summer. Now there's not much here besides the flamingo-pink Rio movie theater and a few mediocre restaurants, but on the outskirts of town a wonderful country inn serves fantastic dinners to its lodgers (see the Huckleberry Springs Country Inn review, below).

*LODGINGS*

**Huckleberry Springs Country Inn ★★** Dispersed on this resort's secluded 60 acres are four very private cottages surrounded by towering redwoods. Everyone's favorite is the barrel-shaped cabin aptly named Cherry Barrel, but all of the units have skylights, decks, wood-burning stoves, queen-size beds, stereos, TVs with VCRs and access to a video library, and two-person hammocks hanging between the trees. A short walk through the redwoods takes you to the main house with its comfortable sofas, sun-splashed window seats, and intriguing collection of games. The swimming pool overlooks a ravine, and there's a non-chlorinated spa tucked among the trees a short distance up the hill. The most recent addition is a massage center offering rubdowns for guests (by appointment only).

Among the inn's main attractions are its gourmet multi-course meals—an optional $25 per person for dinner—served in the solarium. Proprietor Suzanne Greene's cooking emphasizes local ingredients: organic greens and vegetables from nearby farms, salmon and crab from Bodega Bay, and spring lamb from a local rancher. Although the menu changes nightly, expect a meal that starts with an appetizer such as tomato-fennel soup, followed by a Sonoma greens salad with a champagne vinaigrette. You'll have a choice of two entrees, which might include roast pork loin stuffed with cashews and sun-dried cherries in a rosemary and sherry sauce, and a pasta plate such as angel hair with bay shrimp, halibut, scallops, roasted red peppers, and onions in a wine sauce. For the sweet finale, you might be lucky enough to get the traditional strawberry shortcake topped with crème de cassis whipped cream. The inn's full country breakfasts are equally delicious, and they're included in the room rates. ■ *8105 Old Beedle Rd (take Tyrone Rd off the Bohemian Hwy and follow the signs), Monte Rio; (707) 865-2683 or (800) 822-2683; mail: PO Box 400, Monte Rio, CA 95462; hucksprgs@netdex.com; $$$; beer and wine; MC, V; checks OK; breakfast, dinner (both meals are for guests only) every day.* &

▼

Monte Rio

*Lodgings*

▲

## LODGINGS

**Applewood** ★★★ Set on a forested hillside, this 1922 California Mission Revival mansion—formerly the country home of a wealthy banker—is one of the Russian River Valley's finest accommodations, with an atmosphere far more relaxed than you would expect at such an elegant hotel. Filled with high-quality antiques and original watercolor and oil paintings, the 16 secluded guest rooms look out onto the surrounding redwoods, apple trees, and vineyards. All of the rooms have private baths, TVs, telephones, and fresh flowers; seven come with either a spa tub or shower-for-two. Room 1, decorated in soothing forest green colors and English oak, features French doors that open onto a private patio and garden; room 4 has a Louis Philippe cherry-wood sleigh bed and a sitting room framed by huge, curved bay windows. On the second floor are two comfortable sitting rooms with fireplaces, and a beautiful rose-colored dining room with high arched ceilings and French doors that open onto the pool terrace. Beyond the garden there's a swimming pool and a Jacuzzi.

▼

**Pocket Canyon**

*Lodgings*

▲

A breakfast of eggs Florentine, French toast, and other well-prepared dishes is served on tables topped with crisp linens and fresh flowers in the **Applewood Restaurant**. Tuesday through Saturday evenings the Applewood's talented chef David Frakes (a graduate of the California Culinary Academy who worked for a few years with celebrity chef Gary Danko when he presided at San Francisco's Ritz-Carlton) takes over the restaurant, offering informal though dazzling prix-fixe, four-course dinners, with a choice of appetizers, entrees, and desserts. Dinner might start with a tender corn and scallion cake topped with shrimp, tomato, and jalapeño salsa and a dollop of lime cream, followed by a mesclun salad with feta, toasted walnuts, and a balsamic-watermelon vinaigrette. Entrees vary from sautéed halibut with caramelized roasted bell peppers, a white-corn ragout, and herbed basmati rice with cumin butter to pan-seared pork loin with fried Torpedo onions, braised bok choy, and a mango-tarragon reduction sauce. Spend the remainder of the night—the candlelit table is yours for the evening—lingering over coffee and Applewood's blackberry crème brûlée with minted berry compote or perhaps a plate of warm chocolate-chip cookies topped with fudge sauce, coffee caramel, and French vanilla ice cream. ■ *13555 Hwy 116 (1 mile S of Guerneville), Pocket Canyon, CA 95446; (707) 869-9093; stay@applewoodinn.com; www.applewoodinn.com; $$$; beer and wine; AE, DIS, MC, V; checks OK (but not for advance deposits); dinner Tues–Sat (by reservation only; seatings are at 6:30pm, 7:15pm, and 8pm).*

The longtime residents of Guerneville—one of the busiest logging centers in the West during the 1880s—have seen their town undergo a significant change of face in every recent decade. First it was a haven for bikers—the leather, not the Lycra, sort—then it became a hangout for hippies. Now it's a summer mecca for Bay Area gays and naturalists attracted by the beauty of the redwoods and the Russian River. The town is a good launching spot for nature expeditions and touring the area's wineries. **Korbel Champagne Cellars**, overlooking the vineyards and the Russian River, is one of the region's most popular wineries and offers free tastings of its bubbly; 13250 River Road, (707)887-2294. **Armstrong Woods State Reserve** boasts a peaceful grove of spectacular ancient redwoods and a variety of hiking trails; 17000 Armstrong Woods Road, (707)869-2015. Equestrians should saddle up at **Armstrong Woods Pack Station**, which offers 1½-hour and half- and full-day **horseback rides** with gourmet lunches as well as overnight camping rides; (707)579-1520. From May to October, you can rent **canoes**, **kayaks**, and **paddleboats** at **Johnson's Beach**, just under the main bridge; (707)869-2022. Johnson's Beach is also home to the wildly popular **Russian River Jazz Festival**, held every September; (707)869-3940. Another crowd-pleaser is the annual **Stumptown Days Parade and Rodeo**, which takes place on Father's Day weekend; (707)869-1959. For a good, simple meal, grab a bite at **Burdon's**, 15405 River Road, (707)869-2615, or **Sweet's River Grill**, 16521 Main Street, (707)869-3383.

Guerneville

*Lodgings*

### LODGINGS

**Santa Nella House** ★★ This century-old Victorian farmhouse, hidden just off Highway 116, is one of the better B&Bs in the valley—and it's only a short walk from the Russian River. Santa Nella's four turn-of-the-century guest rooms are decorated with antiques, old quilts, and dried flowers, and each has a private bathroom and fireplace. The Blue Room is a large, airy chamber with a view of the redwoods, and is equipped with a queen-size bed and a brass day bed. Proprietors Ed and Joyce Ferrington may remind you of your parents as they encourage you to eat ungodly amounts of Joyce's delicious waffles or eggs Benedict. In the evening everyone relaxes on the wraparound porch, and they'll want to hear all about your day. (Of course, if you're not in the mood to socialize, you can always hide out in the outdoor hot tub.) ■ *12130 Hwy 116 (1½ miles S of town), Guerneville, CA 95446; (707)869-9488; $$; MC, V; checks OK.*

**The Willows** ★ The Willows prides itself on its convivial, hang-loose atmosphere. You can steal away in a canoe off the inn's private dock on the Russian River whenever you like, or fire up the outdoor barbecue, pitch a tent for the night on the property, and even lie out in the buff on the private beach if you so desire. An immense lawn sweeps down from the back of the lodge to the shores of the Russian River, the perfect site for kicking back in a lawn chair on those many warm Russian River Valley afternoons. The 13 guest rooms are simply decorated with wood furnishings and flowered quilts. The least expensive units are on a par with your average no-frills motel room—basic, but equipped with a TV, VCR, and phone. The pricier rooms have views of the river and the grounds. All guests receive a continental breakfast and have full use of the library, which is dominated by a grand piano. There's also an outdoor hot tub and sauna. ■ *15905 River Rd (½ mile E of the green bridge downtown), Guerneville; (707) 869-2824 or (800) 953-2828; mail: PO Box 465, Guerneville, CA 95446; $$; AE, DIS, MC, V; no checks.*

## CAZADERO

*LODGINGS*

**Guerneville**
—|—
*Lodgings*
▲

**Timberhill Ranch Resort** ★★★★ More than a decade ago, when two Marin couples—Tarran McDaid and Michael Riordan and Barbara Farrell and Frank Watson—decided to give up the 9-to-5 grind of city life and create their own inn from the ground up, they had no idea their accomplishments would be honored with numerous awards, including a rare four-star ranking by *Mobil Travel Guide* in 1997. The honors continue to roll in for this secluded resort, perched high above the rugged Sonoma Coast and surrounded by the 6,000 wilderness acres of Salt Point State Park. The Timberhill Ranch offers 15 elegant cedar cottages scattered throughout 80 private acres, each with plush carpeting, a wood-burning fireplace, a private deck, hand-made quilts, a stocked minibar and refrigerator, and vases brimming with colorful fresh flowers. Elsewhere on the estate are Timberhill's two championship tennis courts, a 40-foot heated pool, a Jacuzzi, and Brandy, a friendly Australian Shepherd who looks after Timberhill's three pygmy goats and four miniature horses (this is, after all, a ranch).

Included in the very expensive lodging rate (rooms start at about $365 and go way up) are a continental breakfast, delivered to your doorstep at your requested hour, and an outstanding six-course dinner for two, served on candlelit tables set with fine china, crystal, and silver in the open, airy dining room of the **Timberhill Ranch Restaurant**. The restaurant's prix-fixe menu changes daily, and locally grown produce (much of it from Timberhill's own gardens) often influences

the chef's creations. Fresh fish, fowl, and Timberhill's house-baked breads, pastries, and desserts are always featured. A typical dinner may begin with gingered quail ravioli topped with brandy cream, followed by a black-bean and cumin soup, a mixed-greens salad with grapes, walnuts, and a caramelized shallot vinaigrette, a lemon-lime sorbet, and a choice of four or five entrees, such as roast leg of lamb with mint gravy, grilled swordfish set on a bed of caper relish, roast Long Island duck with a currant-chutney glaze, and pan-fried Dungeness crab cakes with a side of red-pepper mayonnaise. The delectable desserts may include a baked pear Normandy tart or a tri-colored chocolate mousse. The restaurant, open to the public by reservation only, also serves lunch and Sunday brunch.
■ *35755 Hauser Bridge Rd (from Hwy 1, take Myers Grade Rd for almost 14 miles to Hauser Bridge Rd and bear right), Caza-dero, CA 95421; (707)847-3258 or (800)847-3470; timber@ mcn.org; www.timberhillranch.com; $$$; full bar; AE, DC, MC, V; checks OK; brunch Sun, lunch Mon–Sat, dinner every day.* 占

## JENNER

About 16 miles north of Bodega Bay on Highway 1 is what seems to be every Northern Californian's "secret" getaway spot: Jenner. Built on a bluff rising from the mouth of the Russian River, the tiny seaside town consists of little more than a gas station, three restaurants, two inns, and a deli, which means the only thing to do in town is eat, sleep, and lie on the beach—not a bad vacation plan. Perhaps Jenner's best attrac-tion, however, is its location—it's 2 hours closer than Mendo-cino to the Bay Area, yet has the same spectacular coastal scenery and a far better selection of beaches.

▼

**Jenner**

▲

One of the major highlights of the Jenner area is beautiful **Goat Rock Beach**, a popular breeding ground for harbor seals. Pupping season begins in March and lasts until June, and orange-vested volunteers are usually on hand to protect the seals (they give birth on land) from potentially menacing dogs and passersby. They answer questions about the playful animals, and even lend out binoculars for a closer look.

A sinuous 12-mile drive north of Jenner on Highway 1 leads to the mildly interesting **Fort Ross State Historic Park**, a semi-restored redwood fortress built by Russian fur traders in 1812. If you decide to cough up the $6 parking fee, plan to spend about an hour here and start with a short history lesson in the Fort Compound (offered at 11:30am, 1:30pm, and 3:30pm in the summer, and noon and 2pm in the winter). End your visit with a walk down to the cove and beach; (707)847-3286.

A great day trip from Jenner is the scenic drive along Highway 101 to **Salt Point State Park**. There are all kinds of things to do here, including skin diving, searching for tide pools off rocky beaches, hiking through coastal woodland and wildflower-filled meadows, and poking around the 3,500-acre park for wild berries and mushrooms—simply pull your car over anywhere along Highway 1 and start walking. At the north end of the park on Kruse Ranch Road is the 317-acre **Kruse Rhododendron Preserve**, a forested grove of the wild pink and purple flowers that grow up to 18 feet tall in the shade of a vast canopy of redwoods. Peak blooming time varies yearly, but April or early May is usually the best time to see the world's tallest *Rhododendron californicum*; (707)847-3221.

## RESTAURANTS

**River's End** ★★ Don't bother looking for a better restaurant or bar in the area; for more than 20 years owner/chef Wolfgang Gramatzki's oceanside establishment has been the local favorite. Who'd have guessed you could order roasted baby pheasant in tiny Jenner? Rum-roasted saddle of pork, a pricey rack of lamb for two, and straight-off-the-boat fish specials give you an idea of what to expect for dinner. Lunch is more down to earth, with reasonably priced burgers and sandwiches. Most tables have a wonderful view of the ocean, as does the small outside deck—the perfect spot for a glass of Sonoma County wine. ■ *1104A Hwy 1 (just N of town), Jenner; (707)865-2484; $$$; full bar; MC, V; no checks; lunch, dinner every day June to Sept (hours vary Sept to May).* &

▼

**Jenner**

▲

**Sizzling Tandoor** ★ When the weather is warm and sunny, Sizzling Tandoor is the best place on the Sonoma Coast to have lunch. This Indian restaurant is perched high above the placid Russian River, and the view, particularly from the outside patio, is fantastic. Equally great are the inexpensive lunch specials: huge portions of curries and kabobs served with vegetables, soup, *pulao* rice, and superb *naan* (Indian bread). Even if you don't have time for a meal, drop by and order some warm *naan* to go. ■ *9960 Hwy 1 (at the S end of the Russian River Bridge, S of town), Jenner; (707)865-0625; $; beer and wine; AE, DIS, MC, V; no checks; lunch, dinner every day (closed Mon in the winter).* &

## LODGINGS

**Jenner Inn & Cottages** ★ When people say they stayed at the cutest little place in Jenner, they're talking about Jenner Inn & Cottages. There are 16 guest rooms here, each dispersed within a cluster of cottages and houses perched above the Russian River or the ocean. The houses are subdivided into separate suites that are rented out individually, and all have private baths, separate entrances, and antique and wicker furnishings; many units also have kitchens, fireplaces, hot tubs, and private decks or porches. The rose-covered Rosewater Cottage, a honeymooners' favorite, sits right beside the Russian River estuary and is warmed by a stone fireplace (as well as the king-size bed and hot tub). The adorable Pelican Suite is also a newlyweds' favorite, with big bay windows overlooking the water. An extended continental breakfast, served in the main lodge, is included in the room rate. In addition to the bed-and-breakfast accommodations, the inn rents out six private vacation homes located along the river, within Jenner Canyon, or overlooking the ocean. Note: Don't expect the Ritz if you opt for the lower-priced rooms, which are far from fancy but still a great deal for oceanfront property. ■ *10400 Hwy 1 (1 mile N of the Hwy 116/Hwy 1 junction downtown), Jenner; (707) 865-2377 or (800) 732-2377; mail: PO Box 69, Jenner, CA 95450; innkeeper@jennerinn.com; www.jennerinn. com; $$; AE, MC, V; checks OK.*

## MENDOCINO COAST

There are four things first-time visitors should know before heading to the Mendocino coast. First, be prepared for a long but beautiful drive; there are no quick and easy routes to this part of the California coast, and no public transportation. Second, make your hotel and restaurant reservations as far in advance as possible, because everything books up solid during the summer and on holidays. Third, bring warm clothing. You might as well forget about packing only shorts and T-shirts— regardless of how broiling it is everywhere else. A windless, sunny, 80-degree day on the Mendocino coast is about as rare as affordable real estate. Fourth and finally, bring lotsa money and your checkbook. Cheap sleeps, eats, and even banks are few and far between along this stretch of shoreline, and many places don't take credit cards (though personal checks are widely accepted).

So where exactly is the Mendocino coast? Well, it starts at the county line in Gualala and ends a hundred or so miles north at the sparsely populated stretch known as the Lost Coast. The focal point is the town of Mendocino, but the main center of commerce—and the area's only McDonald's, if you can believe it—is in Fort Bragg, 15 miles up the coast. Compared to these two towns, every other part of the Mendocino coast is relatively deserted—something to consider if you're looking to escape the masses.

Spring is the best time to visit, when the wildflowers are in full bloom and the crowds are still sparse. Then again, nothing on this planet is more romantic than cuddling next to the fireplace on a winter night, listening to the rain and thunder pound against your little cottage as you watch the waves crash against the cliffs, so don't rule out a trip in the colder months, either. Actually, when you get down to it, any time you have a few days off is a good enough excuse to pack your bags and head for the coast, reminding yourself why you don't live in Idaho.

For additional information about the Mendocino coast, including upcoming events, visit the area's Web site at www. mendocinocoast.com.

## SEA RANCH

### *LODGINGS*

**Sea Ranch** ★★★ An upper-middle-class ritual among Northern California families and friends is to rent a vacation home along the 9-mile coastal stretch of the ritzy residential development called Sea Ranch. Begun in the 1960s by the land-hungry Castle and Cooke Co. of Hawaii, Sea Ranch is undoubtedly one of the most beautiful seaside communities in the nation, due mostly to rigid adherence to environmentally harmonious (or "organic") architectural standards for its extravagant homes. Approximately 300 homes are available as vacation rentals, managed by eight or nine rental companies, with prices ranging from as low as $165 to as high as $550 for two nights. There's also a lodge and restaurant within Sea Ranch, but your best bet is to get your own house and full kitchen for only a few dollars more. ■ *On Hwy 1 (between Stewarts Point and Gualala), Sea Ranch; contact Sea Ranch Rentals at (707)785-2579; mail: Sea Ranch Rentals, PO Box 88, Sea Ranch, CA 95497; $$–$$$; no credit cards; checks OK.*

▼

**Mendocino Coast**

▲

## GUALALA

The southernmost town in Mendocino County, Gualala also happens to have the most mispronounced name in Mendocino County. Keep the G soft and you end up with "wah-LAL-ah," the Spanish version of *walali*, which is Pomo Indian patois for "water coming down place." The water in question is the nearby Gualala River, a placid year-round playground for kayakers, canoeists, and swimmers.

Once an industrious, lively logging town, Gualala has been tamed considerably since the days when loggers would literally climb the saloon walls with their spiked boots. Though a few real-life suspender-wearing lumberjacks still end their day at the Gualala Hotel's saloon, the coastal town's main function these days is providing gas, groceries, and hardware for area residents. On its outskirts, however, are several excellent parks, beaches, and hiking trails; combine this with the region's glorious seascapes, and suddenly poor little mispronounced Gualala emerges as a serious contender among the better vacation spots on the North Coast.

One of the most enjoyable, healthy, and rewarding activities in Gualala—if not in all of California—is **river and sea** kayaking. It's the ultimate form of escapism around here—effortlessly paddling your safe, silent, and unsinkable craft anywhere you please, sneaking up on river otters and great blue herons. The placid Gualala River is ideal for beginner kayakers, and either Adventure Rents, (707)884-4FUN or (888)881-4FUN, or Gualala Kayak, (707)884-4705, will transport single and two-person kayaks to and from the river and provide all the necessary gear and instruction. (Adventure Rents also carries canoes and bicycles, including tandems.) You don't need any experience for river kayaking, and all ages are encouraged, so why not give it a try?

Other popular pastimes in and around Gualala include **golfing**, **hiking**, and **bird-watching**. Open to the public, the award-winning Sea Ranch Golf Links is a challenging Scottish-style course designed by Robert Muir Graves. Originally built as a 9-hole oceanside course, the Links expanded to a full 18 holes in August 1996. It's located along the Sea Ranch's northern boundary at the entrance to Gualala Point Regional Park, and is open daily; (707)785-2468. Of the six public beach access points along Highway 1 between the south end of Sea Ranch and Gualala, the one that offers the most bang for the $3 parking fee is 195-acre **Gualala Point Regional Park**. The park has 10 miles of trails through coastal grasslands, redwood forests, and river canyons, as well as picnic sites, camping areas, and excellent bird and whale watching along the mostly deserted beaches; (707)785-2377.

## RESTAURANTS

**St. Orres Restaurant** ★★★  St. Orres Restaurant is one of Gualala's star attractions, and one of the main reasons people keep coming back to this region. The constantly changing prix-fixe dinner menu focuses on wild game: dishes range from wild turkey tamales to tequila-marinated quail or sautéed medallions of venison. Self-taught chef Rosemary Campiformio's dark and fruity sauces and sublime soups are perfectly suited to the flavorful game, a distinctly Northern California rendition of French country cuisine. St. Orres' wine cellar stores a sizable selection of California wines. ■ *36601 Hwy 1 (2 miles N of Gualala on the E side of Hwy 1), Gualala; (707)884-3335; www.saintorres.com; $$$; MC, V for hotel guests only, otherwise no credit cards; checks OK; breakfast (guests only) every day, dinner every day.*

**The Old Milano Hotel Restaurant** ★★  If you can get over the odd feeling that you're dining in somebody's former living room (which you are), you're bound to enjoy a candlelight dinner in the Old Milano's small, wood-paneled, Victorian dining room. Chef Brian Knutson serves his guests such tantalizing entrees as spice-crusted rack of Sonoma spring lamb, seared sea scallops in a ruby red vinaigrette, and a wonderful puff pastry appetizer filled with sautéed wild mushrooms. The menu changes weekly, but always includes fresh seafood, thick steaks, and fancy fowl. Come early and spend some time basking on the sun porch overlooking the ocean, and be sure to request a table by the fireplace. ■ *38300 Hwy 1 (just N of the Food Company, ¾ mile N of town), Gualala; (707) 884-3256; $$$; beer and wine; MC, V for hotel guests only, otherwise no credit cards; checks OK; breakfast (guests only) every day, dinner every day (reservations requested).*

**The Food Company** ★ For fine dining in Gualala, go to the St. Orres or the Old Milano. For every other kind of dining, come here. Open all day, every day, the Food Company is a cross between a deli, bakery, and cafe, serving fresh-baked breads, pastries, and sandwiches alongside an ever-changing menu of meat pies, pastas, quiches, tarts, meat loafs, stuffed bell peppers, moussaka, enchiladas, and lord knows what else. It's sort of like coming home from school for dinner—you never know what's going to be on the table, but you know it's probably going to be good. On sunny afternoons, the cafe's garden doubles as a picnic area; throw in a bottle of wine from their modest rack, and you have the makings for a romantic—and inexpensive—lunch. ■ *38411 Hwy 1 (½ mile N of Gualala at the corner of Hwy 1 and Robinsons Reef Rd), Gualala; (707) 884-1800; $; beer and wine; MC, V; checks OK; breakfast, lunch, dinner every day.*

### LODGINGS

**The Old Milano Hotel** ★★★ Overlooking the sea above Castle Rock Cove, this picturesque Victorian bed and breakfast, built by the Lucchinetti family in 1905, is featured on the National Register of Historic Places. If you can drag yourself away from the veranda with the knockout ocean view and through the front door, you'll find six small yet elegant bedrooms upstairs (all with shared baths) and a downstairs suite replete with antique furnishings and a private bath. All but one of the rooms (the Garden View Room) feature fantastic views of the sea. Elsewhere on the 3-acre estate are the Vine Cottage, located in the gardens and furnished with a brass bed, reading loft, wood-burning stove, and private bath; the Caboose, a genuine railroad caboose converted into the quaintest, coziest, and most private room at the inn (if not on the coast) with its wood-burning stove and small deck; four new cottages with fireplaces, ocean views, and hot tubs or showers for two; and a cliff-side Jacuzzi reserved for only two at a time. A full breakfast, included in the room rate, may be served in your room, on the garden patio, or by the fire in the parlor. ■ *38300 Hwy 1 (just N of the Food Company, ¾ mile N of town), Gualala, CA 95445; (707) 884-3256; $$$; beer and wine; MC, V for hotel* *guests only, otherwise no credit cards; checks OK; breakfast (guests only) every day, dinner every day (reservations requested).*

**St. Orres** ★★★ In the early '70s, a group of young architects and builders, inspired by the Russian architecture of the early Northern California settlers, took their back-to-the-land dreams to Gualala and created this dazzling copper-domed inn from redwood timbers scrounged from old logging mills and dilapidated bridges. Located just off Highway 1 and within walking distance of a sheltered, sandy cove, St. Orres consists of eight small, inexpensive rooms in the main lodge (two with great ocean views and all with shared baths) and 11 private cottages scattered throughout the 42 acres of wooded grounds. The best cottage is the ultra-rustic and surprisingly affordable Wild Flower Cabin, a former logging-crew shelter furnished with a cozy sleeping loft, a wood-burning stove (topped with cast-iron skillets), an adorable outside shower overlooking the woods, and even a gaggle of wild turkeys waiting for handouts at your doorstep. Another top choice: the gorgeous Sequoia Cottage, a solid-timbered charmer tucked into the edge of the forest. It has an elevated king-size bed, skylight, soaking tub, wet bar, private deck, and wood-burning fireplace. Start the day with a complimentary full breakfast (delivered to the cottages in baskets), spend the next few hours lolling around the nearby beaches, and have dinner at St. Orres's superb restaurant (see review, above). End the day at your private dacha, snuggled in front of the fireplace and listening to the distant roar of the ocean. Reserve a table for dinner when you make your room reservation; breakfast comes with the room, but dinner doesn't, and the restaurant is almost always booked.
■ *36601 Hwy 1 (2 miles N of Gualala on the E side of Hwy 1), Gualala; (707)884-3335; mail: PO Box 523, Gualala, CA 95445; www.saintorres.com; $ (lodge), $$$ (cottages and restaurant); MC, V for hotel guests only, otherwise no credit cards; checks OK; breakfast (guests only) every day, dinner every day.*

## POINT ARENA

Fifteen miles north of Gualala is Point Arena, one of the smallest incorporated cities in California. Once a bustling shipping port, the three-block-long city is now home to only 400 or so people, mostly transplants from larger cities who have set up shop along Main Street with neither the desire nor the intention of making much money. They're just here to enjoy the quiet small-town life.

Since there is no direct inland road to Point Arena, few tourists pass through, ensuring that the city will never become as overloaded as Mendocino. Yet this ain't no cow town either. It has one of the hottest restaurants on the North Coast, historic lodgings, and even poetry readings at the local bookstore.

So if you're tired of the crowded Mendocino scene yet want to spend a relaxing weekend on the coast, there's no better alternative than little Point Arena.

A cross between a bookstore, cafe, coffeehouse, and impromptu community center is **Bookends**, the dream-come-true enterprise of co-owner Alix Levine, an admitted bibliophile and town mother. Located within a beautifully restored Main Street edifice, Bookends is the perfect place to start your day, whether you're staying in Point Arena or just passing through. Tofu scrambles and house-baked pastries are served for breakfast until 2pm on weekends, and an eclectic lunch menu featuring everything from croissant sandwiches to veggie stir-fries is offered until the doors close at 9pm (6:30pm in the winter). On sunny days, warm your bones on the outdoor patio; 265 Main Street, (707)882-2287.

While you're here, be sure to take a tour of the **Point Arena Lighthouse**. Built in 1870 after 10 ships ran aground here on a single stormy night, the fully operational lighthouse had to be rebuilt after the 1906 earthquake, but now it's solid enough for visitors to trudge up the six-story tower's 145 steps for a standout view of the coast (that is, if the fog has lifted). The dazzling, 6-foot-wide, lead-crystal lens is worth the hike alone. The lighthouse is open 11am to 3:30pm weekdays and 10am to 3:30pm weekends in the summer (11am to 2:30pm daily in the winter), and is located at the end of scenic Lighthouse Road, about 5 miles northwest of downtown Point Arena off Highway 1. The parking/tour/museum fee is only a few bucks; (707)882-2777.

Near Point Arena but virtually isolated is the 5-mile sweep of shore, dunes, and meadows that comprise **Manchester State Beach**. Though several access roads off Highway 1 lead to the beach, the closest one to Point Arena also happens to be the best: the 10- to 15-minute walk across the dunes from the parking lot is a leg-burner, but it's a small price to pay for your own private beach. Take the Stoneboro Road exit west off Highway 1, 2 miles north of the turnoff to Point Arena Lighthouse; (707)882-2463 or (707)937-5804.

## RESTAURANTS

**Pangaea** ★★★★ After stints as the exalted chef of the local St. Orres and the Old Milano Hotel Restaurants, Shannon Hughes opened her own place in tiny Point Arena to the relief of every innkeeper in the city ("Finally, a restaurant in town I can recommend," says one). Although it's a relative newcomer to the area, Pangaea is already the talk of the North Coast, particularly when Hughes goes off on one of her international tangents and astounds patrons with exotic menu items à la Indonesia, Nigeria, and other far-reaching latitudes. Not that she's above chicken and dumplings (i.e., the free-range Rocky

Range chicken stewed in savory sage gravy) or even a good ol' American burger (beef from Marin County's hormone-free Niman-Schell Farms, fresh-baked buns, Thai chile sauce, organic greens, and house-made ketchup). Even the restaurant's neo-bronze decor and hand-blown Mexican glassware are dazzling works of art. Go Shannon. ■ *250 Main St (downtown, across from Bookends), Point Arena; (707)882-3001; $$; beer and wine; no credit cards; checks OK; dinner Wed–Sun (winter hours may vary).* &

## LODGINGS

**Coast Guard House** ★★ Poised high above Arena Cove, this historic Cape Cod–style cottage was originally built by the Life-Saving Service in 1901 to lodge crew members. Beacon lamps, anchors, and a sea captain's hat tossed haphazardly on a table evoke memories of Point Arena's seafaring past, but the inn's Arts and Crafts interiors remain simple and uncluttered. The six guest rooms have all-cotton linens and fluffy down comforters and are stocked with organic soaps, shampoo, conditioner, and body lotion. The Surfman Cove Room, with windows on three sides, has a beautiful view of the ocean and cove, a wood-burning stove, and a sunken Japanese tub. Top choice is the separate Boathouse Cottage, a replica of the original Generator House (except for the spa tub for two, Swedish wood-burning stove, and private patio overlooking the cove). An ocean-view hot tub is available for guests. Breakfast, served by amiable innkeepers Mia and Kevin Gallagher, is included with the room. ■ *695 Arena Cove (off Iversen Ave, 1 mile W of town), Point Arena; (707)882-2442 or (800)524-9320; coast@mcn.org; mail: PO Box 117, Point Arena, CA 95468; www.coastguardhouse.com; $$$; MC, V; checks OK.*

## ELK

Once known as Greenwood, this tiny former logging town was renamed Elk by the postal service when someone realized there was another town in California called Greenwood. For a such a small community (population 250) it sure has a booming tourist trade: six inns, four restaurants, and one authentic Irish pub. Its close proximity to the big tourist town of Mendocino, a mere 30-minute drive up the coast, is one reason for its popularity. Elk's paramount appeal, however, is its dramatic shoreline; the series of immense sea stacks here create one of the most awesome seascapes on the California coast.

## RESTAURANTS

**Harbor House Restaurant** ★★★ The four-course prix-fixe dinners served at the Harbor House Restaurant change nightly, but they always begin with a small, hot-from-the-oven loaf of bread that's perfect for sopping up the chef's delicious soups, such as the tomato-basil or Indian spice-spinach. The salad, made from homegrown vegetables, might be a combination of greens tossed with an herb vinaigrette or sprouts mixed with olives, water chestnuts, and a toasted sesame-seed dressing. The seafood is harvested from local waters, and the meats and cheeses come from nearby farms. Expect to find entrees such as ravioli stuffed with crab, fennel, and shiitakes in a Pernod cream sauce or seared sea scallops on roasted-yellow-pepper rouille with Spanish basmati pilaf. Many of the fine wines offered are locally produced. To take full advantage of the restaurant's spectacular view, beg for a window table (alas, you can't reserve a particular table). The only seating (which is very limited when the inn is full) is at 7pm and reservations are required. ■ *5600 Hwy 1 (in the Harbor House Inn, at the N end of town), Elk; (707)877-3203; mail: PO Box 369, Elk, CA 95432; $$$; beer and wine; no credit cards; checks OK; dinner every day.*

**Greenwood Pier Café** ★  Most of the herbs and vegetables served in this cafe come straight from the elaborate gardens behind the restaurant, and all of the breads and pastries are baked on-site. Try the walnut-corn waffle for breakfast and the black bean chili with polenta for lunch. Dinner items on the daily changing menu range from baked salmon in puff pastry to fresh summer veggies with baked polenta. Prices are very reasonable, and the ambience is pleasantly informal and relaxed. ■ *5926 Hwy 1 (in the center of town), Elk; (707)877-9997; www.elkcoast.com/greenwoodpier; $$; beer and wine; AE, MC, V; local checks only; breakfast, lunch, dinner every day May 15 to Oct 31 (Fri–Mon Nov 1 to May 15).*

## LODGINGS

**Greenwood Pier Inn** ★★★  What separates this cliff-top wonder from the dozens of other precariously perched inns along Highway 1 are its rooms' fantastic interiors and the brilliant flower gardens gracing the property. The inn offers 11 guest rooms, including three detached cliff-hanging suites (Cliff-house and the two Sea Castles) and the separate Garden Cottage. Most of the units have private decks with stunning views of Greenwood Cove, and all guests have access to a hot tub on the cliff's edge. The whimsical, avant-garde decor and tile and marble detailing in most of the rooms are the work of proprietor/artist Kendrick Petty. Some units also feature Kendrick's colorful airbrush collages, and all the rooms have private baths, fireplaces or wood-burning stoves, and stereos. The elegantly rustic Cliffhouse is a favorite, with its expansive deck, marble fireplace, Jacuzzi, and Oriental carpets. While the suites and castles are rather expensive, the rooms in the main house are moderately priced. Room rates include a continental breakfast delivered to your doorstep, and you can even have dinner from the cafe (see review, above) brought to your room. ■ *5926 Hwy 1 (in the center of town), Elk; (707) 877-9997; mail: PO Box 336, Elk, CA 95432; www.elkcoast.com/greenwoodpier; $$–$$$; beer and wine; AE, MC, V; local checks only; breakfast, lunch, dinner every day May 15 to Oct 31 (Fri–Mon Nov 1 to May 15).*

**Harbor House Inn** ★★★  In 1985, Helen and Dean Turner converted this palatial redwood house—perched on a bluff above Greenwood Landing—into the Harbor House Inn, adding six guest rooms, four cottages, and an exceptional restaurant (see review, above). Top picks are the Harbor Room, a romantic boudoir with a fireplace and a breathtaking view of the cliffs and surf, and the Lookout Room, a smaller, less expensive unit with a small private balcony that overlooks Greenwood Landing. Any old room will do, however, since you will probably want to spend most of your time relaxing in the fabulous garden or down at the private beach. Breakfast and dinner are included in the room rates. ■ *5600 Hwy 1 (at the N end of town), Elk; (707) 877-3203; mail: PO Box 369, Elk, CA 95432; $$$; beer and wine; no credit cards; checks OK; dinner every day.*

▼

## ALBION

A renowned haven for pot growers until an increase in police surveillance and property taxes drove most of them away, Albion is more a free-spirited ideal community than an actual town. You'll know you're there when you cross a white wooden bridge; it was built in 1944 (steel and reinforced concrete were unavailable during World War II) and it's the last of its kind on Highway 1.

### *RESTAURANTS*

**Albion River Inn Restaurant** ★★  Chef Stephen Smith presides over the Albion Inn's ocean-view dining room, where fresh local produce complements such dishes as braised Sonoma rabbit, grilled sea bass, and rock shrimp pasta. The extensive wine list has a good selection of hard-to-find North Coast labels. Arrive before nightfall to ooh and aah over the view. ■ *3790 Hwy 1 (on the NW side of the Albion bridge), Albion; (707) 937-1919 or (800) 479-7944; ari@mcn.org; www.albionriverinn.com; $$$; full bar; AE, MC, V; checks OK; dinner every day.* Ᏹ

**The Ledford House Restaurant** ★★  It's rare when an ocean-view restaurant's food is as good as the view, but owners Lisa and Tony Geer manage to pull it off, serving Provençal-style cuisine in a wonderfully romantic cliff-top setting. The menu, which changes monthly, offers a choice of bistro dishes, such as Antoine's Cassoulet (lamb, pork, garlic sausage, and duck confit slowly cooked with white beans), rack of lamb, and roast duckling. Vegetarian entrees and soups are always featured as well. With a view like this, a window table at sunset is a must. After dinner, saddle up to the bar and listen to the live music, which is featured nightly. ■ *3000 Hwy 1 (take the Spring Grove Rd exit W off Hwy 1), Albion; (707) 937-0282; $$$; full bar; AE, DC, MC, V; checks OK; dinner Wed–Sun.* ♿

### LODGINGS

**Albion River Inn** ★★★ After a long period of ups and downs, this modern seaside inn, poised high above Albion Cove where the Albion River meets the sea, is now one of the finest on the California coast. All 20 of the individually decorated New England–style cottages are equipped with antique and contemporary furnishings, private baths, queen- and king-size beds, fireplaces, and a bodacious array of potted plants. The clincher, though, is the private spa tub for two that overlooks the headlands and ocean. (All rooms have the same ocean view, but all do not have the spa tubs, so be sure to ask for one—it's well worth the added expense.) Breakfast, served in the restaurant (see review, above), is included in the rates. ■ *3790 Hwy 1 (on the NW side of the Albion bridge), Albion; (707) 937-1919 or (800) 479-7944; mail: PO Box 100, Albion, CA 95410; ari@mcn. org; www.albionriverinn.com; $$$; full bar; AE, MC, V; checks OK; dinner every day.* ♿

## LITTLE RIVER

Once a bustling logging and shipbuilding community, Little River is now more like a precious suburb of Mendocino. The town does a brisk business handling the tourist overflow from its neighbor 2 miles up the coast. Vacationers in the know reserve a room in serene Little River and make forays into Mendocino for dining and shopping.

Just south of Little River off Highway 1 is the gorgeous **Van Damme State Park**, a 2,337-acre preserve blanketed with ferns and second-growth redwoods; (707) 937-5804. The park has a small beach, a visitors center, and a campground, but among its main attractions are the 15 miles of spectacularly lush trails—ideal for a stroll or a jog—that start at the beach and wind through the redwood-covered hills. Fern Canyon Trail is the park's most popular route, an easy and incredibly scenic 2½-mile hiking and bicycling path that crosses over the Little River. You can also hike or drive (most of the way) to Van Damme's peculiar Pygmy Forest, an eerie scrub forest of waist-high stunted trees. To reach the Pygmy Forest by car, follow Highway 1 south of the park and turn up Little River Airport Road, then head uphill for 2¾ miles.

## RESTAURANTS

**Heritage House Restaurant** ★★★ The Heritage House Restaurant was once considered the premier restaurant on the Mendocino coast, but after years of resting on its laurels it fell far from grace, losing many of its customers to better (and far less expensive) restaurants such as Cafe Beaujolais. But the wheel turns, and with the new addition of award-winning chef de cuisine Lance Dean Velasquez (voted Best New Chef in America by *Food & Wine* magazine in 1996), the Heritage House Restaurant is back in the running among the North Coast's finest restaurants. Velasquez's menu changes seasonally, and might include winter beef stew with smoked bacon, turnips, and potatoes, or grilled Bradley Ranch New York strip with horseradish smashers and Jack Daniels sauce. Gone are the prix-fixe menu, the mandatory coat-and-tie rule, and the exorbitant prices. As always, dinner is served in several elaborate dining rooms, many reminiscent of a swank men's club, but the most spectacular is the main dining area, a domed room featuring a pastel fruit-and-flower fresco painted by local artist Stefan Kehr. Wine director William Harris's wine list ranks among the top in the country. Reservations are required for dinner. ▪ *5200 Hwy 1 (in Heritage House inn, S of Van Damme State Park), Little River, CA 95456; (707)937-5885 or (800)235-5885; www. heritage-house-inn.com; $$$; full bar; MC, V; checks OK; breakfast Mon–Fri, brunch Sat–Sun, dinner every day (closed Thanksgiving through Christmas and Jan 2 to President's Day in Feb).* &

▼

**Little River**

*Lodgings*

▲

## LODGINGS

**Glendeven Inn** ★★★ A few years ago Glendeven was named one of the 12 best inns in America by *Country Inns* magazine, and rightly so. Jan and Janet deVries' stately 19th-century farmhouse resides among 2½ acres of well-tended gardens and heather-covered headlands that extend all the way to the blue Pacific. The 10 spacious rooms and suites feature an uncluttered mix of country antiques and contemporary art that show off Janet's interior-design skills and Jan's fine carpentry work. For the ultimate in luxury, stay in the Pinewood or Bayloft Suites in the Stevenscroft Annex—each has a sitting parlor, a fireplace, and a partial view of the ocean. The cozy East Farmington Room, with its private garden deck and fireplace, is another good choice. Above the Glendeven Gallery, the inn's fine-arts boutique, sits the fabulous Barn House Suite, a two-story, redwood-paneled house ideal for families or two couples. After breakfast, which is included with your room, walk to the beautiful, fern-rimmed canyon trails in nearby Van Damme State Park. ▪ *8221 Hwy 1 (2 miles S of Mendocino), Little River, CA 95456; (707)937-0083 or (800)822-4536; www.innaccess.com/gdi/; $$$; AE, MC, V; checks OK.*

**Heritage House** ★★★ Immortalized as the ultimate bed-and-breakfast lodge in the movie *Same Time, Next Year*, Heritage House has a history well suited to Hollywood melodrama: its secluded farmhouse was used as a safe house for smugglers of Chinese laborers during the 19th century, for rumrunners during Prohibition, and for the notorious bandit "Baby Face" Nelson during the '30s. Since 1949, however, the Dennen family has opened the three guest rooms in the main building, the 63 cottages, and the detached 1877 farmhouse to a considerably tamer crowd. Heritage House sits on a cliff overlooking a rocky cove, surrounded by 37 acres of cypress trees, bountiful flower and vegetable gardens, and expansive green lawns. The best rooms are the cliff-hanging Same Time and Next Year Cottages with their king-size beds, fireplaces, and extraordinary ocean views (the Next Year Cottage also has a Jacuzzi tub). Room rates used to include breakfast and dinner at the **Heritage House Restaurant** (see review, above), but the management has since dropped this requirement (and, accordingly, lowered the room rates). The lodge is closed for parts of the winter, so call ahead and be sure to make reservations far in advance. ■ *5200 Hwy 1 (S of Van Damme State Park), Little River, CA 95456; (707)937-5885 or (800)235-5885; www. heritage-house-inn.com; $$$; full bar; MC, V; checks OK; breakfast Mon–Fri, brunch Sat–Sun, dinner every day (closed Thanksgiving through Christmas and Jan 2 to President's Day in Feb).* ♿

**Stevenswood Lodge** ★★★ Stevenswood Lodge is for people who want the comforts of a modern hotel—cable television, telephone, refrigerator, honor bar—without feeling like they're staying at a Holiday Inn. As it works out, not many Holiday Inns are surrounded on three sides by a verdant 2,400-acre forest, or located just a quarter-mile from the Mendocino shoreline, or embellished with sculpture gardens and contemporary-art displays throughout the grounds. Built in 1988, the lodge's one wheelchair-accessible room and nine suites are outfitted with hand-crafted burl-maple furniture, large windows with striking vistas (some with a partial ocean view), private bathrooms, and access to several shared decks. The Pullen Room has a particularly pleasant view of the forest and gardens. Recent additions to the lodge include a restaurant offering gourmet breakfasts to guests and the public, as well as two spas set within the forest canyon (one spa is available to all guests and the other is private and may be reserved by guests on an hourly basis). ■ *8211 Hwy 1 (2 miles S of Mendocino), Little River; (707)937-2810 or (800)421-2810; mail: PO Box 170, Mendocino, CA 95460; info@stevenswood.com; www. stevenswood.com; $$$; AE, DIS, MC, V; checks OK, breakfast every day.* ♿

**The Inn at Schoolhouse Creek** ★★ Whereas most small inns located along the Mendocino coast have to make do with an acre or less, the Inn at Schoolhouse Creek has the luxury of spreading its nine private, immaculate cottages amidst 10 acres of beautiful flower gardens, lush meadows, and cypress groves. As a result, the instant you pull into the driveway you feel like you've gotten away from it all and have entered a more tranquil environment. Most of Schoolhouse Creek's cottages sleep two, though a few can fit small families. Our favorites are the turn-of-the-century cottages, particularly the very quaint Cypress Cottage with its own private yard graced by an inviting pair of Adirondack chairs. ■ *7051 N Hwy 1 (just S of town), Little River, CA 95456; (707)937-5525 or (800)731-5525; www. innatschoolhousecreek. com; $$; MC, V; checks OK.* ♿

**Little River Inn and Restaurant** ★★ Set on a 225-acre parcel of ocean-front land, the Little River Inn is an ideal retreat for those North Coast travelers who simply can't leave their golf clubs or tennis rackets at home; it's often jokingly referred to as the poor man's Pebble Beach. Susan McKinney, her husband Mel, and brother Danny own and operate the inn and restaurant (as well as the nine-hole golf course, driving range, putting green, and two lighted championship tennis courts). All of the estate's 65 rooms and cottages offer spectacular ocean views, many feature fireplaces, and some also have Jacuzzis (and if you prefer to relax indoors, check out the inn's extensive video library). The antique-filled rooms in the main Victorian house are preferable to the north wing's motel-style units, which suffer from uninspired decor.

The **Little River Inn Restaurant** is a casual place for breakfast or dinner, but, oddly enough, is the only room at the inn without an ocean view. Chef Silver Canul maintains the house tradition of using mostly local products: fresh fish from nearby Noyo Harbor; lamb, beef, and potatoes from the town of Comptche; and greens and vegetables from local gardens. For breakfast try the popular Ole's Swedish Pancakes. ■ *7750 Hwy 1 (across from the Little River Market and Post Office, S of Mendocino), Little River, CA 95456; (707)937-5942 or (888)466-5683; lri@mcn.org; www.littleriverinn.com; $$$; full bar; MC, V; checks OK; breakfast, dinner every day.* ♿

**Rachel's Inn** ★★ Strategically sandwiched between Van Damme State Park and the Mendocino headlands is Rachel Binah's 1860s Victorian farmhouse, one of the best bed and breakfasts on the Mendocino coast. Each of the six rooms and three suites has a queen-size bed with a fluffy comforter, a private bath, and original artwork (including some by Rachel); six rooms also have fireplaces. The Parlor Suite is the most luxurious and spacious of the lot, although it's subject to highway noise and the hubbub of people eating breakfast on the other side of its French doors (not a good combo for late sleepers). A quieter unit is the Blue Room, with a balcony overlooking the back garden, meadow, and trees, or the Mezzanine Suite, which comes with a private sitting room, balcony, fireplace, and views of the park meadows. The inn's main attraction is Rachel, a vivacious innkeeper who spends her time campaigning to protect our nation's coastline from offshore oil drilling when she's not busy welcoming guests or preparing one of her grand breakfasts. ■ *8200 N Hwy 1 (2 miles S of Mendocino), Little River; (707)937-0088 or (800)347-9252; mail: PO Box 134, Mendocino, CA 95460; www.rachelsinn.com; $$$; MC, V; checks OK.* &

## MENDOCINO

The grande dame of Northern California's coastal tourist towns, this refurbished replica of a New England-style fishing village—complete with a white-spired church—has managed to retain more of its charm and allure than most North Coast vacation spots. Motels, fast-food chains, and anything hinting of development are strictly forbidden here (even the town's only automated teller is subtly recessed into the historic Masonic Building), resulting in the almost-passable illusion that Mendocino is just another quaint little coastal community. Try to find a parking space, however, and the illusion quickly fades; even the 4-hour drive fails to deter hordes of Bay Area residents.

Founded in 1852, Mendocino is still home to a few anglers and loggers, although writers, artists, actors, and other urban transplants now far outnumber the natives. In fact, Mendocino County is rumored to have the highest percentage of Ph.D.s of any rural county in the country. Spring is the best time to visit, when parking spaces are plentiful and the climbing tea roses and wisteria are in full bloom. Start with a casual tour of the town, and end with a stroll around Mendocino's celebrated headlands. Suddenly the long drive and inflated room rates seem a trivial price to pay for visiting one of the most beautiful places on earth.

To tour Mendocino proper, lose the car and head out on foot to the **Tote Fête Bakery** at 10450 Lansing Street at Albion Street, (707)937-3383. Fuel up with a double capp and cinnamon bun, then throw away your map of the town and start walking—the shopping district of Mendocino is so small it can be covered in less than an hour, so why bother planning your attack? One must-see shop is the **Gallery Bookshop & Bookwinkle's Children's Books**, one of the best independent bookstores in Northern California with a wonderful selection of books for kids, cooks, and local-history buffs; it's located at Main and Kasten Streets, (707)937-BOOK. Another is **Mendocino Jams & Preserves**, a town landmark at 440 Main Street that offers free tastings—à la cute little bread chips—of its luscious marmalades, dessert toppings, mustards, chutneys, and other spreads; (707) 937-1037 or (800)708-1196.

As with many towns that hug the Northern California coast, Mendocino's premier attractions are provided by Mother Nature and the Department of Parks and Recreation, which means they're free (or nearly free). **Mendocino Headlands State Park**, the grassy stretch of land between the village of Mendocino and the ocean, is one of the town's most popular sites. The park's flat, 3-mile trail winds along the edge of a heather-covered bluff, providing spectacular sunset views and good lookout points for seabirds and California gray whales. The headlands' main access point is at the west end of Main Street—or skip the footwork altogether and take the scenic motorist's route along Heeser Drive off Lansing Street.

About 2 miles north of Mendocino off Highway 1 is the worst-kept secret on the coast: **Russian Gulch State Park**, a veritable paradise for campers, hikers, and abalone divers. After paying a $5 entry fee, pick up a trail map at the park entrance and find the path to **Devil's Punch Bowl**—a 200-foot-long, sea-carved tunnel that has partially collapsed in the

*Mendocino*

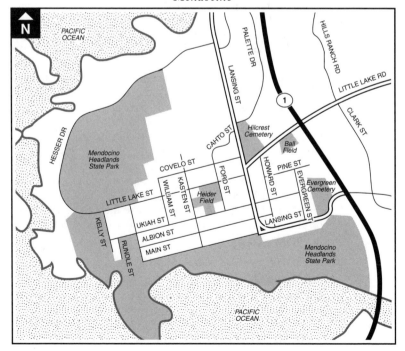

center, creating an immense blowhole that's particularly spectacular during a storm. Even better is the 5½-mile round-trip hike along **Falls Loop Trail** to the **Russian Gulch Falls,** a misty 35-foot waterfall secluded in the deep old-growth forest; for more park information call (707)937-5804.

If you have a passion for plants and flowers, spend a few bucks on the admission fee to the **Mendocino Coast Botanical Gardens,** located 2 miles south of Fort Bragg, at 18220 Highway 1, (707)964-4352. The nonprofit gardens feature 47 acres of plants—ranging from azaleas and rhododendrons to dwarf conifers and ferns—as well as a picnic area, retail nursery, gift store, and the popular Gardens Grill restaurant (see review under Fort Bragg).

The black sheep of Mendocino's hiking trails is **Jug Handle State Reserve's Ecological Staircase Trail.** Perhaps people think it's not worth the effort because it's free and "educational," but this 5-mile round-trip trail is a wonderful hike and gets surprisingly little traffic. The attraction is a series of naturally formed, staircase-like bluffs—each about 100 feet higher and 100,000 years older than the one below it—that differ dramatically in ecological formation: from beaches to headlands to an amazing pygmy forest filled with waist-high, century-old trees. The trail entrance is located on Highway 1, 1½ miles north of the town of Caspar, between Mendocino and Fort Bragg; (707)937-5804.

After a full day of adventuring, why not top off the evening with a little nightcap and music? If you appreciate classical tunes and warm snifters of brandy, take a stroll down Mendocino's Main Street to the elegant bar and lounge at the **Mendocino Hotel and Restaurant** (see review, below) at 45080 Main Street, (707)937-0511. If blue jeans and baseball caps are more your style, hang out with the guys at **Dick's Place,** which has the cheapest drinks in town and the sort of jukebox-'n'-jiggers atmosphere you'd expect from this former logging town's oldest bar; 45080 Main Street, next to the Mendocino Hotel, (707)937-5643. For a rowdy night of dancing and drinking, head a few miles up Highway 1 to **Caspar Inn,** the last true roadhouse in California where everything from rock and jazz to reggae and blues is played live Thursday through Sunday nights starting at 9:30pm; take the Caspar Road exit off Highway 1, 4 miles north of Mendocino and 4 miles south of Fort Bragg, (707)964-5565.

## RESTAURANTS

**Cafe Beaujolais** ★★★ Cafe Beaujolais started out as the finest little breakfast and lunch place in Mendocino. Then, over the years, owner Margaret Fox (author of two best-selling cookbooks, *Cafe Beaujolais* and *Morning Food*) and her husband, Chris Kump, managed to turn this modest Victorian house into one of the most celebrated restaurants in Northern California. Unfortunately, now that Margaret and Chris spend half their time in Austria running their recently inherited castle-cum-bed-and-breakfast-inn (not to mention tending to their newly adopted baby), the kitchen doesn't always turn out such stellar four-star fare as it once did, but the food is still quite good. When chef Kump is in town he usually takes charge of the kitchen, where his weekly changing dinner menu might feature entrees such as roast free-range chicken with kumquat sauce and chickpea pancakes; salt cod bouillabaisse with local rockfish, mussels, and shrimp; or Niman-Schell steak served with yellow mashed potatoes and green beans. Listed under "Of Course" are a sinful array of desserts such as the chocolate hazelnut *fragilite*, a soft nut meringue layered with ganache (a rich semisweet chocolate icing) and served with Frangelico whipped cream. Try to avoid sitting in the bustling bench section, which has itsy-bitsy tables; rather, opt for the enclosed atrium overlooking the garden. ■ *961 Ukiah St (at Evergreen St, on the E end of town), Mendocino; (707)937-5614; www. cafebeaujolais.com; $$$; beer and wine; DIS, MC, V; checks OK; dinner every day.*

**MacCallum House Restaurant ★★★** Using the freshest ingredients—seafood straight from the coast, organic meats and produce from neighboring farms and ranches—chef/owner Alan Kantor whips up some wonderful North Coast cuisine. Entrees on the seasonally changing menu may range from roasted Pacific salmon with saffron-pistachio risotto and arugula pesto to pan-seared duck confit with huckleberry-honey vinegar sauce. Lighter and less expensive fare, such as the delicious pan-charred rock-cod tacos with handmade corn tortillas, are served at the adjoining **Grey Whale Bar & Cafe**, a nice alternative for those who wish to forgo a formal dinner in the elegant dining room. The MacCallum House also hosts a weekend brunch, offering such treats as Grand Marnier French toast with pistachio butter and organic maple syrup. ■ *45020 Albion St (between Kasten and Lansing Sts), Mendocino; (707)937-5763; $$$; full bar; MC, V; checks OK; brunch Sat–Sun, dinner every day (closed Jan to mid-Feb).*

**955 Ukiah Street Restaurant ★★★** This relatively unknown Mendocino restaurant is described by local epicureans as "the sleeper restaurant on the coast." The powers behind the restaurant's doors are Jamie and Peggy Griffith, who have managed to turn 995 Ukiah into a serious (and slightly less expensive) rival to its more famous neighbor, Cafe Beaujolais. The dramatic interior, with its split-level dining room, 20-foot ceilings, rustic wood-trimmed walls, and elegant table settings, sets the mood for the haute cuisine, which might include seared pork loin stuffed with prosciutto, crispy duck

**Mendocino**

*Restaurants*

served with ginger-apple brandy sauce, and a thick swordfish steak resting in a red chile-tomatillo sauce. The upstairs section can get cramped and a little noisy, so try to sit downstairs—preferably at the corner window table—where the vaulted ceiling imparts a comfortable sense of space. ■ *955 Ukiah St (next to Cafe Beaujolais), Mendocino; (707) 937-1955; $$$; beer and wine; MC, V; checks OK; dinner Wed–Sun.* ♿

**The Mousse Café ★★** Rising triumphantly from its ashes—literally—this small, popular cafe has made an amazing comeback after burning to the ground a few years back. Formerly known as the haunt for Mendocino's confessed chocoholics, the Mousse has switched to a more substantial (read healthier) menu that makes the most of local and organic meats, herbs, and vegetables (the caesar salad, fashioned with a perfect balance of Parmesan and a robust smack of garlic, is particularly good). The result? Make a reservation, because there's usually a waiting list for dinner. Of course, dessert (especially the chocolate kind) is as good as it ever was. ■ *390 Kasten St (at the corner of Albion St), Mendocino; (707) 937-4323; $$; beer and wine; no credit cards; checks OK; brunch Sun, lunch, dinner every day (closed in Jan).*

**Mendocino Café ★** The Mendocino Café is one of the last vestiges of the Mendocino of the '60s. Everyone from nursing mothers to tie-dyed teenagers to Gap-clad couples queues up for the cafe's eclectic mix of Asian and Mexican specialties, served fresh and fast. The hands-down winner is the Thai burrito, a steamed flour tortilla filled with brown rice, sautéed vegetables, a healthy dash of the cafe's fresh chile sauce, and a choice of smoked chicken, pork, or beef. The hot Thai salad, spicy nachos, and barbecued half chicken are also good bets. Xenophobes needn't worry: there's also good ol' American food like salads, steaks, and fresh fish, as well as macaroni and cheese for the kids. If the weather's mild, grab a table on the deck. ■ *10451 Lansing St (at the corner of Albion St), Mendocino; (707) 937-2422; $; beer and wine; DC, DIS, MC, V; checks OK; brunch Sat–Sun, lunch Mon–Fri, dinner every day.*

### LODGINGS

**Agate Cove Inn ★★★** Completely renovated in 1995 with light pine furnishings and "casual country" decor, the cottages at Agate Cove offer seclusion, privacy, and views that in-town B&Bs just can't match. All but one of the 10 cottages have good views of the ocean, king- or queen-size beds, TVs with VCRs (and a free video library), wood-burning stoves, and private decks. In the morning you'll find the *San Francisco Chronicle* on your doorstep, and you can peruse the paper at your leisure over a bountiful country breakfast in the main house's enclosed porch. ■ *11201 N Lansing St (½ mile N* of downtown), Mendocino; (707)937-0551 or (800)527-3111; mail: PO Box 1150, Mendocino, CA 95460; www.agatecove. com; AE, MC, V; checks OK.

**Cypress Cove** ★★★ Hidden among the cypress trees that encircle the bluff across the bay from Mendocino is Suzanne and Jim Hay's Cypress Cove, a pair of bright, modern suites stacked atop each other in a fashion that results in one of the best views of the Mendocino Coast. Each abode is lavishly appointed with a wood-burning fireplace, fully equipped kitchen, spa tub, separate shower, stereo, and TV with a VCR, but it's the stellar views from the large bay windows and private deck that will make you fall instantly in love with this place. Trust us: if you're looking for a romantic weekend retreat, this is where you want to be. ■ *On Chapman Dr (off Hwy 1 at the S end of Mendocino Bay; call for directions), Mendocino; (707)937-1456 or (800)942-6300; mail: PO Box 303, Mendocino, CA 95460; jimbay@mcn.org; www.cypresscove.com; $$$; MC, V; checks OK.*

**Joshua Grindle Inn** ★★★ The most authentic of Mendocino's many New England-style B&Bs, this masterpiece was built in 1879 by the town's banker, Joshua Grindle. Startlingly white against a backdrop of wind-whipped cypress trees, the two-story beauty has lovely bay windows and a wraparound front porch trimmed with gingerbread arches. There are five Early American rooms in the clapboard house (including one with a whirlpool tub and fireplace), two in the cottage, and three in an old-fashioned water tower set back in the trees. Top picks are any of the cute water-tower rooms or the Library Room with its country-pine furnishings, four-poster bed, and 19th-century hand-decorated tiles encircling the fireplace. All of the rooms have sitting areas and private baths. The large front lawn and garden, equipped with a pair of Adirondack chairs and a redwood picnic table, is an ideal place to relax in the sun. ■ *44800 Little Lake Rd (at the road's E end), Mendocino; (707)937-4143 or (800)GRINDLE; mail: PO Box 647, Mendocino, CA 95460; joshgrin@joshgrin.com; www.joshgrin.com; $$$; MC, V; checks OK for reservations only if received 1 month in advance.*

**The Stanford Inn by the Sea ■ Big River Lodge** ★★★ Hats off to Joan and Jeff Stanford, the environmentally conscious couple who turned this parcel of prime coastal property and the former Big River Lodge into something more than a magnificent resort. It's a true ecosystem, a place where plants, animals, and people coexist in one of the most unforgettable lodging experiences in California. Upon entering the estate you'll see several tiers of raised garden beds, where a wide variety of vegetables, herbs, spices, and edible flowers are organically grown for local grocers and restaurants. Watching your every move as you proceed up the driveway are the

Stanfords' extended family of 14 curious llamas, which, besides providing an endless source of entertainment, do their part in fertilizing the gardens. Guests may also bring along their own menagerie of critters, be it a pet dog, cat, parrot, or iguana—it's all part of the Stanfords' commitment to animal equality. Also on the grounds is a gigantic, plant-filled greenhouse that encloses a grand swimming pool, sauna, and spa. And if all this doesn't provide you with enough diversions, there's also a mountain-bike and canoe shop on the property; you can borrow a bike and pedal along several tree-lined trails or slip into a canoe and paddle through the Big River's pristine estuaries.

The inn's 23 rooms and 10 suites display a mixture of styles, from units with dark wood walls, deep burgundy furnishings, and four-poster beds to sun-streaked suites with pine-wood interiors, country antiques, and sleigh beds topped with down comforters. All of the rooms feature decks with ocean views, fireplaces or Waterford stoves, TVs with VCRs, telephones, and sitting areas. The isolated, utterly romantic River Cottage sits right on the water's edge—an ideal honeymooners' hideaway. A cooked-to-order full breakfast, afternoon snacks, and evening wine and hors d'oeuvres are included in the price. ■ *At Hwy 1 and Comptche-Ukiah Rd (¾ mile S of town), Mendocino; (707) 937-5615 or (800) 331-8884; mail: PO Box 487, Mendocino, CA 95460; stanford@stanfordinn.com; www.stanford@ stanfordinn.com; $$$; AE, DC, DIS, MC, V; checks OK.*

**John Dougherty House** ★★ This classic saltbox is a wonderful example of why so many movies supposedly set in New England (*The Russians Are Coming, Summer of '42*) are actually filmed in Mendocino. The John Dougherty House features authentic Early Americana throughout: stenciled walls, Early American furniture, and all-cotton linens on the beds. Innkeepers Marion and David Wells have given each of the six rooms touches of individual charm, but your first choice should be one of the spacious two-room suites: the Starboard Cottage, Port Cottage, or everyone's favorite, Kit's Cabin—a small private cottage hidden in the flower garden. All of the rooms have private baths, and most have a TV, a small refrigerator, and a wood-burning stove. An expansive breakfast including homemade bread and scones is served next to a crackling fire. ■ *571 Ukiah St (just W of Kasten St), Mendocino; (707) 937-5266 or (800) 486-2104; jdhbmw@mcn.org; mail: PO Box 817, Mendocino, CA 95460; www.innaccess.com/jdh/; $$$; MC, V; checks OK.*

**Mendocino Farmhouse** ★★ Once you emerge from deep within the redwood forest surrounding Marge and Bud Kamb's secluded estate, you know you're going to be very happy here. First to greet you is one of the Kambs' friendly farm dogs, followed by their can't-pet-me-enough cats, and finally the instantly likable Kambs themselves. All five rooms—filled with antique furnishings and fresh flowers from the surrounding English gardens—have private baths, queen- and king-size beds, and, if you listen carefully, echoes of the nearby ocean; all but one have fireplaces as well. A real country breakfast (straight from the chicken coop) is served each morning at tables-for-two in the sitting room, after which the dog gives free lessons in the meadow on how to loll around in the sunshine. ■ *43410 Comptche–Ukiah Rd (from Hwy 1 just S of Mendocino, turn E on Comptche–Ukiah Rd, drive 1½ miles to Olson Lane, and turn left), Mendocino; (707)937-0241 or (800)475-1536; mail: PO Box 247, Mendocino, CA 95460; mkamb@mcn.org; www.innaccess.com/mfh/; $$; MC, V; checks OK.*

**Mendocino Hotel and Restaurant** ★★ The Mendocino Hotel, built in 1878, combines modern amenities—telephones, full bathrooms, room service—with turn-of-the-century Victorian furnishings to create a romantic yesteryear setting with today's creature comforts. The hotel's 51 rooms—all decorated with quality antiques, patterned wallpapers, and old prints and photos—range from inexpensive European-style rooms with shared baths to elaborate garden suites with fireplaces, king-size beds, balconies, and parlors. Suites 225A and 225B, on the hotel's third floor, have wonderful views of Mendocino Bay from their private balconies. Other favorites are the deluxe rooms with private baths, particularly rooms 213 and 224, which face the water. Breakfast and lunch are served downstairs in the verdant **Garden Cafe**; at dinner, chef Colleen Murphy's California-style cuisine, which might include pan-seared ahi tuna, double-baked pork chops, and prime rib au jus, is offered in the adjacent **Mendocino Hotel Restaurant's** Victorian dining room. Budding sommeliers should inquire about the hotel's Winemaker Dinners, featured one Sunday a month from October through May. ■ *45080 Main St (between Lansing and Kasten Sts), Mendocino; (707)937-0511 or (800)548-0513; mail: PO Box 587, Mendocino, CA 95460; mdohotel@ mcn.org; $$$; full bar; AE, MC, V; checks OK; breakfast, lunch, dinner every day.*

▼

**Fort Bragg**

▲

## FORT BRAGG

Even Fort Bragg, Mendocino's bad-boy cousin to the north, hasn't been able to escape the relentless approach of gentrification. Originally built in 1855 as a military outpost to supervise the Pomo Indian Reservation, it's still primarily a logging and fishing town, proud of its century-old timber-and-trawler heritage. But not a year goes by in Fort Bragg without yet another commercial fishing vessel being converted into a whale-watching boat (the ultimate insult) or an unemployed logger trading his chain saw for a set of carving knives.

Fort Bragg's two largest festivals best exemplify the sociological split: **Paul Bunyan Days** on Labor Day weekend features a big parade, log-cutting races, and a demolition derby (of all things), while the annual **Whale Festival**, held the third Saturday of March, includes ranger-led talks about the cetaceans, a Whale Run, and a beer- and chowder-tasting contest. Whether this is progress or not is debatable, but, hey, at least you have a choice.

There are plenty of interesting things to do in and around Fort Bragg. If you've visited all of Mendocino's boutiques and still haven't shrugged the shopping bug, Fort Bragg's downtown area has enough shops and galleries—all within walking distance of each other—to keep you entertained for hours. Another dangerous place for a credit card is the **Fort Bragg Depot**, a 14,000-square-foot marketplace with more than 20 shops and restaurants, as well as a historical logging and railroad museum; 401 Main Street at Laurel Street, (707)964-8324.

After you've dragged your feet up and down Fort Bragg's streets, give your tired dogs an extended rest aboard the city's popular **Skunk Train** (so named because the odoriferous mix of diesel fuel and gasoline once used to power the train allowed you to smell it before you could see it). Depending on which day you depart, a steam- or diesel-electric-engine train will take you on a scenic 8-hour round-trip journey through the magnificent redwoods to the city of Willits and back again (or you can take the 3½-hour round-trip excursion to Northspur). Reservations are recommended, especially in the summer; 100 Laurel Street Depot, (707)964-6371.

One of the prettiest—and largest—public beaches on the Mendocino Coast is **MacKerricher State Park**, located 3 miles north of Fort Bragg off Highway 1. The 8-mile shoreline is the perfect place to while away an afternoon (plus it's free). The park's highlight is the **Laguna Point Seal Watching**

*Fort Bragg*

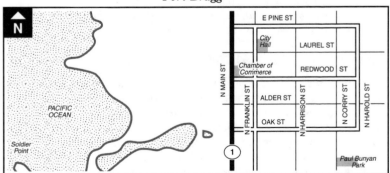

**Station**, a fancy name for a small wood deck overlooking numerous harbor seals sunning themselves on the rocks below; (707)937-5804. English and western **horseback riding** on the beach and into the redwoods is offered by Ricochet Ridge Ranch, 24201 North Highway 1, (707)964-PONY or (888)873-5777. Prices range from about $35 for a two-hour beach ride to $200 for an all-day private beach/redwoods trail ride and lunch.

Certainly among the most exciting things to come to Fort Bragg in years is the **Warehouse Repertory Theatre**, one of the hottest new theater groups in Northern California. What possessed this group of professional actors and producers— most of whom came from much bigger cities with much bigger salaries—to make the pilgrimage to the Mendocino coast? Ashland II: If a quaint little town on the Oregon border can become world-renowned, they figured, surely this one can, too. Visit their Web site at www.theatre@warerep.org, or call the 24-hour reservation and information line at (707)961-2940 for a listing of performances ranging from modern comedies to Shakespearean classics.

If you're passing through between December and April, be sure to watch the migrating California gray whales and humpback whales make their annual appearances along the North Coast. Although they're visible from the bluffs, you can practically meet the 40-ton cetaceans face to face by boarding one of the **whale-watching** boats in Fort Bragg. The *Tally Ho II* charter offers 2-hour tours for about $20 per adult, departing from the Old Fish House on North Harbor Drive in Fort Bragg; (707)964-2079. Another great way to get out on the ocean is to book a trip on one of the numerous **fishing charters** that depart from Noyo Harbor. For approximately $45 per person, which includes pole and bait, Anchor Charter Boats will take you on a 5-hour salmon- or bottom-fishing trip (whale-watching excursions are also available). No experience is necessary, and gear, instruction, and fish-cleaning services are provided; (707)964-4550.

## RESTAURANTS

**Gardens Grill** ★★ The perpetually packed parking lot is a dead giveaway to the popularity of this relatively new restaurant, located in the Mendocino Coast Botanical Gardens (for information on the gardens see Mendocino, above). The romantic alfresco seating on the elevated deck overlooking the flower gardens is the main attraction. Though the lengthy lunch menu leans heavily toward salads and sandwiches, it's the grill's fajita that takes first prize. Dinner entrees range from fresh local fish, such as pan-seared salmon with fennel ragout, to vegetarian dishes and applewood-grilled New York steak served with mashed potatoes. ■ *18220 Hwy 1 (in the*

*Mendocino Coast Botanical Gardens, S of town), Fort Bragg; (707) 964-7474; $$; beer and wine; MC, V; checks OK; brunch Sun, lunch Mon–Sat, dinner Thurs–Mon. &*

**North Coast Brewing Company** ★★ If Norm Peterson of *Cheers* died and went to heaven, he'd end up here, permanently hunched over the bar within easy reach of his own ever-flowing tap of the North Coast Brewing Company's Scrimshaw Pilsner (a Gold Medal winner at the Great American Beer Fest, the Super Bowl of beer tastings). To his right would be a bowl of the brewery's tangy Route 66 Chili, on his left a hearty plate of beef Romanov (made with braised sirloin tips, fresh mushrooms, and Russian Imperial Stout), and in front of his brewski a big platter of fresh Pacific oysters. This homey brew pub is the most happening place in town, especially at happy hour, when the bar and dark wood tables are occupied by bois-terous locals. The pub is housed in a dignified, century-old redwood structure, which in previous lives has functioned as a mortuary, an annex to the local Presbyterian Church, an art studio, and administration offices for the College of the Red-woods. Beer is brewed on the premises, in large copper vats displayed behind plate glass. A pale ale, wheat beer, stout, pil-sner, and a seasonal brew are always available, though first-timers should opt for the inexpensive four-beer sampler—or, heck, why not indulge in the eight-beer sampler?—to learn the ropes. You'll like the menu, too, which offers above average pub grub as well as more exotic fare ranging from Mayan roast pork to seafood crêpes. ■ *444 N Main St (just S of the Grey Whale Inn), Fort Bragg; (707) 964-3400; $$; beer and wine; DIS, MC, V; checks OK; lunch, dinner Tues–Sun. &*

**The Restaurant** ★ One of the oldest family-run restaurants on the coast, this small, unpretentious Fort Bragg landmark is known for its good dinners and Sunday brunches. The eclectic menu offers dishes from just about every corner of the planet: blackened New York strip steak, sweet-and-sour stir-fry, Livorno-style shellfish stew, and even scampi-style crab cakes. The comfortable booth section is the best place to sit if you want to keep an eye on the entertainment—courtesy of ebul-lient chef Jim Larsen—in the kitchen. ■ *418 N Main St (1 block N of Laurel St), Fort Bragg; (707) 964-9800; $$; beer and wine; MC, V; checks OK; brunch Sun, lunch Thurs–Fri, dinner Thurs–Tues.*

**Viraporn's Thai Café** ★ When Viraporn Lobell opened this tiny Thai cafe in 1991, Asian-food aficionados on the North Coast breathed a communal sigh of relief. Born in northern Thai-land, Viraporn attended cooking school and apprenticed in restaurants there before coming to the United States. After moving to the North Coast with her husband, Paul, she worked for a while at Mendocino's most popular restaurant,

Cafe Beaujolais. A master at balancing the five traditional Thai flavors of hot, bitter, tart, sweet, and salty, Viraporn works wonders with refreshing Thai classics such as spring rolls, satays, phad thai, lemongrass soup, and a wide range of curry dishes. ■ *500 S Main St (off Hwy 1, across from PayLess), Fort Bragg; (707)964-7931; $; beer and wine; no credit cards; checks OK; lunch Mon–Fri, dinner every day.*

## LODGINGS

**Grey Whale Inn** ★★ Wide doorways and sloped halls are the only vestiges of this popular inn's previous life as the town hospital. Owners Colette and John Bailey have successfully transformed this stately four-story building into one of the more comfortable and distinctive inns on the coast. Decorated with quilts, heirlooms, and antiques, the 14 large guest rooms have private baths and wonderful views of the town or sea. Reserve one of the two penthouse rooms: Sunrise offers a view of the town, pretty wicker furniture, and a double whirlpool bath, while Sunset opens onto a private deck overlooking the ocean. Another good choice is the spacious Campbell Suite, which comes with a marble gas-log fireplace, a TV with a VCR, a microwave oven, and a refrigerator. There's also a large rec room with a pool table and a TV. The full buffet breakfast (with trays for carrying your food back to bed, if you prefer) is included in the rates. ■ *615 N Main St (at 1st St and Hwy 1), Fort Bragg, CA 95437; (707)964-0640 or (800)382-7244; gwhale@mcn.org; www.innaccess.com/gwi; $$; AE, DIS, MC, V; checks OK.* &

## WESTPORT

If you've made it this far north, you're either lost or determined to drive the full length of Highway 1. If it's the latter, then you'd best stock up on a sandwich or two at the **Westport Community Store & Deli**, at 37001 North Highway 1, Westport, (707)964-2872, because you still have a loooong way to go.

## LODGINGS

**DeHaven Valley Farm and Restaurant** ★★★ This remote 1875 Victorian farmhouse, with its sublime rural setting and access to a secluded beach, comes complete with a barnyard menagerie of horses, sheep (including one that thinks it's a horse), goats, and donkeys. If the animals aren't enough to keep you amused, try a game of croquet or horseshoes, do a little bird-watching or horseback riding, or take a meditative soak in the hot tub set high on a hill overlooking the ocean. The inviting parlor has deep, comfortable couches, while the five guest rooms in the house and the three nearby cottages are decorated with colorful comforters and rustic antiques;

some even have fireplaces. In the morning, you'll wake to such treats as apples pancakes or potato-artichoke frittatas. The small **DeHaven Valley Farm Restaurant** offers a commendable prix-fixe four-course menu that might include entrees like roasted pork tenderloin with apple horseradish or seafood baked in filo dough with roasted pepper aioli, and a killer apple strudel for dessert. ■ *39247 Hwy 1 (1.7 miles N of town), Westport, CA 95488; (707) 961-1660; www.dehaven-valley-farm.com; $$; beer and wine; MC, V; checks OK; dinner Sat and any day 6 or more people make a reservation.*

**Howard Creek Ranch** ★★★ Located off a remote stretch of Highway 1 near the tiny town of Westport, this isolated 40-acre ranch appeals to travelers who really want to get away from it all. You'll revel in the peace and quiet of this rustic retreat, which Mendocino County has designated as a historic site. For more than two decades, proprietors Sally and Charles Grigg have been renting out three cabins, four guest rooms in the farmhouse, and four rooms in the renovated carriage barn. Set back just a few hundred yards from an ocean beach, the farmhouse and barn are on opposite sides of Howard Creek, connected by (among other routes) a 75-foot-long swinging footbridge. The rooms in the farmhouse feature separate sitting areas, antiques, and homemade quilts, while the barn units—each one handcrafted by Charles Grigg, a master builder with a penchant for skylights—have curly-grain redwood walls and Early American collectibles. The separate Beach House, with its freestanding fireplace, skylights, king-size bed, large deck, and Jacuzzi tub, is a great romantic getaway. A hot tub and sauna are perched on the side of a hill, as are Sally's guardian cows, sheep, llama, and horses. In the morning, Sally rings the breakfast bell to alert her guests that it's eatin' time—and the fare is definitely worth getting out of bed for. Note: Pet dogs are welcome with prior approval. ■ *40501 Hwy 1 (3 miles N of town), Westport; (707) 964-6725; mail: PO Box 121, Westport, CA 95488; www.HowardCreekRanch. com; $$; AE, MC, V; checks OK.*

▼

**Westport**

*Lodgings*

▲

# REDWOOD EMPIRE

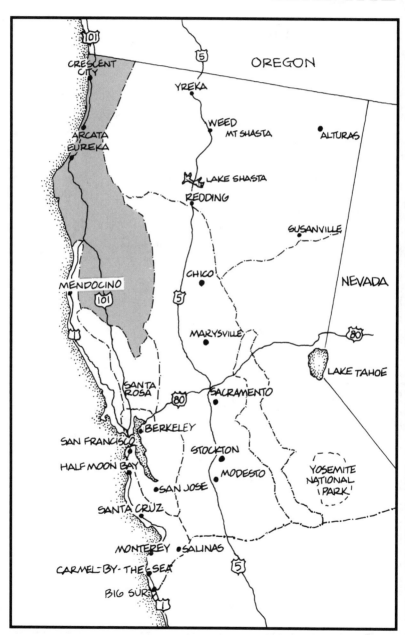

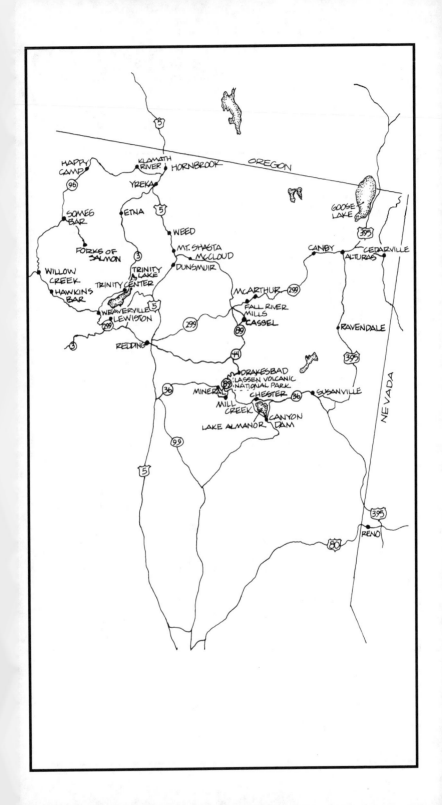

# Redwood Empire

*North on Highway 101 from Redwood Valley to
the Oregon border, with side trips to Shelter Cove,
Petrolia, Dinsmore, and Mad River.*

## REDWOOD VALLEY

### RESTAURANTS

**Broiler Steak House** ★★ The Broiler is more than a steak
house—it's a temple to meat. If you arrive without a reservation, expect to wait awhile in the giant cocktail lounge—a
good place to catch up on the latest Western fashions. Eventually you'll be ushered into the inner sanctum, where, if you're
a true believer, you'll order a juicy steak grilled (to your exact
specifications, of course) over an oakwood pit. All entrees
include a mammoth baked potato with butter, sour cream, and
chives, plus a garden-fresh dinner salad the size of your head.
■ *8400 Uva Dr (from Ukiah, drive 7 miles N on Hwy 101, take
the West Rd exit, and turn left), Redwood Valley; (707) 485-7301;
$$; full bar; AE, DIS, MC, V; checks OK; dinner every day.* &

## WILLITS

### RESTAURANTS

**Tsunami** ★★ Tsunami offers simple, healthy Japanese- and
Polynesian-inspired preparations made with organic vegeta-
bles, chicken, seafood caught right off the Mendocino coast,
and other fish such as shark, mahi-mahi, and ono, which are
flown in fresh daily. Purists may scoff at the sushi dishes,
which are all made with cooked seafood, but they've probably
never tried peddling raw fish to the locals. Still, fish this fresh
deserves to be raw. If you're a strict vegan, start with the
soothing miso soup, followed by the crisp tempura vegetables
and the Cajun tofu cubes. ■ *50 S Main St (on Hwy 101, near
Commercial St), Willits; (707) 459-4750; $; beer and wine; no
credit cards; checks OK; lunch Mon–Fri, dinner every day.* &

### LODGINGS

**Emandal Farm** ★ Since 1908 this thousand-acre working farm
situated along the Eel River has been a popular summer get-
away for Bay Area families who long for a stint on the farm.
The second and third generations of the Adams family own
and run Emandal Farm, and they happily let children and their
parents help with the daily chores, such as feeding the pigs,
milking the goats, tending the garden, and gathering eggs in

the chicken coop. The fruits of their labor are often presented hours later at mealtime. In addition to helping out on the farm, guests may enjoy the Adamses' private sandy beach on the river or explore trails meandering through the valley. At night a campfire circle inevitably forms, where parents struggle to remember old skits, ghost stories, and campfire songs.

The 13 rustic, redwood one-bedroom cabins and 4 two-bedroom cabins are nestled under a grove of oak and fir trees. They're not equipped with much—just single- and queen-size beds, cold spring water, and electricity (and *that's* it). The bathrooms and showers are housed in a separate, communal facility. The Adams family prepares a healthy, hearty breakfast, lunch, and dinner, which are included in the price. Expect to find fare like omelets stuffed with garden-fresh vegetables, spaghetti and meatballs, barbecued chicken (most likely the bird your child befriended earlier in the day), and home-baked bread. The farm is usually open to guests for weeklong stays in August and for weekend trips only in September; the schedule often changes, so call for an update. ▪ *16500 Hearst Post Office Rd (16 miles E of town; call or write for directions), Willits, CA 95490; (707)459-5439 or (800)262-9597; emandel@ pacific.net; www.pacific.net:80/~emandel/; $$ (includes meals); no alcohol (guests may bring beer and wine into the cabins); MC, V; checks OK; breakfast, lunch, dinner every day (typically open late July to late Sept).*

## GARBERVILLE

### RESTAURANTS

**Woodrose Cafe ★** This late-blooming flower-child coffee shop is the social center of Garberville—a place to eavesdrop on local gossip from a booth, table, or counter stool. Colorful artwork by local artists hangs on the plain white walls, and in back there's a small outdoor patio perfect for basking in the sun and wolfing down healthy (some would say hippie) fare such as omelets, granola, vegetarian garden burgers, organic-fruit shakes, and chunky, vegetable-based soups served with sourdough garlic bread. Organic produce is used whenever possible. Although the service is sometimes slow (especially on the patio), everything is skillfully and tastefully prepared, and you'll certainly leave feeling well nourished. ▪ *911 Redwood Dr (from Hwy 101, take the Garberville exit), Garberville; (707)923-3191; $; beer and wine; no credit cards; checks OK; breakfast every day, lunch Mon–Fri.*

### LODGINGS

**Benbow Inn ★★** From its sophisticated afternoon tea to its beautifully cultivated gardens of primroses, narcissus, tulips, and roses, this elegant Tudor-style inn built in 1926 is a little slice of England nestled in the redwoods. A National Historic Landmark, the inn (named after the family who built it) has housed such luminaries as Herbert Hoover, Eleanor Roosevelt, and Charles Laughton. The inviting lobby features a huge fireplace surrounded by comfortable sofas, Oriental carpets, and grandfather clocks, and the cherry-wood wainscoting in the hallway adds to the inn's formal elegance. The 55 guest rooms vary in size and amenities; the deluxe accommodations include private patios and Jacuzzis, fireplaces readied with kindling, and VCRs (there's a large movie library at the front desk). The least expensive rooms are small but comfortable, and while they don't have the frills of the other rooms, they are tastefully decorated with antiques.

The aristocratic dining room is lined with carved-wood and marble sideboards, and the large-paned windows provide a great view of the river and gardens. The menu changes frequently but always features seafood, beef, pasta, and poultry dishes. Dinner entrees might include fresh salmon, grilled chicken breast marinated in lime and herbs, and honey-miso-roasted pork loin served with black-eyed peas. Breakfast and lunch are served daily, and on Sunday the Benbow offers a sumptuous champagne brunch. Of course, as British etiquette dictates, tea and scones are served daily from 3pm to 4pm. The inn hosts many special events throughout the year, including a Nutcracker Christmas celebration, a New Year's dinner dance, a summer Shakespeare on the Lake festival, and a fall Murder Mystery Weekend. The Benbow has been a popular destination for years, though some guests have recently complained that the inn's staff is not as attentive as it used to be and the dining room's host can act more aristocratic than his exclusive surroundings merit. ■ *445 Lake Benbow Dr (from Hwy 101, take the Benbow Dr exit), Garberville, CA 95542; (707) 923-2124; $$$; full bar; AE, DIS, MC, V; checks OK; brunch Sun, breakfast, lunch Mon–Sat, dinner every day (lunch is not served from mid-Sept to mid-May, except on holidays; open mid-Apr to Dec 31).*

## REDWAY

### RESTAURANTS

**The Mateel Cafe** ★★ With its delicious, healthful food and lively atmosphere, the Mateel has become a social and cultural magnet for the southern Humboldt region. Lunch and dinner are served in three areas: the main dining room, which has high-backed wooden booths and a modest collection of watercolors by local artists; the African-style Jazzbo Room, decked out in giraffe decor; and the covered patio, the preferred spot on warm days and nights. A worldly selection of food is served here, ranging from roast rack of lamb to seafood linguine,

Louisiana tiger prawns, Thai tofu, and fresh seafood specials of the day. All entrees are served with appetizers, soup or salad, and house-made pita bread. If you're not up to one of the full meals, try a stone-baked pizza (there are more than 20 toppings to choose from) or a gourmet salad, such as the Napa cabbage, spinach, and chicken salad topped with tomatoes and almonds and a curry dressing. This is one of the few places in town that remains open all afternoon—perhaps in an effort to woo those numerous Humboldt County marijuana smokers suffering from a severe case of the munchies. ■ *3342 and 3344 Redwood Dr (from Hwy 101, take the Redway exit to downtown), Redway; (707)923-2030; $; beer and wine; no credit cards; checks OK; lunch, dinner Mon–Sat.*

## SHELTER COVE

### RESTAURANTS

**Cove Restaurant** ★★ At the north end of a small runway for private planes, this rather remote restaurant—selected by *Private Pilot* magazine as one of the nation's premier fly-in lunch spots—is situated in an A-frame beach house with two-story-high picture windows, an outdoor dining area, and a spectacular view of this untamed region of California known as the Lost Coast. The menu's offerings are wide ranging and well prepared: charbroiled steak cut to order, Cajun-style fish (we're talking right out of the water), grilled chicken, juicy hamburgers, and piles of fresh shellfish. All meals are served with a creamy clam chowder, a shrimp or green salad, and house-made bread. Desserts range from fresh fruit pies (snatch a slice of the wonderfully tart wild huckleberry if it's available) to chocolate mousse and cheesecake. ■ *210 Wave Dr (off Lower Pacific Dr), Shelter Cove; (707)986-1197; $$; full bar; MC, V; local checks only; lunch, dinner Thurs–Sun.*

### LODGINGS

**Shelter Cove Ocean Inn** ★★ Snoozing seals, grazing deer, and migrating whales are just some of the sights you'll see in Shelter Cove, the Lost Coast's only oceanside community. Once you leave Highway 101 in Garberville, prepare to navigate along 24 miles of steep, twisting tarmac that passes through rocky grasslands and patches of forest before reaching the cove (good brakes are a must). At the end of the journey you'll reach the Shelter Cove Ocean Inn, a handsome Victorian-style facility built smack-dab on the shoreline. The inn, which is popular with recreational pilots who can park their planes within walking distance, offers two spacious suites with sitting rooms and Jacuzzi tubs. Two smaller rooms upstairs have private baths and balconies. All rooms have an ocean view, but the panorama from the suites is definitely worth the extra expense. Since the B&B is in such a remote location, a home-cooked breakfast, lunch, and dinner may be delivered to your room upon request. Serious R&R is the theme here: lie on the sun deck overlooking the ocean, play a round of golf across the street, or walk to the nearby black sand beach, cause there ain't nothin' to do around here except relax. ▪ *148 Dolphin Dr (from Shelter Cove Rd, turn right on Upper Pacific Dr, left on Lower Pacific Dr, then right on Dolphin Dr), Shelter Cove, CA 95589; (707)986-7161; $$; AE, MC, V; checks OK.* &

## PETROLIA

### LODGINGS

**Lost Inn Bed and Breakfast** ★ As you wind along Old Mattole Road through the sleepy hamlet of Petrolia, keep a lookout for an old green tractor with a hand-painted sign that reads, "Welcome! You have just found the Lost Inn." Once you've spotted it, drive up the circular driveway lined with flowers, fruit trees, and rustic antiques, and prepare to be greeted by a friendly entourage of cats, dogs, and chickens. They belong to Gail and Phil Franklin, the friendly keepers of this remote country inn, the only B&B in the Mattole Valley. There are just two guest rooms here: a large two-room suite with a queen bed, glassed-in porch, and private entrance (parties of three or four also may rent an adjoining suite), and a much smaller room with a queen bed and couch, added in 1998. Breakfast, including eggs from their chickens and organic fruit from their trees, is served either in your room or on the porch. Solitude is this inn's selling point (you can't get any more away-from-it-all without a backpack) and it comes at a very reasonable price. You can even bring your pooch, and the Pacific Ocean is only 5 miles away. ▪ *On Old Mattole Rd (1 block from the Petrolia General Store), Petrolia; (707)629-3394; mail: PO Box 161, Petrolia, CA 95558; $; no credit cards; checks OK.*

Myers Flat

*Lodgings*

▲

## MYERS FLAT

### LODGINGS

**Myers Inn** ★ The two-story, wood-framed Myers Inn, constructed in 1860 and restored in 1906, sits just outside Humboldt Redwoods State Park in Myers Flat, a hamlet reminiscent of a cardboard-cutout saloon town. As you work your way to the inn's front desk you'll pass through a spacious lobby with a player piano, Victrola, and sofas arranged around a restored Rumford fireplace. Ten comfortable, sparkling clean guest rooms—all with private baths—have been renovated with an eye toward upscale country charm. Verandas encircle the building on both floors, providing every room with a balcony that has a view of the town, mountains, and forest. Although the inn is close to the highway, the nearby Eel River and redwoods seem to absorb most of the noise. The forest also provides plenty of superb hiking and biking trails. A continental breakfast is served to guests at the B&B, and for dinner many dine at the popular **Knights Restaurant**, (707)943-3411, across the street, which serves reasonably priced classic American fare such as steak, prime rib, and fresh seafood, including lobster. ■ *12913 Old Redwood Hwy/Ave of the Giants (in town), Myers Flat; (707)943-3259; mail: PO Box 173, Myers Flat, CA 95554; www.northcoast.com/myersinn/; $; AE, MC, V; no checks.*

## REDCREST

### RESTAURANTS

**Eternal Treehouse Cafe** ★  Located in the tiny town of Redcrest on the scenic Avenue of the Giants, the Eternal Treehouse is an all-American cafe right down to the chocolate malts, housemade pies, and country western music flowing out of the kitchen. Photos of family, friends, and passers-by even line the walls of the restaurant. This family-run cafe serves the best biscuits and gravy in the county, as well as wholesome daily specials such as corned beef and cabbage served with potatoes, carrots, and a choice of soup or salad—all for less than the price of a movie. ■ *26510 Ave of the Giants (from Hwy 101, take the Redcrest exit), Redcrest; (707)722-4247; $; no alcohol; MC, V; checks OK; breakfast, lunch, dinner every day.*

## SCOTIA

### LODGINGS

**Scotia Inn** ★★  This landmark three-story hotel constructed entirely of redwood is the pride of Scotia, one of the last company-owned towns in America. In fact, the whole town is built of redwood—no surprise once you discover the town's owner is the Pacific Lumber Company. The Scotia Inn has 2 guest rooms downstairs and 10 spacious rooms on the second floor, each gussied up with antiques and balloon drapery. The inn's private bathrooms are equipped with showers and claw-footed tubs. The bridal suite boasts a king-size bed draped with a beautiful crocheted half-canopy, plus a separate room with a hot tub.

The elaborate dining room, handsomely decorated in rust, green, and burgundy, is lit by brass chandeliers. The well-prepared lunches and dinners feature locally grown vegetables, berries, and fowl. Traditional American fare such as steak, prime rib, pheasant, and seafood are offered alongside Greek, Italian, and French entrees. Saturday and Sunday are ethnic nights, when you might find specials like Greek-style

mustard lamb or Thai-roasted pork loin. The wine list is excellent. For classic, hearty steak house fare, dine at the inn's
**Steak n' Potato Pub.** ■ *On Mill Street (directly across from the
mill; from Hwy 101, take the Scotia exit), Scotia; (707) 764-
5683; mail: PO Box 248, Scotia, CA 95565; www.scotiainn.com;
$$; full bar; MC, V; checks OK; dining room: brunch Sun, lunch
Wed–Sat, dinner Wed–Sun; pub: lunch every day May 1 to Oct
31, dinner every day year-round.*

## DINSMORE

### RESTAURANTS

**The Weekender Cafe** ★  All the proceeds of this homey, volun-
teer-run cafe support the local fire department and its three
secondhand engines. Neighbors donate the homemade rolls,
muffins, breads, pies, cakes, cookies, soups, relishes, salads,
and even the fresh flowers decorating every table. Most of the
ingredients come from local pastures, chicken coops, and gar-
dens (including sun-ripened tomatoes and sweet, freshly
picked carrots and celery) and are prepared in a family-size
kitchen behind the five-stool counter. For breakfast the staff
whips up waffles, pancakes, freshly made Danish pastries,
homemade biscuits and gravy, and a variety of egg dishes.
This is the kind of place where you help yourself to the coffee,
and if the vinyl chairs get too uncomfortable you can always
take a seat on the couch in front of the fire. ■ *On Hwy 36, near
mile marker 4400 (1½ miles E of Dinsmore, between Bridgeville
and Mad River), Dinsmore; (707) 574-6521; $; no alcohol; no
credit cards; checks OK; breakfast, lunch every day.*

## MAD RIVER

### LODGINGS

**Journey's End Resort** ★  This remote resort is settled on the
edge of little-known Ruth Lake, a well-hidden manmade lake
that's a 1½-hour winding drive from the coast. Created in 1962,
the lake is frequented by serious anglers in search of its siz-
able trout and black bass, which explains why a good number
of guests at Journey's End are fisherfolk (and the rest are typ-
ically water-skiers and jet-skiers). The motel's four no-frills
guest rooms are clean and warm, equipped with two firm
double beds and a bathroom with a shower. A cabin on the
premises sleeps up to eight people and is supplied with a dish-
washer, stove, refrigerator, and towels—all you need to bring
is food. Evening entertainment is left to the imagination rather
than the networks, and if that doesn't work, there's a game-
filled pub with a satellite TV. The resort also has a grocery
store, a laundry, and basic fishing and boating supplies.

The food at **Journey's End Restaurant** is the gastronomical equivalent of insulated underwear—it's intended to ensure survival amid the elements and not much more. Fortunately no frozen, packaged, or pretend nourishment is served here, and there's no fat- and cholesterol-free sissy fare, neither. Expect to get John Wayne-size rations prepared by wilderness wives and mothers. The house specialty is pizza made from scratch, but the majority of the dinners are range-fed (rib-eye, top sirloin, New York) and served with house-made fries, sautéed mushrooms, and grilled onions. For lunch you'll find burgers no smaller than a quarter pound as well as hot dogs and chicken. The hearty morning meals are designed to keep you fueled for the rest of the day. ▪ *200 Mad River Rd (at the NE end of Ruth Lake, 10 miles S of Hwy 36), Mad River, CA 95552; (707)574-6441; $$; seasonal full bar (Feb to Oct only), beer and wine (year-round); AE, DIS, MC, V; no checks; breakfast Sat–Sun, lunch every day, dinner Thurs–Sun (call for the winter schedule).*

## FERNDALE

Even if Ferndale isn't on your itinerary, it's worth a detour off Highway 101 to stroll for an hour or two down its colorful Main Street, browsing through the art galleries, gift shops, and cafes that are strangely reminiscent of Disneyland's "old town." Ferndale, however, is for real, and hasn't changed much since it was the agricultural center of Northern California in the late 1800s. In fact, the entire town is a National Historic Landmark because of its abundance of well-preserved Victorian storefronts, farmhouses, and homes. What *really* distinguishes Ferndale from the likes of Eureka and Crescent City, however, is the fact that Highway 101 doesn't pass through it—which means no cheesy motels, liquor stores, and fast-food chains.

For a trip back in time, view the village's interesting memorabilia—working crank phones, logging equipment, and a blacksmith shop—at the **Ferndale Museum**, 515 Shaw Street at Third Street, (707)786-4466. Not officially a museum but close enough is the **Golden Gate Mercantile** at 421 Main Street. Part of this general store hasn't been remodeled (or restocked) in 50 years, giving you the feeling that you're walking through some sort of time capsule or movie set. Far less historic but equally engrossing are the pedal-powered entries in the **World Championship Great Arcata to Ferndale Cross-Country Kinetic Sculpture Race** on display at the **Kinetic Sculpture Museum** at 580 Main Street at Shaw Street (no phone). The dusty, funky museum is unlike anything you've ever seen.

Another worthy Ferndale attraction is the leisurely drive along scenic **Centerville Road**. The 5-mile excursion starts at the west end of Main Street downtown and passes through several ranches and dairy farms on the way to the Centerville Beach County Park. If you continue beyond the park and past the retired naval facility, you'll be rewarded with an incredible view of the Lost Coast to the south. On the way back, just outside of town on the north side of the road, keep an eye out for **Fern Cottage**, a restored 1865 Victorian farmhouse built by the late state senator Joseph Russ, one of the first Ferndale settlers. Tours of the farmhouse are by appointment only; call caretaker Greg Martin (who's also an accomplished organic gardener) at (707)786-4835.

In keeping with its National Historic Landmark status, Ferndale has no movie theaters. Rather, it has something better: the **Ferndale Repertory Theatre**. Converted in 1972 from a movie theater, the 267-seat house hosts live performances by actors from all over Humboldt County. The revolving performances run pretty much year-round and range from musicals to comedies, dramas, and mysteries. Tickets are reasonably priced and, due to the popularity of the shows, reservations are advised; 447 Main Street, (707)786-5483. For more information on Ferndale's upcoming event and activities, visit the town's Web site at www.victorianferndale.org/chamber.

## RESTAURANTS

**Curley's Grill** ★★ Longtime restaurateur and Ferndale resident Curley Tait decided it was finally time to open his own business, so in April 1995 he filled the 460 Main Street vacancy (former home of the Bibo and Bear Restaurant) with Curley's Grill, and it's been a hit ever since. The reason? Curley doesn't fool around: the prices are fair, the servings are generous, the food is good, and the atmosphere is bright and cheerful. Sure bets are the grilled polenta with Italian sausage, fresh mushrooms, and sage-laden tomato sauce, or the moist tortilla-and-onion cake served with a tangy onion salsa. Indulge in the house-made breads and desserts, too. On sunny afternoons, request a seat on the shaded back patio. ■ *460 Main St (between Washington and Brown Sts), Ferndale; (707)786-9696; $; beer and wine; DIS, MC, V; checks OK; lunch, dinner every day.* &

**Stage Door Café** ★ Ferndale's top soup 'n' sandwich shop is the tiny Stage Door Café, run by Barbara and Jerry Murry. Barbara does most of the cooking, while Jerry—a real character—takes the orders and directs the foot traffic. Daily specials are posted in the front window; if one of them happens to be Orange Wonder soup, Ferndale tradition requires that you order a bowl of this puréed concoction, made from a secret recipe (hint: carrots are the key ingredient). Other top picks are the Cloverjack Melt (locally made Jack cheese, bacon, and a fried or poached egg layered on sourdough toast), Ferndale scramble, and honey-almond granola topped with fresh fruit. If you can't find a seat inside, order your food to go and dine alfresco at an outside table or on one of the many benches lining the town's main drag. ■ *451 Main St (next to the Ferndale Theatre), Ferndale; (707) 786-4675; $; no alcohol; no credit cards; checks OK; breakfast, lunch Fri–Tues.*

## LODGINGS

**The Gingerbread Mansion** ★★★ The awe-inspiring grande dame of Ferndale, this peach-and-yellow Queen Anne inn is a lavish blowout for Victoriana buffs. Gables, turrets, English gardens, and architectural gingerbread galore have made it one of the most-photographed buildings in Northern California. The mansion has been through several reincarnations since 1899, including stints as a private residence, a hospital, a rest home, an apartment building, and even an American Legion hall before Ken Torbert converted it into a B&B in 1983. All 10 guest rooms have queen- or king-size beds and private baths. The Fountain Suite boasts a grand view of Ferndale and the garden, twin claw-footed tubs for side-by-side bubble baths, a canopied bed, a fireplace, and a fainting couch. The corner Rose Suite has a wonderful view of Ferndale village through a cut-out gingerbread veranda, stained-glass windows, two fireplaces, hanging plants, and a vast, mirrored bathroom that's as big as the bedroom. For the ultimate in luxury, though, reserve the new Empire Suite, an orgy of marble and columns with twin fireplaces and a lavish bathing area. In the morning all guests awaken to a sumptuous breakfast in the formal dining room that overlooks the garden. An extravagant afternoon tea is served in one of five parlors, each handsomely furnished with Queen Anne, Eastlake, and Renaissance Revival antiques. ■ *400 Berding St (at Brown St, 1 block S of Main St), Ferndale; (707) 786-4000 or (800) 952-4136; mail: PO Box 40, Ferndale, CA 95536; kenn@humboldt1. com; www.gingerbread-mansion.com; $$$; AE, MC, V; checks OK.*

**The Shaw House Bed and Breakfast Inn** ★★★ This Carpenter Gothic beauty, the oldest house in Ferndale, is modeled after the titular manse of Hawthorne's *House of the Seven Gables*. It was built in 1854 by Ferndale founder Seth Louis Shaw and is listed on the National Register of Historic Places. Owners Norma and Ken Bessingpas meticulously restored the house and filled it with books, photographs, baskets, antiques, and all manner of memorabilia; the couple also added a gazebo and a fish pond to the inn's well-tended acre. Each of the six guest rooms has a private bath (although three of the bathrooms are down the hall), and most have bathtubs and showers. Three units—the Honeymoon Suite, the Garden Room, and the Wisteria Room—have balconies overlooking the garden, and the Shaw Room, under the central gable, features the original bed Shaw and his bride slept in during their honeymoon (though the mattress is new, of course!). In the morning, guests feast on Norma's homemade breakfast fare, which may include oven-baked Dutch babies and cheddar French toast served with dried-fruit syrup specked with apricots and currants. After breakfast, ride around town on a vintage bicycle from Ken's collection. ■ *703 Main St (just E of the downtown area), Ferndale; (707)786-9958 or (800)557-SHAW; mail: PO Box 1125, Ferndale, CA 95536; $$$; AE, MC, V; checks OK.*

## EUREKA

Named after the popular gold-mining expression "Eureka!" (Greek for "I have found it"), this town is the largest city on the North Coast (population 30,000). The heart of Eureka is **Old Town**, a 13-block stretch of shops, restaurants, and hotels, most of which are housed in painstakingly preserved Victorian structures; it's bordered by First and Third Streets, between C and M Streets. One of the finest Victorian architectural masterpieces is the multi-gabled-and-turreted **Carson Mansion**, built of redwood in 1886 for lumber baron William Carson, who initiated the construction to keep mill workers occupied during a lull in the lumber business. Although the three-story, money-green mansion is closed to the public (it's now a snooty men's club), you can stand on the sidewalk and click your Kodak at one of the state's most-photographed houses; it's located on the corner of Second and M Streets. For more Old Town history, stroll through the **Clarke Memorial Museum**, which has one of the top Native American displays in the state, showcasing more than 1,200 examples of Hupa, Yurok, and Karok basketry, dance regalia, and stonework; 240 E Street at Third Street, (707)443-1947. A block away, there's more Native American artwork, including quality silver jewelry, at the **Indian Art & Gift Shop**, which sells many of its treasures at reasonable prices; 241 F Street at Third Street, (707)445-8451.

Eureka

If you need a good book at a great price, stop by the **Bootlegger**, a marvelous bookstore in Old Town with thousands of used paperbacks (especially mysteries, westerns, and science fiction), as well as children's books and cookbooks; 402 Second Street, (707)445-1344. Or if purple potatoes, cylindra beets, and other fancy foods are on your shopping list, then you're in luck, because you'll find them at the **farmer's markets** held weekly from May through October in Eureka and Arcata. Most of the produce is grown along the local Eel and Trinity Rivers, and is sold at bargain prices at the Eureka Mall (on Highway 101 at the south end of Eureka) on Thursday from 10am to 1pm; in Eureka's Old Town on Tuesday from 10am to 1pm; and at Arcata Plaza on Saturday from 9am to 1pm.

Better yet, why not spend the day picking produce directly from the North Coast's small farms? Call the North Coast Growers Association at (707)441-9999 for a free copy of the "Farmers Market Directory & Farm Trails Guide," an annotated map of 13 local family-run farms that encourage visitors to drop by and purchase their products—vegetables, fruit, herbs, flowers, plants, and more—directly from the dirt.

Before you leave Eureka, be sure to take a bay cruise on skipper Leroy Zerlang's *Madaket*, the oldest passenger vessel on the Pacific coast. The 75-minute narrated tour—a surprisingly interesting and amusing perspective on the history of Humboldt Bay—departs daily from the foot of C Street in Eureka, and gets progressively better after your second or third cocktail. For more information, call Humboldt Bay Harbor Cruise at (707)445-1910. Afterwards, stroll over to the **Lost Coast Brewery** for a fresh pint of Alleycat Amber Ale and an order of onion rings; 617 Fourth Street, between G and H Streets, (707)445-4480.

*Eureka*

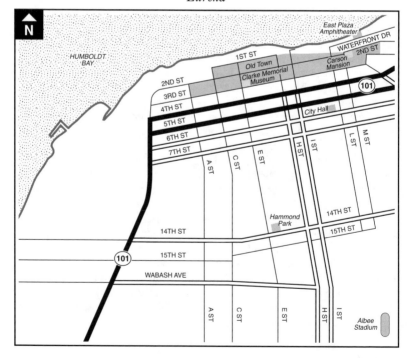

**Restaurant 301** ★★★ Chef Rodger Babel, who prides himself on using ultra-fresh ingredients, collects many of the herbs and vegetables used at Restaurant 301 (located on the first floor of Hotel Carter, see review), from the hotel gardens and gets seafood direct from local fisheries. Diners, seated at windowside tables overlooking the bay, may order from either the regular or the prix-fixe five-course dinner menu. A recent meal started with a savory satay of grilled marinated quail, followed by a garden-fresh salad topped with warmed chèvre, roasted hazelnuts, and a pear vinaigrette, and an entree of tender grilled medallions of filet mignon served with smoked oyster dressing and a green peppercorn glaze. For dessert, Christi Carter's fresh rhubarb tart drizzled with lemon-curd sauce is superb. Restaurant 301's impressive 1,200-bottle wine list received an award of excellence from *Wine Spectator* magazine. ■ *301 L St (at 3rd St in Old Town), Eureka; (707) 444-8062 or (800) 404-1390; $$$; full bar; AE, DC, DIS, MC, V; checks OK; breakfast (by reservation only for non-guests), dinner every day.* Ꮠ

**Los Bagels** ★★ Simply put, this is Eureka's best bagel shop. For more details, see the review of the Los Bagels branch in Arcata. ■ *403 2nd St (at E St in Old Town), Eureka; (707) 442-8525; $; no alcohol; no credit cards; local checks only; breakfast, lunch Wed–Mon.* Ꮠ

**Tomaso's Tomato Pies** ★ This family-style Italian pizza parlor reeks so divinely of baked garlic and olive oil that you can smell it a block away. Top of the list of Tomaso's favored fare are the calzone and the spinach pies, both guaranteed to make garlic lovers (and their dining partners) swoon. Be prepared for a 30-minute wait—it's the price you pay for such fresh ingredients. Other popular plates include the chicken cannelloni and the square pizza with a whole-wheat crust. For a proper Italian finale, order a Cremosa: a blend of milk, soda water, and whipped cream infused with a fruity Torani Italian syrup. ■ *216 E St (between 2nd and 3rd Sts in Old Town), Eureka; (707) 445-0100; $; beer and wine; AE, DIS, MC, V; local checks only; lunch Mon–Sat, dinner every day.* Ꮠ

**Samoa Cookhouse** Visiting the Eureka area without a stop at the Samoa Cookhouse is like visiting Paris without seeing the Eiffel Tower. This venerable dining spot is the last surviving cook house in the West (it's been in operation for more than a century) and a Humboldt County institution, where guests are served lumber-camp-style in an enormous barnlike building at long tables covered with checkered cloths. Few decisions are required—just sit down, and the food will come until you say uncle. Breakfast typically features sausages, biscuits, scrambled eggs, and potatoes as well as a choice of French toast, hash browns, or pancakes (not to mention all the coffee and OJ you can drink). Lunch and dinner include potatoes and the meat-of-the-day, which might be ham, fried chicken, pork chops, roast beef, barbecued chicken, or fish. Mind you, the food isn't great (except for the delicious bread, which is baked on the premises), but there's plenty of it. And just when you think you're about to burst, along comes the fresh-baked pie. After your meal, spend a few minutes waddling through the adjoining logging museum. ■ *On Cookhouse Rd (from Hwy 101, take the Samoa exit—R St—in downtown Eureka, cross the Samoa Bridge, and turn left on Samoa Rd, then left on Cookhouse Rd), Eureka; (707)442-1659; $; no alcohol; AE, DIS, MC, V; checks OK; breakfast, lunch, dinner every day.*

## LODGINGS

### Carter House ■ Hotel Carter ■ Carter House Cottage ★★★★

What is now one of the finest accommodation-and-restaurant complexes on the upper North Coast started serendipitously in 1982, the year Eureka residents Mark and Christi Carter converted their newly built dream home—a four-story, five-bedroom Victorian reproduction—into an inn. Not only did they turn out to be some of the area's best hosts, but the Carters actually reveled in their newfound innkeeper roles. Once word got around that the Carter House was *the* place to vacation, they were flooded with folks who wanted a room. In 1986, Mark, a former builder, added the 23-room Hotel Carter across the street (its design is based on the blueprints of a historic 19th-century Eureka hotel), and four years later he refurbished the Carter House Cottage, an adjacent three-bedroom Victorian mansion built in 1890.

The trio of inn, hotel, and cottage offers a contrasting array of luxury accommodations, ranging from rooms with classic Victorian dark-wood antique furnishings in the house and cottage to a softer, brighter, more contemporary decor in the hotel. The decor varies from guest room to guest room, but some boast marble fireplaces, imported antiques, two-person whirlpool bathtubs with views of the marina, immense four-poster beds, double-headed showers, entertainment centers, and kitchens. Amenities include baskets filled with wine and specialty foods, concierge services, overnight dry cleaning and shoe shining, a videotape and CD library, tea-and-cookie bedtime service, and wine and hors d'oeuvres in the evening. Also included in the room rate is an outstanding full breakfast featuring fresh-baked tarts, muffins, cinnamon buns, breads, fresh fruit, an ever-changing array of entrees, juices, and strong coffee. The highly acclaimed **Restaurant 301** (see review), formerly known as the Carter House Restaurant, is located on the first floor of Hotel Carter and is widely regarded as one of the North Coast's top restaurants. ■ *301 L St (at 3rd St in Old Town), Eureka, CA 95501; (707)444-8062 or (800)404-1390; carter52@carterhouse.com; www.carter52@carterhouse.com; $$$; full bar; AE, DC, DIS, MC, V; checks OK; breakfast (by reservation only for non-guests), dinner every day.* ♿

**An Elegant Victorian Mansion** ★★★ This inn is a jewel—a National Historic Landmark lovingly maintained by owners Doug "Jeeves" Vieyra and Lily Vieyra. If you're a fan of Victoriana, be prepared for a mind-blowing experience. Each of the four guest rooms upstairs has furnishings reflecting a different period, place, or personage. The light-filled Lillie Langtry Room, named for the famed 19th-century chanteuse who once sang at the local Ingomar Theatre, has an impressive four-poster oak bed and a private bath down the hall. The French country-style Governor's Suite sleeps up to three, has a private bath, and offers a distant view of the bay. The Vieyras have an incredible array of old (1905-1940) movies and a collection of popular music from the same era, which guests often enjoy in the common room. Then there's Doug's obsession with antique autos—he's frequently seen motoring (with guests on board) in his 1928 Model A Ford or one of his other two old Fords. Doug and Lily are incredibly attentive hosts; they'll lend you bicycles, show you the way to their Finnish sauna and Victorian flower garden, pore over road maps with you, and make your dinner reservations. Lily, trained as a French chef (and Swedish masseuse), prepares a morning feast. ■ *1406 C St (at 14th St), Eureka, CA 95501; (707)444-3144; www.bnbcity.com/inns/20016; $$; MC, V; no checks.*

Redwood
Empire
▼
Arcata
▲

## ARCATA

Home to the **California State University at Humboldt**, a liberal arts school, Arcata is like most college towns in that everyone tends to lean towards the left. Environmentalism, artistry, good beads, and good bagels are indispensable elements of the Arcatian philosophy, as is a cordial disposition towards tourists, making Arcata one of the most interesting and visitor-friendly towns along the North Coast.

The heart of this seaside community is **Arcata Plaza**, where a statue of President McKinley stands guard over numerous shops and cafes housed in historic buildings. A walk around the plaza—with its perfectly manicured lawns, hot dog vendor, and well-dressed retirees sitting on spotless benches—is enough to restore anyone's faith in small-town America. At the plaza's southwest end is its flagship structure, **Jacoby's Storehouse**, a handsomely restored 1857 brick pack-train station that now holds shops, offices, and restaurants; 791 Eighth Street at H Street. If you need a new book, the **Tin Can Mailman** is a terrific used-book store with 130,000 hard- and soft-cover titles, including a few collector's items; 1000 H Street at 10th Street, (707)822-1307.

You can see (and touch!) three-billion-year-old fossils and view various California flora and fauna exhibits at Humboldt State University's **Natural History Museum** at 13th and G Streets downtown; (707)826-4479. For a wide range of first-run and classic college flicks, queue up at the **Arcata Theatre**, 1036 G Street at 10th Street, (707)822-5171, or the **Minor Theatre**, 1013 H Street at 10th Street, (707)822-5171, both of which offer a wide range of films at starving-student prices (the daily matinees are particularly cheap). After the flick, savor a pitcher of Red Nectar Ale at the **Humboldt Brewing Company** (brewery tours are offered, too) at the corner of 10th and G Streets next to the Minor Theatre; (707)826-BREW.

Once you've toured the downtown area, it's time to explore Arcata's numerous parks and preserves. A 2-minute drive east of downtown on 11th Street will take you to Arcata's beloved **Redwood Park**, a beautiful grassy expanse—ideal for a picnic—complemented by a fantastic playground that's guaranteed to entertain the tots. Surrounding the park is the **Arcata Community Forest**, 600 acres of lush second-growth redwoods favored by hikers, mountain bikers, and equestrians; before you go, pick up a free guide to the forest's mountain-biking or hiking trails at the **Arcata Chamber of Commerce**, 1062 G Street at 11th Street, (707)822-3619.

On the south side of town is the **Arcata Marsh and Wildlife Preserve**, a 154-acre sanctuary for hundreds of egrets, marsh wrens, and other waterfowl. Get the free self-guided walking tour map of the preserve, which doubles as

*Arcata*

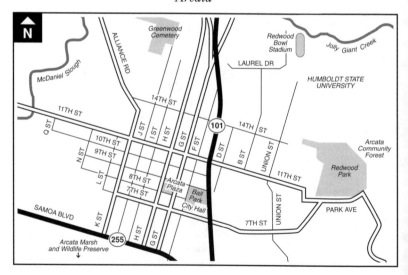

Arcata's integrated wetland wastewater treatment plant; maps are available at the Chamber of Commerce (see above). Each Saturday at 8:30am the Audubon Society gives free 1-hour guided tours of the preserve—rain or shine—at the cul-de-sac at the foot of South I Street; (707)826-7031.

The best way to spend a summer Sunday afternoon in Arcata is at the **Arcata Ballpark**, where only a few bucks buys you nine innings of America's favorite pastime hosted by the Humboldt Crabs semipro baseball team. With the brass band blasting and the devoted fans cheering, you'd swear you were back in high school. Most games are played Wednesday, Friday, and Saturday evenings in June and July. The ballpark is located at the corner of Ninth and F Streets in downtown Arcata, but don't park your car anywhere near foul-ball territory; (707)822-3619.

## RESTAURANTS

**Abruzzi** ★★ Named after a region on the Italian Adriatic, Abruzzi is located on the bottom floor of the 140-year-old Jacoby Storehouse, an old brick complex that's been converted into the historic Arcata Plaza shopping mall. If you have trouble finding the place, just follow your nose: the smell of garlic and fresh bread will soon steer you to Chris Smith and Bill Chino's friendly spot, where you'll be served an ample amount of artfully arranged food. Meals begin with a basket of warm bread sticks, focaccia, and a baguette, followed by such highly recommended dishes as pasta carbonara, linguine *pescara* (prawns, calamari, and clams tossed in a light Sicilian tomato sauce), or any of the fresh seafood specials. The standout dessert is the chocolate paradiso—a dense chocolate cake set in a pool of champagne mousseline. Smith and Chino also own the **Plaza Grill** on the third floor of the same building—a great place to finish off the evening by sipping a glass of wine in front of the fireplace. ■ *791 8th St (at H St in the Arcata Plaza), Arcata; (707)826-2345; $$; full bar; AE, DIS, MC, V; checks OK; dinner every day.* &

**Arcata**

*Restaurants*

▲

**Folie Douce** ★★ To say Folie Douce just serves pizza is like saying Tiffany's just sells jewelry. *Designer* pizza is more like it. Try the Thai chicken pizza—marinated bits of breast topped with fontina, mozzarella, bean sprouts, and mushrooms—which is cooked in a wood-fired oven. Other toppings you won't find in your standard Pizza Hut include chèvre, Brie, and wild mushrooms. If pizza doesn't set your heart aflutter, indulge in brandy-flambéed filet mignon topped with Roquefort cheese and green peppercorns or the moist Monk's Chicken, a full boneless breast sautéed in butter, flambéed in brandy, and simmered in white wine, mustard, and cream. Locals love this festive, brightly painted place, so reservations—even for early birds—are strongly recommended. ■ *1551 G St (between 15th and 16th Sts), Arcata; (707)822-1042; $$; beer and wine; DIS, MC, V; checks OK; dinner Tues–Sat.* ₲

**Los Bagels** ★  In 1987 bagel companies all over the country sent their doughy products to NBC's *Today Show* to vie for the title of Best Bagel. The verdict: the best bagel outside of New York City was made by Los Bagels in Arcata. This emporium is a popular town hangout, where you'll see lots of folks scanning the morning paper while they munch on bagels layered with smoked salmon, smoked albacore, or lox. Try some fresh-baked challah or, if you're feeling particularly adventurous, a poppyseed bagel topped with jalapeño jam and cream cheese, or a multigrain bagel smeared with hummus or guacamole. Owing to Los Bagels' brisk business, the owners opened a second location in Eureka. ■ *1061 I St (between 10th and 11th Sts), Arcata; (707)822-3150; $; no alcohol; no credit cards; local checks only; breakfast, lunch Wed–Mon.* ₲

## LODGINGS

**The Lady Anne** ★★  Just a few blocks from Arcata Plaza in a quiet residential neighborhood, this exquisite example of Queen Anne architecture has been painstakingly restored by innkeepers Sharon Ferrett and Sam Pennisi (who, by the way, was once Arcata's mayor). Five large and airy guest rooms are each decorated with antiques, burnished woods, English stained glass, Oriental rugs, and lace curtains. Romantics should book the Lady Sarah Angela Room, which boasts a four-poster bed and a beautiful bay view. Families often request the Cinnamon Bear Room, which is chock-full of teddy bears and will sleep up to four with its king-size and trundle beds. The inn's two parlors are stocked with several games, as well as a grand piano and other musical instruments that you're welcome to play. When the weather is warm, relax on Lady Anne's veranda or head out to the lawn for a game of croquet. Breakfast (beg for the Belgian waffles) is served in the grand dining room, which is warmed by a roaring fire in the winter. ■ *902 14th St (at I St), Arcata, CA 95521; (707)822-2797; $$; MC, V; checks OK.*

▼

Arcata

*Restaurants*

▲

# TRINIDAD

In the early 1850s Trinidad was a booming supply town with a population of 3,000; now it's one of the smallest incorporated cities in California, encompassing a little rocky bluff that a handful of anglers, artists, retirees, and shopkeepers call home. A sort of Mendocino-in-miniature, cute-as-a-button Trinidad is known mainly as a sportfishing town: trawlers and skiffs sit patiently in the bay, awaiting their owners or tourists eager to spend an afternoon salmon fishing. Scenery and silence, however, are the town's most desirable commodities; if all you're after is a little R&R on the coast, Trinidad is among the most peaceful and beautiful areas you'll find in California.

There's plenty to see and do in the Trinidad region. Five miles north of Trinidad off Patrick's Point Drive is **Patrick's Point State Park**, a 640-acre oceanside peninsula with lush, fern-lined trails that wind through foggy forests of cedar, pine, and spruce. The park was once a seasonal fishing village of the Yurok Indians. Nowadays it's overrun with campers in the summer, but it's still worth a visit. Stroll down **Agate Beach** (keep an eye out for the semiprecious stones), climb the stone stairway up to the house-size **Ceremonial Rock**, and admire the vistas from the **Rim Trail**, a 2-mile path along the cliffs where you can sometimes spot sea lions, harbor seals, and gray whales. In 1990 descendants of the original Native American settlers reconstructed an authentic Yurok village within the park, and visitors are welcome. A map and guide to all of the park's attractions are included in the $5-per-vehicle day-use fee; call (707)677-3570 for more details.

If the long drive on Highway 101 has you feeling cramped, unwind for a spell at Trinidad's **Demonstration Forest**. A self-guided trail—virtually unknown and almost always deserted—leads through a lush, peaceful redwood forest and takes about 20 minutes to complete. A picnic area hidden near the parking lot is the perfect spot for a leisurely lunch in the cool shade. From Highway 101, take the Trinidad exit and head north on Patrick's Point Drive for about a mile.

▼

**Trinidad**

▲

The **Humboldt State University Marine Laboratory** features various live marine life displays, including a touch tank and tide pools; it's open to the public daily and is located at Edwards and Ewing Streets downtown, (707)826-3671. Then again, why not catch your own sea critters? A day spent **sportfishing** off Trinidad's bounteous coast is more fun and much easier than you probably think. You simply drop your pre-rigged line into the water, reel it in when something's tugging on the other end, and throw your catch in the burlap sack at your feet. The crew does all the dirty work of cleaning and cutting your fish, and Katy's Smokehouse (see below) will take care of the rest. Trinidad's two sportfishing charter boats are the 36-foot *Jumpin' Jack*, (707)839-4743 or (800)839-4744; and the 45-foot *Shenandoah*, (707)677-3625. Both charters offer morning and afternoon trips daily from Trinidad Pier, and walk-on customers are welcome. The 5-hour salmon or rockfish hunt costs about $60 per person, which includes all fishing gear. One-day fishing licenses can be purchased on board. If you're lucky enough to reel in a lunker salmon, haul it up to **Katy's Smokehouse**, just up the road from the pier at 740 Edwards Street, (707)677-0151. Katy herself will smoke it up and wrap it to go—or even send it via UPS to your home. Her salmon jerky ain't bad, either.

*RESTAURANTS*

**Larrupin' Café** ★★★ Trinidad's finest restaurant—looking very chic with its colorful urns full of exotic flowers—draws crowds with its creative seafood dishes and fantastic pork ribs doused with a sweet and spicy barbecue sauce. Often, oysters, mussels, and crab are served the same day they're plucked from Humboldt Bay. Every meal comes with a red- and green-leaf salad tossed with a Gorgonzola vinaigrette and an appetizer board stocked with gravlax, pâté, dark pumpernickel, apple slices, and the house mustard sauce. For your choice of a starch, order the tasty twice-baked potato stuffed with locally made cheese, sour cream, and scallions. Finish off your feast with a slice of pecan-chocolate pie topped with hot rum sauce. Reservations are recommended year-round. ▪ *1658 Patrick's Point Dr (from Hwy 101, take the Trinidad exit and head N on Patrick's Point Dr), Trinidad; (707)677-0230; $$; beer and wine; no credit cards; checks OK; dinner every day in the summer (Thurs–Sun only from Labor Day to Memorial Day).* &

*LODGINGS*

**The Lost Whale Bed and Breakfast Inn** ★★★ The Lost Whale isn't just a place to stay overnight, it's a destination in itself—particularly for families with small children. The traditional Cape Cod-style building, constructed in 1989, stands alone on a 4-acre grassy cliff overlooking the sea, with a private stairway leading down to miles of deserted rocky beach. Proprietors Suzanne Lakin and Lee Miller manage to give romancing couples lots of space and solitude, yet they also have created one the most family-friendly inns on the California coast. Five of the inn's eight soundproof rooms have private balconies or sitting alcoves with views of the Pacific, two rooms have separate sleeping lofts, and all have private baths and queen-size beds. Lakin and Miller also rent out two furnished private homes that can accommodate up to six people each: a spectacular beach house that overlooks the ocean, and a charming farmhouse set on 5 acres that's equipped with a whirlpool tub, a fireplace, a kitchen, and a laundry room. After a day on the inn's beach or at neighboring Patrick's Point State Park, relax in the outdoor hot tub while listening to the distant bark of sea lions or looking out for whales. Kids can romp around on the playground—which has a small playhouse with its own loft—or play with the menagerie of pygmy goats and rabbits roaming the inn's 1½-acre plot up the street. Lakin and Miller take great pride in their huge breakfasts—casseroles, quiches, home-baked muffins, fresh fruit, locally smoked salmon served with vegetables from the garden—and provide plenty of snacks throughout the day and evening. ▪ *3452 Patrick's Point Dr (from Hwy 101, take the Seawood Dr exit and* *head N for 1¾ miles on Patrick's Point Dr), Trinidad, CA 95570; (707)677-3425 or (800)677-7859; 1miller@northcoast. com; www.lost-whale-inn.com; $$$; AE, DIS, MC, V; checks OK.*

**Trinidad Bay Bed and Breakfast** ★★ Perched on a bluff overlooking Trinidad's quaint fishing harbor and the rugged California coast, this Cape Cod-style inn is the dream house of innkeepers Carol and Paul Kirk, Southern California transplants who fell in love with the area while visiting Arcata more than a decade ago. They offer four guest rooms and two great suites. Both suites have private entrances, comfortable sitting rooms, spectacular views of Trinidad Bay, and breakfast-in-bed service. The Mauve Suite has a large brick fireplace, wrap-around windows, and a king-size bed; the Blue Bay View Suite upstairs offers more privacy (its entrance is outside of the inn), a telescope for whale watching, a king-size bed, and the best bay view in town. The Kirks' expanded continental breakfast features fresh and baked fruit, homemade breads served with lemon-honey and molasses butter, muffins (pear-ginger, cranberry-orange, fruit-bran), and locally made cheeses. ■ *560 Edwards St (from Hwy 101, take the Trinidad exit to Main St, and turn left on Trinity St), Trinidad; (707)677-0840; mail: PO Box 849, Trinidad, CA 95570; www.visitormags.com/ trinidadbay; $$$; MC, V; checks OK.*

▼

## ORICK

The burl art capital of the world, Orick looks more like a huge outdoor gift shop than a town. What's burl art, you ask? Well, take a sizable chunk of redwood, do a little carving here and there with a small chain saw, and when it resembles some sort of mammal or rodent, you have yourself a piece of burl art. There are thousands of burl pieces to choose from here, ranging from the Abominable Burlman to Sasquatch and the Seven Dwarfs. Several roadside stands have viewing booths where mesmerized tourists watch the redwood chips fly. Orick is also the southern entryway to **Redwood National and State Parks**; 1 mile south of town off Highway 101 is the **Redwood Information Center**, where visitors can pick up a free park map and browse through geologic, wildlife, and Native American exhibits; open daily 9am–5pm, (707)464-6101, extension 5265. Of course, the best way to experience the park and its magnificent redwoods is on foot. The short **Fern Canyon Trail** leads through an incredibly lush fern grotto. The **Lady Bird Johnson Grove Loop** is an easy, 1-hour self-guided tour that loops 1 mile around a gorgeous grove of redwoods. Closer to shore is the **Yurok Loop Nature Trail** at Lagoon Creek, located 6½ miles north of the Klamath River bridge on Highway 101; the 1-mile self-guided trail gradually climbs to the top of rugged sea bluffs—with wonderful panoramic views of the Pacific—and loops back to the parking lot. But the summa cum laude of trails is the **Boy Scout Tree Trail**, a 6-mile round-trip hike through a cool, damp forest brimming with giant ferns and majestic redwoods. You may also want to visit the aptly named **Tall Tree Grove**, featuring the world's tallest tree: a 368-foot giant. For more information about the Redwood National and State Parks, visit their Web site at www.nps.gov/redw.

### RESTAURANTS

**Rolf's Park Café** ★  After decades of working as a chef in Switzerland, Austria, San Francisco, and even aboard the presidential ship SS *Roosevelt*, the trilingual Rolf Rheinschmidt decided it was time to semi-retire. He wanted to move to a small town to cook, and towns don't get much smaller than Orick—population 650. So here among the redwoods Rheinschmidt serves good bratwurst, wiener schnitzel, and crêpes Suzette. His specialty is the marinated rack of spring lamb, and he has some unusual offerings such as wild boar, buffalo, and elk steak (the truly adventurous should get the combo platter featuring all three). Each dinner entree includes lots of extras: hors d'oeuvres, a salad, vegetables, farm-style potatoes, and bread. And ever since the debut of Rheinschmidt's German Farmer Omelet—an open-faced concoction of ham, bacon, sausage, mushrooms, cheese, potatoes, and pasta, topped with sour cream and salsa and garnished with a strawberry crêpe—breakfast in Orick has never been the same. ■ *On Hwy 101 about 2 miles N of Orick; (707) 488-3841; $$; beer and wine; MC, V; local checks only; breakfast, lunch, dinner every day in the summer (typically open Mar through Nov).* &

▼

**Orick**

▲

## KLAMATH

From the looks of it, the town of Klamath hasn't recovered since it was washed away in 1964, when 40 inches of rain fell within 24 hours. All that remains are a few cheap motels, trailer parks, tackle shops, and boat rental outlets, kept in business by the numerous anglers who line the mighty Klamath River, one of the finest salmon and steelhead streams in the world. The scenery around the river is extraordinary; smack in the middle of the Redwood National Forest, the area has some incredible coastal drives and trails that even the timid and out-of-shape can handle with aplomb.

Stretch out your legs at the lofty **Klamath Overlook**, which stands about 600 feet above an estuary at the mouth of the Klamath River. A short but steep trail leads down to a second overlook that's ideal for whale-watching and taking photographs. To get there, take the Requa Road turnoff from Highway 101, north of the Klamath River bridge. For more hiking recommendations, read about **Redwood National and State Parks** in Orick (above).

One of the premier coastal drives on the Redwood Coast starts at the mouth of the Klamath River and runs 8 miles south towards **Prairie Creek Redwoods State Park**. If you're heading south on Highway 101, take the Alder Camp Road exit just south of the Klamath River bridge and follow the signs to the river mouth. North-bound travelers should take the Redwood National and State Parks Coastal Drive exit off the Newton B. Drury Scenic Parkway. Campers and cars with trailers are not advised. The narrow, partially paved drive winds through stands of redwoods, with spectacular views of the sea and numerous turnouts for picture-taking (sea lions and pelicans abound) and short hikes. Keep an eye out for the World War II radar station, disguised as a farmhouse and barn.

## LODGINGS

**Requa Inn** ★  The Requa Inn was established in 1885, and since then it has gone through several owners, three name changes, one relocation, and a major fire that burned it to the ground in 1914 (it was rebuilt the same year). But this venerable riverside inn is still going strong. The 10 spacious guest rooms are modestly decorated with antique furnishings and have private baths with showers or claw-footed tubs; 4 offer views of the lower Klamath River. The inn's highlight is the cozy parlor downstairs, where guests bury themselves in plump armchairs and read beside the wood-burning stove. If you're the outdoorsy type, there are plenty of enticements just outside: sandy riverside beaches, myriad hiking trails in nearby Redwood National and State Parks, and, of course, fishing in the wonderful Klamath. If you'd rather luxuriate indoors, make an appointment for the tender ministrations of the inn's massage therapist.

**Klamath**

*Lodgings*

Aside from being the only decent lodge in the greater Klamath area, the **Requa Inn Restaurant** is one of the only two decent restaurants in the region. The dining area is simple yet dignified, with views overlooking the Klamath River and a wonderful parlor for sipping an after-dinner drink by the fireplace. The no-nonsense, pricey menu of steak, chicken, and fresh seafood obviously caters to Klamath's well-heeled anglers. On Friday and Saturday nights in the summer, the best entrees are the seasoned prime rib and the grilled salmon and halibut. Be sure to leave room for the fresh-baked blackberry cobbler topped with vanilla ice cream. Breakfast is included in the room rate. ■ *451 Requa Rd (from Hwy 101, take the Requa Rd exit and follow the signs), Klamath, CA 95548; (707) 482-8205; $$; beer and wine; DIS, MC, V; checks OK; breakfast (for guests only) every day, lunch Mon–Fri (in the summer only), dinner every day.* &

Because it's the northern gateway to the popular **Redwood National and State Parks** (for park highlights see Orick, above), one might assume Crescent City would be a major tourist mecca, rife with fine restaurants and hotels. Unfortunately, it's not. Cheap motels, fast-food chains, and mini-malls are the main attractions along this stretch of Highway 101, as if Crescent City exists only to serve travelers on their way someplace else. The city is trying, however, to enhance its image, and if you know where to go (which is anywhere off Highway 101), there are actually numerous sites worth visiting in the area and several outdoor-recreation options that are refreshingly non-touristy. You won't want to make Crescent City your primary destination, mind you, but don't be reluctant to spend a day lolling around here, either; you'd be surprised what the town has to offer besides gas and groceries.

For starters, take a side trip to the **North Coast Marine Mammal Center**. This nonprofit organization was established in 1989 to rescue and rehabilitate stranded or injured marine mammals. Staffed by volunteers and funded by donations, the center is the only facility of its kind between San Francisco and Seattle, providing emergency response during environmental disasters and assisting marine researchers by collecting data on marine mammals. The center is open to the public daily year-round, and visitors are welcome to watch the volunteers in action, make a donation, and buy a nature book or two at the gift shop; located at the north end of Crescent City Harbor at 424 Howe Drive in Beach Front Park, (707)465-MAML.

Other interesting local sites include the operational **Battery Point Lighthouse**, built in 1856 on a small island off the foot of A Street. Guided tours of the lighthouse and the light-keeper's living quarters are offered Wednesday through Sunday from 10am to 4pm, tide permitting (you have to cross a tide pool to get there), April through September; (707)464-3089. Next, head to the **B Street Pier** (at the south foot of B Street), rent a crab net ($5) and fishing pole ($5 including tackle) from Popeye's bait shop (no phone), and do some fishing and crabbing off the city's 800-foot-long pier. Crabbing is simple: throw the prebaited net into the water (don't forget to tie the other end to the pier), wait about 10 minutes, then pull it up and see what's for supper. Because it's a public pier, you don't even need a fishing license.

If you're not one to get your hands dirty, take a shoreline tour along **Pebble Beach Drive** from the west end of Sixth Street to Point St. George. You're bound to see a few seals and sea lions at the numerous pullouts. End the tour with a short walk though a sandy meadow to Point St. George, a relatively deserted bluff that's perfect for a picnic or beach stroll. On a clear day, look out on the ocean for the **St. George Reef Lighthouse**, reportedly the tallest (146 feet above sea level), deadliest (several light-keepers died in rough seas while trying to dock), and most expensive ($704,000) lighthouse ever built.

One of the prettiest picnic sites on the California Coast is along **Enderts Road** at the south end of town. Pack a picnic lunch at Alias Jones cafe (see review, below), and stop by a liquor store for a bottle of Chianti. Drive 3 miles south on Highway 101 from downtown, and turn right on Enderts Road (across from the Ocean Way Motel), and continue 2⅓ miles. Park at the Crescent Beach Overlook, lay your blanket on the grass, admire the ocean view. Type-A personalities can drive to the end of Enderts Road and take the 1.2 mile round-trip hiking trail to Enderts Beach. In the summer, free 1½- to 2-hour ranger-guided **tide pool and seashore walks** are offered when the tides are right, starting at the beach parking lot. For specific tour times, call (707)464-6101, extension 5265.

Crescent City's best-kept secret, however, is the **Lake Earl Wildlife Area**, a gorgeous habitat replete with deer, rabbits, beavers, otters, red-tailed hawks, peregrine falcons, bald eagles, songbirds (some 80 species), shorebirds, and migratory waterfowl who share these 5,000 acres of pristine woodlands, grasslands, and ocean shore. Hiking and biking are permitted, but you'll want to make the trip on foot with binoculars in hand to get the full effect of this amazing patch of coastal land. To get there, take the Northcrest Drive exit off Highway 101 in downtown Crescent City and turn left on Old Mill Road. Proceed 1½ miles to the park headquarters at 2591 Old Mill Road (if it's open, ask for a map) and park in the gravel lot. Additional trails start at the end of Old Mill Road. For more information, call the Department of Fish and Game at (707)464-2523.

## RESTAURANTS

**Alias Jones** ★★ Just when you were about to give up on Crescent City cuisine, along comes the answer to "Where's a good place to eat around here?" This small, lively cafe and bakery does just about everything right, including whipping up savory sandwiches, salads, burgers, and breakfast items—all at inexpensive prices. For breakfast, try the pesto omelet with herb cream cheese and mozzarella, and wash it down with a nonfat banana-berry tofu smoothie. A lunch favorite is the hot zucchini, mushroom, cream cheese, and tomato sandwich served on a roll. Bakery items are made from scratch, and the espresso drinks are all standard doubles—*zzzing!* ■ *983 3rd St (between I and J Sts), Crescent City; (707)465-6987; $; no alcohol; no credit cards; checks OK; breakfast, lunch Mon–Fri.*

**Beachcomber Restaurant** ★ Ever since Jim's Bistro closed, it's been difficult to find a good place to eat dinner in Crescent City. The Beachcomber is the most-nominated spot. If you can get past its tired nautical theme and blue Naugahyde booths, it does a fair job of providing fresh seafood—halibut, red snapper, ling cod, chinook salmon—at reasonable prices. Set right on the beach, the Beachcomber also specializes in flame-broiled steaks, cooked to your specification on an open barbecue pit. Friday and Saturday are prime-rib nights. Ask for a booth by the window, and start the evening with the steamer-clam appetizer: 1½ pounds of the North Coast's finest. ∎ *1400 Hwy 101 S (2 miles S of downtown), Crescent City; (707)464-2205; $$; beer and wine; MC, V; local checks only; dinner Thurs–Tues.* &

### LODGINGS

**Crescent Beach Motel** ★ Crescent City has the dubious distinction of being the only city along the coast without a swanky hotel. There is, however, an armada of cheap motels, the best of which is the Crescent Beach Motel. A new color scheme of brown, beige, and green has improved the interiors considerably, and all but 4 of the 27 rooms are within steps of the beach. Most units have queen-size beds and color TVs. The small lawn area and large sun decks overlooking the ocean are great venues for kicking back and enjoying some true R&R. Another perk: you can get a seafood dinner at the **Beachcomber Restaurant** (see review, above), which is right next door. ∎ *1455 Hwy 101 S (2 miles S of downtown), Crescent City, CA 95531; (707)464-5436; $; AE, DIS, MC, V; no checks.* &

# NORTH
# MOUNTAINS

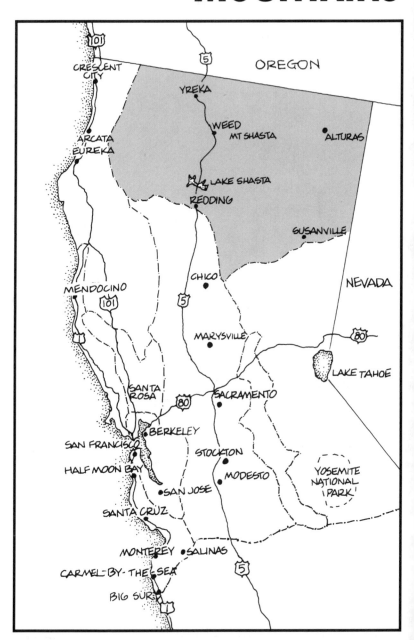

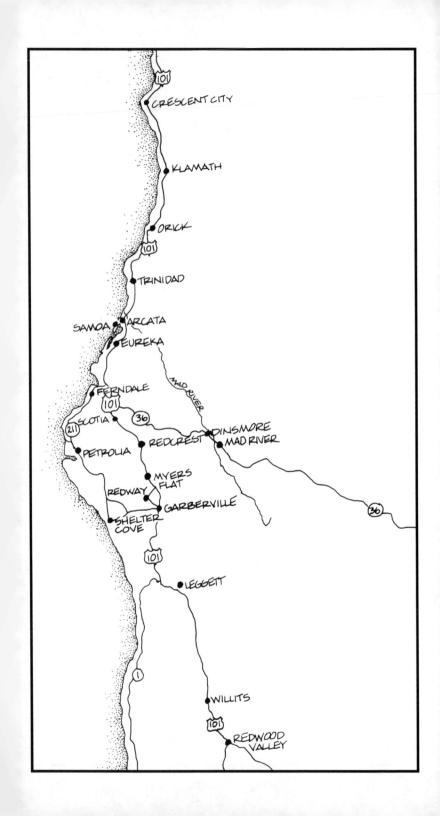

# North Mountains

*A tour of the North Mountains region from
Redding to Willow Creek, then north to the Klamath River
and south to Mount Shasta. After side trips to Fort Jones,
Etna, and Coffee Creek, continue to Cedarville, Susanville,
Lake Almanor, and Lassen Volcanic National Park. Note:
Some establishments in the North Mountains' remote
regions close during the winter. Call before you travel.*

## REDDING AND THE SHASTA LAKE AREA

As you drive north to Redding up the flat, uninspiring Interstate 5 corridor, snow-topped Mount Shasta first appears as a white smudge at the end of the highway. Venture a little closer and the imposing volcano soon dominates the horizon. This unforgettable sight heralds your approach to the gateway to California's northern mountains: Redding. Step out of your car, and you'll feel as though you've stepped back in time to a simpler (and frequently less expensive) way of life. Redding isn't known so much for what's here as for what's near: prime fishing, hiking, boating, waterskiing, mountain biking, rock climbing, camping, and river rafting.

**Whiskeytown Lake**, west of Redding, offers great beaches and windsurfing and sailing opportunities; for information call the visitors center at (530)246-1225. About 20 minutes north of Redding is **Shasta Lake**, the largest reservoir in California and an ideal place for fishing, waterskiing, or just lounging with a good book in the sun on a houseboat. To fully appreciate Shasta Lake's 370 miles of shoreline, view the lake by boat. And while you're at it, keep your eye on the sky for a glimpse of the mighty **bald eagle**, the largest bird of prey in North America. Shasta Lake is currently the home of at least 18 pairs of the endangered birds—the largest nesting population of bald eagles in California. For information about other lake attractions and houseboat rentals, call the **Redding Convention and Visitors Bureau** at (800)874-7562.

If you're heading up to Shasta Lake on Interstate 5, the monolithic 3,640-foot-long **Shasta Dam** is a great place to pull over for a lengthy pit stop. Shasta is the second-largest and second-tallest concrete dam in the United States (it contains enough concrete to build a 3-foot-wide sidewalk around the world) and one of the most impressive civil engineering feats in the nation. The visitors center and viewing area are rather ho-hum, but the free 45-minute tour of the dam is outstanding. It kicks off with a speedy elevator ride into the chilly bowels of the 15-million-ton, 602-foot-high structure—definitely not recommended for claustrophobes. Dam tours are held from 9am to 4pm daily; call (530)275-4463 for information and winter and holiday hours (from Interstate 5, take the Shasta Dam Boulevard exit and follow the signs).

About 10 miles north of the dam is another popular attraction: guided tours of the impressive, crystal-studded stalagmites and stalactites in the **Lake Shasta Caverns**. Getting there is an adventure in itself; after you pull off the highway and check in at cavern headquarters, you'll have to hop aboard a ferry for a 15-minute trip across Shasta Lake, then climb onto a bus for a white-knuckle ride up to the caverns (open daily year-round); from Interstate 5, take the Shasta Caverns Road exit and follow the signs, (530)238-2341. And anglers take note: the stretch of the **Sacramento River** between Shasta Lake and Mount Shasta is one of the top spots in the country for **trout fishing**, so don't forget to pack the rod and reel. For tips on touring the area north of Shasta Lake, see the Mount Shasta section in this chapter.

In the town of Redding, the 6-mile-long **Sacramento River Trail** meanders along the riverbanks and over a stress-ribbon concrete bridge—the only bridge of its kind in the country. This section of the river also offers good year-round urban fishing for steelhead, trout, and salmon; for information about where to cast your line, call Redding's world-class fly-fishing store, the Fly Shop, (800)669-3474. Another local attraction is **The Redding**

*Redding*

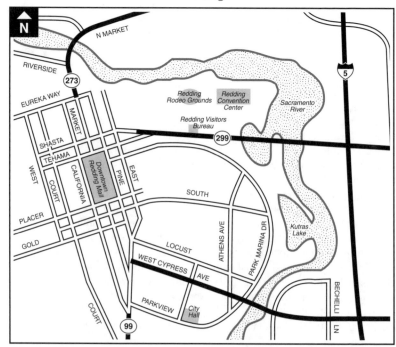

Museum of Art and History, which has local-history exhibits and a fine collection of Native American baskets; 56 Quartz Hill Road, (530)243-8801. Next door is the Carter House Natural Science Museum, a funky, spirited place that houses live animals as well as those that have spent some time with a taxidermist (rest assured that *only* animals that died accidentally or of natural causes got the glass-eye treatment). Kids will also find plenty of hands-on activities to keep them amused; 56 Quartz Hill Road, (530)243-5457. For an extensive selection of newspapers, magazines, and other good reading material, The Redding Bookstore is second to none in this part of the state; 1712 California Street, (530)246-2171. The bookstore also houses the Downtown Espresso and Coffee Roasting Company, so you can get a good cup of joe to go along with that terrific travel tome you're now reading.

## RESTAURANTS

**Nello's Place** ★★★ The exuberant Italian murals and the bright Campari umbrellas hanging from the ceiling add a playful touch to this traditional, romantically lit Italian dinner house. Nello's menu and Italian and California wine list are vast and wide-ranging. For starters, try the golden deep-fried artichoke hearts or the clams steamed with garlic and white wine. Entrees include a meaty lasagne, rich Chicken Rossini (a boneless chicken breast stuffed with prosciutto, mozzarella, and provolone in a brandied stock-reduction sauce), and the house specialty: *bistecca pizzaiola*, a New York steak with caramelized red onions, garlic, mushrooms, and a dash of marinara. Top off the meal with the dazzling crêpes Suzette. To ensure that your evening ends on a romantic note, Nello's bestows a red carnation upon every *signorina e signora* at dinner's end. For romance on the cheap, try the early bird special served from 5pm to 6:30pm, a four-course Italian dinner for just over 11 bucks. ■ *3055 Bechelli Lane (near Hartnell Ave), Redding; (530)223-1636; $$; full bar; AE, DIS, MC, V; local checks OK; dinner Tues–Sat.* &

**Buz's Crab** ★★ Every day the bounty of the North Coast is hauled over the hills into California's parched interior to Buz's seafood market. With Naugahyde booths and Formica tables, this ain't no pretty place for a romantic dinner for two, but Buz's earns its stars for doing what it does perfectly. The seafood baskets offer much more than your standard fish 'n' chips: you'll find everything here—from stuffed prawns, oysters, scallops, and clam strips to calamari, catfish, Cajun halibut, and crisp potato rounds. From December to May, order the fabulous crab (just plucked from the boiling crab pots on the patio) along with a slab of Buz's fresh-baked sourdough bread. ■ *2159 East St (N of W Cypress Ave and Pine St), Redding; (530)243-2120; buzscrab@snowcrest.net; www. snowcrest.net/buzscrab/index.html; $; beer and wine; MC, V; local checks only; lunch, dinner every day.* &

**Cheesecakes Unlimited & Cafe** ★★ Cory Gabrielson and Nicholas Parker started Cheesecakes Unlimited as a wholesale cheese-cake business, then opened a small cafe that offers light meals—so now you can have your cake and eat croissant sandwiches and freshly made salads, too. A couple of winners are the Mexican chicken salad tossed with tomatoes, bell peppers, red onions, tortilla strips, and a cilantro salsa vinaigrette, and the prawn and pasta salad seasoned with a roasted garlic and herbed vinaigrette dressing. Of course, the New York–style cheesecakes (lemon, chocolate-chocolate, raspberry, almond amaretto, and mocha Bailey's) are the kind you'd never want to pass up—or even share with your mate. ■ *1334 Market St (just N of the downtown mall), Redding; (530)244-6670; $; beer and wine; AE, DIS, MC, V; checks OK; lunch Mon–Fri.* &

**Jack's Grill** ★★ A 1930s tavern, Jack's Grill is a beloved institution in Redding—so beloved, in fact, that few even grumble over the typical 2-hour wait for a table on the weekend. But be forewarned: this is a carnivores-only club, specializing in huge, juicy 1-pound steaks, tender brochettes, and thick steak sandwiches. The meaty meals are served with garlic bread, a green salad, a potato, and coffee. Jack starts cooking at 5pm, and hungry folks get there early. ■ *1743 California St (S of the downtown mall, between Sacramento and Placer Sts), Redding; (530)241-9705; donalcon@ aol.com; $$; full bar; AE, DIS, MC, V; local checks only; dinner Mon–Sat.* &

## LODGINGS

**Tiffany House Bed and Breakfast Inn** ★★ Perched on a hill above town, Brady and Susan Stewart's beautifully refurbished Cape Cod–style home offers three guest rooms and a cottage, a swimming pool, and a fine view of Mount Lassen. The Victorian Room, dressed in black-and-mauve rose-print walls, features charming cupola windows and a claw-footed bathtub. If you're an early bird, you'll appreciate the blue and white Tierra Room and the larger Oak Room, which both offer great sunrise views. All three rooms have a queen-size bed and a private bath. Guests are welcome to lounge in the antique-filled music parlor, where old-time sheet music is stacked on the piano. Another parlor houses a game table and a fireplace, an ideal retreat on cool nights. If you prefer total privacy (and can fork over a few more bucks), rent the attractive guest cottage, where you can bask in the luxurious indoor spa. ■ *1510 Barbara Rd (off Benton Dr), Redding, CA 96003; (530)244-3225; tiffanyhse@aol.com; www.sylvia.com/ tiffany.htm; $$; AE, DIS, MC, V; checks OK.*

## LEWISTON

### *RESTAURANTS*

**Lewiston Hotel** ★ Built in 1863 as a stage stop, the Lewiston Hotel is home to one of California's oldest continuously operating restaurants. As you might expect in a 19th-century country establishment, guns, animal furs, photos, and a large collection of street signs adorn the walls. An equally eclectic display is featured on the seasonal menu: prime rib (some of the region's best), steaks, game, fresh fish, housemade pasta, and a good beet, broccoli, and kidney bean salad are typically offered. Nelly Kaufman is both co-owner (with her husband) and the one wearing the chef's toque. ▪ *On Deadwood Rd (1 block from the bridge), Lewiston; (530)778-3823; $; full bar; DIS, MC, V; checks OK; dinner Thurs–Sun.*

### *LODGINGS*

**Old Lewiston Inn** ★★★ Innkeepers Connor and Mary Nixon ran a travel lodge in the Amazon for 13 years before trading up to a bed and breakfast in the wilds of Trinity County. Their B&B has seven guest rooms: three small rooms in the 1875 Baker House and four rooms in the adjoining inn (most have private baths). A favorite is the Baker House's Herbert Hoover Room, where the 31st president once slept. The inn accommodations have less history but more elbow room, with private entrances and decks overlooking the Trinity River. The Old Lewiston Inn also has a hot tub for unwinding after a hard day of touring the towns or fishing for trout. ▪ *On Deadwood Rd (½ block from the bridge), Lewiston; (530)778-3385 or (800)286-4441; mail: PO Box 688, Lewiston, CA 96052; nixons@snowcrest.com; www.ffa.com/ california/oldlewiston.html; $$; MC, V; checks OK. &*

Weaverville

## WEAVERVILLE

Founded nearly 150 years ago by gold miners, the little rural town of Weaverville (population 4,000) is the largest town in Trinity County (an area the size of Rhode Island and Delaware combined). While cruising through the historic downtown district, keep your peepers open for the peculiar outdoor spiral staircases that grace many of the homes—they're remnants of the days when each floor was owned by a different person. For a bit of Gold Rush and Weaverville history, stroll down Main Street and visit the small **Jake Jackson Museum**, 508 Main Street, (530)623-5211. Adjacent to the museum is **Joss House State Historic Park**, site of the oldest Chinese temple in the United States. The well-preserved temple was built by immigrant Chinese miners in 1874 and is worth a peek (and the nominal entrance fee); call (530)623-5284 for information on temple tours.

National forest blankets 70 percent of Trinity County, which includes the stunning Trinity Alps to the north. The area is chock-full of good fishing spots, especially on the **Trinity River**, **Trinity (aka Clair Engle) Lake**, and **Lewiston Lake**. Mountain bikers, hikers, and horseback riders flock to the scenic 50-mile **Weaver Basin Trail**, which circles Weaverville. Another town highlight is the grueling **La Grange Classic Mountain Bike Race**, typically held the first weekend in June. To find out more about this mountain town's activities, call the **Trinity County Chamber of Commerce** at (530)623-6101 or (800)487-4648, and for information about hunting, fishing, and backpacking in the area, visit the helpful staff at Brady's Sport Shop, located on the ground floor of the Weaverville Hotel at 201 Main Street, (530) 623-3121.

## RESTAURANTS

**La Grange Cafe ★★★**  Named after a nearby mine, La Grange Cafe serves the best food in town. Start your dinner with chef/owner Sharon Heryford's exceptionally fresh salad tossed with an Italian dressing and chunks of blue cheese. Then sink your teeth into her charbroiled marinated steak served with black bean chili, or try the tender Duane's Chicken accompanied by a wheat pilaf. An excellent and moderately priced wine list boasts more than 100 selections. And then there's the sweet stuff: divine desserts, such as berry cobbler, banana cream pie, and old-fashioned bread pudding, are made on the premises. ■ *315 N Main St (on Hwy 299), Weaverville; (530)623-5325; $$; full bar; AE, DIS, MC, V; checks OK; breakfast, lunch, dinner every day.* &

**Noelle's Garden Cafe ★★**  This snug, cheerful cafe, now located in an old two-story house, has a phalanx of windows and a sunny outside deck. Proprietress Noelle Roget's specialties include Austrian strudel (a flaky puff pastry filled with shrimp, veggies, and cheeses) and a hefty veggie melt served with her home-fries spiced with garlic and onion. The seasonal dinner menu may include such dishes as a perfectly cooked lime-marinated halibut or a vegetable stir-fry prepared with jumbo shrimp, chicken, or fresh vegetables. She also offers an array of baked desserts, and if the espresso cake is up for grabs, take it. ■ *252 Main St (1 block W of Oregon St), Weaverville; (530)623-2058; $; no credit cards; checks OK; breakfast, lunch every day Memorial Day to Labor Day (breakfast, lunch Tues–Sat Labor Day to Memorial Day), dinner Fri–Sat year-round.*

## LODGINGS

**Red Hill Motel ★**  The Red Hill's 14 well-maintained auto-court units (cabins with small covered garages) would have made a great set for a '40s film noir starring Ida Lupino and Humphrey Bogart. (If you've forgotten your film history lessons, auto-courts were a prominent feature of flicks in those days.) So put on your best Bogart fedora and step back in time by booking a night or two at these one- or two-bedroom cabins, decorated with authentic pre–World War II furnishings (except for the remote-control satellite TV, of course). Owners Patty and Willie Holder are doing a good job of restoring and refurbishing this jewel, surrounded by a rolling green lawn and ponderosa pines. Spend the day reeling in rainbow trout on the Trinity, then prepare your catch for supper at Red Hill's fish-cleaning station. Or kick back in a lawn chair under the pines and think about the good ol' days, when life was simpler, the fish were bigger, and folks were named Claudette, Clark, Ida, and Humphrey. The friendly Red Hill folks permit pets, too. ■ *On Red Hill Rd (across from the U.S. Forest Service station on Main St, at the N end of town), Weaverville; (530)623-4331; mail: PO Box 234, Weaverville, CA 96093; redhill@ snowcrest.net; www.redhillresorts.com; $; AE, MC, V; checks OK.* &

**Weaverville Hotel** This hotel has been in operation since 1861— a few fiery interruptions notwithstanding (it burned to the ground several times in the town's early days). The eight guest rooms, located on the second floor, are a bit spare, but they're a good choice for the budget-conscious traveler who likes historic surroundings with that morning cup of coffee. All rooms have private baths; most have TVs. Register at Brady's Sport Shop on

*Weaverville*

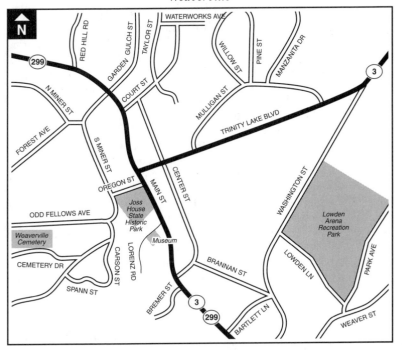

the ground floor, a gold mine of information about hunting, backpacking, and fishing in the area. ■ *201 Main St (in the center of town), Weaverville; (530)623-3121; mail: PO Box 537, Weaverville, CA 96093; $; MC, V; checks OK.*

## WILLOW CREEK

### *RESTAURANTS*

**Cinnabar Sam's** ★ If you travel between the Pacific coastline and Redding, be sure to stop for a bite at Cinnabar Sam's. A popular hangout for rafters and kayakers, this restaurant is decked out in Western memorabilia: antique gas pumps, old photographs, and movie posters from the golden days—even the salad bar is in a claw-footed tub. A favorite breakfast dish is the Claim Jumper: ham, scrambled eggs, hashbrowns, onions, bell peppers, sausage, and cheese. For lunch or dinner, try the popular do-it-yourself fajitas, the behemoth hamburger, the sirloin steak, or the barbe-cued ribs. On those sweltering summer days, head for the patio and toss back one of Sam's cooling fresh-fruit drinks. ■ *19 Willow Way (at Hwy 299, at the E end of town), Willow Creek; (530)629-3437; $; beer and wine; AE, DIS, MC, V; checks OK; breakfast, lunch, dinner every day.* &

## FORKS OF SALMON

### *LODGINGS*

**Otter Bar Lodge** ★★★ Surrounded by a pond and acres of mowed green grass, this seven-bedroom ranch-style lodge features oak floors, French doors, and lots of glass—all in an effort to bring the outdoors indoors. Two living rooms, two kitchens, a sauna, and a hot tub are also available to guests. The cedar-roofed, white-washed rooms have private decks and down comforters on the beds, and some are stocked with good books. Reserve the roman-tic Tower Room, an upstairs retreat lined with windows offering views of the fir trees, or try one of the three cabins.

Otter Bar Lodge doubles as a world-class kayaking school and offers some of the most beautiful mountain biking trails in the state. You can also take a three-day guided horseback trip into the Trinity Alps or grab your rod and reel and go fish; guides are even available to help you discover what's biting and where. The food is terrific—no ranch-style meat and potatoes here. Instead, look for paella, snapper Veracruz, and other sophisticated delights on the ever-changing menu. Breakfast offerings include veggie omelets, homemade granola, and berry pancakes. Six-night stays are required (and the seventh night is free), although shorter visits are available in April. All meals are included in the weekly rate. ■ *On Salmon River Rd (15 miles E of Somes Bar), Forks of Salmon; (530)462-4772; mail: PO Box 210, Forks of Salmon, CA 96031; otterbar@aol.com; $$$; no credit cards; checks OK (open Apr 1 to Sept 30).*

## HAPPY CAMP

Happy Camp used to be a lot more, well, happy. Nowadays, the town is dependent on the uncertain fortunes of lumbering, fishing, and tourism; some locals jokingly suggest a different adjective might be in order. Sleepy Camp, anyone?

### RESTAURANTS

**Indian Creek Cafe** ★  It may be a small cafe in one of the most sparsely populated corners of California, but Indian Creek has one of the state's largest menus. Youngsters in tow will definitely be happy campers, because there's something for everyone here—from breakfast sandwiches and subs to chicken, steak, seafood, and barbecued turkey platters. Still not satisfied? Take a look at the separate Mexican and vegetarian menus, and ask about the daily specials. ■ *106 Indian Creek Rd (near 2nd Ave), Happy Camp; (530)493-5180; $; beer and wine; AE, DC, DIS, MC, V; local checks only; breakfast, lunch, dinner every day.* ♿

## KLAMATH RIVER

### LODGINGS

**Beaver Creek Lodge** ★★  One of the better lodges on the Klamath River, Beaver Creek has five knotty pine cabins, well-groomed grounds, and a coveted riverfront location. Four cabins sleep up to three people each; a larger unit accommodates as many as five. All units have kitchens, and you can pick up groceries in town, only 2 miles away. Consider bringing along your golf clubs and plaid pants—a golf course is nearby. ■ *16606 Hwy 96 (2 miles E of town), Klamath River, CA 96050; (530)465-2331; $; no credit cards; checks OK.*

Yreka

*Restaurants*

## YREKA

Once a boomtown, Yreka now mines gold from tourists who visit the town's **Historic District**; city maps are available at the **Yreka Chamber of Commerce** at 117 West Miner Street, (530)842-1649. In the summer, take a scenic round-trip train ride on the **Yreka Western Railroad**, (530)842-4146, to the historic town of **Montague**, where you can poke around the museum in the 1887 railroad depot and get a snack at the 1904 **Opera Restaurant** at 170 South 11th Street, (530)459-5794.

### RESTAURANTS

**The Old Boston Shaft** ★  You won't get the shaft at this Yreka restaurant, where a generous three- to four-course meal costs about $35 for two. What a deal! Swiss chef/owners Erich Gisler and Max and Erich Schuler specialize in hearty beef and veal dishes. Try their Veal Zingara, prepared with tomato, ham, and mushrooms, or the Veal à la Swiss, made with tomato, Swiss cheese, asparagus, and hollandaise. The wine list is basic but won't blow your budget. ■ *1801 Fort Jones Rd (W of I-5 at the Fort Jones/Hwy 3 exit), Yreka; (530)842-5768; $; full bar; AE, DIS, MC, V; local checks only; lunch Mon–Fri, dinner Mon–Sat.* ⌖

## FORT JONES

### *LODGINGS*

**The Wild Goose** ★★  Furnished with family heirlooms and antiques, this 1890 country Victorian house has been rebuilt from the ground up by owners Terry and Cindy Hayes. The two rooms on the second floor were designed for the care and comfort of guests, and each has an antique double bed and a private bathroom. Step out onto the second-story veranda for a view of the village of Fort Jones and the distant Marble Mountains. The Wild Goose goes wild over breakfast, so bring your appetite to the table and prepare yourself for fresh breads and muffins, homemade granola, fresh-squeezed juice, French toast with poached pears, and warm morning puddings. ■ *11624 Main St (off Hwy 3), Fort Jones; (530)468-2735; mail: PO Box 546, Fort Jones, CA 96032; $; no credit cards; checks OK.* ⌖

## ETNA

### *RESTAURANTS*

**Sengthong's** ★★★  Folks from Redding to Yreka sing the praises of this unpretentious restaurant hidden in one of the most remote areas of California. Born in Vietnam, Sengthong Phelps lived in Laos and Thailand before making her way to this sparsely populated corner of Siskiyou County. Now she and her husband, Don, run this small restaurant and work hard at blending the cuisines of the three countries Sengthong left behind. You can see (and taste) the Laotian influence in the savory sticky-rice balls. Also don't miss the Thai hot-spiced beef and the thick seafood stew bubbling with fresh fish, clams, scallops, and prawns. ■ *434 Main St (off Hwy 3, in the center of town), Etna; (530)467-5668; $; beer and wine; no credit cards; checks OK; lunch Wed–Fri, dinner Wed–Sun.*

### *LODGINGS*

**Bradley's Alderbrook Manor** ★★  Recently restored, this Victorian mansion set on 3 acres of oaks and alders has been lovingly furnished by Dr. Joyce Bradley with memorabilia from her travels around the world. The downstairs guest room has a private bathroom, the two rooms on the second floor share a bath, and a four-bed dorm shares a bath with Bradley. Alder Creek runs through the property, and downtown Etna is just a short walk away. Equestrians can board their horses here, and Diana, the assistant innkeeper, will take care of other manageable pets at her house nearby. ■ *836 Main St (near Church St), Etna, CA 96027-0489; (530)467-3917; joybrad@snowcrest.net; $; no credit cards; checks OK.* &

## COFFEE CREEK

South of Etna on Highway 3 is the postage-stamp-size town of Coffee Creek, which supposedly got its name from a miner's pack train that spilled coffee into the town's creek, although some claim the name came from the spring runoff, which colors the creek brown. Whatever the case, this town dates back to the Gold Rush days of the 1850s. There aren't many places to dine around here, but your best bet is the **Forest Cafe** on Highway 3 at Coffee Creek Road, (530)266-3575. Venture a little farther south and you'll see **Trinity Lake** (also known as **Clair Engle Lake** in honor of an environmentally conscious local politician), a popular haunt of anglers and other lovers of the great outdoors.

### *LODGINGS*

**Ripple Creek Cabins** ★★ Set amid tall pines and cedars where Ripple Creek enters the Trinity River, all seven of Jim and Michele Coleman's well-furnished cabins have amply stocked kitchens (Wow! Corkscrews and garlic presses!) and private baths. Most of the cabins accommodate two to six people. There's also a four-bedroom house for rent—ideal for a family reunion or retreat. Diversions include table tennis, bicycles, a volleyball and badminton court, and a swimming hole. For a $10 fee, you can even bring your pooch along. ■ *On Eagle Creek Loop (off Hwy 3), Coffee Creek; (530)266-3505 or (510)531-5315; mail: Rte 2, Box 4020, Trinity Center, CA 96091; RippleC2JPG@www.travelsphere. com; www.TravelSphere.com/916; $; no credit cards; checks OK.* &

## GAZELLE

### *LODGINGS*

**Hollyhock Farm Bed & Breakfast** ★★★ Mount Shasta looms beyond this B&B's front yard like some giant ghostly apparition, giving Hollyhock Farm one of the most impressive views in the country. Though this 1902 Normandy-style stone farmhouse is easily overlooked, its charm and setting make it a required stop for visitors to the North Mountains. Downstairs are the Blue Room (painted blue, of course) with a king-size bed and a private bath, and the Sierra Room with twin beds and a bathroom that's shared with the owner. The upstairs suite includes a queen-size bed, a daybed in the sun room, and a private bath. For the ultimate in privacy, stay in the guest house behind the inn, equipped with a queen-size bed, twin bed, kitchenette, and private bath. Owner Beth Pokorny has tastefully furnished all the rooms with antiques and lace curtains. She'll even house your canine companions in her kennel and your horses at the farm. Breakfast is served whenever you'd like it. ■ *18705 Old Hwy 99 (just west of I-5; from Yreka take the Grenada/Gazelle exit; from Weed take the Edgewood/Gazelle exit), Gazelle; (530)435-2627; mail: PO Box 152, Gazelle, CA 96034; $–$$; MC, V; checks OK.* ♿

## WEED

Nestled on the north flank of Mount Shasta, this little lumber town doesn't offer much to the tourist, except, perhaps, the popular "I got high on Weed, California" T-shirt.

### LODGINGS

**Stewart Mineral Springs ★** Hidden in a forested canyon at the end of a twisting country road, Stewart Mineral Springs is a great place to commune with nature and unwind from the rigors of daily life. To ensure you get the R&R you deserve, start off with a visit to the bathhouse, located across the creek at the end of the footbridge, for a detoxifying mineral bath, a sauna, and maybe even a plunge in the creek or the large pond. You can sleep in one of the two inexpensive but spiritually enriching tepees (bring your own bedding) or in one of the five more comfortable (though spartan) little cabins with kitchens. If you plan to cook in your cabin, buy foodstuffs before you get to this remote locale— convenience stores and burger emporiums are (thankfully) not a part of the scenery here. The five-bedroom A-frame is perfect for large groups of up to 10 people, and there are 10 modest motel rooms. Camping and RV sites are available, too. ■ *4617 Stewart Springs Rd (call for directions), Weed, CA 96094; (530)938-2222; $; DIS, MC, V; checks OK (open Mar 1 to Nov 15).* ♿

## MOUNT SHASTA

Magnificent, snowcapped Mount Shasta soars 14,162 feet into the sky and it is the largest volcano (by mass) in the contiguous 48 states. Shasta is a dormant volcano; it's not dead, just sleeping until it decides to blow its snowy stack—something it hasn't done since the late 1700s. Although an eruption may seem long overdue, fear not; geologists constantly monitor movement within the volcano and claim they will be able to predict an eruption early enough for you to pack your bags and skedaddle.

Shasta is only the fifth-highest peak in the state, but unlike its taller cousins, which are clustered with other large mountains, this volcano stands alone, a position that seems to intensify its grandeur. "Lonely as God and white as a winter moon" is how author Joaquin Miller described this solitary peak in the 1870s. The mountain dominates the horizon from every angle, and on clear days it's visible from as far away as 150 miles.

Some Native Americans who lived in its shadow believed Mount Shasta was the home of the Great Spirit and vowed never to climb its sacred slopes, which they viewed as an act of disrespect. Today, men and women from around the world pay tribute to the volcano by making the spectacular trek to the top. This is not a mountain for novice hikers, however; its many tremendous crevasses have swallowed careless climbers, and its extreme, unpredictable weather at high altitudes makes expert equipment a must. But with some basic **mountain climbing** instruction and a good study of Shasta's various routes, physically fit adventurers can safely reach its stunning summit ("It's just like climbing stairs nonstop from 9 to 5," says one veteran climber). You can buy a good map of the mountain and rent crampons, an ice ax, and sturdy, insulated climbing boots at the Fifth Season sports store, staffed by experienced and helpful mountaineers; 300 North Mount Shasta Boulevard at Lake Street, (530)926-3606 (store), (530)926-5555 (mountain report). If you're eager to climb Mount Shasta but you don't know a crampon from a tampon, take an all-day lesson in basic mountain-climbing skills from the folks at Shasta Mountain Guides, (530)926-3117. And whether you're a beginner or an expert climber, visit the **Mount Shasta Ranger District Office**, which gives out up-to-date climbing literature as well as friendly advice. Get your free (but mandatory) hiking permit while you're there, so the rangers will know how long you'll be on the mountain (permits are located in a small booth outside the front door); 204 West Alma Street off North Mount Shasta Boulevard, (530)926-4511. You also must sign off on your permit *after* you return from your climb so a rescue team won't be sent out to find you.

▼

**Mount Shasta**

▲

If all this climbing sounds a wee bit intimidating, there *is* an easier way. For the last decade, many folks have made their way up Mount Shasta via a chairlift (though it doesn't reach the peak) and their way down on skis. **Mount Shasta Ski Park** offers mostly intermediate runs with nary a mogul in sight, and the lift tickets won't require a second mortgage on your home. Ski Park also has a ski and snowboard rental/repair shop, restaurant, snack bar, and ski school. In the summer, the resort provides naturalist-led walks, mountain biking trails accessible by chairlift (bike rentals are available, too), and an indoor recreational climbing wall for people of all ages and abilities; it's located at the end of Ski Park Highway off Highway 89, 10 miles east of Interstate 5, (530)926-8610 (ski resort), (530)926-8686 (snow report). About a quarter-mile down the highway is the **Nordic Lodge**, a cross-country ski center with several miles of groomed tracks; located on Ski Park Highway, (530)926-8610.

If you prefer to admire Mount Shasta from afar, visit **Castle Crags State Park**, one of California's geologic wonders. The park's enormous 6,500-foot spires of ancient granite are visible from the highway, but they deserve a much closer look. If you're anxious to really stretch your legs, hike up the park's moderately strenuous 2.7-mile **Summit Dome Trail** to the base of the crags—the view of Mount Shasta alone is worth the trip. Less adventurous souls can stroll along the 1-mile **Root Creek** or **Indian Creek Trails** or picnic among the pines and wildflowers; from Interstate 5, take the Castle Crags State Park exit, about 13 miles south of Mount Shasta, (530)235-2684.

For another unforgettable experience, splurge on a guided **whitewater rafting** trip down the mighty **Klamath River**. Daredevils can soar down the narrow, steep chutes appropriately called Hell's Corner and Caldera, while saner souls (including children) can navigate the much-less-perilous forks. Prices for one-day trips range from $70 to $100 (multiday trips are also available). Call the Turtle River Rafting Company for more details at (530)926-3223.

While the town of Mount Shasta (population 3,700) caters to the thousands of thrill-seekers and naturalists who make the long journey here every year, it also has its share of New Agers and metaphysical folks (the Creative Harmonics Institute, Ascended Master Teaching Foundation, Shasta Buddhist Abbey, and the Temple of Cosmic Religion are all here). In fact, for years, Mount Shasta has been hailed by spiritualists as one of the seven "power centers" of the world. Although city council members are loath to admit it (and you certainly won't see the words *channeling*

or *crystal* in any chamber of commerce brochure), a large percentage of visitors are spiritual pilgrims who have come from around the world to bask in the majestic mountain's mysterious energy. If you're interested in learning about the mountain's alleged mystical powers, visit the delightfully funky **Golden Bough Bookstore**, where the staff can give you the spiritual lowdown and direct you to tapes, books, and all matter of info on the topic; 219 North Mount Shasta Boulevard at Lake Street, (530)926-3228.

If you've had enough spiritual enlightenment and are no longer excited about hanging by your nails from cliffs for fun, the town of Mount Shasta offers two good (and safe) attractions that won't even make a dent in your billfold: the free **Sisson Museum** showcases changing exhibits on local history, nature, geology, and Native American life, and its adjacent **Mount Shasta Fish Hatchery**, the oldest hatchery in the West, keeps thousands of rainbow and brown trout, including a few biggies, in the holding ponds. For only a quarter you can get some fish food and incite a fish-feeding frenzy; take Lake Street across the freeway, turn left on Hatchery Road, and head to 3 North Old Stage Road, (530)926-2215 (hatchery), (530)926-5508 (museum). For more information on Shasta's attractions, see the Redding and the Shasta Lake Area section at the beginning of this chapter or contact the **Mount Shasta Visitors Bureau** at 300 Pine Street at Lake Street, (530)926-4865.

**Serge's Restaurant** ★★★ This classical French restaurant framed with lace curtains is Mount Shasta's best—and it's even more memorable because of the view of the grand volcano from the deck. The menu changes seasonally, and starters often range from garlicky escargots and prawns sautéed with Pernod to a classic caesar salad and a sublime onion soup gratiné. Entrees might include a perfectly grilled 9-ounce New York steak with Provençal herbs or scallops and prawns in a light Chablis sauce served over a puffed pastry shell. Mount Shasta is a hotbed of vegetarianism, so meatless dishes always make an appearance, such as the manicotti stuffed with toasted walnuts, mushrooms, and eggplant and drizzled with a lemon-thyme tomato sauce. Desserts are whipped up daily and often include a rich, heavenly chocolate mousse and a cheesecake topped with a savory berry sauce. ■ *531 Chestnut St (1 block E of Mt Shasta Blvd), Mount Shasta; (530)926-1276; $$; beer and wine; AE, DIS, MC, V; local checks only; dinner Wed–Sun.* ♿

**Lily's** ★★ Even with new owners at the helm, this popular place offers very good California cuisine with an ethnic flair. Start your dinner with spicy Thai noodles, kung pao shrimp, or baked Brie, and follow that with an entree of prime rib, Chicken Rosie (a chicken breast browned in butter and simmered with raspberries, hazelnut liqueur, and a hint of cream), or the terrific enchiladas *suizas* stuffed with crab, shrimp, and fresh spinach. Lunch offerings are equally varied and imaginative, and if you're looking for something a little different from the usual breakfast fare, try Lily's cheesy polenta fritters. ■ *1013 S Mt Shasta Blvd (from I-5, take the Central Mt Shasta exit), Mount Shasta; (530)926-3372; $; beer and wine; AE, DIS, MC, V; local checks only; breakfast Mon–Fri, brunch Sat–Sun and holidays, lunch Mon–Fri, dinner every day.* ♿

▼

**Mount Shasta**

*Restaurants*

▲

**Acacia Restaurant, Bar and Grill** ★ When the dinner bell rings, Acacia's faithful clientele comes running for entrees like Chicken Bombay, a tender breast of chicken in a coconut curry sauce sprinkled with cashews and raisins; hearty jambalaya studded with chicken, shrimp, and sausage; juicy barbecue pork ribs; and vegetarian curry pie. Several tables are set outside for dining alfresco when the weather's warm, and if you're a football fan, you might want to chow down while watching the big games on the big-screen TV. All-American standards are served for breakfast and lunch, but Acacia's calling card is definitely dinner. Live reggae, rock 'n' roll, classical guitar, or soft jazz bands perform on Saturday night. ■ *1136 S Mt Shasta Blvd (from I-5, take the Central Mt Shasta exit), Mount Shasta; (530)926-0250; $; full bar; AE, DIS, MC, V; breakfast, lunch, dinner every day in the summer (breakfast Sat, brunch Sun, lunch, dinner every day in the winter).* ♿

**Michael's Restaurant** ★  Michael and Lynn Kobseff have been running this estimable little restaurant since 1980, which makes them old-timers on the ever-changing Mount Shasta restaurant scene. Some of their best lunchtime offerings are the crisp, greaseless fried zucchini appetizer, the french fries, and a terrific teriyaki turkey sandwich. Their Italian dinners will satisfy those with lumberjack-size appetites, especially the combination ravioli and linguine plate. The small but varied wine list features several bargains. ■ *313 Mt Shasta Blvd (from I-5, take the Central Mt Shasta exit), Mount Shasta; (530) 926-5288; $; beer and wine; AE, DIS, MC, V; local checks OK; lunch, dinner Tues–Sat.* ♿

## LODGINGS

**Mount Shasta Ranch Bed and Breakfast** ★★★  This 70-year-old bed-and-breakfast inn with gabled windows and hip roofs offers large rooms, large baths, large views, and even large breakfasts. In addition to five guest rooms in the main building, the Mount Shasta Ranch B&B has five rooms in a converted carriage house and a two-bedroom cottage. The main house, decorated with colorful country decor, has the largest guest rooms (four of them sleep up to four people each), plus huge private bathrooms sporting original 1920s fixtures. The carriage house's five units are smaller and share two bathrooms, but have great views of Mount Shasta and the rugged Siskiyous. Come morning, indulge in a hearty breakfast that might include cream-cheese-filled waffles with fresh fruit toppings, crêpes bursting with local blackberries, plump sausages, a fresh fruit salad, and good strong coffee. Afterwards, curl up with a book in front of the main lodge's gargantuan stone fireplace, or work off those waffles by hiking, swimming, playing a few rounds of table tennis, or golfing at the nearby course. ■ *1008 W. A. Barr Rd (S of the fish hatchery), Mount Shasta, CA 96067; (530) 926-3870; alpine@macshasta. com; $$; AE, DIS, MC, V; checks OK.*

**Mount Shasta Resort** ★★★  If you think people who live to hit little golf balls should get a life, you'll have second thoughts when you see the incredibly scenic Mount Shasta Resort. The prospect of spending all day on a rolling green lawn and breathing in clean air under the towering presence of Mount Shasta is alluring—even to those who have never heard of Tiger Woods. The 50 one- and two-bedroom Craftsman-style chalets have all the creature comforts, and they're located on the forested shore of Lake Siskiyou, where you can swim, fish, sailboard, kayak, canoe, or rent paddleboats. What? Left your putter at home? Don't despair. You can buy a new one here or consider such pastimes as fishing, hiking, mountain biking, or skiing—they're all within putting distance of the resort. Two-night minimum stays are required for Friday and Saturday in the summer and on major holidays. Chalet rentals vary seasonally. Ask about the special golf packages offered from May through September (weather permitting) and the ski packages and romantic getaway deals available in the winter. The clubhouse restaurant serves good California cuisine, and there are several great restaurants nearby in town and in Dunsmuir. ■ *1000 Siskiyou Lake Blvd (from I-5, take the Central Mt Shasta exit, go W on Old Stage Rd, veer onto W. A. Barr Rd, and turn left on Siskiyou Lake Blvd), Mount Shasta, CA 96067; (530) 926-3030 or (800) 958-3363 (reservations only); msresort@ macshasta.com; www.mountshastaresort.com; $$–$$$; AE, DC, DIS, MC, V; local checks only.* &

**Strawberry Valley Inn** ★★ Hosts Chuck and Susie Ryan have incorporated the privacy of a motel and the personal touches of a B&B to create this terrific 14-room inn surrounded by a lush garden and towering oaks. Guest rooms are individually decorated with color-coordinated fabrics, and if you prefer lots of room to romp, ask for a two-room suite. A buffet breakfast featuring fresh fruit, granola, oatmeal, waffles, and pastries is set up next to the inn's stone fireplace (and those who want to dine in private may take a tray to their room). Complimentary wine is poured at the cocktail hour every evening. ■ *1142 S Mt Shasta Blvd (from I-5, take the Central Mt Shasta exit), Mount Shasta, CA 96067; (530) 926-2052; $; AE, DIS, MC, V; checks OK.* &

## DUNSMUIR

When a Southern Pacific train ran off the tracks in 1991 and spilled an herbicide in the Sacramento River, it killed all aquatic life for 45 miles along the river. And it darn near killed Dunsmuir. But this pretty, historic railroad town has a population of 2,300 resilient residents who are bringing the place back with a vengeance. Using a financial settlement from Southern Pacific, the townsfolk have gussied up their community and hope to make Dunsmuir a major California tourist destination. They may just succeed. In addition to the beautiful natural surroundings, stylish gift shops and restaurants have sprung up on the city's streets (particularly on Dunsmuir and Sacramento Avenues). Furthermore, trophy-size wild trout now abound in the Sacramento River, and the community slogan is "The Upper Sac is back." Fortunately, not all of the tourists are coming to Dunsmuir by car, thanks to the Amtrak train that stops here daily. Call the **Dunsmuir Chamber of Commerce and Visitors Center** at (800) DUNSMUIR for the nitty-gritty.

### RESTAURANTS

**Cafe Maddalena** ★★★★ Had chef/owner Maddalena Sera built her restaurant in San Francisco, it would have been a great success among the city's culinary cognoscenti. Thank goodness she didn't, because Dunsmuir is a perfect (though surprising) place for her cafe. Dining at this small, intimate restaurant (which was even designed and built by Sera) is similar to eating at a four-star restaurant in some little European village. Sera is from Sardinia, an island west of the southern Italian peninsula, so expect superb Italian cuisine with subtle differences in flavors and ingredients than what you'd find on the Italian mainland. For example, Sardinians are particularly fond of using fish in their fare, and instead of incorporating Parmesan cheese into many of their dishes they prefer to use the sharper flavored pecorino (cheese made from sheep's milk). Sera cooks everything herself from behind a counter in the corner of her cafe, which only holds a dozen tables. When the weather is warm, she also sets out a couple of tables in her Italian herb garden. The small scale of her restaurant enables Sera to consistently whip up delicious fare night after night. Her seasonal one-page menu is always satisfying but quite simple: appetizers, salads, pizza, pasta, and a fresh fish and meat dish of the day. Don't pass up the menu's mainstays: the Gallega Salad, made with shrimp, parsley, garlic, and thinly sliced potatoes with a lemon dressing, and the Pasta Marco, fresh fettuccine with shrimp, tomatoes, herbs, and cream wrapped in dough and baked in the pizza oven. Everything is made daily, including the breads and desserts. The wine list is small but carefully selected and reasonably priced. Cafe Maddalena is, unfortunately, only open half the year. ■ *5801 Sacramento Ave (one block W of Dunsmuir Ave), Dunsmuir; (530) 235-2725; $$; beer and wine; MC, V; local checks only; dinner Thurs–Sun (open May to mid-Dec only).* ✦

**The Old Rostel Pub and Cafe** ★★　Built by German emigrant Herman Rostel in 1892, this lively pub and cafe across the street from the Dunsmuir train station is popular with locals, anglers, and history buffs. Mr. Rostel would have appreciated the labor of love that went into the restoration of his building by proprietors Tim and Joan Elam. They used all of the original wood to create a warm, friendly restaurant with a wraparound deck that overlooks the historic train yard. Expect a mix of very good traditional German and not-so-traditional vegetarian dishes. For a breakfast that'll fuel your butt right up Shasta, order the Rostel Mess: baby red potatoes and grilled veggies smothered with cheese and a pair of eggs. A wide variety of sandwiches, soups, and a tasty black bean chili are offered for lunch, and dinner selections range from the grilled balsamic vegetable platter served with polenta to the aptly named Hog Heaven platter—a savory concoction of pan-fried pork chops and linguiça sausage with cabbage, bacon relish, and house-made applesauce. In addition to imported and domestic microbrews, there are nine Pacific Northwest microbrews on tap. In the summertime, inquire about the outdoor concerts. ■ *5743 Sacramento Ave (one block W of Dunsmuir Ave), Dunsmuir; (530) 235-2028; rostel@macshasta.com; www.rostelpub. com; $; beer and wine; DIS, MC, V; checks OK; breakfast, lunch, dinner every day (breakfast, lunch, dinner Wed–Sun in the winter).* ✦

**Railroad Park Resort/The Caboose Motel** A must for railroad buffs but a maybe for everyone else, the Railroad Park Resort's funky Caboose Motel offers quiet, comfortable lodgings in a boxcar and 23 refurbished cabooses from the Southern Pacific, Santa Fe, and Great Northern Railroads. Most have king- or queen-size beds with small bay windows or rooftop cupolas. The Boxcar (room 20) is decorated in country antiques and has a small private patio. Motel management also rents out four cabins. All guests have access to the pool and Jacuzzi—not to mention a great view of nearby Castle Crags. Guests may bring along their small pets, too. And if you're a big prime rib fan you're in luck: that's the specialty of the Railroad Park Resort Restaurant. ■ *100 Railroad Park Rd (1 mile S of town), Dunsmuir, CA 96025; (530)235-4440; $ (lodgings), $–$$ (restaurant); full bar; AE, DIS, MC, V; checks OK; dinner Wed–Mon (dinner Fri–Sun in the winter).* &

## McCLOUD

A company-built milltown, McCloud bills itself as "the quiet side of Mount Shasta." And true to its motto, this is a relatively sleepy place, but its many sumptuous B&Bs attract a lot of anglers, hikers, and other nature lovers who spend their waking hours in the great outdoors, as well as those bleary-eyed city folk who long for little more than a warm bed and some solitude. Whatever your attraction to this neck of the woods, you can introduce yourself to the area in style by hopping aboard the **Shasta Sunset Dinner Train**, which follows a historic turn-of-the-century logging route. The steep grades, sharp curves, and a unique switchback at Signal Butte are still part of the route, though passengers now ride in cars handsomely restored in wood and brass. As you nosh on a very good dinner in your railcar, you'll be treated to views of Mount Shasta, Castle Crags, and the Trinity Alps. The 40-mile, 3-hour journey is run by the McCloud Railway Company from April to December, and costs about $70 for adults and $45 for children under 12, which includes dinner. Special-event train trips are scheduled throughout the year; call (530)964-2142 or (800)733-2141 for more details.

**McCloud**

In the summer, you can watch—or, better yet, join—the McCloud locals as they kick up their heels every weekend from May to September in the town's two air-conditioned dance halls. Dancing—especially square dancing—is a favorite pastime here, so if you want to promenade your partner or swing to the beat (not to the heat), call (530)964-2578 for the latest schedule. This part of the North Mountains is also extraordinarily rich in outdoor recreational opportunities; see the Mount Shasta section for details.

**McCloud Bed and Breakfast Hotel** ★★★★  Built in 1916, the McCloud Bed and Breakfast Hotel has earned a highly coveted spot on the National Register of Historic Landmarks. Its meticulous restoration was completed in 1995, and now the hotel offers 14 beautiful guest rooms gussied up with antiques, decorator fabrics, and, in many cases, tall four-poster beds. Each room also has a private bath. Stay in one of the luxe suites decked out with a whirlpool bath, sitting area, canopy bed, and balcony and you may never want to leave your room. Gourmet breakfasts of fresh fruit, house-made bread, and a hot dish are served in the lobby area (though if you're staying in a suite, you can have the meal delivered to your room). If you happen to tire of McCloud's numerous outdoor attractions, kick back in the hotel lobby's comfortable chairs and sofas and borrow one of the many books, games, and puzzles stashed here. The hotel also offers picnic-lunch tours of the surrounding area in the comfortable hotel van. And car collectors take note: a 20 percent discount on the room rate is given to anyone arriving at the hotel in a pre–World War II auto. ▪ *408 Main St (from exit off Hwy 89, follow signs to the historical district), McCloud; (530)964-2822 or (800)964-2823; mail: PO Box 730, McCloud, CA 96057; mchotel@telis.org; www.mchotel.com; $$–$$$; DIS, MC, V; checks OK.* &

**Hogin House** ★★★  Many innkeepers try, but few have managed to create the relaxing ambience and charm of a country B&B as well as Angie and Rich Toreson have. Located just outside downtown McCloud, their small, delightfully cluttered two-story Victorian house was built in 1904 for the town doctor. The four guest bedrooms are decorated with antique toys, colorful quilts, calico fabrics, and country-style wallpaper. You can curl up in front of the fire in the sitting room or spend a leisurely morning in the airy sun room. An expanded continental breakfast of fresh fruit, cereal, homemade breads and muffins, juice, coffee, and tea may be served in the dining room, on the porch, or on the lush lawn that sweeps down toward the center of town. ▪ *424 Lawndale Ct (at W Colombero Dr), McCloud; (530)964-2882 or (530)964-3125 (proprietor's office); mail: PO Box 550, McCloud, CA 96057; $; MC, V; checks OK.*

**McCloud Guest House** ★★  Built in 1907 for McCloud timber baron J. H. Queal, this stately two-story mansion became the McCloud River Lumber Company's guest house after Queal's death in 1921. Herbert Hoover, Jean Harlow, and various members of the Hearst family dallied here in the '20s and '30s, but soon afterward the house fell into disrepair. Restored as a country inn and restaurant, McCloud Guest House reopened its doors in 1984. Downstairs in the lobby and dining room are delicately wrought cabinetry, beveled glass, antique wallpaper, and a massive stone fireplace. Upstairs you'll find a game room furnished with the house's original light fixtures and a magnificent antique carved billiards table. The inn's spacious five guest rooms have four-poster beds and antique furnishings. A continental breakfast including a fresh fruit cup is served every morning, and the inn's restaurant serves well-prepared dinners of charbroiled beef, chicken, veal, pasta, and seafood to the public several nights a week. ■ *606 W Colombero Dr (at the W end of town), McCloud; (530)964-3160; mail: PO Box 1510, McCloud, CA 96057; $$; beer and wine; MC, V; checks OK; dinner Wed–Sun (call for winter hours).*

## CASSEL

### *LODGINGS*

**Clearwater House** ★★★★  This fine turn-of-the-century farmhouse is the only fishing lodge in California officially approved by Orvis—that old-money purveyor of gentlemanly fishing and sports equipment. Created by former wilderness and fishing guide Dick Galland, the inn features seven rooms (all with private baths) decorated in the style of an English angling lodge with fish and game prints on the walls, Oriental rugs on the hardwood floors, and cherry-wood tables set for family-style meals. Pick up pointers on the art of fly-fishing at a three-day (Sunday through Tuesday) fishing class, or attend Galland's "Mastering the Art of Fly-Fishing" five-day program. Meals are included in the room rate—and they're the best you'll find for miles around. Expect traditional breakfasts, picnic lunches, and well-prepared country-style dinners featuring fare like barbecued ribs, roast pork loin, and various pastas. A tackle shop and tennis courts round out the amenities. ■ *At the intersection of Hat Creek and Cassel/Fall River Rds, Cassel; (415)381-1173; mail: PO Box 90, Cassel, CA 96016; d1trout@aol.com; www.clearwatertrout.com; $$; beer and wine; MC, V; checks OK (open Apr 30 to mid-Nov).*

## FALL RIVER MILLS

### *LODGINGS*

**Lava Creek Lodge** ★★  The panoramic view of the southern Cascades from Mount Lassen to Mount Shasta is Lava Creek's trump card. Set well back from the main road at the end of a country lane, the lodge has eight modest guest rooms with private baths, and most offer lake views. But the best accommodations are actually in the woods: seven small, comfortable cabins were recently renovated and all have private baths. Rates include either two or three country-style meals served in the lodge's knotty pine dining room. Lava Creek is located in one of the country's best trout-fishing areas, so take advantage of this golden opportunity: rent one of the lodge's boats and hire their fishing guide so you can tell the folks back home how you reeled in the big one. Hunting guides are available during duck season, too. Also nearby is the

Fall River Golf Course, one of Northern California's best. ■ *On Eastman Lake (at the end of Island Rd), Fall River Mills; (530)336-6288; mail: Glenburn Star Rte, Fall River Mills, CA 96028; $$–$$$ (includes meals); beer and wine; MC, V; checks OK; breakfast, lunch, dinner every day for guests only (closed in Feb).* &

## ALTURAS

### RESTAURANTS

**Nipa's California Cuisine** ★ You won't find seared tuna in loquat sauce here. Nipa's version of California cuisine is actually spicy Thai food—and it's the finest fare of any kind in Modoc County. Located in an old drive-in burger joint that's been transformed into a contemporary cafe decorated with Thai artifacts, Nipa's serves such classic favorites as Tom Yum Kung, a fragrant soup packed with prawns and mushrooms; phad Thai, a satisfying dish of pan-fried noodles with prawns, chicken, egg, bean sprouts, green onions, and a sprinkling of ground peanuts; and a spicy, succulent, red curry dish made with prawns, chicken, or beef simmered in coconut milk. Wash it all down with a deliciously sweet Thai iced tea. ■ *1001 N Main St (1 block S of Hwys 299 and 395), Alturas; (530)233-2520; $; beer and wine; MC, V; local checks only; lunch, dinner every day.*

### LODGINGS

**Dorris House** ★★ A room with a view is a standard feature of this two-story, turn-of-the-century ranch house, named for the brothers who founded Alturas in 1870. Set on a sage-covered plain at the edge of Dorris Lake, just below the towering Warner Mountains, the property is a favorite stop for migratory birds (not to mention patrons who migrate here for a respite). Hosts Karol and Mary Woodward have decorated their immaculate inn's four guest rooms with family antiques and comfortable furnishings, making the rooms a pleasant home-away-from-home. Longtime residents of Alturas, the Woodwards know all the choice spots for hiking, fishing, bird-watching, and picnicking, so be sure to ask them for touring tips. Breakfast, served in the homey kitchen, is simple but very good, and might include moist zucchini nut bread, sweet bran muffins, or a dazzling fruit platter. ■ *On County Road (CR) 57 (3 miles E of Hwy 395; on CR 56, turn right at CR 57 and drive 1 mile), Alturas; (530)233-3786; mail: PO Box 1655, Alturas, CA 96101; $; no credit cards; checks OK.*

## CEDARVILLE

North of Alturas, Highway 299 turns east and crosses the narrow, little-known, and seldom visited **Warner Mountains**, where antelope often graze. Then the highway descends into the aptly named **Surprise Valley**, an oasis for overland trail emigrants after the rigors of the Nevada desert, and Cedarville, a little old-fashioned town of a bygone time. As one local poet put it, Cedarville is "where the pavement ends, and the West begins."

Isolated by the Warner Mountains on one side and the western edge of the Great Basin on the other, Cedarville attracts an interesting mix of travelers: in addition to the usual hunters, fly fishers, history buffs, and bird and wildlife watchers, you'll find paleontologists and paleobiologists drawn to the plentiful animal and plant fossils found in this part of the Great Basin. Whatever lured you here, there are lots of hot springs to help rejuvenate those weary bones after a day of exploring. To find out what's currently happening in the area, visit the friendly folks at **Great Basin Books**, 540 Main Street, (530)279-2337. In addition to selling books, this shop houses Floating Island Publications, a publisher of limited-edition poetry and prose.

### *RESTAURANTS*

**Country Hearth Restaurant & Bakery** The Country Hearth should be called "The Country Heart" for all the love owner Janet Irene puts into the meals served in her homey, pine-paneled dining room with its wood-burning stove. Bite into her good hamburgers served on toasted, fresh-baked rolls, or try the nightly special "country-cooked meal," which might feature pork chops or fried chicken. Irene makes all the breads, rolls, pastries, and desserts, which you can purchase for the trip home, too. ■ *551 Main St (S of Hwy 299), Cedarville; (530)279-2280; $; beer and wine; no credit cards; checks OK; breakfast, lunch, dinner every day.* ♿



### *LODGINGS*

**J. K. Metzker House Bed and Breakfast** ★★ Built in 1860 by town founder William Cressler, this pretty clapboard house with its white picket fence and rose-lined walkway was the residence of Cressler's descendants until 1990, when it was acquired by Judy Metzker Topol. Topol named the B&B in honor of her great-great-great grandfather who followed the Oregon Trail and settled in the Surprise Valley. After that long trek, Mr. Metzker surely would have appreciated snoozing in the comfort of one of the four guest rooms, three upstairs and one downstairs. Each room has a private bath and a queen-size bed (the downstairs bedroom also has twin beds). Innkeeper Michael Sykes, who owns Great Basin Books next door, hurries over every morning to set out a buffet breakfast of cereals, yogurt, fresh fruit, and bagels, and with advance notice he'll also make sure there are low-fat and low-cholesterol treats. In the winter, snuggle up in the cozy parlor, which has a Franklin fireplace and a piano. In the summer, relax on the front porch and listen to the crickets. ■ *520 Main St (turn right onto Main St from Hwy 299), Cedarville; (530)279-2650 or (530)279-2337; mail: PO Box 341, Cedarville, CA 96104; $; no credit cards; checks OK.* ♿

*LODGINGS*

**Spanish Springs Ranch ★★★** Buckaroo wannabes should pack up their cowboy boots and head on out to this 70,000-acre working cattle ranch. For city slickers who have a hankering to join a horse drive, this is the place—you can even learn how to castrate the animals if you're so inclined! Authentic Western lodgings are scattered across the property, and whether you want to slumber in ultimate comfort or rough it on the range, the choice is yours: accommodations vary from log cabins, Western-style suites, and a historic homestead to turn-of-the-century ranch houses. You can saddle up and ride the trails, fish in stocked ponds, hike and camp in the wilderness, or swim in the pool. The smallest cowpokes should check out the ranch's "dudeo," a junior rodeo where kids can learn to ride those easier-to-mount four-legged creatures: sheep. In the winter, cowboys and cowgirls can cross-country ski, ice skate (when the lake freezes), and whoop it up on sleigh rides. Of course there are such traditional ranch activities as barbecues and campfires, plus a petting zoo for the kids. Meals are served family style in the ranch's dining room, and you can sip a cocktail in the lounge, or hoist a cold one in the Old West Beer and Wine Bar. Inquire about the special vacation packages, including the fall and spring cattle roundups. Children under age 3 stay for free. ■ *On Hwy 395 (40 miles N of Susanville and 6 miles S of Ravendale); (800) 272-8282; mail: PO Box 70, Ravendale, CA 96123; $$–$$$ (includes meals); beer and wine; AE, DIS, MC, V; checks OK.* &

SUSANVILLE

*RESTAURANTS*

**St. Francis Cafe ★** You won't hear anybody asking "Where's the beef?" in this cafe. Located in the 80-year-old St. Francis Hotel, the St. Francis Cafe has been owned and operated by the Goni family since 1946; their specialty is prime rib, indisputably the best (and the largest servings) in the area. If you're not at the door by 6pm on Friday and Saturday, you may be out of luck because the prime rib sells quickly. (Strict vegetarians should try their luck elsewhere.) They also offer a hearty 10-ounce New York steak sandwich, and freshly made soups and salads served Basque-style in tureens and large bowls. The adjacent hotel bar, the Round-Up Room, features Picon Punch on its list of spirits—a tasty Basque drink that transforms even the grumpiest cowboy into a very friendly dude. ■ *830 Main St (at Union St), Susanville; (530) 257-4820; $$; full bar; MC, V; no checks; lunch, dinner Mon–Sat.* &

**Grand Cafe** The art deco light fixtures in this time warp of a restaurant are the real McCoy. Owned by the Sargent family since 1921, this green stucco building is furnished with green-and-black tiles, dark wooden booths, and a long Formica counter. There's also a nickel jukebox (it doesn't work, so save your nickel) and a small lamp with a pull chain in each booth. At the counter, wooden chairs on ornate iron bases have clips to hold diners' hats. The mounted deer staring from the walls were shot by a Sargent in the '30s—back when a tuna sandwich was a mere 35 cents (and even now, they're not charging a whole lot more). For breakfast, try the sweet buckwheat hotcakes. At lunchtime, soup, house-baked bread, and a chocolate malt are your best bets.
■ *730 Main St (near Gay St), Susanville; (530)257-4713; $; full bar; no credit cards; checks OK; breakfast, lunch Mon–Sat.* &

## CHESTER

### *RESTAURANTS*

**Creekside Grill ★★★** This fine restaurant has upped the ante in the Chester cuisine game. Owners Don and Tracy Darue have taken a comfortable place with lots of natural wood and a great stone fireplace and fashioned it into a restaurant that attracts tourists and locals alike. A graduate of the prestigious California Culinary Academy in San Francisco, Tracy does the cooking (all dishes are prepared fresh daily) while her husband Don does everything else. A recent meal included a crisp baby greens and romaine salad tossed with red onions, Gorgonzola, and a red wine vinaigrette; grilled prawns marinated in rosemary and garlic; lasagne made with fresh pasta, roast turkey, spinach, four cheeses, and a marinara sauce; and a tender grilled pork tender-loin seasoned with rosemary, garlic, and sage and served with roasted garlic mashed potatoes and glazed carrots. The wine list is well edited and there is a trio of microbrews on tap. The changing dessert list is small but select: tiramisu, an exceptional carrot cake, and Tracy's signature diet-busting delight—alternate layers of white chocolate–walnut cake and chocolate cake, filled with a mocha mousse and glazed in a dark chocolate ganache. As the restaurant's name implies, there is a creek lined with aspens here, and a beautiful deck perched creekside provides alfresco dining. ■ *278 Main St, Chester; (530)258-1966; $–$$; beer and wine; MC, V; local checks only; lunch, dinner every day in the summer (lunch, dinner Wed–Sun in the winter).* &

**Ernest and Jessie's Coffee Lounge and Tea Room ★** Don't let the rather stark facade of this establishment deter you. If you're looking for a spot to have a cup of tea, an espresso, or an informal breakfast or lunch, this friendly place with its eclectic collection of pretty furniture and colorful plants is perfect. The highlights of the breakfast menu are the Eggspresso (scrambled eggs cooked with the steam of an espresso machine), the pastries, and the seven kinds of waffles. Lunch specials might include corn chowder, artichoke quiche, and a house-baked lemon or apple pie. The ambience is so pleasant that you could sit here for hours and read a book (or even write one, for that matter). ▪ *346 Main St, Chester; (530)258-2238; $; no alcohol; no credit cards; checks OK; breakfast, lunch every day (dinner Thurs–Sat in the summer only).* &

## LODGINGS

**The Bidwell House Bed and Breakfast Inn** ★★★ The beautifully restored Bidwell House, fronted by a yard of aspens and cottonwoods, looks out over mountain meadows and the broad expanse of Lake Almanor. The former home of Chico pioneer John Bidwell, it was opened as a B&B in 1991. The 14 guest rooms (most have private baths) are furnished with antiques and a few have wood-burning stoves; seven units are equipped with Jacuzzi tubs. A cottage that sleeps up to six people makes an ideal family retreat. Be sure to show the kids the Bidwell House's pretty, enclosed downstairs porch gussied up with wicker furniture, a Gibson Girl sketchbook, and antique doll buggies and tricycles. The inn's manager is a creative pastry chef, so guests are treated to delicious breakfast dishes such as fresh fruit crêpes and frothy frappés, served in the airy dining room. The Bidwell recently started serving gourmet dinners by reservation only, so call ahead for specifics. If you're around in September, don't miss the popular cowboy poetry reading—it's a hoot. ▪ *1 Main St (E end of town), Chester; (530)258-3338; mail: PO Box 1790, Chester, CA 96020; $$; MC, V; checks OK.* &

**The Cinnamon Teal** ★★★ From the carved pineapple finials on the four-poster beds to the vintage floral wallpapers and colorful quilts, no touch has been spared to make this bed and breakfast feel as homey as a visit to Grandma's—that is, if Grandma has excellent taste in fabrics. Comfy, plumped-up feather beds are the crowning glory of each of the four guest rooms. Two of the rooms have private baths; one suite, located in a separate building with a private entrance and bathroom, has a living room, a wood-burning stove, and cable TV. The spacious sitting room in the 1930s-vintage main house is a comfortable place to read and relax. The 1-acre grounds stretch over a lush lawn and through an apple and pear orchard to the banks of the Feather River's north fork. ▪ *227 Feather River Dr (near Main St), Chester; (530)258-3993; mail: PO Box 1517, Chester, CA 96020; $$; no credit cards; checks OK.*

# LAKE ALMANOR

## *RESTAURANTS*

**BJ's Bar-B-Que & Deli** ★ Barbecue basics—beef, pork, and chicken—reign at this unassuming roadside spot. The ribs are thick, tender, meaty, and slathered with a tangy sweet sauce, and the baked beans and barbecued pork sandwiches are good, too. Get plenty of napkins for this deliciously messy fare and eat it on the sunny, enclosed porch to the left of the front door. Prime rib takes a turn on the rotisserie Friday and Saturday nights, and it's so popular you'll need reservations. ■ *3881 Hwy A-13 (Hamilton Branch), Lake Almanor; (530)596-4210; $; beer and wine; no credit cards; checks OK; lunch, dinner Tues–Sun (closed Jan to March).* ᔟ

**Wilson's Camp Prattville & Carol's Cafe** ★ Certainly the oldest and funkiest place at Lake Almanor, Camp Prattville has been around since 1928, when it was founded by Frank and Nettie Wilson. Daughter-in-law Carol Wilson Franchetti now runs the restaurant, which offers breakfast, lunch, and dinner in a small dining room crowded with knickknacks. The menu is prodigious, and breakfasts are served until 1pm. Sandwiches and french fries are among the better offerings, but save room for dessert, especially the terrific bread pudding with applejack hard sauce and the house-made pies with delicate, flaky crusts and supreme fillings. When the weather is warm, eat lunch at one of the picnic tables on the deck overlooking the lake. ■ *2932 Almanor Dr W (on the lake's W shore), Lake Almanor; (530)259-2464; $; beer and wine; MC, V; checks OK; breakfast, lunch, dinner every day (closed mid-Oct to Apr).* ᔟ

**Lake Almanor**

*Lodgings*

## *LODGINGS*

**Dorado Inn** ★★ What sets the Dorado apart from the other resorts along Lake Almanor's commercialized east shore are the spectacular Mount Lassen and lake views from the decks outside the cottages. All of the Dorado's six cottages (four two-bedroom cottages and two one-room units) are near the water's edge, and they have fully equipped kitchens, private bathrooms, electric heat, and wood-burning stoves. In addition to soaking in the view, most visitors spend their time either sunbathing and lounging lakeside or boating, fishing, and swimming. ■ *4379 Hwy 147 (on the lake's E shore), Lake Almanor, CA 96137; (530)284-7790; $$; no credit cards; checks OK.* ᔟ

### RESTAURANTS

**St. Bernard Lodge ★★** In 1912, the St. Bernard Lodge was constructed to house workers building the dam at Big Meadows (now known as Lake Almanor), and in 1929 it was picked up and moved to its present location, where it started a new life as a public lodge. Now the St. Bernard is primarily a restaurant, though if you overindulge on the booze or the food (or just ask very politely), chances are that owner Don "Smokey" Stover will rent you one of his seven comfortable rooms upstairs. Most Mill Creek residents come to the St. Bernard for its juicy hamburgers: a half-pound patty of lean chuck served on a fresh-baked bun (all breads are baked on-site). You can also sink your teeth into prime rib, steak, fried chicken, and fried or sautéed fish. Before your meal, sip a cocktail in the antique bar with painted glass windows; afterward, head outside for a stroll along the deck and around the trout pond. ■ *On the S side of Hwy 36 (10 miles W of Chester), Mill Creek; (530)258-3382; mail: Rte 5, Box 5500, Mill Creek, CA 96061; $$; full bar; MC, V; checks OK; breakfast, lunch Sat–Sun, dinner Thurs–Mon (Fri–Sun in the winter). & restaurant only*

▼

### LODGINGS

**Mill Creek Resort ★★** If it's peace and solitude you're after, look no further. The Mill Creek Resort makes you feel as though you've stepped back in time to a quieter, gentler, and infinitely more affordable era (somewhere around 1925). A picture-postcard general store and coffee shop serve as the resort's center, and nine housekeeping cabins are rented on a daily or weekly basis. The units are clean and homey, with vintage '30s and '40s furniture. Seclusion is one of the main charms of the place, though it's not far from cross-country skiing trails and Lassen Volcanic National Park. Pets are welcome. ■ *On Hwy 172 (3 miles S of Hwy 36), Mill Creek; (530)595-4449; mail: Mill Creek, CA 96061; $; no credit cards; checks OK.* &

## LASSEN VOLCANIC NATIONAL PARK

Surprisingly, many Californians have never even *heard* of Lassen Volcanic National Park, much less been there. In fact, it's one of the least crowded national parks in the country, forever destined to play second fiddle to its towering neighbor, Mount Shasta. This is reason enough to go, since the park's 108,000 acres (including 50 beautiful wilderness lakes) are practically deserted, even on weekends.

The heart of the park is 10,457-foot **Lassen Peak**, the largest plug-dome volcano in the world (its last fiery eruption was in

1915, when it shot debris 7 miles into the stratosphere). For decades Lassen held the title of the most recently active volcano in the continental United States; it lost that distinction in 1980, when Washington's Mount St. Helens blew her top. The volcano also marks the southernmost end of the Cascade Range, which extends to Canada. A visitors' map calls the park "a compact laboratory of volcanic phenomena"—an apt description of this pretty but peculiar place. In addition to wildflower-laced hiking trails and lush forests typical of many national parks, parts of Lassen are covered with steaming thermal vents, boiling mud pots, stinky sulfur springs, and towering lava pinnacles—constant reminders that Mount Lassen is still active.

Lassen Park's premier attractions in the summer and fall are sightseeing, hiking, backpacking, and camping (sorry, no mountain bikes allowed). The $5-per-car entrance fee, valid for a week, gets you a copy of the "Lassen Park Guide," a handy little newsletter listing activities, hikes, and points of interest. Free naturalist programs are offered daily in the summer, highlighting everything from flora and fauna to geologic history and volcanic processes. If you have only a day here, spend it huffing up the mountain on the **Lassen Peak Hike**, a spectacular 2½-mile zigzag to the top. Most hikers can make the steep trek in four to five hours—just don't forget to bring water, sunscreen, and a windbreaker. Another great—and much easier—trail is the 3-mile **Bumpass Hell Hike**, named after a mid-19th-century tour guide. Poor ol' Kendall Bumpass lost a leg on this one, but that was long before park rangers built wooden catwalks to safely guide visitors past the pyrite pools, steam vents, seething mud pots, and noisy fumaroles that line the trail.

▼

**Lassen Volcanic National Park**

▲

Mount Lassen attracts a hardier breed of tourists in the winter, when the park's main thoroughfare is closed and the chief modes of transportation are snowshoes and cross-country skis. Smaller roads are plowed only from the north and south park entrances up to the ranger stations, and on sunny weekends parking lots are filled with families enjoying every kind of snow toy imaginable. On Saturday afternoons from January through March, a loquacious naturalist will take anyone who shows up at the Lassen Chalet by 1:30pm on a free, two-hour eco-adventure across the park's snowy dales. You must be at least eight years old, warmly dressed, and decked out in boots. Free snowshoes are provided (although a $1 donation for shoe upkeep is requested) on a first-come basis. Pack a picnic lunch. The chalet is at the park's south entrance, 5 miles north of the Highway 36/89 junction. For more details, call park headquarters at (530)595-4444.

For the best lodgings and restaurants near the park, see the Mill Creek, Drakesbad, and Lake Almanor sections in this chapter.

*LODGINGS*

**Drakesbad Guest Ranch ★★★★**   Hidden in a high mountain valley inside Lassen Volcanic National Park, the Drakesbad Guest Ranch is probably the worst-kept secret in California. This mountain retreat has a waiting list for its 19 rooms that's several months (and sometimes a year or two) long. Fortunately, plans made that far in advance often change, and May and June are good times to call to take advantage of cancellations. At night, kerosene lamps cast a warm yellow glow over the rustic accommodations since there's no electricity, except in the lodge. The tables, chairs, and bedsteads are made of smooth-sanded logs and branches. There are a half-dozen pleasant rooms upstairs in the main lodge, but you might prefer one of the four quieter cabins at the edge of the meadow, a good place to watch wildlife. Half of the lodge's guest rooms and all the cabins have their own sink and toilet, but showers are in a shared facility. If you want a private bathroom, inquire about the two-room duplex (rented to a minimum of four people) or one of the eight rooms in the bungalows.

**Drakesbad**

*Lodgings*

▲

Breakfast, lunch, and dinner (included in the price of lodging) are exceptionally good for national park food. The breakfast buffet includes fresh fruit, hot and cold cereals, buttermilk pancakes, and excellent sausages. For lunch you can eat at the buffet or order a picnic lunch. Dinner is a fancier affair starting with soup or a fresh wild greens salad, followed by an entree such as roasted rosemary chicken with Monterey Jack polenta or vegetarian eggplant Napoleon; dessert might be a white chocolate mousse cake. The popular Wednesday night cookouts feature barbecued steak and chicken, plus pasta and an assortment of salads.

During the day, explore the wonders of Lassen—you can even do it on horseback. One of the ranch's star attractions is the thermal swimming pool, fed by a natural hot spring and open 24 hours a day. The pool is particularly romantic at night when the steam swirls around you and your partner and rises into the star-studded sky. ■ *On Hwy 36 (about 17 miles N of Chester; call for directions), Drakesbad; (530)529-9820; mail: California Guest Services, 2150 N Main St, Ste 5, Red Bluff, CA 96080; calguest@ mci.com; $$ (includes meals); beer and wine; MC, V; checks OK (closed mid-Oct to mid-June, depending on weather conditions).* ⅛

# SIERRA NEVADA

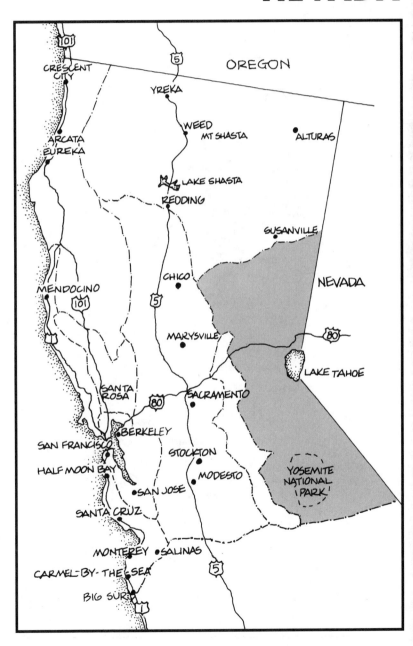

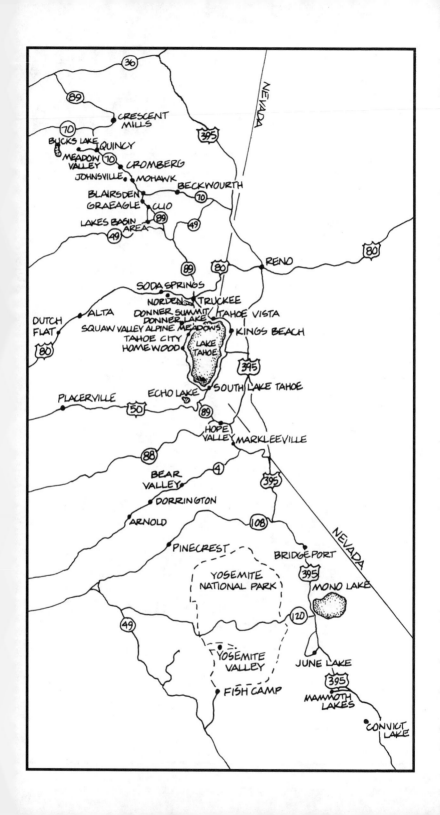

# Sierra Nevada

*A north-to-south sweep of the Sierra Nevada mountain range beginning at Quincy and continuing to Convict Lake, including excursions to the Lakes Basin Area, Lake Tahoe, Yosemite National Park, Mono Lake, and Lake Tahoe's major ski resorts. Note: The 559 area code in this chapter goes into effect November 14, 1998. Until that date, use area code 209.*

## QUINCY

### RESTAURANTS

**The Loft** ★★ Nestled in the heart of downtown Quincy, the archetypal all-American small town that could have served as the setting for a John Wayne Western, this restaurant is a great spot for noshing while watching the passersby on Main Street. At lunchtime, patrons sit on the Loft's little patio surrounded by a white picket fence or in the small ground-floor dining room and order a classic burger, a bowl of chili, or perhaps one of several low-fat, low-calorie dishes, such as pasta primavera or Mandarin chicken. Dinner is served upstairs in a more formal dining room, where the food is dressed up, too: entrees range from prime rib (on Friday and Saturday only) and filet mignon wrapped in bacon to beer-battered prawns, broiled salmon, and a half-dozen pasta plates. On Wednesday and occasionally Friday nights a band performs in the bar. ■ *384 W Main St (downtown, across the street from Serkins Bar), Quincy; (530)283-0126; $; beer and wine; AE, DIS, MC, V; checks OK; lunch, dinner Mon–Sat.* &

**Morning Thunder Cafe** ★ With its stained-glass window, vine-laced trellis, and macramé plant holder, the Morning Thunder Cafe may look a bit like a hippie haven, but those details are just leftovers from its impetuous youth. Breakfast has always been the draw here, with dishes like biscuits and gravy, huevos rancheros, and three-egg spinach, cheese, and mushroom omelets. The portions are huge, and the biscuits are as large as a prizefighter's fist. The restaurant also serves lunches of enormous hamburgers and freshly made soups (the delicious Boston clam chowder has become such a hit that the cafe's regulars insist on having it every Friday). ■ *557 Lawrence St (downtown), Quincy; (530)283-1310; $; beer and wine; AE, MC, V; checks OK; breakfast, lunch every day.* &

**Moon's** A popular local hangout since the mid-'70s, Moon's is a roomy, ramshackle, rustic wooden building with four separate dining areas, including a formal dining room and an open-air patio covered with lush plants. The strong scent of garlic and yeast is a dead giveaway to the house specialties: pizza and pasta. The thick lasagne, heavily laden with sausage, and some of the beef entrees, featuring only certified Angus beef, are among the kitchen's best efforts. Another favorite is the Mushrooms St. Thomas—a spinach, mushroom, and Italian-sausage casserole. Moon's is ideal for families, offering something to suit just about all tastes. ■ *497 Lawrence St (at Plymouth St), Quincy; (530)283-0765; $; beer and wine; AE, MC, V; checks OK; dinner Tues–Sun.* ⅃

## LODGINGS

**The Feather Bed** ★★ This 1893 Victorian inn, proudly punctuated with colonnades on its teal and peach front porch, features five cozy, turn-of-the-century country–style guest rooms with private baths. There are also two quaint little cottages set behind the house. Floral-print wallpaper and beautiful patchwork quilts give the rooms a homey, old-fashioned feel. Some rooms have those terrific, deep, claw-footed soaking tubs; others have gas fireplaces. After refueling on the full breakfast served in the dining room, borrow a bike from proprietors Bob and Jan Janowski and take a spin around Quincy. You can also easily walk from the Feather Bed to the heart of the quaint town. ■ *542 Jackson St (at Court St, 1 block from Hwy 70), Quincy; (530)283-0102 or (800)696-8624; mail: PO Box 3200, Quincy, CA 95971; www. innaccess.com/tfb; $$; AE, DC, DIS, MC, V; checks OK.* ⅃

**New England Ranch** ★★ A working ranch with cattle and horses grazing on 88 acres of pastureland in the American Valley, this handsome English country–style ranch house has been updated and restored with a mix of fine antiques and pretty, modern furnishings. Its original owner, Daniel Cates, arrived from Boston in 1852, and the area's first store and blacksmith shop were on his property. Now the proprietor is Barbara Scott, who offers two very comfortable, well-appointed guest rooms with private baths and views of the lush countryside. Scott serves a full breakfast of home-baked goods, fresh farm eggs, and locally grown fruit. You are welcome to stable your horse here, or if you're a city slicker without a Black Beauty, Scott can arrange a horseback-riding tour of the area for you. If your idea of a good time doesn't include anything that requires a saddle, borrow a mountain bike instead. Peaceful and quite pleasant, this is a place where you'll definitely feel as though you've gotten away from it all. Well-behaved pets can come, too. ■ *2571 Quincy Junction Rd (at the junction of Chandler Rd; coming from the N, take a left on Chandler Rd—on the northern outskirts of Quincy—and drive 3 miles), Quincy, CA 95971-9311; (530)283-2223; neranch@psln.com; www.newengland ranch.com; $$; AE, MC, V; checks OK.*

## MEADOW VALLEY

*RESTAURANTS*

**Ten-Two** ★ The road to this restaurant is 10.2 miles away from the town of Quincy, hence the name. Ten-Two is built right over a rushing flume, and although it's off the beaten track, many Quincy residents make the trek here for dinner. The menu offers sturdy standbys such as fish and chips and a grilled chicken burger with a mound of freshly made fries or onion rings, as well as fancier fare like a chicken breast dressed with capers and pine nuts and grilled Szechuan salmon topped with a delicate, secret sauce culled from an old Chinese cookbook. Service is casual, friendly, and attentive. When the weather is warm, consider dining on the deck. ■ *8270 Bucks Lake Rd (10.2 miles E of Quincy), Meadow Valley; (530)283-1366; $$; full bar; MC, V; checks OK; dinner every day.* ⅄

## CROMBERG

*RESTAURANTS*

**Cromberg**

*Restaurants*

**Mount Tomba Inn** ★★ Mount Tomba Inn is a genuine, landmark roadside dinner house that has managed to survive and thrive since 1936 in a sparsely populated area where businesses regularly go belly-up. The place is a hoot. It's not only a restaurant, it's a shrine to John Wayne. The walls are papered with Wayne's mug, and every dish is named after one of the Duke's movies (well, except for the nameless vegetarian plate). Take a seat at the long bar, pardner, and order a tall one, or sit in front of the stone fireplace as you wait for a table. Mount Tomba's specialty is prawns—big, meaty, tender prawns, the way Duke would have liked 'em. You can get them deep fried, boiled with drawn butter, or sautéed in garlic butter, olive oil, lemon, and white wine. And of course, no John Wayne shrine would be complete without every cut of beef, from filet mignon (named after *The Quiet Man* flick because the slabs of meat are "known for their tenderness") to prime rib (aka *True Grit*, a reference only the author of the menu understands). For those who like innards, there's calf liver and onions. Diners also can choose from several chicken and fish dishes. Included in the price of every cowboy-size dinner is an excellent made-from-scratch soup (served in a large tureen), a nothing-special tossed green salad, a basket of warm bread, rice or a baked potato with all the trimmings, coffee, and a choice of sherbet, vanilla ice cream, or a chocolate sundae. Aren't you glad you don't have to mount a horse after all that eatin'? ■ *Off Hwy 70 (½ mile E of town, 17 miles from both Quincy and Portola), Cromberg; (530)836-2359; $–$$; full bar; DIS, MC, V; checks OK; dinner Tues–Sun Apr to Oct (Fri–Sun Nov to Mar).* ⅄

**Twenty Mile House ★★★** Take the Old Cromberg Road back in time to Twenty Mile House. Set on the middle fork of the Feather River, this inn has been a tranquil haven for travelers since 1854, when it served as a stagecoach stop. The two-story brick building is set amid 250 acres of wildflowers, evergreens, and wildlife, and only an occasional train rumbling by on the Feather River route disturbs the silence. The house has been carefully restored with New England pine paneling, decorative fretwork, and carved Victorian furnishings. It offers three guest bedrooms with private bathrooms, including the Old Parlor Room, which has a private porch entrance, a double brass Victorian bed, and a wood-burning fireplace, and the Old Trading Post Room, which also has its own entrance, and boasts two doubles and a twin bed. Tucked into the nearby forest across Jackson Creek is a cabin with a double and a twin bed, a fully equipped kitchen, a bathroom with a claw-footed tub, and a large deck that faces the creek.

Anglers are particularly partial to Twenty Mile House, since 2 miles of the Feather River—designated a National Wild and Scenic River—run through the inn's private property. Proprietor Barbara Gage has stocked the river with wild and native trout, though she limits the number of fly-fishers to four per day (and they're restricted to catch-and-release fishing). Breakfast is served in the country kitchen or on the front porch of the Old General Store next door, which has been restored and is now used as a local meeting and activities hall. ■ *On Old Cromberg Rd (1 mile S of Hwy 70, 7 miles N of Graeagle, 18 miles SE of Quincy), Cromberg; (530)836-0375; mail: PO Box 30001, Cromberg, CA 96103; $$; no credit cards; checks OK.*

**Cromberg**

*Lodgings*

▲

## JOHNSVILLE

This tiny, charming town, established by the Sierra Buttes Mining Company in the 1870s, is a California treasure. It was built for the gold miners and their families who didn't want to live next to the brothels and gambling centers in the nearby mining camps. Surrounded by the densely forested **Plumas–Eureka State Park**, Johnsville is a mix of old, abandoned miner's shacks and restored ones that serve as private residences. In between the historical buildings are some new homes, most built to meet the Johnsville Historical Society's strict design guidelines. As you drive down Main Street, note the striking old barn-red **Johnsville Hotel**, now a private home, and the toylike firehouse across the street with a bell in its steeple and a horse-drawn fire wagon inside. Among the many wonderful artifacts at the **Plumas–Eureka State Park Museum** are a working blacksmith shop and a five-story 60-stamp mill where gold was processed. A nearby campground area straddles pretty **Jamison Creek**, and across the street from the museum is the diminutive **Moriarity House**, a

completely restored miner's home with furnishings and equipment used by the 10-member Moriarity family in 1901. For
museum and campground information, call (530)836-2380.

A mile up Johnsville's main road is the **Plumas–Eureka Ski
Bowl**, a quaint, no-frills downhill ski resort for beginner and
beginner-intermediate skiers. There are two poma lifts, and hidden
behind the one-room lodge is a rope tow—ideal for teaching the
tots how to snowplow; open in the winter on Wednesdays, weekends, and holidays, weather permitting, (530)836-1009.

## RESTAURANTS

**The Iron Door** ★★ Johnsville supports one business, and this is it.
The Iron Door restaurant has occupied the century-old general
store and post office building since 1961, and it hasn't changed
much since then. The bar and dining room are decorated with
antique farm equipment, lanterns, floral wreaths, and Gibson
Girl–style hangings, and behind the bar is a drawing of the last
miner in Johnsville, who worked his claim on Jamison Creek until
the 1950s. The Iron Door's soups are thick and hearty, and the
main bill of fare is heavy with beef, lobster, and fowl. And since
the restaurant's owner is from Bavaria, you can also bite into several excellent—and authentic—schnitzels. A good selection of
beer and wine rounds out the offerings. Ask for a seat on the
pleasant, enclosed front porch, where the paned windows are
draped with hop vines in the summer. ■ *5417 Main St (in Plumas–
Eureka State Park, 5 miles W of Graeagle), Johnsville; (530)836-
2376; $$; full bar; MC, V; no checks; dinner every day (open Apr to
Nov).* ♿

## MOHAWK ■ BLAIRSDEN ■ GRAEAGLE

The tiny towns of Mohawk, Blairsden, and Graeagle sit cheek by
jowl, so to speak—each is located less than a mile from the other.
In Mohawk, an old lumber town at a crossroads on the middle
fork of the Feather River, there's not much left except an old, well-
maintained little cemetery; a deteriorating but interesting log
cabin that was once the town's stage stop; and the funky little
**Mohawk Tavern**, (530)836-2610, a friendly watering hole
adorned with signs labeling it the Mohawk Convention Center
and City Hall. Blairsden boasts the area's only nursery, as well as
a car-repair garage, a hardware store, several restaurants, and a
great bakery, **The Village Baker**, (530)836-4064.

About a quarter mile south of Blairsden is the picturesque
little city of Graeagle, a former company town of the California
Fruit Growers Exchange. Fruit Growers once had a lumber mill
here that made wooden boxes for storing its produce, but the old
mill is gone and the millpond has been converted into a family
swimming area with grassy banks, gravel beaches, brown trout,
and paddleboat rentals; in the winter, the pond is often a resting

ground for flocks of Canada geese. Graeagle modestly bills itself the "Home of the World's Finest Golf Clubs" (there's a custom golf-club store here) and there are five **golf courses** in the area; for golfing information, call or stop by Williamson Realty in the Graeagle Village Center on Highway 89, (530)836-0112. Other outdoor recreational activities include tennis, hiking, and horseback riding. The rest of the town consists of a little grocery store, a tearoom, an antique shop, and a handful of other small businesses—and most are located in former company houses painted barn-red with white trim. For more information and a brochure on the area, call the **Plumas County Visitors Bureau** at (800)326-2247. If you're looking for a place to stay, numerous condos that double as vacation homes are available for rent; call (530)836-0313 or (530)836-2525 for rental information.

## RESTAURANTS

**Grizzly Grill Restaurant and Bar** ★★★ Owners Jim and Lynn Hagen are true pioneers in this neck of the woods: they've introduced baby greens, sun-dried tomatoes, and Asiago cheese into the meat and potato belt. Can you believe *that*? Next thing you know they'll be hosting martini and cigar nights. Their light, woodsy, and relaxed restaurant is a fine spot to have dinner or just a drink at the long bar staffed by a congenial crew. The Grizzly's menu will warm a yuppie heart: a baby greens salad with walnuts, blue cheese, and a vinaigrette dressing; New England crab cakes with a red bell-pepper cream garnish; and a tasty caesar salad. And that's just for starters. Among a number of very good pasta selections is a terrific linguine with wild mushrooms, sun-dried tomatoes, scallions, fresh basil, olive oil, and balsamic vinegar. Main courses range from a perfectly grilled Norwegian salmon with a sweet onion confit to a zesty cassoulet brimming with French lentils, vegetables, chicken, pork, and sausage in a white wine sauce. The small, daily dessert menu often holds some gems, and there is an extensive wine list. ■ *250 Bonta St (near the junction of Hwys 70 and 89), Blairsden; (530)836-1300; $–$$; full bar; MC, V; checks OK; dinner every day April 1 to Oct 1 (Tues–Sun Oct 1 to Christmas, then closed Christmas to April 1. Days may vary slightly—call ahead).*

## LODGINGS

**Feather River Inn** ★★ Back in the '20s and '30s, when train-trip vacations were all the rage, the Feather River Inn was one of the prime destinations in the High Sierra. The palatial, rustic 1914 lodge is located off Highway 70 in a quiet woodland area, and it now functions primarily as a conference center operated by the University of the Pacific in Stockton. The inn is reserved for con-

ference groups (ranging from 15 to 150 people), but other guests are often accommodated on a space-available basis (non-conference reservations are taken no more than 30 days in advance). A half-dozen attractive chalets, which hold six to eight rooms each, and seven cabins are rented to guests. All accommodations are quite rustic, and some share bathrooms; the plain-Jane units are equipped with two twin beds and a double bed or just one twin and perhaps a small dresser or desk. Some of the rooms look out at the inn's nine-hole golf course and the surrounding mountains. The inn's broad veranda, its roof supported by enormous tree-trunk columns and rafters, faces the ninth green and lovely pine trees. The inn also has a swimming pool and volleyball, basketball, and tennis courts. Conference attendees are offered a buffet-style breakfast, lunch, and dinner, but other guests must dine in the nearby towns, unless the resort is holding one of its grand holiday Sunday brunches, which are open to the public.
■ *65899 Hwy 70 (½ mile NW of town), Blairsden; (530)836-2623; mail: PO Box 67, Blairsden, CA 96103; $; AE, DC, DIS, MC, V; checks OK; breakfast, lunch, dinner every day (for conference attendees only), Sun brunch (for the public on holidays only); open mid-Apr through Oct.*

**River Pines Resort** ★★ Set alongside the Feather River, a National Wild and Scenic River, this resort is a popular family retreat that folks return to year after year. It's fun and affordable, and it offers enough activities to keep any hyperactive vacationer entertained. River Pines offers a large pool and Jacuzzi with a poolside bar and snack bar, trout fishing, table tennis, shuffleboard, and horseshoes. It's also only a quarter mile from a stable with horseback riding excursions; nearby are several tennis courts and five golf courses. The resort has 62 units, including 18 one- and two-bedroom cabins constructed of stacked cedar. Each cabin has a fully stocked kitchen and a private bathroom; the one-room cabins have either a queen-size bed or two twins, while the two-room cabins have a queen, two twins, and a futon that folds out into a double bed. The resort's other rooms are reminiscent of a standard motel, with knotty-pine walls and comfortable, albeit plain, furnishings; some rooms have kitchens and sitting areas, too. Lunches of hamburgers, hot dogs, and pizza are served poolside at the umbrella-topped tables or at the pool bar. The popular **River House Restaurant** serves very good American dinners, including pasta, chicken, pepper steak, prime rib, and, on special occasions, wild game. ■ *8296 Hwy 89 (at the NE end of Graeagle, on the Feather River's S side), Graeagle; (530)836-0313 or (800)696-2551; mail: PO Box 249, Clio, CA 96106; $$; full bar; DIS, MC, V; checks OK; lunch every day, dinner Thurs–Tues.* &

## BECKWOURTH

### RESTAURANTS

**Beckwith Tavern and Restaurant** ★★ If you're in the mood for a beef dinner in the company of cowboys, gallop over to the Beckwith Tavern. This bar and restaurant was built of logs in the 1930s and named after the town—which was originally named after pioneer James Beckwith. Decades later, someone discovered that Beckwith often signed his name "Beckwourth" (which he thought worthier), so the town changed its name. On weekends, this place fills up fast with people who travel for miles to fork into the tender prime rib, the fat pepper steak (the house specialty), or the rib steak that hangs over the plate's edge. There were crazy times when cowboys went wild here, but things have settled down since then, and now the Beckwith is a family place run by Karl Baumann (who originally owned the popular Iron Door restaurant in Johnsville). Take a gander at the long bar, which has been branded by local ranchers. ■ *81059 Hwy 70 (5 miles E of Portola), Beckwourth; (530)832-5084; $$; full bar; MC, V; checks OK; dinner Thurs–Tues (Fri–Tues in the winter, weather permitting).* ᕒ

## CLIO

### LODGINGS

**White Sulphur Springs Ranch Bed and Breakfast** ★ Owned by descendants of the McKenzie family since 1867, the White Sulphur Springs Ranch was once a main stop on the Truckee–Quincy stagecoach route. It's located in Clio, formerly known as Boozetown, thanks to the 13 saloons and 14 bordellos that once dominated its streets. The ranch's large restored wood-frame house with a two-story porch offers six guest rooms decorated with period antiques. All the rooms share bathrooms except the Fern Room, which has its own bath, a queen-size bed, and easy access to the swimming pool and patio. The Marble Room has marble-topped antique furniture, a double bed, and views of Mohawk Valley and the pool area, while the Chestnut Room boasts a rare chestnut bedroom suite with matching chairs, a queen-size bed, and a private balcony. Guests wake up to a hearty ranch breakfast of eggs, potatoes, fruit, and freshly ground coffee. During the day, you can dive into the inn's huge 78-degree mineral water pool or head over to the beautiful Whitehawk Ranch for a round of golf. In the evening, unwind on the front porch and watch the sun set over the Mohawk Valley. Avid golfers should ask about the B&B's golf packages with Whitehawk Ranch and the other four courses in the area. ■ *On Hwy 89 (2 miles S of town), Clio; (530)836-2387 or (800)854-1797; mail: PO Box 136, Clio, CA 96106; www.graeagle.com/marketplace/whtssbb; $$; DIS, MC, V; checks OK.* ᕒ

## LAKES BASIN AREA

The scenic **Gold Lake Road**, which starts several miles south of Graeagle and ends at Highway 49 just east of Sierra City, is a spectacular 14-mile-long stretch of tarmac that zigzags through verdant valleys dotted with farms, historic buildings, deer, cows, and horses, and passes nearly a dozen sky-blue lakes (there are 30 lakes within the basin), most of them either visible from the highway or within easy walking distance. The **Lakes Basin Campground**, located right off the road, offers 24 sites available on a first-come, first-served basis; call the Mohawk ranger station for details at (530)836-2575. Most of the lodges in the basin are quite rustic, and folks around here like it that way. Whether you fancy horseback riding through meadows rife with wildflowers, fishing in roaring rivers, hiking through magnificent red-fir forests, or mountain-biking on rugged, hilly trails, you'll find it all here. The lakeside lodges book up quickly, so make reservations well ahead of time or else try your luck at catching a last-minute cancellation. Bear in mind that the seasonal resorts tend to have a high turnover of chefs, so menus and the quality of the fare may change considerably from one season to the next. In the winter, the basin closes and the unplowed road becomes a haven for snowmobilers.

### RESTAURANTS

**Sardine Lake Resort** ★★★ When the stress of daily life begins to take its toll and you long for an escape to some peaceful, far-from-it-all retreat, some places quickly spring to mind. Sardine Lake is one of those places. The towering, craggy peaks of the Sierra Buttes are mirrored in this lake, where the tranquil forest is a restorative for even the most frazzled city folk. The resort's proprietors, Dorothy and Chandler Hunt, take full advantage of the splendid setting, serving cocktails before dinner on a small gazebo that juts over the lake. The food is good—perhaps the best in the Plumas–Eureka area—with a small but nicely rendered selection of meat, seafood, and poultry dishes. Restaurant reservations are a must—make them several weeks in advance. Unfortunately, the resort's nine cabins are often filled by a long list of returning clients, so the chance of getting a cabin reservation is, as one frustrated lad put it, "downright impossible." ■ *At the end of Sardine Lake Rd at Lower Sardine Lake (off Gold Lake Rd, 2 miles N of Hwy 49), Lakes Basin Area; (530)862-1196 (summer), (916)645-8882 (winter); mail: PO Box 216, Sierra City, CA 96125; $$; full bar; no credit cards; checks OK; dinner Fri–Wed (open mid-May to mid-Oct).* &

**Gray Eagle Lodge** ★★★ Gray Eagle Lodge is set in the heart of spectacular scenery at the northern edge of the Lakes Basin Area. Ironically, there isn't a lake nearby, but you will see a lovely stream, a waterfall, and Sierra trails trimmed with wildflowers. The resort's 18 refurbished cabins have small decks, private baths, wall-to-wall carpeting, mini-refrigerators, and queen- or king-size beds with electric blankets and comforters. Seven of the units have two bedrooms, and some are set alongside Graeagle Stream.

Breakfast and dinner are included in the room rates and are served in the impressive lodge's dining room. Constructed of enormous sugar-pine beams, the light-filled, high-ceilinged lodge, with its tall windows and rock fireplace, is all that a grand mountain lodge ought to be. Sit back in the cushy couches or at the small bar and enjoy an aperitif before dinner. The Gray Eagle's menu changes often, but the food is usually quite good. Dinner might include a carrot-curry soup with fresh ginger, a mixed baby greens salad with roasted walnuts and crumbled Roquefort cheese, and an entree of grilled swordfish with papaya-and-bell-pepper chutney accompanied by potato pancakes and French green beans. The extensive wine list features primarily California labels and is the best in the Lakes Basin Area. You can also get the full array of espresso drinks, and the coffee is made from locally roasted beans. If you're not staying at the lodge, dinner reservations are required. ■ *On Gold Lake Rd (5 miles S of Hwy 89), Lakes Basin Area; (530)836-2511 or (800)635-8778; mail: PO Box 38, Graeagle, CA 96103; www.graeagle.com/lodge; $$ (includes breakfast and dinner); full bar; MC, V; local checks only; breakfast (for guests only), dinner (by reservation only) every day (lodge and restaurant are open from May to Oct).* よ

**Packer Lake Lodge** ★★ What separates the 1926 Packer Lake Lodge from its neighbors in the Lakes Basin Area is its combination of good food and—at a 6,218-foot elevation—great scenery. The tall pines, gently rippling waters, and profusion of wildflowers provide an atmosphere of serene seclusion. Accommodations are in 14 simply furnished cabins, ranging from rustic, lakeside log cabins with shared bathrooms to three-room buildings with kitchens and private baths. Each cabin has its own rowboat, too. The single-room main lodge features a large stone fireplace, a tiny store that primarily sells candy bars and fishing supplies, a full bar, a reading and games nook, and a small dining room. Dinner fare includes steak, baby back ribs, pasta, and the "you-catch-it-and-clean-it-and-we'll-cook-it" trout special. ■ *On Packer Lake Rd (off Sardine Lake Rd, 4½ miles N of Hwy 49), Lakes Basin Area; (530)862-1221 (mid-May to Oct), (415)921-5943 (Oct to mid-May); mail: PO Box 237, Sierra City, CA 96125; $$; full bar; MC, V; checks OK; breakfast, lunch, dinner Wed–Mon (lodge and restaurant are open mid-May to Oct).*

**Gold Lake Lodge** ★ Gold Lake Lodge is in the heart of the Lakes Basin Area (at an elevation of 6,620 feet) and within hiking distance of stunning High Sierra scenery, wildflower-filled meadows, and numerous lakes ideal for water play. Bear Lake is the closest (a one-third of a mile hike), and Gold Lake is a 5-minute drive by car. Eleven tidy little cabins line the edge of a pretty meadow and a stand of old-growth red fir trees. Most of the cabins sleep three to four people; each of the seven standard cabins has a private bathroom, and the other four more rustic units share a detached bathing facility just a skip across the lawn. Every cabin has electricity, a small front patio with a table and chairs, and housekeeping service. Breakfast and dinner are included in the rates, and meals are served in the lodge's dining room (open to non-guests, too), which is furnished with a nickel-plated Franklin stove, picnic tables, and wagonwheel chandeliers. Dinner specials range from lasagne and pot roast to lobster and fried chicken, and the lodge's sun tea is the perfect antidote to a hot summer day. ■ *On Gold Lake Rd (7 miles S of Hwy 89), Lakes Basin Area; (530)836-2350 (July 1 to Sept 30), (530)836-2751 (Oct 1 to June 30); mail: PO Box 25, Graeagle, CA 96103; www. plumasnews.com; $$–$$$ (includes breakfast and dinner); beer and wine; MC, V; checks OK; breakfast, dinner every day (lodge and restaurant are open July 1 to Sept 30).* &

**Salmon Lake Lodge** ★ You can't drive to this 1920s resort; instead, you have to drive to the north shore of Salmon Lake, telephone the lodge to send over a ferry, then hop aboard the boat to cross the lake (or you can hike a little less than a mile around the lake's splendid western rim). The 10 tent cabins offer canvas roofs, rough-wood walls, built-in double beds and single bunks, mini-refrigerators, and electric stoves; you need to bring a sleeping bag, towels, dishes, cooking gear, an ice chest, and groceries (showers and a washing machine—but no dryer—are available in a separate building). The three ridge-top cabins with their beautiful high-mountain views are the favorites, and each has a fully equipped kitchen (bring towels, bedding, and food). Also highly sought after is the lakeshore cabin, which has its own dock. Salmon Lake is great for swimming and boating, and row-boats, sailboats, canoes, and kayaks are provided to guests at no extra cost. You can also paddle a boat or take a barge to a lake island for a biweekly barbecue. ■ *At the end of Salmon Lake Rd (off Gold Lake Rd, 3 miles S of Gold Lake, 6 miles N of Hwy 49), Lakes Basin Area; summer mail (Memorial Day to Oct 15): PO Box 121, Sierra City, CA 96125, (530)842-3108; winter mail (Oct 16 to Memorial Day): PO Box 73012, Davis, CA 95617, (530)757-1825; $$; no credit cards; checks OK (open June to mid-Oct, weather permitting).* &

▼

Lakes Basin
Area

*Lodgings*

▲

*See Skiing the Sierra Nevada at the end of this chapter for Truckee area ski information.*

This popular little city packed with quaint shops, restaurants, and some terrific bed-and-breakfast inns started out in the mid-1800s as a railroad-lumber town with the construction of the first transcontinental railroad over Donner Summit. Its transformation from a dirty, run-down, one-horse town to a bustling city began in the 1970s. Today visitors arrive by car, bus, or the eastbound or westbound Amtrak passenger trains that stop at the yellow depot. If you need hiking, rock-climbing, and cross-country skiing guidebooks or topographical maps and hiking supplies, stop by **Sierra Mountaineer**, housed in the stone building that was once a livery and garage; located on Bridge Street at Jibboom Street, (530)587-2025. Another notable shop is the **Bookshelf at Hooligan Rocks**, one of the Sierra Nevada's best bookstores (it's named after a nearby outcropping of rocks where miscreants were once tarred and feathered); 11310 Donner Pass Road, at the west end of the Safeway shopping center, (530)582-0515 or (800)959-5083. The Bookshelf also has a separate children's bookstore called **Kidsshelf**, (530)582-5437, at the opposite (east) end of the shopping center. In the summer, popular Truckee attractions include the **Cannibal Car Cruise** in June, the **Fourth of July Parade**, and the **Truckee Championship Rodeo** in August. The **Truckee River Regional Park**, one-half mile south of town on Highway 267, has softball diamonds, picnic tables, tennis courts, and an outdoor amphitheater offering music programs (many are free) throughout the summer.

▼

**Truckee**

▲

In December, when snow blankets the wooden boardwalks and bright little white lights twinkle in the windows of the century-old facades along Commercial Row, Truckee truly looks like a picture from a fairy tale. All winter long the town swarms with skiers who take advantage of its proximity to many first-rate

*Truckee*

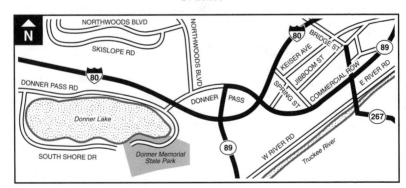

alpine and cross-country ski areas. Others brave the freezing temperatures to engage in such winter activities as the **Sled Dog Races** in February and the 10-day winter carnival called **Snowfest** in March. For more information on the town, call the **Truckee Chamber of Commerce** at (530)587-2757.

## *RESTAURANTS*

**Jordan's** ★★★ Housed within an austerely attractive Queen Anne Victorian house on the town's main drag, Jordan's is a relatively new Truckee restaurant dishing out terrific fare. The Italian pastas are particularly noteworthy, including the sausage, broccoli, and sweet pepper fusilli; the rigatoni puttanesca; and the spaghetti topped with scampi in a white wine and lemon butter sauce. You say you've had a hard day on the slopes and to hell with noodles, you want meat? Then try the braised lamb shank with garlic mashed potatoes or the peppered roast filet of pork with a sun-dried cherry and port wine sauce, or perhaps the chefs could just singe the rib-eye steak with caramelized onions and wild mushrooms and toss it your way. The wine list is small but carefully edited, with primarily California wines and a sprinkling of Italian labels. If you're a wine connoisseur and would like to splurge on Jordan's best bottles, ask for the reserve list of rare wines and champagnes. The desserts, such as apple crisp and crème brûlée, aren't as well-executed as the entrees, but they'll certainly satisfy your sweet tooth. ■ *10292 Donner Pass Rd (1 block west of Commercial Row), Truckee; (530)587-7815; $$; beer and wine; MC, V; local checks only; dinner every day (closed on Tues Apr 1 to June 30 and Sept 1 to Nov 30).* &

**The Passage** ★★★ Tucked inside the landmark Truckee Hotel (see review, below), the Passage offers consistently well-prepared food, thanks to owner/chef Steven Frisch, who has been wearing the chef's toque here since 1993. A Mediterranean salad with feta cheese, kalamata olives, dolmas, and roasted peppers, plus a grilled Thai chicken salad tossed with oranges, grilled green onions, fried pasta, and cilantro, lend an international flavor to a lunch menu of burgers (ahi tuna, veggie, and build-your-own), sandwiches, and pastas. Dinner entrees are ambitious as well as delicious: try the smoked Cornish game hen prepared with a Cognac, black-peppercorn, and lemon reduction sauce; the grilled Black Angus top sirloin steak marinated in tequila with Anaheim chiles and garlic mashed potatoes; or the vegetarian waffle made with seasonal veggies, potatoes, carrot purée, grilled tomatoes, and chèvre and served with an infused basil oil "syrup." The ever-changing dessert tray might feature such treats as mixed-berry cobbler and vanilla-bean crème brûlée—well worth an extra hour on the Stairmaster. The Passage's wine list has won at least a dozen awards of excellence from *Wine Spectator* magazine. ■ *10007 Bridge St (in the Truckee Hotel, at Donner Pass Rd),*

*Truckee; (530)587-7619; $$; full bar; MC, V; checks OK; brunch Sat–Sun, lunch Mon–Fri, dinner every day.* &

**Cottonwood** ★ Cottonwood stands high on a hill on the south side of Truckee at the base of what was once California's first ski jump. The ski jump is long gone, but the restaurant affords a great view of the bright lights of Truckee from its spacious dining room. The eclectic seasonal menu ranges from Southwestern to Creole and Mediterranean fare. Begin the evening by sharing a garlic-slathered whole-leaf caesar salad meant to be eaten with your fingers—it's one of the best dishes on the menu. Entrees might include a braised free-range rabbit with andouille sausage and white beans; firecracker prawns in a very spicy chile sauce with julienned vegetables and udon noodles; a seafood stew of shellfish, prawns, scallops, and boudin sausage in a saffron-tomato broth served over linguine; Creole chicken étouffée with andouille sausage; and fusilli with roasted duck, prosciutto, goat cheese, and cracked pepper. If available, the fresh berry-apple crisp à la mode makes a sweet finale. A jazz combo plays in the bar every Saturday night, and on those warm summer evenings be sure to dine on the deck. ▪ *10142 Rue Hilltop (above town, right off Hwy 267 at Hilltop Lodge, just beyond the railroad tracks), Truckee; (530)587-5711; ctnwood@telis.org; $$; full bar; MC, V; checks OK; dinner every day.* &

▼

▲

**Truckee Trattoria** ★ Conveniently located right off Interstate 80, this good, casual Italian cafe focuses primarily on pastas—and garlic! Appetizers include garlic soup, baked Brie with garlic, and bruschetta topped with—what else?—more of the stinking rose, plus olive oil, tomato, and basil. For a main course, try the fettuccine with tender strips of chicken, wild mushrooms, broccoli, and tomatoes in a garlic cream sauce or the capellini with plump shrimp, artichoke hearts, tomatoes, and spinach in a white wine and garlic sauce. Desserts often include gelato, tiramisu, biscotti, and strawberry Napoleon. Savor an espresso and hit the road again, well fed and raring to go. Truckee Trattoria is both intimate (read small) and popular (despite its steep prices), so you should make a reservation. ▪ *11310-1 Donner Pass Rd (at the W end of the Safeway shopping center), Truckee; (530)582-1266; $$; beer and wine; DIS, MC, V; checks OK; dinner Wed–Mon.* &

**Andy's Truckee Diner** Andy's classic diner is a fairly recent addition to the Truckee scene, but it feels like it's been here forever. Perhaps that's because the 1940s diner had an earlier life in West Chester, Pennsylvania, where it lived on the rails until it was relocated and restored here by the Carey family in 1995. Open 24 hours a day, this is a great place to congregate when you're meeting folks in Truckee, and the copious menu will surely offer something to please even the most persnickety diner. Breakfast features fairly standard diner fare: omelets, pancakes, waffles,

French toast, and, if you're not planning to eat again for a day or two, a hefty platter of chicken-fried steak smothered with country gravy. Burgers, dogs, and diner classics like a hot turkey sandwich with mashed potatoes, your basic BLT, and a Philly cheese steak on a roll are offered for lunch. The homey dinner entrees range from the roast turkey plate with all the fattening trimmings to Chris's killer meat loaf and the beef or turkey pot pie. Andy's kitchen crew proudly mash their potatoes by hand, make their own soups, and have a full fountain churning out shakes, malts, banana splits, and a variety of other diet-busting desserts. ▪ *10144 W River St (junction of Hwy 267), Truckee; (530)582-6925; $; beer and wine; MC, V; checks OK; breakfast, lunch, dinner every day (open 24 hours).* ⅊

### LODGINGS

**Richardson House** ★★★★ Perched on a hill overlooking downtown Truckee and the Sierra Nevada, the lavishly restored Richardson House (built in 1886) sets the standard that other B&Bs in the area will have to strive for. Its eight beautiful guest rooms are elegantly appointed with plush carpeting, color-coordinated drapes and wallpaper, vintage fixtures, feather beds and comforters, and claw-footed tubs. Six rooms have private bathrooms and two adjoining suites share a bath. Some units have fireplaces, and Aunt Klara's Room offers every convenience for wheelchair-bound patrons. The vittles are first-rate, too. Soufflés, quiche, French toast, pancakes, hot cereal, and freshly baked scones are just some of the treats typically offered at the buffet breakfast. And if you ever manage to get hungry again, there's a 24-hour snack bar. Guests are welcome to lounge in the parlor, which has a player piano, a stereo with a CD player, and cable TV with a VCR, or spend your time outdoors among the fountains, sundials, and native aspens on vintage wicker furniture. There's even a pretty gazebo in the garden—the perfect place for exchanging wedding vows (ask about the special wedding packages). Discount plans are also available for skiers, which include lift tickets and bus transportation to nearby ski resorts. ▪ *10154 High St (at Spring St), Truckee; (530)587-5388 or (888)229-0365; mail: PO Box 2011, Truckee, CA 96160; $$–$$$; AE, DIS, MC, V; checks OK.* ⅊

**The Swedish House Bed and Breakfast** ★★★ Proprietors Louise and Bob Showen transformed a building that has had several past lives since 1885—first it was a boarding house, then a restaurant, and eventually a bootleg liquor operation—into a charming 11-room European inn. Louise's father ran one of the largest hotels in Gothenburg, Sweden; she's now carrying on the family trade, and what a great job she and her husband have done. The rooms are lovely, with custom furniture and fabrics and sparkling, private bathrooms with new claw-footed tubs and pedestal sinks.

The inn also has a convenient ski storage space. And what else would you expect at the Swedish House B&B but a delicious breakfast of authentic Swedish pancakes garnished with lingonberries? Guests who arrive by public transportation (the train and bus stations are nearby) receive a $10 discount per night. And if that isn't enough to lure you here, bear in mind that most of Truckee's shops and restaurants are just a stroll away. ■ *10009 E River St (at Bridge St), Truckee, CA 96161; (530) 587-0400 or (888) 302-0400; $$; AE, DIS, MC, V; no checks.* &

**The Truckee Hotel** ★★ Built in 1873, this handsome hotel is one of the oldest operating hotels in the Sierra Nevada. The original building was destroyed by a fire in 1909, but it was rebuilt with a steam heating system—the first hotel in the region to boast such a convenience. In 1992 and 1993, owners Karen and Jeff Winter renovated the place, and their hard work was acknowledged by the California Heritage Council with an award for historic restoration. The hotel's showpiece is the new Victorian-style parlor, a grand room with oak wainscoting, etched-glass doors, brass ceiling fans and light fixtures, and a marble fireplace. Upstairs there are 37 guest rooms with antique dressers, glass chandeliers, and full-, queen-, or king-size beds, many with elaborately carved wooden headboards; 8 rooms have private baths and the other 29 have basins and share bathrooms. The multiple configurations of rooms and suites can accommodate one to five people, and the units at the back of the hotel facing north—away from the railroad tracks and the bustling main street—are the quietest. Included in the rate is an expanded continental breakfast of hot and cold cereals, warm breads, and fresh fruit, served in the parlor. The hotel also houses the very good **Passage** restaurant (see review, above), which serves brunch, lunch, and dinner. ■ *10007 Bridge St (at Donner Pass Rd), Truckee; (530) 587-4444 or (800) 659-6921; mail: PO Box 884, Truckee, CA 96160; truckeeh@sierra.net; www.truckeetahoe.com/truckeehotel; $-$$; AE, MC, V; checks OK.*

## DONNER SUMMIT ■ DONNER LAKE

*See Skiing the Sierra Nevada at the end of this
chapter for Donner area ski information.*

A whirl of white in the wintertime, the Donner region was named after the 89 members of the ill-fated Donner party, who journeyed by wagon train to the area in October 1846. They had come from the Midwest and were bound for the West Coast, but were trapped here by an early winter storm. The **Emigrant Trail Museum** in **Donner Memorial State Park** tells their grim story of starvation, cannibalism, and (for some members) survival. Nowadays the snow-blanketed Donner region is a major downhill and cross-country ski destination in the winter, and in the summer the long fingers of its sparkling azure lake are dotted with sailboats, dwarfed by the imposing forested slopes and granite palisades. Donner Lake is a great fishing and boating retreat (a public boat ramp is on the west side), and a public beach rims the east end of the lake. The 350-acre state park, located at 12593 Donner Pass Road (south of Interstate 80), also offers campsites, picnic tables, and hiking trails; for general park information call (530)582-7894 or (530)582-7892, and for camping reservations call (800)444-7275.

## LODGINGS

**Donner Country Inn** ★★ Can you believe it . . . a B&B that wasn't restored from another lifetime? Donner Country Inn was built in 1986—a rarity for this part of the state, where 19th-century architecture is de rigueur. The attractive and comfortable inn, decorated with country pine furnishings and Laura Ashley prints, sits in a grove of pine trees just across the road from Donner Lake. Its five guest rooms have private entrances and baths, queen-size beds with down comforters, and wood-burning stoves. Breakfast, served in the main house's spacious second-floor living/dining area or on the sunny deck, includes an entree such as sour-cream waffles, plus fresh fruit, muffins, and croissants. There's a minimum two-night stay and advance reservations are required. ■ *10070 Gregory Pl, Donner Lake; (530)587-5574 or (925)938-0685; mail: PO Box 11243, Truckee, CA 96162; $$; no credit cards; checks OK.*

**Loch Leven Lodge** ★ If you want to get away from the crowds in Tahoe but would like easy access to the area's restaurants and shops, this quiet, simple lodge might be for you. Each of its eight small units faces beautiful Donner Lake and all but one have a kitchen. You can bask in the sun on the 5,000-square-foot redwood deck or put on your lime-green pants and head over to the Astroturf putting green (clubs and balls are provided). The lodge also has picnic tables, lawn chairs, a barbecue, a spa, and a rowboat. The rooms on the lower level offer the best lake views, but they don't offer the most privacy (passersby occasionally walk by the exposed windows). If you're traveling with the gang, reserve the two-level townhouse that sleeps eight and has a fireplace, a fully equipped kitchen, a living room with a queen-size hideaway bed, an upstairs bedroom, and an adjoining bunk room with four single beds. ■ *13855 Donner Pass Rd (from I-80, take the Donner Lake exit and turn left on Donner Pass Rd; it's 1½ miles from I-80), Donner Lake; (530)587-3773; mail: PO Box 162, Truckee, CA 96160; $$; no credit cards; checks OK.*

## NORDEN

*LODGINGS*

**Clair Tappaan Lodge** This is no place for wimps, but those hardy souls who want to meet new people, limit expenses, and don't mind a few housekeeping tasks should pack their bags and hike on in. Built by Sierra Club volunteers in 1934, Clair Tappaan Lodge is a massive, rustic three-story structure near Donner Summit. Guests carry their own bedding and luggage 100 yards uphill from the road to a building that accommodates up to 140 people. Dorm-style rooms vary from two-person cubicles with thin walls to family bunk rooms and a men's and a women's dorm (psst . . . the romantically inclined should note that all beds are single bunk beds). The pine-paneled living room is warmed by a rock fireplace in the winter, and a library, hot tub, and resident masseuse help keep you relaxed. Breakfast, lunch, and dinner are included in the room rate, and you're expected to help with basic caretaking chores such as dishwashing or mopping the floors. Guests get a hot breakfast and sack lunches to take skiing or hiking (tracks, slopes, and trails are close by). The dinners here are casual, healthy, and filling affairs served family style. They might include chips and salsa, a tossed green salad, warm cornbread, chili con carne (and a vegetarian version), and, for dessert, big melt-in-your-mouth brownies. Inquire about Clair Tappaan's numerous outdoor recreational opportunities and classes (prices vary), which range from cross-country skiing (ski rentals are available), fly-fishing, and wine-tasting to fort building for kids and family hikes. ■ *19940 Donner Pass Rd (from I-80, take the Soda Springs/Norden exit; it's 2.4 miles E of the highway), Norden; (530) 426-3632; mail: PO Box 36, Norden, CA 95724; jeff.hartley@ sierraclub.org; $; no alcohol (but a liquor license is pending); MC, V; checks OK.*

## SODA SPRINGS

*RESTAURANTS*

**Engadine Café** ★★★ Within Royal Gorge's Rainbow Lodge (see review, below) is the charming and cozy Engadine Café, which boasts a large fireplace that's ablaze continuously on those freezing Sierra winter nights. Some of the best food in the region is served here. Breakfasts are planned for folks with hearty let's-scale-a-mountain appetites and feature a wide range of choices, from a belly-packing stack of whole-wheat pancakes to three-egg omelets bursting with smoked ham, mushrooms, scallions, and Swiss cheese accompanied by a pile of country fries. Lunches at the Engadine are simple and satisfying and might include pasta with fresh eggplant, tomato, and mushroom sauce; a juicy burger with all the fixin's; and a luscious (and messy) sandwich Provençal with grilled vegetables, sun-dried tomatoes, artichoke hearts, and melted provolone on a toasted sourdough roll. In the evening the kitchen turns out an eclectic mix of terrific fare such as Swiss fondue for two, roast rack of lamb breaded with pistachio nuts and basted with Dijon mustard, and several daily seafood specials. Wednesday dinners are all-you-can-eat pasta feasts—a great way to carbo load for the next day's skiing or hiking trip. ■ *On Rainbow Rd at the Yuba River (½ mile W of I-80), Soda Springs; (530)426-3661; info@royalgorge.com; www.royalgorge.com; $$; full bar; MC, V; no checks; breakfast, lunch, dinner every day (weather permitting).*

### LODGINGS

**Royal Gorge's Rainbow Lodge ■ Wilderness Lodge ★★** The 1922 Rainbow Lodge was built of hand-hewn pine timbers and local granite at a bend in the Yuba River. The owner of the popular Royal Gorge cross-country ski resort, the largest cross-country center in the United States, bought this charming retreat several years ago. The lodge's 32 simple, pine-paneled rooms come with either a private bath, shower, and sink or just a sink (with a bath down the hall). Rooms 12, 14, 23, and 24 overlook the river. Oversized chairs and sofas fill the lounge, where guests often read or play Monopoly by the fire. Within the lodge is the very pleasant **Engadine Café** (see review, above), which serves some of the best food in the region and is open to non-guests, too. Breakfast is included with a night's stay.

Royal Gorge also offers cross-country skiers accommodations in its **Wilderness Lodge**, a handsome wood lodge with a huge stone fireplace that's tucked away in a remote part of the cross-country course. Guests arrive at the lodge by jumping aboard an open sleigh pulled by a Sno-Cat. The private knotty-pine guest rooms are equipped with bunks or double beds covered with floral-print comforters. (For details on the skiing opportunities here, see Skiing the Sierra Nevada at the end of this chapter.) ■ *On Rainbow Rd (from I-80, take the Rainbow Rd exit and drive ½ mile W), Soda Springs; (530)426-3871, (530)426-3661, or (800)500-3871 (outside Northern California only); mail: PO Box 1100, Soda Springs, CA 95728; info@royalgorge.com; www.royalgorge. com; $$ (includes breakfast); full bar in main lodge, beer and wine at Wilderness Lodge; MC, V; no checks; breakfast, lunch, dinner every day (main lodge open year-round, Wilderness Lodge open during ski season only).*

## DUTCH FLAT

### RESTAURANTS

**Monte Vista Inn ★** For about 60 years, the Monte Vista has been a roadhouse catering to locals—and to travelers lucky enough to find it. The comfortable inn is built of logs and indigenous stone,

▼
▲

with a wood-burning stove in the bar and large sofas near the pet-rified-wood fireplace in the lounge. Kerosene lamps light the wooden dining tables and old farm implements hang on the walls. The kitchen prepares generous portions of California cuisine, ranging from mesquite-grilled rack of lamb to scampi sautéed with fresh mushrooms and garlic. They also smoke their own ribs and chicken using local fruit wood. You can admire the dozen or so freshly baked pies sitting neatly on the counter along the dining-room wall, which taste as good as they look (the black-berry pie is tangy with lemon). Live music livens up the bar on the weekend. ▪ *Off I-80 at the Dutch Flat exit (9 miles E of Colfax), Dutch Flat; (530) 389-2333; $$; full bar; MC, V; local checks only; breakfast, lunch Sunday only, dinner every day.* ⅃

## LAKE TAHOE

*See Skiing the Sierra Nevada at the end of this chapter for Lake Tahoe area ski information.*

Frontiersman Kit Carson was guiding General John Frémont's expedition across the Sierra Nevada in 1844 when he stumbled on an immense, deep-blue body of water, a lake so vast the native Washoe Indians were calling it *tahoe* ("big lake"). Carson was the first white man to see Tahoe, North America's largest alpine lake and the eighth-deepest in the world (its deepest point is at 1,645 feet). If completely drained, Tahoe would cover the entire state of California with 14 inches of water.

The California/Nevada border runs straight through the heart of the lake, leaving its west side in California and its east side in Nevada. Despite this east/west state division, the lake is more commonly referred to in terms of its north and south shores. The South Shore area is the most populous and urban, where you'll hear all those slot machines ringing and coins tinkling. If you'd rather steer clear of the one-armed bandits, head for the North Shore. There you'll find fewer casinos (and tourists) and more of everything else, including Tahoe's best alpine and cross-country ski resorts, first-rate restaurants, and luxurious lodgings.

Despite all its great skiing, Tahoe is actually most crowded in the summer, when thousands flock here to cool off at the lake (although what constitutes public shoreline versus private water-front is still a matter of heated debate between home owners and county supervisors). Warm-weather activities abound: boating, waterskiing, bicycling, hiking, rock climbing, hot-air ballooning, horseback riding . . . you name it. Unfortunately, the area pays dearly for its myriad attractions, in the form of tremendous traffic jams, water and air pollution, and a plethora of fast-food joints and condos erected before tough building restrictions were imposed. Despite these glaring scars, Lake Tahoe remains one of the pre-mier outdoor playgrounds of the West, dazzling visitors with its soaring Sierra peaks and twinkling alpine waters.

For a grand introduction to the area, take a leisurely 72-mile drive around the lake itself. Highways 50, 89, and 28 hug the shore, providing gorgeous views from the car. Several stellar sights merit pulling over for a closer look, so be prepared to stop and haul out your camera (or camcorder) along the way. Topping the not-to-be-missed list are **Emerald Bay** (off Highway 89 on the West Shore), one of the most photographed sights in the world; **Cave Rock Tunnel**, the 200-foot-long, drive-through granite tunnel along Highway 50 on the East Shore; and **Sand Harbor State Park** (off Highway 28 on the East Shore), one of the lake's prettiest—and least visited—beaches. Allow about three hours to loop around the lake, or longer if you're traveling on a summer weekend, holiday, or when the road is covered with snow.

Once you've circled the lake, make a quick stop in Tahoe City at the **Tahoe North Visitors & Convention Bureau** and sort through the mountain of brochures on local attractions ranging from indoor wall climbing to ice skating and horseback riding. If you plan to hike or ride bikes here, load up on the free trail maps, too. This is also the place to visit or call if you're having trouble finding a hotel room or campsite (a common problem during peak seasons) or need information on ski packages; 950 North Lake Boulevard, above McDonald's, Tahoe City, (530) 581-6900 or (800) 824-6348.

The hot summer weather brings a phenomenal array of lakeside activities, many of which don't cost a dime. Day hikers should head for the trail next to the visitors center on the West Shore; the center is located on Highway 89, just north of Fallen Leaf Road and 3 miles north of South Lake Tahoe, (530) 573-2674. It's the starting point for several well-marked trails, ranging from an easy half-mile stroll to a 10-mile, leg-burning trek. Serious mountain bikers shouldn't miss huffing up and down the famous 24-mile **Flume Trail**, which provides fantastic views of the lake; the trailhead begins at **Nevada State Park** on the lake's eastern shore. Casual and asphalt-only pedalers can vie with in-line skaters, joggers, and strollers for room on North Tahoe's 15-mile-long paved trail, beginning at **Sugar Pine Point State Park** on the West Shore and stretching north along the lake to **Dollar Point** on the North Shore. There's also a 3½-mile paved trail that parallels the **Truckee River** and passes through Tahoe City; the trail starts at the turnoff to Alpine Meadows ski resort on Highway 89. For the truly lazy (or crazy) rider, **Northstar-at-Tahoe** and **Squaw Valley USA** ski resorts offer miles of pedal-free trails accessible by chairlift or cable car—simply let the lifts tote you and your bike up the mountains, then spend the day cruising (or careening like a deranged daredevil) down the slopes.

If you weren't able to pack all your recreational toys, Porter's Ski & Sport in Tahoe City has the best prices in town for outdoor rental equipment—everything from bikes to skates to rackets, as well as a full line of snow skis, waterskis, and snow boards; 501 North Lake Boulevard, Tahoe City, (530) 583-2314.

To try your luck at blackjack or spinning the big wheel, make the short drive to **Nevada**, where the folks in the casinos will be delighted to see you. Although the North Shore's casinos are more subdued and less glitzy than the South Shore's high-rolling highrises, the dealers are still adept at taking your money. If you're a greenhorn, this is a good place to learn the ABCs of the games, especially during off-hours. North Shore **casinos** include the Tahoe Biltmore Hotel, (702) 831-0660; Cal-Neva Lodge and Casino, (702) 832-4000; Hyatt Regency Lake Tahoe, (702) 831-1111; and Crystal Bay Club Casino, (702) 831-0512. (For recommended South Shore casinos, turn to the South Lake Tahoe section in the following pages.)

North Lake Tahoe also offers a few nocturnal alternatives to the dice and the slots. You can dance any night of the week at **Pierce Street Annex**, which caters primarily to a thirtysomething crowd but attracts swingers of all ages; 850 North Lake Boulevard, behind Safeway, Tahoe City, (530) 583-5800. **Humpty's**, on the other hand, resembles (and smells like) a college-town hangout, though this is where you'll find some of the area's top dance bands and the cheapest drinks; 877 North Lake Boulevard, across from Safeway, Tahoe City, (530) 583-4867. During the ski season, the lounge of the **River Ranch Lodge** (see review under Tahoe City) has a raging après-ski scene, with ski bums from all over kicking back and chowing down on cheap hors d'oeuvres.

## SQUAW VALLEY

### LODGINGS

**PlumpJack Squaw Valley Inn** ★★★ Restaurateurs Bill Getty (yes, of *the* Getty family) and Gavin Newsom, the brains—and money—behind the highly regarded PlumpJack Cafe in San Francisco, have teamed together to create Tahoe's most stylish and sophisticated hotel and restaurant. Though it lacks the big-dollar toys offered by its competitor across the valley (the Resort at Squaw Creek; see review, below), the PlumpJack Squaw Valley Inn is undeniably more stylish. The entire hotel bears a strong resemblance to the San Francisco restaurant, draped in muted tones of taupe and soft greens, and highlighted with custom metal work that imparts a handsome industrial-deco theme. Guest rooms are loaded with comforts, ranging from plush hooded robes and terrycloth slippers to thick down comforters atop expensive mattresses. The hotel boasts mountain views from each of its 60 rooms, as well as a swimming pool, two spas, a retail sports shop, ski rentals and storage, complimentary parking, and room service from the terrific cafe from 7am to 10pm.

The adjoining **PlumpJack Cafe** is the latest showcase for award-winning chef Maria Helm, who oversees the kitchen both here and at the sister restaurant in San Francisco. Though dinner prices have dropped to slightly under $20 an entree after guests balked at the original outrageous prices, none of PlumpJack's typically high standards have diminished. Expect impeccable service regardless of your attire (this is, after all, a ski resort) and tempting menu choices that might include risotto with shiitake mushrooms and fava beans (with Chianti, of course), roasted rabbit atop a golden potato purée, and a fabulous dish of braised oxtails paired with horseradish mashed potatoes and carrots. Those already familiar with PlumpJack in San Francisco know that the reasonably priced wine list is among the nation's best.
■ *1920 Squaw Valley Rd (off Hwy 89), Squaw Valley; (530) 583-1576 or (800) 323-7666; mail: PO Box 2407, Squaw Valley, CA 96146; $$$; full bar; AE, DC, DIS, MC, V; checks OK; breakfast, lunch every day, dinner Thurs–Tues (food is served at the bar only on Wed night).* &

**Resort at Squaw Creek** ★★★ The $130-million Resort at Squaw Creek—Tahoe's only super-luxury resort hotel—is a paradise for skiers, golfers, and tennis players. Tucked away in an inconspicuous corner of Squaw Valley, the nine-story resort opened in 1990, offering a plethora of amenities—from parking valets, a concierge, and room service to children's activity programs, a shopping promenade, three swimming pools, a fitness center and spa, cross-country ski trails, an equestrian center with stables, and even an ice-skating rink. Furthermore, it's only a stone's throw from the Squaw Creek chairlift, which accesses the entire Squaw Valley USA ski area. In the summer, golfers may tee off at the resort's 18-hole championship golf course designed by Robert Trent Jones Jr., while tennis buffs may rally at the Peter Burwash International Tennis Center.

The 405 rooms, suites, and bi-level penthouses feature custom furnishings, original artwork, minibars, closed-circuit televisions, and telephones with speakerphones. Unfortunately, the resort suffers from a design flaw: the hotel rooms are in one (unattractive) building and the front desk, restaurants, and other facilities are in another, so guests are forced to walk outdoors—even in the middle of a wicked winter storm—to reach either building. Ask about the midweek package deals, which can knock a hefty amount off the normally exorbitant rates. In addition to a deli, pub, game lounge, and outdoor cafe, the Resort at Squaw Creek offers three restaurants: the elegant **Glissandi**, which serves French-American cuisine, the continental restaurant **Cascades**, and the **Ristorante Montagna**, where you can dine alfresco on wood-oven-baked pizzas, rotisserie-grilled meats, and house specials such as the *agnello alla griglia*—an oakwood-roasted rack of lamb with grilled vegetables and a Provençal sauce. ■ *400*

Sierra
Nevada

▼

Squaw Valley

*Lodgings*

Squaw Creek Rd (off Hwy 89), Squaw Valley; (530)583-6300 or
(800)327-3353; mail: PO Box 3333, Squaw Valley, CA 96146; rr-
rsc@worldnet.att.net; www.squawcreek.com; $$$; full bar; AE, DC,
DIS, MC, V; checks OK; breakfast, lunch, dinner every day. &

## ALPINE MEADOWS

### LODGINGS

**River Ranch Lodge** ★★ Established in 1888 as the Deer Park Inn,
this historic lodge was a popular watering hole for passengers
traveling by narrow-gauge railway. In 1950 the old building was
razed and replaced with the rustic, wood-shingled lodge that now
stands on the banks of the picturesque Truckee River. The River
Ranch's best rooms feature private balconies that overlook the
river as it winds its way from Lake Tahoe to the town of Truckee,
then east to Pyramid Lake in Nevada. All 19 rooms have private
baths, antique furnishings, TVs, and phones. Rooms 9 and 10, the
farthest from the road, are the top choices because they're qui-
eter and have the best river views from their private decks. In the
winter, the lodge is a skier's paradise, a mere 10-minute drive
from both Squaw Valley USA and Alpine Meadows ski resorts
(the Alpine Meadows stay-and-ski packages are outstanding); in
the summer, guests relax under umbrellas on the huge patio
overlooking the river, watching rafters float by while they munch
on barbecued chicken and sip iced tea. A continental breakfast is
included in the surprisingly reasonable rates.

The River Ranch's spectacular circular cocktail lounge, which
cantilevers over the river, has been a locals' haven for years and
is an immensely popular après-ski spot for those who have been
schussing the slopes of Alpine Meadows and Squaw Valley. Also
a big hit is the handsome **River Ranch Lodge Restaurant**, which
serves fresh fish, such as mountain rainbow trout sautéed with
lemon butter, steaks, a full New Zealand rack of lamb, and some-
thing you probably don't cook at home: wood-oven-roasted Mon-
tana elk loin with a dried bing cherry-port sauce. Be sure to ask
for a table overlooking the water or, during the summer, on the
large, heated outdoor patio next to the rushing river. ■ *On Hwy 89
(at Alpine Meadows Rd, 3½ miles from Lake Tahoe and Tahoe
City), Alpine Meadows; (530)583-4264 or (800)535-9900; mail:
PO Box 197, Tahoe City, CA 96145; $$; full bar; AE, MC, V; checks
OK; lunch every day (Memorial Day to Labor Day only), dinner
every day.* &

## TAHOE CITY

### RESTAURANTS

**Christy Hill** ★★★ Perched high above the lake in one of the most
romantic fireside settings in Tahoe, the venerable Christy Hill
restaurant has weathered droughts, recessions, and even a

change of ownership, yet still retains its title as one of the finest—and most expensive—restaurants in Tahoe City. The menu, presided over by chefs Claudio Mejia and Lisa Joakimides, changes seasonally, but always offers a wide selection of fresh seafood—Fanny Bay oysters, broiled salmon, baked halibut—and choice-cut meats ranging from broiled Australian lamb with a honey, cracked-pepper, and mint demiglace to farm-raised New Zealand venison served with blackberry-sage sauce and wild mushroom compote. Christy Hill's experienced servers know the menu and extensive wine list well, so don't hesitate to seek their advice. Dessert is a wonderful excuse to extend your evening here; try the warm summer fruit cobbler with house-made vanilla ice cream or the chocolate pot de crème with crème chantilly. Arrive before sunset to admire the spectacular view. ■ *115 Grove St (off Hwy 28/N Lake Blvd, behind the Village Store), Tahoe City; (530)583-8551; $$$; beer and wine; AE, MC, V; checks OK; dinner Tues–Sun.* &

**Wolfdale's ★★★** Chef/owner Douglas Dale is well known for his innovative California cuisine that's often accented with Japanese touches. His short, frequently changing menu offers an intriguing mix of truly one-of-a-kind, light, and beautifully arranged dishes that vary from very good to sublime. Everything

*Tahoe City*

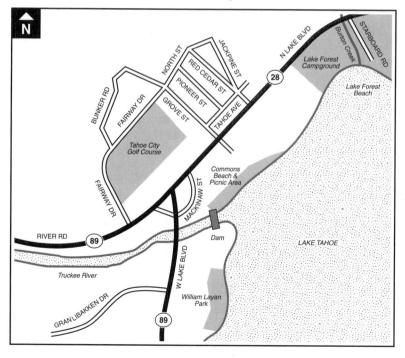

served in this casually elegant restaurant—from the herb-kissed focaccia to the savory sausages, smoked fish, and divine desserts—is prepared on the premises. You might begin your meal with a cured-salmon salad or a vegetable spring roll with a Thai curry-ginger sauce, followed by grilled Columbia River sturgeon with mushroom duxelles and tomato coulis or roasted quail stuffed with fennel sausage and onions served on a bed of kale. Many of Wolfdale's regular patrons dine at the small bar, and in the summertime you can sit outdoors and enjoy the view of Lake Tahoe through the trees. ■ *640 N Lake Blvd (on Hwy 28, downtown), Tahoe City; (530)583-5700; $$$; full bar; MC, V; no checks; dinner Wed–Mon (every day in July and Aug).*

**Fire Sign Cafe** ★★  This converted old Tahoe home has been a favorite breakfast stop for locals since the late 1970s. Just about everything here is made from scratch, including the coffee cake and muffins that accompany generous servings of bacon and eggs. Even the savory, thinly sliced salmon used in the cafe's legendary eggs Benedict is smoked on the premises. Popular lunch items include the garden burger, the chicken burrito, the grilled turkey sandwich with green chiles and cheese, and a scrumptious raspberry cobbler. In the summer, dine on the deck under the pines. Expect a long wait on weekends. ■ *1785 W Lake Blvd (on Hwy 89, 2 miles S of town), Tahoe City; (530)583-0871; $; beer and wine; MC, V; local checks only; breakfast, lunch every day.*

**Jake's on the Lake** ★★  If you're in the mood for steak and seafood, Jake's serves some of the best in Tahoe. One link in a wildly popular California and Hawaii chain, this handsome lakefront restaurant offers consistently good food and service, provided in part by a candidate for California's most affable bartender, who's known simply as Montana. Specialties include rack of New Zealand lamb and fresh fish, such as the favored flame-broiled ahi tuna served with garlic mashed potatoes and red bell pepper beurre blanc. The small seafood bar, which serves light fare like Cajun prawns, rock shrimp quesadillas, and grilled artichokes, is ideal for a quick, inexpensive meal (if you're lucky enough to get an unoccupied stool). And the terrific Hula Pie dessert (an Oreo-cookie crust topped with mounds of macadamia-nut ice cream smothered with fudge sauce and whipped cream) is worth the splurge in calories. ■ *780 N Lake Blvd (on Hwy 28, downtown), Tahoe City; (530)583-0188; $$; full bar; AE, MC, V; no checks; brunch Sun, lunch Mon–Sat June 15 to Sept 15 (lunch Sat only Oct to May), seafood bar opens at 2:30pm June 15 to Sept 15 (and at 4:30pm Oct to May), dinner every day.*

**Rosie's Cafe** ★★  Most folks who spend a few days or more in North Lake Tahoe eventually wind up at Rosie's for breakfast, lunch, dinner, drinks, or all of the above. This humble Tahoe institution serves large portions of traditional American fare—sandwiches, steaks, burgers, salads—but the two dishes that tourists always return for are the hearty Yankee pot roast (the perfect dish for those cold winter nights) and the crisp Southern-fried chicken, both served with mashed potatoes and gravy and a side of sautéed vegetables. Live music is featured every Tuesday night—an event that shouldn't be missed if you care to witness mountain folk at their rowdiest. ■ *571 N Lake Blvd (on Hwy 28, downtown), Tahoe City; (530)583-8504; $$; full bar; AE, DC, DIS, MC, V; no checks; breakfast, lunch, dinner every day.*

**Za's ★★** When the front half of the "PIZZAS" sign fell off this restaurant long ago, the owner decided it was an auspicious omen and renamed the place Za's. Sure enough, Za's turned out to be a hit. In fact, it's one of the most popular restaurants in Tahoe, serving very good Italian food at bargain prices. The herbed bread, baked fresh daily and stacked under hanging braids of garlic, is wonderful, especially when dipped in the accompanying pool of olive oil. Start with the caesar salad or the baked polenta with wild mushrooms and Marsala sauce, and follow that with the golden-brown calzone stuffed with fresh vegetables and moz-zarella or the smoked-chicken fettuccine with fresh artichoke hearts and a garlic-cream sauce. Wash it all down with a tumbler of Chianti, but skip the lackluster desserts. There are only a dozen tables, so during peak hours you'll have to join the line of salivating patrons snaking out the door. ■ *395 N Lake Blvd (on Hwy 28, across from the fire station), Tahoe City; (530)583-1812; $; beer and wine; MC, V; no checks; dinner every day.*

**Bridgetender Tavern and Grill ★** Any bar that has Jaegermeister on tap is worth a visit. The fact that the Bridgetender has 20 other beers on tap and great burgers is icing on the cake. Tahoe's fore-most tavern, a rough-hewn log-and-stone structure built around a trio of healthy ponderosa pines, is frequented by folks who know each other on a first-name basis. The menu is basic—burgers, salads, sandwiches, and various appetizers like pork ribs and deep-fried chicken strips—but the food is filling and cheap. In the summer the outside patio is always packed with giddy tourists unaware of the effects of alcohol at high altitudes. ■ *30 W Lake Blvd (on Hwy 89 at Fanny Bridge, downtown), Tahoe City; (530)583-3342; $; full bar; DIS, MC, V; no checks; lunch, dinner every day.*

## LODGINGS

**Sunnyside Restaurant & Lodge ★★★** Restored about a dozen years ago, this beautiful mountain lodge has 23 rooms, each with a deck. All but four have an unobstructed view of Lake Tahoe, and the best of the bunch are the bright and airy lakefront units (suites 30 and 31 and rooms 32 to 39). A complimentary conti-nental breakfast buffet is served every morning, and in the after-noon locals and visitors assemble for lunch, dinner, or a drink on the huge redwood deck overlooking the lake. The **Chris Craft**

Dining Room serves well-prepared California cuisine and specializes in fresh seafood, such as Hawaiian ahi and baked salmon with Roma tomatoes, fresh basil, and Gorgonzola. In the winter the lodge attracts a sizable après-ski crowd, which watches Sunnyside's ski flicks while munching on the inexpensive food at the bar. ■ *1850 W Lake Blvd (on Hwy 89, 2 miles S of town), Tahoe City; (530)583-7200 or (800)822-2SKI; mail: PO Box 5969, Tahoe City, CA 96145; $$$; full bar; AE, MC, V; no checks; brunch Sun (summer only), lunch every day (summer only), dinner every day.* &

**The Cottage Inn** ★★  This is one of the more appealing places to stay in Tahoe City. Each of the inn's 15 cabins has Swedish-pine furniture, a stone fireplace, a private bath with a ceramic-tile shower, a thick, colorful quilt on the bed, and a TV with a VCR. A full country breakfast, included in the price, may be served at your doorstep, at the family-style tables in the dining room, or on the outside deck. After breakfast, kick back in the comfortable sitting room in front of the large stone fireplace, in the Scandinavian sauna, or at the nearby beach and dock. ■ *1690 W Lake Blvd (on Hwy 89, 2 miles S of town), Tahoe City; (530)581-4073 or (800)581-4073; mail: PO Box 66, Tahoe City, CA 96145; $$; MC, V; checks OK.*

## HOMEWOOD

### RESTAURANTS

**Swiss Lakewood Restaurant** ★★  This handsome Swiss-style edifice, first opened in 1920, is the home of the oldest operating restaurant in Lake Tahoe. Its current owners, Helga and Albert Marty, continue the tradition of offering fine French-Continental cuisine in a traditional Swiss setting (think knotty-pine walls covered with clocks, old photographs, and Swiss cowbells). Though the menu changes frequently, among the secrets of the Martys' unwavering success are their perfectly executed sauces, such as the tangy caper-lemon-mustard sauce drizzled over their delicate crab cake appetizer or the tasty Madagascar green-pepper sauce poured over the hearty Black Angus pepper steak flambé, which is prepared at your table with fiery aplomb. And, but of course, there's the cheese fondue for two, served on weekdays and throughout the week in the winter. For dessert, consider the Grand Marnier soufflé or the cherries jubilee flambé for two. ■ *5055 W Lake Blvd (on Hwy 89, 6 miles S of Tahoe City, next to Ski Homewood), Homewood; (530)525-5211; $$$; full bar; AE, MC, V; no checks; dinner Tues–Sun.*

### LODGINGS

**Chaney House** ★★★  Built in the 1920s, the European-style Chaney House features 18-inch-thick stone walls, Gothic arches, and a massive stone fireplace that extends to a cathedral ceiling.

Each of the four individually decorated rooms has a private bath and a queen- or king-size bed. The attractive Honeymoon Hideaway is a detached, very private unit with a full kitchen. Gary and Lori Chaney—two of Tahoe's more vivacious and friendly innkeepers—serve an elaborate breakfast on the patio (weather permitting) overlooking their private beach and pier. Lori likes to get creative in the kitchen—she often whips up such treats as French toast stuffed with cream cheese and topped with hot homemade blackberry sauce and crème fraîche, or a scrumptious concoction of scrambled eggs mixed with artichokes, vermouth, and cheese. The Chaney House books up quickly, so make your reservations at least a month in advance. ■ *4725 W Lake Blvd (on Hwy 89, just N of Ski Homewood), Homewood; (530)525-7333; mail: PO Box 7852, Tahoe City, CA 96145; www. tahoecountry.com/wslodging/chaney.html; $$; MC, V; checks OK.*

**Rockwood Lodge** ★★★ Innkeepers Louis Reinkens and Constance Stevens bought this native stone and timber house in 1984 and, after a meticulous refurbishing, opened it as a bed and breakfast a year later. Although you may be disconcerted by their requirement that you remove your shoes before entering, all is forgiven when your feet sink into the plush, cream-colored carpet. The lodge, located just across the street from the lake, has five rooms, each furnished with antiques, feather beds, and down comforters covered in Laura Ashley fabrics. Terrycloth robes hang in the bedroom closets, and the extravagant private bathrooms feature brass fixtures, hand-painted tiles, and double showers. The top choice is the Rubicon Bay Suite, which has a beautiful four-poster bed and a partial view of the lake, though every room in this B&B is splendid. In the evening guests often play backgammon and sip cordials by the fireplace in the sitting room. A generous breakfast is served at 9am in the dining room or on the outdoor patio. ■ *5295 W Lake Blvd (on Hwy 89, next to Ski Homewood), Homewood; (530)525-5273 or (800)LE-TAHOE; mail: PO Box 226, Homewood, CA 96141-0226; rockwood@ inreach. com; www.home.inreach.com/rockwood; $$$; no credit cards; checks OK.*

**Tahoma**

*Lodgings*

## TAHOMA

### *LODGINGS*

**Tahoma Meadows Bed & Breakfast** ★★ Missy Sandeman and her husband, Bill (a retired professional football player who played for the Dallas Cowboys and the Atlanta Falcons), are two of the sweetest people you will ever meet and they own and operate the finest moderately priced B&B in Lake Tahoe. Tahoma Meadows Bed & Breakfast consists of 11 private cabins perched on a gentle forest slope amongst sugar pines and flowers. Missy, a talented watercolor painter, has individually decorated each cozy cabin with her framed paintings of bucolic settings. All rooms have a private bath, a discreetly placed TV, and comfy king-size, queen-size, or twin beds; four have gas-log fireplaces. The cheery Sunflower and Fox Glove Cabins are the favorites, and they're both equipped with grand claw-footed soaking tubs. The largest cabin, Columbine, sleeps six and is ideal for families seeking privacy and plenty of elbow room. A full breakfast is served at the main lodge, upstairs from the independently owned Stoneyridge Cafe. Nearby activities include skiing at Ski Homewood, fly-fishing at a private trout-stocked lake, and sunbathing on the lakeshore just across the street. ■ *6821 W Lake Blvd (on Hwy 89, 8½ miles from Tahoe City), Tahoma; (530)525-1553 or (800)355-1596; mail: PO Box 810, Homewood, CA 96141; sandytahoe@telis.org; www.tahoecountry.com/wslodging/tmeadows.html; $$; AE, DIS, MC, V; checks OK.*

## TAHOE VISTA

### RESTAURANTS

**Le Petit Pier** ★★★ One of Tahoe's more exclusive French restaurants is elevated just above the shore with a dazzling view of the lake. Order from the prix-fixe *menu gastronomique* or the à la carte menu, both of which feature such mouth-watering appetizers as escargots in Roquefort butter, warm foie gras with truffle sauce, and oysters on the half shell. The exquisite entrees range from seafood (swordfish with ginger raspberry sauce) and fowl (grilled breast of duck in a zinfandel sauce) to beef (medallions of veal with shiitake mushrooms) and a superb rack of lamb. Le Petit Pier also has an extensive California and European wine list. When making a reservation, request a table by the window and be sure to arrive before sunset—you don't want to miss this view, which extends clear across Lake Tahoe. ■ *7238 N Lake Blvd (on Hwy 28 at the W end of town), Tahoe Vista; (530)546-4464; $$$; full bar; AE, DC, DIS, MC, V; local checks only; dinner every day Memorial Day to Labor Day (Wed–Mon in the winter).*

**Sunsets On The Lake** ★★★ Rare in Tahoe is a lakeside restaurant serving food that's equal to the spectacular view. Yet even the Kodak Moment beyond the window panes is humbled by Chef Lew Orlady's fantastic braised lamb shank, a hefty hunk of tender lamb with shiitake mushrooms, caramelized vegetables, and garlic mashed potatoes—one of the best lamb dishes in Tahoe. If the duck is among the daily specials, you're in luck: each tender slice of this expertly prepared fowl explodes with flavor. Another superb entree is the enormous serving of house-baked focaccia stuffed with succulent wood-fried mushrooms, roasted chiles, goat cheese, glazed red onions, and sun-dried tomato aioli. Just about every dish on the large Northern Italian/California menu is a winner, which explains the carloads and boatloads of patrons

(Sunsets' "boat valet" will even clean your boat and top off its tank while you dine).

Built with gleaming beams of pine, the restaurant has a rustic and romantic ambience, enhanced with a large fireplace, white-linen-draped tables, and, of course, a panoramic lake view. When the snow melts, the heated outdoor deck is open for dining and drinks (request a blanket for an especially cozy sunset cocktail hour). Granted, Sunsets is a bit of a drive from Tahoe City, but it's worth the trek. Reservations are strongly recommended. ■ *7320 N Lake Blvd (on Hwy 28 at the E end of town), Tahoe Vista; (530) 546-3640; $$; full bar; AE, DC, DIS, MC, V; no checks; lunch every day mid-June to mid-Sept, dinner every day year-round.* &

**The Boulevard Cafe & Trattoria** ★★ The breads, pastas, and just about everything else on the Boulevard's menu are made here, in the North Shore's only Italian trattoria. It's a small, casual, road-side restaurant run by talented chef Daniel Paolillo. Start with a bottle of wine from the extensive Italian list and the baked polenta or grilled eggplant appetizer. Then sink your fork into one of the delicious entrees, such as ravioli stuffed with crabmeat, osso buco (braised veal shank), filet mignon with Gorgonzola and sun-dried tomatoes, rack of lamb, or one of the several seafood specials. Top it all off with a dish of the delectable house-made ice cream. In the summer, dine on the small patio among the pines. ■ *6731 N Lake Blvd (on Hwy 28, 1½ miles W of Hwy 267), Tahoe Vista; (530) 546-7213; $$; beer and wine; MC, V; local checks only; dinner every day.*

### LODGINGS

**Franciscan Lakeside Lodge** ★ The best of the area's motel scene, the Franciscan offers access to a private beach and pier, mooring buoys, a heated swimming pool, volleyball nets, a croquet set, horseshoe pits, a children's play area, and nearby tennis courts, ski areas, and a golf course. Its 51 plain but adequate units feature one or two bedrooms, full kitchens, private bathrooms, TVs, phones, and daily housekeeping service. The lakeside rooms have large porches overlooking the water (and, of course, they're the first to get booked, so make your reservations early). ■ *6944 N Lake Blvd (on Hwy 28, 1 mile W of Hwy 267), Tahoe Vista; (530) 546-7234, (530) 546-6300, or (800) 564-6754; mail: PO Box 280, Tahoe Vista, CA 96148; $$; AE, MC, V; checks OK.*

## KINGS BEACH

### RESTAURANTS

**Log Cabin Caffe** ★ Originally a summer home, the funky Log Cabin Caffe is now *the* place to have breakfast in Lake Tahoe. The owner's penchant for freshness is what makes the Log Cabin such a hit: croissants and muffins are baked every morning, the orange juice is fresh-squeezed, and the fluffy Belgian waffles are topped with fresh fruit and nuts. The large lunch menu features everything from fresh vegetable soup and tofu burgers to pizza, pasta, and sliced turkey-breast sandwiches filled with cranberries and cream cheese. Behind the restaurant near the lakeshore is a picnic area where you can cool off with ice-cream sundaes and sodas, served from 11am to 11pm throughout the summer. ■ *8692 N Lake Blvd (on Hwy 28, ⅓ mile E of Hwy 267), Kings Beach; (530)546-7109; logcabin@telis.org; $; beer and wine; MC, V; checks OK; breakfast, lunch every day.* ♿

## SOUTH LAKE TAHOE

Three premier attractions separate sassy South Lake Tahoe from its sportier northern counterpart: glitzy casinos with celebrity entertainers, several sandy beaches, and the massive **Heavenly Ski Resort**, the only American ski area that straddles two states. If 24-hour gambling parties or schussing down the slopes of Heavenly is your idea of paradise, then you're in for a treat (see the ski resort's review in Skiing the Sierra Nevada at the end of this chapter).

Most of the weekend warriors who flock here on Friday afternoons book their favorite lodgings weeks—if not months—in advance. Follow their lead and plan early. For long-term stays, consider renting a condo with a group of friends.

As soon as you roll into town, stop at the **South Lake Tahoe Chamber of Commerce**, where you'll find an entire room filled with free maps, brochures, and guidebooks to the South Lake region. And if you risked traveling to Tahoe without a hotel reservation, ask the staff to help you find a room; 3066 Lake Tahoe Boulevard, (530)541-5255.

In the summer, droves of tourists and locals arrive by bike, car, or boat at **The Beacon** restaurant and bar (see review, below) to scope out the beach, babe, and bar scene—easily the best on the lake. In addition to Jamison Beach, the other popular public beaches are **Nevada Beach**, which has spectacular views of Lake Tahoe and the Sierra Nevada (on Elk Point Road, 1 mile east of Stateline, Nevada), and **El Dorado Beach**—not as pretty, but much closer to town (off Lakeview Avenue, across from Pizza Hut, in downtown South Lake Tahoe).

Tahoe's brilliant-blue lake is so deep it never freezes, so it's navigable even in the dead of winter. Capitalizing on that fact, the *Tahoe Queen,* an authentic Mississippi stern-wheeler regularly used for scenic lunch and dinner cruises, doubles as a ferry for South Shore skiers who want to explore the North Shore's resorts. Skiers hop aboard at the base of Ski Run Boulevard in South Lake. The 25-mile ride takes about 2 hours, disembarking at the West Shore's tiny town of Homewood, where a waiting shuttle transports riders to **Squaw Valley USA** ski resort. Passengers return to South Lake the same way they came; however, on the trip back the bar is open, the band is playing, and the boat is rockin'. The round-trip fare is reasonable, and for an extra fee skiers can fill up on a big breakfast on the morning ferry. Reservations are required; call (530)541-3364 for more details.

The South Lake's number one nighttime entertainment is—you guessed it—the casino. The three top guns on this side of the lake are **Harrah's**, **Caesars Tahoe**, and **Harveys**, which are squeezed next to each other on Highway 50 in Nevada and burn enough bulbs to light a small city. Even if you can't afford to gamble away your money, stroll through the ruckus to watch the high rollers or gawk at those "just-one-more-try" players mesmerized by the flashy money machines. If you want to try your luck, a mere $10 can keep you entertained for quite a while on the nickel slots. Or spend the night kicking up your heels on the dance floor at **Nero's 2000 Nightclub** in Caesars; 55 Highway 50, Stateline, Nevada, (702)588-3515. Or visit **Turtle's Sports Bar and Dance Emporium** in the Embassy Suites; 4130 Lake Tahoe Boulevard, South Lake Tahoe, (530)544-5400.

For more than a century, **Walley's Hot Springs Resort** in Nevada has been the place for South Lake residents to unwind after a hard day of skiing or mountain biking, even though it's about an hour-long drive from town. For less than the price of a pair of movie tickets, you can jump into the six open-air pools (each is set at a different temperature) and watch ducks and geese at the nearby wildlife area. If a good soak doesn't get all the kinks out, indulge in a rubdown at the resort's massage center. No children under 12 are allowed in the resort; 2001 Foothill Boulevard, 2 miles north of the east end of Kingsbury Grade, near Genoa, Nevada, (702)782-8155.

## RESTAURANTS

**Evan's American Gourmet Café** ★★★ This is not the most attractive restaurant in Lake Tahoe, nor does it boast a stunning lake view, but the food at this family-run establishment is its raison d'être. When you enter the small, softly lit dining room, host Candice Williams warmly greets you while chef Evan Williams creates his masterpieces in the kitchen. The ever-changing menu features an eclectic and impressive mix of Italian, Caribbean, Oriental, and Southwestern cuisine, and the wine list, with nearly 300 labels, is equally engaging. A recent repast featured a baked-polenta Sabarin appetizer (polenta ringed with a Marsala sauce, house-smoked chicken breast, mushrooms, and mozzarella cheese), followed by fork-tender sautéed veal medallions served with prawns, morels, apple-smoked bacon, and fresh tomatoes. After dinner, Candice, who's also the pastry chef, tempts diners with her lavish desserts: frozen white-chocolate-mousse torte, tiramisu, or perhaps a decadent cheesecake. ■ *536 Emerald Bay Rd (on Hwy 89, 1 mile N of the Hwy 50 junction, at 15th St), South*

Lake Tahoe; (530)542-1990; $$$; beer and wine; MC, V; no checks; dinner every day.

**The Beacon** ★★ On a warm summer afternoon there is no better place on the lake to sit outside, sip on a frosty Rum Runner (a blend of light and dark rums and seven juices), and say to yourself, "*This* is the life." Located right on Jamison Beach, the Beacon is where locals arrive by car, bike, or boat to bask in the sun, chow down a bucket of steamed clams, and gawk at the tourist scene. The lunch fare is mostly salads, hamburgers, sandwiches, and the like, whereas dinner specialties include fresh seafood, such as blackened salmon with Cajun spices, or a New York steak sautéed in a green-peppercorn sauce. In the summer the Beacon shakes with live jazz, reggae, country, and rock 'n' roll. ■ *1900 Jamison Beach Rd (off Hwy 89, 2½ miles N of the Hwy 50 junction, at Camp Richardson), South Lake Tahoe; (530)541-0630; $$; full bar; AE, DIS, MC, V; no checks; brunch Sat–Sun, lunch, dinner every day.*

**Samurai** ★★ Despite Tahoe's far-from-the-sea location, there is decent seafood in the area, and you'll certainly find some of the freshest sea creatures at Samurai, one of the best Japanese restaurants in South Lake Tahoe. Settle down at the sushi bar for some hamachi or tekka maki, or take a table in the dining room where you may order such traditional Japanese dishes as tempura, teriyaki, seafood yosenabe (fresh vegetables, tofu, noodles, mushrooms, bamboo shoots, and various seafood stewing in a soy-sauce and lemon broth), and tonkatsu (deep-fried breaded pork cutlets). You may also dine at the Japanese *robata* (a table around a volcanic-rock fireplace), or, if you're with a large party, request a private tatami room. ■ *2588 Hwy 50 (1½ miles E of the Hwy 89 junction), South Lake Tahoe; (530)542-0300; $$; beer and wine; AE, MC, V; no checks; dinner every day.*

**Scusa! on Ski Run** ★★ Don't let the restaurant's tacky casino lights and "Pasta Power" sign scare you away. Though the decor leaves much to be desired, this is the place where South Lake Tahoe foodies come for Italian fare. As soon as you're seated, order the terrific rosemary-and-garlic bread, served with extra-virgin olive oil. Then peruse the varied menu for a favorite Italian dish, which might include the fettuccine alfredo tossed with shrimp, mussels, clams, scallops, and calamari or the golden calzone stuffed with lightly cooked fresh vegetables, artichoke hearts, ricotta cheese, and a savory marinara sauce. Desserts are simple but satisfying, and the wines are fairly priced. ■ *1142 Ski Run Blvd (off Hwy 50), South Lake Tahoe; (530)542-0100; $$; beer and wine; AE, DIS, MC, V; no checks; dinner every day.* &

**Sprouts Natural Foods Cafe** ★★ You don't have to be a granola-loving long-haired type to figure out that Sprouts is among the best places to eat in town. If the line out the door isn't a big enough hint, then perhaps a bite of the marvelous mayo-free tuna sandwich (made with yogurt and lots of fresh veggies) will make you a convert to feel-good food. Owner Tyler Cannon has filled a huge culinary hole in this area with the South Lake's premier vegetarian hangout. Almost everything is made on the premises, including the soups, tempeh burgers, sandwiches (try the Real Tahoe Turkey), huge burritos, muffins, fruit smoothies (a meal in themselves), coffee drinks, and fresh-squeezed juices. Order at the counter, then scramble for a vacant seat (outdoor tables are coveted) and listen for one of the buffed and beautiful servers to call out your name and deliver your tray of earthy delights. This is also an excellent place to pack a picnic lunch for a skiing, hiking, or mountain biking expedition. ■ *3123 Harrison St (on the corner of Hwy 50 and Alameda St), South Lake Tahoe; (530)541-6969; $; beer and wine; no credit cards; local checks only; breakfast, lunch, dinner every day.*

**The Red Hut** ★ This all-American coffee shop, complete with an L-shaped Formica counter, booths, and a bubble-gum machine, has become so popular the owners have added a waiting room. The Red Hut's success is based primarily on its good coffee, hefty omelets with a variety of fillings, friendly waitresses, and, best of all, low prices. Lunch follows the same big-and-cheap all-American formula with a menu of mostly burgers and sandwiches. While the food isn't anything to swoon over, it beats the buns off the fast-food chains down the street. ■ *2723 Hwy 50 (¼ mile S of Al Tahoe Blvd, 3½ miles from Stateline, Nevada), South Lake Tahoe; (530)541-9024; $; no alcohol; no credit cards; no checks; breakfast, lunch every day.*

## LODGINGS

**Christiania Inn** ★★ Located only 50 yards from Heavenly Ski Resort's main chairlift, this European-style bed-and-breakfast inn, built in 1965 as a Scandinavian ski dormitory, has four suites that are frequently occupied by honeymooners. Each suite has a wood-burning fireplace, a dry sauna or a whirlpool, and a king-size bed (one even sports a mirror over the bed). A continental breakfast and an afternoon Cognac are included in the rates.

The elegant and expensive **Christiania Inn Restaurant** offers continental cuisine, such as pan-seared spring venison with red currant cabernet sauce, boneless breast of Long Island duck with black currant sauce, and Chilean sea bass with fresh fruit salsa. Guests with lighter appetites may order from the appetizer menu in the lounge. ■ *3819 Saddle Rd (off Ski Run Blvd, at the base of Heavenly Ski Resort), South Lake Tahoe; (530)544-7337; mail: PO Box 18298, South Lake Tahoe, CA 96151; thechris@ sierra.net; www.christianainn.com; $$; full bar; MC, V; local checks only; dinner every day.* ᕦ

**Lakeland Village Beach & Ski Resort** ★★ Although many of Lakeland Village's light-brown, two-story wood buildings are located on busy Highway 50, the 19-acre resort has more than 1,000 feet of beachfront property, two tennis courts, and two swimming pools—all beyond the sight and sound of the traffic. The Village's 208 units, ranging from studios to five-bedroom town houses, are individually owned. Interior decor varies, but the owners are required to meet the strict standards set by the resort's management. The most desirable town houses front the lake, and they get booked quickly during peak season—some also command hefty $600-per-night rates. The studio rooms in the main lodge and the one-bedroom suites are the least expensive, starting at about $100. All units have fireplaces, fully equipped kitchens, and daily housekeeping service. ▪ *3535 Lake Tahoe Blvd (between Ski Run Blvd and Fairway Ave), South Lake Tahoe, CA 96150; (530)544-1685 or (800)822-5969; lakeland@sierra.net; www. lakeland-village.com; $$$; AE, MC, V; checks OK.* ♿

**Richardson's Resort** ★ Richardson's, a popular family retreat, seems worlds away from the high-rise casinos and bustle of South Lake Tahoe, yet it's actually just a few miles outside of town. After leasing this Forest Service property in 1985, the owners restored the 65-year-old log lodge and upgraded the inn and cabins. The lodge, graced with a stately stone fireplace in the lobby, offers 29 sparsely furnished rooms with private baths and is only a five-minute walk from the lake. Even closer to the water are 39 homey cabins named after classic American cars and the small seven-room Beach Inn (the rooms are slightly larger than the main lodge's and they have lake views, TVs, and telephones). The best cabins are near Jamison Beach and are usually reserved far in advance (only some of them are available to rent in the winter). In the summer the resort provides guests with an ice-cream parlor, a general store (which includes beer and wine in its inventory), camping facilities, hiking and biking trails, volleyball nets, horseshoe pits, and equipment rentals for almost anything that floats or rolls. Another perk: One of South Lake's best restaurants and bars, The Beacon (see review, above), is just a short walk away. Staying at Richardson's Resort is sort of like being at camp again, and it's a great place to take the kids. ▪ *At Jamison Beach Rd and Hwy 89 (2½ miles N of the Hwy 50 junction), South Lake Tahoe; (530)541-1801 or (800)544-1801; mail: PO Box 9028, South Lake Tahoe, CA 96158; $$; full bar; AE, MC, V; no checks.* ♿

## HOPE VALLEY

### *LODGINGS*

**Sorensen's Resort** ★★ This resort's cluster of 30 cabins, nestled among the meadows and aspen groves of alpine Hope Valley, offers first-rate cross-country skiing in the winter, prime hiking and llama treks in late spring and summer, and a terrific display of colors in the fall, when the aspens turn vibrant shades of yellow, gold, and red. There's good trout fishing here, too. Accommodations range from inexpensive, rustic-but-comfy cabins to grand, modern chalets. Norway House, a 13th-century Norwegian home with a hand-carved wooden facade and a sod roof, was actually built in Norway and transported here. It features a large open-loft bedroom, a kitchen, and a living room, and is ideal for groups of up to eight people. The country decor, with quilts and vintage furniture, is attractive and unfussy. The cozy, creekside Waterfir Cabin with its brass bed, kitchen, wood-burning stove, natural-stone hearth, and deep wooden bathtub is the best choice for couples. If you rent one of the three smaller, less-expensive cabins (Piñon, Lupine, and Larkspur, which, unlike the others, don't have kitchens), breakfast is included in the cost of your stay. There are also fully furnished homes for rent, which are ideal for families because the kids can explore the log playhouse and dip a fishing pole into the stocked fish pond. Sorensen's Country Cafe is open only to guests for breakfast, lunch, and dinner. The food is a cut above most mountain-resort fare, with good breakfasts of quiche, waffles, and fresh fruit, and your basic steak, pork chops, and pasta for dinner. Sorensen's also recently acquired the nearby **Hope Valley Store and Cafe**, which offers a modest menu of hot dogs, hamburgers, fries, and similar fare from May through Labor Day—a good place for a quick, inexpensive meal. ■ *14255 Hwy 88 (5 miles NW of Woodfords), Hope Valley, CA 96120; (530)694-2203 or (800)423-9949; $$; beer and wine; AE, DIS, MC, V; checks OK; breakfast, lunch, dinner every day.*

## MARKLEEVILLE

This tiny mountain town's claim to fame is the annual **Death Ride Tour of the California Alps**, a grueling 128-mile bike trek over five mountain passes (15,000 feet of climbing) that's renowned among bicyclists as one of the top 10 cycling challenges in America. The tour, limited to the first 2,500 prepaid applicants, is held in mid-July; call the Alpine Chamber of Commerce for more information at (530)694-2475, or send email to alpcnty@telis.org.

The only place worth visiting in Markleeville is the **Cutthroat Bar**, located in the Alpine Hotel and Cafe downtown. Belly up to the bar, order a whiskey or two (skip the food), and contemplate why the owners decided to hang a collection of brassieres from the bar's ceiling. (By the way, women are encouraged to add their bras to the display; payment is a free Cutthroat Bar T-shirt. Whoopee!) Just outside of town is the popular **Grover Hot Springs State Park**, where you may soak in the ugly but soothing cement mineral pools year-round (bathing suits are required); open 9am to 9pm daily in the summer, and 2pm to 9pm weekdays and 9am to 9pm weekends in the winter; located 4 miles west of Markleeville at the end of Hot Springs Road, (530)694-2248.

## RESTAURANTS

**Villa Gigli** ★★★ Located on a remote hillside in the tiny Sierra town of Markleeville is Gina and Ruggero Gigli's Villa Gigli, the quintessential mom-and-pop cafe that's situated alongside their modest home of 25 years. Every Friday, Saturday, and Sunday morning, Ruggero, who was raised in a small town in the hills of Tuscany, rolls pasta dough, bakes breads, and stuffs cannelloni in preparation for his two dozen or so nightly guests, most of whom have traveled hours to get here and made reservations weeks in advance—it's that special. In his spare time Ruggero creates prints from Gina's intaglio etchings, which adorn the restaurant's walls along with the wine labels of their numerous friends' Napa Valley wines. The menu usually consists of three pasta dishes (such as lasagne al forno, tagliatelle with tomato sauce, or cannelloni), one meat dish, one salad, a dessert, and fresh-brewed coffee. Sparse, yes, but when you consider that Ruggero makes all the breads, pastas, sauces, and desserts by hand, without assistance and in his tiny kitchen, it's amazing there are any choices. Prices are surprisingly low: an entree with a bottle of the house red costs about half as much as you'd pay in other three-star establishments in the Sierra Nevada. In the summer, Ruggero often cooks on his wood-burning barbecue on the deck, where guests dining alfresco can watch him prepare their main course.

The Giglis also rent out a small house on Markleeville's main street: **Grandma's House** is a modest three-bedroom, two-bath abode that sleeps up to eight people. It's simply decorated but exceptionally clean and comes with a fully stocked kitchen, a laundry room, cozy down comforters, a small yard, and views of Markleeville Creek from most of the rooms. The Giglis occasionally rent out each room for about $75 a night to dinner guests who have overindulged on beer and wine, but prefer to rent the entire home (and it's a bargain if you have a large group). ■ *145 Hot Springs Rd (about ¼ mile W of downtown), Markleeville; (530)694-2253; mail: PO Box 307, Markleeville, CA 96120; $$; beer and wine; no credit cards; checks OK; dinner Fri–Sun.* ♿

## BEAR VALLEY

*See Skiing the Sierra Nevada at the end of this chapter for Bear Valley area ski information.*

Tucked away in the central Sierra Nevada some 7,000 feet above sea level is the small town of Bear Valley, home of the popular **Bear Valley Ski Company** and the **Bear Valley Cross-Country Area**. In the summer, more than 100 miles of the cross-country ski trails become prime mountain biking territory.

**Bear Valley Lodge and Restaurant** ★★ Bear Valley Lodge, the center of this small mountain community, is a full-service, year-round resort catering to families and sports enthusiasts. There are cross-country and downhill ski facilities nearby (ask about the great skiing/lodging package deals here), and plenty of mountains, trails, lakes, and streams to explore. Another bonus is the resort's high, 7,000-foot elevation, which helps keep the scorching summer heat at bay. There are 53 guest rooms (including three suites), a restaurant and bar, a pizza parlor, a heated swimming pool (open in the summer only), two outdoor hot tubs, and a host of rejuvenating treatments at the lodge's spa. **Bear Valley Lodge Restaurant**, catering to a mostly captive audience, offers standard American fare—steak, fish, chicken, pasta, salads—and a children's menu. White tablecloths and candles set the mood in the dining room, although the dress code is casual. ■ *On Bear Valley Rd, Bear Valley; (209)753-BEAR; mail: PO Box 5440, Bear Valley, CA 95223; $$; full bar; AE, MC, V; checks OK; dinner every day.*

**Lake Alpine Lodge** ★ This quaint Sierra resort situated on Lake Alpine was built in the '20s and remodeled in the '30s. It features lodgepole-pine pillars, a fireplace so large you can walk into it, and a game room equipped with a pool table and video games. Seven of the eight rustic, fully equipped cabins have kitchens and outdoor barbecues, and all come with a shower, a deck, and a view of the lake. The lodge also offers "upscale camping" via three tent cabins, each furnished with four twin beds, a barbecue ring, and access to public bathrooms (available mid-June through Labor Day only). The **Lake Alpine Lodge Cafe** serves breakfast, lunch, and dinner in the summer (pancakes, burgers, sandwiches, et cetera), and there's a small saloon as well as a convenience market that sells bait, tackle, and camping equipment. Boats and mountain bike rentals are available, too. ■ *On Hwy 4 (at Ebbets Pass/Lake Alpine), Bear Valley; (209)753-6358; mail (May to Oct only): PO Box 5300, Bear Valley, CA 95223; mail (Nov to Apr only): PO Box 579, Big Sur, CA 93920; $$; full bar; MC, V; local checks only; breakfast, lunch, dinner every day mid-June to mid-Sept (breakfast, lunch, dinner Sat–Sun only from Memorial Day weekend to Father's Day and mid-Sept until the first snow; lodge open Memorial Day weekend to Columbus Day).*

▼

**Dorrington**

*Lodgings*

## DORRINGTON

*LODGINGS*

**The Dorrington Hotel and Restaurant** ★★ A few miles from magnificent Calaveras Big Trees State Park sits the Dorrington Hotel, built in 1860 and used as a stagecoach stop, a depot for stockmen, and—because of its 5,000-foot elevation—a summer resort where people could beat the heat. The country hotel, surrounded by some of the largest pines and sequoias in California, has been gussied up with lace curtains, period wallpaper, and decorative pillows. The five antique-filled rooms, which share bathrooms, have brass beds with homemade quilts. Complimentary sherry and fruit are available in the lounge, and a continental breakfast is served in your room. The hotel's casual dining room offers Northern Italian–style dinners. ■ *3431 Hwy 4, Dorrington; (209) 795-5800; mail: PO Box 4307, Dorrington, CA 95223; $$; beer and wine; MC, V; checks OK; dinner Thurs–Mon.*

## ARNOLD

### *LODGINGS*

**Lodge at Manuel Mill** ★★★ Linda and Ray Johnson's remote bed-and-breakfast lodge cantilevers over Old Mill Pond in the Stanislaus National Forest. Originally the site of a century-old lumber mill (with its own short-line rail system and a steam-powered engine), the 43-acre resort opened in 1989 as a Western frontier-style lodge with a massive stone fireplace, a mallard-print couch, and splashes of Native American decor. It has five comfortable, individually furnished guest rooms, each with a private bath, a wood-burning stove, and a separate entrance from the deck that overlooks a stocked 3½-acre pond. There is a rowboat for anglers and romantics (or romantic anglers) and plenty of open space for hikers and mountain bikers. Room rates include a full breakfast and a complimentary bottle of wine. ■ *On Dunbar Rd (off Hwy 4), Arnold; (209) 795-2622; mail: PO Box 998, Arnold, CA 95223; $$; MC, V; checks OK.*

▼

**Dorrington**

*Lodgings*

▲

## PINECREST

### *RESTAURANTS*

**Steam Donkey Restaurant** ★ Named after a steam-powered logging machine used to drag timber from the woods to the railroad, this popular barbecue house is usually packed with Sonorans, who make the 32-mile trek up to Dodge Ridge every weekend for the Steam Donkey's highly rated ribs, steaks, and chicken. Many of the regular patrons are ex-loggers, who likely feel right at home amid all the logging memorabilia scattered throughout the restaurant. ■ *421 Pinecrest Lake Rd (off Pinecrest Ave and Hwy 108), Pinecrest; (209) 965-3117; $; full bar; MC, V; checks OK; lunch Sat–Sun (every day in the summer), dinner every day.*

## YOSEMITE NATIONAL PARK

*See Skiing the Sierra Nevada at the end of this chapter for Yosemite area ski information.*

What was once the beloved home of the Ahwahneechee, Miwok, and Paiute Indians is now a spectacular international playground for four million annual visitors. Designated a national park in 1890, thanks in part to Sierra Club founder John Muir, 1,170-square-mile Yosemite is only slightly smaller than the state of Rhode Island. During the peak season, however, Yosemite seems more like a 1,200-square-*foot* park. Crowds more typical of Disney World clog the 7-square-mile valley for a glimpse of some of nature's most incredible creations, including 4,500-foot-high **El Capitan**, the largest piece of exposed granite on earth, and 2,425-foot-high **Yosemite Falls**, the highest waterfall in North America and fifth highest in the world.

To avoid most of the crowds, visit in the spring or early fall, when the wildflowers are plentiful and the weather is usually mild. You can virtually escape civilization by setting up a tent in Tuolumne Meadows, where numerous trails wind through the densely forested and sparsely populated high country. This grande dame of national parks is most dazzling, and least crowded, in the winter, the time of year Ansel Adams shot those world-renowned photographs of the snow-laced valley. Unfortunately, most of the hiking trails will be inaccessible at this time of year and the drive may be treacherous. Snow and ice limit access to the park, and many of the eastern passes are closed; call (800) 427-ROAD for highway conditions. Those who do brave the elements, however, will be rewarded with a truly unforgettable winter vista.

No matter what the time of year, visitors to Yosemite National Park must pay its friendly rangers a $20-per-car entrance fee. In return, you receive a seven-day pass, a detailed park map, and the "Yosemite Guide," a handy tabloid featuring the park's rules, rates, attractions, and current exhibits. One of the best ways to sightsee on the valley floor is by bike. Curry Village, (209) 372-8319, and Yosemite Lodge, (209) 372-1208, have bike stands that rent one-speed cruisers (and helmets) daily. More than 8 miles of paved bicycle paths wind through the eastern end of the valley, but bicycles (including mountain bikes) are not allowed on the hiking trails.

Day hikers in the valley have a wide variety of trails to choose from—some boring, some mind-blowing—and all are well-charted on the visitors' map. The best easy hike is the **Mirror Lake/Meadow Trail**, a 2-mile round-trip walk (5 miles if you circle the lake) that provides a magnificent view of Half Dome. More strenuous is the popular hike to **Upper Yosemite Falls**, a 7.2-mile round-trip trek with a spectacular overview of the 2,425-foot drop. (Note: Don't wander off the trail or you may join the unlucky souls who have tumbled off the cliffs to their deaths.) The grand-daddy of Yosemite hikes is the very steep ascent to the top of 8,840-foot-tall **Half Dome**, a 17-mile, round-trip, 10- to 12-hour-long thigh-burner that requires Schwarzenegger-like gusto and the nerve to hang onto climbing cables anchored in granite—clearly not a jaunt for everyone. But those who reach the top are rewarded with stunning valley views. When the snowstorm season hits, most hiking trails are closed, and many people haul out their snowshoes or cross-county skis for valley excursions, or snap on their alpine skis and schuss down the groomed beginner/ intermediate hills of **Badger Pass Ski Area** (see Skiing the Sierra Nevada at the end of this chapter for more details).

If you'd rather keep your feet firmly planted on lower ground, tour the **Yosemite Valley Visitors Center**, which houses some mildly interesting galleries and museums. The center's **Indian Cultural Museum** hosts live demonstrations of the native Miwok and Paiute methods of basket weaving, jewelry making, and other crafts. Nearby are a reconstructed Miwok–Paiute village, a self-guided nature trail, and an art gallery showcasing the master photographer whose name is almost synonymous with this place: Ansel Adams.

Unless bumper-to-bumper traffic is your idea of a vacation in the woods, skip Yosemite Valley during summer weekends and join the rebel minority who know there's more than one way to view the area. **Glacier Point**, a rocky ledge 3,215 feet above the valley floor, has what many consider one of the best vistas on the continent: a bird's-eye view of the entire valley and a panoramic expanse of the High Sierra. The view is particularly striking at sunset and under a full moon. The point is located at the end of Glacier Point Road, open only in the summer.

At the southern entrance to the park, 35 miles south of the valley, lies **Mariposa Grove**, home to some of the planet's largest and most ancient living things. The most popular attraction is the 2,700-year-old **Grizzly Giant**, the world's oldest sequoia. Pick up a self-guided trail map in the box at the grove trailhead or attend one of the free ranger-led walks, offered regularly; check the "Yosemite Guide" for current schedules.

Due north of Yosemite Valley is the famous **Tioga Pass** (Highway 120), the highest automobile pass in California, which crests at 9,945 feet (and is closed in the winter). The ideal time to tour the 60-mile-long east-west stretch is in early summer, when the meadows are dotted with wildflowers and you can occasionally spot some wildlife lingering near the lakes and exposed granite slopes. Numerous turnouts offer prime photo opportunities, and roadside picnic areas are located at Lembert Dome and Tenaya Lake. This is also the route to **Tuolumne Meadows**, the gorgeous subalpine meadows along the Tuolumne River. The meadows are a popular camping area (half the campsites are available on a first-come, first-served basis and half require reservations) and the base for backpackers heading into Yosemite's beautiful high country.

Backpackers are required to obtain a wilderness permit in person. The permits are free, but only a limited number are distributed; call (209)372-0740 for more information. The 3½-mile hike to **May Lake** is a favorite route for backpackers, and the 6-mile hike to the **Glen Aulin High Sierra Backpacker's Camp** offers a spectacular spot for pitching a tent. Five clusters of canvas cabins (for four to six occupants) are available to backpackers in the High Sierra region; prices average $150 for two per night and include breakfast, dinner, and a shower. These cabins are booked through an annual lottery each fall; call (559) 454-2002 for details.

If you've always wanted to backpack in Yosemite but don't have the equipment or experience, here's your chance. Call **Southern Yosemite Mountain Guides** at (559) 658-TREK and ask for a free brochure of their guided and catered backpacking adventures, which range from leisurely weekend family outings to challenging two-week treks. Guided mountain bike tours, fly-fishing excursions, and rock-climbing clinics are also available. If you're partial to viewing Yosemite by car, pick up a copy of the *Yosemite Road Guide* or the *Yosemite Valley Tour* cassette tape at the Yosemite Valley Visitors Center. It's almost as good as having Ranger Rick in the back seat of your car. City slickers might also want to consider seeing the park on horseback. The thrill (and ease) of riding a horse into Yosemite's beautiful backcountry just might make it worth the splurge. Select a stable in Yosemite Valley, Wawona, or Tuolumne Meadows, then call (209) 372-8348 or (209) 372-8427 to make a reservation.

While the sightseeing in Yosemite is unparalleled, the dining is not. Bring as much of your own food as possible, because most of the park's restaurants offer mediocre (or worse) cafeteria-style food; the only exception is the lofty Ahwahnee Restaurant (see review, below), but you'll have to fork over a bundle to eat there.

Park accommodations range from less than $15 per night for a campsite to more than $200 nightly for a room at the Ahwahnee Hotel (see review, below). Reservations (accepted no more than eight weeks in advance) are required for most Yosemite camp-sites—only a few are available on a first-come, first-served basis. The valley campsites near the Merced River offer easy access to the park's most sought-after attractions but not much in the way of privacy. Moderately priced motel rooms are available at the valley's bare-bones but adequate **Yosemite Lodge** (a quick walk from Lower Yosemite Falls). Spartan cabins (some are nothing more than wood frames with canvas covers, others are heated in the winter) offer inexpensive alternatives to camping, and they're popular with families. There are also 69 tent cabins at **Tuolumne Meadows Lodge**. For camping reservations call (800) 365-CAMP; for reservations at all other Yosemite National Park accommodations call (559) 252-4848.

Vacation-home rentals (with full kitchens) can also be reserved, but they cost a pretty penny; for more information call **Yosemite West Condominiums** at (209) 372-4240, and for rental reservations call (800) 640-9099.

Additional information on Yosemite National Park is available on the park's Web page at www.yosemitepark.com.

**Ahwahnee Hotel** ★★★  The majestic Ahwahnee Hotel stands regally against the soaring cliffs of Yosemite. It is among the most idyllic hotels in California, with a VIP guest list that ranges from Winston Churchill and John F. Kennedy to Greta Garbo and Queen Elizabeth. Built in 1927 with native granite boulders and redwood-hued concrete at a cost of $1.5 million, the multitiered six-story building blends comfortably into its surroundings. The lobby, dressed in a Native American motif, is oversized in all dimensions: thick-beamed high ceilings, walk-in fireplaces worthy of a medieval castle, and opulent chandeliers suitable for an opera house. For some folks, the contrast between the hotel's rustic mountain venue and its upscale image—overeager bellhops and a dress code that requires men to wear a jacket and tie at dinner—might be a bit much. The 123 rooms are spacious, with double or king-size beds and large bathrooms; a few even boast a view of Half Dome. If money's no object, request one of the hotel's luxury suites or private cottages.

The **Ahwahnee Restaurant**—an immense and impressive chamber highlighted by 50-foot-tall, floor-to-cathedral-ceiling leaded windows—is more noteworthy for its ambience than for its food (arrive well before nightfall to admire the view). Starched white tablecloths, tall candles, and a pianist tickling the ivories manage to give the colossal room a warm, almost intimate feel. The food is certainly the best in the region, but don't expect a gourmet affair; while the prices are equal to those of San Francisco's finer restaurants, the quality of the food is not, so stick to the simpler preparations such as the grilled salmon. Those in the know apply far in advance for tickets to the Bracebridge Dinner, a three-hour feast held every Christmas that 60,000 people try to sign up for—though, alas, only 1,750 gain admission. ■ *In Yosemite Valley, Yosemite National Park; (559)252-4848 (hotel), (209)372-1489 (restaurant); mail: 5410 E Home Ave, Fresno, CA 93727; www. yosemitepark.com; $$$; full bar; DC, DIS, MC, V; checks OK; brunch Sun, breakfast, lunch, dinner every day.*

**Wawona Hotel** ★  Four miles from the park's entrance, the Wawona—the Ahwahnee Hotel's more rustic cousin—is the oldest resort hotel in the state. A pair of century-old white buildings, adorned by pillars and a veranda, face an expansive manicured lawn, giving the Wawona the look of an antebellum mansion (you almost expect to see Scarlett O'Hara gracing the entryway). The majority of its 104 rooms are small, and about half of them have private bathrooms. This National Historic Landmark's biggest drawback is its lengthy distance from the park's most popular attractions. The giant sequoias in the nearby Mariposa Grove are inviting, but they don't compare to the cliffs and vistas elsewhere in Yosemite. Amenities include a nine-hole golf course, a tennis court, a riding stable, and a 1917 "swimming tank." For all its pretensions, the **Wawona Hotel Dining Room** offers little more than upscale institutional food. Your best bet is to drive to the town of Fish Camp for dinner. However, the Wawona's year-round Sunday brunch and the Saturday-evening summer lawn barbecues are a treat. ■ *On Hwy 41 (SW corner of the park, 27 miles from Yosemite Valley), Yosemite National Park; (209)375-6556; mail: 5410 E Home Ave, Fresno, CA 93727; $$; full bar; DC, DIS, MC, V; checks OK; breakfast, lunch Mon–Sat, brunch Sun, dinner every day Apr 1 to Dec 31 (breakfast, lunch Fri–Sat, brunch Sun, dinner Thurs–Sat Jan 1 to Mar 31); barbecue dinners on Sat only July 4 to Labor Day.* ⬧

## FISH CAMP

### *RESTAURANTS*

**Narrow Gauge Inn** ★★ An attractive old inn and restaurant nestled in the thick of the Sierra National Forest at a 4,800-foot elevation, the Narrow Gauge is one of the Mariposa Grove area's best restaurants. You'll find down-home service here, as well as views of Mount Raymond and a cozy country ambience enhanced by oil-burning table lamps and a crackling fire. The inn's specialties include pork tenderloin with a fruit-and-nut stuffing topped with an apricot-brandy glaze, and scallops sautéed in a champagne cream sauce with mushrooms. All dinners include a housemade soup or salad, fresh vegetables, and a rice or potato dish. There's a well-edited wine list, too. The inn offers 26 rooms with private balconies; ask for one of the four creekside rooms, which have particularly splendid views. Narrow Gauge also offers a heated black-bottom swimming pool and a spa. ■ *48571 Hwy 41 (4 miles S of Yosemite National Park's south gate), Fish Camp, CA 93623; (559)683-7720; ngi@sierratel.com; $$; full bar; DIS, MC, V; checks OK; dinner Thurs–Mon (open mid-Apr to Oct 31).*

**Fish Camp**

*Lodgings*

### *LODGINGS*

**Tenaya Lodge** ★ What Tenaya Lodge lacks in charm and originality, it makes up for in location—it's just 2 miles from the entrance to Yosemite National Park. Built in 1990, the lodge has 244 rooms, all with mountain and forest views, private baths, and tasteful Southwestern decor. The lodge's showpiece is the immense front lobby, with its stone floors, high ceiling, huge fireplace, and Native American motif. Amenities include outdoor and indoor pools and a small fitness center with a steam room, sauna, and whirlpool. **Sierra Restaurant** offers breakfast and such classic Cal-Ital entrees as grilled swordfish, New York strip steak, and fettuccine primavera for dinner. The **Parkside Deli** specializes in picnic lunches to go, as well as pizza, hot and cold sandwiches, and a half-dozen steak, fish, and chicken entrees. You can sign up for mountain bike rentals, tours of Yosemite, the children's Camp Tenaya, and other outdoor activities at the lodge's events desk. ▪ *1122 Hwy 41 (2 miles S of Yosemite National Park's southwest gate), Fish Camp; (559)683-6555 or (800)635-5807; mail: PO Box 159, Fish Camp, CA 93623; www.tenayalodge.com; $$$; full bar; AE, DC, DIS, MC, V; checks OK; breakfast, lunch, dinner every day.*

## BRIDGEPORT

### LODGINGS

**The Cain House: A Country Inn** ★★ James Stuart Cain made his fortune as the principal landowner in the rough-and-tumble boomtown of Bodie (known in its day as the wickedest town in the West). However, later generations of Cains (perhaps weary of Bodie's sanitation problems and the proliferation of whorehouses) moved over the hill to the comparatively genteel cowtown of Bridgeport. Set in one of the most picturesque valleys in the eastern Sierra, Bridgeport is backed by granite peaks in the west and by round sage- and piñon-covered desert hills in the east. This modest turn-of-the-century inn, owned by the obliging Marachal Gohlich, is a tribute to Cain. It combines European elegance with a Western atmosphere, and each of the seven individually decorated guest rooms has a private bath, a king- or queen-size bed with a quilt and down comforter, and a TV tucked inside an armoire. Top choice is the Candelaria Room, with its handsome oak furnishings, extra-large tiled bathroom, private outside entrance, and a view of the eastern Sierra. In the morning expect good, dark coffee (a rare treat on this side of the Sierra) and a full breakfast, including house-made muffins. ▪ *340 Main St (at the N end of town), Bridgeport, CA 93517; (760)932-7040 or (800)433-CAIN; $$; AE, DIS, MC, V; checks OK.*

## MONO LAKE

Set at the eastern foot of the craggy Sierra Nevada and ringed with fragile limestone tufa spires, this hauntingly beautiful 60-square-mile desert salt lake is a stopover for millions of migratory birds that arrive each year to feed on the lake's trillions of brine shrimp and alkali flies (mono means "flies" in the language of the Yokuts, the Native Americans who live just south of this region). While numerous streams empty into Mono (pronounced "MOE-no") Lake, there is no outlet. Instead, the lake water evaporates, leaving behind minerals washed down from the surrounding mountains. The result is an alkaline and saline content that is too high for fish but ideal for shrimp, flies, and swimmers (the brackish water is three times saltier than the sea). Right off Highway 395 is the **Mono Basin Scenic Area Visitors Center**, a modern, high-tech edifice that would make any taxpayer proud. The center offers scheduled walks and talks, and it has an outstanding environmental and historical display with hands-on exhibits that will even entertain the kids; open daily in the summer and Thursday through Monday in the winter, (760)647-3044. After touring the visitors center, head for the **South Tufa Area** at the southern end of the lake and get a closer look at the tufa formations and briny water.

## RESTAURANTS

**The Mono Inn** ★★ Back in business and better than ever is the latest incarnation of the historic Mono Inn, a popular respite for travelers to the Mono Lake region since 1922. After years of neglect, the inn was recently purchased by the Adams family (relatives of legendary photographer Ansel Adams), who hired architect Peter Bolin to revamp the aging structure to include a restaurant, an arts and crafts gallery, and a lounge, yet still retain the rustic charm and stellar views of Mono Lake. Proprietor Sarah Adams (Ansel's granddaughter) oversees the upper-level gallery/lounge and lower-level dining room, while chef Linda Dore—formerly of the highly reputable Anything Goes Cafe in Mammoth Lakes—runs the kitchen. Dore prepares hearty California-style cuisine ranging from pan-seared Black Angus top sirloin with brandied green peppercorn mustard sauce to prime rib (on Friday and Saturday nights only), sautéed salmon fillets, grilled prawn brochettes, and the Vegetarian's Delight, fresh seasonal vegetables roasted and tossed in a red Thai curry sauce and served over basmati rice. There's also a good wine list. Be sure to arrive early to admire the gallery (featuring *original* Ansel Adams photographs) and the panoramic view from the cocktail lounge— and beg for a dinner table near the window, particularly on moonlit nights when Mono Lake is most dazzling. ■ *On Hwy 395 (4 miles N of Lee Vining), Mono Lake; (760)647-6581; mail: PO Box 969, Lee Vining, CA 93541; www.adamsgallery.com and www.thesierraweb. com; $$; full bar; AE, CB, DIS, MC, V; checks OK; restaurant: dinner Wed–Mon mid-Apr to Oct (Thurs–Sun Dec to mid-Mar); gallery: 9am to 8pm Wed–Mon mid-Apr to Oct (10am to 8pm Thurs–Sun Dec to mid-Mar).* &

## JUNE LAKE

## RESTAURANTS

**Carson Peak Inn** ★★ This barn-red building, located a few miles past the town of June Lake, has led several former lives, most recently as an American Legion headquarters, dance hall, and pizza parlor. Now it's one of the better restaurants in the area, serving hearty dinners such as steak-and-lobster brochette and a melt-in-your-mouth filet mignon smothered with sautéed mushrooms. Many regulars come for the Australian lobster tail (a rarity in these parts). Fish, chicken, and pork are served broiled, deep-fried, pan-fried, or barbecued. Dessert is an ice-cream sundae or sherbet. ■ *On June Lake Loop (off Hwy 395), June Lake; (760)648-7575; $$$; beer and wine; MC, V; checks OK; dinner every day.*

*See Skiing the Sierra Nevada at the end of this chapter
for Mammoth area ski information.*

At the base of 11,053-foot **Mammoth Mountain** are nearly a dozen alpine lakes and the sprawling town of **Mammoth Lakes**—a mishmash of inns, motels, and restaurants primarily built to serve patrons of the popular Mammoth Mountain Ski Area. Ever since founder Dave McCoy mortgaged his motorcycle for $85 in 1938 to buy his first ski lift, folks have been coming here in droves (particularly from Southern California) to carve turns and navigate the moguls at one of the best downhill ski areas in the United States. In addition to skiing, this section of the eastern Sierra Nevada has been famous for decades for its fantastic fishing holes. In fact, the trout is king here, and several fishing derbies celebrate its royal status. This natural kingdom is no longer the exclusive domain of anglers and skiers, however. Word has gotten out about Mammoth's charms, attracting every kind of outdoor enthusiast and adventurer to this spectacular region in the heart of the High Sierra.

▼

**Mammoth
Lakes**

▲

Whether you've migrated to the Mammoth area to ski, fish, golf, play, or simply rest your weary bones, stop by the **Mammoth Lakes Visitors Center/Ranger Station** on Highway 203, just before the town of Mammoth Lakes; (760)924-5500. You'll find wall-to-wall maps, brochures, and day planners, as well as copies of the Forest Service's excellent (and free) "Winter Recreation Map" and "Summer Recreation Map," which show the area's best routes for hiking, biking, sledding, snowmobiling, and cross-country skiing. If you need to rent ski gear or practically any other athletic and outdoor equipment, visit the bustling Kittredge Sports shop on Main Street, next to the Chevron gas station, in Mammoth Lakes; (760)934-7566.

Once you've unpacked your bags, it's time to lace up your hiking boots and explore. A top attraction is **Devil's Postpile National Monument**, one of the world's premier examples of basalt columns. The 60-foot-tall, slender rock columns rise 7,560 feet above sea level and were formed nearly 100,000 years ago when molten lava from the erupting Mammoth Mountain cooled and fractured into multisided forms; they've become such a popular attraction that between June 15 and September 15, rangers close the access road to daytime traffic and require visitors without a special permit to travel by shuttle. Shuttles pick up riders every 15 minutes at the Mammoth Mountain Ski Area parking lot on Minaret Road, off Highway 203 West, and drop them off at a riverside trail for the less-than-half-mile walk to the monument; (760)934-2289. After you've seen the Postpile, follow the trail for another 2 miles to the beautiful **Rainbow Falls**, where the San Joaquin River plunges 101 feet over an ancient lava flow into a deep pool, often creating rainbows in the mist. If you follow the trail to Red's Meadow, you'll be at one of the entrance points to the 228,500-acre **Ansel Adams Wilderness**, a popular backpacking destination highlighted by the jagged **Minarets**, a series of steep, narrow volcanic ridges just south of massive Mount Ritter.

True to its name, the Mammoth Lakes area boasts 10 lakes (none of which, oddly enough, are named Mammoth). The largest and one of the most striking is **Lake Mary**, and even though it's set high in the mountains, it's easy to get to: head west on Main Street, which turns into Lake Mary Road, drive past Twin Lakes, and continue on until you see it. Numerous hiking trails at Lake Mary lead to nearby smaller, less crowded lakes, including **Horseshoe Lake**, a great place for swimming (the water is slightly warmer than in neighboring lakes). Trout fishers frequently try their luck at Lake Mary, although most anglers prefer to cast their lines in **Convict Lake**, where you can rent a boat and stock up at the Convict Lake Resort's tackle shop; from Highway 395 a few miles south of town, take the Convict Lake Road exit, just south of Mammoth Lakes Airport, (760)934-3800. Another hot spot for snagging some meaty trout is **Hot Creek**, the most popular catch-and-release fishery in California (on average, each trout is caught and released five to six times a month). Only a few miles of the creek are accessible to the public—the rest is private property; on Hot Creek Hatchery Road, just off Highway 395 at the north end of Mammoth Lakes Airport, (760)934-2712 or (800)367-6572.

**Mammoth
Lakes**

**Mountain biking** is another hugely popular sport here in the summer, when the entire Mammoth Mountain Ski Area is transformed into one of the top bike parks in the country. The national Norba mountain bike championship race takes place here, too, on Minaret Road, off Highway 203 West; call (760)934-0606 or (800)367-6572 for details. You can buy an all-day pass to 60 miles of single-track trails and a gondola that will zip you and your bike up to the top of the mountain. From there it's downhill all the way (be sure to wear a helmet), with trails ranging in difficulty from the mellow "Paper Route" ride to the infamous "Kamikaze" wheelspinner. If you don't want to pay to ride a bike, there are dozens of great trails in the area where mountain bikes are permitted.

With winter comes an onslaught of downhill skiers, who journey here to schuss the slopes of **Mammoth Mountain Ski Area** (see Skiing the Sierra Nevada at the end of this chapter for more details). Unfortunately, it can be one of the country's most *crowded* ski areas, particularly on weekends, when more than 10,000 Los Angelenos make the lengthy commute. (Tip: About 90 percent of the skiers arrive on Friday night and leave Sunday afternoon, so come on a weekday.) If you've ever seen the several-mile-long traffic jams converging on the ski area's parking lot, then you know why veteran Mammoth skiers always park their wheels in town and take the shuttle to the resort. These shuttles are not only convenient, they're free. And no matter where you're staying in Mammoth Lakes, a Mammoth Area Shuttle (MAS) stop is most likely nearby. The ubiquitous buses run from 7am to 5:30pm daily during the ski season, and they swing by their stops every 15 minutes to shuttle skiers to one of the resort's three entrances. For more info, call (760)934-0687.

Mammoth Lakes also has mile upon mile of perfectly groomed cross-country ski trails, winding through gorgeous stretches of national forest and immense meadows. Nordic skiers of all levels favor the **Tamarack Cross-Country Ski Center** at Tamarack Lodge in Twin Lakes, which offers 25 miles of groomed trails, extensive backcountry trails, lessons, rentals, and tours; it's on Lake Mary Road, 2½ miles southwest of town, (760)934-2442.

Dozens of natural hot springs dot the Mammoth area, although most of the remote ones are kept secret by tourist-weary locals who probably wouldn't make you feel very welcome even if you discovered one. The more accessible springs, how-ever, definitely welcome visitors, including the free **Hot Creek Geologic Site**, where the narrow creek feeds into a series of arti-ficial pools—some only big enough for two, others family size. These pools are equipped with cold-water pipes that usually keep the water temperature toasty yet not unbearably hot. The Forest Service discourages soaking in the pools because of sporadic spurts of scalding water—yes, there *is* a small risk of getting your buns poached—but most people are more concerned about whether or not to show off their birthday suit (swimsuits are optional). Open daily from sunrise to sunset; take the Hot Creek Hatchery Road exit off Highway 395 (at the north end of Mammoth Lakes Airport) and follow the signs. Call the Mam-moth Lakes Visitors Bureau (see below) for more details.

Granted, life is often one big outdoor party in Mammoth Lakes, but when the annual **Mammoth Lakes Jazz Jubilee** swings into gear in July, hold on to your Tevas—nearly everyone in this toe-tapping town starts kicking up their heels when a dozen world-class bands start tootin' their horns. This three-day jazz extravaganza usually happens the first weekend after the Fourth of July, and opening day is free (after that it's about $25 or more per day). A much more sedate but definitely worthwhile musical event is the annual **Sierra Summer Festival**, a tribute to everything from chamber to classical music that begins in late July and winds down in early August. For more details on all of Mammoth's year-round activities, call the **Mammoth Lakes Vis-itors Bureau** at (760)934-8006 or (800)367-6572, or visit its Web site at www.visitmammoth.com.

## RESTAURANTS

**Nevados** ★★★ Mammoth's finest restaurant is packed almost every night with an equal split of locals and Los Angelenos on their annual ski or summer holiday. Ebullient owner/host Tim

Dawson darts about the small dining room and adjacent bar, seating guests, opening wine, and making sure everyone's enjoying themselves. The entrees are so utterly satisfying—and reasonably priced—that nary a complaint is heard about the food or service (that is, if you keep in mind that your server is a skier first, waiter second). A cheerful trompe l'oeil of a European village is painted on the dining room walls, and melds well with the often crowded and boisterous dinner scene. Though all menu items are available à la carte, for only a few dollars more you can enjoy a prix-fixe three-course meal with any dish on the three-part menu. A recommended trio is the strudel appetizer of wild mushrooms and rabbit with roasted shallots and grilled scallions, followed by an entree of braised Provimi veal shank with roasted tomatoes and garlic mashed potatoes and, for dessert, a fantastic warm pear and almond tart sweetened with caramel sauce and vanilla bean ice cream. Other commendable choices include the potato-crusted crab cake with citrus vinaigrette, roasted rosemary rack of lamb, sesame-crusted rare ahi tuna, and orange-scented breast and leg of duckling. Skip the less than satisfactory crème brûlée, however. ■ *On Main St (at Minaret Rd), Mammoth Lakes; (760)934-4466; $$; full bar; AE, DIS, MC, V; checks OK; dinner every day.*

**The Mogul** ★ Your server skillfully charbroils fresh fish, shrimp, and steak under your watchful eye here at the Mogul, the steak house voted Mammoth's best by *Mammoth Times* readers several years in a row. Owner Dan Haydon has added rooms to this ever-expanding restaurant many times over the past two-dozen years, and has brightened it up with shades of rose and green. The restaurant's success is based in part on the Haydon family's recipes for such favorites as baked beans (his mother's dish) and sweet Cinnamon Charlotte (his grandma's dessert), which is a cupcake topped with ice cream and cinnamon sauce. ■ *1528 Tavern Rd (1 block S of Main St off Old Mammoth Rd), Mammoth Lakes; (760)934-3039; $$; full bar; AE, DIS, MC, V; no checks; dinner every day.*

## LODGINGS

**Sierra Lodge** ★★ Unlike most lodges in the area, Sierra Lodge, built in 1991, has no rustic elements in any of its 35 spacious rooms. The decor here is quite contemporary: soothing earth tones, framed modern prints, track lighting, blond wood furnishings, and big comfy beds. Amenities include cable TV, telephones, kitchenettes, and partial mountain views from your private balcony. After a hard day of skiing, relax your bones in the lodge's outdoor Jacuzzi, then kick back by the fireplace for a game of backgammon in the cozy Fireside Room. Skiers are pampered with their own ski locker; all guests enjoy free covered parking and a continental breakfast. But wait, there's more: free

▼

▲

shuttle service right outside the front door, and Mammoth's best restaurant, Nevados (see review, above), is within easy walking distance. You'll like the Sierra Lodge's friendly staff, too—a team that definitely has its act together. ■ *3540 Main St (at Sierra St), Mammoth Lakes; (760)934-8881 or (800)356-5711; mail: PO Box 9228, Mammoth Lakes, CA 93546; $$; MC, V; checks OK.* &

**Tamarack Lodge Resort** ★★  Built in 1924 by the movie-star Foy family of Los Angeles, the 6-acre Tamarack Lodge sits at an elevation of 8,600 feet on the edge of Twin Lakes, 2½ miles above Mammoth Lakes. Come summer or winter, it's an extremely romantic retreat, nestled deep within the pines and overlooking a serene alpine lake. In 1986 Dave and Carol Watson started upgrading the resort's 11 rooms and 25 cabins with pine furnishings and soft-hued fabrics. Rooms 1, 2, and 7 have a view of the lake; some of the rooms have private baths. The cabins range from studios to three-bedroom suites that sleep up to nine people, and a few have wood-burning fireplaces (the best units are the lakefront cabins—Fisherman's, Lakeside, and numbers 8, 36, and 37). The rustic **Lakefront Restaurant**, with its fringed lamps, lace curtains, and antique furnishings, offers the most romantic dinner setting in Mammoth Lakes. Its constantly changing menu may feature such well-prepared fare as grilled salmon with ginger, wild-berry duckling, and rack of New Zealand lamb. In the winter, the lodge opens the Tamarack Cross-Country Ski Center, which offers 25 miles of groomed trails, extensive backcountry trails, lessons, rentals, and tours. ■ *On Twin Lakes Rd (off Lake Mary Rd, 2½ miles above town), Mammoth Lakes; (760)934-2442 or (800)237-6879; mail: PO Box 69, Mammoth Lakes, CA 93546; tamarack@qnet.com; www.tamarack.com; $$; beer and wine; DIS, MC, V; checks OK; breakfast, dinner every day.*

▼

**Mammoth
Lakes**

*Lodgings*

▲

**Mammoth Mountain Inn** ★  This inn is a popular haven for downhill skiers—it's just steps away from the chairlifts at Mammoth Mountain Ski Area—and in the summer the guests are primarily mountain bikers, fly fishers, hikers, and horseback riders. The 214 rooms have a predictably humdrum decor and the walls are thin, but they come with all the usual amenities such as telephones, TVs, and queen-size or double beds. Your best bet is to rent a junior suite in the refurbished section that has a view of the ski area. Other perks include a whirlpool spa, child-care facilities, and shuttle-bus service. The only downside is the 10-minute drive into town, but if your goal is to ski-till-you-drop, you can't get any closer to the slopes. The hotel's **Mountainside Grill**—a semiformal restaurant serving pasta, seafood, lamb, chicken, and prime rib—and **Dry Creek Lounge** are open year-round. ■ *On Minaret Rd (at Mammoth Mountain Ski Area, 4 miles from downtown), Mammoth Lakes; (760)934-2581 or (800)228-4947; mail: PO Box 353, Mammoth Lakes, CA 93546; www.mammothmtn.com; $$$; full bar; AE, MC, V; checks OK; breakfast, lunch, dinner every day.*

*RESTAURANTS*

**The Restaurant at Convict Lake** ★★★ The anglers who toss their lines into Convict Lake to catch rainbow and German brown trout have kept this restaurant a secret for many years. Their secret, however, is slowly slipping out, as others have begun to journey here for a meal at this glorious lakeside locale. The lounge's open-beam ceiling and bare wood floors are warmed by a wood-burning stove and overstuffed chairs and sofas. Some patrons make a meal out of the appetizers at the bar, while others settle into the cozy booths in the elegant dining area, where a free-standing fireplace with a glistening copper chimney glows in the center of the room. The chef's specials might include Chilean sea bass with mango-pineapple-cilantro relish or lamb loin in a hazelnut-and-rosemary sauce. Popular entrees from the seasonal menu include beef Wellington, local Alpers trout, and duck confit flavored with sun-dried cherry sauce and garnished with candied orange zest. For dessert try the tasty meringue topped with kiwi fruit and whipped cream or the banana flambé. ■ *At Convict Lake (from Hwy 395 take the Convict Lake exit; 3½ miles S of Mammoth Lakes), Convict Lake; (760) 934-3803; $$$; full bar; AE, DIS, MC, V; checks OK; dinner every day.*

▼
Skiing the
Sierra
Nevada

▲

## SKIING THE SIERRA NEVADA

When the Golden State's denizens gear up for the ski season, they all usually have one destination in mind: Lake Tahoe, the premier winter playground for deranged daredevils and cautious snowplowers alike. Whether you're a 6-year-old hotshot schussing down chutes and cornices, a 60-year-old granddaddy trekking through cross-country tracks in a serene Sierra valley, or someone in between, the Tahoe region will surely please you. A smorgasbord of downhill slopes encircles the famous twinkling alpine lake, while the cross-country ski trails are some of the most scenic and challenging in the country.

Top on the list of cross-country favorites is the North Shore's **Royal Gorge**, the largest cross-country ski resort in the United States, with 200 miles of trails for skiers of all levels, 9,172 acres of skiable terrain, an average annual snowfall of more than 650 inches, 10 warming huts (for defrosting those frozen fingers and toes), and two lodges (see review of Royal Gorge's Rainbow Lodge and Wilderness Lodge, above); take the Soda Springs exit off Interstate 80, (530) 426-3871. More experienced Nordic skiers should head over to **Eagle Mountain** (one of the area's best-kept secrets), which offers 47 miles of challenging trails with fantastic Sierra vistas; from Interstate 80, exit at Yuba Gap, turn right, and follow the signs, (530) 389-2254 or (800) 391-2254. The South Shore's choicest cross-country tracks are at **Sorensen's Resort** in Hope Valley (see review in the preceding pages), and they're open to the public at no charge. You'll find more than 60 miles of trails winding through the Toiyabe National Forest—plenty of room for mastering that telemark turn and escaping the Tahoe crowds. Rentals, lessons, tours, and trail maps are available at the **Hope Valley Cross-Country Ski Center**, located within Sorensen's Resort. From Highway 50 in Myers, take Highway 89 South over the Luther Pass to the Highway 88/89 intersection, turn left, and continue for a half-mile to Sorensen's. For more details, contact the ski center at (530) 694-2266.

Farther south is the **Bear Valley Cross-Country Area**, with 56 miles of groomed Nordic track (one of the largest track systems in America); located off Highway 4, (209) 753-2834. **Yosemite Cross-Country Ski School**, at Badger Pass Ski Area, offers rentals, lessons, and excursions on 90 miles of groomed trails (there's a total of 350 miles of cross-country trails in the park); located off Highway 41, (209) 372-1244. There are also two major cross-country ski centers at **Mammoth Mountain Ski Area**, where LA folk flock on winter weekends (located off Highway 395); for more information, call the Mammoth Lakes Visitors Bureau at (760) 934-8006 or (800) 367-6572.

For downhill thrill-seekers, Lake Tahoe offers a plethora of first-rate resorts that cater to every age, ability, and whim. Families fare best at **Northstar**, while serious skiers find the most challenging terrain at **Squaw Valley USA**, **Kirkwood**, **Heavenly Ski Resort**, and **Alpine Meadows**. If you plan to stay overnight, call the **Tahoe Visitors Bureau** at (800) TAHOE-4-U for the low-down on ski-package deals. Although most Northern Californians rarely tote their skis beyond Tahoe's sunny slopes, a host of top-notch ski resorts dot the landscape south of the lake, including one of the state's best: **Mammoth Mountain Ski Area**. Aside from Mammoth, these south-of-Tahoe ski spots are often less crowded and less expensive than their lakeside counterparts. Here's a roundup of the Sierra's major downhill ski areas, from the outer reaches of North Lake Tahoe to as far south as Badger Pass, just outside Yosemite National Park.

## LAKE TAHOE SKI RESORTS

**Alpine Meadows** A favorite among locals, Alpine has runs on a par with Squaw Valley's best, but without the holier-than-thou attitude of the Squaw staff. Alpine also has the West's first six-passenger high-speed chairlift, and, bowing to the popularity of snowboarding, the resort has lifted its ban on snowboarders. The ski/lodging combo packages offered by River Ranch Lodge in Alpine Meadows (see the lodge's review, above) are often out-standing. ■ *Off Highway 89, (530) 583-4232 or (800) 441-4423.*

**Boreal** Small and easy, Boreal is a good beginner's resort. It's also one of the few places in the Lake Tahoe area that offers night skiing (open until 9pm), and, thanks to its extensive snowmaking equipment, is usually one of the first ski areas to open. ■ *Off Interstate 80, (530)426-3666.*

**Diamond Peak** Located in Incline Village on the Nevada side of Tahoe's North Shore, this small, family ski resort *guarantees* good skiing—if you don't like the conditions, you may turn in your ticket within the first hour for a voucher that's good for another day. ■ *From Highway 28, exit on Country Club Drive and turn right on Sky Way and drive to Incline Village, (702)832-1177.*

**Donner Ski Ranch** Just up the road from Sugar Bowl is Donner, whose best attribute is its price—a ski pass is about half the cost of its neighbors'. And despite its small size, this unpretentious ski area has a lot to offer skiers of all levels: tree skiing, groomed trails, and a few steeps and jumps, not to mention convenient parking and a cozy, down-home lodge. ■ *Take the Soda Springs exit off Interstate 80, (530)426-3635.*

**Granlibakken** Tiny and mainly for tots, this is a great place to teach kids the fundamentals. Later, when you'll surely need a libation, you won't have far to go to find the Tahoe City nightspots. ■ *Off Highway 89 at the junction of Highway 28, (530)583-4242 or (800)543-3221.*

**Heavenly Ski Resort** South Lake Tahoe's pride and joy has something for skiers of all levels. Heavenly is so immense it straddles two states (California and Nevada); those in the know park on the Nevada side to avoid the crowds. ■ *Off Highway 50, (702)586-7000 or (800)2-HEAVEN.*

**Kirkwood** When skiing conditions just don't get any better, Tahoe locals make the pilgrimage over the passes to where the snow is the deepest and the skiing is the sweetest. Kirkwood also offers some very tempting ski/lodging packages. ■ *Off Highway 88, (209)258-6000.*

**Northstar-at-Tahoe** Northstar is consistently rated one of the best family ski resorts in the nation, due to its numerous amenities. It also has the dubious honor of being called "Flatstar" by the locals because of its penchant for grooming. It's a completely self-contained ski resort (you'll find everything from lodgings to stores to a gas station here), so you can park your car and leave it in the same spot for the duration of your stay. ■ *Off Highway 267, (530)562-1010 or (800)GO-NORTH.*

**Sierra-at-Tahoe** Formerly named Sierra Ski Ranch, Tahoe's third-largest ski area is a good all-around resort, offering a slightly better price than most comparable places in the area. It's not

Sierra
Nevada

▼

Skiing the
Sierra
Nevada

*Lake Tahoe
Ski Resorts*

▲

## Lake Tahoe Ski Resorts

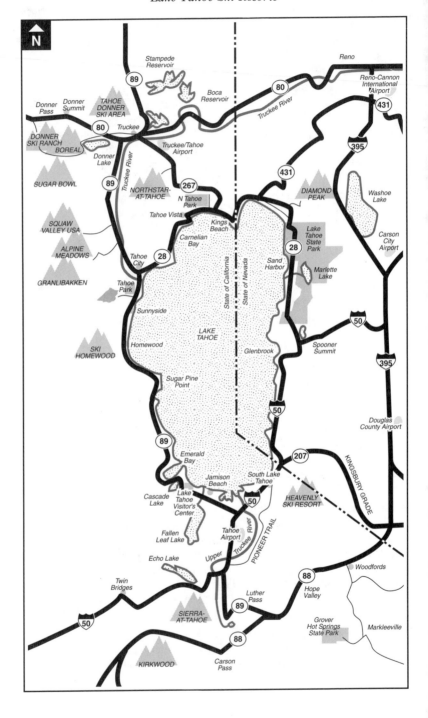

worth the drive from the North Shore, but it's a good alternative to Heavenly Ski Resort if you want a change of venue near the South Shore. ■ *Off Highway 50, (530)659-7453.*

**Ski Homewood** This underrated midsize resort has a little of everything for skiers of all levels, and it sports one of the best views of Lake Tahoe. Midweek specials often knock down the price of a ticket by as much as 50 percent (call ahead for quotes), easily the best deal in town. ■ *Off Highway 89, (530)525-2992.*

**Squaw Valley USA** Site of the 1960 Winter Olympic Games, Squaw is a resort that people either love (because it has everything a skier could hope for) or hate (because the staff here *knows* it has everything). Squaw offers some of the country's most challenging terrain, intensive ski-school programs, top-of-the-line chairlifts, night skiing from 4pm to 9pm, and a snowboard park, plus a variety of non-skiing activities including ice skating, swimming, and even bungee jumping. Unfortunately, the resort tends to attract the most obnoxious snowboarders and most egotistical skiers in North America. ■ *Off Highway 89, (530)583-6985 or (800)545-4350.*

**Sugar Bowl** Here's another good all-around midsize ski resort, with about 50 runs. Sugar Bowl's top feature is its accessibility—it's the closest resort from the valley off Interstate 80, about 30 minutes closer than Squaw Valley USA (and several bucks less a pass, thank you). Whether it's worth the drive from the North Shore, however, is questionable. ■ *Take the Soda Springs exit off Interstate 80, (530)426-9000.*

▼

Skiing the
Sierra
Nevada

*South-
of-Tahoe
Ski Resorts*

▲

**Tahoe Donner Ski Area** If you're a beginner or a beginner/intermediate skier and are staying on the North Shore, Tahoe Donner is a viable option, offering short lift lines, no car traffic, and relatively low prices. ■ *From Interstate 80, take the Donner State Park exit, turn left on Donner Pass Road, and left on Northwoods Boulevard, (530)587-9444.*

### SOUTH-OF-TAHOE SKI RESORTS

**Badger Pass Ski Area** Badger Pass, 23 miles from Yosemite Valley, keeps its predominantly intermediate ski runs well manicured and offers some unique family activities such as daily snowshoe walks led by a ranger/naturalist, and ice skating in the shadow of Half Dome. ■ *Off State Route 41, (209)372-8430.*

**Bear Valley Ski Company** Nestled in the small town of Bear Valley, this is one of the undiscovered gems of downhill skiing in Northern California. The eighth-largest ski area in the state, Bear Valley Ski Company has a network of 60 trails for skiers of all levels, serviced by 11 lifts that can accommodate 12,000 skiers per hour. Considering the relatively inexpensive lift tickets and the diversity of the terrain, Bear Valley offers one of the best deals in the state. ■ *Off Highway 4, (209)753-2301.*

**Dodge Ridge Ski Area** This small ski resort in the tiny town of Pinecrest has a decades-long reputation as a friendly, low-key ski area that's short on frills but high on family conveniences such as a top-ranked children's ski school. Its lift lines are often short, and Dodge Ridge is the closest ski resort to the Bay Area (it's just above Sonora and Columbia). More advanced skiers, however, would be happier driving the few extra miles to Bear Valley for more challenging terrain. ▪ *Off State Route 108, (209)965-3474.*

**June Mountain** Purchased by Mammoth Mountain Ski Area owner Dave McCoy in 1986, June Mountain offers skiers a calmer and less-crowded ski experience than its colossal cousin across the valley. It may be about one-fifth the size of Mammoth, but June also offers great skiing—wide bowls, steep chutes, forested trails—with the added attraction of a spectacular Sierra view from its two peaks: 10,050-foot Rainbow Summit and 10,135-foot June Mountain Summit. ▪ *On June Lake Loop off Highway 395, (760)648-7733.*

**Mammoth Mountain Ski Area** Mammoth vies with Heavenly for the title of largest ski resort in the state, and it's LA's prime weekend ski destination. What makes it so great? The numbers speak for themselves: 8 to 12 feet of consistently deep snowpack, 31 chairlifts, a 70 percent chance of sunny skies, 150 runs, 1,800 employees, 3,100 vertical feet, 3,500 acres of skiable terrain, up to 15,000 skiers a weekend, and more than 30,000 hotel beds. ▪ *Off Highway 395; for ski-resort information, call the Mammoth Lakes Visitors Bureau at (760)934-8006 or (800)367-6572.*

▼

Skiing the
Sierra
Nevada

South-
of-Tahoe
Ski Resorts

▲

# GOLD
# COUNTRY

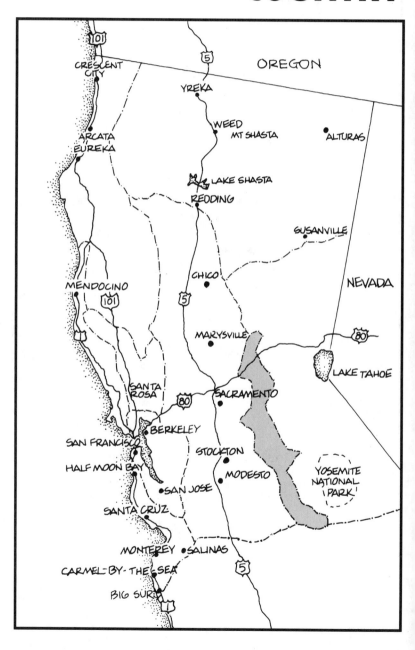

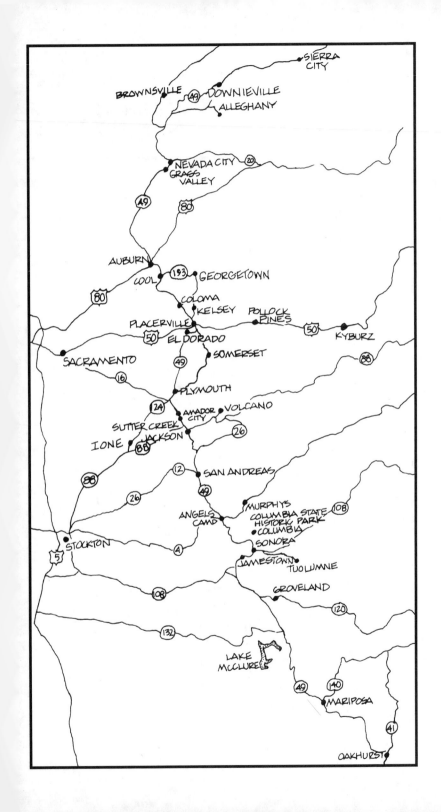

# Gold Country

*A southward exploration down the Gold Rush Highway (Highway 49) from Sierra City to Oakhurst, with occasional diversions into the hills and the edge of the Central Valley. Call ahead to make sure your desired destination is open, especially in the winter. Note: The 559 area code in this chapter goes into effect November 14, 1998. Until that date, use area code 209.*

## GOLD COUNTRY

By 1849, word had spread throughout the United States, Europe, and other corners of the globe that gold miners were becoming millionaires overnight in California. In just one year, more than 80,000 eager souls stampeded across water and land to reach the hilly terrain now known as the Gold Country and the Mother Lode. By 1852, more than 200,000 men were working the mines. Many of the "49ers" had to fight for their claims to the land, claims that left the average miner with little more than dirt and grime in his pocket. Crime and starvation were rampant, and when the exhausted miners put away their picks and pans for the night, most sought comfort in drinking, gambling, and prostitutes. It was a wild and heady time that brought riches to relatively few, but changed the Golden State forever.

You can follow in the miners' footsteps (geographically, at least) by cruising along the aptly numbered **Highway 49**, the zigzagging, 321-mile Gold Rush road that links many of the mining towns. You'll find some of the most authentically preserved towns in the northern Gold Country, including **Grass Valley**, where more than a billion dollars in gold was extracted, and **Nevada City**, former home of one of the region's more famous miners, President Herbert Hoover.

The rolling hills of the southern Gold Country are honeycombed with mysterious caverns and abandoned mines, including the deepest gold mines on the continent. The mining boom went bust by 1860, and most of the Gold Rush towns were abandoned by the 1870s. Some have survived by mining for tourist dollars instead, and as a result it's not always easy to steer clear of tourist trappings. Most people journey to this area for the fishing, camping, hiking, rafting, and mountain biking, though some still come to pan for gold. Yep, there are precious nuggets in those hills and mountain streams, and you can hire a prospector to show you how and where to try your luck. But bear in mind that all that glitters is not gold (there's plenty of fool's gold in these parts), and your chances of hitting the jackpot are much better in Reno.

*RESTAURANTS*

**Herrington's Sierra Pines Resort** ★★  In a log and wood-paneled dining room on the gorgeous north fork of the Yuba River, the Herrington family serves house-baked bread and their specialty: fresh trout reeled right out of their trout pond. The evening menu also offers New York steak and such specials as filet mignon wrapped in bacon, stuffed shrimp, and clam and shrimp fettuccine. For dessert, don't pass up the fresh berry cobbler or the Harvey Wallbanger cake. The Herringtons serve breakfast, too, which might include strawberry pancakes, eggs Benedict, or biscuits and gravy.

If you can't get a room at the High Country Inn (see review, below), try one of the 21 motel-style units here; all have covered decks and most have views of the Yuba River. If you have a group of three or more, inquire about the two apartments—each has a bedroom with two double beds, a fully equipped kitchen, and a living room with a Franklin fireplace. ■ *On the S side of Hwy 49 (at the W end of town), Sierra City; (530)862-1151 or (800)682-9848; mail: PO Box 235, Sierra City, CA 96125; www.quikpage. com/H/herrington/; $$; full bar; DIS, MC, V; checks OK; breakfast, dinner every day (restaurant open 3rd week in Apr to Oct 15; lodgings open Apr 1 to Nov 1 or until the pipes freeze).*

▼
**Sierra City**

*Restaurants*
▲

**Mountain Shadows** ★  British owner/chef Beryl Kelley offers a menu that reflects her English roots: breakfasts of bacon, broiled tomatoes, bangers (those wonderful sausages that snap when you chomp down on them), fried bread, and mushrooms, and lunches of fish and chips and bangers and mash (that's English for mashed potatoes, Yank). Not in the mood for a slice of merry ol' England? Don't despair, Kelley also serves classic American meals—from fried eggs and toast to juicy hamburgers with all the fixings. (She used to work in the kitchens of the popular Packer Lake Lodge and Sardine Lake Resort in nearby Gold Lakes Basin, so she's definitely learned a thing or two about making good American fare.) Mountain Shadows is housed in a century-old clapboard building that was originally a livery stable. When the weather's warm (typically from spring to late fall), ask for a table on the deck where you can get a peek at the mountains. ■ *224 Main St (right on Hwy 49), Sierra City; (530)862-1990; $; beer and wine; no credit cards; checks OK; breakfast, lunch Wed–Mon.* ᕕ

*LODGINGS*

**High Country Inn** ★★★  Aspen flutter in the breeze along the north fork of the Yuba River, the backdrop to this welcoming four-room inn. Mother Nature's handiwork is reason enough to stay here, but the high point of the High Country Inn is the spectacular view of the Sierra Buttes from its deck. Proprietors Marlene and Calvin Cartwright's comfortable living room, furnished with sofas and ottomans clustered around a massive stone fireplace, boasts a great view of the buttes, too. For a room that takes full advantage of the gorgeous mountain scenery, ask for the Sierra Buttes Suite, which encompasses the entire second floor, with a cathedral ceiling, a king-size bed, and a fireplace; the bathroom is almost a suite of its own, with a 6½-foot-long antique bathtub and a dressing room stocked with cozy flannel nightshirts and terrycloth robes. Grandma's Quilt Room, which has a queen-size bed and space for an optional rollaway, offers a view of the Yuba River; the Golden Pond Room, also equipped with a queen-size bed, has a river vista and a deck with yet another view of the buttes. Families often opt for the spacious Howard Creek Room because it has two double beds and room for a rollaway.

The High Country Inn is well-known for its gourmet breakfasts (included in the room tab), a feast that might include a choice of a half-dozen fruit juices, pears poached in wine, housebaked peach-pecan nutbread, strawberry-yogurt bread, individual mushroom soufflés, and Marlene's special spice-pumpkin pancakes or her Scandinavian aebleskivers (ask about her clever technique for making these light-as-a-feather puff pancakes). The Cartwrights get on the good side of their guests by setting a tray of coffee and tea outside each room by 7am for those who want to get an early start. Dozens of nearby hiking and cross-country ski trails wind through Tahoe National Forest to more than 30 mountain lakes that offer great trout fishing. The Cartwrights will happily advise you about local activities, including mountain biking, horseback riding, and snowmobiling. If the inn is booked and you want to stay in Sierra City, try Herrington's Sierra Pines Resort (see review, above, under Restaurants). ■ *100 Green Rd (5 miles E of town, on the S side of Hwy 49 and Gold Lake Rd), Sierra City; (530) 862-1530 or (800) 862-1530; mail: HCR 2, Box 7, Sierra City, CA 96125; $$; MC, V; checks OK.*

Downieville

## DOWNIEVILLE

This scenic little mountain town at the junction of the Yuba and Downie Rivers hasn't changed much since the 1850s: venerable buildings still line the boardwalks along crooked Main Street and trim homes are cut into the canyon walls above. Downieville's population hovers around 350 now, though during its heyday 5,000 prospectors panned the streams and worked the mines here. The lusty gold camp even had the dubious distinction of being the only place in California where a woman was lynched.

A former Gold Rush–era Chinese store houses the **Downieville Museum** (open daily in the summer, and on weekends in the spring and fall); 330 Main Street, no phone. The **Sierra County Courthouse** displays gold dug out of the rich **Ruby**

**Mine**, 100 Courthouse Square, (530)289-3698, and next door stands the only original gallows in the Gold Country. For more Gold Rush history and lore, check out the **Sierra County Historical Park**, just north of Sierra City, where the restored **Kentucky Mine** and a stamp mill still stand (open Wednesday through Sunday in the summer, and on fall weekends); on Highway 99, 1 mile north of Sierra City, (530)862-1310.

For local news and current Downieville events, pick up a copy of the *Mountain Messenger*, a weekly newspaper published since 1853. To tour this scenic area by bicycle, visit the folks at the Coyote Adventure Company and ask them to plan a **mountain-bike tour** for you (bike rentals are available, too); at the corner of Main and Nevada Streets, (530)265-6909.

## RESTAURANTS

**The Downieville Bakery and Cafe** ★★ Housed in the historic Cray-croft Building (which, by the way, is where Juanita, the afore-mentioned hangee, unsuccessfully fled to avoid the lynching mob), this bakery and cafe is engulfed daily by the heavenly aroma of owner/baker/chef Tom Byg's handcrafted breads and pastries. Take a seat in the small, six-table restaurant for a great cup of joe and a pastry, or choose from a wide lunchtime array of sandwiches, soups, and salads. Try the spicy black bean and roasted garlic soup or the delicious veggie sandwich with roasted eggplant, kalamata olives, fresh spinach, feta, and pesto on a house-baked French roll. Dinners are simple but good, especially the meats from the rotisserie: roasted herb chicken, barbecued ribs, lamb, and prime rib. The wine list is small but select and rea-sonably priced. Don't leave without a loaf of Byg's popular sun-dried tomato and black-olive bread. ■ *On Hwy 49 (at the Jersey Bridge, just off Main St), Downieville; (530)289-0108; $–$$; beer and wine; no credit cards; checks OK; breakfast (pastries and coffee), lunch, dinner every day Memorial Day to Labor Day (break-fast, lunch, dinner Thurs–Mon Labor Day to Memorial Day).* &

## LODGINGS

**Sierra Shangri-La** ★★ Sierra Shangri-La sits beside the Yuba River at the base of Jim Crow Canyon, once the site of a mining camp called Crow City. The comfortable lodge has three guest rooms with brass bedsteads, but it's the seven riverside cot-tages—with roomy decks, patios, kitchens, barbecues, and wood-burning stoves—that keep people coming back year after year (making it difficult to get a reservation in the summer). The one-room La Vista Cabin, with its choice setting at the elbow of the river, is the hands-down fave. If you need lots of space, ask for the two-bedroom Cedar Ridge Cabin With the Great Room. It sleeps up to nine people, has a large (30-foot-by-30-foot) living room/dining room with a stone fireplace, and is great for family reunions, retreats, and really spiffy pajama parties. In the summer, bring some charcoal, food, and a bathing suit, and you'll be set. Some of the most sparkling swimming holes on the Yuba are right outside the cottage doors. ■ *On Hwy 49 (2½ miles E of town), Downieville; (530)289-3455; mail: PO Box 285, Downieville, CA 95936-0285; sierrashangra@telis.com; www.sierrashangrila.com; $$–$$$; MC, V; checks OK (open year-round, weather permitting).*

## BROWNSVILLE

If you're driving anywhere near this remote region of the Gold Country, consider making a reservation for a tour of the **Renaissance Vineyard & Winery**, a spectacular 365-acre winery with rose gardens fit for a queen's palace. Located in the village of Oregon House, Renaissance is at an elevation of 2,300 feet and is one of the largest mountain vineyards in North America. It is owned and operated by a wealthy religious group known as the Fellowship of Friends. The visitors' schedule is subject to change, but tours and tastings are usually available on Friday and Saturday and appointments are essential, even if you just want to smell the roses; 12585 Rice's Crossing Road, 7 miles south of Brownsville (call for directions), Oregon House, (530)692-3104 or (800)225-7582. If you're in town on the weekend, the best place for a bite in Brownsville is at **Lottie Brennan's Bakery & Eating Establishment**, which serves an eclectic mix of great food, although (much to the chagrin of the locals) the restaurant is now open only for lunch on Saturday and brunch on Sunday. Don't miss Brennan's aebleskivers (Scandinavian pancakes with cardamom, Grand Marnier syrup, and French custard) or her sumptuous Swedish princess cake with marzipan; 9049 La Porte Road, (530)675-1003.

### LODGINGS

**Mountain Seasons Inn** ★ This delightful two-story 1854 farmhouse, with a wraparound open-air sun porch and herb and flower gardens, is a colorful olfactory retreat—part decorative dried-herb and flower shop (for guests only) and part bed-and-breakfast inn. Owner Nancy Ault offers three quiet rooms (one with a twin bed, two with queen-size beds) modestly decorated with antique mahogany and pine armoires and fluffy comforters. Although there is only one shared bathroom for guests, Ault rarely rents out more than two rooms at once so you don't have to worry about a crowded commode. The simple breakfast buffet of fruit, cereals, muffins, and juice may be savored on the porch or in Ault's lovely rose garden. ■ *9067 La Porte Rd (downtown), Brownsville; (530)675-2180; mail: PO Box 59, Brownsville, CA 95919; $; no credit cards; checks OK.*

Established in 1849 when miners found gold in Deer Creek, Nevada City occupies one of the most picturesque sites in the Sierra foothills. When the sugar maples blaze in autumn, the town resembles a small New England village, making it hard to believe this was once the third-largest city in California. This is also B&B heaven, and with so many beautifully restored houses to choose from, you'll have a tough time selecting a favorite. To understand the lay of the land, put on your walking shoes and pick up a free walking-tour map at the chamber of commerce; 132 Main Street at Coyote Street, (530)265-2692. Town highlights include the **National Hotel** (see review), where the cozy Gold Rush–era bar is ideal for a cocktail or two, and the white, cupola-topped **Firehouse Number 1 Museum**, featuring Gold Rush memorabilia, a fine Chinese altar from a local 1860s joss house, and relics from the infamous and ill-fated Donner Party; 214 Main Street at Commercial Street, (530)265-5468.

Sixteen miles north of Nevada City, up the steep and winding North Bloomfield Road, is the 3,000-acre **Malakoff Diggins State Historic Park**, home of the world's largest hydraulic gold mine and a monument to mining's devastating results. During the Gold Rush days, nearly half a mountain was washed away with powerful jets of pressurized water, leaving behind a 600-foot-deep canyon of minaret-shaped, rust-colored rocks—eerily beautiful to some, but an eyesore to most. The destructive hydraulic mining didn't stop until a court order was issued in 1884, by which time the runoff had turned San Francisco Bay a murky brown.

*Nevada City*

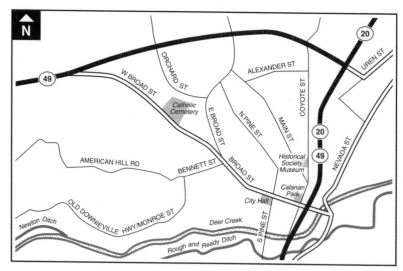

Overlooking the park is the semirestored mining town of **North Bloomfield**, where you can hike along a 3-mile loop trail that shows hydraulic-mining memorabilia. Park rangers lead tours on weekends year-round (every day in the summer) and rent out campsites and replicas of miners' cabins; for more details call the park at (530)265-2740.

If you've ever visited downtown Nevada City or Grass Valley on a weekend, you know how hard it is to find a parking spot (and to think you came here to get away from it all!). This time, why not leave the car at the inn and let Gold Country Stage's drivers do all the navigating? A couple bucks buys you an all-day shuttle pass good for both towns as well as rides to major attractions in outlying areas. Call (530)477-0103 for a free map and riders' guide. And as long as you're not driving, consider an afternoon of beer-tasting: you can sample some of the Gold Country's finest microbrews at the **Nevada City Brewing Company**. Free tours and tastings are offered Friday from 1pm to 5pm, Saturday from 10am to 4pm, and by appointment (or whenever you can talk the staff into taking a break to show off their suds); 75 Bost Avenue at Searls Avenue, (530)265-2446.

*RESTAURANTS*



**Kirby's Creekside Restaurant & Bar ★★★** This attractive restaurant is perched precariously over Deer Creek, a mild-mannered stream most of the time, but when the heavy rains of '97 hit, the creek turned into a savage torrent that filled Kirby's restaurant halfway to the ceiling. Fortunately, after the water drained, the popular restaurant quickly bounced back and patrons were soon dining alfresco on the sunny deck again. The fare here is excellent. You can choose from the lunch menu's large selection of salads and sandwiches, or indulge in the risotto of the day or a healthy serving of meat loaf with garlic mashed potatoes. Dinner is a more elaborate affair kicked off with appetizers such as fresh pumpkin ravioli in a chardonnay cream sauce or steamed mussels in a chardonnay-tomato coulis. For your next course, select from one of a half-dozen pasta dishes and entrees such as braised beef in a red wine sauce, smoked stuffed pork chops, or roasted leg of lamb. Prix-fixe multicourse dinners are also available. Kirby's takes its wine list as seriously as its food and maintains a very good selection. The wine and beer bar offers live music Wednesday through Saturday. ■ *101 Broad St (at Sacramento St), Nevada City; (530)265-3445; $$; beer and wine; AE, MC, V; checks OK; brunch Sun, lunch Mon–Sat, dinner every day.* ♿

**Country Rose Cafe ★★** Within this tall, stately brick building you'll find chef/owner Michael Johns cooking some mighty fine French country fare. Michael is in charge of dinner, and his son, Dave, presides over lunch. The afternoon offerings often include a savory salmon-cucumber sandwich served on a baguette with an herb spread, ratatouille, beef stroganoff, and a delicate salmon quiche. For dinner, expect plenty of fresh fish, rack of lamb, beef tournedos, and a range of well-prepared poultry entrees. Fortunately, sunny days are in abundance here, enabling diners to sit on the cafe's pretty walled-in garden patio. The wine and beer lists are terrific, and more than a dozen wines are poured by the glass. ■ *300 Commercial St (at Pine St), Nevada City; (530) 265-6248; $$; beer and wine; AE, MC, V; local checks only; lunch, dinner every day.* &

**Cirino's** ★ Nevada City folk come to ever-popular Cirino's for its large, family-style Italian dishes, including the veal piccata prepared with a tangy lemon caper sauce and the penne pasta with salmon, leeks, and dill. Each belly-packing dinner comes with garlic focaccia, soup (a thick Boston clam chowder is served on Friday) or salad, and a choice of spaghetti with a marinara sauce, spaghetti *aglio-olio* (with garlic and olive oil—simple, but delicious), or fettuccine alfredo. Expect a large, loud, bustling environment that's kid-friendly and full of the wonderful aroma of roasted garlic. Cirino's also has an extensive Italian wine list. ■ *309 Broad St (just past Pine St), Nevada City; (530) 265-2246; $$; full bar; AE, DIS, MC, V; local checks only; lunch, dinner every day.*

**Cowboy Pizza** ★ Cowboy Wallie, the founder of this pizza joint, gussied up the place with cowpoke kitsch—you'll see everything from a Gene Autry *Singing Cowboy* poster to the official emblem of the Manure Movers of America. But before you even walk through the door of this wacky place, you'll smell the garlic loaded onto the Gilroy Pizza, cooked in an old stone-floor oven. If you prefer the stinking rose in moderation, bite into the Greek vegetarian version (artichoke hearts, feta, black olives, fresh tomatoes, garlic, and oregano) and you'll soon be bucking for more. You can wash down your slices with a pint or two of an all-natural microbrew. Tip: Locals know it's best to place an order in advance—otherwise, you'll have to wait a bit. For some peculiar reason, Chinese fortune cookies are served at the end of every Cowboy Pizza meal. ■ *315 Spring St (near the Miners Foundry Cultural Center), Nevada City; (530) 265-2334; $; beer and wine; no credit cards; checks OK; dinner Wed–Sun.* &

## LODGINGS

**Emma Nevada House** ★★★★ Although it was built in 1856, the immaculately restored Emma Nevada House (the childhood home and namesake of 19th-century opera star Emma Nevada) is one of the newer stars in Nevada City's fine array of bed-and-breakfast inns. Many of the home's antique fixtures such as the gas-lit chandeliers, claw-footed bathtubs, transoms, and doors have been refurbished and modernized, and the six guest rooms have private baths and new queen-size beds. One of the preferred units is Nightingale's Bower, a room on the main floor with bay windows, an antique stove, elegant Italian bedding, and a Jacuzzi. Another popular choice is the romantic Empress's Chamber, decorated in ivory and burgundy hues, with a French antique bed and armoire, a wall of windows, a sitting area, and a Jacuzzi. A full breakfast of fresh fruit, juices, muffins or scones, an entree such as onion-caraway quiche or pumpkin waffles, plus Emma's special cobbler is served in the dining room and sun room overlooking the garden. There's a minimum stay of two nights on weekends from May through December and on holidays. ■ *528 E Broad St (on the right side of the Y), Nevada City, CA 95959; (530) 265-4415 or (800) 916-EMMA; emmanev@oro.net; www.riese.com/emma. htm; $$–$$$; AE, DC, MC, V; checks OK.*

**Grandmère's Inn ★★★★** Generally considered the grande dame of Nevada City's hostelries, Grandmère's Inn is indeed a showplace, with quite a history to boot. This three-story colonial revival mansion was once owned by Aaron and Ellen Clark Sargeant, and Susan B. Anthony was a regular guest. A suffragette, Ellen helped champion women's rights while Aaron authored the legislation that ultimately allowed women to vote; he was also a major catalyst in the founding of the transcontinental railroad. The mansion is set amid old terraced gardens and offers seven guest rooms. The downstairs suite is the finest, with blond hardwood floors, a sitting area, an antique gas fireplace, and a private porch. If you've brought the family along, ask for Gertie's Room, which has a private garden entrance, a kitchen, and a bathroom with a tub and shower. The wonderful breakfast spread consists of hot dishes, baked goods, and fresh fruits. ■ *449 Broad St (at Bennett St), Nevada City, CA 95959; (530) 265-4660; www.virtualcities. com/ons/ca/g/cag9503.htm; $$$; MC, V; checks OK.*

**The Red Castle Historic Lodgings ★★★★** A towering, four-story red brick manse detailed with lacy white icicle trim, the Red Castle is a gothic revival gem. The seven guest rooms (three of them are suites) have either a private porch or a garden terrace. The oft-photographed Garden Room on the mansion's entry level is furnished with a canopy bed, French doors, and two mannequin arms that reach out for your towels in the bathroom. Equally embracing is the Rose Room, with its four-poster bed and Jessie Wilcox Smith illustrations. Smaller quarters are upstairs on the former nursery floor, where the tissue dispensers are fashioned from wicker fishing creels. As you climb still higher, the stairs get narrower and steeper until they stop at the three-room Garret Suite, where the private veranda provides a superb view of Nevada City. The Red Castle's ever-changing breakfast (prepared by an in-house chef) is a feast. ■ *109 Prospect St (call for directions), Nevada City, CA 95959; (530) 265-5135; www.virtualcities. com/ons/ca/g/cag9507.htm; $$$; MC, V; checks OK.*

**Gold Country**

**Nevada City**
*Lodgings*

**Deer Creek Inn** ★★★ Set on the banks of pretty Deer Creek, which was famous in the Gold Rush days as a "pound-a-day" source for gold panners, this Queen Anne Victorian house has been completely restored and attractively decorated as a bed-and-breakfast inn. The five guest rooms have either king- or queen-size four-poster or canopy beds with down comforters, private baths with marble or claw-footed tubs, and private verandas. If you're contemplating getting engaged, you might be interested to know that Winifred's Room has been the site of at least a half-dozen marriage proposals (perhaps it's the romantic veranda overlooking the creek that inspires couples to commit?). In the morning, guests are treated to a gourmet breakfast of fresh fruit, eggs Florentine, baked onion potatoes, French toast, and beverages, served on the deck overlooking the creek and rose garden or in the formal dining room. Afterwards, it's time to pan for gold in the creek, fish for trout, play a game of croquet, or just lounge in a hammock with a good murder mystery. Wine and hors d'oeuvres are served each evening. A two-night minimum stay is requested on weekends. ■ *116 Nevada St (at Broad Street), Nevada City, CA 95959; (530)265-0363 or (800)655-0363; www.virtualcities.com/ons/ca/g/cag9501.htm; $$–$$$; MC, V; checks OK.*

**Downey House** ★★★ The exterior of the impeccably restored Downey House wears a traditional cloak of respectability; inside, however, its personality is more contemporary. Each of the six pastel guest rooms features built-in beds, comfortable reading chairs, and an aquarium. Guests may make themselves at home in the upstairs sun room, which opens onto an expansive view of Nevada City, or in the downstairs garden room, where there is a phone, a cookie jar full of brownies, coffee, tea, and soft drinks. Before bedtime, expect some candies from the local sweet shop. The buffet breakfast often features quiche, chiles rellenos, cinnamon rolls, fresh fruit, and freshly squeezed orange juice. ■ *517 W Broad St (just beyond the historic district at Bennett St), Nevada City, CA 95959; (530)265-2815 or (800)258-2815; www. virtualcities.com/ons/ca/g/cag9502.htm; $$; MC, V; checks OK.*

**Kendall House** ★★★ This sunny bed and breakfast is graced by Southern hospitality. Set amid a 2-acre garden with apple trees, the four-room inn is a quiet, serene, and comfortable escape for city dwellers—and it's only two blocks from downtown Nevada City. The Garden Room downstairs is a private retreat that's near the large heated swimming pool and garden. If you prefer to wake up in the morning sun, try the French Country Room. Some folks prefer staying in the cottage (a converted barn), which now sports a tiled kitchen, a breakfast nook, a wood-burning stove, and a private deck with built-in seating and a view of the pool and fruit trees. Ask proprietor Ted Kendall, an avid jogger, for the lowdown on the best local running trails. Jan Kendall's scrump-

tious three-course breakfast makes for a fine morning send-off.
■ *534 Spring St (just S of W Broad St), Nevada City, CA 95959; (530)265-0405; kenhouse@netshell.net; www.virtualcities.com/ons/ ca/g/cag5501.htm; $$–$$$; DIS, MC, V; checks OK.* ⅃

**Piety Hill Inn** ★★★ Originally built in 1933 as an auto court, Piety Hill Inn has been imaginatively and charmingly restored and redecorated by owners Joan and Steve Oas. The inn consists of nine cottages clustered around a grassy, tree-shaded courtyard and garden. Each of the one-, two-, and three-room cottages has a kitchenette stocked with complimentary hot and cold beverages, at least one king- or queen-size bed, a private bath, cable TV, and air conditioning. One unit also has a wood-burning stove. Between 8:30am and 10am (you pick the exact time), the innkeeper delivers a breakfast basket filled with juice, fresh fruit, and lemon poppyseed bread or orange sourdough French toast. Guests are free to linger in the lodge-style living room, soak in the gazebo-sheltered spa nestled among cedars, and barbecue on the outdoor grills. The larger cottages are rented by the week in the summer. ■ *523 Sacramento St (2 blocks SE of Hwy 49), Nevada City, CA 95959; (530)265-2245 or (800)443-2245; www.virtual cities.com/ons/ca/g/cag9506.htm; $$–$$$; AE, MC, V; checks OK.*

**Flume's End Bed and Breakfast Inn** ★★ This eclectic building originally served as a quartz mill and later as a brothel. Nowadays its patrons are a more respectable sort, who tend to spend their time strolling along the terraced gardens on the 3-acre lot or relaxing indoors with a good book. Visitors here are never far from the namesake Gold Rush–era flume—or from the refreshing and restorative sound of rushing water in Gold Run Creek. (Gold panners, bring your gear and prepare to get wet! Locals say the creek, which flows by an old mine, is generous with flecks of gold.) Decks, large and small, are everywhere at Flume's End, and there's even a patio next to the creek. Of the six guest rooms, the scenic Creekside Room, perched dramatically above the creek (the water deceptively appears to flow underneath the room), is one of the most popular. The inn's attic has been converted into a mini-suite known as the Penthouse Room, a good choice if you like to be awakened by the early morning sun. Flume's End also rents out a charming creekside cottage equipped with a kitchenette and a wood-burning stove—it's a popular haunt of honeymooners. ■ *317 S Pine St (at Spring St), Nevada City, CA 95959; (530)265-9665 or (800)991-8118; www.virtualcities.com/ons/ca/ g/cag8501.htm; $$–$$$; MC, V; checks OK.*

▼

**Nevada City**

*Lodgings*

▲

**Parsonage Bed and Breakfast Inn** ★★ Once home to the ministers of the Nevada City Methodist Church, the Parsonage is quiet and unassuming—and an essential stop for California history buffs. Owned and operated by a great-granddaughter of California pioneer Ezra Dane, the Parsonage is something of a living museum. Deborah Dane lovingly maintains the home, which is decorated with collections from three generations of Californians—everything from a Turkish pillow chair to Chinese rice-paper-and-silk peacock screens. All six guest rooms have private baths and are furnished with the family's museum-quality heritage antiques, including Deborah's great-grandparents' impressive bedroom set. The Mouse House, a cute cottage that was originally an old woodshed, is set apart from the inn, making it ideal for honeymooners seeking privacy or for couples with a particularly rambunctious young child. ■ *427 Broad St (call for directions), Nevada City, CA 95959; (530) 265-9478; www.virtualcities.com/ons/ca/g/cag9504.htm; $$; MC, V; checks OK.*

**National Hotel** The 42-room National Hotel is truly a California institution. It opened in the mid-1950s, and is the oldest continuously operating hotel west of the Rockies. President Herbert Hoover slept here, as did entertainers Lotta Crabtree and Lola Montez. Heck, even former governor Jerry Brown spent the night, though presumably he slept in a four-poster bed and not on the floor. PG&E was founded here and had its first office in this building. Sure, the place shows its age, and the decor (particularly the carpets) is a mishmash from every era from the 1850s to the 1950s. But, hey, such color keeps the fastidious and faint of heart away, and that ain't all bad. Plus, there's lots to see—take a look at the original office with cubbyholes for storing room keys, the innumerable photos, the baby grand piano that sailed around the Horn, or the exhaustive cocktail shaker collection on the perimeter of the bar and dining room. The 42 guest rooms are furnished with exquisite antiques, and all but 8 units have private bathrooms. The National also has a swimming pool and a dining room serving perfunctory American fare. The hotel's bar features live music on Friday and Saturday. ■ *211 Broad St (center of town), Nevada City, CA 95959; (530) 265-4551; $–$$; full bar; AE, MC, V; checks OK; breakfast, lunch, dinner every day.* &

## GRASS VALLEY

Once known for rich quartz mines, Cornish pasties, and Gold Rush entertainers like dancers Lola Montez and Lotta Crabtree, Grass Valley has a historic and slightly scruffy downtown that's a pleasure to explore, as well as elegant bed-and-breakfast inns and good restaurants. Stop at the chamber of commerce for a free walking-tour map of the town and two terrific brochures listing more than two dozen scenic walking, hiking, and mountain biking trails; 248 Mill Street, (530) 273-4667 or (800) 655-4667. As you tour the town, be sure to stop at the 10-ton **Pelton Waterwheel** (at 30 feet in diameter, it's the world's largest) on display at the exemplary **North Star Mining Museum**. The museum building was once the powerhouse for the North Star Mine (open daily from May through October); located at the south end of Mill Street at McCourtney Road, (530) 273-4255. Just outside of town is the 785-acre **Empire Mine State Historic Park**, the oldest, largest, and richest gold mine in California; its underground passages once extended 367 miles and descended 11,007 feet into the ground. A museum occupies a former stable, and the impressive granite and red brick **Empire Cottage**, designed by San Francisco architect Willis Polk in 1897 for the mine's owner, is a prime example of what all that gold dust could buy; 10791 East Empire Street, (530)273-8522.

In the 1870s and 1880s, long after the peak gold-mining days had passed, hordes of miners from the depressed tin mines of Cornwall, England, moved here and began mining ore deposits. They were nicknamed "Cousin Jacks," and their mining talents helped keep the town of Grass Valley alive and bustling while other Gold Rush cities died. These ore miners also introduced their beloved Cornish pasty to the town settlers, which you can still sample at Mrs. Dubblebee's Pasties (see review). If you're tired of driving and jockeying for weekend parking spots, spend a couple of dollars for an all-day pass on a Gold Country Stage shuttle, which will take you to the highlights of Grass Valley and Nevada City, among other areas. Call (530)477-0103 for a free map and riders' guide.

After touring Grass Valley, head about 5 miles west on Highway 20 for a pleasant side trip to the tiny town of **Rough and Ready**, which once chose to secede from the Union rather than pay a mining tax. Then continue on Highway 20 for another couple of miles and turn north on Pleasant Valley Road; 15 miles up the road is **Bridgeport**, home of California's longest covered bridge. Built in 1862, the bridge provides a good spot for dangling your fishing line—or pretending you're Clint and Meryl in a scene from *Bridges of Madison County*.

*Grass Valley*

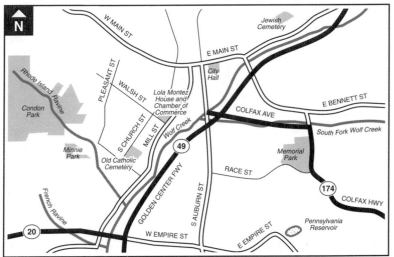

**The Stewart House** ★★★ An elegant, classic Victorian manse on the edge of downtown Grass Valley, the Stewart House was built in 1891 by the owner of the local sawmill (which once stood next door) and now it's one of the town's best restaurants. Tantalize your taste buds with an appetizer of seared peppercorn-encrusted tuna carpaccio with a sweet pepper and wasabe aioli, escargots served in mushroom crowns, French onion soup, or an asparagus salad with a balsamic vinaigrette. The entrees are equally delicious, whether you order the seafood special of the day, stuffed pork tenderloin in a port wine sauce, breast of duck in a brandied apricot sauce, range quail, rack of lamb, or filet mignon with a bordelaise sauce. The carefully edited wine list includes more than 70 selections. On Friday and Saturday (and occasionally Sunday), diners are treated to the music of the beautiful grand piano in the main salon. ■ *124 Bank St (off S Auburn St), Grass Valley; (530) 477-1559; mrsaute@aol.com; $$; AE, MC, V; local checks only; lunch Tues–Fri, dinner Tues–Sun.*

**Main Street Cafe & Bar** ★★ Contemporary, casual, and colorful, the Main Street Cafe is appreciated for its standard but accomplished American lunch menu, featuring a variety of burgers (try the Holy Creole burger slathered with Jack cheese, caramelized onions, mushrooms, and roasted red pepper pesto), sandwiches, and salads. At dinnertime the kitchen offers more challenging entrees: specials might include salmon poached in a fennel-spiked court-bouillon with mashed potatoes studded with rock shrimp and a champagne-dill sauce; grilled rib-eye steak with garlic mashed potatoes and chili-fried onions; or the house signature dish, pan-seared sturgeon atop rock-shrimp potatoes with a pinot noir reduction sauce and horseradish cream. The full bar maintains a good selection of beers and an extensive wine list in addition to an array of spirits. There's also an espresso menu with a variety of excellent coffee drinks including the locally famous "hot nut" beverage: a combo of hazelnut flavoring, espresso, and steamed milk topped with whipped cream. Live entertainment is offered Wednesday through Saturday. ■ *213 W Main St (across from the Holbrooke Hotel), Grass Valley; (530) 477-6000; mainstre@ av.net; $$; full bar; AE, DIS, MC, V; checks OK; lunch Mon–Sat, dinner every day.* &

**Tofanelli's** ★★ Tofanelli's is one of Grass Valley's cultural and culinary meeting places. And when people convene here for lunch, they often order the restaurant's famous veggie burger. The tostadas also make a very good lunch, including the version topped with marinated chicken breast (or marinated tofu), brown rice, the house pinto beans, greens, carrots, and tomatoes. Tofanelli's whips up several vegetarian dishes, but the kitchen can also turn out a mean hamburger and Reuben sandwich. Each week the chefs prepare a new dinner menu, which might feature char-

▼

**Grass Valley**

*Restaurants*

▲

broiled chicken breast with sun-dried tomatoes and a balsamic cream sauce, spring vegetables with orange chipotle (smoked jalapeño chile) sauce, as well as the favored vegetarian lasagne with three cheeses, fresh spinach, and house-made marinara. Be sure to save room for Katherine's Chocolate Cake, complemented perfectly by one of Tofanelli's dozen coffee or espresso drinks. On the weekend, indulge in the bounteous brunch served in the garden room and courtyard. ■ *302 W Main St (next to the Holbrooke Hotel), Grass Valley; (530)272-1468; $; beer and wine; AE, MC, V; checks OK; brunch Sat–Sun, lunch Mon–Fri, dinner Mon–Sat.* &

**Mrs. Dubblebee's Pasties** Thanks to the miners who emigrated here from Cornwall, England, today's hungry visitors can feast on a genuine British legacy: the Cornish pasty, a traditional butter-crust beef-and-vegetable pie. William Brooks, founder of Mrs. Dubblebee's Pasties, patented the Billy Brooks Pie Machine now used to make pasties worldwide. Try the traditional British beef pie (the Cornish pasty), or the less traditional but still tasty spinach pasty with mushrooms and three cheeses, or the spicy Olé pasty. The untraditional versions are made from family recipes by current owner (and Brooks's granddaughter) Janine Clark. Pick up some pasties and a few squares of Scottish shortbread and have a picnic at nearby Empire Mine State Historic Park. Mrs. Dubblebee's closes at 6pm during the week and at 5:30pm on weekends. ■ *251-C S Auburn St (next to the Veterans' Memorial Building, downtown), Grass Valley; (530)272-7700; $; no alcohol; no credit cards; checks OK; lunch, early dinner every day.*

## LODGINGS

**The Holbrooke Hotel** ★★★ Mark Twain slept here. And so did entertainers Lola Montez and Lotta Crabtree, as well as the notorious gentleman-bandit Black Bart. Other heavyweight visitors to this historic Gold Rush hostelry include champion boxers Gentleman Jim Corbett and Bob Fitzsimmons and political prizefighters Ulysses S. Grant, Benjamin Harrison, Herbert Hoover, and Grover Cleveland. But don't be intimidated; despite its rugged Gold Rush grandeur, the 140-year-old brick Holbrooke Hotel is a relaxed and accommodating establishment. Many of the 27 guest rooms have private balconies, and all offer antiques, cable TVs tucked away in armoires, and contemporary bathrooms with those delightful (though not so contemporary) claw-footed bathtubs. A continental breakfast is served in the library. The Holbrooke's Golden Gate Saloon is the best bar on Main Street, so light sleepers should request a suite far from the libations. The venerable hotel restaurant, **Arletta's**, is excellent. Lunch offerings range from a club sandwich to a Chinese chicken salad, and dinner entrees include house-made mushroom ravioli, roast breast of chicken with shrimp mousse, great seafood specials, and prime rib. Save room for one of the terrific desserts of the day. ■ *212 W Main St (between S Church and Mill Sts), Grass Valley, CA 95945; (530)273-1353 or (800)933-7077; holbroo1@ nccn.net; www.holbrooke.com; $$; full bar; AE, DC, DIS, MC, V; checks OK; champagne brunch Sun, lunch Mon–Sat, dinner every day.* ♿

**Murphy's Inn ★★★** Once the personal estate of North Star and Idaho Mines owner Edward Coleman, Murphy's Inn has become one of Grass Valley's premier B&Bs. Marc and Rose Murphy established this well-known, highly regarded inn more than a decade ago, and now proprietors Ted and Nancy Daus are running the show. A topiary garden with bubbling fountains, a fish pond, and a giant 140-year-old sequoia surrounds the elegant Victorian mansion. The main house has remained true to its 19th-century origins with its downstairs parlors and a bold brass-fronted fireplace, but the kitchen has taken a more contemporary turn. And in true Victorian style, all eight guest rooms are tastefully gussied up in an understated floral motif. Breakfast is a feast. ■ *318 Neal St (at School St, 1 block from Main St), Grass Valley, CA 95945; (530)273-6873 or (800)895-2488; www.virtualcities. com/ons/ca/g/cag9601.htm; $$–$$$; AE, MC, V; checks OK.*

▼
**Grass Valley**

---

*Lodgings*

▲

## AUBURN

The Gold Country's largest town, Auburn is sprawled on a bluff overlooking the American River and has been the seat of Placer County since 1850. Nowadays, Auburn serves mainly as a pit stop for vacationers headed for Lake Tahoe. Its few noteworthy sights, including **Old Town** and the impressively domed **Placer County Courthouse**, 101 Maple Street, (530)889-6550, are best seen out the car window as you head toward the far more congenial towns of Grass Valley and Nevada City to the north. But if you're here to stretch your legs or get a bite to eat (there are some very good restaurants), stroll by the numerous bustling shops and restaurants that grace Old Town's streets. Many of these enterprises are housed in historic Gold Rush buildings, including the **Shanghai Restaurant**, a Chinese establishment that has been open continuously since 1906 and displays a wonderful collection of memorabilia in its bar (where part of the movie *Phenomenon* was filmed with John Travolta); 289 Washington Street, (530)823-2613. A gigantic stone statue of Claude Chana, who discovered gold in the Auburn Ravine in 1848, marks the historic section. Other Old Town highlights include the whimsical firehouse (on Lincoln Way at Commercial Street), the former 1852 Wells Fargo Bank (on Lincoln Way, 1 block south of the firehouse), and the post office that first opened its doors in 1849 (on Lincoln Way at Sacramento Street). The north and middle forks of the **American River** in the **Auburn State Recreation Area** are popular destinations for gold panners, swimmers, picnickers, and rafters. The

---
**I**

recreation site also has great camping sites, hiking trails, equestrian trails, and mountain biking routes; on Highway 49, 1 mile south of Auburn, (530)885-4527.

## RESTAURANTS

**Le Bilig** ★★★★ The sign in front of the modest building says "Bail Bonds," but open the correct door and you will discover what looks like a slice of the French countryside. This small jewel-box restaurant with 10 rough-hewn pine tables is the creation of husband-and-wife team Marc and Monica Deconinck. Marc is an accomplished and dedicated chef from Lille in northern France, and his specialty is hearty, rustic French comfort food—not unctuous, sauced French fare or prissy nouvelle cuisine. The menu changes every few months to accommodate available ingredients (and to keep the chef from getting bored). In the winter, Deconinck might be dishing out a definitive French onion soup or ham hocks with lentils; in the early spring look for his lamb shanks roasted with fennel and thyme-scented tomatoes. There are also a few house specialties served nearly year-round: *pissaladière* (a Niçoise-style caramelized-onion pizza with fresh goat cheese, olives, and pine nuts), steak with Belgian fries, and Brittany-style whole-wheat or buckwheat crêpes with savory fillings like poached fresh salmon. The wine list has some rarities and bargains, including reasonably priced French wines from the '70s and '80s. A few divine desserts are offered, such as the classic tarte Tatin served warm with crème fraîche. For a great culinary treat, visit Le Bilig on the second Sunday of each month when the Deconincks serve a prix-fixe French Country feast. ■ *11750 Atwood Rd (off Hwy 49, 1 block W of the Bel Air Shopping Center, at the N end of town), Auburn; (530)888-1491; $$; beer and wine; MC, V; checks OK; dinner Wed–Sat and the second Sun of each month.* &

*Restaurants*

**Bootlegger's Old Town Tavern & Grill** ★★★ Located in a handsome old brick building in the heart of Auburn's historic center, Bootlegger's offers a large, eclectic seasonal menu that's so chock-full of interesting choices you'll want to come back several times to sample them all. Lunchtime winners include the oven-roasted eggplant sandwich layered with peppers, caramelized onions, tomatoes, capers, and basil aioli; the spicy Creole chicken gumbo; and the delicate Maryland-style crab cakes. For dinner, choose from an extensive list of pastas; grilled steak, ribs, lamb, or chicken; Southern fried chicken; Mom's Meat Loaf; prime rib; or veal scaloppini. If that isn't enough to stimulate your appetite, Bootlegger's features special-occasion theme menus, such as the Oktoberfest selection of sauerbraten, schnitzel, and wursts. Whew! ■ *210 Washington St (in Old Town), Auburn; (530)889-2229; bootleg@ix.netcom.com; www.bootleggers.com; $$; AE, DIS, MC, V; checks OK; lunch Tues–Sat, dinner Tues–Sun.* &

**Latitudes** ★★★  Latitudes, which owner/chefs Pat and Pete Enochs call their "world kitchen," is located in a lovely Victorian building just above Auburn's Old Town. Most of their cuisine is truly adventurous and wide-ranging (for example, you might find an African dish sharing the menu with a Cajun specialty), and this is a reflection of their desire to encourage people to try foods from other cultures. A recent lunch included a terrific tofu Florentine (tofu grilled with cashews, green onions, and spinach), a tenderloin fajita (pepper-coated tenderloin strips grilled with vegetables and red wine served in a sun-dried tomato tortilla with lettuce and caesar dressing), and a first-rate burger served with the best fries in town. Dinner is equally rewarding with a juicy fillet of fresh Atlantic salmon, gingered prawns, East Indian curried tofu, and a fork-tender filet mignon. The extensive wine and beer lists feature brands from around the world. And as if the great food weren't enough, Latitudes often has live music in its downstairs bar, especially on Saturdays. ■ *130 Maple St #200 (across from the courthouse), Auburn; (530)885-9535; latitudes@neworld.net; $$; full bar; AE, MC, V; local checks only; brunch Sun, lunch Mon–Fri, dinner Wed–Sun.*

## LODGINGS

▼
**Auburn**
───────────
*Restaurants*
▲

**Power's Mansion Inn** ★★  Built at the turn of the century by a California state assembly member who owned the Hidden Treasure Mine, the charming, pink Power's Mansion Inn, located on a hill in the heart of downtown Auburn, has 11 antique-filled guest rooms with big brass beds and private baths. Ask for the Anniversary Room, which has a fireplace to keep you cozy on cool nights, or the Honeymoon Suite, where you can kick back with your honey in the sunken, heart-shaped Jacuzzi-for-two, then dry off in front of the roaring fireplace. Innkeepers Arno and Jean Lejnieks serve a full breakfast in the attractive dining room. ■ *164 Cleveland Ave (between Lincoln Way and High St; call for directions), Auburn, CA 95603; (530)885-1166; $$–$$$; AE, MC, V; checks OK.*

## COOL

### RESTAURANTS

**The Nugget** ★  The Nugget isn't the fanciest restaurant around, but it's a good place to stop for a meal if you're traveling along Highway 49 between Coloma and Auburn. Attentive service and hearty servings are this coffee-shop-style restaurant's strong points, and the menu's best bets are its German dishes, such as the bockwurst, *rundstueck* (warm pork roast on a French roll with homemade gravy), or one of a dozen schnitzels. Wash it all down with one of the 40 beers. ■ *At the intersection of Hwys 49 and 193, Cool; (530)823-1294; $$; beer and wine; AE, DIS, MC, V; local checks only; breakfast, lunch every day, dinner Tues–Sun.* &

## GEORGETOWN

When the tent city located here burned in 1852, this mountain town was rebuilt with much wider streets, which are now graced by a few noteworthy old buildings: **I.O.O.F. Hall** (at Main Street and Highway 193), **Georgetown Hotel** (6260 Main Street), and the **American River Inn**, which had an earlier life as a boardinghouse (see review, below). In the spring, spectacular displays of wild Scotch broom cover the Georgetown hillsides.

### LODGINGS

**American River Inn** ★★  This is the hotel that gold built. In the nearby community of Growlersburg, the gold nuggets were so big they growled as they rolled around the miners' pans. One nugget taken from the Woodside Gold Mine (which has tunnels running underneath the inn) weighed 126 ounces—the equivalent of winning the Super Lotto today. Innkeepers Will and Maria Collin have done an exemplary job of maintaining the inn's 25 guest rooms, which are spread out between three well-appointed buildings dating back to the 1850s. The best room is number 18, which takes up a generous portion of the second floor of the handsome Queen Anne house. If it's unavailable, ask for one of the two honeymoon suites in the main house that overlook the Victorian gardens. The hotel has a pool and spa, as well as bicycles, a putting green, horseshoes, table tennis, badminton, a driving range, and a croquet ground. If you arrive in Georgetown by plane, take advantage of the inn's free airport limo. ■ *At the corner of Main and Orleans Streets, Georgetown; (530)333-4499 or (800)245-6566; mail: PO Box 43, Georgetown, CA 95634; $$; AE, DIS, MC, V; checks OK.* &

Coloma

## COLOMA

As every California schoolchild knows, the Gold Rush began here when carpenter James Marshall found traces of the precious metal at John Sutter's sawmill on January 24, 1848. A full-scale working replica of the famous sawmill and other gold-related exhibits are displayed at **Marshall Gold Discovery State Historic Park**, a 280-acre expanse of shaded lawns and picnic tables that extends through three-quarters of the town; on Highway 49, (530)622-3470. Stop at the park's small **Gold Discovery Museum** for a look at Native American artifacts and James Marshall memorabilia, and pick up the self-guided tour pamphlet outlining the park's highlights; (530)622-1116.

Coloma is silly with tourists and river rafters on summer weekends, so try to plan your visit during the week, when you can picnic in peace and float down the **American River** without fear of colliding into others.

**Coloma Country Inn** ★★★ Every weekend, adventure-seeking innkeepers Alan and Cindi Ehrgott offer their guests and other visitors one of the thrills of their lives: whitewater rafting trips down the south fork of the American River (Class III), and hot-air balloon rides for a one-of-a-kind, bird's-eye view of the Gold Country. Visitors who have nerves of steel may find innkeeper-cum-pilot Alan's whitewater-ballooning trips more enticing: all you have to do is jump into the hot-air balloon, and Alan will take your breath away as he swings the balloon's carriage within inches of the river, then soars 2,000 feet back into the sky.

Of course, you don't have to take your feet off the grounds of this intimate 1852 hotel, set in the heart of the lovely Marshall Gold Discovery State Historic Park. The Coloma Country Inn has seven guest rooms (including a two-bedroom suite), and despite the wild weekend adventure trips, it is a tranquil retreat. Every day ends in a most civilized manner with iced tea and homemade cookies in the garden gazebo. After tea, you can indulge in such restful pastimes as feeding the ducks, paddling a canoe around the pond, or strolling through the gold-discovery exhibits in the park. ▪ *345 High St (in Marshall Gold Discovery State Historic Park), Coloma; (530)622-6919; mail: PO Box 502, Coloma, CA 95613; $$; no credit cards; checks OK.*

▼

**Coloma**

*Lodgings*

▲

## PLACERVILLE

One of the first camps settled by miners who branched out from Coloma, Placerville was dubbed Dry Diggins because of a lack of water. Its name was changed to Hangtown in 1849 after a series of grisly lynchings; it became Placerville in 1854 to satisfy local pride. Home to an unassuming array of gas stations, budget chain hotels, and 24-hour coffee shops, Placerville doesn't have much to offer visitors except some Gold Rush–era relics, Old Town gift shops, and its famous "Hangtown fry"—a concoction of bacon, eggs, and oysters popular with early miners—which nowadays is dished out at the **Bell Tower Cafe** at 423 Main Street, in Old Town, (530)626-3483.

Among the town's historical highlights is the brick-and-stone **City Hall**, which was built in 1860 and originally served as the town's firehouse; 487 Main Street, (530)642-5200. Another note-worthy edifice is **Milton's Cary House Hotel** (see review, below), where Mark Twain once lodged; 300 Main Street. Across the street, note the dangling dummy that marks the location of the town's infamous hanging tree. A mile north of downtown Placerville is **Gold Bug Park**, home of the city-owned **Gold Bug Mine**; guided tours of the mine lead you deep into the lighted shafts; located on Bedford Street, call (530)642-5238 for tour details. **El Dorado County Historical Museum**, adjacent to the county fairgrounds, showcases Pony Express paraphernalia, an original Studebaker wheelbarrow, a replica of a 19th-century general store, a restored Concord stagecoach, plus other mining-era relics (open Wednesday through Sunday); 104 Placerville Drive, (530)621-5865.

Every autumn, droves of people—about a half-million each year—come to a small ridge just east of Placerville called **Apple Hill Orchards**. What's the attraction? Why, apples, of course. Baked, fried, buttered, canned, candied, and caramelized apples, to name just a few variations. Dozens of apple vendors sell their special apple concoctions, and on weekends the atmosphere is positively festive, with everyone basking in the alpine sunshine while feasting on such treats as hot apple pie à la mode. In September and October (peak apple-harvest season), it's definitely worth a stop. From Highway 50, take the Carson Road exit and follow the signs.

## RESTAURANTS

**Zachary Jacques ★★★★** The decor at Zachary Jacques may be Western, but the cuisine is definitely French Country and it's superb. Owner/chefs Christian and Jennifer Masse offer a seasonal menu that recently featured a savory platter of shellfish sautéed in a saffron-garlic broth served with aioli; fresh rabbit in a white wine and coarse-grain mustard sauce; and roasted venison with a green peppercorn sauce. On Wednesday nights the house specialty is cassoulet, the classic French stew of white beans, duck, sausage, and lamb that takes days to prepare and is rarely served in American restaurants. Finding the perfect bottle of wine to accompany your order is never a problem: Zachary Jacques's wine list, which received an award of excellence from the highly respected *Wine Spectator* magazine, features more than 300 French and American labels. In June, July, and August the restaurant hosts popular wine tastings featuring French and local foothill wines as well as canapés topped with cheese, fruit tartlets, and other French hors d'oeuvres. When the weather is warm, dine on the deck ringed with pine trees. ■ *1821 Pleasant Valley Rd (3 miles E of Diamond Springs), Placerville; (530)626-8045; www.eldorado-mall.com; $$$; beer and wine; AE, MC, V; no checks; dinner Wed–Sun.* &

**Lil' Mama D. Carlo's ★★** This pleasant, unpretentious Italian restaurant across from the city courthouse features old-fashioned food based on the recipes of four generations of a Neapolitan-American family. Start your meal with a bowl of the hearty minestrone soup (made fresh daily), followed by such favorites as linguine in light clam sauce or made-to-order cioppino. The pasta entrees are smothered in rich, flavorful sauces, such as *carciofini*, a light cream-based sauce with artichoke hearts, fresh tomatoes, and garlic. Aside from one imported Chianti, the wine list features El Dorado County wines. ■ *482 Main St, Placerville; (530)626-1612; twinoaks@pacbell.net; $$; beer and wine; MC, V; local checks only; dinner Tues–Sun.* &

**Sweetie Pies** ★★ Stop for lunch at this cute little house on Main Street and order one of the freshly made soups served with house-baked sourdough bread. Or you might fancy a slice of the vegetable quiche and a freshly tossed garden salad. Whatever you choose, save room for the pie. Better yet, eat dessert first—it's *that* good. Don't miss the knockout thick, rich olallieberry pie or the rhubarb pie filled with tart chunks of the real thing. Other sweet-tooth delights include cream pies, poppyseed cake, lemon tea cake, and cinnamon and pecan rolls. Should you need more than a sugar rush to get you pumped, various coffee drinks ought to do the trick. Breakfast at Sweetie Pies is sweet and simple: coffee, tea, pastries, muffins, and, of course, pies. ■ *577 Main St, Placerville; (530)642-0128; $; beer and wine; MC, V; checks OK; breakfast every day, lunch Mon–Sat.* &

## LODGINGS

**Chichester–McKee House** ★★ This gracious Victorian home, built in 1892 by lumber baron D. W. Chichester, was the finest house in Placerville at the time and the first to have the luxury of indoor plumbing. Today the refurbished home still has the look and feel of the late 1800s—except, of course, for its updated plumbing. All four guest rooms have Victorian-era bedsteads, stained glass, and fireplaces trimmed with carved wood and marble. A polished Pullman basin adds a touch of elegance to the Yellow Rose Room, a favorite. You won't find televisions in the guest rooms of this B&B, but the grand old house offers something even better: a library. And despite the location on occasionally busy Spring Street, all is peaceful inside Chichester–McKee. ■ *800 Spring St (on Hwy 49, ½ block N of Hwy 50), Placerville, CA 95667; (530)626-1882 or (800)831-4008; inn@innercite.com; www.el-dorado.ca.us/ ~inn/; $$; AE, DIS, MC, V; checks OK.*

**Combellack Blair House** ★★ A spectacular sight, the recently renovated Combellack Blair House is trimmed with gingerbread and guarded by a white picket fence. White wicker furniture graces the large front veranda and a love swing hangs on the back porch. (Sounds like the setting for a Hallmark commercial, right? But wait—there's more.) Just off the porch you'll see a gazebo, a rose garden, and a little waterfall in a rock garden. Of course, proprietors Marlene and Loren DeLaurenti have made sure the Queen Anne Victorian theme continues inside—from the sweeping spiral staircase to the rich wood moldings and the floral carpets. The four guest rooms have private baths and queen- or king-size beds and are tastefully appointed. Unfortunately, the house fronts a relatively busy street. ■ *3059 Cedar Ravine Rd (from Hwy 50, take the Bedford St exit, turn left on Main St and right on Cedar Ravine Rd), Placerville, CA 95667; (530)622-3764; $$; MC, V; checks OK.*

▼

**Placerville**

*Restaurants*

▲

**Historic Cary House Hotel** ★ Originally built in 1857, refurbished in the late 1980s, and redecorated in 1997, the Cary House is a historically significant Victorian inn centrally located on Main Street. The four-story brick building was the headquarters of the Wells Fargo stage lines during the Gold Rush, and according to local lore, $90 million worth of bullion was once dumped on the hotel's porch before it was transported to the U.S. Mint in San Francisco. Years later, newspaper editor Horace Greeley used the same porch to give an impassioned presidential campaign speech to miners. All 31 of the simple, comfortable guest rooms are decorated with antiques and have received a fresh coat of paint and new beds and drapes; each has a private bath, a remote-control TV, and a phone. Many units have kitchenettes, and six overlook the street, though old Hangtown ain't as noisy and rambunctious as it was in its wild youth. Who is? ■ *300 Main St (between Bedford and Spring Sts), Placerville, CA 95667; (530)622-4271; $$; AE, DC, DIS, MC, V; no checks.* ♿

## POLLOCK PINES

### RESTAURANTS

**The Haven** ★ This modest restaurant of polished wood and stained glass just may be the best-kept secret in the mountains. While most out-of-towners don't know it exists, the Haven is famous among locals for its scallops, stir-fry (a great mix of chicken, beef, or shrimp with water chestnuts, broccoli, and other tenderly cooked veggies), thick-cut steaks, and mountainous salads. During the summer, eat outside among the fragrant pines and fuchsia blossoms. In the winter, call and ask about the weather conditions before driving up here; the restaurant is at a 4,000-foot elevation, well above the snow line, and chains might be required. ■ *6396 Pony Express Trail (½ mile W of Safeway), Pollock Pines; (530)644-3448; cesario@cwnet.com; $$; beer and wine; MC, V; local checks only; lunch, dinner every day (closed the last 2 weeks in Dec).*

**Pollock Pines**

*Restaurants*

**Weird Harold's** ★ Tucked under a grove of towering ponderosa pines, this pale blue chalet-style restaurant serves thick cuts of prime rib and hefty platters of steak, pasta, and fresh seafood, such as lobster, Dungeness crab, scampi, and scallops. The competent, witty servers make you feel warm and welcome, though the decor—pine wainscoting, dull carpeting, an old steel fireplace—could be described as '70s funk. In the winter, find out if you'll need chains to navigate the trail before driving here. ■ *5631 Pony Express Trail (at the W end of town), Pollock Pines; (530)644-5272; $$; full bar; AE, MC, V; checks OK; dinner every day.* ♿

*LODGINGS*

**Strawberry Lodge** ★★ Wedged between the giant conifers and granite headwalls of Lake Tahoe's southwestern rim, Strawberry Lodge has been the headquarters for a cornucopia of year-round outdoor activities for more than a century. You can downhill or cross-country ski in the winter (Tahoe's third-largest ski resort, Sierra-at-Tahoe, is just 10 minutes up the road), rock climb, bike, hike, swim, fish, ride horses, attend the great quintet of summer music festivals, or gamble at the casinos in nearby South Lake Tahoe. Named for the wild strawberry patches that once covered the area, the lodge has 45 rooms (most with private baths) that often get booked up during the peak of summer and winter (and they do a fierce wedding business). The rooms overlooking the river are the quietest. Mind you, they aren't lavish (and have no TVs or phones), but then neither is the price, especially if you opt for the fantastic weekend and midweek specials. (Smoking is not allowed in any of the rooms.) Families or small groups might prefer the River House, a cabin at the edge of the American River's south fork. The Strawberry Lodge's dining room offers fresh-baked bread, steaks, chicken, seafood, and a daily pasta special. ■ *17510 Hwy 50 (43 miles E of Placerville, 9 miles E of Kyburz), Kyburz, CA 95720; (530) 659-7200; $; full bar; AE, MC, V; no checks; breakfast, lunch, dinner every day (closed Tues–Thurs the last 3 weeks of Apr and for a month from mid-Oct to mid-Nov).*

## EL DORADO

Three miles south of Placerville on Highway 49 sits the small town of El Dorado, whose denizens tolerate but in no way cultivate tourism. In fact, most travelers pass right on through—except for those who know about **Poor Red's** (see review, below), a bar and restaurant that may not look like much from the outside (or the inside, for that matter), but is known throughout the land for its famous cocktail.

*RESTAURANTS*

**Poor Red's** It's not often that small-town bars garner an international reputation, but this Cheers of the Gold Country has had its name translated into more tongues than a Robert Ludlum novel. It all started one night when the proud new owners of a gold-colored Cadillac asked the bartender to whip up a commemorative drink to celebrate their purchase. Grabbing the only thing behind the bar that was gold-colored (Galliano liqueur), the bartender dusted off the bottle, added a shot of this and a jigger of that, and eureka!—the frothy Golden Cadillac was born. By alchemic accident, this tiny Golden State saloon soon become the largest user of Galliano in North America (as the gilded plaque, sent from

Italy and proudly displayed behind a glass showcase, attests). Legend has it that during Poor Red's golden era, dozens of bottles were emptied per day as celebrities, dignitaries, and plain folks all queued up at the door for a chance to squeeze inside. Nowadays things are a bit more placid, with ranchers in baseball caps and boots politely ordering from a memorized menu of barbecued steak, ham, chicken, and pork (in fact, Dorothy, the lunchtime waitress, has been scribbling the same orders in her notepads for nearly two decades). Nothing, down to the placement of the coat rack, ever changes here—just ask Mike, Poor Red's friendly, loquacious bartender, as he whips up his umpteenth Golden Cadillac. ■ *6221 Pleasant Valley Rd (downtown), El Dorado; (530)622-2901; $; full bar; AE, DIS, MC, V; checks OK; lunch Mon–Fri, dinner every day.* &

## SOMERSET

### *LODGINGS*

**Fitzpatrick Winery and Lodge** ★★ If you've never experienced true Irish hospitality, reserve a night at Brian and Diana Fitzpatrick's country-style winery and lodge to see (and taste) for yourself why Irish eyes are always smiling. Sitting atop a hill with a commanding 360-degree view of the countryside, their lodge has five guest rooms: French Basque, Irish, Old Fairplay, the Wine Maker's Suite, and the Log Suite. Guests may also dive into the new 25-meter lap pool, and bask in the sun on the expanded deck, where meats and breads are often cooked on the outdoor wood-fired oven. A full breakfast and complimentary glasses of the Fitzpatricks' wine are included in the room rate. Don't miss the monthly theme dinners, ranging from Algerian fare to Alice in Culinary Curryland. ■ *7740 Fairplay Rd (off Mount Aukum Rd, 6 miles SE of town), Somerset, CA 95684; (530)620-3248 or (800)245-9166; www.fitzpatrickwinery.com; $$; beer and wine; DIS, MC, V; checks OK; dinner once a month (call for the current schedule).* &

## PLYMOUTH

### *LODGINGS*

**Indian Creek Bed and Breakfast** ★★★ Part of Indian Creek's popularity is simply a matter of location—it's right off Highway 49 and conveniently close to Amador County's Shenandoah Valley wineries. But it's not just the location that keeps folks coming back. Steve Noffsinger and Lena Stiward run this beautiful B&B on 10 wooded acres outside Plymouth, where you can meditate by the artesian-fed pond, explore a secret gold mine, sunbathe on your private deck, or drink whiskey in the way-cool Cowboy Bar (bring your own booze, though, 'cause they don't have a liquor license). Indian Creek B&B was originally built in 1923 by Hollywood producer Arthur Hamburger, who entertained such celebrity guests as John Wayne. Hence the playful (but tastefully done) cowboy/Indian theme running throughout the lodge, including the handsome log-framed living room with its cathedral ceiling and massive stone fireplace. Indian Creek offers four guest rooms (all with private baths, queen-size beds, air conditioning, and ceiling fans), and the top gun is the decidedly feminine Margaret Breen room, which has French doors that open onto a private deck. Cowboy wannabes may prefer the Way Out West Room festooned with real cowboy toys. After a bounteous gourmet breakfast, rest yer tired dogs by the pool or in one of the shaded two-person hammocks—it's a fantastic place to unwind from the hustle and bustle of daily life. ▪ *21950 Hwy 49 (3 miles N of town), Plymouth, CA 95669; (209) 245-4648; $$; DIS, MC, V; checks OK.*

## AMADOR CITY

Amador City is the smallest incorporated city in California. Lined with false-fronted antique and specialty shops, this block-long town is a good place to stop, stretch your legs, window-shop, and eat dinner.

*LODGINGS*

**Imperial Hotel** ★★★ Proprietors Bruce Sherrill and Dale Martin restored this century-old brick hotel in 1988, striking a marvelous balance between elegance and whimsy. One of the best examples of their playful talent is on display in the Oasis Bar: a fresco fantasy of a Saharan oasis complete with palm trees, belly dancers, and camels. The six upstairs guest rooms house numerous antiques as well as hand-painted furnishings by local artist John Johannsen. Room 5 is one of the quietest, but room 1 is everyone's favorite, with its high ceiling, queen-size canopy bed, giant windows, and French doors that open onto a private balcony overlooking Main Street (granted, you have to put up with some traffic noise, but the old brick hotel is located on a slow curve, so no one's going terribly fast). Breakfast is served downstairs, in your room, or on the patio or balcony.

The elegant **Imperial Hotel Restaurant** is under the domain of talented executive chef Rhonda Uhlmann, who prepares first-rate California cuisine, including oven-baked polenta with tomato fondue and wild mushrooms, grilled apricot- and sage-glazed pork tenderloin, and poached salmon in a basil champagne cream sauce. On warm summer evenings request a table on the back patio, but forget about finding a seat on New Year's Eve—there's already a two-year waiting list to join the Imperial's legendary end-of-the-year bash. ▪ *14202 Hwy 49 (downtown), Amador City; (209) 267-9172 or (800) 242-5594; mail: PO Box 195, Amador City, CA 95601; brucesherrill@imperialamador.com or dalemartin@ imperialamador.com; $$; full bar; AE, DC, DIS, MC, V; checks OK; brunch Sun (Feb 1 to Oct 1), dinner every day.*

"Big Four" railroad baron Leland Stanford made his millions at Sutter Creek's Lincoln Mine, then used his wad to invest in the transcontinental railroad and fund his successful campaign to become governor of California. Sutter Creek is the self-proclaimed "nicest little town in the Mother Lode" and was named after sawmill owner John Sutter. It boasts some beautiful 19th-century buildings that you can admire from the street, including the landmark **Knight's Foundry**, the last water-powered foundry and machine shop in the nation (81 Eureka Street off Main Street, no phone), and the **Downs Mansion**, the former home of the foreman at Leland Stanford's mine (this private residence is on Spanish Street, across from the Immaculate Conception Church). Also worth exploring: the Asian furnishings and Native American and Mexican folk art at the **Cobweb Collection**, 83 Main Street, (209) 267-0690; the contemporary and traditional American handicrafts at **Fine Eye Gallery**, 71 Main Street, (209) 267-0571; and the prints, watercolors, and stone carvings at **Sutter Creek Gallery**, 35 Main Street, (209) 267-0228.

## RESTAURANTS

**Zinfandels** ★★★ Zinfandels has filled the vacancy left by the Pelargonium restaurant—and what a welcome newcomer it is. Chef Greg West, a six-year veteran of Greens (San Francisco's most famous vegetarian restaurant), has teamed up with pastry chef/baker/wife Kelley West to provide their version of light (but not meatless) California cuisine to the southern Gold Country. The Wests' menu changes weekly, incorporating the best local farm produce and seasonal ingredients. A recent meal began with two terrific appetizers: a charbroiled chicken and portobello mushroom salad sprinkled with toasted almonds, Parmesan, and a chipotle chili dressing, and crisp polenta topped with mushrooms, garlic, shallots, applewood-smoked bacon, and fresh herbs and cream. For the main course, standouts included a butternut squash risotto with pancetta, leeks, crimini mushrooms, and spinach; petrale sole with a citrus-ginger beurre blanc; and cannelloni filled with lamb sausage, chard, and smoked mozzarella. Zinfandels also offers a well-edited list of locally produced wines, and the chef thoughtfully highlights the perfect wine to accompany each dish on the menu. There are even a couple of very reasonably priced "Just for Kids" plates available. The only sour note here is the rather blasé decor (one tires of the cozy country theme rather quickly); otherwise, Zinfandels is strongly recommended, particularly if prime rib and baked potatoes just aren't your thing. ■ *51 Hanford St (downtown), Sutter Creek; (209) 267-5008; Wild4Zin@ aol.com; $$; beer and wine; MC, V; checks OK; dinner Tues–Sun.*

### The Foxes in Sutter Creek Bed and Breakfast Inn ★★★

For nearly two decades Pete and Min Fox have run the finest B&B in Sutter Creek. An immaculate garden fronts the Gold Rush–era foundation, and from there it only gets better. Each of the seven guest rooms is furnished with antiques, including massive, elaborate Victorian headboards and armoires that seem too priceless to actually use. All of the rooms have private baths, and four have fireplaces. The Garden Room is a favorite because it boasts a private entrance and a view of the garden and dogwood trees. What helps account for this B&B's popularity is the breakfast experience: you get to choose your meal from the Foxes' menu (special dietary requests are accommodated, too) and the hearty spread is delivered with the morning paper on a silver platter to your room or at the garden gazebo. Located on Main Street, the inn is only steps away from Sutter Creek's shops and restaurants. Expect a two-month waiting list for weekend stays during peak seasons. ■ *77 Main St (downtown), Sutter Creek; (209) 267-5882 or (800) 987-3344; mail: PO Box 159, Sutter Creek, CA 95685; foxes@cdepot.net; www.foxesinn.com; $$; DIS, MC, V; checks OK.*

### Grey Gables Inn ★★

This adorable Victorian retreat is run by Roger and Sue Garlick, two ever-friendly British expatriates dripping with genuine hospitality. Surrounded by terraces of colorful, meticulously manicured gardens, their two-story inn has eight plushly carpeted guest rooms named after British poets and writers. Sue's favorite, the Byron Room, is bedecked in hues of deep green and burgundy, which pairs well with the dark wood furnishings and Renaissance Revival bed. Aside from the king bed in the Brontë Room, all of the boudoirs have queen-size beds, gas-log fireplaces, large armoires, air conditioning, and private baths (a few with claw-footed tubs). A bounteous breakfast, delivered on fine English bone china, is served either in the formal dining room (adjacent to the Victorian parlor) or in your room. And in true English fashion there is an informal tea every afternoon from 3pm to 4pm, and wine and cheese is served daily from 6pm to 7pm. The only caveat to this English Eden is that the house abuts heavily traveled Highway 49, though the rooms are soundproofed. On the flip side, Sutter Creek's shops and restaurants are only a short walk away. ■ *161 Hanford St (on Hwy 49, at the N end of town), Sutter Creek, CA 95685; (209) 267-1039 or (800) 473-9422; greygables@cdepot.net; www.cdepot.net/greygables; $$; AE, DIS, MC, V; checks OK.* &

### The Gold Quartz Inn ★

If you enjoy the ambience of a B&B but are reluctant to give up the comfort and privacy of a hotel, the Gold Quartz Inn is a good compromise. Both the strengths and the weaknesses of this 24-room Queen Anne replica stem from its relative newness. On the plus side, the Quartz Inn delivers all the amenities you'd expect in a new hotel: king-size beds, modern bathrooms, cable TV, telephones, even hair dryers. On the other hand, you'll have to make some aesthetic sacrifices to pay for these luxuries. The inn is plunked on the outskirts of town (aka suburbia), and the furnishings are reminiscent of Macy's "Country Living" collection. That said, the emphasis here is on privacy: separate room entrances, parlor seating that discourages mingling, and individual breakfast tables (full breakfast and afternoon tea are included in the rate). The idea is, you're here to be with your partner and to eat to your heart's content (in fact, the innkeepers encourage guests to make frequent raids on the buffet, which is stocked with a seemingly endless progression of goodies). ▪ *15 Bryson Dr (at Hwy 49, just S of town), Sutter Creek, CA 95685; (209)267-9155 or (800)752-8738; $$; AE, DIS, MC, V; checks OK.* &

**Sutter Creek Inn** ★ One of the first B&Bs in California, proprietor Jane Way's inn is still as popular as ever, which is somewhat mystifying considering that the decor is stuck in the '70s—not a particularly good era for interior design. A major plus about this complex, however, is how intimate and relaxed it feels; with 17 guest rooms, you'd expect the place to feel overrun on a busy weekend, but it doesn't. Part of the secret is the layout: only three rooms are in the main house, with the other 14 in remodeled buildings scattered around the grounds behind hedges and under grape arbors. Two new deluxe rooms—the Storage Room and Carriage House—are equipped with cable TV, fireplaces, and tubs for two. Four of the guest rooms feature Way's fabled swinging beds, which hang from chains bolted to ceiling beams. Unquestionably, the best room in the house is the cozy living room, with its large library, piano, and eclectic selection of magazines and board games. A large breakfast is served family style in the kitchen at 9am sharp. Should you wish to indulge in a handwriting-analysis session or, better yet, a massage, it's available here by appointment. ▪ *75 Main St (between Keyes and Hayden Sts), Sutter Creek; (209)267-5606; mail: PO Box 385, Sutter Creek, CA 95685; info@suttercreekinn.com; www.suttercreekinn. com; $$; AE, DIS, MC, V; checks OK.*

Gold Country
|

▼

Volcano

▲

## VOLCANO

This tiny town with fewer than 100 residents is so wonderfully authentic that it borders on decrepit (it doesn't get more Gold Rush–genuine than this, folks). During the heady mining days, this unusually sophisticated town built the state's first library and its first astronomical observatory. Nowadays you can see some preserved buildings and artifacts, including a Civil War cannon. An outdoor amphitheater, hidden behind stone facades along Main Street, is the site of popular summer theatricals performed by the **Volcano Theatre Company**; 1 block north of the St. George Hotel, (209)296-2525. And at nearby **Indian Grinding**

Rock State Historic Park you'll find an enormous limestone outcropping—the largest of its kind in America—dotted with thousands of holes created by generations of native Miwoks who ground their acorn meal on the rock here. The park also has a fine Indian artifacts museum and a replica of a Miwok ceremonial roundhouse; located off Pine Grove/Volcano Road, 1½ miles north of Highway 88, (209)296-7488. After touring the town, take the side trip up winding Ram's Horn Grade to cool off in the funky, friendly bar at the **St. George Hotel** (see review, below). Or, in early spring, picnic amid the nearly half-million daffodils (and more than 100 varieties) in bloom on **Daffodil Hill**, a 4-acre ranch 3 miles north of Volcano (follow the signs on Ram's Horn Grade; there is no phone).

## *LODGINGS*

**St. George Hotel**  In its heyday in the 1860s, the burgeoning village of Volcano offered a tired miner his choice of 17 hotels. Those whose pockets held the largest nuggets chose the St. George. Although its elegance has faded considerably over the last century, this three-story hotel wrapped with balconies entwined with trumpet vine and wisteria is still a gold mine for anyone spending an evening in this little town. By modern standards, the 14 guest rooms in the main building are not even slightly luxurious: they share four bathrooms, lack air conditioning, and are not heated—which has led to many a miserable experience for unwary winter travelers. The rooms in back have great views of the garden, but heat up quickly in the early morning summer sun; your best bet is to ask for a balcony room in front. Avoid the six rooms with baths in the modern annex (built in 1961)—they're dingy and dark. On Saturday nights, Sara Gillick, a fourth-generation Volcanoan and St. George's cook for more than 40 years, prepares slabs of prime rib fit for a prospector-size appetite. The reasonable room rates include breakfast and dinner for two in the hotel dining room, which is open to the public for dinner by reservation only. Please note that at the time this book went to press, the St. George was sold, so hotel and restaurant hours and details are subject to change. ■ *2 Main St (can't miss it), Volcano; (209)296-4458; mail: PO Box 9, Volcano, CA 95689; $$; full bar; AE, MC, V; checks OK; breakfast Sat–Sun (Thurs–Mon for guests only), dinner by reservation only Wed–Sun (call for winter hours).*

**Volcano**

## JACKSON

Just beyond an enormous Georgia Pacific lumber mill lies Jackson, the seat of Amador County. Jackson hides most of its rowdy past behind modern facades, but old-timers know the town (once called "little Reno") as the last place in California to outlaw prostitution. For a trip back in time, take a gander at the **National Hotel**, which has been in continuous operation since 1862 and has built up quite a guest list: Will Rogers, John Wayne, Leland Stanford, and almost every other California governor in the last century stayed here. Ragtime tunes and classic oldie sing-alongs are played on the grand piano, and guests register for the spartan rooms with the bartender through a wooden cage at the back of the saloon; 2 Water Street at Main Street, (209)223-0500.

A sight Gold Rush buffs shouldn't miss is the **Amador County Museum**, which has scale models of the local hard-rock mines. It's open Wednesday through Sunday; 225 Church Street, (209)223-6386. There's also **Kennedy Tailing Wheels Park**, site of the Kennedy and Argonaut Mines, the Mother Lode's deepest. Though these mines have been closed for decades, their head-frames and huge tailing wheels (some are 58 feet in diameter) remain to help show how waste from the mines was conveyed over the hills to a settling pond. The park is also home to the white, picturesque **St. Sava's Servian Orthodox Church**, built in 1894 and surrounded by a cemetery; to reach the park, take Main Street to Jackson Gate Road, just north of Jackson (there is no phone). If you're a wannabe gold panner, hire a guide to take you to **Roaring Camp Mining Company** on the Mokelumne River, where you can try your luck and enjoy a cookout; call (209)296-4100 for more information.

▼

▲

## RESTAURANTS

**Upstairs Restaurant & Streetside Bistro** ★★  Chef Layne McCollum, who learned his trade at the California Culinary Academy, presides over this two-story restaurant housed in a handsome Gold Rush–era building made of exposed brick and petrified wood. The bright, cheery Streetside Bistro—tastefully furnished with wrought iron furniture, tile flooring, and colorful oil paintings—offers quiche, soups, salads, and gourmet sand-wiches such as smoked pork loin with red chile pesto for lunch until about 2:30pm; afterwards, it remains open for wine, house-roasted espresso drinks, and appetizers. For dinner, take the stairway to the Upstairs Restaurant, a long, narrow room of exposed brick and glass furnished with a dozen blond wood tables topped with fresh flowers and oil lamps. McCollum's small, contemporary American menu features a half-dozen entrees and some daily specials that might include pasta puttanesca prepared with tomato-basil fettuccine, a medley of smoked vegetables grilled with pesto, shrimp scampi sautéed in lemon-garlic sauce, or a grilled boneless breast of duck topped with blackberry-ginger sauce. Whether you're staying in Jackson or just passing through, this is the best place in town to rest and refuel. ■ *164 Main St (downtown), Jackson; (209)223-3342; $$; beer and wine; DIS, MC, V; checks OK; lunch, dinner Tues–Sun.*

**Mel and Faye's Diner** ★  Mel and Faye have been churning out good eats at their highway-side diner since 1956, and the place is still a favorite, primarily because you pay small prices for big burgers. Mel chops the onions himself for his special Moo-Burger, a sloppy double cheeseburger smothered in onions and a special sauce that will stick with you for the rest of the day. The shakes are thick enough to properly clog your straw, but skip the pies. ■ _205 Hwy 49 (at Main St, at the bottom of the hill), Jackson; (209) 223-0853; $; beer and wine; no credit cards; local checks only; breakfast, lunch, dinner every day._

_LODGINGS_

**Court Street Inn** ★★  Dave and Nancy Butow's pretty 1872 Victorian inn, with its tin ceilings, redwood staircase, and marble fireplace, has earned a well-deserved spot on the National Register of Historic Places. A two-minute stroll from Main Street, the inn's seven guest rooms (all with private baths) are loaded with vintage furnishings. The Rose Court Room, one of the largest in the house, has an adjoining sitting room that's perfect for a lazy read of the morning paper. The rustic Indian House is a private two-room cottage with a wood-burning fireplace, a piano, cushy furniture, a porch swing, and an enormous 61-inch TV with VCR and cable that's discreetly tucked away for those who prefer to ignore such electronic entertainment centers. On warm summer mornings, a bounteous Butow breakfast is served on the back garden patio—a perk that guests like as much as the inviting hot tub. ■ _215 Court St (just off Church St), Jackson, CA 95642; (209) 223-0416 or (800) 200-0416; court_st_inn@msn.com; www.isgnet.com/ctstinn/; $$; AE, DIS, MC, V; checks OK._

## IONE

_LODGINGS_

**The Heirloom Bed and Breakfast Inn** ★★★  One of the most charming B&Bs in the Gold Country is run by business partners Patricia Cross and Melisande Hubbs, who have turned this Southern antebellum mansion into one of the ultimate bed-and-breakfast experiences. The English garden? Breathtaking. The sitting room? Captivating. The rooms? Immaculate. The breakfast? Delicious. The price? Surprisingly, this is one of the lowest-priced B&Bs in the region, which makes it more than worth your while to pull out the map and search for Ione, a former supply center during the booming Gold Rush days. Each of the inn's six guest rooms is cleverly named to correspond to its seasonal advantages. The Summer Room is shaded by a 150-year-old walnut tree; the Springtime Room's private balcony overlooks the garden; and the Winter Room has a fireplace, an extra-long tub, a colonial four-poster bed, and handmade quilts. The Rooms For All Seasons are in a detached two-unit cottage built of handcrafted

16-inch-thick rammed-earth walls (which maintain pleasant temperatures year-round), framed by California cedars, redwoods, and pines, and topped with an honest-to-God sod roof. Each cottage unit has a wood-burning stove, too. For the ultimate in luxury, guests may have their breakfast served in bed (although this isn't an option for guests in the cottage) or, if you prefer, outside on the veranda or in the dining room. And no matter how many times you stay at the Heirloom, the proprietors promise never to prepare you the same breakfast twice. Golf buffs will be happy to know that the 18-hole Castle Oaks Championship Golf Course is only a block away. ■ *214 Shakeley Lane (downtown), Ione; (209)274-4468; mail: PO Box 322, Ione, CA 95640; $$; AE, MC, V; checks OK.* ♿ *cottages only*

## SAN ANDREAS

In 1883, the law finally caught up with the famous gentleman-bandit Black Bart at this former grungy mining camp. The legendary stagecoach robber was famous for being extremely polite to his victims and leaving poetry at the scene of his numerous crimes. He served five years in San Quentin prison and was never heard from again after his release in 1888. There isn't much to see in San Andreas, the seat of the Calaveras County government, except for the very good **Calaveras County Historical Museum**, full of gold-mining relics, Miwok Indian artifacts, and the courtroom where Black Bart was convicted; 30 North Main Street (in the old courthouse), (209)754-6579.

*LODGINGS*

**Robin's Nest** ★ If you need a pleasant place to spend the night in this foothill whistle-stop, the accommodations in this nine-room, 100-year-old Queen Anne Victorian building (the best-looking in town by a long shot) are quite cozy. The inn's five upstairs rooms, carved into the sloping rooflines of the very large converted attic, are bright and airy. Downstairs, the spacious Snyder Suite features a 7-foot-long bathtub and a brass shower. The Carriage Room, with a private entrance, phone, and TV, is favored by business clientele. Innkeepers Bill and Karen Konietzny's bountiful breakfasts start with a seasonal fruit soup, followed by fresh-baked rolls and breads (don't pass up the sticky buns), an egg dish such as eggs Benedict or a soufflé, and a dessert. ■ *247 W Saint Charles St (facing Hwy 49, between Russells and Church Hill Rds), San Andreas; (209)754-1076 or (888)214-9202; mail: PO Box 1408, San Andreas, CA 95249; www.touristguide.com-b&b/ca/ robinsnest; $$; AE, DIS, MC, V; checks OK.*

## ANGELS CAMP

Cruise right through the overcommercialized and truly uninspiring town of San Andreas, and you'll eventually pull into Angels

Camp, made famous by Mark Twain's short story "The Cele-brated Jumping Frog of Calaveras County." Every year on the third weekend in May, thousands of frog fans flock to the **Calaveras County Fair** to witness the **Jumping Frog Jubilee**, one of the premier frog-jumping contests in the world. The festival takes place at the county fairgrounds, 2 miles south of town, (209)736-2561, and features a rodeo, carnival rides, live music, and—for those of you who forgot to bring one—frogs for rent. *Ribbit.*

## RESTAURANTS

**Camps** ★★★  A bit hard to find, Camps is ensconced within a sprawling golf resort on the western fringes of Angels Camp, but it's definitely worth seeking out. Executive chef Jean Paul Lucy's fusion cuisine pairs local produce with European, Asian, and Caribbean cooking techniques. A French chef in *Angels Camp*? Yep—and this sleepy little Gold Rush town will soon become one of Northern California's newest destination retreats as savvy developers take advantage of its blue skies, balmy weather, and soothing vistas. Fortunately, Camps's architects have adopted a Julia Morganesque approach to their low-impact design, building this high-ceilinged restaurant/clubhouse from locally mined rhyolite, painting it in natural earth tones, and adding furnishings like natural leather armchairs, wicker, and antique woods. Then there's the food: everything from a wildflower salad with American field greens, toasted pine nuts, and a raspberry hazelnut vinaigrette to crisp roasted duck with kumquat and sun-dried cherries or perhaps a marinated demi-rack of lamb grilled with an essence of sweet bay and thyme. Sounds good, is good. Come see for yourself, and request a table on the veranda. Oh, and PGA wannabes shouldn't forget their golf clubs. ▪ *676 McCauley Ranch Rd (½ mile W of the junctions of Hwys 4 and 49, off Angel Oaks Dr), Angels Camp; (209)736-8181; $$$; full bar; MC, V; checks OK; breakfast Fri–Sat, brunch Sun, lunch Mon–Sat, dinner Wed–Sun.* ♿

**B of A Cafe** ★★  Owner Katherine Reese, who also runs the Cooper House Bed and Breakfast Inn (see review, below), has done a bang-up job of converting this 1936 Bank of America building into a bright, lively cafe that attracts crowds of tourists and locals alike. Using leftover artifacts, she adorned her cafe's walls with polished teller windows, partially removed the second floor to add balcony seating, and converted the vault into a wine tasting room. ("If anyone shuts the vault door I'm done for," Katherine admits, "because I don't know the combination.") Lunch items range from gourmet baby greens salads and a country-style quiche of the day to roasted eggplant sandwiches with herbed mayonnaise on multigrain bread. For dinner the chef caters to local meat eaters with her juicy lemon-rosemary chicken and marinated baby back ribs—both slow-cooked in a rotisserie oven—and sliced pork loin marinated with an Australian maple-syrup-based sauce. There's always a daily fresh fish, pasta, and

▼

**Angels Camp**

▲

vegetable dish on the menu, too, and all entrees are served with
fresh bread, soup or salad, and Kathy's Famous Herbed Roasted
Red Potatoes. B of A (which Reese says stands for Bistro of
Angels) also offers inexpensive Basque-style dinners—steak,
chicken, or lamb with tureens of soup, salad, and pasta—on
Sunday night, but be sure to make a reservation because the
seats get booked up fast. ■ *1262 S Main St (near the intersection
of Hwys 4 and 49), Angels Camp; (209)736-0765; $$; beer and
wine; MC, V; local checks only; lunch Wed–Mon, dinner Thurs–Sun.*

*Gold Country*

*LODGINGS*

**Cooper House Bed and Breakfast Inn** ★   This 1911 restored
Craftsman-style bungalow was originally built for Dr. George P.
Cooper, a former Angels Camp physician, to serve as both his
home and his office. The small B&B, the only one in town, is nes-
tled in a quaint garden setting well away from the main highway.
The names of the three suites (Zinfandel, Cabernet, and
Chardonnay) are indicative of the influence the winemaking com-
munity has had on this town. All of the rooms have private baths.
A commanding greenstone-and-quartz fireplace in the living
room beckons on cold nights. An expanded continental breakfast
is served in the morning and complimentary wines and appe-
tizers are served each afternoon. ■ *1184 Church St (from Main
St, turn E on Raspberry Lane), Angels Camp; (209)736-2145 or
(800)225-3764 ext. 326; mail: PO Box 1388, Angels Camp, CA
95222; $$; DIS, MC, V; checks OK.*

▼

**Murphys**

▲

## MURPHYS

Gingerbread Victorian homes peek from behind white picket
fences and tall locust trees border the streets of Murphys, a
former trading post set up by brothers Dan and John Murphy in
cooperation with local Native Americans (John married the
chief's daughter). It's worth taking the detour off Highway 49 just
to stroll down Murphys' tree-lined Main Street or better yet, to
sample a pint of **Murphys Brewing Company's** outstanding
Murphys Red, served on tap at the Murphys Historic Hotel and
Lodge (see review, below).

Eighteen miles northeast of Murphys on Highway 4 is **Calaveras Big Trees State Park**, a popular summer retreat that offers
camping, swimming, hiking, and fishing along the **Stanislaus
River**; (209)795-2334. Many of the numerous caverns in the area
were discovered in the mid-1800s by gold prospectors and can
now be toured, including **Mercer Caverns**, (209)728-2101, which
has crystalline stalactites and stalagmites in a series of descend-
ing chambers; **Moaning Cavern**, (209)736-2708, where a 100-foot
stairway spirals down into a limestone chamber so huge it could
house the Statue of Liberty; and **California Caverns**, (209)736-
2708 (reservations required), the West's first commercially
developed cave and the largest single cave system in Northern

485

California (it has yet to be fully explored). For more information on the caverns, plug into the Web site at www.caverntours.com.

## RESTAURANTS

**Grounds** ★★ River Klass, a handsome young transplant from the East Coast, opened this fantastic coffeehouse and cafe in 1993. Many locals have become addicted to the Grounds' potato pancakes (served with every made-to-order omelet), and lunch favorites include the grilled eggplant sandwich stuffed with smoked mozzarella and fresh basil and the sausage sandwich on house-baked bread. The dinner menu changes frequently, but recent winners were the fettuccine topped with sautéed shrimp, halibut, and mussels in a garlic cream sauce; a juicy pot roast with steamed red potatoes; oven-roasted sweetheart ham with glazed yams; and a good ol' New York steak with caramelized onions and half-mashed red potatoes. To spice things up a bit, Klass serves only Mexican food on Mondays. The long, narrow dining rooms are bright and airy with pine furnishings, wood floors, and an open kitchen. On sunny days, request a table on the back patio. Reservations are strongly recommended for dinner. ■ *402 Main St (downtown), Murphys; (209) 728-8663; $$; beer and wine; DIS, MC, V; checks OK; breakfast, lunch, dinner Thurs–Mon.* &

## LODGINGS

**Dunbar House, 1880** ★★★ Without question, Dunbar House is among the finest B&Bs in the Gold Country. Century-old gardens adorn this lovely Italianate home built in 1880 by Wills Dunbar, a superintendent for the Union Water Company, for his bride. The lush grounds are complemented by a two-person hammock, a gazebo, a rose garden with benches, and a swing. All four guest rooms are furnished with wood-burning stoves, heirloom antiques, down pillows and comforters, and vases of fresh flowers for dashes of vibrant color. The Cedar Room offers a private sun porch and a two-person whirlpool bath, while the Sugar Pine two-room suite comes with English towel warmers, a CD/stereo system, and a balcony perched among the elm trees. For breakfast, fresh juices, coffee, housemade pastries, and a main dish such as the fabulous concoction of crab and cheese atop an English muffin are served in your room, at the dining room table, or in the gorgeous garden. ■ *271 Jones St (just off Main St), Murphys; (209) 728-2897 or (800) 692-6006; mail: PO Box 1375, Murphys, CA 95247; dunbarhs@goldrush.com; www.dunbarhouse.com; $$; AE, MC, V; checks OK.*

**The Redbud Inn** ★★ A town in great need of luxury accommodations, Murphys hadn't celebrated the opening of a new inn in more than a century until October 1993, when the Redbud opened its doors. Proprietors Pam and Steve Hatch have been busy ever since, and their painstaking attention to detail is evident in each of the 13 individually decorated guest rooms. All are exquisitely furnished with brass or antique beds, family heirlooms and mementos, antique baths and sinks, fireplaces, wood-burning stoves, and original artwork. The immaculate Anniversary Suite features a private balcony, a wet bar, a double-sided fireplace, a peach-and-white king-size bed, and an enormous, inviting spa tub. Guests are treated to a full breakfast and, in the evening, hors d'oeuvres and locally produced wine. You can also pamper yourself with a massage or an herbal bath at the Redbud by appointment. The inn's only drawback is the lack of scenery—it's located in a small shopping complex. ■ *402 Main St (in the Miner's Exchange Complex), Murphys, CA 95247; (209)728-8533 or (800)827-8533; innkeeper@redbudinn.com; www.redbudinn.com; $$; DIS, MC, V; checks OK.* &

**The Trade Carriage House** ★★ Two blocks from downtown Murphys in a quiet residential neighborhood stands Charlie and Cynthia Trade's pride and joy: the Trade Carriage House. Guarded by fruit trees, strawberry patches, and a white picket fence, this two-bedroom cottage has a full kitchen, a private veranda, a queen-size and a double bed with down comforters, and a profusion of wicker and antique furnishings. Small, cozy, and charming, it's the winsome hideaway that every city dweller would like to own for romantic weekend retreats. The Trade Carriage House is also near the Gold Country's best attractions—wineries, state parks, ski areas, golf courses, and caverns. ■ *600 Algiers St, Murphys; (209)728-3408 or (800)800-3408 (days), (209)728-3909 (evenings); 230 Big Trees Rd, Murphys, CA 95247; sales@realtyworld-murphys.com; www.realtyworld-murphys.com; $$; no credit cards; checks OK.*

**Murphys Historic Hotel and Lodge** ★ When this hotel opened in 1856, who could have known what kind of characters would pass through its doors? The illustrious guest register includes Ulysses S. Grant, Mark Twain, Horatio Alger, and Black Bart, to name just a few. Although its days of housing dignitaries are long past, this national- and state-registered landmark still maintains its hold as Murphys' social center. Any time of day or night you'll find a few locals here hunched over stools and voicing their opinions and politely ignoring the tourists who stop in for a bed or a drink or both (try the terrific Murphys Red draft). The main building has nine historic guest rooms that reflect turn-of-the-century lifestyles (that is, no phones, televisions, or private baths), while the newer building offers 20 modern rooms with private bathrooms. In the dining area you'll find huge platters of chicken, beef, seafood, and pasta, but the lackluster service and mediocre cuisine usually discourages most visitors from coming back (especially now that the estimable Grounds restaurant is just down the street). ■ *457 Main St (downtown), Murphys; (209)728-3444 or (800)532-7684; mail: PO Box 329, Murphys, CA 95247; $$; full bar; AE, DC, DIS, MC, V; checks OK; breakfast, lunch, dinner every day.*

▼

**Murphys**

*Lodgings*

▲

Some mighty fortunate 49ers unearthed a staggering $87 million in gold in this former boisterous mining town, once the state's second largest city (it was only two votes shy of becoming the state capital over Sacramento). But when the gold no longer panned out in the late 1850s, Columbia's population of 15,000 nearly vanished. In 1945, the entire town was turned into **Columbia State Historic Park**, a true Gold Country treasure. This is the Mother Lode's best-preserved park, filled with historic facades and mining artifacts. Follow the free, short, self-guided park tour, and don't miss the **Wells Fargo Express Office**, a former stagecoach center, and the restored **Columbia School-house**, which was in use until 1937. Big-time Gold Rush buffs who want more area history should pick up the inexpensive walking-tour booklet at the visitors center or sign up for a guided mine tour. For a more leisurely view of the park, hop aboard one of the horse-drawn stagecoaches. And to learn how to pan for gold, ask about the **Matelot Gulch Mining Company's** free lessons or call park information at (209)532-4301.

### RESTAURANTS

▼

**Columbia**

▲

**Columbia House Restaurant** ★ This American restaurant has had its ups and downs over the years, but locals still come to Columbia House for its hearty breakfasts: bacon and eggs, biscuits and gravy, and buttermilk pancakes that would make any miner feel at home. Lunch is just as filling, with basic fare such as soup, chili, burgers, sandwiches, steak, and chicken, which should all be washed down with the locally made sarsaparilla. ■ *On the corner of State and Main Sts, Columbia; (209)532-5134; $; beer and wine; MC, V; local checks only; breakfast, lunch every day, group dinners by reservation only.*

### LODGINGS

**City Hotel** ★★★ City folk who frequented this opulent hotel in 1856 called it the Gem of the Southern Mines. Predictably, the building has gone through several incarnations since then, including stints as a gold-assay shop and a dance hall. When the town was turned into a state historic park in 1945, visitors once again returned to this venerable landmark. In the '70s, nearby Columbia College obtained grant money to renovate the structure and turn it into a hotel-hospitality training center, and now students assist the staff here. The lobby is fitted with period settees and marble-top tables, and six of the ten high-ceilinged rooms face a central parlor, the setting for an elaborate continental breakfast. Rooms 1 and 2 have balconies overlooking Main Street. All of the rooms have half-baths, with showers down the hall, and the hotel provides comfy robes, slippers, and wicker baskets full of toiletries to ease the trip.

The **City Hotel Restaurant** is a rarity—a culinary palace in the heart of a state park. Inside, it's decked out with red velvet drapes, oil paintings, and antique furniture topped with crisp linens and flowers. If this is Hotel Hospitality Class 101, these are 4.0 students—the serving staff even dresses in period costumes. You may order from the small prix-fixe or à la carte menus featuring peppered filet of beef and giant house-smoked shrimp with garlic-herb butter and sour-cream mashed potatoes, seared salmon steak with dill hollandaise and a crisp cucumber-mint salad, or perhaps walnut-crusted rack of lamb with pomegranate sauce and yam and mushroom croquettes. For dessert, diners who can wait 30 minutes will be justly rewarded with a lemon soufflé crowned with Grand Marnier sauce. California vintages feature prominently on the wine list. While you wait for your dinner table, spend some time in the hotel's saloon, called What Cheer. Reservations are essential on weekends and recommended during the week. ■ *On Main St (between Jackson and State Sts), Columbia; (209)532-1479 or (800)532-1479; mail: PO Box 1870, Columbia, CA 95310; info@cityhotel.com; www.cityhotel.com; $$ (hotel), $$$ (restaurant); full bar; AE, DIS, MC, V; checks OK; brunch Sun, dinner Tues–Sun.*

**Fallon Hotel** ★★ In 1988, this 1850s hostelry was beautifully refurbished to a more elegant 1890s splendor with embossed wallpapers, antique oak furnishings, ornate porcelain basins, and pull-chain toilets. It's a far cry from the building's early days as a courthouse, a bakery, and ultimately a sparsely furnished miners' rooming house. The adjoining Fallon Theatre (still in operation) was built right before the turn of the century. Just like the staff at the City Hotel (see review, above), some of the workers here are hospitality trainees from Columbia College. Fallon Hotel's 14 bedrooms are quite small, so request one of the five larger balcony rooms. Robes, slippers, and baskets brimming with soap, shampoo, and towels make the walk to the showers down the hall practically painless. A continental breakfast, served in the ice cream parlor, is included in the room rate. ■ *On Washington St (at Parrots Ferry Rd), Columbia; (209)532-1470; mail: PO Box 1870, Columbia, CA 95310; info@cityhotel.com; www.cityhotel.com; $$; AE, DIS, MC, V; checks OK.*

Sonora

## SONORA

When the traffic starts to crawl along Highway 49, you're probably closing in on Sonora. In 49er days, Sonora competed with Columbia for the title of wealthiest city in the southern Mother Lode. Today, it is the Gold Country's largest and most crowded town and the Tuolumne County seat. If you have time to spare, search for a parking space along Washington Street (no easy feat on weekends), feed the meter, and take a look at the well-preserved 19th-century **St. James Episcopal Church**, at the top of

Washington Street, and the **Tuolumne County Museum**, located in the century-old jail at 158 West Bradford Street, (209)532-1317. If you really have time to kill, take a leisurely drive along the picturesque **Detour Route 108**, which heads west into the Sierra Nevada over Sonora Pass, and through several scenic alpine communities.

### RESTAURANTS

**Good Heavens: A Food Concern** ★★ According to local lore, this historic building lined with old-fashioned paintings once housed a coffin-maker downstairs and a bordello upstairs. For the last dozen years, however, it's been the setting for a delightful boutique cafe noted for its very good daily lunch specials, including a divine mushroom, spinach, Monterey Jack, and turkey sausage crêpe topped with a creamy lemon sauce and served with a Parmesan-pasta flan and fresh steamed vegetables. Standard menu items include house-made soups and salads and a creative selection of sandwiches and hamburgers. Each meal starts with fresh herb-and-cheese biscuits and a choice of owner/chef Don Hartwell's wonderful freshly made jams, such as tart orange marmalade with walnuts or rich raspberry-chocolate (and for Good Heavens' sake, don't leave without purchasing a jar or two). Even *Gourmet* magazine wants the recipe for Hartwell's butter cake, but he has politely declined since he hopes to publish his own cookbook someday. ■ *49 N Washington St (downtown), Sonora; (209)532-3663; $; beer and wine; no credit cards; checks OK; lunch Tues–Sun.*

*Sonora*

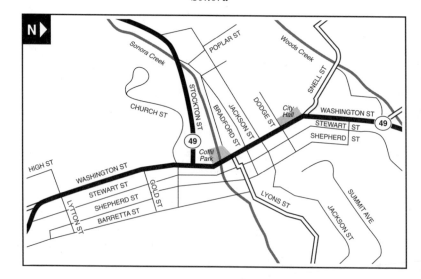

**North Beach Cafe** ★★ Terry La Torre, a longtime local and a progeny of San Francisco restaurateurs, has turned this former auto parts store into one of Sonora's most popular restaurants. Part of his success is due to his skillful cooking, but the crux of his customers come simply to bask in La Torre's infectious pomposity. Part Falstaff, part Orson Welles, the well-rounded, mustachioed La Torre can usually be found draped in chef's whites, expounding to his adoring staff as he deftly flips a New York steak on his mesquite grill. (Sitting at the counter facing the open kitchen is not for the timid or introverted, since La Torre will inevitably impale you with offhanded inquiries.) The simple lunch menu features chicken and steak sandwiches, burgers, soups, and salads, while the predominantly Italian dinner menu offers a dozen or so pastas, fresh fish, veal, chicken, and steak. Standout dishes are the pork tenderloin and the triangle tip in mushroom sauce. The pasta and fish plates, such as the petrale sole in lemon butter, tend to get drowned with La Torre's sauces, but prices are so low—and his histrionics so entertaining—that it's hard to complain. ■ *14317 Mono Way/Hwy 108 (from central Sonora, drive 3 miles E on Hwy 108 to John's Sierra Market and turn into the parking lot), Sonora; (209)536-1852; $$; beer and wine; no credit cards; checks OK; brunch Sun, lunch Mon–Sat, dinner every day.* &

**Banny's** ★ Nancy Hoffman, innkeeper at the Ryan House B&B around the corner (see review, below), has been sending her guests here for years and has yet to hear a complaint about the food. As for the decor, well . . . peach-colored walls with forest-green trim, charcoal-colored carpet, and cheap floral tablecloths topped with glass evoke a tired, slightly tacky ambience. Yet everybody in town agrees that chef/owner Rob Bannworth is a darn good cook, and you certainly can't complain about the reasonable prices he charges for a braised veal shank with wine beans and applewood-smoked bacon ragout; pan-roasted duckling with currants, chile, and a red wine glacé; and marinated rack of lamb grilled with mint and roasted garlic. Expect to pay almost *half* of what you'd pay in the San Francisco Bay Area for fare of equal quality. Decor aside, Banny's is a good bet. ■ *83 S Stewart St, Suite 100 (in Old Town), Sonora; (209)533-4709; $$; beer and wine; DIS, MC, V; checks OK; lunch Mon–Sat, dinner every day.* &

## LODGINGS

**Barretta Gardens Inn** ★★ Expansive gardens of native flowering shrubs surround this small country inn on a hillside southeast of downtown Sonora. The wraparound porch is perfect for curling up with a good book (or your honey) in spring or autumn. Winter conversation takes place on soft sofas around the fireplace in the comfortable living room. Barretta Gardens has five guest rooms, and the most impressive is the pretty Christy Room, fashioned after a late 18th-century Italian suite. The innkeepers greet guests in the afternoon with a beverage, and treat them the following morning to a generous breakfast of apple puff pancakes, freshly baked muffins, and fresh-squeezed juices served in the dining room or, when it's warm, on the porch. Try not to miss the inn's wonderful view of the sunset. ■ *700 S Barretta St (a few blocks E of Washington St), Sonora, CA 95370; (209)532-6039 or (800)206-3333; barretta@mlode.com; www.sonnet.com/dancers/bandb/ barretta; $$; AE, MC, V; checks OK.*

**Lulu Belle's Bed and Breakfast** ★★ One of the few Gold Country B&Bs that welcome families, Denise Morris's century-old Victorian is surrounded by a spacious lawn and rose garden that beckon guests to an afternoon siesta outdoors. Located only a few blocks from historic downtown Sonora, the inn has five guest rooms—two inside the main house and three in a quiet carriage house—all with private baths. The Parlor Suite, perfect for honeymooners, is gussied up in red velvet and crystal with a queen-size brass bed, a bathtub, and an adjoining parlor. The furnishings throughout the rest of the house are in keeping with the casual, unstuffy atmosphere. Impromptu concerts take place in the music room when guests take their turn at the flute, piano, organ, and guitar. A full country breakfast is served in the dining area or on the patio if weather permits. ■ *85 Gold St (off Washington St, downtown), Sonora, CA 95370; (209)533-3455 or (800)538-3455; lulubelle@goldrush.com; www.lulubelle.com; $$; AE, DIS, MC, V; checks OK.*

**Ryan House, 1855** ★★ When Dennis and Susan Ryan came to the United States in 1855 from Cork, Ireland, to escape the potato famine, they settled in booming Sonora and built their dream house, which stayed in the family until the early 1980s. It is now a picture-perfect B&B owned by Guy and Nancy Hoffman that retains its authentic 19th-century architectural details—everything from the square nails to the handmade windows (with original glass, no less!). The only drawback is its small size, but the three guest rooms have unexpectedly high ceilings, cheerful wallpaper, antique furnishings, queen-size beds with handmade quilts, and private baths. In 1992, the Hoffmans converted the attic into a spacious three-room suite with a parlor, a gas-log cast-iron stove, a two-person soaking tub, a queen-size brass-and-iron bed, and a pleasant view of downtown Sonora (it's a popular choice among honeymooners). Guests often gather around the library's gas-log fireplace to sip complimentary sherry and port. In the morning, if the weather's nice, breakfast is served in the rose garden; otherwise, the repast is enjoyed in the formal dining room. Be sure to sample Nancy's special scones—so good they were featured in *Country Inns* magazine. ■ *153 S Shepherd St (2 blocks E of N Washington St), Sonora, CA 95370; (209)533-3445 or (800)831-4897; www.ryanhouse.com; $$; AE, MC, V; checks OK.*

**Serenity** ★★ It's not easy to find this secluded inn, tucked away at the end of a country road on 6 acres of mixed forest just outside Sonora. The antique-filled house combines the gracious atmosphere of the past with the modern conveniences of the present. Guests may entertain themselves with board games, cards, and the books that fill a small sunlit upstairs library. A wraparound veranda encourages nothing more strenuous than basking in the sun and waiting for the deer to visit. Proprietor Charlotte Hoover's four-course gourmet breakfast is whipped up in her cavernous kitchen and often consists of treats like gingerbread, mushroom-crust quiche, and fruit cobbler. All four guest rooms have private baths and color-coordinated floral furnishings, as well as a private sitting area; two even have a remote-control gas-log fireplace. If you don't mind the short drive to town for dinner, chances are you'll be perfectly happy at this serene B&B. Plus, the Stanislaus National Forest and Phoenix Lake are only 15 miles away. ■ *15305 Bear Cub Dr (6 miles E of downtown, off Phoenix Lake Rd), Sonora, CA 95370; (209) 533-1441 or (800) 426-1441; serenity@mlode.com; www.serenity-inn.com; $$; AE, DC, DIS, MC, V; checks OK.*

## TWAIN HARTE

### LODGINGS

**McCaffrey House Bed & Breakfast Inn** ★★★ Located in the Stanislaus National Forest, Michael and Stephanie McCaffrey's gorgeous, sprawling three-story country home was built specifically as a B&B, and it's one of the top 10 in the Gold Country. Nowhere else in this region will you find such a winning combination of amenities, style, and service for such reasonable prices. Each of the seven immaculate guest rooms has its own bath with a shower and tub, an individually controlled thermostat, access to a video library of 400 movies, and a private phone and modem jacks. All but two units have private decks. But it's the details that make the difference: a nearby creek to lull you to sleep; a view of the forest from your deck; queen-size quilts handmade by the Amish of Lancaster County, Pennsylvania; a black iron stove in every room; exceptional gallery-quality art adorning the walls; TVs with VCRs stored in pinewood armoires; a library of paperbacks that are yours to keep—and more.

In the summer, breakfast and hors d'oeuvres, wine, and sparkling cider are served on the huge redwood deck, which surrounds the house and overlooks the verdant hollow. Winter attracts families of skiers, who opt for McCaffrey House's bargain ski packages to nearby resorts. Every room in this B&B is a winner, but top honors go to the Evergreen and Burgundy boudoirs, which have unobstructed views of the forest. The McCaffreys and their gaggle of pets are all incredibly friendly—reason enough to return again and again. ■ *23251 Hwy 108*

*(11 miles E of Sonora), Twain Harte; (209)586-0757 or (888)586-0757; mail: PO Box 67, Twain Harte, CA 95383; innkeeper@sierra getaway.com; www.sierragetaway.com; $$; AE, MC, V; checks OK.* &

## JAMESTOWN

Jamestown has been preoccupied with gold since the first fleck was taken out of Woods Creek in 1848; a marker even commemorates the discovery of a 75-pound nugget. For a fee, you can pan for gold at troughs on Main Street or go prospecting with a guide. But gold isn't Jamestown's only claim to fame. For decades, this two-block town lined with picturesque buildings has been Hollywood's favorite Western movie set: scenes from famous flicks like *Butch Cassidy and the Sundance Kid* were shot here, and vintage railway cars and steam locomotives used in such TV classics as *Little House on the Prairie, Bonanza,* and *High Noon* are on display at the **Railtown 1897 State Historic Park**. You can view the vehicles at the roundhouse daily or ride the rails on weekends from April to October and during holiday events, such as the Santa Train in December; located on Fifth Avenue at Reservoir Road, near the center of town, (209)984-3953.

### RESTAURANTS

**Smoke Cafe ★★** One of Jamestown's liveliest restaurants, the Smoke Cafe is named after a 1920s baseball pitcher from the Cleveland Indians who, after a career of smoking fast balls down the pipe, opened this ex-slot-machine saloon. Creative Mexican fare dominates the menu, and favored dishes include the black

*Jamestown*

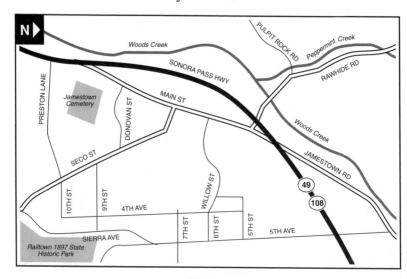

bean burritos, flautas, fajitas, spicy corn chowder, and a powerful garlic soup made with beef broth and sprinkled with croutons and Jack cheese. For a nightcap, ask bartender John Aldabe to make you the Smoke's award-winning After Burner, a potent concoction of Kahlúa, cinnamon, schnapps, and Absolut Peppar. ■ *18191 Main St (downtown), Jamestown; (209) 984-3733; $; full bar; DIS, MC, V; checks OK; dinner Tues–Sun.* ⟂

**Kamm's** ★ Since numerous Chinese were among the miners in search of big gold nuggets, you'd think there would be more remnants of their culture in this part of the state—particularly in the form of Chinese food. But Chinese restaurants are few and far between in the Gold Country. Kamm's is one of the better ones. You'll see a mix of locals and tourists here ordering from the large selection of mild Cantonese dishes and the spicier Hunan and Mongolian fare. ■ *18208 Main St (downtown), Jamestown; (209) 984-3105; $; beer and wine; MC, V; local checks only; lunch Mon–Fri, dinner Mon–Sat.* ⟂

## LODGINGS

**Jamestown Hotel** ★★ Built at the turn of the last century and converted into a hospital in the 1920s, this two-story brick charmer with its Western facade and wood veranda was transformed into a country inn more than a decade ago. Upstairs, each of the eight engaging guest rooms—named after female Gold Rush personalities—are furnished with antiques and private Victorian baths with brass showers. The romantic one-room Lotta Crabtree Suite is furnished with lots of wicker, floral fabrics, and a claw-footed tub. And it's rumored that the fiery Lola Montez haunts her suite, complete with a black iron bed and a claw-footed tub. The huge wood deck at the end of the hall is an ideal spot for a game of backgammon and an iced tea. Downstairs is the handsome saloon, with a fabulous bar that's worth a gander even if you're just passing through. The dining room serves commendable country-style cuisine with a contemporary flair, such as prime rib and pepper steak. ■ *18153 Main St, Jamestown; (209) 984-3902 or (800) 205-4901; mail: PO Box 539, Jamestown, CA 95327; jthotel@ sonnet.com; www.sonnet.com/jthotel; $$; full bar; AE, DC, DIS, MC, V; checks OK; brunch Sun, lunch Mon–Sat, dinner every day.*

**National Hotel** ★★ The restoration of the 1859 National Hotel was so impressive that both the Tuolumne Visitors Bureau and the Tuolumne County Lodging Association bestowed awards for its new look. The restorers of the nine guest rooms did an admirable job of blending 19th-century details (handmade quilts, lace curtains, brass beds) with 20th-century comforts (private bathrooms). The saloon, with its handsome redwood bar, is the best place in town to catch up on local gossip. A generous continental breakfast includes cereals, house-made muffins, hard-boiled eggs, fresh fruit, fresh-squeezed juices, coffee and tea, and the morning paper.

Brunch, lunch, and dinner are served to the public in the handsome old-fashioned dining room, replete with antiques, old photos, and Gold Rush memorabilia. You'll find an extensive array of hearty steak, prime rib, chicken, seafood, and pasta dishes, as well as numerous fine wines and house-made desserts. On sunny days or warm summer nights, ask for a table in the Garden Courtyard, draped by a century-old grape arbor. ■ *77 Main St, Jamestown; (209)984-3446 or (800)894-3446; mail: PO Box 502, Jamestown, CA 95327; national@sonnet.com; www.national-hotel.com; $$; full bar; AE, DC, DIS, MC, V; checks OK; brunch Sun, lunch Mon–Sat, dinner every day.*

## TUOLUMNE

### *LODGINGS*

**Oak Hill Ranch** ★★★ Proprietors Jane and Sanford Grover's son designed this elegant Victorian replica to house more than a quarter-century's worth of collected treasures, including an ornate, multicolored stained-glass window, heirloom furniture, elaborate fireplace mantels, and a mahogany balustrade acquired from an old Victorian mansion. Quintessential B&B hosts with more than 15 years of experience, the Grovers even dress in Victorian costume when they serve your lavish country breakfast in the dining room or gazebo. There are four guest rooms, and top honors go to the Queen Anne–era Eastlake Room, furnished with antiques. The Canopy Room, albeit small, has a private deck overlooking the pond and trees, and families will feel right at home in the Cow Palace, a former milking barn converted into a private cottage that sleeps up to six and has a kitchen. At a 3,000-foot elevation, the Oak Hill Ranch affords a wondrous view of the woods and mountains. And anglers take note: A private pond stocked with bass ("Big ones!" says Sanford) is literally steps from the porch. ■ *18550 Connally Lane (off Apple Colony Rd), Tuolumne; (209)928-4717; mail: PO Box 307, Tuolumne, CA 95379; $$; no credit cards; checks OK.*

## GROVELAND

### *LODGINGS*

**Groveland Hotel** ★★ Constructed in 1849, the adobe Groveland Hotel is one of the Gold Country's oldest buildings; an addition was erected some 65 years later to serve as a rooming house. Several years ago, the hotel underwent a million-dollar renovation, adding a modern conference center and a saloon. Despite the costly upgrades, the place still manages to retain some of the charm of yesteryear. Its 17 guest rooms aren't large, but down comforters and private baths make them quite comfortable, and

they're furnished with attractive European antiques. The best
rooms are the two-room suites equipped with Jacuzzis and fireplaces. The old-fashioned hotel restaurant, a sea of polished
woods, serves American classics such as rack of lamb, baby back
ribs, fresh fish, and pasta. ▪ *18767 Main St, Groveland; (209) 962-
4000 or (800) 273-3314; mail: PO Box 481, Groveland, CA 95321;
peggy@groveland.com; www.groveland.com; $$; beer and wine; AE,
DC, DIS, MC, V; checks OK; dinner every day (Tues–Sun in the
winter).* &

**Berkshire Inn** ★ By the time you reach this Tudor-style B&B, you
will have driven over the foothills and into the mountains. Most
guests come for a weekend of boating, golfing, or hiking at
nearby Pine Mountain Lake Recreation Area, or stop for a night
on their way to Yosemite. Perched on 20 wooded acres, the Berk-
shire Inn has six large bedrooms and four suites with private
entrances (some also have decks). Guests share access to the
large gazebo overlooking the countryside. Other perks include
complimentary wine and a large continental breakfast. ▪ *19950
Hwy 120 (2 miles E of town), Groveland; (209) 962-6744 or
(800) 679-6904; mail: PO Box 207, Groveland, CA 95321; $$; AE,
DIS, MC, V; checks OK.*

**Hotel Charlotte** ★ Charlotte DeFerreri, an ambitious Italian immigrant, built this hotel in 1918 and soon afterward annexed a small
store next door for her dining room. Here she served the men
working on the Hetch Hetchy Water Project, a dam constructed
to collect water for San Francisco after the city's supply was
depleted during the massive 1906 fire. Today the roadside hotel
serves gold panners and folks on their way to Yosemite. Each of
the 11 guest rooms is pleasantly dressed up with an iron bed-
stead, lace curtains, and floral wallpaper; eight rooms have private baths. Country dinners featuring steak, chicken, fresh fish,
and the Saturday night prime-rib special are offered in the dining
room. ▪ *18736 Main St, Groveland; (209) 962-6455 or (800) 961-
7799; mail: PO Box 787, Groveland, CA 95321; $; full bar; AE,
DC, MC, V; no checks; dinner every day (dinner Fri–Mon in the
winter).*

## MARIPOSA

The town clock in the two-story **Mariposa County Courthouse**
has been marking time since 1866. Another town landmark is **St.
Joseph's Catholic Church**, built in 1863, and behind it lies the
entrance to the **Mariposa Mine**, discovered by Kit Carson in
1849 and later purchased by John C. Frémont, who owned most
of the land around these parts.

Two miles south of Mariposa is the **California Mining and
Mineral Museum**, a state geology center. One wing showcases
20,000 glittering gems and minerals; another holds artifacts and

photos that tell California's mining story; 5007 Fairgrounds Road, (209) 742-7625.

A side trip off Highway 49 leads to **Hornitos** (Spanish for "little ovens"), a name that refers to the shape of the tombs on Boot Hill. This formerly lawless burg is nearly a ghost town, though it was once a favorite haunt of Gold Country *bandido* Joaquin Murrieta, whose pickled head was turned over to state authorities in a glass jar for a $1,000 reward in 1853. Weathered old buildings (saloons, fandango halls, and gambling dens) stand around the plaza, some flaunting bullet holes from bygone battles.

## RESTAURANTS

**Charles Street Dinner House ★★**  This 18-year-old landmark isn't as formal as its name might suggest. Rather, it's a hoot—a fun, funky place where the Old West reigns over decor, food, and service. The waitstaff are dressed in period costume and look as though they just stepped out of the historic photos on the wall. Although the culinary offerings—steaks, chops, chicken, seafood—are fairly typical, they are skillfully prepared and well presented. Nightly specials might include broiled chicken breast, rack of lamb, scampi, or prime rib, and all dinners are served with soup and salad. Charles Street Dinner House's latest addition is a 2,000-bottle wine cellar offering an impressive array of vintages. This restaurant is a local favorite, so reservations are recommended on weekends. ■ *5043 Charles St (at Hwy 140 and 7th St), Mariposa; (209) 966-2366; www.yosemite.net/mariposa/restaurants/ csdh; $$; beer and wine; AE, DIS, MC, V; local checks only; dinner Wed–Sun (closed in Jan).*

## LODGINGS

**Meadow Creek Ranch ★★**  A stage stop in the 1850s, this refurbished ranch house is one of the most secluded bed-and-breakfast inns in the Gold Country—a good choice for those looking for serious solitude. There are only two guest rooms, each decorated in an Early American style. The Garden Gate Room, located in an annex to the main house with a private entrance, offers a queen-size bed, sitting area, private bath, and a patio that overlooks the meadow. The cozy Country Cottage, a converted chicken coop that has been beautifully decorated in mahogany, has a queen-size bed imported from Austria, a private bath with a claw-footed tub, and a sitting area. As you enjoy that early morning cup of coffee, wander around the waterwheel and arbor or take a seat on the patio and soak in the scenic surroundings. A hearty breakfast is served family style in the ranch house's spacious dining room. Meadow Creek is usually closed during the winter and reopens on April 1. ■ *2669 Triangle Rd (about 11½ miles S of town on Hwy 49), Mariposa, CA 95338; (209) 966-3843; www.sierranet.net/web/meadow/; $$, AE, DIS, MC, V; checks OK (closed in the winter).*

**Mariposa Hotel Inn** ★ Located in downtown Mariposa, this two-story building is featured on the National Register of Historic Places and was once the LeGrand stage stop, serving stagecoach passengers in the early 1900s. Attractively restored in an Early American style complete with lace curtains, it has five individually decorated rooms with private baths, cable TV, and air conditioning. A continental breakfast is served on the rear garden veranda overlooking the pines. ■ *5029 Hwy 140 (at 6th St), Mariposa; (209)966-4676 or (800)317-3244; mail: PO Box 745, Mariposa, CA 95338; hotelinn@yosemite.net; www.yosemite.net/ mariposa/mhotels/hotel_inn/; $$; AE, DIS, MC, V; checks OK.*

## OAKHURST

### RESTAURANTS

**Erna's Elderberry House** ★★★★ Vienna-born Erna Kubin-Clanin selected this Oakhurst hillside more than a decade ago as the site for her now-famous restaurant and inn. The location is reminiscent of a corner of Provence, and, indeed, after indulging in one of her meals you'll think you've been transported to some European gastronomical paradise. Ever since *The New York Times* praised Erna's Elderberry House as "one of the most elegant and stylish restaurants in the nation," epicureans from around the world have made the pilgrimage to the elaborate Mediterranean-style dining room ensconced among pine trees and elderberry bushes. The prix-fixe dinner is a six-course affair that changes daily. A meal might begin with crab cakes dressed with a cilantro-cucumber sauce or salmon with Madeira gelée and tarragon mayonnaise, followed by a delicate consommé, a dramatic array of salads, and roasted veal medallions with Pernod sauce and pear chutney or perhaps a combination of pork, duck sausage, and veal schnitzel. The sweet finale might be a Sacher torte. Order a bottle of wine from sommelier Renée-Nicole Cubin's award-winning list to match the vintage to the course. Erna also runs the spectacular Château du Sureau (see review, below). ■ *48688 Victoria Lane (off Hwy 41, just W of town), Oakhurst; (559)683-6860; www.integra.fr/ relaischateaux/sureau; $$$; full bar; AE, MC, V; brunch Sun, lunch Wed–Fri, dinner Wed–Mon (closed Jan 2–23).* ♿

**Oakhurst**

*Lodgings*

### LODGINGS

**Château du Sureau** ★★★★ In 1991, when the opulent Château du Sureau was completed (*sureau* is French for "elderberry"), Erna Kubin-Clanin was able to offer her guests a magnificent place to stay after indulging in the exquisite cuisine at her Elderberry House (see review, above). Erna's desire for perfection doesn't stop in the kitchen, as you'll instantly notice once you see the château's massive chandeliers and 19th-century paintings, the cathedral windows framing grand Sierra views, and the imported tiles that complement the limestone baths. The nine guest rooms come replete with goose-down comforters, canopy beds, antiques, Provençal fabrics, tapestries, fresh flowers, and even a CD sound system. The elegant Thyme Room is designed to easily accommodate wheelchairs; the Mint Room has a private entrance for those seeking seclusion; and the Saffron Room has a breathtaking Napoleon III–era bedroom set made of ebony and inlaid ivory. A European-style breakfast is served to all château guests in the cozy dining room or alfresco on the patio. Elsewhere on the grounds lie a fountain, a swimming pool, and a giant outdoor chess court with 3-foot-tall pieces. There's even a tiny chapel where wedding bells occasionally ring. All this luxury comes at a price, of course. But both the Elderberry House and Château du Sureau are one-of-a-kind Gold Country finds—and just about as precious and rare as those golden nuggets in the surrounding countryside. ■ *48688 Victoria Lane (off Hwy 41, just W of town), Oakhurst; (559)683-6860; mail: PO Box 577, Oakhurst, CA 93644; www.integra.fr/relaischateaux/sureau; $$$; full bar; AE, MC, V; brunch Sun, lunch Wed–Fri, dinner Wed–Mon (closed Jan 2–23).* ♿

**Yosemite Gateway Inn** ★  Across town from the Château du Sureau, this Best Western motel's lures (besides the inexpensive prices) are the indoor and outdoor pools that keep the kids entertained while Mom and Pop soak in the spa. Some of the 119 rooms have kitchens, and all have cable TV, phones, and air conditioning. Other amenities include a fitness center, a sun deck, and a laundry room. The **Viewpoint Restaurant** serves better food than you would expect to find at a chain motel. House-made cinnamon rolls, a large salad bar, and tiny, warm loaves of honey-wheat bread are just a few of the selections that lift it a notch above the commonplace. ■ *40530 Hwy 41 (1 mile E of the intersection of Hwys 49 and 41), Oakhurst, CA 93644; (559)683-2378 (inn), (209)683-5200 (restaurant); $; full bar; AE, DC, DIS, MC, V; no checks.* ♿

# CENTRAL VALLEY

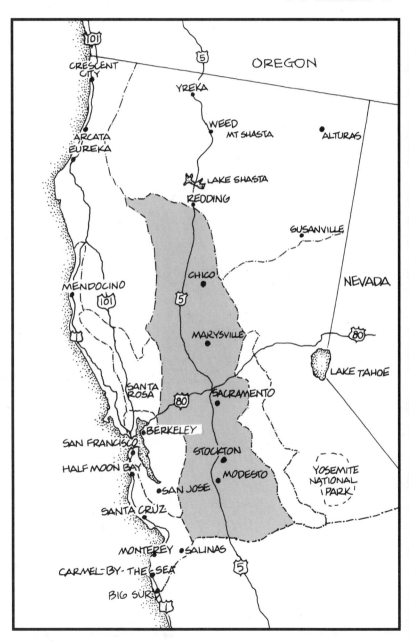

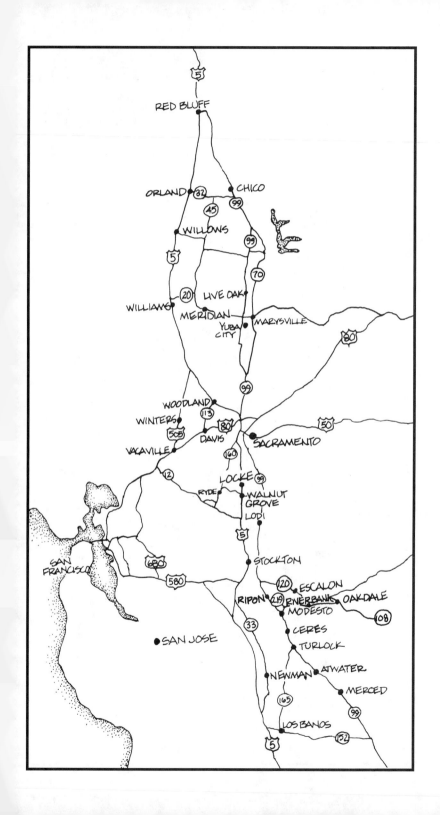

# Central Valley

*A south-to-north tour from Los Banos to Red Bluff along two major routes, Interstate 5 and Highway 99, with side trips to Davis, Vacaville, Marysville, and other valley towns.*

## LOS BANOS

Surrounded by four major highways—Interstate 5 and Highways 152, 33, and 165—the sleepy town of Los Banos calls itself the "Crossroads of California." A more accurate nickname would be "California Pit Stop," since it's nearly impossible to drive through this sparsely populated part of the state without stopping for something—food, gas, or simply to use *los baños.* If you decide to hang around town for a while, you can see remnants of America's halcyon days at the soda fountain at **Los Banos Drugs**, which looks like a set for *Happy Days,* right down to the cherry phosphate; 601 J Street at Sixth Street, (209)826-5834. And if you're overcome with the urge to visit a herd of tule elk, **San Luis National Wildlife Refuge** won't let you down; it's off Highway 165, 8 miles north of Los Banos, (209)826-3508. At the opposite end of town are the **San Luis Reservoir** and **O'Neill Forebay,** a mecca for boaters and water-skiers during the summer; off Highway 152, 12 miles west of Los Banos.

### RESTAURANTS

**España's Mexican Restaurant** ★ Located on cattle baron Henry Miller's Canal Farm Ranch, España's offers a full range of traditional Mexican dishes such as house-made tamales, enchiladas, tacos, and flautas, plus a small selection of steak, chicken, and seafood entrees. Try the *sopa de albóndigas* (meatball soup), the Baja-style salmon with Cajun spices, or the delicate crab enchiladas, and wash it down with a pitcher of margaritas. Most of España's entrees are available to go, too. ■ *1460 E Pacheco Blvd (E of Hwy 165), Los Banos; (209)826-4041; $; full bar; AE, DIS, MC, V; local checks only; lunch, dinner every day.* &

**Wool Growers Restaurant** ★ This old-time Basque restaurant, run by the Iturbide brothers, is a Los Banos institution. If you've never experienced a real Basque feast, it's a great place to start. The meals always begin with a steaming bowl of spicy vegetable soup served with a side of beans (which you may mix into your soup if you like), a tossed green salad, and a lamb stew appetizer. Then comes the meat of the meal: steak, chicken, lamb chops, or prime rib with a side of fries or

503

chicken-sautéed rice. Red wine (the pour-and-gulp variety) is always served with your dinner, too (it's a Basque tradition). The feast isn't final until you get the last course: a cup of vanilla ice cream or slices of Monterey Jack cheese. The question is, will you be able to wolf it all down? ■ *609 H St (between 6th and 7th Sts), Los Banos; (209)826-4593; $; full bar; no credit cards; no checks; lunch, dinner Tues–Sun.* &

## NEWMAN

### *RESTAURANTS*

**Marty's Inn** ★ A favorite on the west side of Stanislaus County, Leonard and Amelia Silvey's rustic, wood-paneled steak house has a mellow, lodgelike atmosphere and a simple menu that has kept its unpretentious clientele satisfied since 1955. Your best bet here is the steak sandwich—a generous slab of beef on a French roll. Marty's barroom, however, is the main attraction, especially on a typical sizzling-hot summer day when the heavenly margaritas are flowing. ■ *29030 Hwy 33 (just S of town), Newman; (209)862-1323; $$; full bar; MC, V; local checks only; lunch Thurs–Fri, dinner Tues–Sun.*

## MERCED

Merced has claimed the title "Gateway to Yosemite" for more than a century, and the majority of its visitors are San Francisco Bay Area residents just passing through. Those who stop long enough to look around usually end up at **Applegate Park**, a 23-acre greenbelt with more than 60 varieties of trees, an immaculate rose garden, a small, free zoo, and, in the summer, amusement rides to whirl and twirl you and the kids; it's located between M and R Streets. On Thursday evening local farmers sell their fresh produce from 6pm to 9pm on Main Street (between N and K Streets), a good place to buy picnic basket ingredients. One of the more interesting sights in the area is the **Old Courthouse Museum**, the pride and joy of Merced and a monument to the early settlers of the Great Central Valley; 2222 N Street, (209)723-2401.

### *RESTAURANTS*

**The Mansion House** ★★ This aging grande dame with her brick facade and large, white-pillared porch may have seen more glamorous days in years past, but now the house has an unabashedly casual interior and serves as the site of one of Merced's better restaurants. Occasionally, on weekends, live jazz or acoustical guitar tunes drift through the pink-hued dining rooms and into the broad, glassed-in veranda overlooking the yard. The menu features a wide variety of Italian dishes—veal, pasta, fish—as well as mesquite-grilled chicken and steak. The Mansion House hosts a popular weekend brunch, highlighted by owner Heather Vann's delicate sour-cream-and-cream-cheese blintzes and cinnamon-sprinkled French toast served with warm maple syrup. ■ *455 W 20th St (at Canal St), Merced; (209) 383-2744; $$; full bar; AE, DIS, MC, V; checks OK; brunch Sun, lunch Mon–Fri, dinner Tues–Sat.*

**Branding Iron Restaurant** ★ This paean to the American Beef Council has delighted Mercedites for nearly half a century, thanks in part to chef Bob Freitas, who has presided over the kitchen for almost three decades. Owners Kara and Greg Parle have added to the Branding Iron's Old West ambience by decorating its rough-hewn redwood walls with registered livestock brands from all over California. Dinner begins with soup and salad, followed by such carnal delights as a thick cut of choice prime rib seasoned with coarse-ground pepper, garlic, rosemary, and thyme, and a large baked potato with all the fixin's. If your stomach (or waistline) will allow it, finish the evening with a sweet treat from the well-stocked dessert tray. ■ *640 W 16th St (next to the Santa Fe Railway Depot), Merced; (209) 722-1822; $$; full bar; AE, MC, V; local checks only; lunch Mon–Fri, dinner every day.* ♿

### LODGINGS

**Ramada Inn** ★ Your best bet for lodging in Merced is the impeccably clean Ramada Inn, managed by Russian hosts Anatol and Igor Shliapnikoff. Although the inn's exterior is painted a garish pink and green, within its 61 capacious mini-suites you'll find attractive cherry-wood furnishings, brass lamps, love-seat sofa beds (in addition to regular beds), large showers, and coffee-makers. Each room has satellite TV and pool access (a *must* in the scorching summer months), and all are within steps of the bar in the Denny's-like restaurant that shares the lodge's parking lot. ■ *2000 E Childs Ave (off Hwy 99), Merced, CA 95340; (209) 723-3121; $; full bar; AE, DC, DIS, MC, V; no checks; breakfast, lunch, dinner every day.* ♿

## ATWATER

### RESTAURANTS

**Out To Lunch** ★★ Word got out a long time ago about the delicious thick sandwiches that emerge from this little veranda-wrapped cottage. Almost anything piled between the warm, sweetly spiced slices of house-made zucchini bread is a good bet, including the crunchy veggie sandwich with cream cheese, cucumbers, bell peppers, shredded carrots, avocado, and sprouts. Two other great choices are the English muffin topped with sautéed mushrooms, Jack cheese, and crumbled bacon, and any of the house-made quiches. No alcohol is served here, but you're welcome to bring your own bottle of wine. If you're en route by car from Los Angeles to the Sacramento area (or vice versa), this is one of the best places for a lunch break—and it's just a minute away from the highway. ■ *1301 Winton Way (at Drakely St; from Hwy 99, take the Applegate exit), Atwater; (209)357-1170; $; no alcohol; MC, V; checks OK; lunch Mon–Fri year-round, dinner Fri only from Memorial Day to Labor Day.* &

## TURLOCK

### *RESTAURANTS*

**El Jardín** ★★ If you ignore the Wells Fargo Bank sign across the street, you could easily imagine you were basking in the sun at a cozy cantina on the plaza in Guadalajara. True to its name, El Jardín has a fragrant, colorful flower garden surrounded by several outdoor tables—*the* place to sit when the weather is mild. El Jardín's pride and joy, however, is the wildly colorful "Matador Mosaic" flooring that encompasses the entire restaurant. The authentic south-of-the-border fare— all offered at south-of-the-border prices—includes such house specials as the Milanesa breaded beef fillet with fresh green salsa and the tender and tasty *pollo a la parilla* (grilled chicken breast). For *los niños* there are kid-size enchiladas, quesadillas, taquitos, burritos, and tostadas served with rice and beans that will beat a Happy Meal any day of the week. If you're in the mood for a late breakfast (the kitchen doesn't open until 11am), stop by for huevos rancheros, steak, scrambled eggs with chorizo, and other Mexican standards. ■ *409 E Olive St (1 block W of Golden State Blvd, 1 block N of Main St), Turlock; (209)632-0932; $; beer and wine; V; no checks; late breakfast (starting at 11am), lunch, dinner every day.* &

## CERES

### *RESTAURANTS*

**La Morenita** ★ This restaurant brought fajitas to the Modesto area and it still serves the best in this part of the valley. The chicken and beef fajitas come with fresh tomatoes and peppers sizzling in a cast-iron skillet, ready to be rolled up in fresh-baked tortillas. Other good dishes are the flautas, chicken mole, Mexican chicken salad, and Milanesa beef fillet served with green salsa and guacamole. Expect to wait for a table at this typically crowded restaurant, especially on weekends. La Morenita also serves Mexican and American breakfasts at very reasonable prices. ■ *1410 E Hatch Rd (from Hwy 99 take the Hatch Rd exit and head E), Ceres; (209)537-7900; $; beer and wine; AE, DIS, MC, V; local checks only; breakfast, lunch, dinner every day.*

*RESTAURANTS*

**Deva Café & Bistro** ★★ If you're looking for a good, reasonably priced breakfast, lunch, dinner, or simply a decent cup of coffee, head directly for Deva, a swank, very popular little cafe in Modesto's downtown district. Large framed prints of Renoir, Van Gogh, Monet, and other Impressionists adorn mustard-colored walls lined with dark-wood trim, and bentwood furnishings cover the painted cement floor. Several spinning ceiling fans keep everything cool and breezy in the dining room on sweltering summer days, and when the temperatures aren't soaring into the triple digits you can dine alfresco on the sidewalk. The wildly eclectic menu offers everything from the Provence Scramble (eggs scrambled with roasted red peppers, olives, onions, capers, tomatoes, and Asiago cheese) and house-made honey-raisin and roasted-cashew granola for breakfast to curried rice salad, Ravoux meat loaf served on focaccia, and Cajun dark roux gumbo with jumbo shrimp and andouille sausage for lunch and dinner. Deva also boasts a good selection of beer on tap. ■ *1202 J St (at 12th St), Modesto; (209) 572-3382; www.ainet.com/deva; $; beer and wine; MC, V; checks OK; breakfast, lunch every day, dinner Mon–Sat.* ♿

**Hazel's** ★★ This old pink house, converted about 30 years ago into a restaurant, is a favorite romantic weekend retreat for many Modesto residents. It may pale next to the hoity-toity culinary castles in San Francisco, but in this part of the valley Hazel's is the place to be for a candle-lit dinner. Owner Jeff Morey, a graduate of the California Culinary Academy, maintains original owner Hazel Saylor's time-honored menu, featuring dishes as simple as liver and onions topped with sautéed mushrooms and as deluxe as the rich lobster Macedonia. Hazel's version of cannelloni, stuffed with seasoned veal, chicken, and mushrooms, is still a lunchtime favorite. The wine list is well edited and reasonably priced, with several selections available by the glass. ■ *513 12th St (between E and F Sts), Modesto; (209) 578-3463; $$; full bar; AE, DC, DIS, MC, V; local checks only; lunch Tues–Fri, dinner Tues–Sat.* ♿

**Tresetti's World Caffe** ★★ Located a few blocks from City Hall, this popular hangout attracts a steady gaggle of lawyers, lobbyists, politicians, and other professionals who congregate at the stylish galvanized steel and polished-wood wine bar. The adjacent high-ceilinged dining room is equally chic with its burgundy drapes, matching cement floor, pale yellow walls, a glass facade overlooking downtown Modesto, and only a dozen tables. The chef strives for a global culinary theme, focusing on classic dishes from around the world—a heady pursuit that doesn't always result in well-executed fare. At a recent meal, the paella had all the right ingredients—prawns, scallops, mussels, sausage, saffron rice—but as a whole was woefully short on flavor. Other dishes fared better, such as the tender grilled lamb loin chops in a reduced balsamic sauce, and the grilled New York steak served with cumin-laced mashed potatoes. In short, your best bet here is to buy American. Tresetti's also has the largest assortment of single-malt whiskeys and ports in the valley. ▪ *927 11th St (at J St, adjacent to Tresetti's Wine Shop), Modesto; (209)572-2990; $$; full bar; AE, DIS, MC, V; checks OK; lunch, dinner Mon–Sat.* ♿

### *LODGINGS*

**Doubletree Hotel Modesto** ★ Towering 14 stories above the Modesto landscape, the Doubletree is the Central Valley's premier business/luxury accommodation. Guests are pampered with such amenities as a spa, sauna, sun deck, heated outdoor pool, weight room, two restaurants, two bars, and extensive conference facilities. Each of the 258 dull but comfortable guest rooms (including six suites) are equipped with a remote-control TV, three telephones with a fax/PC data port, a king- or queen-size bed, a separate desk and table, a coffeemaker, an iron and ironing board, and a hair dryer. A free shuttle will whisk you to the Modesto airport; if you have your own wheels take advantage of the free parking in the sheltered lot. ▪ *1150 9th St (at K St), Modesto, CA 95354; (209)526-6000 or (800)222-TREE; www.doubletreehotels.com; $$$; full bar; AE, DC, DIS, MC, V; checks OK; breakfast, lunch, dinner every day.* ♿

## RIPON

### *RESTAURANTS*

**Christopaolo's** ★★ If there were ever a reason to roll your wheels into Ripon, this is it. Owner Christopaolo Bonora has kept many of the original fixtures in this handsome, high-ceilinged 1886 edifice, including the marvelous exposed brick walls, intricate mahogany woodwork, and an authentic dumbwaiter. The menu offers a large array of Italian dishes such as *nocetta di maiale ai porcini* (pork loin sautéed with porcini mushrooms and wine), spaghetti Bolognese, and *zuppa di pesce*, an Adriatic fisherman's stew laden with a variety of shellfish and chunks of fresh fish. Grilled items, such as center-cut rib steak, salmon, and a half-chicken, are also available. The small wine bar offers a smart selection of California wines—a good reason to arrive a little early. ▪ *125 E Main St (at Stockton Ave), Ripon; (209)599-2030; $$; beer and wine; AE, DIS, MC, V; checks OK; lunch Wed–Fri, dinner Wed–Sun.* ♿

## RIVERBANK

### *RESTAURANTS*

**El Ranchito** ★★ A good way to tell whether a Mexican restaurant's food is *truly* authentic is to sample the refried beans—nothing has the taste or the texture of hand-mashed *frijoles*, which is what you'll find at this family-run landmark that's been in business for more than a quarter of a century. In addition to the refried beans, the locals keep coming back for the tasty tamales, chicken mole, flautas, and the all-time favorite, *camarones al mojo de ajo* (jumbo prawns marinated in garlic sauce), which are served Friday through Sunday only. Fresh fish (a rarity in these parts), such as grilled halibut and mahi-mahi, are also offered on the weekend. El Ranchito is just a short drive from Highway 99, making it a great roadside stop.
■ *3048 Atchison St (at 1st St), Riverbank; (209)869-0196; $; full bar; no credit cards; checks OK; lunch, dinner Wed–Mon.* &

## OAKDALE

Oakdale would be just another sleepy Central Valley cow town were it not for the monolithic **Hershey Chocolate Factory** located on the south side of the city. Believe it or not, some 150,000 annual visitors line up for the free 30-minute tours of the chocolate-making plant, offered Monday through Friday from 8:30am to 3pm (excluding major holidays). Tours depart from the Hershey Visitors Center, which has a few low-tech displays on the history of Milton Hershey's chocolate empire, but it's mostly crammed with Hershey teddy bears, Hershey coffee mugs, Hershey toy trucks, Hershey beer mugs, Hershey sweatshirts, Hershey . . . well, you get the point; 120 South Sierra Avenue, at the intersection of Yosemite Avenue and East F Street, (209)848-8126. Another town highlight is the Saturday **Oakdale Livestock Auction**, which is best enjoyed with a big piece of pie from Cheryl's Cafe; for more details see the review of Cheryl's, below.

### *RESTAURANTS*

**Cheryl's Cafe** ★ Every Saturday, ranchers from all around come to the Oakdale Livestock Auction to bid on a heifer or two and talk business over a Cattleman's Sandwich (beef, of course) and a slice of pie. While the auctioneers are taking bids on various farm animals, Cheryl and her crew are busy making omelets, pouring coffee, and slicing pies in the cafe adjoining the auction room. Though Cheryl's omelets are held in high regard in these parts, the real treat is the auction itself: if you've never been to one, prepare to be dazzled by the entire spectacle, right down to the 2,000-indecipherable-words-a-minute bidding procedure. The whole event, from cafe to corral, will take about an hour of your time, but it's an hour you'll never forget (especially if you scratch your itchy nose and suddenly become the dumbstruck new owner of a 600-pound Black Angus). The cafe is open on Saturday only. ■ *6001 Albers Rd (S of town, just past the Hershey Chocolate Factory), Oakdale; (209)847-1033; $; no alcohol; no credit cards; no checks; breakfast, lunch, dinner Sat only.* &

**H-B Saloon ■ Bachi's Restaurant** ★  For a real Central Valley experience, don your shitkickers and cowboy hat and head for the H-B saloon, a decidedly funky old bar and restaurant festooned with faded photos of ranches and rodeos, mounted game, old-fashioned tack, branded wainscoting, and other mementos of ranching life. During any time of the day or night you'll find aging cattlemen in baseball caps and cowboy hats playing shuffleboard or poker in the saloon, drinking $1 beers, listening to Johnny Cash on the jukebox, and doing their best to ignore the occasional wayward tourists. Dinner, served family style in the adjacent **Bachi's Restaurant**, will satisfy even the hungriest cowboy: choose from rib-eye steak, pork chops, lamb chops, chicken, baby back ribs, halibut, or, on Friday and Saturday only, prime rib. Each inexpensive meal includes red wine, soup, salad, french fries, bread, beans, potato salad, *and* ice cream. Near the end of your meal you'll begin to appreciate the thick-cushioned banquettes as you sink deeper and deeper with every bite of the good ol' American grub. ■ *401 East F St (next to the Hershey Chocolate Factory), Oakdale; (209)847-2985; $; full bar; MC, V; local checks only; lunch Mon–Fri, dinner Wed–Sat.*

## STOCKTON

The birthplace of Caterpillar tractor inventor Benjamin Holt and, more recently, heartthrob rock star Chris Isaak, Stockton used to be a simple blue-collar town—home to a multicultural mix of European, Mexican, and Asian immigrants who worked the fields, stockyards, and docks. As the Deep Water Channel was being dredged to accommodate grain carriers during the 1930s, however, this inland city was gradually transformed into an international seaport, growing by leaps and bounds, particularly over the last decade (as did the crime rate and gang activity). Despite suburbanization and its inherent problems, agriculture is still king here—fruit stands continue to dot the roadsides from April to October, and fresh local produce still draws crowds to Stockton's **farmers markets**. The open-air markets offer superb produce and are held on Thursday and Sunday from 8:30am to 1pm in the Weberstown Mall parking lot at March Lane and Pacific Avenue, in front of Sears; Friday from 10am to 2pm in Hunter's Square downtown, by the courthouse; and Saturday from 7am to 11am underneath the freeway, across from St. Mary's church. For more information on the farmers markets call (209)943-1830. If you're in town on Friday, Saturday, or Sunday, don't miss the huge outdoor **flea market** (open from 8am to 5pm), where everything that can be sold *is* sold. Great ethnic food stands and a summertime carnival for kids are additional flea-market attractions; 3550 North Wilson Way, off Highway 99, (209)465-1544.

## RESTAURANTS

**Nena's Restaurant** ★ Owner Maria Elena Reyes (also known as Nena) came to California as a farmworker from Mexico. She and her husband, Jesús, saved their money and opened a tiny cafe on the south side of Stockton. Nena's was an instant hit, especially with Stockton's large Latino population. The restaurant became so successful that the couple moved it to bigger digs in a central part of town, where the crowds still come for the saucy stews (*campechana, chile verde,* and *chicana*) and the *birria* (shredded beef, goat, or lamb simmered for hours in a light, spicy barbecue sauce and wrapped in steamed corn tortillas). Live Latin music is played on Friday, Saturday, and Sunday nights. ■ *1064 E Waterloo Rd (at Solari St), Stockton; (209)547-0217; $; full bar; AE, DIS, MC, V; local checks only; breakfast, lunch, dinner every day.* &

**Primavera Ristorante** ★ Anna and Francesco Piccione's traditional Italian restaurant features tables topped with crisp linens and candles, and a host of waiters spouting Italian accents. Anna makes most of the pasta herself; particularly good are the tagliatelle mixed with salmon, scallops, and a garlic cream sauce and the spinach fettuccine tossed with a piquant tomato sauce. ■ *856 W Benjamin Holt Dr (in the SE corner of Lincoln Center, at Pacific Ave), Stockton; (209)477-6128; $$; beer and wine; AE, MC, V; no checks; lunch Tues–Fri, dinner Tues–Sat.*

**Yen Ching** ★ Ornate wall carvings and bright red partitions set the mood for the authentic Peking, Hunan, Sichuan, and Mandarin Chinese cuisine served here. Standout entrees include the Shandong steamed bread, dumplings, noodles, and the various meat dishes perfected by former owner Kin Fo Ju (a native of China's Shandong province) and now prepared by his sons Billy, Jack, and Tom. Other popular dishes include the spicy string beans, eggplant with garlic sauce, house chicken (crunchy bites of batter-fried chicken served in a sweet-and-spicy sauce with vegetables), and hot braised fish à la Yen Ching (a whole fish sautéed with green onions and topped with a ginger sauce). ■ *6511 Pacific Ave (in the SE corner of Lincoln Center, at Benjamin Holt Dr), Stockton; (209)957-0913; $; beer and wine; MC, V; no checks; lunch, dinner Tues–Sun.*

**Yoneda's Japanese Restaurant** ★ Owner Kunio Yoneda takes great pride in his culinary ancestry. Born into a family of chefs, he attended the Tsugi Cooking School in Osaka, then crossed the Pacific to open his own restaurant in a modern shopping center on the outskirts of Stockton. The pleasantly decorated dining room retains a hint of old Japan, with mounted Japanese swords, silk wall hangings, and colorful paper lanterns dangling behind the sushi counter. Yoneda offers a wide selection of sushi and sashimi, as well as the traditional sukiyaki, tempura, and teriyaki dishes and a good mix of vegetarian entrees. ■ *1101 E March Lane (in the Calaveras Square shopping center on the NW corner of March and West Lanes), Stockton; (209) 477-1667; $; beer and wine; AE, MC, V; local checks only; lunch Tues–Fri, dinner Tues–Sun.* &

## LODGINGS

**Stockton Hilton** ★ Tucked away in a quiet corner of Stockton, this five-story hotel with 198 one- and two-bedroom suites is certainly nothing to swoon over, but it offers the most pleasant (and safest) accommodations you'll find in town. The executive rooms on the south side of the hotel have small balconies overlooking a series of canals. Beat the sweltering summer heat by jumping into the hotel pool, or, better yet, stay indoors and order a frosty beer in the bar. The hotel has two restaurants: Atrium Café serves standard American breakfast dishes, and The Grill offers sizzling steaks, seafood, and other traditional American fare. Room service, a spa, and free access to the athletic club across the street round out the Hilton's amenities. ■ *2323 Grand Canal Blvd (from I-5 take the March Lane exit and head E), Stockton, CA 95207; (209) 957-9090 or (800) 444-9094; $$$; full bar; AE, DC, DIS, MC, V; checks OK; breakfast, lunch, dinner every day.* &

▼
**Stockton**

*Restaurants*

▲

LODI

## LODGINGS

**Wine and Roses Country Inn** ★★★ This ivy-covered 1902 farmhouse is surrounded by 5 acres of cherry trees, rose gardens, and towering 100-year-old deodara cedars, and innkeepers Del and Sherri Smith have covered the interior of their B&B with flowers and lace. In the rose-toned sitting room, camelback couches and wing chairs are clustered around a wide fireplace that's always blazing in the winter. The inn's 10 guest rooms (named after songs) have queen-size beds, turn-of-the-century decor, and handmade comforters. One of the most romantic boudoirs is "White Lace and Promises," a two-room honeymoon suite with a terrace and French doors.

Sherri, a graduate of the California Culinary Academy in San Francisco, sprinkles fresh edible flowers on the morning's gourmet breakfast, served in the sunny dining room. For lunch try her classic caesar salad or the chicken *vol-au-vent* (chicken dressed in a cheese sauce and served in a puff-pastry shell). The dinner menu might offer a fresh, tenderly poached salmon topped with a citrus salsa or filet mignon with sundried tomato garlic butter. Order a bottle of one of the increasingly popular Lodi wines to round out the meal. The inn hosts special events including musical and theatrical productions in the garden on Fridays and Saturdays between June and September. During these fêtes a grand buffet is served in place of the regular menu and reservations are suggested. ■ *2505 W Turner Rd (5 miles E of I-5, 2½ miles W of Hwy 99), Lodi, CA 95242; (209)334-6988; www.winerose.com; $$; full bar; AE, DC, DIS, MC, V; local checks only; breakfast (for guests only) every day, brunch Sun, lunch Tues–Fri, dinner Wed–Sat.* &

## SACRAMENTO RIVER DELTA

Flat as a flour tortilla, the Sacramento River Delta is made up of thousands of miles of rivers, canals, and sloughs, snaking through tule grass and farmland. Kept at bay by massive levees, most of the rivers are slightly higher than the surrounding farmland—all diked and drained former wetlands. The delta contains half of the freshwater runoff in California, although by the time it meanders through the valley's agribusiness, its freshness is debatable. The delta is dotted with quaint, old-fashioned little island towns connected by drawbridges and ferries. You'll find a good, if pricey, Sunday brunch in the delta at **Grand Island Mansion**, a Gatsby-esque inn with 58 rooms and a private bowling alley and cinema, located on the west end of Grand Island, 3 miles west of Highway 160, at 13415 Grand Island Road, (916)775-1705. For a true delta experience, rent a houseboat and cruise the water for a few days alongside snowy egrets, sandhill cranes, and Swainson's hawks. **Houseboat, ski-boat**, and **wave-runner rentals** are available several miles north of Stockton off Interstate 5 at Herman and Helen's Marina at the west end of 8 Mile Road, (209)951-4634 and www.houseboats.com, and Paradise Point Marina, 8095 Rio Blanco, (209)952-1000 and (800)752-9669 (reservations).

## RYDE

### LODGINGS

**The Ryde Hotel** ★★ Originally built as a boardinghouse, this four-story, pink stucco inn on the banks of the Sacramento River became famous as a speakeasy during Prohibition, when roadsters filled with flappers bounced down the delta's dusty streets in search of jazz and illicit liquor. The inn now has 32

guest rooms decorated in a 1920s art deco style with a pink, gray, and mauve color scheme. They all have ceiling fans and some have private bathrooms. The 209-210 suite features a small sitting room and a bedroom with wonderful views of pear orchards, the inn's nine-hole golf course, and the Sacramento River. The Master Suite at the corner of the hotel also overlooks the water, orchards, and golf course. In late 1997, the hotel changed hands, and renovations were in progress.
■ *14340 Hwy 160 (3 miles S of Walnut Grove), Ryde; (916) 776-1318; mail: PO Box 43, Ryde, CA 95680; $$; full bar; MC, V; checks OK; brunch Sun (Mar to Jan), dinner Fri–Sat (Apr to Nov).*

## WALNUT GROVE

### RESTAURANTS

**Giusti's** ★★ Egisto Giusti opened this restaurant alongside the Mokelumne River in 1910 after immigrating here from Lucca, Italy. Today you'll find his grandson Mark Morais continuing the family tradition of serving good food in an old-fashioned, laid-back atmosphere. Except for the 1,500 baseball caps hanging from the ceiling, Giusti's looks as if it has been frozen in time for the last 50 years. You're in luck if you arrive on a Thursday, Giusti's Italian night, when Mark's wife, Linda, makes a wonderfully rich Italian-sausage lasagne and linguine with clam sauce topped with fresh steamed cockles or New Zealand clams. The fresh seafood is always a good bet. ■ *14743 Walnut Grove–Thorton Rd (4 miles W of I-5), Walnut Grove; (916) 776-1808; $; full bar; no credit cards; checks OK; brunch Sun from Mother's Day to Labor Day, lunch Tues–Sun from Labor Day to Mother's Day (Tues–Sat from Mother's Day to Labor Day), dinner Tues–Sun year-round.*

## LOCKE

Locke was the first town in the United States built solely by Chinese laborers for Chinese residents (even though the Chinese businesspeople and workers who built it were forbidden to own any of the land). During its heyday at the beginning of the century, Locke was a town of gambling houses, opium dens, and speakeasies. Now the tiny town is owned by a Hong Kong corporation, and the businesses are much tamer (and certainly more legal) than in years past. Note the old wooden sidewalks lining the streets, a remnant of Locke's early days.

### RESTAURANTS

**Al the Wops** ★ Al Adami bought this former Chinese restaurant in 1934 and it has been known ever since as Al the Wops. When Al died in 1961, his bartender Ralph Santos Sr. took over this venerable and legendary delta institution. Ralph, in

turn, was succeeded by his son in 1981, who changed the
name of this restaurant to Al's Place—a more politically correct moniker. Alas, the name change didn't go over too well, in
part because people drove the phone company crazy asking
for "Al the Wops" and got very surly when the name didn't
come up in the database. In June 1995, Ralph's nephews,
Lorenzo and Steve Giannetti, took over the place and, by popular demand, reinstated the old name. Everything else here
remains pretty much the same. The bar area is still awash in
old business cards and one-dollar bills thumbtacked to the
ceiling, and used signs, memorabilia, and lots of other weird
stuff still covers every inch of the walls. The low-ceilinged
dining room in the back of the building is furnished with long
tables and benches—just as it was in the '30s. The food is
simple but adequate and the assorted tourists, boaters, and
local characters who hang out here like it that way. For lunch,
try Al's traditional steak or chicken dishes or one of the newer
menu items: hamburgers and cheeseburgers. Al's dinners are
limited to chicken and New York steaks (12 or 18 ounces)
served with a side of spaghetti or french fries. A bowl of homemade minestrone soup is available, too. ■ *13943 Main St (the
first street off the levee), Locke; (916)776-1800; $; full bar; no
credit cards; checks OK; lunch, dinner every day.* &

## SACRAMENTO

▼

Sacramento

▲

Sacramento has long been regarded as the second-class step-
sister of San Francisco, but with its increasing number of sky-
scrapers, upscale restaurants, and swanky hotels (not to
mention the NBA's Sacramento Kings and the new Sacramento Monarchs, a women's NBA team), California's capital
city is no longer the sleepy little valley town folks whiz
through on their way to Lake Tahoe. Located 90 miles northeast of the Bay Area, the city is best known for its dual status
as the seat of state government and the epicenter of California's biggest industry: agriculture (locals affectionately call
Sacramento the Big Tomato, Sacratomato, and the River City).
But disregard any disparaging words you may have heard
about this agricultural hot spot: there are no cows (or even
cowboy hats) within city limits, and most of the city slickers do
not pick tomatoes for a living.

A former Gold Rush boomtown, Sacramento sprang up
where the American and Sacramento Rivers meet—a tourist
area now known as Old Sacramento. In 1839 Swiss immigrant
John Sutter traversed both rivers, built his famous fort, and
established his colony called New Helvetia ("New Switzer-
land"). But his hopes that the thriving colony would evolve into
his own vast empire were dashed when gold was discovered
up near his sawmill in 1848. Sutter's colonists deserted New

## Sacramento

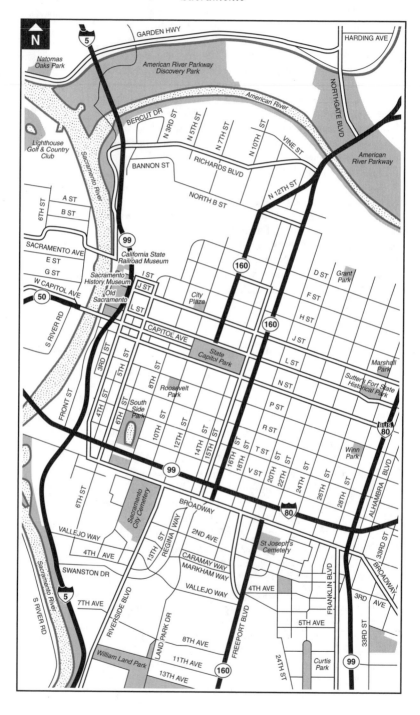

Helvetia to search for the precious nuggets, and as word of the
gold discovery spread, thousands more wound their way to
the hills above Sacramento to seek their fortune. Ironically,
Sutter himself never prospered from the Gold Rush and he
died a bitter, penniless man.

Today, Sacramento is home to more than a million people,
many of whom play politics with the capital crowd or practice
law. They dote on their spectacular Victorian homes and fine
Craftsman-style bungalows, and are justly proud of the tree-
lined streets and thick carpets of grass that surround their
houses and parks.

In the scorching summer months, when thermometers often
soar above three digits for days, many folks beat the heat by
diving into swimming pools, chugging around the delta on a
houseboat with a fishing pole in hand, or floating down the
American River in a raft or inner tube. Once the sun sets, however, things cool off dramatically, and Sacramentans often enjoy
their dinners alfresco. Winters are punctuated by the famous
tule fog—so thick it can block the sun for weeks at a time. But
as all ski buffs know, Sacramentans always get the jump on
their Bay Area neighbors racing to the snowy slopes of Lake
Tahoe, thanks to the city's proximity to the Sierra Nevada.

To best appreciate the Big Tomato, start your tour of the
town in **Old Sacramento** (aka Old Sac), the historic district.
Perched along the Sacramento River, the four-block-long
stretch is filled with dozens of restaurants, gift shops, and
saloons. An Old Sac highlight is the **California State Railroad Museum**, a grand monument to the glory days of loco-
motion and the Big Four and the largest museum of its kind in
the nation; 125 I Street at Second Street, (916)323-9280. The
granddaddy of Old Sac attractions is the **Sacramento Dixieland Jubilee**, the world's largest Dixieland jazz festival,
which attracts thousands of toe-tappers and bands from
around the world each Memorial Day weekend, (916)372-
5277. One mile south of this historic district is the **Towe Ford
Museum of Automotive History**, which boasts the largest
antique Ford collection in the world; 2200 Front Street,
(916)442-6802. Nearby is the **Crocker Art Museum**, home of
the region's largest art collection, including a fine selection of
contemporary California art by local talents who made the big
time such as Wayne Thiebaud and Robert Arneson. The
museum also holds a stunning collection of European master
drawings; 216 O Street at Third Street, (916)264-5423. Also of
special interest to art lovers is **La Raza Galleria Posada**, a
Chicano, Latino, and Native American arts center located in a
beautifully restored Victorian house. Within this complex are
a cultural center, a contemporary-art gallery, a bookstore, and
a gift shop stocked with wonderful Mexican folk arts; 704 O
Street at Seventh Street, (916)446-5133.

A few blocks northeast of the gallery is the awe-inspiring **State Capitol**, restored in the 1970s to its original turn-of-the-century magnificence with $67.8 million in taxpayers' dollars (so come see what you paid for). You may wander around the building on your own, but you really shouldn't miss the free tours given daily every hour between 9am and 4pm. Tours include an overview of the legislative process and, if you're lucky, a chance to see the political hotshots in action. Tickets are handed out a half hour before the tour on a first-come, first-served basis in the basement of room B-27 in the Capitol; it's located on 10th Street, between L and N Streets, (916)324-0333. While you're getting your tickets, pick up a copy of the "State Capitol Tree Tour" brochure and after your indoors tour you can saunter through marvelous **Capitol Park** and admire more than 340 varieties of trees from around the world.

If you're a big history buff, step back in time by strolling through **Sutter's Fort**, where you can view the restored self-contained community that Sutter built in the wilderness in 1839. On the same grounds is the **California State Indian Museum**, with artifacts from more than 100 California Indian tribes, including one of the finest basket collections in the nation; it's located between K and L Streets and 27th and 28th Streets, (916)445-4422 (fort), (916)324-0539 (museum).

## MUSIC, DANCE, AND THEATER

**The Sacramento Community Convention Center** is the regular venue for the local symphony, as well as big-name jazz and classical groups and dance troupes; 1421 K Street, (916)264-7777, (916)264-5181 (box office). Just up the road is the **Crest Theater**, a refurbished art deco palace that hosts rock, folk, reggae, and World Beat concerts and runs classic movies; 1013 K Street, (916)442-7378.

Sacramento has a thriving live theater scene, and two top venues are the **Sacramento Theater Company**, 1419 H Street, (916)446-7501, and **B Street Theater**, co-founded by TV and film star Timothy Busfield (of *thirtysomething* fame) and his brother, Buck; 2711 B Street, (916)443-5300. One of the city's most popular summer pastimes is the **Music Circus**—an annual festival of Broadway musicals presented under a big-top tent. Every July and August the Sacramento Light Opera Association continues this 50-year-old summer musical tradition by reviving the music of Cole Porter, the Gershwins, and Stephen Sondheim using professional casts from Broadway and Hollywood; 1419 H Street, (916)557-1999.

## RECREATION

Sacramento's two most notable natural attractions are not its 105-degree heat in the summer and its tule fog in the winter, but its two rivers: the boat-filled, bustling, brown

**Sacramento River** and the raft-filled, sparkling blue **American River**.

For cyclists and joggers, nothing beats the **American River Parkway**, a 5,000-acre nature preserve with a 22-mile-long, pothole-free bike trail, which starts in Old Sac, runs along the Sacramento River to the American River, and follows the water all the way to the town of Folsom. You can **rent a bike** for about $15 a day at City Bicycle Works, 2419 K Street at 24th Street in midtown, (916)447-2453. In the sweltering Sacramento summers many locals and visitors alike abandon their bikes for a leisurely **raft trip** down the American River. American River Raft Rentals has all the equipment and information you'll need for this refreshing, delightful trek, (916)635-6400. If you're cruising through town during the last two weeks of August, set aside a hot day or night to visit the **California State Fair**, Sacratomato's grandest party. The carnival rides and games are predictably head-spinning and not for the faint of stomach, but everyone agrees the livestock exhibits and wine tastings (featuring winners of the prestigious State Fair wine competition) are worth the admission price. Other fair highlights include daily horse races, nightly rodeos, free nightly concerts by big-name groups of all persuasions, and a wild variety of events ranging from Western art and Web page competitions to the State Fair film festival; located at Cal Expo, off the Interstate 80/Capital City Freeway (north of the American River) at Expo Boulevard. Call (916)263-3000 for more details or visit the State Fair's Web site at www.bigfun.org.

### RESTAURANTS

**Biba** ★★★★ Biba is a study in understated neo-deco design—the sort of place where you'd expect precious, trendy foods to dominate the menu. Fortunately, they don't. Bologna-born chef/owner Biba Caggiano is a traditionalist to the core, and what comes out of her kitchen is exactly what she learned at her mother's elbow: classical Italian cooking based on the finest ingredients available and a painstaking attention to detail. The menu changes seasonally, but expect to find such entrees as grilled shrimp wrapped in basil and Parma ham, melt-in-your-mouth nutmeg-and-ricotta tortellini, angel hair pasta tossed with sun-dried tomatoes, a phenomenal shrimp-studded linguine, duck cooked with port and Italian cherries, and rosemary-infused lamb chops. Biba has an uncanny ability to transform seemingly mundane side dishes, such as carrots, snap peas, mashed potatoes, and white beans, into star attractions, so don't pass them up. If all that weren't enough, the service is superb and the long list of domestic and Italian wines should please even the snootiest wine connoisseur. Top off your marvelous meal with Biba's divine double-chocolate trifle.

In addition to running one of the region's finest restaurants, Biba has written more than a half-dozen books on Italian cooking (her first, *North Italian Cooking*, published by HP Books, has been in print for more than 16 years) and she hosts the popular television show *Biba's Italian Kitchen* on the Learning Channel. ■ *2801 Capitol Ave (at 28th St), Sacramento; (916) 455-2422; biba@infovillage.com; www.infovillage. com/biba/; $$$; full bar; AE, MC, V; no checks; lunch Mon–Fri, dinner Mon–Sat.* &

**Lemon Grass** ★★★★   This elegant restaurant, offering a unique blend of Vietnamese and Thai cooking, keeps getting better and better and is approaching nirvana. Husband-and-wife owners Mai Pham and Trong Nguyen use local organically grown produce, fresh seafood, Petaluma free-range chicken, and little or no oil in many of their culinary masterpieces. The Siamese Seafood Feast, a Thai bouillabaisse, comes bubbling with fresh clams, sea scallops, mussels, and prawns in a spicy, hot-and-sour broth infused with lemongrass, galangal (Thai ginger), kaffir lime leaves, and chiles. Other standout dishes include the fillet of farm-raised catfish cooked in a caramelized garlic sauce, and the Thai green curry, made with slices of chicken breast, bamboo shoots, and peas simmered in a curry-based coconut milk. The wide-ranging dessert menu features such delicacies as Saigon by Night, a blend of Vietnamese espresso, hazelnut syrup, whipped cream, and vanilla ice cream; a silky house-made caramelized Australian ginger ice cream with Grand Marnier sauce; and a banana cheesecake drizzled with warm coconut sauce. Mai's book, *The Best of Vietnamese and Thai Cooking—Favorite Recipes from Lemon Grass Restaurant and Café*, a national best seller, is now in its third edition. She was recently featured in *Martha Stewart Living* and on National Public Radio's program *Fresh Air*. In her spare time she teaches at the Culinary Institute of America in St. Helena. ■ *601 Monroe St (just N of Fair Oaks Blvd, near Loehmann's Plaza shopping center), Sacramento; (916) 486-4891; maipham@ibm.net; $$; full bar; AE, DC, MC, V; no checks; lunch Mon–Fri, dinner every day.* &

**Paragary's Bar and Oven** ★★★★   Paragary's Bar and Oven restaurants (there are three in Sacramento and one in Folsom) are well known for zesty pizzas cooked in wood-burning ovens, mesquite-grilled entrees that typically have a strong Italian accent, and freshly made pastas and desserts. Part of the Randy Paragary empire, each Bar and Oven restaurant has different and wonderfully imaginative menus that change frequently, and the 28th Street branch is the small chain's flagship. Recent offerings included an outstanding mushroom salad tossed with shaved fennel, Parmesan cheese, parsley, lemon juice, and olive oil; house-made butternut-squash ravioli topped with brown butter, sage, and hazelnuts; a calzone stuffed with herbed mozzarella, fresh basil, tomatoes, and Westphalian ham; and a grilled New York strip steak with oven-roasted potatoes, fennel, arugula, and white truffle oil. ■ *1401 28th St (at N St), Sacramento; (916)457-5737; www.paragary.com; $$$; full bar; AE, DC, DIS, MC, V; checks OK; lunch Mon–Fri, dinner every day.* ♿ ■ *2384 Fair Oaks Blvd (between Howe and Fulton Aves), Sacramento; (916)485-7100; $$$; full bar; AE, DC, DIS, MC, V; checks OK; lunch Mon–Fri, dinner every day.* ♿ ■ *2220 Gold Springs Court (at the corner of Sunrise Blvd and Gold Express), Sacramento; (916)852-0214; $$$; full bar; AE, DC, DIS, MC, V; checks OK; lunch Mon–Fri, dinner every day.* ♿

**David Berkley** ★★★ Located in the Pavilions, Sacramento's most upscale shopping mall, David Berkley is essentially a deli-catessen—but, wow, what a deli! Just about everything served here is perfect: perfect salads, perfect sandwiches, perfect produce, perfect desserts. There's even a superior selection of wine and beer, as well as some little boxes of edible flowers you may purchase to make your own perfect salads at home. The deli section offers nearly two dozen different salads every day, including several low-fat options. Try sinking your teeth into the savory smoked-chicken salad, the wild rice and pear salad, or the luscious shrimp, avocado, cucumber, and fresh dill combination. The popular Mendocino Masterpiece sand-wich is piled high with smoked turkey, lappi cheese, Mendocino hot-sweet mustard, sprouts, and tomato slices. David Berkley (named after the owner) also offers a take-out dinner menu, which changes weekly and features four entrees and a selection of side dishes. A take-out meal might include a salad of jicama and orange slices tossed with a citrus vinaigrette; a thick, grilled New York steak crusted with Dijon mustard and horseradish; herbed mashed potatoes; and sautéed baby veg-etables. Finish your feast with an unblemished pear, ripe rasp-berries, an exotic blood orange, or, if you're not counting calories, a decadent cheesecake or tart. Arrive early if you're planning to eat here, since seating is limited (most tables are outdoors) and this place packs 'em in. ■ *515 Pavilions Lane (in the Pavilions shopping center, on the N side of Fair Oaks Blvd, between Howe and Fulton Aves), Sacramento; (916)929-4422; dberkley@spyderwebb.com; $$; beer and wine; AE, MC, V; checks OK; lunch every day.* ♿

**The Fox and Goose** ★★★ You'll see chaps chugging down pints of bitter and having a jolly good time over a game of darts at this bustling British pub, almost as genuine as any neigh-borhood spot you're likely to find in the United Kingdom. Owned by Allyson Dalton, the Fox and Goose is a River City institution, offering a wee bit of everything—beer, breakfast, lunch, and live music—and doing it all wonderfully. There are 13 beers on tap, including brews from England, Ireland, and Scotland. For breakfast choose from a variety of omelets (you may order eggs from free-range chickens for a small additional price) as well as kippers (Atlantic herring), grilled tomatoes, crumpets, and such authentic English treats as bangers and mash; or you can take the California-cuisine route and order the vegetarian pub grill (scrambled tofu mixed with pesto and red onions or curry and green onions). The lunch menu features a wide array of sandwiches and salads as well as a daily soup. The Fox and Goose is famous for its burnt cream (a rich, velvety custard topped with caramelized brown sugar), but the other desserts are equally delectable, such as the English trifle (a sherry-soaked cake layered with custard, Jello, raspberry jam, and Devonshire cream). Be forewarned: this is a popular pub and reservations are not accepted, so arrive a little early, particularly for lunch. At night the place swings to folk, jazz, and bluegrass tunes. ■ *1001 R St (at 12th St, just S of the Capitol), Sacramento; (916)443-8825; www. infovillage.com/fox&goose; $; beer and wine; MC, V; local checks only; breakfast every day, lunch Mon–Fri.* ᕝ

**Morton's of Chicago** ★★★ Morton's is part of a restaurant chain, but it's a golden chain. Although the restaurant has built its reputation on red meat, the truth is, Morton's does practically everything superbly, especially at this Sacramento branch. Expect the best cut, the freshest fish, and the pick of the crop. Sure, the prices are steep, but where else can you find sliced, juicy beefsteak tomatoes (with a luscious blue cheese dressing) all year round? The Cajun-style rib-eye steak, dusted with spices and cooked exactly as you order it, is so flavorful and tender you'll feel sorry for vegetarians. And the grilled swordfish with béarnaise sauce might prompt carnivores to give up beef. Equally wonderful are the vegetables (such as the fresh asparagus topped with hollandaise) and the desserts (like fresh raspberries with sabayon sauce). If you don't think of potatoes as gourmet fare, you've never had one of Morton's Idaho baked spuds—they're guaranteed to change your mind. ■ *521 L St (in the Downtown Plaza shopping center, between 5th and 6th Sts), Sacramento; (916)442-5091; $$$; full bar; AE, DC, MC, V; no checks; dinner every day.* ᕝ

**33rd Street Bistro** ★★★ Recognized as Sacramento's "outstanding new restaurant" in 1996 by the California Capital Chefs' Association, the 33rd Street Bistro was a huge success right from the start and it just keeps getting better. Chef/owner Fred Haines has combined a casual, trendy ambience—a handsome red-brick wall, high ceilings, polished wood floors, and vibrant oversized paintings of vegetables—with terrific food at reasonable prices. You can order the excellent salads in a large or "lite" size, including a knock-out Mediterranean salad tossed with wood-roasted chicken, sweet red peppers, red onions, white beans, and feta. The bistro's signature spinach salad comes with toasted walnuts, chèvre, roasted red onions, and a citrus-shallot dressing. The panini (Italian grilled sandwiches) are large, messy, delicious, and served on wonderful locally baked focaccia. The Puget Sound Panini is a savory mixture of fresh Dungeness crab, Alaskan bay shrimp, artichokes, and Tillamook cheese on crusty sourdough bread. The entrees, called "large plates," include Manilla clams and gulf prawns with spinach and prosciutto rotolo in a tomato basil broth; seasonal vegetable risotto with arugula-flavored butter; and grilled rosemary strip-loin with a Gorgonzola and arugula salad plus crispy onions. The daily soups are always outstanding, and so are the seasonal desserts, including the strawberry shortcake and the plum tart in a shortbread crust. Expect a crowd during peak dining hours—and this is probably not the place for a marriage proposal (or even a proposition), unless you don't mind yelling a bit. Alas, the bistro does not take reservations. ■ *3301 Folsom Blvd (at 33rd St), Sacramento; (916)455-2282; $$; beer and wine; MC, V; checks OK; breakfast, lunch, dinner every day.* &

**Dos Coyotes Border Cafe** ★★ See the review of this restaurant's Davis branch. ■ *1735 Arden Way (at Market Square in the Arden Fair shopping mall), Sacramento; (916)927-0377; $; beer and wine; AE, MC, V; no checks; lunch, dinner every day.* &

**Jammin' Salmon** ★★ Until fairly recently in Sacramento history, it wasn't easy to get a really good meal with a view of any body of water unless it was a mirage. Things have changed. It's now possible to hang out on the banks of the Sacramento River in such charming spots as the small but delightful Jammin' Salmon. Built on a barge, this restaurant gently rocks when boats pass by, creating a rather soothing environment for nibbling on the excellent freshly tossed salads and perhaps the blackened ahi tuna seared with wasabe and Chinese mustard, or the baked polenta torta with wild mushrooms and fontina cheese. The restaurant's produce must be the freshest around—they get it from a farm one-half mile away. Jammin' Salmon has an extensive California wine list as well as a good selection of microbrews and imported beers. Reservations are recommended, particularly for the outside seats, since the floating restaurant can only seat 49 people. The outside dining area is heated on nippy days, and when the weather is warm you can catch the *River Otter* water taxi from Old Sacramento to the restaurant's front door for $7 per person round-trip—or just take it for a short river cruise after you dine; call (916)448-4333 for the water taxi schedule. ■ *1801 Garden Highway (on the river), Sacramento; (916)929-6232; $$; beer and wine; AE, DC, DIS, MC, V; no checks; brunch Sat–Sun, lunch Mon–Fri, dinner every day.* &

**Sacramento**

*Restaurants*

**Rio City Cafe** ★★ Located on the Sacramento River smack dab in the middle of "Old Sac," the city's premier tourist attraction, the Rio City Cafe has a commanding view up and down this Old Man River. The pleasantly light, airy, and attractive dining room also offers a view of the glassed-in kitchen so you can watch the cooks as they sauté and grill the evening's entrees—a scene reminiscent of drones in a busy beehive. But the primo place to eat here is on the capacious deck-with-a-river-view, especially when there's a slight (though rare) river breeze. The fare here is primarily Southwestern with a dash of California and a soupçon of New Orleans. For lunch, expect a large variety of soups, salads, sandwiches, and temptations such as the wild-mushroom filo rolls with baby greens and chipotle aioli or the spicy Cajun jambalaya with chicken, pork, and seafood served over rice. Dinner entrees range from mesquite-broiled New York steak with wild-mushroom and sun-dried tomato salsa to the tequila-citrus-marinated Sonoma Valley chicken with black beans and green chile sauce. The extensive wine list features a thoughtful collection of California vintages. ■ *1110 Front St (between J and K Sts), Sacramento; (916) 442-8226; $$; full bar; AE, DC, DIS, MC, V; no checks; lunch, dinner every day.* &

▼

**Sacramento**

*Restaurants*

▲

**Siam Restaurant** ★ This admirable tiny Thai restaurant located in a redeveloping part of town turns out delicious soups, unusual salads, fiery-hot curry dishes, and seafood entrees such as garlic prawns, sautéed mussels, steamed clams cooked with fresh ginger, and calamari laced with garlic, onion, and chile paste. Other favorites include the drunken noodles (pan-fried noodles mixed with green peppers, vegetables, garlic, mint, and your choice of pork, chicken, or beef), deep-fried pompano with a sweet and sour sauce, and perfectly sautéed asparagus. Cool your fevered mouth with a tasty Thai iced tea, a Thai beer, or a sweet scoop of coconut ice cream. The Siam is always hopping, so reservations are recommended. ■ *5100 Franklin Blvd (at 26th Ave, in the south-central part of town), Sacramento; (916) 452-8382; $; beer and wine; AE, MC, V; no checks; lunch, dinner Tues–Sun.* &

## LODGINGS

**Amber House** ★★★★ Amber House is actually three restored historic homes—two set side by side (a 1905 Craftsman and a 1913 Mediterranean) and one across the street (an 1895 colonial revival). The houses have been exquisitely restored, with many contemporary features added for the modern-day traveler. The 14 guest rooms, named after artists, poets, and musicians, have private, Italian marble-tiled baths stocked with plush robes (11 also have Jacuzzi tubs for two), private phones with voice-mail, cable TVs with VCRs, and CD players. Each room is artfully decorated with a mix of antiques and contemporary furnishings that are as comfortable as they are aesthetically pleasing. The Van Gogh Room offers a spectacular bathroom with a heart-shaped Jacuzzi for two that perhaps even Vincent would have approved of. Guests may enjoy their gourmet breakfast at whatever time they wish, served in their room, the dining room, or in one of the inn's several delightful gardens. Amber House is located on a quiet, shady street eight blocks from the Capitol and is within easy walking distance of a half-dozen of Sacramento's finest restaurants. ■ *1315 22nd St (between Capitol Ave and N St), Sacramento, CA 95816; (916)444-8085 or (800)755-6526; innkeeper@amberhouse.com; www.amberhouse.com; $$; AE, DC, DIS, MC, V; checks OK.*

**Hyatt Regency Sacramento** ★★★★ This is the only lodging in Sacramento that truly feels like a big-city hotel. It boasts a vaulted marble entryway; the nightclub **Busby Berkeley's** on the 15th floor; a sumptuous, light-filled atrium lounge; 500 beautifully appointed rooms with pretty views of palm-tree-lined Capitol Park; and excellent service. The higher-priced rooms on the Regency Level come with a continental breakfast and pre-dinner snacks served in a private lounge. If cost is no object and you want to impress, book the $795-a-night Grand Terrace Suite, which offers a balcony overlooking the park, a Jacuzzi, a baby grand piano, and a luxurious living room. There are two excellent restaurants on the hotel's main floor: **Dawson's**, a chophouse that caters mostly to meat eaters with its prime rib, pepper steak, and filet mignon; and the cross-cultural **Ciao-Yama**, an Italian/Japanese restaurant offering a variety of creative salads, entrees, and desserts. The outstanding artwork displayed throughout the hotel—murals, paintings, and wrought-iron railings and banisters—was created by local artists. ■ *1209 L St (at 12th St, across from the Capitol), Sacramento, CA 95814; (916)443-1234 or (800)233-1234; www.hyatt.com; $$$; full bar; AE, DC, DIS, MC, V; checks OK; brunch Sun, breakfast, lunch, dinner every day.*

**Sterling Hotel** ★★★★ From the outside, this striking, turn-of-the-century Victorian inn with its beautiful garden and manicured lawn immediately draws the attention of all who pass by. Inside, it's a sleek luxury hotel aimed at the upper echelon of corporate travelers. The Sterling's interior is awash in Asian-influenced, neo-Deco flourishes, and the artwork has a decidedly Zen twist. The 16 guest rooms are large, airy, and spotless; each has a marble bathroom equipped with a Jacuzzi, replicas of antique furniture, big, CEO-style desks, and numerous brass fixtures. **Chanterelle**, the hotel's small but highly regarded restaurant, is located on the ground floor with a charming patio for fair weather dining. The menu changes regularly and may feature such fine fare as medallions of veal sautéed with chanterelle mushrooms and served with a port wine demi-glace, or grilled duck breast with pappardelle noodles, green peppercorns, and baby spinach. Sterling House is within walking distance of the Capitol. Its conference room is a refreshing, low-key alternative to the sterile meeting rooms offered in most hotels. ■ *1300 H St (at 13th St), Sacramento, CA 95814; (916) 448-1300 or (800) 365-7660; $$$; full bar; AE, DC, MC, V; checks OK when mailed in advance; brunch Sun, lunch Mon–Fri, dinner every day.* ♿

**Abigail's Bed and Breakfast** ★★★ A 1912 colonial revival mansion operated by Ken and Susanne Ventura, Abigail's is a prime example of home-building and hospitality from an era when both were art forms. It is located in the heart of mid-town's Boulevard Park district, a neighborhood with some of the city's most opulent Victorian homes and fine restaurants. Note the white-pillared entryway (often frequented by a friendly feline named Fiona), the high-ceilinged living room (decked out with chintz sofas and ornate glasswork), and the backyard flower garden graced with a gazebo, waterfall, and hot tub. The five handsome bedrooms are furnished with antiques. The light, airy Aunt Rose Room overlooks the mansions on verdant G Street; the Solarium, the least expensive room, has three walls lined with French windows, a private deck, a garden view, and a detached bath; the Margaret Room offers a queen-size four-poster canopy feather bed draped with fancy fabric, a chaise longue, and a large bathroom with a hand-painted sink and a claw-footed tub. Frittatas, streusels, raspberry-stuffed French toast, and cheese stratas are typically served for breakfast in the banquet-style dining room or in the privacy of your boudoir. ■ *2120 G St (between 21st and 22nd Sts), Sacramento, CA 95816; (916) 441-5007 or (800) 858-1568; $$; AE, DC, MC, V; checks OK.*

## FOLSOM

### *RESTAURANTS*

**Alexander's Meritage** ★★★★ Chef/owner Vincent Paul Alexander already had a wide following as the head chef at one of Sacramento's best restaurants when he took the plunge and opened his own place—and what a fine place it is. French inspired, if not strictly French, Meritage has some appetizers that alone are worth the visit. Try the Atlantic king salmon gravlax on a roasted corn blini with a dollop of caviar, or the baked escargots on a bed of sautéed spinach topped with pine nuts and crispy filo dough. And don't lick the plate. This is a classy joint. The soup on a recent visit was essence of asparagus with a quenelle of salmon and cream cheese swimming gracefully in its midst. Entrees included a fair number of ocean creatures, such as white beluga sturgeon topped with a spicy watercress sauce and baked Pacific halibut dusted with herb bread crumbs and served with a fresh tomato verge sauce. A domestic rack of lamb was stuffed with braised bell peppers and wrapped in a basil mousseline. The wines were equally engaging, especially Meritage's rare cabernets, such as the Beringer Reserve 1992. Desserts included a poached pear in a buttery, flaky pastry sitting in a caramel sauce that was to die for, and a delicately orange-flavored crème brûlée. And, finally, no small feat, the decaf coffee actually tasted like a great French roast. *Mon dieu!* ▪ *6608 Folsom–Auburn Rd, Suite 9 (in the Ashland Station Center), Folsom; (916)988-7000; $$$; full bar; AE, DIS, MC, V; no checks; dinner Tues–Sun.* ᕭ

**Christophe's French Restaurant** ★★★★ It takes guts to open a French restaurant in the Central Valley where, for the most part, California cuisine in all its manifestations is considered the cutting edge. And what's really odd is that four good French (or mostly French) restaurants have located themselves in the foothills around Sacramento—Christophe's and Alexander's Meritage in Folsom, Le Bilig in Auburn, and Zachary Jacques in Placerville. Have all the gourmets and gourmands fled to the hills? Christophe's, the most classically French of them all, has relocated into a lovely new building designed and built from the ground up (a real rarity in this region). The building is open, light, and airy, with a courtyard, a pond, gardens, and a dramatic fountain. Best of all, the tables are so far apart you can actually have a private conversation—a revolutionary concept. Chef/owner Yvan Chalaye offers a traditionally French menu featuring *civet de canard*, duck stewed in Beaujolais with green peppercorns; boeuf bourgignon with mushrooms, carrots, and pearl onions; and pork medallions in a Dijon mustard and cornichon sauce. The awesome wine list includes both French and California labels, and a Rhône blend vintage— Terra Rouge's Chalaye Cuvée—made from vines owned by the Chalaye family. Christophe's notable desserts include an elegant chocolate crème brûlée with a caramelized, crinkly top, fresh fruit tarts, and plums jubilee served over vanilla ice cream with a cabernet sauvignon sauce. *Bon appètit, mon ami.* ▪ *2304 E Bidwell St (between Creekside Dr and Oak Ave), Folsom; (916)983-4883; $$$; full bar; AE, DIS, MC, V; no checks; dinner Tues–Sun.* ᕭ

**Paragary's Bar and Oven** ★★★ See the review of the restaurant's main Sacramento branch. ▪ *705 Gold Lake Dr (near Riley St), Folsom; (916)852-0214; $$$; full bar; AE, DC, DIS, MC, V; checks OK; brunch Sun, lunch Mon–Fri; dinner every day.*

## LOOMIS

*LODGINGS*

**Emma's Bed and Breakfast** ★★★  Perched on a hill overlooking rolling farmlands dotted with grazing horses and llamas doing whatever it is that llamas do, this stately manor situated on 45 acres is impressively furnished and decorated. It has five guest suites with opulent private baths, down-filled duvets, TVs with VCRs, and fax and PC hookups (a contemporary Holmes would quickly deduce that Hewlett-Packard and NEC are nearby). Three of the suites are in the immaculately renovated 1912 farmhouse and two are in a new, matching building next door. The Orchard Suite features mahogany antiques, including a beautiful Louis XV queen-size bed. The upstairs Garden Suite has a canopied iron bed and a Jacuzzi for two in a bathroom brightened with an antique stained-glass window. The Honeymoon Suite offers a king-size iron bed, a dining area for a private breakfast, and a Jacuzzi. The full breakfasts are different every day and include juice, an entree such as German pancakes, and coffee or tea. A separate, newly constructed hall that accommodates up to 150 guests is available for weddings, receptions, and conferences (it even has a kitchen and dressing rooms). Golf carts are also available for guests who want to drive them along the trails through the oaks to find choice picnic areas or good spots for picking the delicious wild blackberries abundant in the summer and fall.
■ *3137 Taylor Rd (between King and Penryn Rds), Loomis, CA 95650; (916) 652-1392; emmas@garlic.com; $$; DIS, MC, V; checks OK.* &

**The Old Flower Farm Bed and Breakfast Inn** ★★★  Set in a bucolic countryside and oozing charm from every 100-year-old board, the Old Flower Farm looks out over (what else?) a flower farm. With its century-old architecture lovingly painted and restored, it looks like a cover shot for *Sunset* magazine. And inside it's even more impressive. Owner Jenny Leonard, a longtime professional decorator, has turned this into a special place, indeed. The living room's focal point is a red Vermont stove set on a rock hearth, which, with the two antique wing-back chairs, a large upright wicker chair, and an overstuffed celadon green sofa, cry out for a good book and a willing reader. Upstairs are three guest bedrooms, each with a queen-size bed topped with overstuffed down pillows and a private bath with a claw-footed tub and shower. The largest unit, the Country Checker Room, is filled with antiques, a white wicker chaise longue, a high poster bed with a Victorian dresser, and red- and white-checked curtains. Adjacent to the main house is the Honeymoon Cottage, decorated in neutral tones with a net-draped queen-size bed. The cottage's living room is furnished with a love seat and a comfortable overstuffed chair and has a lovely view of the B&B's waterwheel and nursery. The innkeeper lives in a separate residence, so the main house is a great place for your friends or relatives to take over. The swimming pool beckons on hot summer days, and Folsom Lake, a mecca for boaters and anglers, is only a 5-minute drive away. Horse stables and a bicycle path are easily accessible from the inn as well. Breakfast consists of fresh fruit, home-made jam, bread and pastries, fresh juice, coffee, and tea. ■ *4150 Auburn–Folsom Rd (halfway between the towns of Auburn and Folsom, at Horseshoe Bar), Loomis, CA 95650; $$–$$$; (916)652-4200; AE, MC, V; checks OK.*

## DAVIS

The **University of California at Davis** (UCD) is this little city's claim to fame, particularly the college's respected veterinary science and enology schools. A former farming town, Davis is also famous for its city officials who pride themselves on finding more ecological ways of living on the planet. For example, to encourage people to move their feet up and down on bicycle pedals instead of gas pedals, the city has built 67 miles of bike lanes and trails. The great minds of Davis get their world-shaking ideas while sipping espresso at **Mishka's Cafe**, 514 Second Street, (530)759-0811, and **Cafe Roma**, 231 E Street, (530)756-1615; they spend their spare hours pawing through the works of other great minds at **Bogey's Books**, 223 E Street, (530)757-6127, and the **Avid Reader**, 617 Second Street, (530)758-4040. The urban-village atmosphere

*Davis*

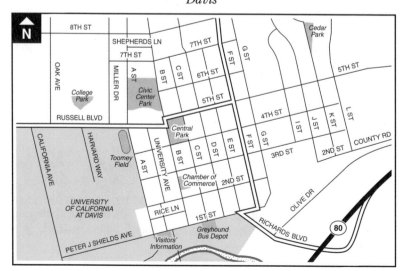

of downtown Davis draws shoppers, diners, and browsers to its charming streets, and on the southeastern outskirts of town is **The Palms Playhouse**, an intimate, down-home spot that features nationally known blues, country, jazz, and folk acts that will save you a trip to Austin; 726 Drummand Avenue, (530) 756-9901.

### RESTAURANTS

**Soga's Restaurant** ★★★   If you didn't know about this exquisite slip of a restaurant you might pass right by it (look for the British telephone booth out front). Word of mouth has transformed the classy, 16-table, wood-paneled restaurant into a bustling establishment where reservations are highly recommended. Owner/chef Matt Soga prepares innovative appetizers such as smoked salmon served alongside cornmeal pancakes smeared with cream cheese, onions, and chives, and medallions of lamb with fresh artichoke hearts, tomatoes, and mushrooms. He also makes a superb, double-thick pork chop that's marinated for 48 hours, roasted to perfection, and served with garlic mashed potatoes and gravy. Another winner is the juicy grilled sea bass served with scallion mashed potatoes and fried leeks. Desserts are simple but heartwarming: strawberry shortcake, warm apple crisp, and lemon-mint sorbet scooped onto a cookie shell and topped with a raspberry purée. ■ *222 D St (between 2nd and 3rd Sts), Davis; (530) 757-1733; chefms@mother.com; $$; beer and wine; AE, DC, DIS, MC, V; local checks only; lunch, dinner Tues–Sat.* ᕦ

**Dos Coyotes Border Cafe** ★★   This distant outpost of Southwestern cuisine is one of the hottest places in Davis. The crowds come for the fresh, consistently good food, such as the house-made salsas (help yourself to the salsa bar), shrimp tacos, and ranchero burritos with marinated steak, chicken, or vegetarian fillings. Equally good are the more unconventional offerings, such as the mahi-mahi taco or the Yucatán salad with marinated charbroiled chicken breast, black beans, red onion, carrots, cabbage, sweet peppers, and corn served on a flour tortilla. If you have room for dessert, sample the light-as-a-feather Santa Fe wedding cookies dusted with powdered sugar. Owner Bobby Coyote has turned his cafe into a howling success—even the branch in Sacramento attracts crowds. ■ *1411 W Covell Blvd #108 (in the Marketplace shopping center, just E of Hwy 113), Davis; (530) 753-0922; $; beer and wine; AE, MC, V; local checks only; lunch, dinner every day.* ᕦ

**The Symposium** ★★   Ancient Greeks cavort across the mural-covered walls of this lively Greek restaurant—and after one taste of the Symposium's deliciously different Greek pizza, you may want to do a bit of cavorting yourself. Niko's Special, a pizza with a thick yet slightly crunchy crust piled high with salami, ham, pepperoni, feta, olives, mozzarella, and mushrooms, is a local legend. If you're not a pizza fan, owner/chefs Nick and Contilo Pandeleon create both Greek-American and pure-Greek dishes ranging from authentic dolmades to savory souvlakia. And, of course, where would a Greek restaurant be without honey-drenched baklava for dessert? The place is usually packed, but try to grab a table in the cozy wood-paneled alcove. ▪ *1620 E 8th St (at M St, near Albertson's), Davis; (530)756-3850; $$; full bar; AE, DIS, MC, V; no checks; lunch Mon–Fri, dinner Mon–Sat.* ⅙

**Crêpe Bistro** ★ Tucked into a row of small shops, the Bach family's tiny, brightly lit cafe is a favorite hangout of the university crowd—and there is always a crowd here. True to its name, the specialty is crêpes—some bursting with succulent meats, others oozing with cheeses or teeming with tender vegetables. A couple of favorites include the crêpe boeuf bourguignon, filled with tender chunks of beef marinated in wine and herbs, and the avocado crêpe, stuffed with cheese, tomatoes, mushrooms, and, of course, lots of avocado slices, with a dollop of sour cream. Getting the freshest ingredients available is one of the Bachs' top priorities, and most of the bistro's herbs are fresh-picked from their backyard garden. For dessert, Papa Bach's lemon cake is a tart treat. ▪ *234 E St (between 2nd and 3rd Sts), Davis; (530)753-2575; $; beer and wine; MC, V; checks OK; brunch Sat–Sun, breakfast, lunch Mon–Fri, dinner every day.* ⅙

## LODGINGS

**Palm Court Hotel** ★★★ This chic, unobtrusive jewel is reminiscent of a fine little boutique hotel. The lobby is small and intimate with a kind of Raffles Hotel look (English with a dash of East Indian) and some very classy antiques artfully scattered about. The 28 suites (all for nonsmokers) have lots of goodies for the serious traveler, including irons and ironing boards, hair dryers, TVs and telephones in every room, and sofa beds (in addition to the beds in the adjoining rooms). The two Palm Suites are the ritziest, with fireplaces, marble bathrooms with whirlpool baths, and full-length balconies. The decor in the rooms has an East Indian/English flair, too, with dark wooden blinds, Regency furnishings in hues of rust, maroon, and gold, and handsome armoires that conceal TVs, honor bars, and refrigerators. It all makes a chap long for a Pimm's Cup and a volume of Rudyard Kipling. ▪ *234 D St (at 3rd St), Davis, CA 95616; (530)753-7100 or (800)528-1234; $$; AE, DC, DIS, MC, V; no checks.* ⅙

## VACAVILLE

### *RESTAURANTS*

**Merchant and Main Grill and Bar ★★**  Belly up to this grill and bar and order the steak sandwich, a juicy, 2-inch-thick slab of charbroiled steak on toasted garlic bread; the rich, buttery, grilled crab-salad sandwich, which is crunchy with onions and celery and delivers a surprising kick of cayenne; or the Asian chicken salad with grilled marinated chicken breast, lemongrass, cilantro, and a ginger, soy, and sesame seed vinaigrette. The house-made desserts are the high point of the meal, an agonizing choice between bread pudding topped with cream and Jack Daniels whiskey sauce or chocolate decadence with raspberry sauce. This restaurant is very popular, so reservations are advised. ■ *349 Merchant St (take the Alamo/Merchant St exit off I-80), Vacaville, CA 95688; (707)446-0368; $$; full bar; AE, DC, DIS, MC, V; local checks only; lunch, dinner every day.* ♿

## WINTERS

### *RESTAURANTS*

**The Buckhorn ★★**  You know you're in serious meat-eating country when you see the glassy eyes of the Buckhorn's small herd of mounted deer, a moose, and a goat gazing down at you. Buckhorn dinners begin with a basket of hot sourdough bread and a mound of whipped butter, followed by such entrees as tender rack of lamb (fresh from farms in nearby Dixon) and certified Angus prime rib roasted with a special blend of spices. There's also a variety of pasta, fresh fish, and seafood dishes, but meat is the Buckhorn's big draw. ■ *210 Railroad Ave (at Main St), Winters; (530)795-4503; www. pagemakers.com/buckhorn; $$; full bar; AE, DC, MC, V; checks OK; dinner every day.*

## WOODLAND

### *RESTAURANTS*

**Morrison's Upstairs ★★**  Tucked into the attic of one of Woodland's most striking buildings, an 1891 Queen Anne Victorian that was originally a luxury apartment house, Morrison's Upstairs combines old-fashioned elegance with a pre-dinner aerobic workout; guests must climb three flights of stairs. (The elevator is an option for those who are easily winded.) Favorite entrees include an abundance of creatively prepared fresh fish dishes, plump beer-batter prawns, fettuccine with prawns in a Parmesan cream sauce, perfectly cooked prime rib, and Steak Morrison, a 12-ounce prime-cut New York strip smothered with mushrooms and shallots. Early birds dining between 5pm and 6pm Monday through Thursday get the same fare at bargain prices. Morrison's wine list is the best in town. ■ *428½ 1st St (at Bush St), Woodland; (530)666-6176; $$; full bar; AE, DC, DIS, MC, V; local checks only; lunch Mon–Fri, dinner every day.* &

**Ludy's Main Street BBQ and Catering** ★ Ludy's is located in a handsome 19th-century stone building next to the beautifully restored Woodland Opera House. From the outside it looks a lot like any small-town restaurant, but step inside and you'll feel as though you've been transported to the heart of Texas. The barnwood walls, wagon wheels and antlers, and that sweet, sweet smell of smoked meat all shout that this is meat eaters' country, pardner. And so it is. There are half-pound charburgers; all kinds of plates and combinations of barbecued chicken, pork ribs, beef ribs, and sausage; plus taters, rings, slaw, and chili. And our green friends aren't totally overlooked—a veggie burger and a wonderful spinach salad are made for their kind. The atmosphere is friendly and casual and everyone seems to be having a good, if messy, time. Ludy's occasionally has live music on the back patio. ■ *667 Main St (downtown), Woodland; (530)666-4400; $; beer and wine; AE, MC, V; local checks only; lunch, dinner every day.* &

## WILLIAMS

### *RESTAURANTS*

**Granzella's, Inc.** ★ This culinary emporium houses everything from a restaurant and an ice-cream parlor to a sports bar and a bakery. Its fine Italian deli is packed with a large selection of wine and beer, olive oils, and Granzella's own exquisite olives (there's even an olive tasting bar). The deli's sandwiches are piled high with fresh meats such as turkey, roast beef, and imported prosciutto, as well as good imported cheeses. In the restaurant, pasta and pizza share the menu with all-American standards, but the pizzas are the favored fare. Try the linguiça pizza, with its rich, tangy marinara sauce and crunchy crust. The ice-cream parlor offers real ice-cream milk shakes and banana splits. ■ *451 6th St (just W of I-5), Williams; (530)473-5496; $; full bar; AE, DC, DIS, MC, V; checks OK; breakfast, lunch, dinner every day.* &

**Louis Cairo's** ★ A popular local dinner house, Louis Cairo's offers the warm atmosphere of a traditional Italian cafe, a large variety of entrees, and a good wine list. Burgundy-checkered tablecloths and matching napkins top the tables of the simple dining room, which is now managed by Louis's daughter, Pattie Jo. This 53-year-old establishment is famous for its fresh garlic bread, which is available as a side order and is used for the wonderful open-faced charbroiled-steak sandwich. ■ *558 7th St (downtown), Williams; (530)473-5927; $; full bar; AE, MC, V; local checks only; lunch, dinner every day.* &

## MERIDIAN

### *RESTAURANTS*

**El Rio Club** ★  Good news! Thanks to the efforts of residents and friends who spent days and nights building a levee of sandbags around the town, the hamlet of Meridian was saved from the '97 flood. Newly renovated and under new ownership, El Rio Club is also alive and thriving. Once you're safely ensconced in the small dining room (beyond the bar haunted by mounted moose, deer, boar, owl, and antelope heads), begin with the roasted garlic and cheese crouton appetizer. Follow that lead with the tasty chicken baked with prunes, olives, and capers or the lamb loin chops prepared with rosemary, pecans, and croutons. All entrees come with fresh veggies, pasta, and a salad. ■ *1198 3rd St (just E of the Sacramento River and S of Hwy 20), Meridian; (530)696-0900; $$; full bar; MC, V; local checks only; lunch Tues–Sat, dinner Tues–Sun.* &

## YUBA CITY

### *RESTAURANTS*

**City Cafe** ★★★  By golly, Yuba City's gone trendy with this chic, little cafe smack-dab in the middle of the town's historic section. Take a seat inside the bistrolike dining room or sit outside in the courtyard in front of the restaurant where you can watch the Yubans stroll. The lunch menu focuses on an assortment of panini prepared with focaccia and herb mayo, including the popular grilled eggplant, sautéed spinach, mild banana pepper, and feta sandwich. There are also a few pastas and a mix of salads, although the Bombay shrimp salad is a bit pricey and skimpy on the shrimpy. Dinner is a more ambitious affair with such items as sautéed duck breast served medium rare with a port wine sauce, and grilled rack of pork with a roasted red pepper and shallot demiglace served with mashed potatoes. City Cafe has a good selection of beer and wine, with many wines available by the glass. While you're in the neighborhood, pop into Chili Cauldron, the cute shop next door, and pick up a bottle of chile sauce (from the selection of hundreds) as a souvenir of the hot time you had in Y.C. ■ *667 Plumas St (at Colusa Hwy), Yuba City; (530)671-1501; $$; beer and wine; DIS, MC, V; checks OK; lunch Mon–Fri, dinner Mon–Sat.* &

**Ruthy's Bar and Oven** ★★  If you're a big breakfast eater, make a beeline to Ruthy's. You'll find such belly-packing fare as French toast made with Ruthy's own cinnamon-raisin bread, terrific whole-wheat and buttermilk pancakes, and creative egg dishes such as the omelet stuffed with Monterey Jack cheese and prawns sautéed in garlic-herb butter. For lunch, head straight for the salad bar or order a sandwich served on house-made bread. Dinner is a more elaborate affair, with interesting appetizers like little chicken quesadillas, tiny New Zealand clams steamed in a garlic and white wine sauce, and spicy Cajun prawns in a garlic red pepper sauce. Entrees vary from house-made fettuccine tossed with house-smoked salmon to a spicy chicken stir-fry. Pick up some freshly baked bread to take home and perhaps a bottle of wine from Ruthy's wine shop, which has the best selection in the area. ■ *229 Clark Ave (in the Hillcrest Plaza mini-mall, S of Franklin Ave), Yuba City; (530)674-2611 or (800)455-LAKE; ruthys@syix.com; $$; full bar; AE, DC, DIS, MC, V; checks OK; brunch Sun, breakfast, lunch, dinner Tues–Sat.* ಓ

## LODGINGS

**Harkey House** ★★  This beige 1874 Victorian Gothic B&B trimmed in blue and red offers four guest rooms with private baths, as well as such diversions as a spa, a chess table, and an antique Chickering piano. The spacious Harkey Suite is swathed in a paisley pattern and has a small sitting room that doubles as a library; a pellet-burning stove keeps the room toasty on chilly winter nights. The soft gray and green Empress Room features an electric fireplace, and a water fountain graces the room. In the solarium-style dining area guests are treated to a full breakfast: Belgian waffles, zucchini croquettes, Canadian bacon, fresh fruit, scones, juice, and coffee. ■ *212 C St (in old downtown, across from the courthouse), Yuba City, CA 95991; (530)674-1942; www.mcn.org/b&b; $$; AE, DIS, MC, V; checks OK.*

## MARYSVILLE

### RESTAURANTS

**Silver Dollar Saloon** ★  As you amble up to the Silver Dollar Saloon, be sure to pay your respects to the massive wooden cowboy standing guard at the entrance. This restaurant and saloon is a lively relic of Marysville's frontier past, with Western memorabilia scattered throughout the building. You can watch 'em cook your order on the open-pit grill here or, heck, even cook it yourself. The Silver Dollar's menu features nothing but meat: terrific grilled steaks and steak sandwiches, grilled chicken, hot ham or pastrami sandwiches, and delectable half-racks of barbecued ribs. Place your order, pour yourself a cup of java, and grab a table. A brothel once occupied the area upstairs, and the warning buzzer used to alert the ladies of the night that the law was on its way still works; nowadays the floor is used for private parties of a more legitimate sort. Friday and Saturday nights the place is packed with cowpokes tappin' their boots to the beat of live country music. ■ *330 1st St (in Old Town, between C and D Sts), Marysville; (530)743-0507; $; full bar; AE, DIS, MC, V; checks OK; lunch, dinner every day.* &

## LIVE OAK

### RESTAURANTS

**Pasquini's** ★★ This roadhouse restaurant has become a regional institution—a favorite detour of locals from Yuba City to Gridley as well as in-the-know interstate travelers. Pasquini's is a warm, welcoming, and sometimes raucous dinner house, where the tables are draped with red-checkered cloths and the favored seats are the two well-padded booths. The menu is as thick as a magazine, and the filling meals are guaranteed to bloat your belly. Select the steak smothered in mushrooms or crusted with cracked pepper, the prime rib, the cioppino (served on Wednesdays only), or the Basque-style lamb grilled with garlic and butter. The wine list offers a respectable collection of California vintages and an Italian Chianti. ■ *6241 Live Oak Blvd (on Hwy 99, about 5 miles N of Yuba City), Live Oak; (530)695-3384; $$; full bar; AE, MC, V; checks OK; dinner Mon–Sat.* &

## ORLAND

### LODGINGS

**The Inn at Shallow Creek Farm** ★★ Who would have thought there'd be an elegant and absolutely peaceful refuge so close to Interstate 5? Mary and Kurt Glaeseman are the proprietors of this gray-and-white, ivy-covered farmhouse surrounded by citrus trees and set at the end of a long drive lined with fruit and nut trees. The inn offers four guest rooms, including the Heritage Room upstairs, a favorite with its striking morning-glory wallpaper and wonderful antiques. The Brookdale Room has twin beds and a wide window overlooking the wild verdant tangle along the creek. If total privacy is what you're after, stay in the four-room Cottage, with a fully equipped kitchen, a sun porch, and a wood-burning stove. Mary serves a breakfast of home-baked breads and muffins, fresh fruit from the farm's orchards, juice, and coffee. When the day turns cold and wintry, sink into one of the overstuffed sofas in front of the roaring fire with a good book and nibble on some Mandarin oranges—a local delicacy. ■ *4712 County Rd DD (take the Chico–Orland exit off I-5, drive 2½ miles W, then turn right on County Rd DD and drive ½ mile), Orland, CA 95963; (530)865-4093 or (800)865-4093; $; MC, V; checks OK.*

# OROVILLE

Oroville has been largely, and undeservedly, overlooked by tourists. This historic Gold Rush town (site of the second major gold discovery after Coloma) and center of a rich agricultural industry (cattle, citrus, nuts, olives) has lots for the traveler to investigate. The **Oroville Chinese Temple and Garden** was built in 1863 to serve the 10,000 Chinese who worked the mines here. It has an extensive collection of tapestries, costumes, and puppets used in Chinese opera, and its lovely gardens, planted exclusively with plants from China, offer a great place for meditation; 1500 Broderick Street, (530)538-2496. The 770-foot-tall **Oroville Dam** is the tallest earthen dam in the country, and **Lake Oroville** is regularly rated as one of the best bass fishing spots in the United States. It is also a houseboaters' paradise, with 24 square miles of surface area and 167 miles of shoreline; to reach the dam and lake from Highway 70, head east on Oroville Dam Boulevard, (530)534-2306. Just south of the dam you can rent a houseboat, ski boat, or wave-runner and find out where to reel in the big ones by visiting the folks at Bidwell Canyon Marina; 801 Bidwell Canyon Road, (530)589-3165. The 640-foot-high **Feather Falls**, the sixth tallest waterfall in the country, is a worthy side trip if you're up for a moderately strenuous hike. Your reward: spectacular views of the falls, the Sacramento Valley, and the Coast Range; for directions and details, call the **Oroville Area Chamber of Commerce** at (530)538-2542.

▼

Berry Creek

*Lodgings*

▲

# BERRY CREEK

## *LODGINGS*

**Lake Oroville Bed and Breakfast** ★★★ "Silent, upon a peak in Darien. . . ." With apologies to Mr. Keats, make that "upon the outskirts of Oroville" and you have a pretty fair description of the Lake Oroville Bed and Breakfast sitting in lonely yellow splendor on 40 acres high above the lake, with views in every direction. Built in 1992 specifically to be an inn (as opposed to a reconfigured residence), the B&B has six guest bedrooms with private entrances and baths, and five of them have whirlpool tubs. The Rose Petal Room is appropriately covered with rose print wallpaper, and a white Battenberg bedspread is draped over the king-size bed, from which you have a view of the lake. The Victorian Room, decked out with Eastlake antique furnishings, also has a king-size bed and a terrific lake view. The Monet Room, Max's Room, the Arbor Room, and the Vine Room all have queen-size beds and views of the surrounding woods. Kick back in the warm and inviting parlor, framed by a fireplace and bay windows, or shoot some pool in the billiards room. The sun room is designed for nothing more strenuous than reading a good book and viewing the gorgeous sunsets. Breakfast is a hearty affair featuring a main course of either quiche, eggs Benedict, crêpes, waffles, or French toast. Proprietors Ron and Cheryl Damberger welcome children and maintain a small play room for them, and they like to host family reunions and other group events, too. A gas grill is available for guests who get so downright relaxed they'd rather barbecue than drive into town for dinner. ■ *240 Sunday Dr (from Hwy 70 take Oroville Dam Blvd/Hwy 162 E for 1.7 miles, turn right at Olive Hwy and continue for 13.5 miles, then turn left at Bell Ranch Rd, bear right, and drive a half mile to Sunday Dr), Berry Creek, CA 95916; (530)589-0700 or (800)455-LAKE; lakeinn@dcsi.net; www.now2000.com/lakeoroville; $$; AE, DIS, MC, V; checks OK.* &

## CHICO

This pretty little college town gained a national reputation when *Playboy* magazine named the **California State University at Chico** (aka Chico State) the number-one party school in the nation. Horrified by this label, most of the local gentry tried to put an end to it by doing away with Chico's biggest college celebration, Pioneer Days—a weeklong beer bust rivaling spring break in Palm Beach. Of course, the college crowds still party hearty here, but they don't take over the town once a year as they used to. When the warm weather rolls in, plan a picnic or a stroll among the trees in the 2,400 acres of pretty **Bidwell Park**. And when the summer temperatures start to soar into the 90s and above, do as the locals do and dive into one of the swimming holes in lower **Big Chico Creek**. Those in search of more vigorous exercise should try the **Chico Wildflower Century**, a 100-mile bicycling marathon held every April. To find out what's currently going on around town, settle in at **Caffe Paulo** with a pastry and espresso and thumb through the *Chico News and Review*, the city's fine alternative-press newspaper; 642 West Fifth Street, (530)343-0704.

### RESTAURANTS

**The Albatross** ★★ Set in a lovely neighborhood of old mansions, the Albatross was a private home before it was converted into a dinner house with several small, casual dining rooms and a wonderfully landscaped garden patio. Despite the waitstaff's aloha attire and the restaurant's tropical decor, you won't find any pounded taro root or papaya salsa on the menu here. What you will find is well-prepared mahi-mahi, fresh salmon topped with champagne butter, and broiled swordfish with tarragon, as well as steak and prime rib. All of the entrees come with steaming hot sourdough and squaw bread and include a trip to the first-rate salad bar. Top off your meal with the ultra-rich Island Pie: macadamia-nut ice cream piled onto a cookie-crumb crust and smothered with fudge, whipped cream, and a sprinkling of almonds. ■ *3312 The Esplanade (N of downtown), Chico; (530)345-6037; $$; full bar; AE, MC, V; checks OK; dinner Tues–Sun.* &

**Cory's Sweet Treats & Gallery ★★** This cheerful little daytime cafe adorned with the work of local artists serves lumberjack-size sandwiches with generous layers of meats such as roast beef, baked ham, and pastrami. All the meats are cooked on the premises and shoveled onto thick slices of house-made bread; there are various vegetarian options, too. For dessert try the lemon bars, the Black Forest cake, or the unusual oat-meal spice cake with caramel frosting. ■ *230 W 3rd St (between Broadway and Salem St, downtown), Chico; (530)345-2955; $; no alcohol; no credit cards; local checks only; breakfast, lunch Tues–Sun.* &

**Kramore Inn ★★** Owner Bill Theller started at the Kramore as a dishwasher, worked his way up to become cook and manager, then bought the place and clearly figured out how to keep his customers happy . . . the inn's food has kept people coming back for more than 20 years. The Kramore specialty is

*Chico*

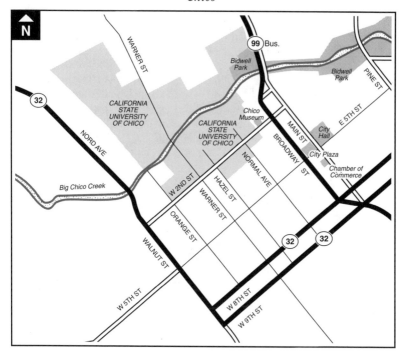

crêpes. You'll find 30 different kinds—everything from a shrimp-and-broccoli combo to the old favorite ham-and-cheese crêpe. There are plenty of vegetarian varieties as well (to keep the conscience as pure as the body), and the Kramore serves organic and pesticide-free vegetables whenever possible. Other good dishes on the lengthy menu are the Italian roast chicken, Hungarian mushroom soup, and the daily stir-fries. The excellent breads, pasta, and ice creams are made locally. For a sweet finale, top off your meal with the decadent chocolate-mousse crêpe. ■ *1903 Park Ave (at W 19th St), Chico; (530)343-3701; jpw@cmc.net; $; beer and wine; AE, DIS, MC, V; local checks only; brunch Sat–Sun, lunch Tues–Fri, dinner Tues–Sun.* &

**Redwood Forest Restaurant** ★★ Come to this kick-back college-town cafe for a good lunch of vegetarian lasagne, enchiladas, or such specials as the Portobello mushroom sandwich and the cashew-chicken-salad croissant sandwich. Don't leave without ordering a slice of the great carrot cake, which is especially good with a cup of java or herbal tea. The dinner menu typically features grilled or poached salmon, filet mignon, and several veggie selections. The Redwood Forest is famous for its wine-tasting bar, offering tastings of four wines each night. ■ *121 W 3rd St (between Broadway and Main St, downtown), Chico; (530)343-4315; $; beer and wine; AE, MC, V; local checks only; lunch Mon–Sat, dinner Wed–Sat.* &

**Sicilian Cafe** ★★ Settle in beneath the vineyard mural, order some good Italian wine, and prepare yourself for a simple but tasty Italian meal. The Sicilian's specialties are its fresh pasta dishes and calamari, which may be ordered fried, sautéed with herbs, or stuffed with baby clams and baked. The house-made cannoli, ricotta cheesecake, and tiramisu are good choices for dessert—and well worth an extra hour in the gym. ■ *1020 Main St (between W 9th and W 11th Sts), Chico; (530)345-2233; $$; beer and wine; AE, DIS, MC, V; checks OK; dinner Tues–Sat.*

### LODGINGS

**Johnson's Country Inn** ★★★★ Set in the heart of a picture-perfect almond orchard, this Victorian-style farmhouse is an ideal place for a wedding, an anniversary, or simply a peaceful retreat—and you'd never guess that it's only 5 minutes from downtown Chico. Built specifically as a B&B in 1992, the inn has four guest rooms, all with private baths. The Icart Room, named after Louis Icart, a Parisian art deco artist, is furnished in a French country style in shades of green, blue, and rose (and it's wheelchair accessible). The Jarrett Room, adorned with paintings by the 1930s San Francisco artist Charles "Dixie" Jarrett, is decorated in soft greens and blues and has a view of the orchard from an upstairs window. Named after a family member, the Sexton Room is decked out in floral hues of rose, beige, and blue with furnishings designed by William Morris, the famous pre-Raphaelite English artist and poet. The romantic Harrison Room, named after the owners' great-great-great-great grandfather, the 23rd president, has an 1860s Victorian double bed, a fireplace, and a private Jacuzzi. All of the rooms have ceiling fans and individually controlled air conditioning. Owners David and Joan Johnson provide a coffee and juice tray for each room early in the morning, then later bring out an ample breakfast of locally made apple sausages, peach French toast, frittatas, and almond coffee cakes (guess where the almonds come from). There's a fireplace in the parlor, parlor games in the garden room, and garden games (horseshoes, croquet) in the garden. Got that? Wine is provided each afternoon to allow guests to decompress from a hard day on the croquet court. ■ *3935 Moorehead Ave, Chico, CA 95928; (530)345-7829; johnson.country.inn@pobox.com; www.pobox.com/~j.c.inn; $$; MC, V; checks OK.* ♿

**The Esplanade Bed and Breakfast** ★ This B&B is located on one of Chico's most beautiful boulevards, The Esplanade, which is lined on both sides with lush lawns, tall trees, and stately Victorian mansions. The charming turn-of-the-century house sits across the street from the famous Bidwell Mansion (the elegant, three-story former home of Chico's founder) and is close to downtown and the university. Five guest rooms are offered here, each with a cable TV and a private bath. Susan's Room is a favorite with its luxurious queen-size poster bed and a great view of the Bidwell Mansion. Natalie's Room is downstairs and has lavender decor, a bay window, and a Jacuzzi in the bathroom decorated with a stained-glass window. Proprietor Lois Kloss pampers her guests with a hearty breakfast in the formal dining room, and she pours everyone a glass of wine each evening in the parlor or on the garden patio. ■ *620 The Esplanade (near Memorial Way), Chico, CA 95926; (530)345-8084; $; MC, V; checks OK.*

## RED BLUFF

### RESTAURANTS

**The Snack Box** ★ Residents of Red Bluff gladly stand in line to eat the jumbo servings of freshly made food offered for breakfast (served all day) and lunch in this pretty little Victorian house. The Snack Box offers well-prepared steak and eggs, buttermilk pancakes, Belgian waffles, biscuits and gravy, and omelets for the morning meal, while hamburgers, deli sandwiches, soup and corn bread, and house-made cobblers and brownies are offered for lunch. Best of all, the price is right. ■ *257 Main St (at Ash St), Red Bluff; (530)529-0227; $; no alcohol; MC, V; local checks only; breakfast, lunch every day.* ♿

**The Faulkner House** ★★   No use looking for the *Absalom,
Absalom* room or the *As I Lay Dying* suite in this 1890 Queen
Anne Victorian, for it was named after a local doctor who prac-
ticed here in the '30s—not the writer. The Faulkner House
features a red-velvet parlor, a casual living room, and a spacious blue dining room. Its four guest rooms are upstairs, and
each has a private bath. The two smallest rooms are often preferred: the octagonal Tower Room is a light-filled corner room
decorated in tan florals, and the Wicker Room is wallpapered
in dark green with mauve roses and has an iron bed draped
with an antique bedspread, wicker accessories, and views of
the shade trees. In the evening owners Mary and Harvey Klin-
gler leave a full decanter of sherry for you in the upstairs
hall. ■ *1029 Jefferson St (off Union St), Red Bluff, CA 96080;
(530)529-0520 or (800)549-6171; $$; AE, MC, V; checks OK.*

# Index

# We Stand By Our Reviews

Sasquatch Books is proud of *Northern California Best Places*. Our editors and contributors go to great lengths and expense to see that all of the reviews are as accurate, up-to-date, and honest as possible. If we have disappointed you, please accept our apologies; however, if a recommendation in this 3rd edition of *Northern California Best Places* has seriously misled you, Sasquatch Books would like to refund your purchase price. To receive your refund:

1) Tell us where you purchased your book and return the book and the book-purchase receipt to the address below.

2) Enclose the original lodging or restaurant receipt from the establishment in question, including date of visit.

3) Write a full explanation of your stay or meal and how *Northern California Best Places* specifically misled you.

4) Include your name, address, and phone number.

Refund is valid only while the 3rd edition of *Northern California Best Places* is in print. If the ownership, management, or chef has changed since publication, Sasquatch Books cannot be held responsible. Postage and tax on the returned book is your responsibility. Please allow six to eight weeks for processing.

Please address to Satisfaction Guaranteed, *Northern California Best Places*, and send to:

Sasquatch Books
615 Second Avenue, Suite 260
Seattle, WA 98104

# Northern California Best Places
## REPORT FORM

Based on my personal experience, I wish to nominate the following restaurant or place of lodging as a "Best Place," or confirm/correct/disagree with the current review.

_____

_____

_____

_____

_____

(Please include address and telephone number of establishment, if convenient.)

## REPORT:

Please describe food, service, style, comfort, value, date of visit, and other aspects of your experience; continue on another piece of paper if necessary.

_____

_____

_____

_____

_____

_____

_____

I am not concerned, directly or indirectly, with the management or ownership of this establishment.

Signed _____

Address _____

_____

_____

Phone Number _____

Date _____

Please address to *Northern California Best Places* and send to:
Sasquatch Books
615 Second Avenue, Suite 260
Seattle, WA 98104
Feel free to email feedback as well: books@sasquatchbooks.com

# About the Authors

**Rebecca Poole Forée** is a writer, editor, and publishing consultant who has contributed to several travel guides, including *Eyewitness California, San Francisco Access, Budget Europe Access,* and *Northern California Cheap Sleeps*. She has worked as an editorial director for Harper Collins Publishers, the editor-in-chief of Foghorn Press, and the senior editor of *Parenting Magazine,* among other positions. She has edited nearly 75 books on everything from sports and travel to history and medicine, and her writing and photography have been published in several newspapers and magazines, including the *San Francisco Chronicle, San Francisco Focus, California Magazine, Sunset,* and *Sierra Magazine*. When she's not sitting in front of her Macintosh, she travels, runs, skis, and rescues and rehabilitates injured seals and cetaceans at The Marine Mammal Center in the Marin Headlands. A native Northern Californian, Rebecca resides in San Francisco.

## Major Contributors

Combining the only three things he's good at—eating, sleeping, and criticizing—**Matthew R. Poole** has found a surprisingly prosperous career as a freelance travel writer. Matthew is a native Northern Californian and author of more than a dozen guides to California and Hawaii. He currently lives in San Francisco and has no intention of writing a novel.

When she isn't busy advising the political hotshots in the California State Capitol, legislative consultant **Mary Anne Moore** travels the globe in search of great getaways, first-class restaurants, idyllic jogging trails, and the world's best bookstores. She is also a freelance writer based in Sacramento.

**Maurice Read**, a Sacramento-based lobbyist, a gourmet cook, and a restaurant critic, spends his free time touring Northern California with his Australian shepherd. Together they hunt for dog-friendly lodgings, great fly-fishing spots, and memorable meals.

A frequent contributor to magazines, newspapers, guidebooks, and on-line media resources, **Mona Behan** is a freelance writer and editor living in Belmont, California.

**Maria Behan** is a fiction writer and freelance journalist specializing in travel, business, and technology writing. She currently divides her time between California and Dublin, Ireland.

Northern California-based writer **Jean Linsteadt** has contributed to *Self, Veggie Life, Family Circle,* and *New York* magazines. She is the author of the 1996 edition of *California Wine Country Access,* a guidebook published by Harper Collins.